MARGARET MEAD
A Life

MARGARET
MEAD

HARVILL PI
8 Grafton Street, Londor

A Life

JANE HOWARD

Harvill Press Ltd
is distributed by
William Collins Sons & Co Ltd
London · Glasgow · Sydney · Auckland
Toronto · Johannesburg

British Library Cataloguing in Publication Data

Howard, Jane
    Margaret Mead.
    1. Mead, Margaret   2. Anthropologists—
    United States—Biography
    I. Title
    306'.092'4   GN21.M36
    ISBN 0–00–272515–0

First published in the UK by Harvill Press, 1984
© Jane Howard 1984
Made and printed in the United States

We have made every effort to trace the ownership of all copyrighted material and to secure permission from copyright holders. In the event of any question arising as to the use of any material, we will be pleased to make the necessary corrections in future printings. Thanks are due to the following authors, publishers, publications for permission to use the material indicated.

Permission to quote from published works of Margaret Mead and Gregory Bateson, and from Margaret Mead's letters included in the Mead Archive of the Library of Congress for the use of all scholars, has been granted by Mary Catherine Bateson, President of the Institute for Intercultural Studies.

The poem "Misericordia" first published in February 1930, by permission of the Editor of Poetry.

Permission to reprint the poem "Measure Your Thread" has been granted by William Morrow & Company.

Permission to reprint portions of poems by Ruth Benedict has been granted by Houghton Mifflin Company.

Permission to reprint songs as translated by Reo Fortune has been granted by E. P. Dutton, Inc.

"Under Which Lyre" by W. H. Auden, Collected Poems, edited by Edward Mendelson, by permission of Random House, Inc.

Permission to reprint portions of poems by Edna St. Vincent Millay, from Collected Poems, Harper & Row, copyright 1922, 1923, 1950, 1951, has been granted by Norma Millay Ellis.

FOR ALICE E. MAYHEW

Contents

Many More Than Both Ways

"RAINBOW CLOUD," said the man who looked like Santa Claus, "will now take lunch orders." The lunches were ordered, by a graduate student in the anthropology department of American University in Washington, D.C., during a two-weekend symposium, in March of 1980, about "The Legacy of Margaret Mead." Many seminars and forums and discussions assessing Mead's life and work have been held since her death, a month and a day before her seventy-seventh birthday, on November 15, 1978. The man who organized this one was Philleo Nash, who was once lieutenant governor of Wisconsin, where he is now a cranberry farmer. Nash and his wife, born Edith Rosenfeld, first met Mead in the early 1930s, when they were both graduate students at the University of Chicago. I mention these particulars because Margaret Mead was a great one, in most respects, for attention to detail.

Deciding to write about Mead's life five years ago, I promised myself that in this book, unlike the three I had written before, the first person singular pronoun would not appear. I mean to keep that promise, as soon as it is understood that Margaret Mead was not my relative, my friend, my employer, or my teacher. (I have never taken any course in anthropology.) I shook her hand at large receptions a time or two, heard her give a couple of speeches, saw her on television programs, and rode on the same train with her once from Philadelphia, but I did not know her or love her, nor did I wince, as some did, at the sound of her voice or the sight of her face.

I felt certain affinities for her, though, especially after I was asked in 1972 by the *New York Times* to review her autobiographical *Blackberry Winter: My Earlier Years*. There I learned that Mead too was the daughter of midwesterners. She too had chosen to settle, after some years in Greenwich Village, on the Upper West Side of New York. She too wore glasses and was unathletic and got up early and was known to fall asleep in public and made a living writing down people's answers to nosy questions, asked in improbable places. She too tried to go everywhere and know everyone and do everything, only she came close to getting away with it.

Blackberry Winter struck me as an engaging book but an evasive one, which asked nearly as many questions as it answered, and did not say enough about how its author managed to shift gears as often as she did, personally and professionally, without destroying her transmission. Could these changes really have been so painless? Could she really have switched husbands and careers with that much grace? These matters did not obsess me, exactly, but in 1979, when Mead was suggested as a subject for the biography I had been saying I wanted to write, as a change from more general subjects, I found that somewhere in the back of my mind I had been perplexed by her all along. If a biographer is not in love with or in awe of his subject, another critic said, "at least he should be puzzled—by the contradictions, by the processes of decision, by the essential quiddity of the hero."

I was puzzled by Mead, and so, it became clear, were hundreds of other people who had mourned her death of pancreatic cancer. She mattered a great deal, it turned out, not just to her professional colleagues but to people who had seen her only on television talk shows, some of whom had never read one of her books and knew not a thing about anthropology, the science that gave her the platform from which she surveyed, scolded, and beamed at the world. Her death stunned total strangers nearly as much as I was to learn it had stunned Mead herself: "she was furious," one of her close friends told me, "to be stopped so soon." Four years later, when a professor in Australia attacked Mead's first field work, in Samoa, the waves of shock were greater still.

This book is not meant to compete with others being written by Mead's intimates and her fellow academics. This is a generalist's portrait, nonpartisan, drawn from books, articles, and correspondence, but most of all from talks on three continents, over five years, with some three hundred of the people whose lives were changed because they knew her. Many of them spoke of her in the present tense and with tears in their eyes, a few with disdain. Some, with reason, felt proprietary about her memory, but none claimed to know the whole Mead. No one did, or ever will. She took care to reveal only what she chose to have known about herself. The fame she sought and won was on her own terms. She was not only one of the most accomplished and most energetically public women of her time, but one of the most enigmatic.

• •

She was a patron saint of the peripheral. She kept an eye out for people on the sidelines, and knew how to make them feel, as one of her numerous young friends put it, "framed and central." Born the year Queen Victoria died, she carried the optimism of the nineteenth century into the chaos of the twentieth, with its bewildering infinitude of choices. Those choices, she declared, need not leave us feeling flummoxed; this era, for all its peril, is a marvelous time to be alive; mankind can have it not only both ways, but many more than both ways. By her own example she made this grand claim seem almost possible. "It isn't fair, your having it all," her male colleagues would complain to her, but she saw no reason to aim for less.

Mead is best known for the trailblazing and controversial work she did in anthropology, the science of man, at a crucial point in its history as well as in her own. *Coming of Age in Samoa*, her first and most famous book, asserted in 1928 that there were ways and ways not only of getting through puberty but of doing almost anything: that it was culture, at least as much as biology, that accounted for the differences, and that biology for humankind is not an imperative, as it is for other creatures, but only the starting point, only a suggestion. That book's spectacular success made Mead's name an immediate and enduring metaphor for steamy things that happened in torrid, languid jungles, and gave her a reputation that she built onto, steadily, in the fifty more years of her life.

Anthropology had attracted Mead in the first place because its borders were so flexible, but even it could not contain her. Nothing could. She made her own rules and lived many lives. She rushed across oceans and continents, time zones and networks and disciplines, knocking down barriers and redefining boundaries. She had three marriages, a child, and innumerable intense friendships. She made a new friend of importance, she once claimed, every two or three months, without ever losing any of her old ones.

Her generosity was staggering. She didn't just write letters of recommendation and maneuver for grants and fellowships; she gave of her time and her attention, and made connections no one else would have imagined. She picked and chose, assembled and combined and juxtaposed, with breathtaking skill. Her idea of a room was one where people looked well together, and they looked best of all if they happened to have been gathered there by Margaret Mead herself. Wealth, as such, did not tempt her. Mead could have been a very rich woman, could probably have been a millionaire, but she acquired only as much money and as many objects as she needed. What she did collect, insatiably, was people. "I never had enough companionship," she said of her childhood, and perhaps in spite of the staggering number of other lives she walked into, she never had enough companionship ever. Her search for new people and new ideas never stopped.

Nobody was indifferent to Margaret Mead. She was loving, scolding, ebullient, irksome, heroic, and at times vindictive. Like most great characters, she was inconsistent. As a young girl she acted like an old lady, and as one of the fabled elders of this century she could be a coquette and even, as one of her friends said, "a brat." She depended, both personally and professionally, on an ingenious and devoted corps of helpers; others put together the squares she knit for afghans, and many of the ideas she sketched for books. For an academic, she had a remarkably unreflective temperament. She was in such a frantic hurry that she rarely stopped moving, but much of the motion was passive: she exercised her body only when people urged her to.

She wasn't beautiful. More people probably wanted to sit on her lap than thought of her erotically. Nor, for all her quick and sometimes brilliant mind, was she a seminal thinker. What made her unique was her energy and her ability to make the most of everything that came her way, even hurricanes, volcanoes, and fractured bones. Because she was so chronically excited, she was exciting, and the excitement was contagious.

"That's Margaret Mead!" people would whisper when they saw her in an airport. When she came to an auditorium to give a lecture, it was as if the seas were parting. Once, in the middle 1970s, Mead was walking in Central Park, not far from her tower office in the American Museum of Natural History, clutching the fifty-one-inch forked thumb stick that in 1960 had become her trademark. A young man whom she never had seen before suddenly and extravagantly knelt at her feet to say, "Dr. Mead, *thank* you." He was thanking her, as many did who knew her only vaguely, from a distance, simply for being Margaret Mead. In so doing he helped to fulfill one of her earliest dreams: to be known for having made a difference in the world.

In all the career that began with Mead's work in Samoa, she focused, more intensely than any anthropologist ever had before her, on matters of gender and women and children. The average child interested her more than the average adult did, and the average woman more than the average man. Wherever she went in her nearly seventy-seven years she called attention to the ordinary, the previously unsung, and she sanctified the mundane. She was religious privately and evangelistic professionally, recruiting generations of newcomers to anthropology, which she transformed almost single-handedly from a cloistered thing into an object of national and global interest. She had no patience for pedants among her colleagues whose usual response, when confronted with a new train of thought, was, "But that's not my *field!*" Such detachment was not for her. The world was her field.

And the world was her family. Her sense of kinship began with the people who conceived her and bred her and saw her through childhood. Where it stopped was one of the secrets she kept to herself. "We are a family," she once said at a conference of anthropologists, "and we will *not* have differences of opinion before strangers." As a self-appointed *materfamilias*, she trusted that she knew what was good for people, often better than they might know for themselves. This well-meant help could seem high-handed.

Once Mead went so far as to warn a close friend not to have children, on grounds that she regarded the friend's husband as a latent homosexual, unsuited for fatherhood. "It was meddlesome of Margaret to tell me that," said the friend, who disregarded the advice and so relished being a parent that she only wished, forty years later, that she and her husband had raised several children instead of one, "but I forgave her."

People were always forgiving Margaret Mead. "I excused things in Margaret," said one of her friends, "that I'd never have excused in myself." She was excused because those whom she allowed to come close could see that for all her deep reserves of common sense, for all that she made the impossible seem accessible, she was just as vulnerable as anybody. Finally, she was a monumental woman, "one of those," as a friend said, who "came by and left their footprints," on a trail that led in more directions than most people would ever dream of going.

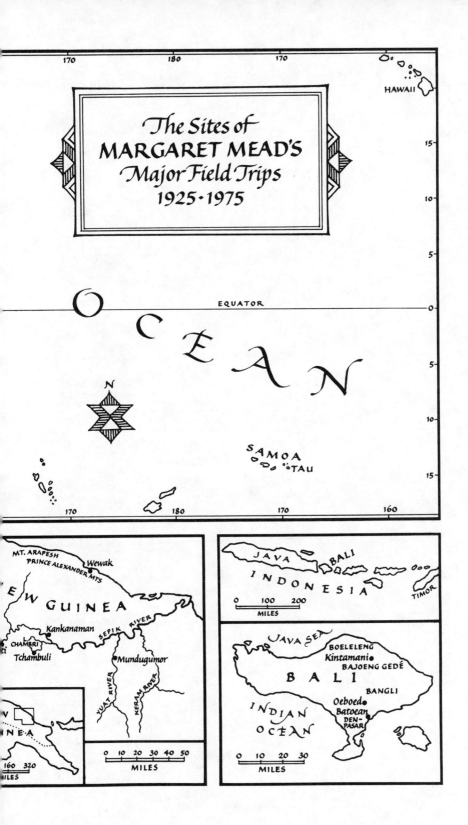

The Sites of
MARGARET MEAD'S
Major Field Trips
1925·1975

HAWAII

EQUATOR

OCEAN

N

SAMOA
TAU

MT. ARAPESH
PRINCE ALEXANDER MTS   Wewak

NEW GUINEA

Kankanaman   SEPIK RIVER

CHAMBRI
Tchambuli   Mundugumor

YUAT RIVER   KERAM RIVER

NEA

160   320
MILES

0 10 20 30 40 50
MILES

JAVA   BALI

INDONESIA   TIMOR

0   100   200
MILES

JAVA SEA
BOELELENG
Kintamani
BAJOENG GEDÉ

BALI

BANGLI

Oeboed
Batoean
DEN-
PASAR

INDIAN
OCEAN

0   10   20   30
MILES

PART ONE

It is not by the direct method of a scrupulous narration that the explorer of the past can hope to depict that singular epoch. If he is wise, he will adopt a subtler strategy. He will attack his subject in unexpected places; he will fall upon the flank, or the rear; he will shoot a sudden, revealing searchlight into obscure recesses, hitherto undivined. He will row out over that great ocean of material, and lower down into it, here and there, a little bucket, which will bring up to the light of day some characteristic specimen, from these far depths, to be examined with a careful curiosity.

—LYTTON STRACHEY
Eminent Victorians (1918)

CHAPTER ONE

"Like a Family of Refugees"

LORD KNOWS they meant well, though they didn't believe in the Lord. Margaret Mead's parents were rational, secular agnostics. "We're the kind of people who read Emerson," said Emily Fogg Mead, and by that she meant the essays, not the poems. They were also the kind of people who had mottoes. The motto of Emily's own father, a midwestern merchant, had been "Do Good Because It Is Right to Do Good." Emily and her husband, Edward Sherwood Mead, who taught at the Wharton School of Commerce of the University of Pennsylvania, had their failings: she could be snobbish, he could philander; but they still maintained as high-minded a household, or rather series of households, as could be found anywhere within a hundred-mile radius of his office in Philadelphia, just across from the university medical school's morgue.

Their children did not grow up with much feeling for what the Spanish call *querencia,* meaning that place in the ring where the bull feels safest from the matador. "In a sense," Mead recalled, "we were like a family of refugees, always a little at odds with and well in advance of the local customs." By the time she reached what would later be called junior-high-school age, she once reckoned, she had lived in sixty houses and eaten food prepared by a hundred and seven cooks. All this moving around was related to Professor Edward Mead's work, part of which was helping to establish extension branches of the university around the state.

Sometimes he moved his family with him; sometimes they spent intervals in places like Hammonton, New Jersey, where Emily Mead, whose spirit was as academic as her husband's, could do research with the families of Italian immigrants.* Hammonton, between Philadelphia

---

* Emily Mead arranged to have a fellowship at Bryn Mawr College in the years she brought up her children, so that she could continue her studies.

and Atlantic City, struck Emily's sister Fanny Fogg McMaster as a lack-luster town, built by uninspired architects, but Emily went there for the people, not the buildings. "She used to take me to weddings all over South Jersey," Mead remembered. "Most of the women were dabbing tears out of their eyes; my mother was always busy taking notes. She taught me not only how to go, but what to look for."

Whenever possible, the Meads chose villages like Holicong, Doyles-town, Buckingham, Lansdowne, and Swarthmore, where the four of their five children who survived infancy could breathe pure country air. So the children grew up inhaling wonderful air, but curiously lack-ing, in the opinion of Luther Cressman, in a sense of nature. Cressman, the first of Margaret's three husbands, met her family when she was six-teen, and came to know them well. If Margaret had had a sense of how things grow and develop, he reflected, "she wouldn't have had the feeling that she could create anything herself." (Or maybe, said some-one well acquainted with both Mead and Cressman, she was by tem-perament urban, and he was not.) Another thing Cressman thought her family lacked was a sense of fun. "Humor," he said, "wasn't exactly run-ning riot in that household. You know," he added after a bit more thought, "I don't think Margaret ever had an honest-to-God childhood."

Mead, in her seventies, had some astonishing early recollections. By the time she was four, she said, she had become "the pivotal family confidante"; her adored paternal grandmother, who lived with the fam-ily, would spend hours brushing young Margaret's remarkably lustrous, remarkably curly blond hair, confiding in her the while about the prob-lems and shortcomings of "poor Emily" and "poor Eddie," in such a way that Margaret sometimes had the confusing feeling that her parents were her children as much as she was theirs. At four, she said, "I was treated as a full person, whose opinions were solicited and treated seri-ously." By the time she was five she had already had "most of the experi-ences other people wait for until they are in college."*

Everyone kept assuring her, Mead wrote in her autobiography, that "there's no one like Margaret." When Margaret's brother and younger sisters came along their mother tried to document their early lives as faithfully as she had her firstborn's, but she had set an impossible stan-dard: thirteen notebooks were filled with accounts of Margaret's deeds as a baby and young child. Margaret, accordingly, grew up with two strong convictions: that being observed was wonderful, and that observing

---

* Well before Margaret knew what the words meant, she learned to say, "in one long difficult utterance: 'My-father-majored-in-economics-and-minored-in-sociology-and-my-mother-majored-in-sociology-and-minored-in-economics.' "

others, far from being anything to feel guilty about, was more wonderful still. She was excited when Woodrow Wilson was elected president in 1912, because she figured that since the Wilsons' summer place in Lavallette, New Jersey, had been right next door to the Meads' home the summer when she was two, the future president almost certainly had to have seen her.

Never did she have enough companionship. Her original family was large and hospitable and in many ways exemplary, but it wasn't enough for Margaret. Maybe no family could have been. It didn't give her a lot of what she needed, which was why Cressman thought she "kept on looking all her life for new mothers, to pick her up when she fell, as she did rather often." Total strangers tended to think of Mead as a mother, and she did her best to oblige them, but she still needed mothering, too, even very late in her life. She also needed, and kept finding, new fathers and brothers and sisters. She never stopped establishing new families, in every way she could think of, and she made a life work of studying the families of others. A big part of her genius was her way of making people feel connected, to her and to one another as well.

No child had ever been delivered before at the West Park Hospital at 46 North Thirty-ninth Street, in Philadelphia, when Margaret was born there on Monday, December 16, 1901. The day was cold; the thermometer never got above 26 degrees. A fierce storm had just stopped raging through all of Pennsylvania, and the papers said that at some points the Susquehanna River had risen twenty-seven feet above its low-water mark, leaving forty thousand people stranded. The United States Senate had just ratified the Panama Canal Treaty, which the *New York Times* called a "personal triumph" for forty-two-year-old Theodore Roosevelt, who in September, after William McKinley's assassination, had become the youngest president in American history.

Signor Guglielmo Marconi had just transmitted the first wireless message across the Atlantic Ocean to Newfoundland, from Cornwall, in southern England, where her subjects were still mourning the death, eleven months earlier, of Queen Victoria. The world had just completed what the *New-York Tribune* solemnly hailed as the "greatest century of recorded time." Rumors of smallpox frightened residents of London, but many terrors seemed tamable. A doctor in Pittsburgh thought he had found a cure for lockjaw. Adrenalin had just been identified. Viceroy Lord George Curzon had toured India expecting to find "wild tribes," but the people he encountered there seemed to him surprisingly civilized.

• •

Philadelphia, Lincoln Steffens reflected two years after Margaret Mead was born, was "the most American of our great cities," in that almost half of its residents were native children of native children, if not of native grandparents, and so were "citizens in the fullest sense, and not easily impressed with claims of inherited wealth." Quaker Philadelphia also had a solid tradition of self-teaching and of inner religion. Churches and public schools were regarded with a skepticism congenial to Margaret's parents when they moved to the city shortly after their wedding on June 1, 1900.

They came from another lively city, Emily's birthplace. They had met there, at the University of Chicago. He was there to work toward his doctorate in political economy. She had enrolled in the fall of 1894, to finish the undergraduate studies she had begun at Wellesley College, in Massachusetts. She had had to drop out of Wellesley when her father's financial reverses caused him to summon her to help out at his temporary headquarters in Cedar Rapids, Iowa.

After a year of drudgery in Cedar Rapids, helping with office and sales work, Emily found a job teaching. Her savings from that and other part-time work, supplemented by a scholarship, allowed her to go back to Chicago and enroll in the university; in the summer quarter of 1896, she met the handsome Mead, who had just graduated from DePauw University, in central Indiana. The first time he saw her on campus, a family story had it, Edward Sherwood Mead decided that Emily Fogg, who was two and a half years his senior, should become his wife.

Soon after they were married, Edward Mead's widowed mother, Martha Ramsay Mead, an eastern Ohioan who had no other children, decided she would make her home with him and his family. This prospect did not entirely please her daughter-in-law, who once told Margaret that her grandmother could "get interested in the most *ordinary* people!" Emily had exalted ideas about the human race but took a stern view of individuals who fell short of her standards. Grandma was more lenient, and more affectionate. Though the parents hovered approvingly over Margaret, and more anxiously over the younger children, they were not demonstrative.

Emily breast-fed Margaret for nine months, but, her daughter said, had "no gift for play, and very little for pleasure or comfort." Edward, on the rare occasions when he reached toward his children, did not have a tender touch. The only time he ever put Margaret's shoes on, the day her only brother was born, he stuffed them onto the wrong feet. Margaret grew up craving even more warmth than she got from her indulgent grandmother. "I loved the feel of her soft skin," she said years later, "but she never would let me give her an extra kiss when I said good night." Perhaps this was because the grandmother, who treated the child as a confidante, had come to regard her as an equal.

"It cannot be said that Sherwood Mead"—as some of his relatives called him—"was of much assistance to his wife," wrote his sister-in-law Fanny McMaster, "during the years when she gave up her interests and ambitions to take care of her family. He was away from home a great deal and absorbed in his own affairs," which reputedly involved other women.

"Father was always attracted to a much rougher sort of life than Mother thought," said Margaret, "and at the same time, he didn't want to be allowed to live it." Mead appreciated his wife's disdain for women who kept poodles and her yearning for houses "with rooms big enough for committees to meet in," but on occasion he felt stifled at home, and tried to escape. Once he tried to escape with a certain redhead, of whom Margaret learned only that he had met her "somewhere in the business world." Edward Mead's mother, learning this, declared that if her son left his wife and children, he would have to say goodbye to her, too. She loved her son, and cherished the rituals they had established: on his birthday, for example, she would always write him a letter, even if the two were sure to be sitting at the same table that evening. But she would not countenance infidelity, and so he stayed put, apparently deciding, as Margaret Mead would write, that "a woman who would ask a man with four children to desert them was a bad woman." So much for the redhead.

"There are only two things you can do as a parent," Mead once said: "Stay alive, and love each other." Her own parents stayed alive and together, but the strongest feeling in their household, she said, was a rule of absolute solidarity among women. The pattern in the families they came from, as in many others in America, was for charming, potentially caddish men, men who needed indulgence and forgiveness, to mate with stern, impressive women who took charge and took care. Sherwood Mead had been a prizewinning debater and a member of Phi Beta Kappa at DePauw, before graduate school; he was the author of five books and numerous articles, and played a big part in organizing the Wharton School. He was also shrewd. His students, as one of them remembered, were obliged to make notes directly in their copies of his textbook, so that the books could not be resold.

"He was the kind of father no kid could contend with," said the political scientist and writer Leo Rosten, who was married to Margaret's youngest sister, Priscilla. "He was an almost classic case of the person who could never come to terms with his own aggression. Instead of saying, 'Oh, damn it!' when something went wrong, he'd just smile that vulpine grin of his. He was a loner, a greatly spoiled only child, with no experience in any way of the real world. He knew facts and tables and statistics, but his humanness was lacking."

The cartoonist William Steig was also a Mead son-in-law, during the years he was married to Margaret's sister Elizabeth. Mead struck Steig as "a pain, a very repressed guy who ate peanuts and got shells all over the floor, while he sat around in a bowler hat reading Veblen." Luther Cressman remembered the Thorstein Veblen and the bowler, too: Mead, he said, would "read Veblen on the porch, with his feet up on the railing and a hat pushed back on his head, while his wife and his mother read his proofs. I respected his status at Wharton, but he always seemed pretty aloof to me."

Edward Mead, Margaret remembered, was "terribly afraid of violence, and terribly afraid something would happen to all of us. He wouldn't let us ride bicycles and he wouldn't let us ride horseback; he was everlastingly overprotective." She usually managed to escape this excessive solicitude, but her brother Richard did not. The boy's most obvious gift was a fine, true voice—he was a tenor when he grew up—but his father only grudgingly let him have music lessons. For years, his Aunt Fanny wrote, Richard tried ineffectually to escape from his father's dominating control. Surely it was easier to be Edward Mead's daughter—especially his first, whom he indulgently nicknamed "Punk"—than to be his only son.

There was never a question of singing lessons for Margaret, who wasn't musical at all, but when she was ten, "Dadda" did complain of her speaking voice, and urged her to try to soften it. If Richard cringed in quiet fear, she did not. When she was disgruntled, the whole world knew it. As a small child she had had a comforting blanket that was referred to as her "shawl," and when the shawl had been washed but was not yet dry enough to be returned to her, she would have what she called a "fit."

These "fits" of anger were frequent, but not lasting. Her childhood, Mead recalled, made her think of the story of the little girl who had been shut up in a closet by her mother, and screamed and screamed and screamed. Abruptly the screaming stopped. Alarmed by the sudden silence, the mother went into the closet to see what had happened.

"I spit on your hat and I spit on your shoes and I spit on your dress," said the child, "and now I'm waiting for more spit!" Margaret was also, by her own admission, a determined slammer of doors. When her father dismissed her from the table for such offenses as having a dirty neck, she made sure to bang all six of the doors between the dining room and her bedroom. Unobtrusiveness was never her style. In Hammonton, where blueberry bushes grew and a flock of chickens squawked outside the house, her Aunt Fanny once came to visit, and observed that her eldest niece "knew everything about the details of the house, and was a constant talker." One day, said the aunt, "some of the chickens were killed and eaten, and Margaret wept when they were brought to the table.

"Her softness of heart was very touching, until she made it plain that it wasn't the killing of the chickens that disturbed her, as the fact that she hadn't been told about it." All her life, wherever she went, she wanted to know everything that was going on, and hated being left out. Nearly seventy years later, revisiting the island of Bali, she was furious one morning to learn that her much younger companions had gone off, without telling her, on what one described as "a last-minute, late-night toot." She ought to have been invited.

Richard was born when Margaret was one and a half years old. When the third Mead child, Katherine, came along three years later, it was Margaret who named her and Margaret who particularly loved her. Soon after Katherine died, at the age of nine months, two more sisters followed, Elizabeth in 1909 and Priscilla in 1911. Elizabeth "was born screaming. She scratched her face horribly and she almost died, and she was very ill when she was about three months old," said Margaret. Still, Elizabeth's arrival so soon after Katherine's death gave Margaret her "abiding faith that what was lost would be found again . . . to this I trace a good deal of my optimism and tendency to put 'Acts of God' in the best light possible." The Law of Compensation, as her mother's hero Ralph Waldo Emerson put it, asked: "Will you gain nothing by the loss? Consider it well; there's no cheating nature."

At times the child Margaret was afraid she might be lost herself. In daydreams so vivid that she could evoke them five decades later, she imagined that robbers or gypsies might capture her, and hold her for just long enough so that she could learn "a whole series of new skills, like languages and painting, and then come home where the important thing would be recognition." She craved recognition all her life. It pleased her, at eleven, to realize that the men who were seated on cracker barrels, venturing comments on all who passed by the country store, most likely were commenting as much on her as on anyone else.

Her elaborate quest for renown, Leo Rosten thought, sprang from something not everybody realized: arrogant though she might seem, surrounded though she usually was with applause and praise, she never had enough recognition, enough affirmation. In a more evolved version of her capture daydream she imagined being taken away not in order to learn new skills but to teach skills she already had to someone else, "to train someone's else's child, who would later be recognized as someone only I could have trained, because no one else could have taught him just that set of things."

Her earliest memories, like most, were random and fragmentary: there was something about ruining a pair of red shoes in the snow at the age of two, something about claiming that a cut on her nose had come from a baby sister's fingernails, rather than from a forbidden penknife. Later she became aware of her grandmother's conviction that children should never have to sit still for more than an hour. What children were expected to do was keep learning, whatever subjects and from whatever teachers might be around. Much of the teaching in this family was done by the parents and the grandmother and any other *ad hoc* tutors who happened to catch their attention.

"Wherever we were living," Margaret said, "Mother would find someone who was a good craftsman to teach us . . . In Hammonton there was a woman who was a magnificent woodcarver, so I learned woodcarving." Elsewhere, for reasons just as coincidental, she studied carpentry, basketry, and how to make clay models. At the age of eight she learned to build a loom, "and so I understood the whole process of weaving. It was educational ideology, but at the period it was very unusual." Unlike many cerebral women who boast that they don't even know how to thread a needle, Margaret Mead carried her knitting with her in the forties, when her own daughter was small, and in the seventies, when her grandchild's generation came along.

Two years of kindergarten were all the official education she had until she reached the fourth grade, and then she went to school for only half-days. Her parents instructed Margaret's teachers to let her leave whenever she liked. Another constant daydream, she said, was "to find a group of contemporaries all of whom were my intellectual equals or superiors." This dream was not to be fulfilled for years, but she systematically made the best of whatever fellowship was available.

Her notion, when she entered a new classroom or any other new environment, was "to find my place in the constellation and find the people who would fit the different roles." Who, if anyone, would be the enemy? Who would need her protection? How did everybody else fit in? In 1980 Mary Catherine Bateson spoke in public of having told her own young daughter, "We don't *have* best friends in our family," but this family rule was apparently not made until after Margaret's childhood. Entering a new classroom, Margaret was aware that "You had to have a best friend, and if the person who was around wasn't very interesting, you turned them into a best friend all the same." She also saw the necessity of attaching herself to teachers, whoever they might be, "and then I romanticized them, though in retrospect they weren't much. I learned Latin from a teacher who had never passed Virgil, and whom I tried to have a crush on because I knew this was the appropriate and rewarding attitude toward one's teachers. It wasn't until I got to Franz Boas"—the celebrated anthropologist who taught her in college and became her mentor—"that I really had a teacher who elicited my total respect, so that I felt he could give me the ground under my feet." Meanwhile, she devoted herself to whoever was at hand.

Since the favorite poet of her fourth-grade teacher, Miss Rinehart, happened to be James Whitcomb Riley, Riley automatically became the favorite poet of Margaret Mead, who decades later, with considerable feeling, could give full recitations of "Little Orphant Annie." She read a great deal. Every December 16, she once told an interviewer, she was given two books as birthday presents: one serious and one frivolous. She read all of Dickens, Scott, George Eliot and Jane Austen, and although Horatio Alger stories and the "Grammar School Boys" series were forbidden, she read them, too, "to study what was wrong with the style."

Margaret could recite all the names of the long string of cooks who had worked for her family, most of whom she later said were "refugees from wretched marriages." This rapid turnover in household help was only partly a consequence of the Meads' uncommonly frequent moves. The mistress of the house, her daughter said, believed in treating servants equitably, "but she was so busy with other things that she paid little attention to the difference between one servant and another."

Work, for Emily as for her eldest daughter, mattered more than anything. Most of the work her mother did fell far short of her early ambitions. Margaret lamented this in a verse, titled "Portrait," that she wrote and dedicated to Emily which was reprinted in a family history.*

* She has a lady's hands, but marred
  By other than a lady's work;
  All intricately traced and scarred

Margaret felt protective as a child toward her mother, and later toward the rest of the world, but she needed protecting, too, especially, as Luther Cressman said, when, metaphorically and otherwise, she fell. She was not so much given to falling down, at least not literally, around the time when she was eleven. Eleven, she often implied in her later years, was her favorite age, her secret, true, spiritual age all her life. "I suppose that intellectually and emotionally I'm my own real age," she remarked when she was well into her middle seventies, "and I'm aware of the extra weight I've added, but I feel as light on my feet now as I did at eleven, and I always have an impulse to jump up and sit on desks like a preadolescent."

Eleven was the age when she menstruated, grew breasts, and began imagining what names she might give her children. She longed at eleven for lace petticoats, she said, but at the same time was determined to keep on wearing bloomers. Bloomers were the proper costume "for climbing trees like a boy, and to permit me to run two miles to a fire and climb the fences." For baseball games she also wore a corset, "one of those cast-iron ones that needed to be buttoned up with button-hooks," so that she could keep on playing after her breasts developed.

She had no special skills as an athlete, but taking charge of games delighted her. In games, one of her playmates testified, she was "a very *affirmative* child." As a boy the literary critic John Hutchens belonged to a gang of children who played with the Meads when they came to visit their Aunt Fanny in the woods west of Chicago. He remembered a particular afternoon of games, "when the young Miss Mead, presiding . . . corrected a small playmate's departure from the rules by rapping him on the head with a baseball bat. The indentation is still there, greatly cherished by this recipient, much as an aging knight might value the memory of Queen Elizabeth I tapping him on the shoulder with a sword. Come to think of it, that might have been the game." His own

---

By little tasks she will not shirk.
Her hair is soft and would have curled
    Did she not bind it up so tight.
She says she does so lest it fall
    Untidily in far-off night.
Her eyes are never still, but flit
    O'er each detail of her ordered room.
To find some new arrangement they
    Relentlessly pierce the candle gloom.
Her voice complaining still is sweet:
    "You never know me as I am,
I only reach the bread and meat,
    I've never time to add the jam."

children, Hutchens said, referred to the protrusion on the back of his skull as the "Margaret Mead Memorial Bump." Mead denied this incident, when she was reminded of it at age sixty-one, but Hutchens insisted it had happened.

For most of Margaret's childhood she was restless and impatient. Not enough happened, in the quiet villages where the Meads lived, to suit her. A contemporary, raised on a New Jersey farm, recalled of her similar childhood that it was "secure, ordered, endless. . . . We did not see many strangers. The voices we heard were few and the faces we saw did not seem to change. Life had a familiar and reassuring rhythm. We did not compare ourselves to others. There was no sense of competition. We just accepted things . . . we knew what to expect and what was expected of us." But Margaret Mead, at eleven as at all other ages, had no need for so heavy a dose of serenity.

Religion would supply some of the excitement she longed for, and also some of the comfort. When Margaret was nine and a half, on May 14 in 1911, she had taken a notebook and written in it, "My name is Margaret Meade*. . . . I have decided to write a diary. But I'm not sure that I won't miss days some times, For I am not very regalar." A year and a half later, four days before her eleventh birthday, she wrote: "Today has been one of the happiest days of my life. I was Baptized this afternoon. Aunt Isobel and Miss Lucia were my Godmothers. I had no godfathers. . . ." Miss Lucia, who remained Margaret's friend all her life, was the daughter of an Anglican clergyman. "Miss Lucia kept a cow," Margaret remembered many years later, "and was the equivalent of a minister's wife. She ran the parish, and she was the kind of person I thought I'd like to be. I needed an anchorage, and the whole idea of a clergyman's daughter seemed ethically appropriate behavior, so I decided I would become an Episcopalian, too."

This decision did not delight Margaret's parents, who scarcely knew, she said, "how to deal with a child who insisted on fasting during Lent. But then agnostics never know what to do with post-agnostics." The Meads' agnosticism ran deep: an uncle had been read out of the Unitarian church for heresy, and Emily Fogg Mead had turned from Unitarianism to Ethical Culture. Margaret's maternal grandfather, the one whose creed was "Do Good Because It Is Right to Do Good," had no need, the Fogg family history said, "for reflection or doubt as to what was right; he was *sure* of what was right."

By the age of ten Margaret had meticulously divided her room

* The family occasionally spelled the name with an added "e" in Mead's early life and before.

"into a pagan half and a Christian half; the pagan half held the Aurora by Guido Reni and a small replica of the Venus de Milo for which I had saved my allowance for a whole winter." In the Christian half were "madonnas, a beautiful carved old prie dieux [sic] bought by accident at an auction, and a small clay jar made from earth from the Holy Land. Around the top were rotogravure reproductions of the murals in the State Capitol depicting the religious sects of Pennsylvania." What she sought in joining the church, she later explained, was not so much a creed as a set of rituals to counterbalance what she called her mother's "overcognitive approach to religion. . . . What I wanted was a form of religion that gave expression to an already existing faith."

Edward Mead treated his firstborn child's baptism with his customary sarcasm. As he galloped the carriage horse through the tollgate taking his family to the ceremony, he yelled, "We're going to *church!*" as if they were rushing to an emergency. Later, when Margaret misbehaved or displeased him, he threatened to have her "unbaptized." She knew this was a joke, of sorts, but it did not amuse her. She took her religion very seriously, and through it found what probably was her first romance. On April 27, 1913, she wrote in her diary, "My highest hope, and greatest wish, has been gratified. I have been to Ham [Hammonton, presumably] and seen Willie. Although I had not seen him for over 2 years. Still, I was no [sic] mistaken in him. He is still the dearest boy in the world to me and always will be . . . I can't express how happy I was to see him kneeling there, in his white cotton and black surplus [sic]. . . .

"I suppose I can't wear a veil when I am confirmed," she wrote in the diary later, "as this church is low Episcopal . . . Willie said it was because of my being Baptised that he was Confirmed, that is, it made him begin to think of those Holy things . . . I had a long talk with Miss Lucia the other day. The more I see of her, the more I love her . . . I've just been reading how the purpose of changing the name of the Protestant Episcopal Church to the American Catholic Church was defeated. I think that's perfectly mean. . . ."

Margaret's handwriting slanted conventionally to the right when she made these early entries in her journal, but around the time she was twelve it changed, and became more vertical. In 1948, when she was thinking of using graphology as a form of personality test, she showed samples of her own early handwriting to an expert, who was convinced that something important had happened to her at the age of twelve. Mead could not quite remember, and in a letter signed "Very lovingly" wrote to ask her godmother whether the important event could have been the breaking of Miss Lucia's engagement. "Can you yourself produce the date without too much uncomfortable introspection? I remember standing in front of the Gardy's house and being very angry because the sunset was still very beautiful."

Elsewhere in her childhood diary Margaret wrote: "I think I will dramitize Castle Blair for us to give [this] summer. If I don't there will be plenty of other things we can give, one of them is the tableau of the Joppa Gate in Jerusilume from Ben Hur." All her life Mead was an indifferent speller and a great enthusiast of pageants. In her fourteenth summer she helped her mother plan a big family Shakespeare festival, in which the children sang madrigals and acted out the casket scene from *The Merchant of Venice*.

She also tended to the eighteen lamps around the family's house in Buckingham, learned to arrange flowers, and tried to cheer her mother, who was suffering postpartum depression after the birth of her fifth and last child. This pretty and exceptionally solemn girl later took the middle name "Ann" so that her initials would justify the nickname "Pam" (and still later said she preferred her original name after all). She was by all accounts the best-looking of the Mead girls but, as Margaret once said, the least energetic: she had rickets as a baby and did not walk until she was nearly two years old.

Priscilla's older sister Elizabeth, later nicknamed Liza, was to become a painter. She had always been "the least like everyone else in the family. From early childhood she had extreme mood swings—everything was either wonderful or terrible." Madeline Rosten Lee, one of Priscilla's three children, recounted a family myth which held that "there had to be a smart daughter and a pretty one, and terrible things happened to the pretty ones." Margaret, obviously the smart one, struck someone else who knew her well as "always being frightened by women who were beautiful and immaculate, like Pam, and always being protective toward temperamental artists, like Liza."

In 1916, Fanny McMaster came to visit her sister's family in Holicong, Pennsylvania, and found her eldest niece "a girl of fourteen, with dresses to her ankles. Skirts had just gone up to the knee in New York, and the child's satisfaction in being 'grown-up' [apparently she did not know of the changed fashion] was almost pathetic." That spring Margaret and three classmates graduated from Buckingham Friends' School—"the room was tastefully decorated for the occasion," according to the local newspaper—and the family moved to Doylestown, where Margaret edited the magazine section of the highly regarded, but for her unchallenging, *Intelligencer*. Impatient to put childhood behind her, she welcomed any distractions.

When the Great War broke out, Margaret threw her energies into another pageant, at Doylestown High School. She made five posters, which illustrated the importance of the themes of Internationalism, Womanhood, Childhood, Vision, and Religion—themes that would preoccupy her, as it happened, all the rest of her life. In an article called "The War in Posters" she wrote, "Before the face of this war, skepticism, atheism, agnosticism all are giving way."*

Margaret also gave a speech in which she said, "Unless the setting star of Germany rose sufficiently above the horizon to enable her to extend a helping hand to Austria, the consequences are too terrible to contemplate." (Her father told her she had "a prize mixed metaphor there, sister, but we'll let it go.") The papers were full of war news. On June 2, 1917, the 1,036th day of the Great War, U-boats were rumored to have been seen off Sandy Hook, New Jersey.

On the evening of that day, Margaret first met Luther Sheeleigh Cressman, a twenty-year-old who had spent three years studying classics at Pennsylvania State College. He had come to Doylestown that weekend to see his older brother George, a science teacher at the high school. George had been invited to speak at the high-school commencement, and also to the Meads' house for dinner. His visiting brother, who stood five feet ten and had coppery red hair and blue eyes, was invited, too. These Cressman boys, Margaret learned, had four more brothers and an Uncle Mark, a Lutheran minister, who had suggested that "Lutie," as his nephew was called, might also choose to become a clergyman. Lutie expressed interest.

The six Cressman brothers had been raised on a farm outside the village of Pughtown, about forty miles from Doylestown. Their father was a country doctor who made house calls and did not badger his patients to pay him when they were short of cash. The Cressmans, unlike the Meads, sent their children to school. The Cressmans did what society expected of them, and with distinction. His childhood, as Luther recalled it, was idyllic and archetypally American. Dr. Cressman said of his wife Florence that she was "as strong as an oak." A noble giant oak

* She went on to wonder: "What have we if we do not kneel and pray, pray with simple faith of this baby at her mother's knee:

'Now I lay me down to sleep
I pray the Lord my soul to keep
God bless my brother gone to War
Across the seas to France so far.
O may his fight for liberty,
Save millions more than little me,
From crual [sic] fate or ruthless blast,
And bring him safely home at last.' "

had arched over the brick house where the boys grew up. When this house burned in April 1917, Luther had been summoned home from the university to run the farm. With the war on and farm workers hard to find, he was not academically penalized. In the fall he could go back and finish his classics studies.

Luther had been pleased to be told, after a physical examination, that he was "just about right." Margaret liked his "precise physical skills and . . . sensitivity to other human beings," traits conspicuously absent in her father. That summer they corresponded, and the next autumn, when Margaret was in her final year at Doylestown High and Luther in his final year at Penn State, they met again. Margaret and another girl, the daughter of a sheriff, were invited to visit the Cressmans at their newly rented large old farmhouse half a mile from Pughtown. The sheriff's daughter, Luther remembered long afterward, was "full of fun and laughter, a perfect foil for Margaret." Since her father's sense of humor was sarcastic, and her mother's nonexistent, Margaret was not much accustomed to levity. But her spirit attracted Luther all the same.

At Christmastime Margaret visited the Cressmans again. Compared with most people she knew, the Cressman boys seemed glamorous. Besides, they might at any moment be shipped off, who knew where, to fight for their country. Undercurrents of war gave the festive weekend an air of urgency. One night Luther and Margaret went ice skating, arm in arm, and he told her the whole story of *Antigone*, which he had been reading in Greek. Another evening, Luther remembered, the young pair "bundled against the cold and went for a walk. The road had been ploughed for sleighs and the snow lay in long high rows on each side. It was bitter cold with no light but that from brilliant stars and some reflection from the snow. We had walked perhaps a quarter mile before we turned to come back to the house.

"We had not been talking much, but as we walked some subtle communication had been going on between us. We stopped, turned facing each other, and when I told her I loved her she replied, 'I love you, too.' She lifted her veil, worn against the cold, and our words were sealed with our kiss. We told no one of our engagement." Margaret Mead, who eleven years later would be known throughout the world for writing about adolescence, saw to it that Christmastime, when she was just sixteen, that she herself would sidestep a lot of the pain most Western people took to be part of growing up.

"I never had to live through that period of being rejected by a man," she said years later. "If you had a man, you weren't continually thinking about them. The insight I had gave me a kind of equilibrium." Her engagement, she said, was "very comfortable and pleasant; it kept me from worrying about men or dates." No broken hearts, no hurt feelings, no uncertainty. She had Luther, but since Luther, as it turned out, would not be around very much, she would not need to discover whatever his shortcomings might be, nor he hers.

Measles prevented Margaret from attending Luther's graduation from Penn State in the spring of 1918. The following August, before Luther went off to the Field Artillery Officers' Training Camp in Fort Taylor, Kentucky, Margaret met him in Philadelphia and went with him to lunch at her mother's club. Next they proceeded to the station from which a train took him south toward all he was to see of the war. As his train departed, Luther looked out the window and saw Margaret walking up the exit ramp toward the street. She did not look back.

At Fort Taylor, just after the Armistice, Luther literally won his spurs and got his commission. Although he missed the war, he had a close brush with the Spanish influenza pandemic. One beautiful autumn Saturday afternoon one of his campmates caught the flu, and by Monday morning "the whole siding was full of coffins. Doctors came up and down and looked into our eyes." Luther's blue eyes showed no signs of disease; he was later discharged with papers that read, "Remarks: Sharpshooter, Sergeant. Service: honest and faithful." Margaret already knew about his being a sharpshooter; he had given her his Penn State medal, which proved that he could fire a Springfield rifle five hundred yards from a prone position. He had also given her his Phi Kappa Phi pin, but later he noticed that she was not wearing either one. "She lost them both, damn her hide," Cressman said, with anger still in his voice sixty years later.

The engagement continued. Margaret had a suggestion about Luther's career as a minister: her Episcopal Church might suit him better than the Lutheran faith of his own childhood. An Army chaplain friend helped him make this change, and in the fall of 1919 he enrolled for the Michaelmas Term at General Theological Seminary, in New York City. As he did so, Margaret, who had hoped to go east to Wellesley College, as her mother had before her, instead headed west for the only campus her father would consent to send her to.

CHAPTER TWO

"Now We're All Bobbed!"

ALTHOUGH DEPAUW UNIVERSITY had not been her first choice, Margaret could hardly wait to get there. Arriving on the central Indiana campus in the fall of 1919, she was eager to find the professors and classes she was sure would stretch her mind, and the new friends who would bedazzle her soul. It never occurred to her that she, who was so solicitous about Richard and Elizabeth and Priscilla, who as a small girl had felt like her own parents' mother, might be found unsuitable for sisterhood.

Rushing parties, at which Greek-letter fraternities and sororities look over possible new members, have traditionally been about as relaxing for their guests as dentists' waiting rooms. The Iota chapter of Kappa Kappa Gamma, however, had hinted an interest in pledging the freshman Margaret Mead. She went confidently to their party wearing an "unusual" dress, as she called it, a dress she had designed herself to suggest a wheat field abloom with poppies. Too late she found out that the dress was all wrong in the eyes of the Kappas, and that her Philadelphia accent sounded stuffy and ridiculous.

"I found the whole evening strangely confusing," Mead wrote later. "I could not know, of course, that everyone had been given the signal that inviting me had been a mistake." And so the curlylocked, golden-haired firstborn of Sherwood and Emily, beloved of her doting grandmother, was suddenly and bewilderingly a pariah. What they had said of her at home proved true here, too: in all DePauw, apparently, there was no one like Margaret.

From home her brother wrote that he hoped Margaret could make the sororities "run after you instead of not want you," and in due course they did, but first Margaret had "to realize the full implications of what it meant to be an unpledged freshman in a college where everything was organized around the fraternities and sororities," especially a college whose main aim seemed to be to turn out worthy Rotarians and garden club members. Had the Kappas foreseen what renown this funny, frumpy little easterner might one day reflect back on them, they might have gritted their teeth and invited Margaret, odd dress and all, to become a member. But it is probably just as well that Margaret Mead was not taught the secret Kappa handshake and the secret Kappa songs, and given a key-shaped Kappa pin to wear above her heart. If she had worn that key, she might not later have felt the need to unlock so many doors and decode so many signals.

But her year at DePauw was not a total loss. True to her custom, Margaret set about picking a best friend, this time an upperclasswoman named Katharine Rothenberger. Katharine was also new to DePauw that fall, having transferred as a junior from Wittenberg, a Lutheran college in Ohio. She came from the Indiana town of Syracuse, where her father was the only undertaker. She and Margaret were both assigned to a dormitory called Mansfield, "where nobody else paid any attention to Margaret," Katharine said, "except for a chaperone named Sophia M. Steese, a stern, straight-backed woman who made all toe the line and who openly disliked Margaret because she couldn't climb a rope or stand up straight."

"She was sweet and bright and quick," Rothenberger said of her new friend, "but so lonely, so lost, and she was different. She appeared to know nothing of the Middle West, and although some of her clothes were striking, made of handkerchief linen and that sort of thing, she didn't fit in. But I could tell that there was a lot there that other people weren't seeing.

"She tried. She went to the Methodist church, because DePauw was a Methodist school, but she would also go to Lutheran communion with me, which she was much stricter about than I was; she'd be careful not to eat or drink before we went. And every night she'd kneel by her bed and say her prayers." Gradually Mead found a few other friends. "There were five of us oddballs," said Rothenberger, "and we formed a little band we called 'The Minority': there were a Negro, a Catholic, Margaret an Episcopalian, I a Lutheran, and David Lilienthal, the only Jew on campus."

In her liberal arts classes Margaret also attached herself to some of the university's more compelling professors, one of whom recalled her as "*that* Mead," and wished aloud that she had stayed at DePauw. Her industry, more than her intelligence, was what most struck her new best friend. "Maybe some of the rest of us had the brains Margaret had," said Rothenberger, "but she knew how to use them. She was too bright, too much ahead, which is one reason the others didn't take to her." All the same, she slowly won campus-wide attention, and proved herself to be a born politician. She campaigned to get Katharine Rothenberger elected vice president of the student body, the first girl ever to hold that office. This campaign, Mead later said, taught her "a few low-level political tricks," among them devising slogans along the lines of: "Wouldn't you rather vote for a nonsorority girl with a knack for organization than for an Alpha Phi?"

Katharine, who later accepted an invitation to pledge Kappa Alpha Theta, was grateful for her campaign manager's cleverness. The two friends, however, did not always agree. They argued about such diverse matters as the shape of Indiana barns, "which Margaret thought were awful, just boxes," and coal strikes in Pennsylvania: "Pennsylvania seemed far away to me; I didn't see how a coal strike there could affect us, but she insisted it would and said, 'You should be concerned!' "

Margaret, in turn, needed to be scolded when she said to Katharine, "I don't see how a *janitor's* daughter could live in the same dormitory with *us!*" Still, the friendship deepened with Margaret's other triumph in her year at DePauw. For the annual May Day pageant she wrote both the words and the music, and cast herself as queen and Katharine as king. Emily Mead came from Philadelphia to see her daughter's show, for which both girls wore lavender. Katharine's mother made her a beautiful suit with a lavender velvet ruff; Margaret wore a lavender dress with a long, full skirt, and put up her hair. Margaret also wrote and planned the winning interclass vaudeville stunt, "The Great God Jupiter Versus the Great God Jazz," which included parodies on "Jada, Jada" and "Old Gray Mare": the final line was "Old Mount Olympus ain't what it used to be, before jazz got there." By this time the Kappas, and other sororities that originally had not even considered bidding Margaret Mead, were having strong second thoughts, but it was too late.

Even though she emerged from social isolation, Margaret increasingly wondered what she was doing at DePauw. It was time to remind her father of his promise to let her transfer to the East after she gave his college a year's try. "Wellesley, where her mother had gone, was probably too expensive," Rothenberger said. "I do remember her talking about Barnard; she liked what she had heard of Dean Gildersleeve, though I believe Margaret was later a thorn in the Dean's flesh when she . . . headed some leftist group."

So the choice was Barnard. Luther Cressman was in New York

City too but the college was more of a lure. "She wasn't madly in love with Luther," so far as Rothenberger could tell, "but she figured she ought to marry someone, and he was the one she was going to marry, and that was that. Her idea was that first she would be a minister's wife, and then a college executive. She thought I ought to be a college executive, too, and that I ought to be more ambitious, but I came from people who didn't have the reach." Rothenberger, who became a history teacher, added, "I minded terribly when Margaret left for New York, but I went to visit her, and she came back to visit me, and we kept in touch all the rest of our lives."

Although Margaret had composed the music as well as the words for the pageant at DePauw, she never claimed she could sing. She admitted, in fact, to a tin ear, which nobody disputed who ever shared a church hymnal with her. (Her composer friend Colin McPhee years later confessed he had taken "malicious pleasure" in her pitiful efforts to answer musical questions she was asked on a radio quiz program.) Nevertheless, she must have done her lusty best, arriving at Barnard in the fall of 1920, to join in a ceremonial song called "Just Up the Banks of the Hudson." The fabled and mighty Hudson, bordering Barnard's campus, and the fabled and mighty city below and all around the college, were much more to Margaret's taste than what she had left behind in Indiana.

A city, as she would write in her final book, *World Enough*, is "A place where there is no need to wait for next week to get the answer to a question, to taste the food of any country, to find new voices to listen to and familiar ones to listen to again. It is that place where one need never be bored, where there is always the possibility of a new encounter that may change one's life . . . where friendships are matters of choice, where the shortest walk can be an experience of surprises and delight."

It is unlikely that Margaret suffered homesickness for Greencastle or for the Pennsylvania and New Jersey villages where she had spent her childhood. The air at Columbia and Barnard when Margaret Mead arrived was exhilarating and purposeful. The war was over and the Wall Street crash and the Depression were too far ahead to imagine. "Those of us in the classes of the twenties," said one of Mead's contemporaries, "never knew that the world was not our oyster. When the crash came, we took it in our stride. The classes of the thirties were quite different." One of Mead's distinguished Barnard contemporaries was Helen Gahagan, who later became a successful actress, married the actor Melvyn Douglas, was elected to Congress, and was slandered as a Communist by Richard M. Nixon, who defeated her for the U.S. Senate in 1950. The Barnard campus in the early 1920s, Douglas wrote, "suited my thirst for drama perfectly." Margaret and her college mates, many of whom lived into their eighties with an energy envied by people half their age, first met in a time of uncommon optimism and a high degree of postwar intellectual ferment.

New Yorkers in the famous twenties paid a nickel to ride the subway to Brooklyn or the ferry to Staten Island, which Edna St. Vincent Millay extolled in one of her verses, "We were very tired, we were very merry—we had gone back and forth all night on the ferry." Many of Margaret's classmates were tired and merry from all-night ferry rides, from dancing the tango and the Charleston, from reading the *Nation* and the *Mercury* and listening to jazz. It was the age of jazz and of the flapper, so called because unbuckled galoshes, like unfastened raccoon coats, tended to flap. The ideal woman of the 1920s was, as Alison Lurie wrote in *The Language of Clothes*, "a daring, even naughty tomboy. The 'flapper' of the 1920s was high-spirited, flirtatious and often reckless in her search for fun and thrills."

The most convincing flapper among Margaret's new friends was Agnes McCall, known as "Bunny," who said things like "I feel so low I have to reach up to shake hands with a snake," and wore a short, elegant red dress with matching stockings. Once Bunny returned from a Yale weekend with some souvenir gin bottles. These bottles were discovered, in the apartment Bunny and Margaret shared with some others, at 606 West 116th Street, by Helen P. Abbott of the Barnard administration, who had stopped there as she gave a tour of the campus to a prospective student's parents. "These girls," Abbott was heard to sputter to the parents, "are a mental and moral muss!"

Margaret Mead enjoyed herself, but nobody mistook her for a flapper. She struck one classmate as "plain, very Yankee, very mature." "She was a very unsophisticated girl without much means," another classmate remembered, "who wore a dark blue skirt with a sort of middy, and a black dress for teas and social events." She also wore her glasses, everywhere she went. When dances were scheduled she busied herself arranging dates between her classmates and Luther's fellow seminarians. "I didn't take my glasses off to look prettier, because it was more important to see people on the other side of the dance floor, keep an eye on people I had brought to the dance. There was always a choice between keeping your glasses on and relating to what happened, or else taking them off."

Bespectacled Margaret waited a long time before bobbing her own

hair, pinning it up meanwhile as she had for years in what were sometimes called "cootie garages," soft wire forms around which long hair
could be rolled. When she finally yielded to the great fashion of the
day that inspired F. Scott Fitzgerald's story "Bernice Bobs Her Hair,"
her classmate Pelham Korteheuer noted in her own diary: "Now
we're *all* bobbed!" adding that the barber had wept "when Margaret's
beautiful wavy golden curls were cut off." Hair was an emotionally
loaded subject: a man friend of Korteheuer's advised her that she had
"lost all her looks" when she had her hair bobbed, and the mother of
another classmate, at first sight of her newly shorn daughter, grew
hysterical.

Most of that bobbed hair was, to use a phrase popular decades later,
squeaky clean. "I seem to remember Margaret and girls in her apartment running around all the time with their heads all foamy from
shampoo, in skirts that showed their bottoms," one classmate said.
Skirt lengths varied. Hobble skirts, briefly in vogue, were "so tight that
you were lucky if you could get into a bus with them"; other skirts were
daringly short.

Dramatic costumes of one sort or another abounded on campus.
Virginia Crocheron Gildersleeve, Barnard's imposing dean and professor of English, usually went everywhere in her cap and gown, and so did
some of the faculty. In the spring many girls who were practicing for
the famous Barnard tradition, the "Greek Games," went around im-
personating horses and discus throwers and Periclean dancers. "But
Margaret and I were kind of far out," said one of her classmates. "We
wouldn't be caught dead in the Greek Games, and how we sneered at
all those girls getting together in the gym—we felt that we were above
that sort of thing."

Mead made herself conspicuous in other ways. When a classmate
exclaimed, "You *work* so hard!" Margaret's reply was: "If you'd been
brought up in my family, you would, too." The specter of her family
was always with Margaret. She knew how scandalized her mother would
be to hear that she had used the word "ain't" on a picket line. The
daughter of teachers, Margaret was determined to do them credit. At
examination time, when most girls strode into exam rooms with a full
fountain pen, she went in with a full ink bottle. Rarely, in any context, was she at a loss for words. "She gave off sparks," remembered a
Mead classmate. "Oh yes, she was sparkly." But by most accounts another student in Margaret's group sparkled even more brilliantly. Léonie Adams had her poetry anthologized when she was still an undergraduate. Léonie Adams got all-A report cards, one of which was
displayed in 606 on the joking premise that it was "typical."

Apartment 21, at 606 West 116th Street, was the first Barnard home for Léonie, Margaret, Bunny, Pelham Korteheuer, Deborah Kaplan, and several other young women, most of whom over the years came to be known as "Ash Can Cats." They got that name from a celebrated Mississippi-born drama teacher, Minor Latham, for whom Barnard's theater was later named. Miss Latham, whose classes were almost a cult for the residents of 606 and certain others, once remarked in her thick drawl to Léonie Adams, "You girls who sit up all night readin' poetry come to class lookin' like Ash Can Cats!"

The name stuck, and it rang with clout. "As soon as I met the Ash Can Cats, it was goodbye to everyone else," Pelham Korteheuer said. "My mother didn't have such a good impression of them, though. When she saw that apartment for the first time she said, 'They aren't very tidy girls; I saw a couple of brushes with hair in them!' But who cared about things like that? When I saw how special Margaret and Léonie and the others were, I was thrilled at the idea of being with them. Only much later did I learn that I might have been a bit damaged by trying to measure up to the excessively high standards of the Ash Can Cats."

The Ash Can Cats were a unique and for the most part an intelligent group. Belonging was a privilege, but a rather amorphous one; "probably at any one point there would not have been agreement about who was and who was not an Ash Can Cat," Louise Rosenblatt said sixty years later. "The group crystalized when we continued to keep seeing one another after my graduation in 1925." As undergraduates, the Ash Can Cats all had other friends and other ties, and their heads were crowded with ideas, jargon, and code words. Their street address, the occupants of 606 West 116th Street were amused to discover, was known as the number of a drug used to treat syphilis.

It was in this period of her life, Margaret recalled, that she "began thinking," in the lofty way undergraduates have of styling their thoughts, "in Jungian terms. I was at that point supposed to be an 'intuitive introvert,' which everybody wanted to be because that was what Jung admired most. And we decided that Luther was a 'sensation extrovert.' . . . He would go along, walk along the street and feel the heat of the sun and the pavement under his feet and say, 'I don't see how you and Léonie live. The rate at which things are going on in your heads all the time! It just tires me to think about it!' That was his reaction to our reports of what we had thought of in the same period of time." The quickness of Mead's mind, as she was first to admit, amazed those around her all her life.

"One of the things that's hard on my secretaries," she said much later, "is that if somebody makes a mistake, I immediately, within thirty seconds, see all the possible consequences of it—how an unanswered letter, or whatever else it might be, could lead to wrecked institutions, sunk ships, dead people." At 606 Margaret had classmates instead of secretaries, though the Ash Can Cats were to impress some observers as the first of what would later be called her "groupies." She confided to her friend Deborah Kaplan the three rules she had formulated for getting along with people: 1) be useful to them; 2) be amusing for them; and 3) build them up in their own estimation. Margaret's strongest flair was for the third of these rules.

"Even though she came here as a sophomore, not knowing a soul," Deborah Kaplan remembered, "Margaret immediately started mothering everybody." She and Léonie Adams agreed that they were first drawn together because of the maternal concern each felt for her younger brothers and sisters. Perhaps so special a bond developed between them because, as Adams speculated, "Having mothered everybody else, we needed mothering ourselves, and mothered each other."

One of the friendships Margaret formed was with the mother of another new student,* not an Ash Can Cat, who had come from the far west with her daughter to act as her chaperone. Margaret often visited this pair in their apartment, also on West 116th Street, and apparently felt more attracted to the older woman. "Margaret fell for my mother, and my mother in turn admired her very much, and thought her a brilliant girl, which in fact she was," said this classmate. "Margaret and I were both transfer students; we made friends when we took the same economics class; we were drawn together because we both were 'brains,' but a brain wasn't all I was—my fiancé had followed me east, which was why my mother came to chaperone me, and my libido was bursting. Margaret's didn't seem to be. She and I drifted apart the next year, when I started getting much more interested in sleeping with men and in seeing the world than in the economic theory of dialectical socialism."

Margaret and Léonie gathered most of those around them into an unofficial, de facto "family," but Léonie took exception to the claim Mead made in *Blackberry Winter*, nearly fifty years later, that this particular kinship system was her own "invention." The original idea for this "family," Léonie Adams said in a Connecticut nursing home on the eve of 1981, "came from the co-op, from a group of girls who had lived together in a cooperative dormitory before Margaret ever came to Barnard. We had thought of one of the members, from the class of 1918, as the 'father,' because she was the least determined.

* Who has asked not to be named.

"Margaret could never accept the fact that this 'family' had existed before she came along. When I told her that it had, she was too taken aback to acknowledge that I might be right." As soon as Margaret was part of the group, apparently, she took control and decided who belonged and who did not, even after her undergraduate years. A younger student named Eleanor Rosenberg joined this same "family" in 1925, after Margaret had graduated, but still by Margaret's decree. "Only Margaret could practice laying on of hands in this new social organization," Rosenberg remembered. "She knew what was good for us. Once she took another friend and me to see [Jean Cocteau's] *Blood of a Poet*, a very Freudian movie with railway cars rushing through tunnels. We were then all of eighteen, if that, and rather innocent, and she thought we should see it."

In college, as in later years, Mead made a point of not limiting her "families" to any one generation, or even any four consecutive classes. As she recalled thirty-five years after her own graduation, in a *Barnard Alumnae Magazine* interview, "We tried to establish a steady chain of relationships through the classes of '21 to '28, seven years, which is better than four, at least." If they could have devised a way of going further, they would have done so.

Aggressive in her femininity as in all other things, Margaret decided that, since she and her friends did not have enough contact with children, she ought to "organize a babysitting setup—not to make money, but so that all our group could share babies, learn the vagaries of parents, and learn the crazy way houses are set up, and what you do about babies." It was at this point in her life that she began to have recurrent dreams about a murdered baby, for whose death she was somehow responsible, "and also dreams," she said, "in which something less than death happens to a child—I categorized badly murdered babies and less serious dreams—a style of dream that makes me think, 'What do I think I ought to have done and haven't done?' " All her life she was beset by the prospect of things she ought to do.

The lost baby sister Katherine may have been on Margaret's mind, but she was attentive toward her surviving sisters, who came periodically to visit her in New York, to have fun and also to do her bidding. Young Priscilla, Pelham Korteheuer remembered, would be dispatched downtown with her or one of the other Ash Can Cats, to do an errand and free her older sister to concentrate on grander matters. Léonie Adams's mother, when she met Elizabeth and Priscilla, declared, "Those girls had better be taken away from Margaret, or she'll do them in."

Richard Mead, enrolled at the Wharton School, also paid visits to his increasingly illustrious sister, and afterward sent enraptured notes of thanks. "I had one grand, glorious, roaring good time," he wrote in November of 1920. "I have written Luther . . . I said ever [sic] nice thing I could and I meant every word of it." In a note the following April he wrote that "Grandma wants me to tell you that April has only 30 days, as she saw that you had invited me to come on the 31st. That is not from me however, for I would come if it were on the 35th." The Meads all exchanged frequent and news-filled letters, but Richard was an especially faithful correspondent.

One of Margaret's enthusiasms was the debate squad. Should the government own railways? Should its immigration policy be exclusive? Should the United States grant immediate independence to the Philippines? The latter topic, debated and lost at Smith College in March of 1922, was reported in a *Barnard Bulletin* column which said that "the most touching moment of The Debate at Smith . . . occurred some ten minutes after its close when Margaret Mead walking across the room paused suddenly, gazed at her feet with a very worried expression and exclaimed, 'Did I debate in these spats? Good Lord!' " The next year Margaret herself edited the *Bulletin*, and wrote an editorial criticizing last-minute newcomers to the squad who seemed to be signing up only in response to rumors that they might be sent to England to debate at Oxford. The trip did not materialize.

Debates, formal and otherwise, delighted Mead all her life. Her friendship with Margaret, Louise Rosenblatt said, was a running debate which lasted until Margaret's death. Debates of an impromptu nature went on at all hours at 606: Was Copland greater than Beethoven? Was *Romeo and Juliet* Shakespeare's effort to prove that all love dies? What should be the fate of Sacco and Vanzetti, the Italian anarchists accused of murder in Massachusetts? How best to mark the amendment allowing women to vote? (This latter question does not appear to have especially preoccupied the Ash Can Cats.)

Who had read the newly published *Ulysses*, or *The Waste Land*, or *Dr. Dolittle*? What to make of the Turkish Question, which had been discussed at one of a series of "Barnard Assemblies" by Ambassador Henry Morgenthau? Margaret was a spirited participant, in arguments over these and all kinds of other matters, but generally only until 10:00 P.M. At that hour, on week nights, she would retire no matter what clamor was going on in the room she and Léonie shared. That room, bigger than the others in the apartment, was the place where the Ash Can Cats gathered, late in the evening, to litter the floor with orange peels as they talked.

"Margaret went to bed at ten," one of her apartment mates remembered, "because tomorrow was another day, and there was never enough time to waste in any day, ever, no matter what went on. She was goal-oriented even when there wasn't any special goal." Margaret's new Barnard friends were learning what Katharine Rothenberger had discovered at DePauw: other people might be as smart as Margaret Mead, or even smarter, but nobody in sight was more industrious or more determined.

On November 7, 1922, in the first semester of Margaret's senior year, she and some other students appeared in the dining hall wearing red dresses, sat down among red flags, red flowers and red candles, and burst into the "Internationale," to honor the fifth anniversary of the Russian Revolution. A letter printed in the next issue of the *Barnard Bulletin* called this spectacle "out of place, highly uncalled for, and in poor taste," to which "L.A.," doubtless Léonie Adams, replied in the following issue defending the Russian Revolution as "a great social experiment . . . courageous, clearsighted, in the main admirable, and which must seem to everyone momentous."

Léonie, who still read the *Bulletin* although she had graduated, had always stuck up for what she thought was courageous and momentous. One night, when the impromptu debate in 606 had to do with the custom of dueling, she took issue with Deborah Kaplan, who charged, from what she considered "a good Hebraic position," that duels were silly and outmoded. Léonie, on grounds that duels were romantic, defended them, and so did the daughter of a southern bishop, who was so vehement on the subject that she all but lunged at Deborah's throat. Through all this hubbub Margaret Mead slept peacefully as usual.

But she did stay awake Saturday nights, to act as proctor for the apartment when the girls came in from their dates at the curfew time of 1:00 A.M. (She couldn't spend Saturday evenings with Luther, because he was busy preparing for Sunday services.) That Margaret should assume this responsibility seemed inevitable. "Who else?" one classmate asked. "She seemed so much older than the rest of us. Actually I was a year her senior, but I always felt younger."

One Saturday night, when a roommate had had to tear herself with particular reluctance from the arms of her beau, Margaret led the others in a melodramatic recitation of Robert Browning's poem "A Woman's Last Word":

> . . . Where the serpent's tooth is,
> Shun the tree—

Where the apple reddens
Never pry—
Lest we lose our Edens,
Eve and I. . . .

Teach me, only teach, Love!
As I ought
I will speak thy speech, Love,
Think thy thought.

Preoccupation with sex was common among Barnard undergraduates. "If you went to Barnard in those days," said someone who did, "you were assumed to be a nymphomaniac." Margaret's classmate Nancy Boyd once wore an organdy frock which prompted another of her friends to exclaim, "*That's* the dress you must lend me to lose my virginity in!" The girl, said Nancy, was "determined, as a matter of principle, to lose it before she was married." But most of the girls were in no rush to marry. "Others of us talked all about men and birth control, and wanted to learn all there was to know, but Margaret, instead of talking, was the only one who was going to *do* something about it—get married, that is."

Margaret did not sneak in through the windows after curfew. Margaret did not flirt with the young men across the courtyard who threw pennies into the windows of 606 when the Ash Can Cats played "I Left My Love in Avalon" or "Apple Blossom Time" on the phonograph. Margaret did put a framed picture of her brother Dick on the desk of a classmate who had no boyfriend, to give her some idea of how it might feel to have an admirer. Margaret did not have to wonder how it felt; Margaret had Luther. An item in a 1922 *Barnard Bulletin* asked, "Did anyone ever hear of traveling on the subway on Sunday with *Jurgen, Human Nature and Conduct* and the Bible under one's arm?" This item probably referred to Margaret, traveling to or from General Theological Seminary. By all accounts, including his own, Luther was Margaret's stalwart and unrivaled fiancé. "If she was sick he would walk two miles to get her ice cream," remembered Katharine Rothenberger, who as often as she could made trips from Indiana to visit her friend Margaret.

Luther and Margaret got together once or twice a week. They went to plays and Gilbert & Sullivan matinées, and introduced their classmates to each other. (Margaret also drew on her brother's pool of Philadelphia friends as blind dates for hers.) A number of Margaret's classmates were not even aware that she had a fiancé. Trysts were fashionable, but engagements were not. Maybe, one alumna speculated, this was "because Dean Gildersleeve, who later was one of the seven delegates from the U.S.A. who signed the charter of the United Nations, made such strong pleas for feminism." Margaret's feminism, then and always, was more instinctive than doctrinaire. Engagement to Cressman, who was safely preoccupied with his own studies several miles downtown, was affirming but not demanding. It not only proved to the world that she was a female desired by a male, but, perhaps more important, it "gave me time," as she said, "for deep, creative friendships with women." All her life she would depend on such friendships, which were intense and enduring.

These friendships, especially those inside the "family," operated according to rules she set down. If this seemed peremptory to the others, then so be it. Generally they followed what Deborah called Margaret's "three Ben Franklinish rules for getting along with people." But one time her friends committed a bad oversight. They forgot the significance of December 16. That they had also overlooked Deborah's birthday in October, and others earlier in the semester, was not relevant, and did not stop Margaret from spending most of the day subtly sulking, in a way her apartment mates did not at first understand. Finally they figured out how they had gone wrong, and after Margaret had retired, at her usual hour of 10:00 P.M., they decided to atone. When they woke her up for a late-night celebration, she was delighted.

"Her need for adulation and approval was boundless," one roommate said, "and so was her feeling for ritual." All Saints' Day had a private significance for Margaret and Léonie Adams which endured as long as Margaret lived. She and Léonie and Pelham, all born in December, also observed for many years their custom of a shared birthday dinner, sometime in that month, at a restaurant on West Tenth Street called Galati's. There, thinking of the most famous lines of their decade's favorite poet, Edna St. Vincent Millay, they would order a candle brought to their table lying on its side, burning at both ends.

They read Millay, they read *Main Street* and *The Age of Innocence* and *Chéri;* they read Dorothy Parker. They knew about the Black Sox baseball scandal, Man o' War's retirement, Warren G. Harding's defeat of James M. Cox, and the new comic strip "Wee Winnie Winkle the Breadwinner." They also alluded, constantly, to the burgeoning new science of psychoanalysis. "Oh, how I wish that I could get back to the pre-Freudian days of fearless forgetfulness," said a fictional cat in a *Barnard Bulletin* column when the *Bulletin's* editor was Margaret

Mead. In an atmosphere so keen on psychoanalysis, there was no such thing as anybody ever just plain forgetting anything.

Sometimes, at the urging of a fellow student named Agnes Piel, Léonie and Margaret and others would try their hand at categorizing people by sexual type. "Agnes was the Grande Amoureuse," said Adams, "and I was something of a masochist—timid, likely to fall for the wrong sort. Margaret did something bad to men, something with a Freudian name—castration, yes, that was it. She did do that to men. She knew it, too. She was full of that stuff, because of the way her brother had been treated." Margaret, another classmate said, "couldn't stand it if I was out with a man."

Perhaps because she seemed so much more forceful than many of the men around her, people glibly applied the word "castrating" to Margaret Mead, from her college years onward. Even after her death, some men shuddered at the mention of her name. But not all. There were those who swore, especially those who knew her late in her life, that as far as they were concerned she was sexy.

"You should have seen the way she operated at seminars," said a man who went to many meetings with Mead in the late 1960s. "Men who generally would chase after anybody's secretary, or any attractive woman who might wander in, would take one first look at Margaret and think, 'Oh my God, a lady intellectual,' but then, as she talked, they'd all end up at her knees. The sex appeal of that mind of hers was absolutely captivating." A handsome and accomplished man thirty years Mead's junior, who met her at a dinner party in 1973, remembered her vividly several years later. "If she had pointed to me and said 'You! You're the one I choose! Come off with me!'" he said, "I would have gone with her. Anywhere."

There were women who seemed to have similar feelings about Margaret, all her life. She grew up at a time when deep involvements between women, sexual and otherwise, were nearly as common as obsessions about losing virginity. At Barnard in the early 1920s, Dean Gildersleeve and several prominent professors were generally assumed to be homosexual. "Once, someone asked all of us Ash Can Cats as a group to go to tea," one of them remembered, "and we wondered why, until we figured that they must have thought we were lesbians. But we weren't, of course, at all."

CHAPTER THREE

"A Companion in Harness"

PLEASED THOUGH Margaret Mead was to bask in the approval of the Ash Can Cats at Barnard, her closest attachment there was not to any fellow student. Her closest attachment there, and one of the closest of her life, was to an instructor, fifteen years her senior, named Ruth Fulton Benedict. Benedict's enthusiasm for anthropology, a discipline she only recently had discovered herself, was so infectious that it set the course of many careers, most notably Margaret Mead's. Eventually Benedict was destined to become one of the most celebrated people in this field, but in 1923, still at work on her own doctoral dissertation, she wrote in her journal that she needed "a companion in harness!" In Margaret Mead she found companionship and love: she found the devoted affection denied her by her aloof husband. During this period Benedict, who for years had been writing poetry, wrote several poems which Mead would include in *An Anthropologist at Work*, her tribute to Benedict. One was called "New Year":

> I shall lie once with beauty,
> Breast to breast;
> Take toll of you, year;
> Once be blessed—
>
> ~~I'll~~ walk your desert quite
> Self-possessed;
> ~~Never~~ Nor once cry pity
> At ~~your worst~~ any jest;
>
> All ~~your~~ thousands of hours, year,
> Be undistressed—
> ~~So I couch~~ When I lie once with beauty
> Breast to breast.*

* Mead included this poem as Benedict had edited the typescript.

Another poem, written January 6, 1923, concludes:

> We have but this: an hour
> When the life-long aimless stepping of our feet
> Fell into time and measure
> Each to the other's tune.

A sonnet, later included in Mead's book, ends with the question:

> —how of this
> Shall we set stars in heaven? Or compete
> With sleep begotten of a woman's kiss?

After her separation from her husband in 1930, Benedict had several love affairs with women, but the first one on whom her affection was lavished may have been the earnest student who as a child had always wished to give her adored grandmother one more good-night kiss. A year before the teacher Benedict ever met the student Mead, she noticed her riding home on a subway from a lecture, arguing and laughing with a group of other girls. Margaret, said someone who knew her in her undergraduate days, was "a missile waiting to be directed—she was going to be *something;* it didn't so much matter what." All her life she had been looking for such direction, taking it where she found it. In grade school she had settled for her teacher Miss Rinehart, who fancied the verses of James Whitcomb Riley. Now, with her roommate Léonie Adams winning prizes for her poetry, Mead was writing mediocre undergraduate poems of her own, exchanging verses with her friends, and considering specializing in literature along with psychology. Benedict, whose language could be beautiful, had entertained such thoughts, too, but her new and lasting obsession was with anthropology, the science that deals with the origins, physical and cultural development, social customs, and beliefs of man.

Anthropology, in the early 1920s, seemed far more alluring to a number of students, including Mead, than other courses listed in the Barnard College catalogue, though it had only one full-time faculty member. Anthropology seemed a new and stirring way of sorting out the ambiguities and contradictions of a world that lurched between what Mead would later recall as the "stupid underbrush of nineteenth-century arguments based on ethnocentric superiority"—of isolationism, Victorianism, and xenophobia—and of the new currents suggested by Freud, Marx, Havelock Ellis, and mechanization.

The mother of a classmate of Mead's wrote a letter home after seeing the World's Columbian Exposition in Chicago in 1893. Reading this letter, which she discovered in 1980, made the classmate "crawl with shame," but it called to her mind why anthropology had seemed so exciting when she and Mead discovered it at Barnard. The letter described one Midway exhibition at the fair that showed "man in his primitive state . . . black, half-clad, flat-headed, big-nosed, protruding lips, a perfect type of brutality and heathenizm," and other examples of somewhat more "advanced" types; ". . . it occurs to you—why—you are the only race not 'on exhibition'—& the whole exhibition is evidently for you—& you are the crowning glory of it all. . . ."*

A quarter of a century later one of the designers of that exhibit would become chairman of the Anthropology Department at Barnard. He also became the most eminent, and controversial, anthropologist in America. The physically slight but formidable Franz Boas had left his native Germany in 1883, at the age of twenty-five, made a lengthy expedition to the Arctic to study Eskimos, helped with the Chicago Fair, and made repeated field expeditions to the Pacific Northwest after teaching first in Worcester, Massachusetts, at Clark University, and later, beginning in 1899, at Columbia. (Simultaneously, for five years ending in 1905, he had also been a curator, as Mead in her time would be too, at the American Museum of Natural History in New York.)

The pacifist stance which the German-born professor adopted in World War I angered some of his colleagues, though Mead would later defend his passionate loyalty to both Germany and the United States" and his belief that the best good of any country can be attained only through the well-being of all countries." Boas had been involved in many controversies. In 1891, after he began the first longitudinal study in America aimed at measuring the same individuals over a period of years, he was attacked in the Worcester press as an "alleged anthropologist," with a "visage seamed and scarred from numerous rapier slashes." (Boas did have a startling appearance: Mead described his "great head and slight frail body, his face scarred from an old duel and one eye drooping from facial paralysis.") He resigned from Clark, where he had

* The letter went on, "You are [aware] how vastly superior is the light of our Christian civilization to the dark and semi-darkness of other lands, how our own race in intellect stands towering above other races, & how grateful one feels that their lot has been cast in such an enlightened clime—& not in the lands that have got it all yet to go through before they catch up—& then one wonders where will our own race be by the time they have caught up— if we go on, in another hundred years, where will we be & how shall we travel—by land or air, how eat, by the now much used method of chewing or shall we 'use a few drops of extract' when we wish a meal? How shall we be writing, or indeed shall we write at all, for talking across the continent is now made so easy. . . . Indeed, one's mind gets in a whirl . . ."

been teaching when he began this study, in a dispute over academic freedom with the university's president, G. Stanley Hall. Hall was an eminent psychologist who shared Boas's interest in human growth but not his view that faculty and students, rather than trustees and non-academic administrators, should make crucial decisions about colleges and universities.

Boas's ideas would inspire Mead and dominate her intellectual approach throughout her life. In 1911, in *The Mind of Primitive Man*, Boas wrote, "There is no fundamental difference in the ways of thinking of primitive and civilized man. A close connection between race and personality has never been established. The concept of racial type as commonly used even in scientific literature is misleading and requires a logical, as well as a biological, function . . . The suppression of intellectual freedom rings the death knell of science." What Boas most "forcibly rejected," the anthropologist Annette Weiner would say, was "*racial determinism.*" But he was embroiled in other controversies. In 1919 he was censured by the American Anthropological Association, and threatened with expulsion, for writing a letter to the *Nation* attacking four anthropologists, whom he did not name, who had carried on espionage activities for the American government while doing anthropological research in Central America. These men, whom he "refused to designate any longer as scientists," had "prostituted science by using it as a cover for their activities as spies."

Anthropology, Boas asserted, could free a civilization from its own prejudices and encourage it "to apply standards in measuring our achievements that have a greater absolute truth than those derived from a study of our civilization alone." The sooner data from other civilizations could be gathered, assessed, and passed on, the better. With Boas, anthropology seemed a thrillingly practical way of studying primitive cultures which were vanishing all over the world. To him, Mead said, anthropology was "a vast panorama which had only been lighted up here and there."

Anthropology, wrote A. L. Kroeber, another Boas student, had "a glowing conviction that it was entering new territory and making a discovery. Its discovery was consciousness of the world of culture, an enormous product and vast influence, with forms and patterns of its own, and a validating principle: relativity. There were far boundaries to this demesne, which included in its totality alike our own and the most remote and diverse human productivities. The vision was wide, charged, and stirring. It may perhaps fairly be called romantic; certainly it emerged historically about at the time point when esthetic romanticism was intellectualizing. The pursuit of anthropology must often have seemed strange and useless to many people, but not one has ever called it an arid or a toneless or a dismal science." Anthropology, Mead was delighted to learn, needed recruits and apprentices, fast, to go forth and study these cultures before they disappeared forever.

Boas's department, Mead wrote, had "tiny, cramped quarters . . . two offices and a seminar room where all the classes were held and where students worked between classes." Perhaps to its chagrin, the department was housed in the Journalism Building. " 'Journalist,' " as Winthrop Sargeant would remark in his 1961 *New Yorker* profile of Mead, "is about as low an epithet as one anthropologist can hurl at another." But the setting wasn't everything, and the chief occupants of the offices were too busy to pay much attention to surroundings. Benedict was finishing "The Concept of the Guardian Spirit in North America," her doctoral dissertation, which concerned the power of religious awe in native American cultures—the methods by which Indian tribes sought the visions that told them what to do. Her own guardian spirit clearly was Boas, who in turn came to rely increasingly on Benedict. He relied on her, among other things, Mead wrote, "to see to it that the precious little bits of money on which people's lives depended got to them in various strange parts of the world . . ."

Benedict had discovered anthropology in 1919 at a series of lectures at the New School for Social Research in downtown Manhattan. She had gone to the lectures for the same reason she had written poems, and considered writing biographies of "restless, highly enslaved women of the past": she felt restless and enslaved herself. Her husband, Stanley Benedict, a professor of biochemistry, had shown some sexual interest in her in 1914, when they married, but now hardly touched her. He had cautioned her, before their marriage, "Your mask is getting thicker and thicker . . . You belong somehow where you never have to wear it . . . You shouldn't have to wear it at all, for it's certain to grow to be a part of you if you do—and then you'll be altogether alone, and it's so *wrong* for you, Ruth."

In anthropology Benedict found, as Mead wrote, "an integrating idea, a rubric under which she could classify both the great achievements of the human spirit and the intractability of that spirit which made some members of each society feel like strangers." Benedict had an abiding feeling for "those who by age or sex or temperament or accidents of life history were out of the main currents of their culture." She had looked and felt like such a person most of her life. In her first year as a Vassar undergraduate, Mead heard Benedict say, five of her most un-

popular classmates asked to room with her "because she looked unhappy. She used to make these castor-oil faces. She was always being
sought out by all sorts of odd people who thought they had found a
soulmate."

As a teacher, she could still seem a painfully shy misfit, but she had
"the rare gift of taking the half-articulate groping interest of a student
and illuminating it with a warmth which was like an accolade." Never
mind that Benedict wore the same dress to class day after day, or that
hairpins were forever escaping from her soft, mousy, graying coiffure.
In Benedict's most halting lectures, as another of her students said to
Mead, there could come, "between the uh and the ah, a bombshell of
light which changed everything."

Instructor and pupil were well met. The older woman, who was
hard of hearing, rarely spoke; the younger—whose "Dadda" had vainly
warned her to quiet down—was extravagantly talkative. Both were attractive to depressed people, Benedict because she seemed depressed
herself, Mead for quite another reason: "They lean on my sense," she
explained much later, "and on the fact that I am *not* depressed." Far
from it: her gusto was such a boon to classroom discussions that she
was exempt from taking the examination, and she was so enthusiastic
in extolling the subject around campus that the registration doubled.
(Thus began her controversial and, some would think, dubious accomplishment of "popularizing" anthropology.)

Theoretically, undergraduates were not supposed to sit in on graduate courses, but Franz Boas was too preoccupied with his own concerns to be fussy about administrative red tape. If his protégée Benedict
had discovered a protégée of her own who wanted to enroll in the
graduate courses, then fine, let her enroll. Mead's anthropological career was therefore the first in America, as far as she knew, to begin before graduate school. Boas, Mead wrote, "spoke with an authority and
distinction greater than I had ever met in a teacher. In the biometrics
course I remember his saying one day, 'I am embarrassed. Some of you
do not know the calculus. I will teach you the calculus.' In the twenty
minutes left of the hour, he did."

Mead admired this man enormously. The Ash Can Cats, her
fiancé, her other classes, and her extracurricular interests had their
claims on her undergraduate time, but Benedict was pulling her into a
circle of other anthropologists, many of them women, who clustered
around Boas and called him "Papa Franz." Boas, a later scholar said,
was "very much the father figure. Ruth and Margaret were his little
girls until the end of their lives. . . . Their activity was messianic; their

duty was to transmit the message." The message was that race, language, and culture varied independently, and did not explain each other, and that the cultural wealth of humanity, created after thousands of years of strong and painful development, needed at once to be transmitted and recorded.

But for all Boas's crucial influence on Margaret Mead, it was Ruth Benedict who was more and more becoming her own guardian spirit, in a closer way than Boas was Benedict's. "I was the child Ruth never had," Mead wrote. "I had all the things she'd have wanted in a child: joy of living, positive affirmation of life—I worried that she'd lose interest in me because of the age discrepancy," but this fear was unfounded. In March of 1923, Margaret's senior year, Benedict wrote in her diary that the younger woman "rests me like a padded chair and a fire place. I say it's the zest of youth I believe in when I see it in her. Or is it that I respond understandably to admiration?" "Lunch with M. Mead," a later entry reads: "—discussed her going into anthropology. I hope she does it . . ." Mead felt committed to psychology for her master's degree, but not, apparently, for her doctorate: "—M. Mead told Dr. Boas today about Ph.D. in Anthropology," Benedict wrote in her journal. "He poured cold water but she arose." Her excitement about anthropology helped to take Mead's mind off physical problems.

One of the poems Margaret published in the *Barnard Barnacle* was called "The Pencilling of Pain":

> As a wayward child, a pencil given,
> Can marr [sic] each picture in a cherished book,
> Pencilling an outline, harsh and clear,
> Changing forever the accustomed look
> Of some fair pictured landscape, . . .
> . . . This Pain hath done to me.
> Threading relentless through all my days,
> No hour of gladness hath he left
> Untouched by outlines, stark and cold.
> So that each hour, of graciousness bereft,
> Is a separate memory—bitter thing.
> I could not list to beauty for an hour
> But Pain would ring that hour with black.
> Nor would I pause before the fragrance of a flower
> But Pain would come behind my back
> And e'er my heart had ceased to sing,
> That hour would broidered be
> By dull thin lines that so distort

> The essence of its beauty, that I'm fain
> To tear in two this life, so marred
> By the pencil lines of Pain.

Benedict's fierce love must have done much to distract Margaret from whatever pain she was alluding to in that poem, which probably was more real than metaphorical. According to Luther Cressman, she told him later that at some point in her adolescence she had needed surgery to relieve extreme menstrual cramps. She also suffered from neuritis so acutely that she sometimes had to wear her arm in a sling. She wore the sling the whole time her classmate Deborah Kaplan went home with her to Pennsylvania, to help Margaret and her mother plan a pageant. Officially presented by the Buckingham Women's Club, this pageant was entitled "The Buckingham Child's Quest."*

"This was a typical example of Margaret's usual talent for making you do something you know you can't do," said Deborah sixty years later. " 'The only people who can get a thing done well,' she used to say, 'are those who think they can't do it.' I certainly didn't think I could do this, but amazingly enough I *did* turn out to have a talent, though I'd never known it before, for choreography. If only those Pennsylvania Dutch had been uninhibited enough to take off their long white stockings and dance in the grass barefoot, the dances might actually have been nice, but I remember them dancing awkwardly in their stockings as clearly as I remember Margaret's sling. What I don't remember is her saying anything about why her arm hurt so."

Margaret's pain may or may not have been connected with the length and lukewarmth of her engagement to Luther, who was diligently at work on West Twenty-third Street toward his degree as a Bachelor of Sacred Theology. Once she confided to a classmate that she was going to marry him only because her family expected her to (although she later said that her family tried to talk her out of such an early wedding). "The most dramatic thing about him," one Ash Can Cat remembered much later, "was the way Margaret said his name: 'Lu-ther.' " His fiancée's undergraduate friends did not, on the whole, seem to find him an imposing presence, which could have been an oversight on their part. At the age of eighty-three Cressman, still a man of considerable charm, recoiled at the description Margaret gave in 1972, in *Blackberry Winter*, of her senior dance, where they "danced all night and in the damp dawn, which took all the curl out of my small ostrich

* In its Epilogue, "The Child of Buckingham, with her hand clasped fast in the hand of Tomorrow, frees the Spirit of the Valley and the Spirit of the People who hold with Today, from the clinging hands of the Past."

feather fan, [and] we walked along Riverside Drive, watching the sky brighten over the river."

"I should think," said Cressman in 1981, "that she'd have remembered more than the curl going out of the fan."

Luther's graduation present to Margaret was a copy of Amy Lowell's *Life of Keats*. Ruth Benedict's was a "no-strings fellowship" of $300, to be used in future professional work. This whimsical and generous gesture, which was to inspire many similar gifts by Mead in years to come, was designed to compensate for a disappointment. Margaret was one of six of her 157 classmates to graduate with honors, and one of twenty elected to the Delta chapter of Phi Beta Kappa; but the Caroline Duror Fellowship, awarded annually to the graduating Barnard senior judged to show "most promise of distinction in her chosen line of work," in 1923 went to Marguerite Loud.

Before adjourning for the traditional Senior Soirée, the whole college stood singing "Beside the Waters of the Hudson." On graduation night, observing another ritual, Margaret stayed up until dawn to have breakfast at a Broadway pancake house. To this breakfast party Margaret's classmate Nancy Boyd brought along a cousin "who was a very square person. We all sat around a table and Margaret was spouting, spouting, spouting, about anything and everything. She left no room for anyone else to say a thing."

The legend next to her photograph in the 1923 Barnard yearbook, the *Mortarboard*, makes the same point: Margaret Mead certainly did like to talk. The legend, in tired doggerel, reads:

> Economics, social science,
> Peggy has advanced idees!
> Discourseful, quite,
> With forceful might
> She ponders immortality.

Nobody at Barnard or anywhere else who knew Margaret ever called her Peggy; perhaps the jingle's author scarcely knew her subject, who is pictured uncharacteristically without her glasses, looking over her right shoulder with a faint trace of a smile. But the sense of the lines is correct.

"More than anything else, she looks purposeful in that picture, doesn't she?" asked Luther Cressman, browsing through the yearbook fifty-eight years after it was published. "She looks as if she were going someplace, doesn't she?

"Well, she was."

CHAPTER FOUR

"Be Lazy Go Crazy"

MARGARET'S FATHER begrudged not a penny of the $10,000 he reckoned that her Phi Beta Kappa key had cost him. Moreover, in what must have been one of the rare flush times of the professor's erratic career as an investor, he made an offer his daughter marveled at fifty years later: he would give her "the equivalent of another ten thousand dollars—all I wanted and a trip around the world—if I wouldn't marry Luther."

Edward Sherwood Mead's estimate of Luther Sheeleigh Cressman waxed and waned. Mead could not have found a better man for his "dear little girl," he wrote in an atypically affectionate letter, than the one she had picked for herself. But that would have been news to Luther. Relations between the two men, who had little in common, were formal at best. One of the reasons Luther appealed to Margaret, she told a friend, was that "He was so different from my father. My father had no empathy at all. He would tell the same story three times and never notice by your face that you'd ever heard it before."

Young Cressman, by contrast, had plenty of empathy, especially for women. The second of six brothers, he was curious about and attentive to women of all ages. Margaret's mother and grandmother both found him charming. But what, they wondered, was the rush? "He'll be riding up to marry you any time you want him to in the next five years," Margaret's grandmother assured her. "You don't have to marry him to keep him."

"But I want to get married," said Margaret, no less defiantly than she had announced in 1912 that she wanted to become an Episcopalian. Her baptism then had seemed to her elders just as unnecessary as her wedding plans seemed in 1923. Part of the appeal of both events, perhaps, was that they were pageants, and a pageant, especially one with herself at center stage, was something Margaret Mead always found hard to resist. ("You should have seen all the long gowns and the fur stole she had in her closet," said one of Mead's last employees. "The fur stole looked like an antique, but she loved it. She really enjoyed getting all dressed up for formal occasions.")

More to the point, Margaret probably wanted to be married for the same reason she had wanted to be engaged: to make it clear to the world, or to herself, or to both, that she was no unclaimed treasure. Ruth Benedict had a husband, most women had one; Margaret Mead may have felt that she ought to have one, too. And one thing was sure: no man in the Commonwealth of Pennsylvania, or anywhere else, was more steadfast than Luther Cressman. He would be there when she needed him. Everyone understood that Margaret was not to be known as Mrs. Cressman. "I'm going to be famous some day," she had declared at the end of a spirited argument with her father, "and I'm going to be known by my own name!" Edward Mead, a relative remembered, was far more "shocked and mortified" by this announcement than Luther Cressman, whose only reaction was to wonder what Margaret would do about the name on her passport.

Luther spent the night of September 2, 1923, his last as a bachelor, in the hotel at Lahaska, Pennsylvania, a short drive from the church where the wedding would be. The next morning his parents and five brothers drove from their Pughtown home in an open touring car, over dusty roads. Not sure just where the hotel was, they stopped at the Meads' house to ask directions. A while later the hotel phone rang. Margaret was calling, and she was frantic.

"Luther," she demanded. "Your family's not coming to the wedding in *those* clothes, are they?"

"No, Margaret," replied her fiancé with a patience not every man could have mustered. "They are changing now."

Luther's brothers were his ushers. Elizabeth and Priscilla Mead, along with Léonie Adams, were their sister's bridesmaids, and Richard sang "Oh, Promise Me." In the glorious words of the *Book of Common Prayer*, Margaret and Luther vowed that they would love, comfort, honor, and keep each other, in sickness and in health; and, forsaking all others, keep only unto each other, so long as they both should live. The farthest thing from Luther's mind, as he heard Margaret speak these vows, was that he was about to become, as she would call him in *Blackberry Winter*, her "student husband"—a term implying something short of a lifetime commitment. "We were *both* students," he pointed out, "she just as much as I. We weren't trying some innovative social experiment, the way she may have wanted it to seem in retrospect; we were getting married the way any other couple would. But all her life Margaret had a way of saying, 'Well, if that isn't the way it was, that's the way it *should* have been.'

"She was the one who was urging marriage," he remembered. "She insisted that between us we had enough income to work it out. We were a very earnest young couple," he said. "Our idea wasn't, 'Let's hang around together until we're out of graduate school,' it was for life." On their wedding day Margaret was three months short of her twenty-second birthday, Luther six weeks short of his twenty-sixth, and both were virgins.

After the morning wedding service the guests went to the Meads' for a reception. The day was fair and everyone mingled in the yard, congratulating the couple. Luther noticed that his father spent some time standing alone, with nobody to talk to. "To the Meads," he said, "we Cressmans were outlanders." But the Meads did arrange for confetti to be thrown at the departing couple. On the road, Luther stopped to pick up a policeman who needed a ride, who sat in the back seat and said, "I see by the evidence here," referring to some traces of confetti, "that something has happened."

"Your inference is correct," said Luther, but Margaret, who thought she had swept all the confetti away, was not pleased. The honeymoon itinerary was leisurely: after a visit with Stanley and Ruth Benedict, at their retreat in New Hampshire, the couple went to a cottage in Hyannis, on Cape Cod. The first two nights, Cressman remembered, "there was nothing doing. Her tightly barred gates," he reflected years later, "were a sign of both psychological fear and hostility to the commitment of marriage.

"But on the third day," Cressman said, "she got very eager to fondle me while I was driving, and I had to tell her, 'Watch what you're doing, or we'll end up in a ditch!' " Before dinner the marriage was consummated, and later "we went to a movie called *Branded*. I remember her snuggling and asking, 'Have you put your brand on me?' "

In the Hyannis cottage the honeymooners had separate bedrooms. "Margaret claimed to have some soul-splitting thinking to do," Cressman said. "She had to review a book about American intelligence by some duffer at Princeton. It couldn't possibly have required any hard thinking to tear that book to pieces, but Margaret, you must understand, never did unimportant things. The real reason she made such a fuss about that review was to dramatize the fact that she was going to give a seminar."

Back in New York, Luther and Margaret moved into their first apartment. She was generous and conspiratorial about handing out keys to couples in need of a place to tryst. One afternoon when Luther came home unexpectedly he found a condom in the bathroom and heard enthusiastic noises from one such couple in the bedroom. This did not offend him. What did offend him, decades later, was reading in *Blackberry Winter* that this marriage had been "unclouded by fear of pregnancy."

"Not *much* we weren't afraid of it," he said. "Only once a month, that's all." Not until *Blackberry Winter*, which Cressman read in 1972, did he learn that a gynecologist had told Margaret, early in her marriage, that a tipped uterus would prevent her from carrying a child. The only thing of the kind he remembered hearing was that surgery for an ovarian cyst, which was thought to cause her exceptionally painful cramps, had removed her hymen. What seems certain, no matter what she heard or did not hear from a doctor, was that Margaret was deciding that she did not want to have children with Luther after all.

The pretty picture she had cherished as a child, of herself as a pastor's motherly wife, was fast fading. Only once did she accompany her husband to the Brooklyn church where he was first assigned. She did not have time, she recalled years later, "to be a minister's wife in the depths of Brooklyn. Besides, Luther was getting more and more interested in sociology, and less and less in the ministry." This was true. When a woman died in childbirth in Cressman's next parish, St. Clement's, in the wretched Manhattan neighborhood called Hell's Kitchen, he felt he could help her survivors more by washing their dishes than by praying.

A crisis of faith loomed for Luther. When one of his former seminary roommates told him he wished to God he could leave the church, Luther could only think, "You poor Devil, or rather, your poor parishioners." In time he became unable to speak the words a priest must speak and to believe that they represented anything more than a magnificent metaphor. So Cressman, after solitary and painful introspection, took the first painful step toward leaving the ministry. He continued his courses at General Theological, but began work at Columbia on the thesis for his next degree, a master's in sociology.*

"During our graduate work our feeling for each other changed," Cressman said. "Centrifugal forces drew us apart. We were both very,

---

* Mead got the title wrong in *Blackberry Winter*. Cressman's dissertation was "Social Comparisons of the Rural Populations of the United States."

very young, and although she didn't think so, she was a lot younger than I. She always knew all the answers."

"Be lazy go crazy, be lazy go crazy, I'll finish that charm off," Mead wrote to Ruth Benedict. Professor William Fielding Ogburn, of the Department of Economics and Sociology, had hired her as an assistant, and she was helping him edit the *Journal of the American Statistical Association*. She was hurrying to finish the essay for her master's in psychology, based on research inspired by her mother's sociological studies in Italian immigrant communities. Her thesis subject suggests what an instinct she had for issues of enduring interest. She gave the Otis intelligence test to 276 Italian children and compared their scores, she wrote, "with the amount of English spoken in the children's homes, *by their parents*."

Intelligence tests, she said, should not be relied on too naïvely. She advised "extreme caution in any attempt to draw conclusions concerning the relative intelligence of different racial or nationality groups on the basis of tests, unless a careful consideration is given the factors of language, education, and social status, and a further allowance is made for an unknown amount of influence which may be logically attributed to different attitudes and different habits of thought." Sixty years later, this issue is still being hotly debated.

When the time came to think about her doctoral studies, Mead assumed at first that she would work with immigrant groups in the United States, as her mother had, and perhaps also, like Benedict, with American Indian tribes. If only they could go to do field work together, Mead wrote to Benedict in the summer of 1924. "I don't like to think of you all alone," Margaret, visiting her parents in Pennsylvania, wrote to her friend, who was doing field work in Zuni, New Mexico. She promised to send along "a few things I've written this summer. . . . They are very bad, but I think it's important for you to see the worst things I am capable of. You are too encouraging."

Fully focused by now on anthropology, Mead decided on the topic for her thesis in an interview with Boas which, as she recalled, took "perhaps three minutes." She would compare different cultural elements within a single area. "You could do this in Siberia," he told her, "but that would mean knowing Russian and Chinese. The Low Countries might be a good place, but that would mean a lot of work with Old Flemish, Medieval Latin, etc. There is not good enough material to use the Algonkian-speaking peoples. You might try Polynesia where you would only need French and German."

Polynesia, meaning "many islands," is part of Oceania. Oceania, as the British anthropologist A. C. Haddon had written in 1914, was "probably that part of the world which most urgently needs ethnological investigation. . . . Intensive study of as many portions of that area as possible would confer an incalculable boon on all present and future students of the history of human culture. If this is not attempted very soon the opportunity will pass away forever." Polynesia, along with Africa, was the object of much excitement among American anthropologists. A New York businessman named Bayard Dominick had given $40,000 to the Bernice P. Bishop Museum, in Honolulu, to help solve "the great Polynesian puzzle" by gathering "data necessary to the understanding of the history of primitive man in the Pacific area."

In her preliminary work Mead concentrated on a comparative scholarly study of Polynesian tattooing, and in 1924 she presented a paper on this subject at the Toronto convention of the British Association for the Advancement of Science. The heady talk she heard from colleagues there about their "peoples" deepened her resolve to find a "people" of her own and to study them, preferably in Polynesia. In Toronto she also discovered Edward Sapir, a friend of Ruth Benedict's who was chief of the division of anthropology in the Geological Survey of Canada, in Ottawa. Twenty-six years earlier, at fourteen, he had won a city-wide competition and been hailed as "the brightest boy in New York City"; and his reputation as an intellectual giant had never since been questioned. Mead found the forty-year-old linguistics scholar "the most brilliant person . . . the most satisfactory mind I ever met." Sapir's severely melancholic wife had just died, leaving him with three children. He and Mead soon developed, as she wrote to Benedict, "such a satisfactory friendship . . . founded on such sure ground of likemindedness."

"It fills me with something like horror and melancholy," Sapir had once written to Benedict, "to see how long and technical a road I must travel in linguistic work, how fascinating its prospect, and how damnably alone I must be. There is practically no one to turn to for either assistance or sympathetic interest."

In Mead, Sapir found a rapt and responsive listener. In Sapir, whom some of his later students would nickname "God," Mead found someone with whom she could discuss the most complicated questions on her mind. Why did cultures differ from each other? Which mattered more, heredity or environment, nature or nurture? Old answers to these questions, based on race, geography, and evolutionary stages, seemed outmoded. How could psychology and anthropology contribute to social psychology? What light could the new fields of psychoanalysis and psychiatry shed on questions such as how to define the word "normal"? Mead admired, among other ideas, Sapir's view that "Cultural anthropology, if properly understood, has the healthiest of all skepticisms about the validity of the concept 'normal behavior.' It cannot deny the useful tyranny of the normal in a given society, but it believes the external form of normal adjustment to be an exceedingly plastic thing."

The "useful tyranny of the normal" might be a splendid thing for most of the human race, but there seemed to be far too much normalcy, for Margaret's taste, in the Cressman-Mead marriage. Luther was thoughtful and thorough and loyal, but the exchanges she was having with other friends, especially Sapir, were magical. One evening the great man came to the young couple's apartment after a concert, along with Ruth Benedict and the poet Louise Bogan and Bogan's husband Raymond Holden. The conversation turned to the Finnish composer Sibelius, whose music, Cressman recalled the others all agreed, "enters the body without passing through the central nervous system." For him this was not a joyous evening.

"They tried to be polite and courteous to me," he said, "but I felt condescended to." His and Margaret's apartment was often crowded with talkative visitors, most of them her friends, full of stories about "their love affairs, which started out like firecrackers on the Fourth of July, but ended up with the fuses all wet."

In the middle of a visit to the Pennsylvania Meads, in the summer of 1925, Margaret left to spend a day in New York, ostensibly to see about a possible job at the American Museum of Natural History. Pliny Earle Goddard, the museum's curator of ethnology, had asked whether she might be interested in working there. Someone, she understood him to say, was needed "to help Americans understand cultural anthropology as well as they understood archaeology."

"That was the year," Mead wrote, "that Roy Chapman Andrews brought back dinosaur eggs from the Gobi Desert, and everything ancient stirred public interest. People were talking about prehistoric American mound builders, the British excavations in Athens, the lively dispute over King Tutankhaman's tomb in Egypt, and Turville-Petre's tremendously exciting find in Palestine—the first Neanderthal skeleton discovered outside Europe." How exhilarating it would be to help excite interest in the equally important work being done by Boas and Benedict and their followers. But at this point Dr. Goddard could only sound

Mead out; no final decision about filling the job could be made until Dr. Clark Wissler, chairman of the department, returned from a business trip to Australia.

The Goddard interview had given Margaret an excuse to go to New York, but the real reason was a date she had that evening to dine with Edward Sapir and then to spend the night with him at a hotel. The story, as Luther Cressman was amused to recall many decades later, was that Sapir, for all his vaunted brilliance, could not remember, checking out of the hotel the next morning, under what name he had registered.

Sapir implored Margaret, who was seventeen years his junior, to divorce Luther, marry him, and "be mama," as she put it much later, "to his three motherless children." But attracted though she felt to Sapir, and tantalized though she was by encounters with him—encounters which did not greatly seem to disturb the ever understanding Luther Cressman—something else attracted Mead even more: the "giant rescue operation" of anthropology which Franz Boas, with Ruth Benedict's help, was leading. If funds could possibly be found, Mead wanted to go somewhere far away to do field work as part of the rescuing. With this in mind, as she wrote later in "Social Organization of Manu'a," she had begun to design "a study to measure the relative strength of old and new elements of culture—to parallel the thesis upon which I was already at work. In this proposal, I hoped to use the psychogalvanometer [an instrument that measures electrical changes in the body stimulated by mental processes]. My field hopes naturally turned to the area which I now knew through literature."

Mead's doctoral thesis would be entitled "An Inquiry into the Question of Cultural Stability in Polynesia." Some elements of culture, theorists held, were more stable than others, and more reliable as indicators of history. Tattooing was one such element. Different Polynesians tattooed their skins according to different designs, techniques, and religious and social rituals. Mead studied five cultures—Hawaiian, Maori, Samoan, Tahitian, and Marquesan—in terms of their tattoos. Then she studied the way they built their houses and canoes, and began to write her thesis. If a field project could be wangled, she expected her task would have to do with what she had been learning in libraries. But Boas came up with an entirely different idea. He suggested that she put aside these comparisons to take on a study of something she had lived through herself but never given any particular thought to: adolescence. This subject, fascinating enough in 1924, would become more so in a century that afforded time to dwell on such matters.

Faye Moskowitz, in a *New York Times* commentary in 1981, called adolescence "a 20th-century invention most parents approach with dread and look back on with the relief of survivors." Much of the popularity of this "invention" can be traced to the psychologist G. Stanley Hall's *Adolescence: Its Psychology and Its Relations to Physiology, Anthropology, Sociology, Sex, Crime, Religion and Education* (1905), which drew on more than sixty studies of physical growth alone. That book, Mead wrote, characterized adolescence "as the period in which idealism flowered and rebellion against authority waxed strong, a period during which difficulties and conflicts were absolutely inevitable."

Teaching under G. Stanley Hall at Clark University, Franz Boas had resented Hall's role in the academic freedom dispute there. He also disagreed with Hall on a theoretical issue: Boas held that the difficulties of adolescence might spring at least as much from culture as from biology. Hall's view, which emphasized biology as the determining factor, seemed narrow and unenlightened to Boas. Enlightenment, in the mid-1920s United States, was in dangerously short supply. John Scopes, a high-school teacher in Tennessee, had been fired from his job for assigning to his classes a textbook that included a thorough account of what in Tennessee was often pronounced "*ee*-volution"—the theory, propounded by Charles Darwin, that human beings are descendants of lower species. Scopes, in assigning the book, had broken a state law which forbade the teaching of any theory that denied the story of the Divine Creation of man as taught in the Bible. Clarence Darrow defended him, with William Jennings Bryan representing the prosecution, in the celebrated "Monkey Trial," the first trial ever broadcast over the radio. In a triumph of oratory over reason, Bryan won the case, though Scopes's conviction was later reversed on a technicality.

Boas was beginning to work out "a broad-ranging plan for the development of American anthropology, a plan which presupposed the theoretical orientation that emerged in the course of his critique of evolutionism in the early 1890s," as the anthropologist George Stocking wrote. He was also developing what Marvin Harris, another eminent anthropologist, called one of his "most important achievements . . . the distinctively American plan of graduate education in anthropology known as the 'four-field approach,' which unites coursework in physical anthropology with studies in anthropological linguistics, archaeology, and cultural anthropology." Boas's major task, Harris added, was "to prove that there is only *one* human nature that allows for an enormous amount of mentally encoded variation."

To be young and energetic and bright in the twenties, recalled another Boas protégée, the anthropologist Ruth Bunzel, was to face stirring choices. "Some of us fled to the freer air of Paris," she said, "and eventually retired. Some of us joined radical movements and sold the *Daily Worker* on street corners, and some of us went into anthropology, hoping that there we might find some answers to the ambiguities and contradictions of our age and the general enigma of human life. . . . It was inconceivable that this cultural upheaval would not be reflected in so sensitive a discipline as anthropology." To this third group it appeared that anthropology could be instrumental not only in influencing and manipulating primitive peoples, but in bringing about "self-confrontation." Perhaps, Bunzel said, the important question was less "How can we change others?" than "How can we change ourselves?" In 1983, Bunzel amended that last question to read "How can we *understand* ourselves?"

Whichever way the question was phrased, it was more and more on Margaret Mead's mind as she turned from her general thesis topic to the new inquiry Boas suggested, into "the relative strength of biological puberty and cultural pattern." The prospect of finding a "people of my own," whose culture might help to disprove Hall's theory, sounded promising. So did Polynesia, which she had studied so much from afar. Deeply attached though she was to Ruth Benedict, who had worked extensively among the Zuni, Mead now had no wish to study American Indians. Any anthropologist could do that; everybody knew the joke about how an Indian family consisted of a father, mother, child, and an anthropologist, and how resentful Indians were becoming, understandably, at the idea of so many "studies" by whites.

The more Mead thought about studying the psychology of adolescence in Polynesia, the more alluring it sounded, especially considering her background in psychology. Students of the soul, G. Stanley Hall himself had written, "should be students of man, and the unanthropological character of American psychology is not only un-American, but scientifically so unnatural that it must be transient. Field work here has a disciplinary and broadening effect, now one of the most urgent needs of our too cloistered and sequestered work. . . . It is precisely psychological study that is most needed for these vanishing races if we would truly know ourselves, and only a profound conviction of the validity and the value of psychic evolution can give the right motivation to this work." If psychology needed anthropology, then the reverse was equally true, and Margaret Mead, who then and always stood on the cusp between the two disciplines, did her best to shove away the barrier between them.

First Mead wanted to conduct her own study on the remote Polynesian archipelago of Tuamotu. When Boas objected that Tuamotu was too inaccessible, she came up with another idea. Suppose she could find a place in Oceania where a boat would stop every three weeks or so, which would make her a little easier to reach? What about American Samoa, an outpost of the United States Navy, where boats called frequently? Dr. George Cressman, Luther's father, had gone to college with the rear admiral in charge of the naval base there. Since that admiral could be counted upon to keep a kindly eye out for her welfare, would Samoa not be as safe a place as any for her to join Boas's "rescue operation"?

"Samoa was not chosen," Mead wrote, "because I had any theoretical or personal preference for it over other Polynesian islands." Nor was adolescence chosen as her topic because it had especially interested her before Boas helped her formulate "the question which sent me to Samoa": "Are the disturbances which vex our adolescents due to the nature of adolescence itself or to civilisation? Under different circumstances does adolescence present a different picture?"

Mead's was not the only project Boas was guiding. During this same period Melville Herskovits carried out early studies of the American Negro, and Otto Klineberg began his decade-long investigation of racial mental differences. They had their tasks; Mead had hers, which was to test Hall's and other views that "rebellion against authority, philosophical perplexities, the flowering of idealism, conflict and struggle" could be ascribed to a period of physical development, rather than to the determinism of culture. The "most important contribution that we hope you will make," Boas wrote to her, "will be the psychological attitude of the individual under the pressure of the general pattern of culture . . . anything that pertains to this subject will be of greatest importance for the methodological development of ethnological research." He also cautioned her not to get sidetracked by "regular ethnological questions" (advice she was to ignore) and not to work "when it is too hot and moist in the daytime. If you find that you cannot stand the climate do not be ashamed to come back. There are plenty of other places where you could solve the same problem on which you propose to work."

The assignment was flatteringly difficult, and Mead's father, finally talked out of his misgivings, agreed to pay her way to the other side of the world and back. The Board of the National Research Council, furthermore, offered her a Fellowship in Biological Science which would pay her $150 a month.

Word came of the fellowship at an auspicious moment: on the eve of May Day, which in 1925, as always, was an important ritual for the Ash Can Cats: their annual expedition to Mosholu Parkway, between Van Cortlandt Park and Yonkers, to gather the makings of the May baskets they traditionally presented to their favorite people. The flowers, the baskets, and the lining for the baskets all had to come from nature: no fair buying anything.

The baskets themselves were woven from willow sprigs, lined with strips of moss, and filled with whatever flowers were available. "We got the fattest violets in this year's crop: spring beauties, marsh marigold, apple blossoms, ferns, and other things of unknown but obviously charming origin," wrote Pelham Korteheuer, who cut the moss in long strips from the rocks: "The result was an even bit of green velvet which Léonie [Adams] called Titania's Carpet. When we dragged our wetness and tiredness and our weeds into Margaret's at eight, we found her at the telephone," receiving a telegram that she had got the fellowship that would help take her to Samoa: "Wasn't that a whopping start for May Eve?"

Then came two more spectacular bits of news: "In burst wild-eyed Louise [Rosenblatt] who had just heard about having been given the Duror money [a Barnard College prize] in addition to the Grenoble fellowship," and, shortly afterward, Léonie announced that on this same day she had received definite confirmation that her book had gone to press. Elated, the Ash Can Cats made their rounds, distributing a total of seven baskets—including one for Ruth Benedict, one for Louise Bogan, and, most ambitiously and excitingly of all, one for Edna Millay herself.

From the Columbia neighborhood the young women made their way through the city down to Greenwich Village. As the last delivery began, Pelham glanced at her wristwatch and "most appropriately it said twelve, exactly midnight when we arrived at Edna St. Vincent Millay's house . . . one of the tiniest houses in the Village . . . Millay's husband, Eugene Boissevain, a charming gentleman who pretended we didn't look like silly street urchins huddled there . . . very graciously asked who was calling. We said, 'No one you know.' Finally Bunny [Agnes McCall] burst out with 'Where is Edna? We want Edna!' " and in due course "the window swung open and a thin reddish bobbed head stuck out—a very beautiful and rapt voice exclaimed 'You sweet things, you darlings, why, this is the loveliest thing that ever happened to me.' "

The Ash Can Cats tried to work up courage to recite a Millay verse in chorus, but instead gaped, whispered among themselves, and stared, until Millay asked who they were. "Oh, just people," Léonie said. Later, when Millay came downstairs to greet the "people," they admitted to being ex-Barnard students who had always liked May Day. So had she, Millay told them, but it had been a long time "since anyone gave me a May basket." When the Ash Can Cats repeated their names, Millay said to their delight that she recognized Léonie Adams's. "Then, as we couldn't bask forever in her presence, magical as it was," wrote Pelham, they made a move to go.

Millay "gravely shook hands with each one, no perfunctory shake but a long, firm, quiet pressure that meant something . . . We fled, calling back, 'Good night and thank you,' and she kissed her hand after us. After that we went to Romany Marie's all in a daze . . ." Pelham ended this letter, "You sympathize with our extravagance of delight, don't you, Marie?" Marie Earle Eichelberger, another Barnard student in the early 1920s and a great friend of Mead's, no doubt did sympathize. Seven years older than Margaret, she had been obliged by a bout with tuberculosis to postpone her education. She was never quite an Ash Can Cat herself, but she always reveled in the pleasures of those who were.

That same spring, Margaret's aunt Fanny McMaster and her husband invited Margaret and Luther to their Rhode Island cottage. Her husband, Fanny wrote in her *Family History*, referred "jocundly" to his "tiny, young-looking niece as 'Old Doc Mead,' " as the two couples "sat in our little living room while Margaret announced that she was going to 'live native.'

"At the time it seemed a wild and adventurous idea." As the four sat talking, Fanny turned to Luther, whom she considered "a quiet young fellow, of some charm," to ask, "What do you think of this?"

"I've got nothing to say," replied Luther, shaking his head. He had applied for a traveling fellowship for the following year, too.

"I wasn't going to blow my top," Cressman said later. "If she wanted to do this, she could. We discussed the possibility of my joining her, but her attitude was that I didn't have the skills or the insight to go there."

Not that Mead's heart was set on going off by herself to the tropics. On the contrary, as she had written to Ruth Benedict, she was "bending all my energies toward persuading Isabel Gordon to go to the South Seas with me." Gordon had been "working on the problem of common ancestry in a Tennessee mountain community" for her dissertation, and returned after taking "genealogies for some 1,000 children and being most weary of it." Going with her "would be far better than go-

ing alone," wrote Mead, but going alone would be better than not going at all, or, it seemed, than going with Luther. Whatever else her
husband was, he was not her idea of a companion in harness.

In preparing for this adventure, as for many of her later ones, Margaret had the devoted and inspired backstage help of Marie Eichelberger. Eichelberger earned her living as a social worker, and had other ties
in the world, but nothing mattered more to "Aunt Marie," as in time
she would be known to Margaret's daughter and to the children of several other people she knew through Margaret, than helping her friend
to achieve her ambitions. Outside this circle, Eichelberger never cared
to discuss what she called "a private friendship"—a friendship that
never faded. Mead always had a way of making friends with people who
felt this same impulse to do what they could to ease her way in the
world.*

In later years Marie Eichelberger would keep Mead's books, handle her financial affairs, act as her attorney. In the summer of 1925 she
scurried around New York helping find appropriate dresses and a little
writing case to take to the tropics. Like most of Margaret's other friends
and kinfolk, she slowly got used to the young woman's decision to head
for the other side of the world. But Edward Sapir was unreconciled, as
he made clear in a poem he wrote to Mead, called "Ariel":

> Of the heedless sun you are an Ariel,
> Rising through cloud to a discovered blue,
> The windy, rocking landmarks travel through
> And clamber up a crazy pinnacle.
> Be wild, oblivious, nor think how fell
> One mocking angel and a frightened crew
> Through all the sunny pools of air into
> The dark and wondrous ritual of Hell.
> For you have footing poised and in your breast
> The interchange of breath, both quick and slow.
> Reckless, be safe. The little wise feet know
> Sun-way and cloud's and sudden earthen aim,
> And steps of beauty quicken into flame
> Wherein you burn up wholly in arrest.

Margaret answered Sapir's message with a verse of her own:

* "You're certainly lucky, Margaret, to have all these slaves," Melville
Herskovits once said when he came to dinner at Margaret's and Luther's
apartment.
"They're not slaves, Mel," said Margaret, "they're people who like to
help me."
"They're slaves all the same," replied Herskovits.

> Measure your thread and cut it
> to suit your little schemes
> Sew the garment tightly, tightly
> And leave no room for dreams
> Head down! Be not seen peeking
> Where the wild geese fly . . .

Like Holly Golightly, in Truman Capote's *Breakfast at Tiffany's*, she was counseling him to "never love a wild thing." Whether Sapir or anybody else liked the idea or not, Margaret Mead was off to Samoa.

"In the summer of 1925," as she would write, "when I said good-bye to my family and my student husband Luther Cressman at the B&O railroad station in Philadelphia and boarded a train that would take five days to reach San Francisco, I had all the courage of complete ignorance. . . . I had never spent a day of my life alone." Although the train took five days to reach San Francisco, she herself got off it sooner, to visit Ruth Benedict. From Gallup, New Mexico, not far from the site of Ruth's Zuni field work, the two friends traveled to the Grand Canyon. Sitting there, watching the canyon colors change, they talked about Sapir's having fallen in love with Margaret. The only way she could end this affair, Margaret speculated, would be to scheme to have him reject her.

"I don't know anybody who would find it harder to invite a rejection," replied Ruth Benedict, who knew Sapir nearly as well as she knew Mead. He had been her principal intellectual support in her troubles with her husband, and he was so important to Franz Boas that Boas had paid his way to a seminar in Europe.

Talks with Sapir, Mead wrote, were "just magnificent. He'd say half a sentence and I'd say half a sentence and things just wound up in fireworks that were delightful." But he was also "terribly vulnerable and desperately unhappy." The eminent psychiatrist Harry Stack Sullivan called his friend Sapir "one of the most articulate of men, a poet, a musician," with "an intellect that evoked reverence, a personality unendingly charming," but said that his genius was "very largely wasted on a world not yet awake to the value of the very great."

The companionship Sapir may have hoped for from Mead was not to be. "As one emancipated young woman once expressed it to me," Sapir would write in a 1928 article that made him sound a little like one of Woody Allen's confused intellectual heroes several decades later, "it would be an insult either to her or her husband to expect fidelity of them. Yet what is more obvious than that jealousy can no more be weeded out of the human heart than the shadows cast by objects can be obliterated by some mechanism that would restore to them an eternal luminosity?"

Mead's departure left Sapir jealous and lonely. Ruth Benedict, returning to her Zuni field work, was dreading the long gaps between letters from her dear friend, but she was resigned. As to Luther Cressman, Margaret wrote him a letter, before she boarded the ship that would take her to Honolulu, on paper from the little writing case Marie had bought. She promised him that she would never leave him—unless she fell in love with someone else. Perhaps she meant to tell him that he, too, should feel free to consider a new partner, if one should happen to come his way.

That letter reached Cressman just before he left for England. He arrived there early in October 1925 to begin a fellowship for study abroad which he had been awarded by General Theological Seminary. His task was to learn all he could about methods of handling delinquency in Europe and about birth control. But the day he found Margaret's letter he had no assurance that anything worthwhile was in store for him. "The young lad, twenty-eight years old, who arrived in England . . . was a deeply troubled person," he wrote later, "one who seemed to have been defeated by life. My marriage seemed to have a very uncertain future; I was [in the process of giving up] my profession as a priest for which I had worked hard and with great expectations; the disillusion was very real after the War when the programs of the government and society seemed to disavow all the ideals which, naïvely or not, many of us had enlisted to fight for (four Cressman brothers among the others).

"My going to Europe had been, I'm afraid, far more a device to facilitate M's Samoan plans than a carefully thought out educational program. . . . In my depressed state it seemed to me sometimes that one of the options was suicide, and while it was more than a passing thought I was not at ease with it as a solution. In this state of mind I arrived in London to start an entirely new kind of year."

His wife, separated by many thousands of miles from him and the other two people who were in love with her, was in a considerably more businesslike frame of mind.

CHAPTER FIVE

Samoa

MARGARET MEAD was a young woman in 1925, but a veteran confidante. She had been listening to other people's secrets since the age of four, when her grandmother commiserated with her about her parents' problems. Now, twenty years later, she traveled 9,000 miles to American Samoa, to hear secrets in a language she had to learn from scratch, as part of a project which would lead to worldwide fame only three years later and make her reputation the subject of impassioned international debate more than than fifty years after that.

Not even Franz Boas could have guessed any of this when Mead described her project in the classic academese of grant applications. What she would learn in Samoa, she hoped, would "add appreciably to our ethnological information on the subject of the culture of primitive women. Owing to the paucity of women ethnologists, practically no ethnological [work] has been done among women as such, and this investigation offers a particularly rich field for the study of feminine reactions and participation in the culture of the group."

She had crossed a continent and an ocean and the Equator to settle in this archipelago, to talk to these Polynesian girls, as part of an enterprise one of her colleagues, Robert Lowie, described as "incomparably subtler than those which usually engage the ethnographer's attention." Ethnography, generally, is the scientific description of customs and habits among mankind. Mead's findings, Boas thought, could prove to "be of greatest importance for the methodological development of ethnological research," though not even he or Ruth Benedict could tell her exactly what to expect or how to proceed. Between them, they worried about the "necessarily rather haphazard character," as Benedict described it, of what Mead would be doing.

Mead should watch out, Boas suggested, for the way "the young girls react to the restraints of custom"; would they be sullenly or sub-missively rebellious, as American and European girls were? Would they be as bashful in the presence of their elders as the girls in most North American Indian tribes? Would they have crushes among themselves? Would they have romantic love affairs with men of whom their parents or their society disapproved?

Much of what she would want to find out, Boas cautioned Mead, could be learned only indirectly; she would have to "be prepared to waste a great deal of time just sitting about getting to know the adoles-cents." Sitting around inactively, he well knew, was not among Mead's talents, and he had, after all, warned her not to be sidetracked, just for the sake of keeping busy, by routine questions that any ethnographer could handle. Anthropology had been generally a matter of males study-ing males, or else of males measuring bones or artifacts or whatever else was around to be quantified. Let others do those things, Mead was told. Her own formidable energies should be focused on a newer idea: "the psychological attitude of the individual under the pressure of the gen-eral pattern of culture."

Boas no doubt expected to be pleased if what she learned were to support his strong and humane suspicion, zealously shared by Benedict, that culture plays as important a role as biology in determining how human beings behave. But he could not predict what Mead would find in Samoa, nor could he send her off with any formula of how to go about her business in this "stone age," as another ethnographer called it, of cultural and psychological anthropology. Procedures and guide-lines did not yet exist. She had to invent her strategy as she went along.

But if Mead had only a dim notion of how to proceed, at least she knew something about where she was going. Many enchanted reports had been written, from viewpoints both scholarly and romantic, by pre-vious visitors to Samoa. "It's all true about the South Seas!" Rupert Brooke had written home from Samoa in 1913. "If you ever miss me, suddenly . . . you'll know that I've got sick for the full moon on these little thatched roofs, and the palms against the morning, and the Sa-moan boys and girls diving thirty feet into a green sea or a deep moun-tain pool under a waterfall—and that I've gone back."

In the late nineteenth century, Robert Louis Stevenson had called Samoa a land of "perpetual song and dance, perpetual games, journeys, and pleasures," of "fine, clean emotions; a world all and always beauti-ful." Henry Adams thought the Samoans "not only the most interest-ing but personally the most attractive race I ever . . . met"; they made him feel "as though I had got back to Homer's time, and were cruising about on the Aegean with Ajax."

Samoa can mean "holy chicken," which is an apt description of the shape of the archipelago in the southwest Pacific Ocean between latitudes 13 and 15 degrees south and longitudes 168 and 173 west. Of the fourteen or so islands in the group, some of them hard to distinguish from rocks, only nine are inhabited and only three are sizable: Savai'i and Upolu, in the independent state of Western Samoa, and Tutuila, the chief island of American Samoa, which President William McKinley had annexed by executive order the year before Mead was born. Tutuila is about twice the size of Manhattan; Mead's sojourn began in its port and capital Pago Pago, pronounced "Pahngo Pahngo," whose harbor is considered the finest in the South Pacific.

If the climate proved too oppressive, as Boas had emphasized to Mead, she should not be ashamed to pack up and come home: her health was more important than anything, and for much of the previous year she had been thin and sickly. In the spring of 1925, Ruth Benedict had been so concerned that she sent Mead to "two doctors of the highest standing, one a neurologist"; their diagnosis was fatigue and their prescription was rest. In a triumph of wishful thinking Benedict let herself muse that Samoa's tropical climate might somehow be a therapeutic contrast to "the strenuous setting she is used to." Louise Bogan tried to console Benedict with the thought that "perhaps Samoa hasn't the aching, tearing kind of tropical oppression that Central America has. Perhaps it's higher and wilder."

Every summary of Mead's first and most famous field trip, beginning with her own account in *Coming of Age in Samoa*, stresses the fact that at not quite five feet three, weighing not quite a hundred pounds, she looked rather like an adolescent herself. In her determination, however, she had the assurance of a matriarch. "I trust Margaret," Louise Bogan said, "to make something out of nothing in almost any circumstances." Others, too, dismissed Mead's plan to study women and children as scarcely more than "nothing." In Honolulu, on her way to Samoa, she was told not to worry if the scholar E. S. C. Handy, who had tutored her in Polynesian, should be doing Samoan field work while she was there; he was concerned with religion and cosmology; there would be no overlap with her study of "low things." Apart from that condescending remark, however, the Hawaiian stop was a delight. "Picture me for these next two weeks," she wrote home, as "the most fortunate of mortals in charming surroundings, with all my needs noiselessly supplied." When she left Hawaii, she later wrote, "A whole group of people [saw me off and put] so many leis around my neck that I had to stagger up the gangplank."

But it was hard for her to sustain the festive mood the day her ship docked in Pago Pago on August 31, 1925. Disconcertingly many other Americans were around, most of them connected with the Navy. In the harbor and on all sides of the island were battleships. "Airplanes scream overhead; the band of some ship is constantly playing ragtime." The fleet was in. It was comforting to know that Dr. Cressman's friend Admiral Stitt would look after Margaret, if need be, but the noisy Navy, for all the security it implied, pushed aside the romantic literary associations.

Nobody paid special attention to Mead at the ramshackle hotel where she stayed in Pago Pago. Somerset Maugham had made this hotel famous in his 1920 story "Rain," describing it as "a frame house of two storeys, with broad verandahs on both floors and a roof of corrugated iron." She spent most of her time studying, in her six largely joyless weeks at the hotel. She was in a hurry to learn enough about Samoan geography and language to get out of Pago Pago. "I received a reasonably frosty reception from the captain who was then governor of Samoa," she wrote, "who told me firmly that I could not learn the language—he hadn't.

"I said, I thought tactfully, because he must have been at least sixty, that it was harder to learn languages after the end of the twenties. This remark did not please." With a few unimportant exceptions, as she wrote home near the end of her stay, most of what she learned was "contained in the Samoan language and not through the medium of interpreters." But her command of Samoan was to become the subject of heated dispute many years later. A flair for languages, colleagues observed, was never one of Mead's strong suits; anthropologists and others who knew Samoan wondered whether she could possibly have learned enough of the language in six weeks' time to carry out so delicate a task.

By October, in any case, she felt confident enough with the language, as she wrote Boas, to proceed to a new site. She proposed to spend the bulk of her research time on Ta'u, one of three small islands in the Manu'a group, about a hundred miles east of Pago Pago. Ta'u, she told Boas, was "the only island with villages where there are enough adolescents, which are at the same time primitive enough and where I can live with Americans. I can eat native food, but I can't live on it for six months; it is too starchy."

Although a government steamer called every three weeks at these islands, they were nevertheless "much more primitive and unspoiled than any other part of Samoa. . . . There are no white people on the island [of Ta'u] except the Navy man in charge of the dispensary, his family, and two corpsmen. There is . . . a cluster of four villages there within a few minutes' walk of each other. The chief, Tufele, who is also district governor of Manu'a, was educated in Honolulu and speaks excellent English and is probably the most cooperative chief in American Samoa."

She was "standing the climate with commendable fortitude," she also assured Boas. She needed all the fortitude she could muster; Samoa has a year-round humidity of 80 percent, with temperatures ranging between 70 and 90 degrees. Furious rains in "drops the size of almonds," as a later visitor, the writer John Koffend, described them, fall five times a day, followed by sunlight drying everything. "Everything molds overnight," this visitor added, "and in all that tropical humidity bacteria thrive, so one must treat at once the most minor cut." The air, Mead wrote home, was fragrant with the "heavy, oppressive odor" of frangipani blossoms . . . mixed on the warm breeze with the odor of slightly fermented overripe bananas," which made her think of beestung grapes. But even more trying than the weather would be the yawning gap between the time she mailed her letters and the time the answers arrived.

The letters that mattered most came from Ruth Benedict, who wrote to her young friend that she would "count off the year with the steamer's coming as the Indians do with their prayerstick plantings." Of a book of verses she had given Margaret, Ruth wrote, "I shall delight in having you feel me speaking them to you. Will you do one thing?—jot down the verses you wish you had or the ones that haunt you brokenly, and I'll send them to you. . . . It will be one of this year's crosses not to be able to have your comments on my verses while they are still fresh in my mind."

"Develop all the expedients you can against weeping," Benedict advised in another letter. "Companionship is only one of them. I've had excellent ones: they range from brushing your teeth and gargling your throat with every onset, to playing you're your own daughter for a year." Margaret thought of another kind of self-discipline: "Imagining what would have been the fate of the very definite personalities I knew—Franz Boas, Ruth Benedict, Léonie Adams, Edward Sapir—if they had been born Samoans." Luther Cressman's name was not on this list. It did not occur to anyone she met in Samoa that Mead might be married; early in her visit she had conferred on her the highly honorary title of taupou, "ceremonial virgin"—which was comparable to the chief's status the Samoans often gave to distinguished male visitors.

Spinsterhood, she found in Samoa and later, is confusing to people in primitive societies. Mary Kingsley, the English explorer, had found the absence of a husband very difficult in her lone travels through West Africa, where she collected specimens for the British Museum in 1893. Rather than admitting she was unmarried, she would explain that she was looking for her husband, and point in the direction she wished to travel. Nearly a century later, a woman anthropologist who had made several expeditions to Bali vowed, "The next time I go back there, I'll either be married or else I'll pretend to be; they can't deal with my being single except to treat me as a minor."

Since she was apparently an unmarried woman, it was unthinkable for Mead to have a house of her own. Where then was she to live? Not with the natives, who, she wrote home, "still live in beehive-shaped houses with floors of coral rubble, no walls except perishable woven blinds which are lowered in bad weather, and a roof of sugar-cane thatch over which it is necessary to bind palm branches in every storm." Some critics would later accuse Mead of something like cowardice, in passing up a chance to learn firsthand about a native household, but she made a persuasive case that it would have been inefficient to live with a native family, where there would be half a dozen people in the same room, "always sitting on the floor and sleeping in constant expectation of having a pig or a chicken thrust itself upon one's notice."

And so, when she arrived in Ta'u on November 9, Mead settled into the household of U.S. Navy Pharmacist's Mate Edward Holt, who, she said in a letter home, was "a tall fair man who reminds me quite a little of Dick in appearance." This household gave her "an absolutely essential neutral base from which I could study all the individuals in the village and at the same time remain aloof from native feuds and lines of demarcation." The household included Holt's wife, their children, and two sailors, one of whom, called "Sparks," had not been educated beyond the third grade. Sparks, Mead wrote, spent his days "fooling with new types of radio apparatus and radio magazines." Soon afterward she would have reason to be grateful that Sparks knew how to fool with those radios.

Mead's first Christmas away, four months after she had sailed from San Francisco, was cheered by a red-paper wreath from the Ash Can Cats, inscribed "Home is where you hang your halo." She was glad hers was hung at the Holts. After even a few hours in a native house, she wrote, she got "a different taste in the mouth, a sense of heavy, almost sticky heat, a feeling as if one's skin were going to fly off in thin gossamer layers." There were odd moments at the Holts': one night she woke under her mosquito netting terrified by the sound "Raw! Rah! Raugh!" which turned out to come from a deaf mute outside, looking for something in the dark. But the Navy-issue food was a welcome contrast to the Samoan dietary staple taro, the "tasteless yet individual carbohydrate," as she described the gray and shiny root, and from breadfruit, which when sliced like parsnips could be delicious, but was still strange.

Just after Christmas, on the first day of 1926, a devastating storm brought ferocious winds and then the proverbial calm, a calm that "lasted only about a minute, but the air seemed chocked full of coconut leaves so stiff they might have been wired. Even the sand was suspended in the embrace of that calm. And then the other edge of the storm . . . hit us, tearing that little calm into a thousand pieces . . . It was pouring rain and the air was full of flying sand, coconuts, parts of tin roofs, and so on."

A week later, when news of the storm reached New York, Ruth Benedict was frantic. Manu'a, she noted in her diary on January 6, had been razed. Three days later and again on January 11 she wrote, "Still no word from M," although she had sent four telegrams of inquiry. Finally, on the twelfth, came a one-word cable: "Well." Ruth wired this news to the Meads and to Marie Eichelberger, and then "took a hot bath like a ritual." Another one-word cable, no doubt transmitted by Sparks the radio man, arrived on January 22, and said simply: "Love."

Ta'u and all the Manu'a islands had been swept clean: nothing remained but the concrete churches and the copra sheds. By great good fortune the only undemolished wooden structure was the house of the Holts, which had lost only part of its roof. From this base Mead could continue with her researches among the young girls. ("I suppose you knew there was going to be a hurricane," Mead's mother wrote her. "There is one every ten years, you say, and you chose this year on purpose.") Boas had warned Mead to "be prepared to waste a great deal of time just sitting about getting to know the adolescents." Boredom, always a great fear, beset her, but she did her best to accustom herself to the rhythms of the quiet island of Ta'u and its four quiet villages.

Lacking a daily routine, especially after the hurricane had disrupted normal life, Mead did her best to spend as much time as she could with her adolescent informants. One Sunday noon she wrote home that in an hour she expected her "good Christian girl, Fealofaina," to "arrive to escort me to the afternoon service in Faleasao, an abominably hot walk, and Solomona [the pastor and political boss who had "presented" Fealofaina to Margaret] warned me to start early because we would be so wet when we got there!

"A whole procession of girls with wet lava-lavas tied as sarongs under their armpits and pails of water slung on poles over their shoulders are returning from bathing in the sea," this letter continued. "The costume problem is blessedly simplified here. I wear only a combination, a slip and a dress and Keds when I go out and walk barefoot in the house. Two little girls have just come in and two more, I see, are coming. Letter writing is over for now and conversation is in order."

The chief subject of these conversations was sex, and the style was necessarily roundabout. Very little of what Mead would report in *Coming of Age in Samoa* came from formal interviews, "but was rather deviously extracted from the directed conversations of social groups, or at formal receptions." She found it useful, she said, "to utilize the Samoan love for pedantic controversy and to propound a question to a group and listen to the ensuing argument."

First she had had to master local etiquette. "Speaking on one's feet within the house is still an unforgivable breach of etiquette," she wrote, "and the visitor must learn to sit cross-legged for hours without murmuring." For Mead, to whom silence never came naturally, this must have been especially trying. "In Samoa I learned to bend nearly double as I passed a seated person of high rank," she wrote years later, "and today when I must pass in front of some one whom I regard with deep respect, I feel a curious itching in the small of my back."

She learned more about the intricacies of Samoan manners. Men, she found, headed the house. Elderly women were supreme in their area, but for the most part women dared not speak in the presence of men on official occasions. This rule did not apply to Mead, who during these visits was obliged to make speeches of effusive gratitude, for which her debating at Barnard stood her in good stead. "America excels with the making of machinery," she told her hosts. "France excels in the making of clothes. From Italy come the greatest singers. But the Samoan people excel the whole world in hospitality." These required speeches, she wrote home, were "no picnic." Nor were sleeping conditions easy on expeditions, called *malagas* (pronounced "malahngas"). At times she had to try to rest on "Samoan feathers," fairly flat small pebbles covered with a sleeping mat woven of pandamus leaves. And once she had to take "a terrible walk over harsh pebbles and mud. Men would lose five pounds on the walk. I started thinking about the shells, and what I would do with the shells—could I make a dress out of them? That kind of highly focused, narrow attention helped me on the walk."

After the hurricane, Mead had somebody new with whom to compare her impressions. Because he could speak more Samoan than any other officer around, the United States Navy sent Chaplain William Edel to Ta'u from Pago Pago as hurricane relief administrator. With a tugboat of goods he had been dispatched to Ta'u for a three-month sojourn, to clear away debris, replant crops, and, he remembered, "get the place back on its feet." (In an enigmatic passage of *Blackberry Winter*, Mead tells of a chaplain she had met at a dance in Pago Pago, soon after her arrival. This chaplain, "thinking I was a tourist with whom he could take liberties, turned over my Phi Beta Kappa key to look for my name. I said, 'It isn't mine.' And this confused things for many months afterward." Mead does not explain what the confusion was, or who had given her the key. Maybe it belonged to Ruth Benedict, who had been elected to Phi Beta Kappa at Vassar in 1909.)

Punctilious about Navy tradition, Edel decided on his first Saturday at the Holts' to hold an official inspection of the pharmacist's mate and Sparks and the other sailor. They were required to put on dress whites and salute the visiting superior officer, who realized only later that this might have made him seem a little stuffy. Edel and his fellow guest Margaret Mead, for all that they both had Phi Beta Kappa keys and had been raised on the eastern seaboard of the United States, were not soulmates. But there they were together, under the roof of the Holts, and they had to make the best of it. Most evenings, after a day in which Edel had led work teams to repair the storm damage and Mead had interviewed her subjects, they and the Holts would play bridge. Occasionally, busy with her notes, Mead would invite Edel to her room and urge him to add whatever he had been learning about Samoan culture to her own observations; "I was deeply in love with the Samoans," he said much later, "and with their way of life." As fast as he spoke his thoughts, Mead took down his words in her notebook. She did not notice that all the while he talked he was holding a fan up before the single naked light bulb in the room, to shield her eyes from the glare.

But if Mead did not thank Edel for this small, repeated courtesy, he nevertheless developed "a high opinion of her intellectual ability, probity, and clarity. She went about her tasks with great enthusiasm and dedication," he remembered, "and sometimes worked for ten or fifteen hours a day." He was particularly impressed with her courage during a post-mortem Caesarian, which he watched from a wary distance and she from the side of the grave. The fetus was cut with a machete from the abdomen of its mother, who had died in the eighth month of her pregnancy, so that it could be buried in her arms and would not return as an avenging ghost.

"If shock is the result of early experiences with birth, death, or sex activities," Mead would write in *Coming of Age*, "it should surely be manifest here . . . where grief for the dead, fear of death, a sense of horror and a dread of contamination from contact with the dead, the open, unconcealed operation and the sight of the distorted, repulsive foetus all combine to render the experience indelible.

"An only slightly less emotionally charged experience was the often witnessed operation of cutting open any dead body to search out the cause of death. These operations performed in the shallow open grave, beneath a glaring noon-day sun, with a frighted [sic], excited crowd watching in horrified fascination, are hardly orderly or unemotional initiations into the details of biology and death, and yet they seem to leave no bad effects on the children's emotional makeup." Mead spoke to Edel about all this, he remembered, "with a frankness I found a little embarrassing," but which readers of Mead's account were to find engrossing. These daring, titillating, distinctly un-Victorian passages, presented in a spirit of academic inquiry, would establish Mead for life as one bravely willing to explain the confusing and defang the dangerous.

Years later, when rumors circulated that Margaret Mead had dallied with native Samoan men during her first field trip, William Edel said he never saw or heard anything of the sort. Liaisons between American Navy men and Samoan women were common enough; "a blind native girl at the far end of the village would call out, 'Come on in, youse guys'—we figured she must once have known a Marine from Brooklyn." But Edel saw no trace of any romance between Samoan males and his fellow house guest, who incidentally never mentioned to him that she had a husband, or that she had ever shared the chaplain's interest in religion.*

One Samoan man, Mead later told Luther Cressman, had in fact made quite clear his willingness to demonstrate his sexual prowess in order to provide her with firsthand knowledge. And though it was rumored she had taken him up on this offer, she abstained, and learned all she could in conversations which persuaded her that Samoans were so familiar with sex, and so given to dealing with sex as an art, that they had produced "a scheme of personal relations in which there are no

---

* They never met again, by Mead's choice. Once, on a visit to New York years later, Edel sent his card up to her museum tower office, with a note that he would like to come say hello. Her reply said that she was busy.

neurotic pictures, no frigidity, no impotence, except as the temporary result of severe illness, and the capacity for intercourse only once in a night is counted as senility."

To Samoans, Mead would write, the concept of celibacy was "absolutely meaningless." A youth of twenty-four who married a virgin was "the laughing stock of the village over his freely repeated trepidation which revealed the fact that at twenty-four, although he had had many love affairs, he had never before won the favours of a virgin." The Ta'u village girls told Mead of their trysts "beneath the palm trees or in the shadow of beached canoes," of what they had done to inspire "ardent love songs, long and flowery love letters," and "the invocation of the moon, the stars and the sea in verbal courtship." They told her of a curious activity called *moetotolo*, sleep crawling, "in which a man stealthily appropriates the favours which are meant for another," practiced at times by "the most charming and good-looking youths of the village." Later Samoanists, finding *moetotolo* a far less playful custom, described it as manual rape.

Coming of Age in Samoa, Mead's report of this field trip, would begin with a portrait of "A Day in Samoa." In the moonlight, she wrote at the end of this tantalizing chapter, men and maidens would dance and "detach themselves and wander away among the trees. Sometimes sleep will not descend upon the village until long past midnight; then at last there is only the mellow thunder of the reef and the whisper of lovers, as the village rests until dawn." She would tell of horseplay between young people, "particularly prevalent in groups of women, often taking the form of playfully snatching at the sex organs." She was satisfied that adolescence, for these girls, "represented no period of crisis or stress, but was instead an orderly development of a set of slowly maturing interests and activities. The girls' minds were perplexed by no conflicts, troubled by no philosophical queries, beset by no remote ambitions.

"To live as a girl with many lovers as long as possible and then to marry in one's own village, near one's own relatives and to have many children, these were uniform and satisfying ambitions." Samoans had no notion of "romantic love as it occurs in our civilization, inextricably bound up with ideas of monogamy, exclusiveness, jealousy and undeviating fidelity."

Mead's far-off husband had no doubt she would establish a degree of empathy with her subjects to which no male could aspire: "Most men of our own culture were and are poor reporters on the nature of women, because they work with a sexist bias." She was doing her best, but she had her own psychological problems, of which lonesomeness was the most acute. "News from Polynesia is apt to come piecemeal," as Robert Louis Stevenson had reported in 1890, "and thus fail of its effect, the first step being forgotten before the second comes to hand."

In future field trips, to places at least as remote, Mead would have access to a telephone, but on her maiden voyage, for word from the world she had left behind, she had to depend on a boat which every several weeks would bring "a huge batch of 70 or 80 letters which I would sit and stare at, spread out on my bed, bracing myself for whatever news they brought, whatever questions they raised." Toward the end of her stay in Ta'u, a letter came from Edward Sapir that must have reminded Mead of the conversation she and Ruth Benedict had as they watched the colors change in the Grand Canyon. Sapir's letter, as she recalled later, said "he didn't want to hurt me terribly, but he had fallen in love with someone else. I made a bonfire of all his letters on a beach in Samoa and that was the end of that." (The bonfire was highly uncharacteristic of Mead: it had been her habit before, and would be ever afterward, to save nearly all the mail she received from anybody.)

Mead got on with her work, and her research notes accumulated. But, "Oh, all the holes there are to patch," she wrote home on March 24, when she had been there four and a half months—"the width of a basket, the height of a post, the name of a feast, how they burn scars, what you really do call your mother's brother and how many fires there were at a death feast. At this stage my work looks exactly like a beaded dress only partly beaded. So there will be no more bulletins. But I have a temporary lull for this one because I've had tonsillitis and am forbidden to walk about until tomorrow."

In patching those holes, Mead was spreading herself too thin, doing work Boas had explicitly instructed her not to do. The incidental ethnography would be reported in a scholarly work, "Social Organization of Manu'a," published in 1930 by the *Bernice P. Bishop Museum Bulletin* in Honolulu. "The specified ethnographic materials in this monograph," she wrote, "were . . . almost bootlegged."

Isolated as Mead was in Ta'u, she did not know that she had happened upon a turbulent period in Samoan history. The year before she arrived, some visiting New Zealand policemen had opened fire on a procession of Samoans, killing a high chief. Though most of her friends were omnivorous readers, none apparently called her attention to an article about Samoan political troubles that appeared in the *Nation* on

April 14, 1926, when Mead was still in Ta'u. The article discussed "abuses and evils" in American Samoa and asserted that the U.S. Navy treated it as a little kingdom, "owned and operated . . . for its own benefit." It charged that the U.S. government, through the Department of the Navy, had destroyed the citizenship of the people of Samoa.*

Nothing Mead saw or heard, it seems, made her think twice about painting an idyllic Samoa in pastel tones, or suggesting that what was true of the remote island of Ta'u must be true of the whole archipelago. As her Samoan visit drew to an end, she wrote home of "a feeling of intense relief. . . . It seemed such a gamble to put a long trip and all the time it took to learn the language into a doubtful venture which might have been hopelessly cut short by illness or hurricane or what not. And when I add to this the assurance which everyone gives me that the last few weeks are always the most fruitful, then truly I have cause for rejoicing."

She had relied upon the friendliness and good will of the Samoans. They could hardly have been friendlier, nicknaming her "Makelita" after one of their dead queens, assuring her that she fit in so well that they took her for one of themselves.† Certainly they had given her a lot to write about.

Two publications would result from this field trip, though Mead's doctoral dissertation was not one of them. One was the "bootlegged" monograph, "Social Organization of Manu'a," and the other, of course, was the phenomenally successful *Coming of Age in Samoa*. That book, to the satisfaction of Franz Boas and later of a huge reading audience, would challenge the accepted idea that adolescence had to be, as Mead put it, "the time of stress and strain which western society made it. . . . Growing up could be freer and easier and less complicated: and also . . . there were prices to pay for the very lack of complication I found in Samoa—less intensity, less individuality, less involvement with life."

Her research, she said, was intended to contribute "to our knowledge of how much human character and human capacities and human

* J. A. C. Gray's *Amerika Samoa: A History of American Samoa and Its U.S. Naval Administration* recounts the trouble that erupted in Samoa when Mead was still there—and which led, on December 28, 1929, to "Black Saturday," when eleven Samoans were shot and killed.
† Raymond Firth was paid a similar compliment by the Tikopians, among whom he did extensive field work in 1927, but he said that they knew as well as he did that he was not really one of them.

well-being of young people depend on what they learn and on the social arrangements of the society within which they are born and reared." In years to come, many other scholars would disagree with Mead's Samoan work, none more vociferously than Derek Freeman, who was an eleven-year-old schoolboy in his native New Zealand at the time of Mead's first field trip.*

After nine months, she left Samoa to sail, by way of Sydney and the Suez Canal and Marseilles, back to the world she had left behind.

* The controversies surrounding Mead's reporting of her work in Samoa, and of Franz Boas's influence on it, are dealt with in Chapter 21 and in the Afterword.

CHAPTER SIX

The Voyage of the Chitral

A. H. Haddon (seated) and W. H. R. Rivers (far left, standing) during their famous 1898 expedition to the Torres Strait, just south of New Guinea. Their work greatly influenced Margaret Mead's and Reo Fortune's generation of anthropologists. Haddon would teach both Fortune and Gregory Bateson at Cambridge.

MARGARET MEAD was heading to Europe on the maiden voyage of the Pacific & Orient liner S.S. *Chitral*. This large liner, which she boarded in Sydney, would stop at a number of ports on its way to Southampton, England. Mead's plan was to disembark at Marseilles to reunite with Luther and her fellow Ash Can Cat Louise Rosenblatt, who had been studying at Grenoble. Later she was to meet Ruth Benedict, and join her at an anthropologists' congress in Rome. Ruth and her husband, Stanley, who would not separate finally for four more years, had spent most of the summer of 1926 touring Europe.

All these reunions would surely be a feast for Mead, after having nobody to talk to but the Holts, sailors like Sparks, Navy officers like Chaplain Edel, and her girlish Samoan informants. The six-week voyage to Marseilles would meanwhile give her time to sort through her notes and plan her report. Her fellow passengers, many of whom were mothers with their daughters and Anglo-Indian children with their nurses, did not look interesting enough to entice her away from her work.

But there, among them, was Reo Franklin Fortune.

Even if the two had found nothing to say to each other, Mead would have been distracted, at least for a moment. This black-haired, blue-eyed, tall young man of Irish, French, and German stock was alive with energy, and clearly and immediately attracted to her. In addition, they had everything to talk about. Fortune, a twenty-four-year-old New Zealand-born scholar, was on his way to Cambridge University in England to study psychology, the subject second closest to Mead's heart. He had been born in the village of Coromandel, once a gold-mining boom town, on March 27, 1903, when Mead was fifteen months old. His name, pronounced "Ray-o," was the Maori term for "logos," or "The Word"; he had been so christened as a compliment both to the original inhabitants of his birthplace and to the profession of his father, Peter Thomas Fortune, who had been a missionary in China at the time of the Boxer Rebellion.

All this was fascinating to Mead, whose mother had told her as a child that New Zealand had the best social legislation in the world. She had studied something of the Maoris of New Zealand, along with other Polynesians, before she settled on Samoa as a destination, and she relished the fiction of the New Zealand-born writer Katherine Mansfield. New Zealand, she later said, struck her early as "a country in which there was an insistence not only that one should not rise above one's fellows—except in excellence—but also that one should not fall below them."

The handsome young New Zealander and the alert young American, neither of whom had expected to find anyone remotely kindred to talk to on their long journey, traded life stories. Reo's early education, like Margaret's, had been eclectic. Since his father's work had been to assist vicars in different parishes around the country, he had gone to four different primary schools. He had begun his secondary education

in 1916 by commuting daily, and with great difficulty, to high school in
the town of Palmerston North. Three years later, at the age of fifty-two,
his father had resigned holy orders and, with a personal capital of forty
pounds, had taken up dairy farming at the village of Paraparaumu,
some thirty miles north of the capital city, Wellington. In 1921, Fortune
enrolled at Victoria University College in Wellington. Too poor to
board there or to attend more than six weeks of the year's scheduled
lectures, he nevertheless completed his year successfully, and went on at
V.U.C. "under exceedingly frugal circumstances" but showing "early
signs of an incredibly quick ear for cracking fiendishly difficult languages."

Like Luther Cressman, Fortune had begun his university career
studying classics. Later, also like Cressman, he had been lured into
other fields: at first philosophy and later psychology, which at V.U.C.
was classified, as logic and ethics also were, as a subdivision of philosophy. In 1923 he had taken a B.A. in advanced philosophy, and the
next year his thesis was submitted by mail to United Kingdom exam-
iners, who in 1925 awarded him an M.A. with first-class honors. Now,
having won one of the first traveling fellowships in the arts awarded in
New Zealand, Fortune was headed for Emmanuel College at Cambridge. In his luggage was the gown his father had worn in his days as
a cleric, which would save him the expense of buying academic robes.
It was just like Reo, his younger brother Barter Fortune said many
years later, to use his father's robes, "on the dual counts of whimsy
and frugality."

When Reo came home from college on a visit, his brother said,
"the whole house would ring with the sound of my father's voice as
he and Reo went at each other hammer and tongs. 'I long to see him
come,' my father would say, 'and I long to see him go.'" Reo could
not see why his father, who had rejected the religious establishment,
could still be conservative politically, so it pleased him "to con-
secrate his father's robes of former religious office to his own brand of
political apostasy." But by the time Reo reached Cambridge, "im-
pecuniosity" had added "a dimension of economic logic to the whimsy."
And "in a more serious vein, although he rejected dogma *qua* dogma,
Reo had deep feeling for the forms of ritual. . . . His father's robes
would have been of some considerable sentimental value to him because, fury of political battle notwithstanding, each had sincere regard
for the other—at a distance."

Reo's most interesting fellow passenger also had a quarrelsome
father and a deep regard for ritual. The two must have talked of these

and many other matters of common interest as the *Chitral* made its slow way across the Indian Ocean and into the Mediterranean. Reo's spirit, which a friend once said "could be with equal facility brilliant or absurd," must have dazzled Margaret Mead, as hers no doubt dazzled him. Both young passengers, as Mead wrote later, were "in a state of profound excitement . . . hungering and thirsting for communication.

"In many ways innocent and inexperienced, Reo was unlike anyone I had ever known. He had never seen a play professionally performed, he had never seen an original painting by a great artist or heard music played by a symphony orchestra. But to make up for the isolation in which he had lived in the days before modern communication, he had read deeply and with delight, ranging through the whole of English literature, and he had eagerly taken hold of whatever he could find on psychoanalysis. It was like meeting a stranger from another planet, but a stranger with whom I had a great deal in common." At this point in their lives both Reo and Margaret were accomplished listeners. A man who studied with Fortune later on recalled his striking ability to "listen to what people said—listening and challenging and arguing. 'But that's not what you said ten minutes ago,' he would tell a student. 'How can you say that? . . . You can't believe *that*, can you?'—all the while laughing at and with you, forcing you to justify and rephrase."

If Fortune's thinking was at times disjointed, six steps ahead of what he was saying, those who cared enough to pay close attention could perceive the connections. Margaret Mead perceived the connections astutely. Since her own undergraduate days, she had learned a lot about listening. From Samoa she had written home of "a curious buzzing noise inside one's head, mostly from the strain of listening." By the time she left Samoa she had learned enough to write a book people would still be arguing about sixty years later; she could surely attend with unfeigned fascination to this odd and exciting fellow passenger, whose concerns so closely matched her own.

One topic they lingered over was their shared admiration for the Cambridge psychology professor W. H. R. Rivers, who, they agreed, was the teacher they would most like to have studied with. Rivers, who had died in 1922, had been a fellow in natural sciences at St. Johns College (which later would figure hugely in Margaret's life). His *Instinct and the Unconscious: A Contribution to a Biological Theory of the Psycho-Neuroses* had so impressed Ruth Benedict that she went to a memorial service for him in New York.*

* Rivers's work was widely influential. *Instinct and the Unconscious*, published in 1920 in Cambridge, dealt at length with traumatic war neuroses

What especially impressed the young *Chitral* passengers was the study Rivers had made of the work of Sigmund Freud, whom he defended by asking: "Are we to reject a helping hand with contumely because it sometimes leads us to discover unpleasant aspects of human nature and because it comes from Vienna?" His ideas about sleep also fascinated Fortune and Mead. Sleep, Rivers had written, was "much more than the negation of psychological activity, and quite apart from the occurrence of dreams, sleep has characters of a positive kind which must be fitted into any scheme of mental happenings which seeks to be abstract and complete . . . disturbed sleep only exhausts the sufferer's strength and makes still more unequal the struggle between fear, horror, or shame, and the forces by which the attempt is made to subdue the ever-rising storm."

Reo Fortune had been studying sleep. His V.U.C. master's thesis, on the subject of dreams, obliged him, as his brother said, to "subject himself to the most rigorous regime of sleep interruption that one could imagine." His excitement about dreams proved contagious; Margaret Mead produced more dreams for him than she ever had in her life. Reo also liked chess. Margaret had no taste for such games—only the isolation of the field could have induced her to play bridge—but for his sake she was soon moving pawns and knights around the chessboard. Between matches she confided that Franz Boas was the ground under her feet, and that in ten years she hoped to do some original work. He didn't need ground under his feet, Reo replied. And he had already done original work.

Reo and Margaret were both too poor to stay in hotels ashore, as some of their fellow passengers did at ports where the *Chitral* called. A strike in Tasmania extended the length of their journey toward Marseilles from six to seven weeks. Probably the two compared notes on their rural childhoods, with Reo telling Margaret how his father applied lessons he had learned in China about the use of animal and human excrement on his dairy farm, and about the disdain he shared with his father for Anglican dogma. At the age of sixteen Reo himself had written:

---

suffered by veterans of World War I. It also mentioned the author's 1908 excursion to Melanesia, where he had marveled at "the great harmony of social life in savage peoples." An earlier book, his *History of Melanesian Society* (1914), had contained "necessary steps toward the construction of a science of social psychology." In 1924, Rivers's *Social Organization* set forth a sixfold classification of social groupings that Robert and Helen Lynd later used in their *Middletown*. A memorial medal dedicated to Rivers was awarded later by Cambridge University to Reo Fortune.

There once was a fellow named God,
A most benignant old sod,
Who, anxious to please us,
Sent us down Jesus
Till the Jews put the bastard in quod.

If Margaret told Reo how at eleven she rejected her own parents' agnosticism, he might have sensed that his irreverent limerick could offend her and told her instead about his admiration for George Bernard Shaw and other socialist thinkers whom his father regarded as unspeakable. He also might have told her how, when he came home from college on vacation, he rode the train to its last stop and then walked the final six miles. But Reo would not have bragged about this. In his younger brother's judgment, he was "excessively modest." He never "went to town on his looks, though maybe he could have. He was . . . modest and honest. Honesty was his besetting sin. He never knew how to bend the word to the prevailing wind. He was possessed of an innate courtliness, but he had no training whatever in the graces of life. . . . He was always a country boy, from an unsophisticated country at that. . . . If he'd try to kiss the vicar's granddaughter, he'd throw her up in the air and she'd break her leg."

When a fancy-dress ball was held on the *Chitral*, Margaret was enterprising about costumes for herself and Reo. They borrowed clothing, washed and pressed for the occasion, from the crew of lascars, sailors who were natives of East India, and decorated themselves with blackface. They learned from an officer, too late, that the ship's captain found these costumes "an intolerable insult."

Their fellow passengers generally left the young couple alone, no doubt assuming, as Mead later wrote, that "we were having an affair. We were not, but we were falling in love, with all the possibility of a relationship that I felt was profoundly unsuitable. Reo was so young, so inexperienced, so fiercely ambitious and so possessively jealous of any fleeting glance I gave another person."

Although she sensed trouble, Margaret was disarmed. Reo was not only passionate about anything or anyone he found interesting, he was dashingly attractive. He was also emotionally needy: he had been turned down, in New Zealand, by a fellow student, named Eileen Pope, to whom he had proposed. Margaret was accustomed to and accomplished at being needed, but in this relationship she, for different reasons, was just as needy as Reo. He distracted her from thoughts of Edward Sapir and Luther Cressman, of how tedious and confusing life had sometimes been in Samoa, of how gravely she sometimes had doubted whether she was accomplishing her mission there, and of how uncertain her future sometimes seemed. It was flattering to hear that she reminded Reo of the "life force incarnate" in George Bernard Shaw's *Man and Superman*. It was flattering, too, to hear that in Reo Fortune's scheme of things there were four kinds of girls, his favorite of which was "the girl whose shoulder straps always slip, who'll dance with you all evening because you want to dance with her."

That, Reo told Margaret, was the kind of girl she seemed to him. That must have been nice to hear after all those months of research notes and bridge games. As someone who knew both Margaret and Reo said, "She must have relished his long, intense, inconclusive but very stimulating arguments. If Luther was too sane and too organized, then Reo was the exact obverse."

Sane and organized Luther was right there at the gangplank when the *Chitral* docked in Marseilles, his blue eyes scanning the descending passengers' faces as he waited for his first glimpse of his wife after many months. He had a long time to wait. Margaret was the last passenger to appear, and she looked embarrassed. She had reason to. This scene, she later said, was one of the few in her life she would have relived differently, given the opportunity. Until the last possible minute she had stayed on board the ship with Reo, who almost succeeded in persuading her to go on with him to England.

CHAPTER SEVEN

"A Dreadful Blue Fit"

BUT MEAD finally did disembark, setting foot for the first time on European soil. Cressman, forgiving her puzzling delay, took her off to "the nicest rooms in all Marseilles." After breakfast, they did what long-parted couples are expected to do, but the earth, to borrow a phrase from their contemporary Ernest Hemingway, did not move.

"Luther," Margaret said afterward, as she sat on his lap, "do you remember that you said you had no objection to my living with someone else if I loved someone who loved me, and it was possible, and that I might go with him to marry him if his love gave me more than yours?"

"Yes," answered Luther.

"Well," said Margaret, "I have found him."

"I haven't changed my mind," Luther declared. "I love you, and my love wants only your greatest happiness."

Yet Margaret herself was not sure how to define her happiness. How, Luther wondered then and later, as he reconstructed the conversation, was anyone else supposed to?

For the moment, with Reo safely on his way to Cambridge, Margaret was glad enough to let Luther show her the South of France. In his year abroad he had paid three visits to Paris, seen Chartres, and in Grenoble bought the first of the berets he would wear for the rest of his life, but, characteristically, he had "saved some of the loveliest of France to see with Margaret." Together, he had planned, they would discover Marseilles, Arles, and Carcassonne, and then wander up the beautiful Loire Valley. After two leisurely months of getting reacquainted, Luther would precede her back to New York to find an apartment. Margaret, meanwhile, would join Ruth Benedict in Rome, at the twenty-second annual Congress of Americanists.

Luther had expected that Margaret's long months in the South Seas might have changed her, but he had not reckoned on her shipboard romance, nor had he envisioned such a "strange girl, doing things I had not known her to do before." Maybe their tour of the South of France should not be à deux; they invited Louise Rosenblatt to join them. For Louise's sake and their own, Luther and Margaret pretended things were all right between them. Only when they reached Paris did Margaret confide to Louise that all was not well with the marriage.

Somewhere in the Loire country a cable reached Luther, who had definitely decided to leave the ministry, offering him a full-time position the following fall teaching sociology at the City College of New York. At once he cabled his acceptance and, "since the month in the Midi had been such torture for us both," decided to return to New York long before he had meant to. He did this not so much to prepare for his teaching as to avoid a confrontation with Reo Fortune, who had written from England that he would be coming to Paris to see Margaret. But as matters turned out, Luther did not get away soon enough. Reo was impetuous. The boy from Coromandel arrived in Paris before the boy from Pughtown had left. One evening as Luther was leaving the hotel where he and Margaret still uneasily shared a room, "I looked up and saw this good-looking lad, taller than I, and told him, 'I'm Luther Cressman; Margaret's expecting you; I'm going out.' Then I spoke to the concierge in French, which Reo did not understand."

Nor did Reo quite understand why Luther invited him to a dinner he gave for Margaret and several of her friends who had gathered in Paris. "He expected me to want to shoot him," said Cressman, "but I was not so juvenile as that. I figured, If this woman doesn't want to be my wife, I'm not going to plead with her. I don't think I have any jealousy in me. Jealousy eats you up. I can be envious, but not jealous." Luther kept to himself the fact that he too had met and become interested in someone new: an Englishwoman nine years his senior named Dorothy Cecilia Loch. Miss Loch, it was clear, had grown fond of the young American, but it was understood that as long as he was someone else's husband, they were not to think of each other as more than friends.

One evening Luther left the Paris hotel to go for a walk. When he returned to the room he found Margaret locked in such a tight embrace with Reo that neither heard him come in. He went back out and walked some more, and did not tell her he had seen her with Reo. The two men were not precisely fighting over Margaret, since Luther was not combative, but she still must have found their rivalry for her

affections at least as confusing as it was flattering. Luther's reasonable-
ness confused matters even more. At one point he told her where in
England she and Reo, if they went there together, could find contracep-
tives, an item they had never had occasion to use on all the long *Chitral*
journey. But Reo, Luther gathered from what Margaret told him, appeared at that time to be impotent. Was Margaret being foolish to
consider Reo? At times she seemed to think so. "She offered to run
away from this with me," said Luther, "but she knew I would never
accept that solution, and that in the end I would pay the piper. She
even burst into tears."

"What should I *do?*" Margaret asked Luther.

"You'll have to decide that," he told her, "for yourself."

Margaret and Louise Rosenblatt saw Luther off at the St. Lazare
railroad station. Again Margaret cried. "I left a weeping girl there,"
remembered Luther. " 'Take care of her, Louise,' I said, and I sat heavy
of heart and bitter as the train rushed toward Cherbourg through the
lovely country where I had been so happy."

In Paris, Margaret and Reo went to museums. One day she took
him to the Trocadéro to show him an exhibit of Oceanic art. The
Samoan collection, which she particularly wanted him to see, was
locked, and so she asked a man nearby, whom she took to be in charge:
"*Est-ce que vous avez les clefs?*" Had he the keys? And then she asked,
"*Parlez-vous anglais?*"

"*Un peu,*" the man answered, with reason: he was Kenneth Emory,
a native of New Hampshire and an anthropologist on the staff of the
Bishop Museum in Honolulu; Mead had barely missed meeting him
on her way to Samoa. From this encounter sprang another of her
lifelong friendships.

Paris helped distract Margaret from the anguish of choosing between
Reo and Luther. She also found time for "ten frantic days in England,"
she later wrote to Emory, "trying to absorb large rooms full of miscellaneous Oceanic ethnography," and no doubt trying to figure out how
she felt about Fortune. In Rome Margaret spent most of her time with
Ruth Benedict, who had cut her hair short in what seemed a "helmet"
of gray, and who the previous winter had acknowledged her deafness by
getting an earphone. At first Ruth struck Margaret as dejected, but they
cheered each other up between sessions of the Congress of Americanists. Mead's month in Italy, she wrote a friend, "culminated with Mussolini's receiving the Congress with a blast of trumpets and a ruffle of
drums and all the Uniforms of the Middle Ages and the best comic
opera combined—for Mussolini, not for us." The two women also went

sightseeing, and had what Margaret described as "one of our most violent disagreements ever, over the ceiling of the Sistine Chapel," whose
outsize demigods repelled Margaret and delighted Ruth.

"I knew you wouldn't like it," Ruth said, and smiled mischievously.
But she did not smile on the Paris day, that same summer, when she
and Margaret sat in a little churchyard across the Seine from the towers
of Notre Dame Cathedral.

"Isn't it unbearable," Benedict asked as they looked up at the
cathedral, "that all this is about nothing?" Mead did not record her
answer to this question.

Reo Fortune had returned to Cambridge to write his thesis, which
would be published as *The Mind in Sleep*. Its theme was that dreams
release thoughts which have been "repressed as the result of waking
conflict," and the author used his own dreams as examples.

Fortune had not quite persuaded Mead to end her marriage. She
sailed back to New York to rejoin Luther Cressman in what he recalled as "a small but nice apartment" at 610 West 116th Street. They
were both products, after all, of solid, middle-class American stock, and
the three notable words in middle America at the time were "mother,"
"home," and "heaven." Motherhood seemed to be out of the question,
but was there hope that this particular home might be more heavenly?

For all that Luther and Margaret were intellectuals, among whose
ranks a fear was growing that marriage might wreck the lives of any
who dared it, the new chance they were giving their own marriage
seemed promising. It seemed so at least to Luther and at least for a
while, in spite of Margaret's probably psychosomatic medical symptoms. He wrote to his friend Miss Loch of the terrible neuritis Margaret had in both arms even before they were married: "She thinks
that . . . affected our relationship. Well, sometimes that part of things
[makes] her pain worse. She is never without it, and her bravery has
been marvelous. But she tends to dramatize situations and give a symbolic importance to them and this year her eyes went bad. She thought
it was I. ["That Samoan eye trouble," Mead herself said in a letter,
"continues to be an expensive and irksome nuisance."] I thought it was
glasses. I sent her to a specialist, and found out I was right." But, he
said, they were working things out quite satisfactorily, and by the
spring of 1927 "were at last very happy."

Work, as always, was a salvation and a distraction. Cressman's
students at C.C.N.Y., who included the future novelist Henry Roth,
were the most impressive he would encounter in his lifelong career as

a teacher. Mead began her first eight-hour-a-day job ever, as an assistant curator at the American Museum of Natural History. For want of a more conventional office, she was relegated to "a kind of cataloguing room up in the sixth floor tower"—a tower that over the years would become the envied headquarters and symbol of her whole independent professional life. She hung patterned tapa curtains, put Samoan mats on the floor, and spread around "many kava cups, now . . . liberally desecrated with cigarette ashes."

Mead's boss, Dr. Clark Wissler, thought that museum work fitted women, she said, "because it was like housekeeping," but she got her housekeeping tasks over with efficiently. She also had "a lot of teaching to do," for a class at Columbia, "which necessitated much learning which I didn't have and had to acquire hurriedly." She devoted all the time she could to her writing projects. She resumed her doctoral dissertation, "An Inquiry into the Question of Cultural Stability in Polynesia," and began her two accounts of field work. Her monograph, "Social Organization of Manu'a," was considerably influenced by Ruth Benedict: "every detail of the phrasing," said Mead, "was thrashed out between us." Most important, she began to summarize her findings about adolescence, which she would write about in *Coming of Age in Samoa*.

In preparing this report for a general audience, which was a daring and innovative way to think of a first account of field work, she had the considerable help of "a spry little man named George Dorsey," who had given up scholarly museum work for popular writing, and married a young wife. Dorsey first suggested that Mead send her Samoa manuscript to Harper & Brothers, where it was rejected. Next it went to an acquaintance of Dorsey's named William Morrow, who had just started a publishing firm. Morrow liked the manuscript very much, but had a suggestion.

"What would you have to say," he wrote to Mead, "if you wrote some more about what all this" (whether the stress of adolescence was or was not biological in origin) "means to Americans?" That sounded like a fine idea to Mead, who had begun to travel all over the city, when her museum work and her writing allowed, giving speeches on just such trains of thought. Outside her tower, around town, she hurried to find out what the stalwarts among her old friends had been doing. Her colleague Ruth Bunzel, at Franz Boas's urging, had written a highly respected book, *Pueblo Potters*, and had also spent a year in Chicago studying with Edward Sapir. Before his remarriage Sapir had tried to enlist Bunzel's help in discouraging Margaret from going to the

South Seas. In this matter as in most others, Bunzel had kept her own counsel. Mead noticed that this was a habit her friend still had.

"You know, Bunny," Margaret remarked to her, "you never ask embarrassing questions."

"I try not to," Bunzel said. "I still find out things, though." And so she did. A short time later Margaret approached her and said, "I just *have* to tell you about Reo," who by this time was reading anthropology at Cambridge under the eminent A. C. Haddon.

"You see, Margaret," said Bunzel after she heard the romantic tale, "how I find things out without asking?"

Léonie Adams also proved a durable confidante. She was full of news and stories. Edmund Wilson so admired her and her work that he had brought F. Scott Fitzgerald around to meet her. Later Wilson wrote that Léonie's "half Latin-American prettiness and obvious purity of spirit called for all [Fitzgerald's] instinct of chivalry. But this lasted only for about three minutes before the sloppy boor took over." Luther was Léonie's friend, too. He was pleased when she recited some of her new poems for him as they rode on a bus down Fifth Avenue to a restaurant where they drank, as he recalled, "a lot of raw red wine."

Though Dorothy Loch was much on Luther's mind, he still did not even mention her to Léonie or any of the other Ash Can Cats, least of all to Margaret, whose spirits were so visibly shaky that her friends remarked how depressed she seemed. "What's this about Margaret thinking that life is strange?" Louise Bogan asked in a March letter to Benedict. "Léonie said she had a dreadful blue fit a while back. And is she really going back to Samoa again soon?"

That rumor proved false; Mead had considered returning to Samoa but in fact would not go back for fifty years. But she was feeling low, and with reason. She could not stop herself from quoting to Luther, with feigned lightheartedness, the final three lines from the thirty-first sonnet of *The Harp Weaver*, which in 1923 had won Edna St. Vincent Millay the Pulitzer Prize:

> And some day, when you knock and push the door,
> Some sane day, not too bright and not too stormy,
> I shall be gone, and you may whistle for me.

In the early summer of 1927, Reo Fortune, who now had his degree in anthropology from Cambridge, made a tour of the great collections of Oceanic art in the museums of Germany. So, not the least bit coincidentally, did Margaret Mead, who wrote to a friend that she had taken her savings, $325, and spent eleven weeks "sopping up all the carefully labelled, carefully exhibited knowledge of nine German cities." She had reached new and proud heights of frugality—"you just never would believe you'd get to the point where you'd hesitate to spend a penny or write a letter because three and a half stamps equalled one meal"—and done "what I could, which was not much, with the German language." But Pelham Korteheuer, her cheerfully digressive traveling companion and fellow Ash Can Cat, spoke fluent German. Pelham was planning to listen to music while Margaret looked at the museum collections.

Preoccupied with her own affairs, Pelham had not kept up with Margaret's, aside from noting that things did not seem promising with Luther. "I was just about to console her on the departure of Edward Sapir," Pelham remembered, "when I learned that sympathetic arm pats weren't needed; she had Reo all lined up." But had she? Where was Reo when the two young women arrived in Germany?

"I haven't heard from him!" Margaret complained, as she "bared her teeth," said Pelham, "and stamped her feet." Had he found someone else? Or had he run out of money? Louise Rosenblatt, on a visit from Grenoble to Reo in Cambridge, had found him "a marvelous host; he came to greet me in a very old, frayed, greenish-black academic robe, the one his father had worn in his days as a clergyman, of course, and I thought 'heavens, if he's so poor I shouldn't have let him invite me here.' "

Reo was late, but he did appear, and this time Margaret would find him, as Louise Rosenblatt recalled him after many decades, "a very intense person with very keen interests, extremely intelligent and attractive, who went about things with a tremendous vigor." Mead's reservations about Fortune vanished. The previous week she had written encouraging letters to Luther. In spite of everything, they would choose an apartment for the academic year 1927-28, and perhaps revisit France the following summer. But now, after three days with Reo in Berlin, she wrote Luther another letter saying they had no future together after all.

"Is it any wonder I am badly smashed and cannot understand her actions?" Luther wrote to a friend. He was fearful that "Ray," as he spelled his rival's name, would "insist on dominating" Margaret, and pained at "the uncertainty of her suffering for oh, how I love her. And she is worth a thousand Rays. . . . Tomorrow," he concluded this letter, dated July 8, 1927, "I must rush to Philadelphia for the funeral of Margaret's grandmother, a gentle, gracious lady of 83 who loved Margaret beyond words. I am glad she did not live to know about this, for it would have broken her heart." Cressman's own heart proved to have healing powers. "Luther," exclaimed Emily Mead as soon as she saw him arriving for her mother-in-law's funeral, "you have it made." He had about him a new maturity. He had even managed to laugh the very day he received Margaret's fateful letter from Berlin. Just as he and a friend were about to go out that evening, they heard on the radio the strains of "Love's Old Sweet Song."

"Come on," said Luther to the friend. "Let's go out for dinner." When he thought about Miss Loch in London, he heard that song in his own head.

On June 25, from Berlin, Margaret wrote her mother a very short note saying she was "having a beautiful time, learning tons and being very busy and diverted the while. Gladys [Reichard, a fellow ethnographer working in Germany] and Papa Franz have overwhelmed me with letters of introduction . . . I am not going to write many letters because I have such a short time and so much to do in it." The most momentous thing she did in that short time was to decide on Fortune.

Reo headed toward his New Zealand home by way of Sydney to continue his studies under A. R. Radcliffe-Brown and to prepare for his first field trip, a six-month Australian National Research Council expedition to Tewara Island, near Dobu in Eastern Papua, which began in late 1927. Margaret returned to New York and her office at the museum, which, she wrote to a friend, had "a map of the world on one wall, and to that I turn, lovingly."

By the fall of 1927, when Mead was back in New York, Cressman had taken a bachelor apartment on Charles Street, in Greenwich Village. This change of address entitled her lawyer to claim, when the time came for their divorce the following summer, that Luther had "without any justified cause abandoned the conjugal domicile."

Mead's new domicile, at 507 West 124th Street, was shared with a succession of whichever Ash Can Cats and other friends were most in need. Eleanor Rosenberg, one of the youngest members of the Barnard-based "family," always felt at home in the different Ash Can Cat apartments around town and over the years "because most of the Ash Can Cats were about my own height—five feet, five-two at the most—and their paintings, more Impressionist than Abstractionist in those days, were at my own eye level."

Mead gave succor and shelter to her friends, but was mainly busy, as always, with her work. In speeches and in the last two chapters of *Coming of Age* ("Our Educational Problems" and "Education For

Choice"), added at her publisher's suggestion, she raised issues that would still be debated long after her death. "What are the rewards," she asked, "of the tiny, ingrown biological family opposing its closed circle of affection to a forbidding world, of the strong ties between parents and children, ties which imply an active personal relation from birth until death?" It was clear that her own strong preference, on paper as later in her personal life, was for "a larger family community, in which there are several adult men and women." Such a community, she wrote, "seems to ensure the child against the development of the crippling attitudes which have been labeled Oedipus complexes, Electra complexes, and so on."

And, she added, "the children must be taught how to think, not what to think." Ideas like these would help find a vast and receptive audience for her book, in which she had also portrayed a romantic paradise of a place where no one ever had acne or blushed from embarrassment or squirmed from frustration. If the Samoans could live so happily, she strongly hinted, perhaps North Americans could too. In the Foreword, Franz Boas urged readers to feel "grateful to Miss Mead for having undertaken to identify herself so completely with Samoan youth that she gives us a lucid and clear picture of the joys and difficulties encountered by the young individual in a culture so entirely different from our own."*

Morrow accepted the manuscript, and Mead continued to think about widening its audience. Maybe she could increase her readership if she published some magazine articles on similar subjects around the time the book came out. Which would be more suitable, she asked her publisher, *Smart Set* or the possibly more literate *Cosmopolitan?* He cautioned her, as others would throughout her professional life, to "take into account the possible attitude of your fellow-scholars whose opinions would count in connection with your further career as a scholar and scientist." Her cavalier attitude about this hazard would impose a lifelong strain on her relations with her academic colleagues.

Morrow's advice reached Mead just after a trip to Hermosillo, in Sonora, Mexico, where she filed for divorce (for which adultery was the only grounds in New York). She claimed no alimony, "in view of the fact," her lawyer said, "that she is in a position to provide for herself all the necessary means of her maintenance." Pointing out that "the

---

* Not for decades to come would counterclaims be made by other scholars that, regardless of what Mead had thought she had found, questions of sex and adolescence were still fundamentally the same in Samoa and America and everywhere else.

characters of husband and wife were incompatible," the document added that "there is not noted any rashness or bad faith on the part of any of the litigants." Indeed there was none; Mead was so solicitous of her new ex-husband as to recommend that he consider marrying their poet friend Eda Lou Walton, who in the event of Margaret's death was to inherit her Indian tree plates and her electric chafing dish.

"She and I would *never* get along, Margaret," Luther answered. "She and I are two negatives."

"I didn't know you noticed things like that," said Margaret.

"I notice a lot more than you give me credit for," said Luther.

The divorce degree, signed by Ignacio A. Navarro on July 25, 1928, allowed Cressman to take part on August 31 in quite another ceremony, in a registrar's office in the South Kensington section of London. Before "an aged registrar wearing steel-rimmed spectacles," Luther Cressman became a husband for the second time. The occasion was "truly somber," Cressman remembered, "until I took my newly married Dorothy really in my arms and gave her a thoroughly impressive kiss. The place did not collapse, but there were small shock waves."

So Margaret was free to rejoin Reo, who had been assured of a second year of research work on the basis of the reports he was making from Dobu. He planned to continue his study of primitive religion in the Admiralty Islands, north of New Guinea. The Admiralties would be as likely a site as any for the work Mead and Fortune had agreed should be her next project: "testing whether one would find among young primitive children the kind of thinking that Freud had identified as characteristic of children, neurotics, and primitives, and that Piaget, taking a clue from Lévi-Bruhl's discussion of prelogicality, had also identified as primitive."

Making the Melanesian expedition a reality was not easy. Anthropological rendezvous, Mead was beginning to learn, were "as complicated to arrange as the storied encounters of separated lovers. Each person has to get separate funds from separate sources and plan life so that the two of you will end up at the same time in the same part of the world with scientific mandates that make it feasible for you to work together in the same place. It takes a fair amount of maneuvering." But Mead was becoming a champion maneuverer.

The Social Science Research Council, which had supported her in Samoa, came through again with a grant for her to study in the Admiralties. The 1927–28 *Annual Report of the Social Science Research Council* listed Mead's project just after Harold Lasswell's. His was "Possible Uses of Psychiatric Methods in the Study of Political Personalities"; hers was "A Study of the Mental Development of Young Children among Primitive People and the Collection of Further Data upon the Behavior of Adolescent Girls among Primitive People." A shorter description of the study she planned was "the thought of the pre-school child," and she realized that there was no point worrying how silly that phrase sounded applied to a place where no schools existed. All that might soon change.*

Pliny Earle Goddard granted Mead a year's leave of absence from the museum, beginning in January 1929, and she made preparations. In August 1928 she revised her Last Will and Testament, bequeathing her manuscript copies of Léonie Adams's poems, her blue glass vase, her Chippendale mirror, and her prayer desk to Ruth Benedict; her silver bowl, her two oriental rugs, her coral necklace, her electric sewing machine, and her pair of silver candlesticks to Marie Earle Eichelberger; her typewriter, her camera, and her clock to her brother; her photograph albums to her father; a variety of things to her mother and sisters, including the "blue and white quilt made of samples of all our great-aunts' dresses" to Priscilla; all her books not otherwise disposed of to Reo F. Fortune of Paraparaumu, New Zealand; and sentimental keepsakes to the Ash Can Cats, the Holts, with whom she had stayed in Samoa, and other friends.

No more than $300, she specified, should be spent on her funeral. She wished to be cremated, and the ashes deposited in the graveyard of the Buckingham Meeting House in Lahaska, Pennsylvania. If a religious service was held over her remains it was to be the Episcopal, "read without any sermon or any sort of comment." Religion was not as important to Mead at this point as it had been, and decades later would be again.

Never for a moment was there a question of Luther's beginning his second marriage in the city where his first had foundered. "It would have been much too hard on Cecilia," he said, "to be eyed and assessed

---

* "Ethnology," Bronislaw Malinowski had written in the foreword to his *Argonauts of the Western Pacific* in 1922, "is in the sadly ludicrous, not to say tragic, position, that at the very moment when it begins to put its workshop in order, to forge its proper tools, to start getting ready for work on its appointed task, the material of its study melts away with hopeless rapidity. Just now, when the methods and aims of scientific field ethnology have taken shape, when men fully trained for the work have begun to travel into savage countries and study their inhabitants—these die away under our very eyes. . . . The need for energetic work is urgent, and the time is short."

by all those people who were part of the cloud of dust following Margaret."*

Washington State Normal School in Ellensburg, a town with a population of eight thousand, halfway between Yakima and Wenatchee, offered Cressman a position teaching social science at twice his C.C.N.Y. salary. At first he hesitated—"primarily, I suppose, because I thought Normal School teaching was work lower in status than college teaching, and the place seemed to be terribly isolated after New York City and London"—but, on reflection, he got over his "silly snobbishness" and in the fall of 1928 headed west with a high heart, high hopes and an equally optimistic bride. She charmed her in-laws, as they did her, when they met in Pennsylvania. The only thing she could not understand was their curious American fondness for corn on the cob.

News of Luther's remarriage startled most of the Ash Can Cats, who had been hearing all about Reo Fortune but had no idea that Dorothy Cecilia Loch had also been waiting in the wings. Reticence was uncharacteristic of Luther, whom one Ash Can Cat recalled as "one of those men who liked to talk to women, was very fond of us and all our friends, and listened to all our business," as they in turn listened to his. But he had kept quiet about Cecilia, as he explained much later, "because everything everyone did was just common gossip in that group. Our apartment was the center for much that went on in those remarkably social times, and I preferred to keep the whole thing private."

Mrs. Cressman, a title which suited Cecilia just fine, did not for decades choose to meet Margaret Mead. But the least Luther could do, Margaret said, was tell her what his new wife was like.

"Oh," he answered naughtily, "sort of a cross between Léonie Adams and Ruth Benedict." And then he and Margaret parted, both traveling vast distances to begin vastly different new lives.

* When they began their new life together, Luther and Dorothy decided to call each other by their middle names, Sheeleigh and Cecilia.

Mead removed her glasses for her graduation portrait in the 1923 *Mortarboard*, the Barnard yearbook.

2

3

Undergraduate Mead helped edit the *Barnard Bulletin* (2); (3) debated (at far right) with two teammates in a match against Smith College; and (4) was a founder of the redoubtable unofficial sorority the "Ash Can Cats." Members included (standing l. to r.) the poet Leonie Adams, Deborah Kaplan, and Mead; (seated) Pelham Korteheuer and Viola Corrigan. (5) Deborah Kaplan alone with Mead, 1921.

4

5

7

6

Luther Cressman (6), a second lieutenant in the United States Army in 1918, was an Episcopal minister when he and Mead were married in 1923. She also formed a strong attachment to Ruth Fulton Benedict (7), who introduced her to anthropology, to Benedict's German-born mentor Franz Boas (8) and to the brilliant linguistics scholar Edward Sapir (9), who implored her, Mead later said, to divorce Cressman and marry him.

8   9

10

11

Reo Fortune (10) had planned to study psychology at Cambridge University, but switched, partly under Mead's influence, to anthropology. In 1927, when this snapshot was taken in Cambridge, they decided to marry. His parents (11), Peter (a minister turned dairy farmer) and Hetty, welcomed their daughter-in-law in rural New Zealand, in the early 1930s.

Mead and Gregory Bateson, three years her junior. They had fallen in love in New Guinea in 1933, had a rendezvous in Ireland the following summer, and were married in 1936 in Singapore, just before beginning their field work in Bali.

13

14

15

Lawrence K. Frank's friendship with Margaret Mead began at a conference, in 1934. They never stopped conferring (16) (here at Cloverly, in New Hampshire). Near the house they shared in Greenwich Village, lived Allen and Sara Ullman (13) (photographed in Paris in 1937). The Ullmans named Mead secular godmother to their daughter Martha, pictured in 1947, at age nine, horseback riding with Jane Belo (15). Belo's interest in Bali first kindled Mead's. The English writer Geoffrey Gorer (14) became so close a friend that Mead referred to him, to her godchildren, as "Uncle Geoffrey."

16

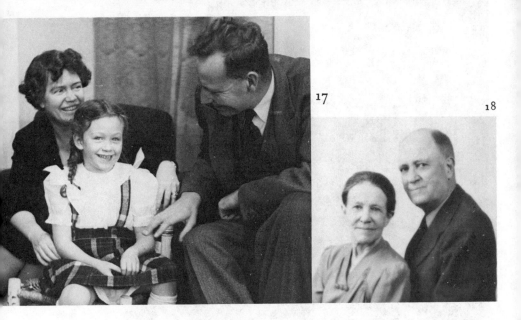

In the middle 1940s Mary Catherine Bateson still had two resident parents (17). Her grandparents Emily Fogg and Edward Sherwood Mead (18), whom she called "Bompa," wished friends a happy new year with a 1945 portrait. Priscilla, Margaret's youngest sister, posed for a 1948 Christmas snapshot with her children Madeline, Philip and Peggy Rosten (19).

For half a century Mead's museum office was this turret (20) overlooking Columbus Avenue and 77th Street. After her fiftieth birthday she had the top removed from the rolltop desk in her office (21) to make more room for work, but in a whimsical moment posed with an artifact (22).

22

20

COURTESY PAUL BYERS

23

Mead dispatched her curatorial duties at the museum with the help of assistants (23) but was more exhilarated by conferences, at which she spent as many as forty days a year. Rhoda Metraux (F), Gregory Bateson (B) and Ray Birdwhistell (D) were among her fellow conferees at this 1963 meeting on families (24).

KEN HEYMAN

24

25

26

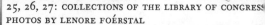
25, 26, 27: COLLECTIONS OF THE LIBRARY OF CONGRESS
PHOTOS BY LENORE FOÉRSTAL

27

29

During Mead's 1953 return to Manus she talked with children (25), got reacquainted with John Killipak (26), who had been a child himself when she and Reo Fortune worked there in 1928, and did her best to console a crying baby (27). Mead was delighted with this model of Peri, her village in Manus (28), which was shown to the Manus political leader Paliau (29) when he visited the American Museum of Natural History.

31

After her friends the Franks moved to Boston, Mead took an apartment in a nearby Greenwich Village house on Waverly Place (30, 31), owned by Rhoda Metraux. Cathy Bateson (32) returned to this house after a sojourn studying in Israel in 1957; her mother and Theodore Schwartz (reflected in mirror) watch her open mail.

30

30, 31: KEN HEYMAN

32

33

34

L KREMENTZ

KEN HEYMAN

The more surrounded Mead was by young people in her classes at Columbia (33) and her office at the museum (34), the happier she was. It pleased her to see former students like the ethnographic filmmaker Timothy Asch (to her left in this 1977 Bali picture) at work on their field sites (35).

RYL BERNAY

35

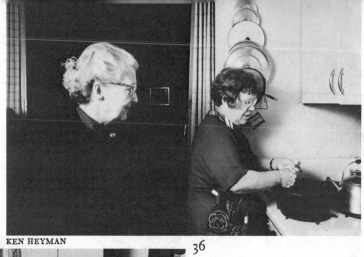

KEN HEYMAN

36

Marie Eichelberger (36), a social
worker and devoted Mead friend
since Barnard days, helped send
her off to Samoa in 1925 and managed her business affairs. Rhoda
Metraux, walking with Mead from
their apartment just a block from
the museum (37), first collaborated
with her in 1942. Philleo Nash,
who met Mead in Chicago in the
1930s, helped to organize a 1976
celebration (38) to honor her fifty
years in anthropology.

37

38

JILL KREMENTZ

INSTITUTE FOR INTERCULTURAL STUDIES

PETER GOLDBERG · 39

COURTESY, JEAN HOUSTON

Already sick with her final illness, Mead sat at a 1977 forum (39) between her museum associate Malcolm Arth and Gregory Bateson. One of her most attentive friends in the last decade of Mead's life was the philosopher Jean Houston (40). Vanni Kassarjian visited her grandmother later in 1977 (41).

40

41

BERYL BERNAY

Wilton Dillon and a delegation of friends brought Mead's forked stick to John Killipak in Manus.

PART TWO

In normal conditions, fieldwork is already enough of a strain: you have to be up at daybreak, and then remain awake until the last native has gone to sleep, and even sometimes watch over him as he sleeps; you have to try to make yourself inconspicuous, while being constantly present; see everything, remember everything, note everything; display an embarrassing degree of indiscretion, coax information out of a snotty-nosed urchin and be ready to make the most of a moment's obligingness or carelessness; or alternatively, for days on end you have to repress all curiosity and withdraw into an attitude of research because of some sudden change of mood on the part of the tribe. As he practises his profession, the anthropologist is consumed by doubts: has he really abandoned his native setting, his friends, and his way of life, spent such considerable amounts of money and energy, and endangered his health, for the sole purpose of making his presence acceptable to a score or two of miserable creatures doomed to early extinction, whose chief occupations meanwhile are delousing themselves and sleeping, and on whose whims the success or failure of his mission depends?

—CLAUDE LÉVI-STRAUSS
Tristes Tropiques

CHAPTER EIGHT

"Now Piyap
Can Write It Down"

Drawing collected by Margaret Mead in Manus, 1928.

"SHE ISN'T PLANNING to be the best anthropologist," Ruth Benedict had been overheard to say of Mead, "but she *is* planning to be the most famous." Mead's twenty-seventh birthday was approaching as she headed for her second South Seas trip and her second marriage, in the fall of 1928. Before she left New York she wrote to Bronislaw Malinowski at the London School of Economics, thanking him for the pioneering he had done in psychological field work and saying she looked forward to his criticisms of the copy her publishers had sent him of her "work of apprenticeship," *Coming of Age in Samoa.* Malinowski's was one of the two biggest names in "social anthropology," as the discipline was referred to in England. The other was A. R. Radcliffe-Brown, now at the University of Sydney, who had approved Reo Fortune's work in Dobu and soon would send him, along with his new wife, Margaret Mead, to the Admiralties.

In San Francisco, after a placid trip across the continent by train, Mead was given encouraging news about her health. A Dr. Jarvis, who had treated Emily Fogg Mead, told her that the persistent trouble she had been having with her arms and lately with her eyes stemmed from a sinus infection. He could cure it, he said, by performing an operation on her nose. This, they agreed, could be done on her return trip. On the *Malolo,* bound for Honolulu, she had a cabin to herself, but her genteel fellow passengers included a Professor and Mrs. Mead to whose stateroom was mistakenly delivered "a ton of Flit," Mead wrote, "which the Flit company has sent me with its compliments for my trip." Already she was a bit of a legend.

In Honolulu she was briefly the house guest of a Barnard classmate who lived in a Waikiki Beach apartment with friends of whom Margaret took a dim view. "I can't *stand* the way you live," she informed her hostess. "Don't you know any people who have *minds?*"

"Look," said the classmate, "this is Waikiki Beach. People aren't *supposed* to have minds here. But some people in Honolulu do." That Margaret knew, from her mother's college friend Mrs. Freer, the wife of the former governor, and from ties she had formed on her way to Samoa with scholars at the formidable Bernice P. Bishop Museum. And so she arranged to move to more elevating and congenial quarters, not a minute too soon to suit her Barnard friend. "The rest of us in that carnal Waikiki paradise just went on as we had been, gulping down liquor and having liaisons," said the friend. "I wouldn't have given Margaret much further thought at all, after her ship sailed on, except for what she did next. Can you imagine what she did next? She wrote to my mother to tell her what a tramp I was, and how loose were my morals!

"Now I'll say this," said the classmate in 1981, with anger still in her voice: "Margaret was right, I was on the wrong track in those days, but what right did she have to tell my mother, and worry her?"

Fortune joined Mead in Auckland, on October 8, and insisted that they be married then and there, instead of waiting, as they had planned to do, until they got to Sydney. Radcliffe-Brown had bet Reo Fortune that Margaret Mead would not really become his wife; perhaps after three years of romantic indecision Fortune decided he could not bear to take chances. On such short notice he could not easily find the right size wedding ring for what one of Mead's later friends would describe as the smallest adult hand he had ever shaken, but finally a jeweler was located who could alter a ring just in time for the couple to reach the registry office before it closed, "and make a dash to the ship before it sailed," Mead later wrote. "So we arrived in Sydney and presented Radcliffe-Brown with a fait accompli." Not until later would she meet Fortune's family in New Zealand.

There was nothing ambiguous about Mead's plans. She knew exactly what she wanted to do: study the minds of primitive children. She knew where it should be done: in the Admiralty Islands. And she knew whom she wanted for a partner: the author of *The Mind in Sleep* and the future author of *Sorcerers of Dobu,* his account of the field work he had just completed. That book, the great Malinowski would say, showed that Fortune had "the ethnographer's supreme gift: he can integrate the infinitely small imponderable facts of daily life into convincing sociological generalizations." Malinowski called it the best, most informative account of field work he knew, and "a book of permanent value."

In the Admiralties, Mead would continue the study she had begun in Samoa of primitive children: she would try to find out how primitive children think. Fortune, meanwhile, would continue the study he had begun in Dobu of primitive religion: he would be concerned with the imponderable aspects of the people's lives—their religion, from which he expected they would be converted—and with their morals. He was strong and keen and amazingly learned about the very things that interested Mead most. If she was not much more attracted to him sexually than she had been to Cressman, maybe that would change in time, or maybe it didn't matter. Professional partnership was the main thing. If all this had happened fifty years later, and she had had to summarize her needs in a classified Personal ad, she could have described herself with the acronym for "divorced white female" and written:

> DWF, 27, Ph.D., bent on global renown, seeks ethnographer husband for extended field work in malaria-ridden tropics. Must be expert climber, linguist, photographer, marksman. Knowledge of classics and psychology helpful, paternal ambitions immaterial.

Fortune met all these requirements and more. He was attentive— to a fault, Mead would find—and, by now, experienced in the field. With the Dobu, a tribe who lived on the island of Tewara in the D'Entrecasteaux group of the Bismarck Archipelago, northeast of Papua New Guinea, he had spent the six months of his first exhaustive field expedition alone.

As a lone Western man, in a context radically different from any he had known, Fortune had fared astonishingly well among the Dobu. Women of the tribe, who were not supposed to have much to do with the opposite sex, had eluded their menfolk to visit Reo's hut and trade the information he wanted for tobacco. The New Zealand farm boy, so new to anthropology, could not have known how rare such a feat was. When he left the island for Christmas of 1927, one of the head men took a boot and a comb of Fortune's to work a magical love charm.

He was lucky it wasn't another kind of charm. Dobuan men came of age awed by the hypnotic powers of sorcery, which some among them could practice. Sorcerers made life hard for Dobuans who got ahead other than by old age and primogeniture, the accepted avenues to success. Fortune had learned all he could about what sorcerers did, and how, at the age of nine or ten, a Dobuan boy had his septum and earlobes pierced, and tight arm bands forced up over his elbows in an agonizing, hour-long procedure initiating him into manhood.

Now, at Radcliffe-Brown's suggestion, Fortune and Mead were heading for an island group between latitudes 1 degree 50 minutes and 2 degrees 25 minutes south and between longitudes 146 and 148 degrees east, to live among fishermen whose houses stood on stilts in sea lagoons, between the reef and the shoreline. There they would begin work leading to their next books—his *Manus Religion* and her *Growing Up in New Guinea*—during what her old admirer Edward Sapir would describe a few months later as "an age of perfectly terrifying loneliness." Working together would protect both from the loneliness they both had experienced on their first field trips, and would teach them more than either could hope to learn alone, or with a partner of the same sex. Sex antagonisms were so strong in Melanesia, Mead would find, "that no member of one sex can hope thoroughly to win the confidence or understand the point of view of the other." She and Reo set forth as if in answer to the question with which Malinowski concluded his *Argonauts of the Western Pacific*: "The study of Ethnography—so often mistaken by its very votaries for an idle hunting after curios, for a ramble among the savage and fantastic shapes of 'barbarous customs and crude suggestions'—might become one of the most deeply philosophic, enlightening and elevating disciplines of scientific research. Alas! The time is short for Ethnography, and will the truth of its real meaning and importance dawn before it is too late?"

The songs Fortune had collected during his field work among the Dobu represented an earthiness that is fairly typical of the tribal world—a combination of sexual simplicity and elegant allegory. One of them went this way:

> Kuyoni child kuyoni
> Undress that I may see
> Undress that I see, see
> Kuyoni her mons of Venus
> White as the pandamus flower
> Undress that I may see.

Another, as Fortune translated it from the Dobuan, went:

Vulvas of evil
A cooking pot full around
full, full around
full, full around
your vulvas we eat
with a crowd of my mother's brothers
a cooking pot full around.

Now, returned to civilization, Fortune was eager to introduce his
bride to his friends in Sydney. "But you've simply *got* to meet Caroline!" he told her, a short time after their boat had deposited them
there. He was referring to Caroline Tennant Kelly, an anthropologist
married to the landowner Timothy Kelly. The genial and hospitable
Kellys were Reo's closest Australian friends, and he could not imagine
why nobody came to the door of this lovely old house near Sydney University, where Caroline had told them they would be that night. He had
been knocking and knocking, to no avail, and so finally he broke in.
The Kellys and the other people inside the house were no noisily rehearsing amateur theatricals that they did not hear Fortune. Such performances, in the opinion of A. R. Radcliffe-Brown, were "the best possible laboratories for anthropologists," which may have been part of the
reason Reo liked the plays of George Bernard Shaw. When the Kellys
were finally found, Caroline was charmed enough with Reo's American
bride to invite the young couple to stay with her: "they hadn't a lot of
money, and were glad to save hotel bills." This hospitable friendship
would last all of Mead's life. On future field trips to the lower half of
the eastern hemisphere she would leave her luggage with the Kellys on
arrival and stop to pick it up later, on the way back north; she would be
succored and would find out, in passing, what was on Australian minds,
particularly the minds of social scientists. Mead grew so attached to
Australians and Australia that she once thought of settling there.

But Radcliffe-Brown himself was not at first so welcoming. Maybe
Fortune's adviser felt a little threatened by the younger man's precocity.
Certainly he seemed irked with Fortune's ambitious young wife when
she showed him a typescript of her monograph "Social Organization of
Manu'a." One point in the monograph, Mead wrote on October 28,
1928, to Ruth Benedict, so angered Radcliffe-Brown "that he was barely
civil to me and didn't introduce me to A. P. Elkin, who has just come
back from the field; and remarked caustically that he'd changed his
mind and thought the book shouldn't be published in England, it being the kind of thing which was more appreciated in America . . . He
really is rather insufferable because he is so sulky and rude whenever he

is crossed . . . he identifies himself with every idea that was ever voiced and any disagreement, tacit or uttered, with his ideas he takes as a slap in the face."

Later Mead sent Benedict articles on "Broken Homes," intended for the *Nation*, and on "Americanization in Samoa," intended for the *American Mercury*. She also mailed some technical writing, the untyped first draft of Fortune's *Sorcerers*, and a letter petitioning the United States Department of Labor to admit Reo Fortune to America, where he planned to go when this expedition was over. Ruth was to have this petition sworn to by two witnesses, along with copies of Reo's application for a fellowship at Columbia University. But all this ambitious planning, meant to simplify life for her husband as well as for herself, could not free Mead from anxiety, particularly about *Coming of Age in Samoa*.

"I dreamed last night that the book had failed completely," she wrote to Benedict, and "that the publishers who were doing the monograph had left out the dedication to you. I know what that means— I'm dissatisfied with the monograph . . . Brown finally said he had no criticism to offer—[that it was] probably the most that could be done with the material." If there was a nervous air of competition among ethnographers in Sydney, there was a reason: one visitor to Australia in 1925 wrote of hearing that "there is a population of 2,000 white people in Papua, of whom 1,782 wrote articles upon anthropology for the Sydney Bulletin."

But Margaret and Reo were going somewhere more dramatic. The next leg of their voyage, from Sydney to Rabaul, was in "a tiny, evil smelling little tub" called the *Marsina*, which took twelve days to reach Rabaul, and whose menu consisted of "eighteen curries, different in name only." On their way north they stopped for an afternoon at Samarai, where "Reo collected a group of his natives and elucidated an obscure point in the Dobuan kinship system."

In Rabaul, the biggest town on New Britain Island and one of the most European in Melanesia, they looked for an interpreter to guide them to and around the island of Manus, where with Radcliffe-Brown's help they had decided they would be working. They hired a youth named Banyalo, who happened to come from the south Manus coast village of Peri. On the way to Banyalo's village they stopped in Lorengau, the capital of Manus, where the two dozen resident white people, Mead wrote home on November 22, "all speak to each other, but hate is rampant. It was better at Pago Pago where they didn't speak to each other." Interracial tension was rampant in Papua, too. Two years earlier, according to Amirah Inglis's *Sexual Politics in New Guinea*, the government had passed a White Women's Protection Act, decreeing that "any New Guinea man who makes advances to a white woman or girl and causes her harm will be punished severely . . . will be sent to prison and will also be beaten with a cane fifty times a day for three days . . . will be put in prison for life and, if the Government wishes, he will be hanged."

Mead and Fortune had no particular fondness for their interpreter Banyalo, nor any more interest in his village than Mead had originally had in Samoa as a place to study adolescence, but if Peri was the young man's home, then Peri was where they would have the least difficulty learning their way around.* As soon as the couple had a fixed address, Mead mailed at-home announcements to her friends. Louise Bogan, who received one of them, wrote to Ruth Benedict, "Margaret is one to be *quite* at home in whatever Mandatory Province!"

There was a lot to learn. They were pioneers. "The ethnologist," Mead wrote, "cannot march upon a native community like an invading army, for that community is going to be not only a source of labor and food, but also the very stuff of his investigation. He must slip in quietly, lower himself or herself as gently as possible into the placid waters of native life, make the unprecedented arrival of an inquiring white person as inconspicuous as possible . . ." Most indigenous people, she wrote, "had only one kind of contact with white people, as inferiors, either as work boys or merely as British subjects dealing with occasional government officials very much on their dignity. The house of a white man, any house in which a white man took up temporary quarters, was forbidden to the native, except in his servant capacity or as cook or house boy.

". . . Into this setting stepped ethnologists who could not work unless all these carefully constructed barriers for the peace of the white invader were summarily shattered. To the native it was as if we hung up a shingle saying, 'We want to be bothered, we aren't like the other white people,' and they responded to this chance of a lifetime with great vigor . . . not until midnight was there any peace." And always there were new customs to learn, new *faux pas* to avoid. They learned slowly, as all field workers must, about the people who would be their informants.

"I shall never forget the panic caused among a group of visitors,

---

* Over the next five decades Mead would come back oftener to Peri than to any other field site of her career.

early in our stay," Mead wrote, "when my husband complied with one person's tentative request that he pronounce my name. Several people almost fell into the sea in their horrified retreat from such blasphemous behavior."

The natives instead referred to Reo Fortune as Moeyap, which means Western Man, and to his wife as Piyap, Woman of the West. "When I arrived among the Manus," Mead wrote later, "they had already been quarreling for thousands of years about how many dogs' teeth somebody had paid to somebody else. They could count way up in the thousands in their heads, but of course you couldn't prove what was in somebody else's head, so it was an endless quarrel.

"So the first thing they said to me when I came along was, 'Ah, now Piyap can write it down. You write down every single transaction and we won't need to quarrel any more.'" Fortune and Mead also found that "it was necessary to construct a house with several exits," as Mead wrote, "so that mothers-in-law could depart as sons-in-law entered, for it is always the women who have to do the running away."

Twenty-one years later, much of America would be singing "Bloody Mary's Chewing Betel Nuts," from the Broadway musical based on James Michener's *Tales of the South Pacific*. This was old news to Mead, who in a 1928 monograph explained that all native women in this part of the world were referred to as "Mary"; that "bloody" was one of the commoner adjectives; and that betel nut, the narcotic most favored by natives, seemed no more odd to them than alcohol did to the man who told her, in Melanesian pidgin: "All the same you fellow longlong around drink-em whiskey, now beer, now brandy, now kirsch, now champagne, now altogether something you fellow savee drink along fashion belong white man." In this Mandated Territory of New Guinea, Mead was discovering "a strange, widely flung culture . . . a new culture bred of the contact of the white man and the native, a culture that is breaking down barriers hundreds, perhaps thousands of years old . . . a strange culture that requires boys whose homes are widely scattered to 'go, go-go-go, two fellow Sunday' (two weeks) to reach the places from which they came, but they speak a common language, Pidgin English or 'talk-boy,' and their canons are homogenous and simple.

"This," Mead wrote, "is the culture of the work boy, the boy who has made, or is about to make 'paper' with the white man, as plantation hand, member of a boat's crew, wharf laborer, or laborer in the gold fields. . . . When they return to their villages, they will be armed with a language of rebuke or contempt which they can shower at will upon their less traveled 'Marys.' . . .

"Pidgin," she went on, "is a stark, unadorned language, without euphemism . . . without delicacy, racy, picturesque, exceedingly adequate, musical when well spoken but withal graceless." This pidgin was new to both Mead and Fortune, who had conducted his work among the Dobuans in their local dialect. His field work there had equipped him superbly for whatever rigors he might find among the seafaring Manus. The Dobuans, by his standards, had been unimpressive sailors, less willing than he had been himself to cross "open seas by canoe, exposed to the full Pacific swell and without any reef to hug, at the rate of forty miles a day, sailing by daylight or by night indifferently."

Mead's luggage for the expedition included "drawing paper for the children—I took a thousand sheets and the supply ran out in the first month—baubles by the gross, beads, toys, balloons, paper flowers, etc., and large and bulky amounts of rice and tobacco. Everything had to be packed into cedarwood boxes with double locks, one of which sang when it was turned like a musical clock to warn the owner of the prowling thief . . . The tobacco had to be unpacked from the telltale crates in which it is shipped from Louisiana, and repacked in ambiguous cedar boxes."*

What was she doing with all that drawing paper? What did she expect to learn about the minds of children? In the back of her own mind as she planned this expedition, Mead later wrote, were two things: the influence of the progressive education movement and "a quick and partial interpretation of the first flush of success in Russian educational experiments," which had caused educators and philosophers to say, "Yes, the child is malleable, he takes the form you wish him to take; therefore, if you train him sufficiently differently from the way his unfortunate parents were trained, in no time at all you will produce

---

* Tobacco, to anthropologists doing field work in many parts of the world, was and still is an essential supply. One husband-and-wife team entering a Guatemalan village were cautioned in advance to take up cigarette smoking in order not to be classified as missionaries. "Without tobacco," as Marjorie Shostak quotes an African informant in her 1981 book Nisa, "you wake up and walk around all day with only half your heart and don't know when the sun rises or sets." Shostak wrote that there was no point in telling Africans tobacco was bad for their health. "They didn't care, or even believe us . . . and argued further that we should give them something that made their life more enjoyable. After all, they cooperated with us, letting us intrude into their lives; we, in turn, should give them something that we could easily get and they badly wanted."

a new generation which will build a new world." This showed, Mead said, that "our premise—the flexibility of human nature—had already been turned to point a social philosophy of cultural change. It was necessary to examine it."

But she found that despite their exposure to social forms different from those that ruled their parents' lives, "when they passed adolescence, the generous gay co-operative Manus children turned into grasping competitive Manus adults. On the basis of the Manus material, we could add a caution: Human nature was malleable, yes; children could be given years of freedom apparently emphasising other values from those which ruled the lives of their fathers and mothers, yes. But there were limits to this malleability. It was no use permitting children to develop values different from those of their society. The adult forms . . . always won. Human nature is flexible, but it is also elastic—it will tend to return to the form that was impressed upon it in earliest years. From this it follows that 'Culture is very, very strong. You cannot alter a society by giving its children of school age new behaviour patterns to which the adult society gives no scope.' "

The question of how primitive children think had concerned Mead since the early days of her friendship with Edward Sapir. She had introduced Sapir to *The Growth of the Mind: An Introduction to Child Psychology*, published in 1924 by the influential psychologist Kurt Koffka. "The only characteristics that are important in the world of primitive peoples," Koffka held, "are generally different from those that are important in our own world. This difference is apparent in primitive drawings and their relation to reality." This was why Mead had packed so much drawing paper.

Assuming, as Mead did, that Freud and Lévi-Bruhl and Piaget and others were correct in claiming that primitive people, civilized children, and neurotics were alike in their patterns of thought, what then were the thought patterns of primitive children? Koffka's book made it clear that many riddles and questions remained unsolved: "The nature of mental development as it has been revealed to us is not the bringing together of separate elements, but the arousal and perfection of more and more complicated configurations, in which both the phenomena of consciousness and the functions of the organism go hand in hand."

The sooner Mead could get to know primitive children, the more productive she would feel. Those who preoccupied her first and most were young males between twelve and thirty, who were more affected than anyone else in the Mandated Territory of New Guinea by the new culture of the pidgin-speaking "talk-boys." The younger children showed her that it was wrong, as she would write in *Growing Up in New Guinea*, to suppose that "all children are naturally creative, inherently imaginative, that they need only be given freedom to evolve rich and charming ways of life for themselves." These children were allowed to play all day long, she said, "but, alas for the theorists, their play is like that of young puppies or kittens. Unaided by the rich hints for play which children of other societies take from the admired adult traditions, they have a dull, uninteresting child life, romping good-humoredly until they are tired, then lying inert and breathless until rested sufficiently to romp again."

During her six months' "concentrated and uninterrupted field work" in "a social setting which I learned to know intimately enough not to offend against the hundreds of name tabus, I watched the Manus baby, the Manus child, the Manus adolescent, in an attempt to understand the way in which each of these was becoming a Manus adult."

While Mead did this, Fortune was concentrating on Manus ancestors. Each Manus household contained the skull of an ancestor, referred to as Sir Ghost. "The Manus are not aware," as Fortune wrote, "that modern Christianity challenges their most formal postulate—that unexpiated sin causes death . . . in cases of malaria, they always have recourse to their oracles to shrive them of their sins, never to the quinine. The government quinine supply is poured into the sea, and application put in for more on occasion in order to please the government."

The ghostly cult, Fortune found, was "fluid and amorphous. It has form, but it is a wide, loose form that follows the recurring accidents of existence. It is a system adjusted to deal with the passage of the individual through time, but in contrast with Manus *rites de passage*, which deal with the steady, healthy progress of the individual life cycle, it is adjusted to emergencies and disasters . . ." Manus virtues, he went on, strikingly resembled the virtues of strict puritan Christianity; the Manus religion embodied "a belief that setting man right with man sets him right also with the supernatural and exemplifies on the lowest level of the ancestor cult the thoroughgoing coalescence of religion and morality that has been characteristic also of the Christian religion."

Among the Manus, Mead whetted an old talent for matchmaking and developed a new one for medicine. In an article she described "a tall, shaggy-headed sorcerer, with one injured eye and a bad case of ringworm, who sought my aid to cure his disfigured skin. Day after day he came to be treated, while I supervised the application by one of the small boys of a stronger lotion than the natives were allowed to have themselves. After about two months Patiliyan was cured, and made me the confidant of his projected elopement with a widow. The wrath of the ghostly husband shook the village and killed an unfortunate woman go-between, and the whole village was thrown into confusion—which was priceless to the ethnologist—all from a steady application of ring- worm medicine to make the lover beautiful and desirable to a much wooed and most excellent maker of pots."

Mead had new medical troubles of her own. In April she had to go to Lorengau to get a pair of crutches for a foot she told her mother was "strained," but in fact, according to her official report of the ex- pedition, was fractured. The whole time she was in Manus, she later wrote, she suffered from malaria, which *Merck's Manual* describes as "an acute, sometimes chronic but often recurrent febrile disease char- acterized by periodic paroxysms of chills followed by high fever, sweat- ing, intra-erythrocytic parasites, splenomegaly, and occasionally jaun- dice." The patient is hot, then cold; the spleen enlarges and the skin may turn yellow. The fevers can last for eight hours; the paroxysms can go on for three days, and in between the paroxysms "the patient usu- ally feels miserable and runs a low-grade fever." And, in areas where falciparum malaria flourishes, as in the South Pacific, it can be fatal. Blackwater fever is the last stage of this kind of malaria.

At one point during this expedition a Manus tribesman, a builder named Lalinge, assured Mead that in case her husband was unkind to her she might regard him, Lalinge, as a brother, but Fortune was kind; he nursed his wife tenderly during her attacks, and she recovered enough to persevere with her work. In general she was impressed with her subjects. "The little bush monkey, naked except for his loin cloth, with pierced septum and ear lobe and scarified back, is sophisticated in the ways of the white man, far beyond the sophistication of many Eu- ropean peasants," she wrote.* "One problem, however, resulted from taking boys up in airplanes, which has produced complications the mis- sionaries did not foresee when they taught their converts 'God he stop on top along sky' "—God, in other words, is in His heaven.

"This dogma did very well until airplanes, familiarly described as 'motor car belong Jesus,' came into such constant use at the gold fields that some masters took their boys up to the fields in a plane rather than send them the seven-day journey up the mule tracks. Then the boys who rode above the clouds looked around for God and did not see him, and so would scratch their heads perplexedly upon alighting."

* Racist though such terms sound by present standards, they were common- place among ethnographers in the early part of the twentieth century. Bron- islaw Malinowski often refers, in his diaries, to "the niggers."

Research was going well, but by early May, as Fortune wrote to Ruth Benedict, they were both looking forward with "overpowering pressure" to getting out of primitive society. He and Benedict had been corresponding because she was so impressed with what she had heard of his work among the Dobuans. She asked permission to use some of his material—along with her own from the Zuni and the Pueblo, and Franz Boas's from the Kwakiutl—in a manuscript she was preparing herself. It would be her celebrated best-seller, *Patterns of Culture*, in which she visualized culture as an integrated whole, and applied to groups the psychological concepts usually reserved for individuals. Fortune replied that he was pleased to oblige, as he and his wife packed up to leave Manus in the middle of July.

On the way to Sydney, Fortune made a side trip from Rabaul to revisit the Dobuans and photograph them for his book. Mead had planned to go with him, but at the last minute followed another impulse. In Rabaul she was introduced to a woman in her sixties named Phoebe Parkinson, whose mother had belonged to a chiefs' family in Western Samoa and whose German father, one of eighteen children, had been the nephew of an American bishop. Another American was supposed to have written Mrs. Parkinson's biography but had not done so.

The same day Fortune left to take his pictures in Dobu, Mead went with Mrs. Parkinson to her home in Sumsum, where she stayed for several weeks to record the story of this curious multicultural life. "Rapport was a matter of seconds," Mead wrote, "for I still spoke polished Samoan," which Mrs. Parkinson rarely got a chance to hear any more. Whether or not Mead ever spoke polished Samoan, later critics charged that Mrs. Parkinson could not have known what she was talking about when she "cleared up" a point about Samoan virginity customs that Mead admitted had "always worried" her.

In Samoa Mead had been told that if a *taupou* (ceremonial virgin) proved not to be a virgin after all, when her husband's talking chief came with his fingers wrapped in white *tapa* to take the tokens of virginity, the girl would be beaten to death. "This punishment seemed too severe for the Samoan ethos," Mead wrote in "Weaver of the Border," her account of these interviews, "but happily, Mrs. Parkinson had the answer for which I had been seeking. . . . 'If the girl is not a virgin she will tell her old women, and they will secretly bring the blood of a fowl or a pig,' and smear it on a mat spread on the ground, which mat was then displayed to all, whereupon the bride's old woman relatives 'rub the blood on their faces and dance and sing and the husband waves it in the air like a flag, and then goes in, behind a *siapo* [bark-cloth curtain] to his wife.' "*

Mead should have looked further, her critics said, for an authoritative answer to the problem of the blood of the *taupou,* instead of relying on an informant who had spent so little time in Samoa.

On this and many other occasions in her career, Mead's haste invited not only skepticism but ire. A story has been told about A. C. Haddon, the founding father of British anthropological field research: "when Haddon read the first ethnographic work of a now famous lady anthropologist," this story went, "he reacted with incredulity. After a while, it is said, he remarked that when he organized the Torres Straits Expedition of 1898, he took out with him three psychologists (W. H. R. Rivers, C. S. Meyers, and William McDougall). He did so in the expectation that psychology was the key to understanding the mind and ways of thought of the native peoples of Australia and New Guinea. Alas, however . . . he was disappointed in this . . . 'But now,' he concluded, 'I see that I should have taken out not a team of psychologists but a lady novelist.' "

It seems beyond question that the "lady novelist"—and it was the term "novelist," not "lady," that must have stung—was Makelita of Ta'u and Piyap of Peri Village.† Mead, enfeebled by her broken foot and her malaria and her neuritis, should probably have just accepted nice Mrs. Parkinson's hospitality, without overestimating her new friend's expertise.

Fortune's photographic expedition was a success even though the sun had shone only three days of his several weeks among the Dobuans. Margaret and he sailed on to Sydney, where he introduced her to Raymond Firth, who had been doing the field work that would lead to his famous *We, the Tikopia.* Mead's appearance surprised Firth: "I expected to see a tall, willowy woman rather like Ruth Benedict," instead of the "dumpy little figure in a raincoat and a hat," who seemed, to Firth, quite persuaded, as her husband also was, that the great Mali-

---

* This account was not published until 1960, along with several other anthropologists' essays collected in Joseph Casagrande's *In the Company of Man.*

† Haddon belonged to a British school of social anthropology which, as Marvin Harris wrote in *The Rise of Anthropological Theory,* "repeatedly expressed [its] opposition to the concept of culture as employed by Malinowski and the Boasians, arguing that it is too vast and shapeless a notion to be of much use for the individual researcher."

nowski had no ideas. Malinowski, Ruth Benedict had intimated in a letter to Margaret, was also "a terrible Don Juan," a notion which fueled Reo's fears that his wife, whom he had seduced from her first husband, might be seduced by someone else.

Apart from his brooding jealousy, Fortune must have felt burdened, as he and Mead sailed on the *Aorangi* from Sydney to Vancouver, Canada, in August 1929. He had his Dobu book to finish and his Manus one unwritten. His wife, however, set him a stirring example. While he was with Margaret, Reo's friends recalled, he was charged with a sense of purpose that he would never regain after they parted. Mead herself admitted to "a tendency to step up the energy of the person I am working for or with." Perhaps, with her help, the dashing, promising name of Reo Fortune could become as much a household word as her own.

Mead fervently hoped so. Letters from New York hinted that *Coming of Age* was being well received, and she already had premonitions that "life was going to be uncomfortable for Reo in a country in which I was at home and already well-known but he was a stranger." Meanwhile, in San Francisco, where they went from Vancouver, Dr. Jarvis operated on Mead's nose "and permitted Reo to be an interested spectator—which, as it turned out, was unwise," she wrote in *Blackberry Winter*, "and I almost died."

With sixteen pieces of luggage, the ethnographers then made their way across America to New York.

CHAPTER NINE

"Climbing at Forty Thousand Feet"

In Manus, Reo and Margaret had lived with an obliging staff of young "bush monkeys" to cook and sweep and make Margaret feel "as much a figurehead as an English queen" in their domestic arrangements. Now, in New York, they had nobody to help clean their walkup apartment four flights above 102nd Street, just west of Broadway. Reo, Margaret wrote, "did not like to see me doing the housework, which he did not intend to help with; yet he felt it was a reproach to him that I had to do it at all.

"As a result, I became expert at tidying up on Sunday morning while appearing to give complete attention to what he was saying. . . . I was always willing to pretend that I never did housework, and I tried to be good-tempered when, after buying food and carrying the package for four blocks and, finally, up three flights of stairs, I was greeted with the suggestion, 'Let's go out to dinner'—which we could not afford."

This *Blackberry Winter* account of his older brother's domestic life rang false to Barter Fortune. "All she'd have had to say was 'Reo, give me a hand'; he may have been obtuse, but he wasn't malicious, nor was he some dithering absent-minded professor. It's so untrue of her to imply that 'he made a slave of me.' He was almost embarrassingly willing to participate in the humdrum work of the world." Indeed, when the Manus field trip was over, Reo had proposed that he and Margaret might settle not in New York but in New Zealand, where if anthropological jobs did not materialize he could support them by working as a common laborer—not a prospect designed to appeal to Margaret Mead.

"There were times," Barter Fortune added, "when you wished to God Reo would stop. But Margaret may have decided it was easier to do the work herself. Putting myself in a woman's skirts, Reo couldn't have been easy to live with." The "man who starred as the Antichrist for Margaret," as Barter's daughter Ann McLean would refer to her uncle Reo, was by all accounts stubborn, sensitive, and unusually intense.

Fortune's career was by almost any standards off to an exceptional start by 1930. *Sorcerers of Dobu* was being edited, and *Manus Religion* was well under way. He had his fellowship at Columbia, and shared an office there with Mead's colleague Ruth Bunzel. He was trying to get used to America, and to the astonishing success, exceeding even Margaret Mead's and William Morrow's wildest dreams, of *Coming of Age in Samoa.*

"It was great good luck to receive, on the same day, the wonderful letters from Havelock Ellis and Dr. Malinowski," Morrow had written to Mead. "We almost staged a celebration when we read them. We got out a bright red band to put around the book with part of Havelock Ellis's comment on the front. That stunt helped the sales materially. . . . You must allow me to take special personal satisfaction in the success of this book. I haven't enjoyed anything so much in years. . . . The only disappointment we have had is with the English market. . . . Isn't it amazing that with the two such comments as those from . . . Ellis and Dr. Malinowski the British publishers haven't been able to see the possibilities? But they will, before I am done with them, however."

Havelock Ellis, celebrated in the 1920s for his own enthusiastic writings about sex, called *Coming of Age in Samoa* "fascinating, valuable, and instructive," adding that "the great master in these fields is Professor Bronislaw Malinowski [author of *Sexual Life of Savages*], and I could not pay higher tribute to Miss Mead than to mention her name in connection with his." Malinowski himself hailed *Coming of Age* as "an absolutely first-rate piece of descriptive anthropology" and "an outstanding achievement."

In the *American Mercury*, H. L. Mencken commented at some length (if imprecisely) about how Mead's "precise, scientific pages" brought the islanders vividly to life. A Samoan "swain," Mencken said, "avoids repression by devoting himself to light and transient loves." Freda Kirchwey advised readers of the *Nation* to read the book, predicting they would "probably be astonished to discover how like a South Sea island that South Sea island can be . . . Sex experience is frequent before marriage, almost to the point of promiscuity."

Mary Austin in *Birth Control Review* wrote, more astutely, "The only quarrel I have with [Mead] . . . is for suggesting that her single limited inquiry could be used as a basis for reliable social conclusions. As for the reviewers who do so make use of it, they are perhaps exhibiting a characteristic American penchant for easy solutions, for quick and formalized methods of disposing of social problems." But A. L. Kroeber, who was one of the founders of the anthropology department at the University of California at Berkeley, made light of complaints that Mead's book was short on data. "Somehow," he wrote to her, "I have confidence that your diagnoses are right even when your facts are few or not printed in full . . . I think you have given us all a mark to shoot at."

A professor in Tennessee wrote her to suggest that she expurgate her final two chapters, which, following her publisher's suggestion, connected her Samoan conclusions with her view of America. Mead replied that out of a total of 297 pages, there were exactly 68 which dealt with sex. Perhaps there was not much sex in her marital life, either. Certainly there was less and less pleasure. Once, when Margaret was running a fever, Reo refused to go to the drugstore for a thermometer. She had to borrow a neighbor's, on which she learned that her temperature was 105 degrees. Fortune, who in Manus had been capable of great tenderness, was now angry. He came from a culture, Mead said, where men pushed women around. Some of her friends wondered whether she had learned this by more than hearsay, and they found some of Fortune's views startling.

"You people don't know how to do things," Fortune told Ruth Bunzel, when a young anthropologist named Henrietta Schmerler, a student of Boas's, was raped and murdered by an Indian while doing field work on an Apache reservation.* "You should just line up ten Indians and shoot them, to show them that they can't get away with this." That, Bunzel gathered, was how colonialist New Zealanders might have dealt with a murderous Maori. Fortune was probably speaking ironically, though his wife and friends did not understand him.

"But Reo was bright and interesting . . . ," said Bunzel, "and I enjoyed his company." Another friend recalled Fortune as a "sweet guy" with an aversion to jargon. Many found him not only intense but attractive. Florette Henri, a Barnard friend who edited Sorcerers, said Reo was "gorgeous, dark, mysterious looking, and very silent," but, "he didn't seem to come to parties." Possibly New York parties made Fortune wish he were back with the Dobuans.

---

* An Apache brave had fatefully misunderstood Schmerler's willingness to ride over the plains with him on his horse. Franz Boas, on a trip to Germany when he heard this news, wrote to Benedict in Mexico: "It is dreadful," he said. "How shall we now dare to send a young girl out like this? And still . . . is it not necessary and right?"

The Ash Can Cats flocked as they always had around Margaret, and so did other New York friends. When they were asked to the 102nd Street apartment for a reunion, Mead would tell them to bring their husbands along, "to have a talk with Reo." The husbands "were supposed to both be there and not be there," said Karsten Stapelfeldt, a commercial artist and photographer who had married Margaret's old friend Pelham Korteheuer. "While the girls had their girl talk, we were to wait in the anteroom—we might as well have been invisible—until it was time to take them home. Some of us played pinochle or poker, but Reo wasn't a poker player. He and Mel Mandelbaum, who had married Deborah Kaplan, couldn't imagine what we were doing."

For all its internal tensions, this household, like Mead's previous one with Cressman, provided a stable refuge for friends with more severe troubles. Ruth Benedict was never far away either, if she could help it, and she was always obliging about Mead's requests. Through Margaret's two marriages and Ruth's separation from her husband, the two women had remained as close as ever, but their professional equation had altered. As Mead's stature grew, the difference between her and Benedict's ages mattered less. Increasingly it was Mead who told Benedict what to do. Benedict once told Esther Schiff Goldfrank, Boas's secretary and another of his protégées, "Whenever Margaret goes out into the field she throws a batch of manuscripts on my desk and says, 'Please get these ready for publication.'"

But Mead gave Benedict presents along with demands. When Ruth was doing field work in Zuni in late October 1929, she woke very early and by 5:00 A.M. was writing a note to thank Margaret, not for the first time, for the "small book of ruminations" Margaret had left behind before she went to Manus. "I saved the little manuscript book like a too scant water supply on a voyage in an open boat," Benedict wrote. "But this morning I waked hours ago with a back and forth rocking restlessness and I took out my flagon. . . . The part of wisdom is, as you say, the hushed watching of experience till it takes on the form it will wear, the wings it will fly with. That's congenial, very, to my feeling about the process of verse—incubation, gestation. And I'd never made half enough of it."

Mead herself had written a poem, "Misericordia," dedicated to Benedict and published in the February 1930 issue of *Poetry*:

Summer, betray this tree again!
Bind her in winding sheets of green;
With empty promises unlock her lips;
Sift futile pollen through her finger-tips.

Curve those tense hands so tightened in disdain,
To eager chalices for falling rain.
Break and elaborate that frozen line
With golden tendril and swift sinuous vine.
Summer, in mercy blur this bare delight
Of chiseled boughs against the winter night.

Eager to build on the momentum of her first book's spectacular success, Mead was hurrying to finish the second, and thinking about what the third should be. Edward Sherwood Mead had warned his daughter, when the stock market crashed, that another war would break out within ten years. Her response was to resolve "to get our field notes written up as quickly as possible, so we can get back to the field to rescue as many cultures as we can before a war comes that may wipe them out altogether."

Her father also advised her to put her royalties from *Coming of Age in Samoa* into the small, safe bank at home in Doylestown, Pennsylvania. This she did. Her royalties for the $3 book amounted to $5,000, and that would go a good long way at a time when a full sit-down lunch cost thirty-five cents, and a grilled-cheese sandwich with a Coca-Cola cost fifteen cents. She took a cut in her $2,500-a-year salary, but for the most part the Great Depression, like her own adolescence, left Margaret Mead unscathed. She was free to concentrate on cultural anthropology. Her evangelism never ceased. She recruited friends, husbands, and strangers into this urgent new discipline. *Coming of Age in Samoa*, as one of her friends reflected, had "put anthropology on the map and caused youngsters to flock to it, the way they flocked to communes in the sixties. It was stylish, chic, and daring to go off on field trips and come back with such marvelous stories to tell."

Mead was also busy polishing the stage presence she had begun to acquire on the Barnard debating team. Karsten Stapelfeldt recalled accompanying Reo and Margaret to a lecture Mead gave to a women's group at a high school in Queens.

"She asked Reo and me to sit in the back row, and we did, but Reo fed me embarrassing questions to put to her during the question-and-answer period. 'Dr. Mead,' I'd get up and say, 'I'm told that if you stick a pin into an effigy you can make someone two hundred miles up the river fall ill; to what do you ascribe this? Is there any rational explanation?' Margaret would get flustered and have to resort to double talk that didn't answer the question at all."

But Mead was not flustered often, nor had she yet become "a cast-iron monument, a figure to be venerated like Douglas MacArthur," which was the way Stapelfeldt came to think of her much later. "She could be abrasive and testy in those early years," he said, "but she was decent and kind, a warm human being. It was refreshing to think of a young woman having done all the things she had done." Her career, as someone else said, was "truly meteoric and hard to duplicate. The conditions simply aren't there any more. She was climbing at forty thousand feet at the age of twenty-five."

And now, as Mead at age twenty-eight continued her climb, Reo Fortune had no choice, and perhaps no wish, but to climb on with her. "I set the pace, as far as writing up was concerned, for both of us," Mead wrote in *Blackberry Winter*. "During the two years we lived in New York, in addition to carrying out our short American Indian field trip [in the summer of 1930 they would go together to Nebraska], we each wrote three major works.* With this much accomplished, we could go back to the Pacific with a reasonably good conscience."

In January 1930 she wrote to the director of the Bishop Museum in Honolulu that "good Pacific material of course must come now from Melanesia, preferably from the mainland of New Guinea," where she and Fortune were eager to spend fifteen to twenty months. "We have firm contacts with government anthropologists and government officials which would make it easy to get our material culture," she said. "This is especially easier on account of Mr. Fortune's British citizenship. . . . Dr. Wissler is willing to let me have an eighteen month or if necessary two year leave of absence, and is of course always most sympathetic to cooperation with Bishop Museum."

Dr. Wissler was still Mead's boss at the "house look-look belonglong," as a museum is called in pidgin. Almost from the beginning of her work at the American Museum of Natural History, Mead had been planning an entirely new Hall of the Peoples of the Pacific, which at first was intended to combine two other exhibits: the old South Sea Island Hall, which Robert Lowie had installed in 1911, and the Philippine Hall, constructed mainly with materials from the St. Louis Exposition of 1904.

On returning from Manus she had convinced the museum's Department of Preparation to construct a miniature model of Peri village, and she also decided what to do with the bowls, arm and ear ornaments, belts, cloths, betel nuts, and spears she had brought back with her in

* Reo Fortune: *The Sorcerers of Dobu*, 1932; *Manus Religion*, 1935; and *Omaha Secret Societies*, 1932. Margaret Mead: *Growing Up in New Guinea*, 1930; *The Changing Culture of an Indian Tribe*, 1932; and *Kinship in the Admiralty Islands*, 1934.

friendly competition with Fortune, who had been collecting for the
Sydney Museum. But collecting was never Mead's forte. "Sometimes
she collected with a vengeance, sometimes not," said Philip Gifford,
who in the 1980s was in charge of plans for the remodeling of the Hall
of the Peoples of the Pacific. "It depended on who she was married to,
what they were doing. From Samoa she brought back one fan, one kava
cup, one tapa cloth which she gave to Ruth Benedict, on whose death
it was given back to the Museum."

"She was never particularly interested in amassing great collections," agreed Junius Bird, a contemporary and colleague of Mead's.
"What made her a legend so early was the way she emphasized details
of a native culture that nobody else would have noticed."

From the start Mead's relationship with the museum was existen-
tial. Each, as time passed, figured how to make the best use of the
other. "I learned very early," she once said, "that I would be a cancer
in any organization if anybody knew what I was doing." Up in her
tower, she was safe from routine distractions and idle prying. Later,
when rank entitled her to a more central and accessible headquarters on
the stately fifth-floor corridor downstairs, she chose to stay put. She
would have been foolish to do anything else.

In years to come much of the work done in that tower was not,
strictly speaking, museum business. Mead took pains to separate her
routine duties as a curator from her independent extra projects. "If I'd
started putting in requisitions for all I was doing through Museum channels," she said, "I'd have been fired, and quite justly. This is what I
think overproductive people don't usually learn: that you remain a tu-
mor, provided you introduce a comparison with other people who have
less vitality, less energy. It's a comparison that is invidious."

Her male counterparts had treated Mead with a mix of wary chivalry and neglect. She scarcely knew the other curators until 1929, when
several of their wives, who had accompanied them on expeditions,
formed the Society of Woman Geographers and asked Mead to join
them—"and then I met my male colleagues, because once a year we
had a Men's Night we invited them to. By joining the Woman Geographers I got to know most of the important men in the Museum very
well, but it was an indirect route." Her contemporary Harry Shapiro,
eventually curator of physical anthropology and later chairman of the
Anthropology Department, suggested the title for her second book,
Growing Up in New Guinea. Originally, he recalled, Mead had been
hired not so much to collect as to write her own research and field

notes, in order to encourage the preservation of cultures that were about
to disappear or be modified.

In due course the museum would get around to lionizing Margaret
Mead, but nothing of the sort was happening in 1930. She was in fact
"quite miffed," an article reported, when the museum that year gave
her her only direct field assignment, to study American Indian women
on a reservation. A committee led by Mrs. Leonard Elmhirst had $750
to spend on a study of such women. Not knowing quite what to do
with this money, Wissler offered it to Mead. Compared with her earlier work this prospect probably seemed insultingly unchallenging, but
Ruth Benedict kindled her interest with a suggestion that the Omaha
Indians, in Nebraska, might be worth study by Margaret and Reo together. "If we would go to the Omaha," Benedict could find field
funds for Reo, so that he could "tackle a problem," Mead wrote, "that
had been bothering her for some time."

The problem Benedict wanted Fortune to tackle, and used her influence to get Columbia to sponsor, had to do with the subject of her
own doctoral dissertation, on folk tales regarding men's visions. Most
tribes' folklore abounded with accounts of these visions, but the Omaha
Indians of Nebraska were an exception. None of their visions had been
recorded, and Benedict wondered why.

Fortune, who had been writing so brilliantly of the spiritual lives
of the Dobu and the Manus, could not have been better equipped to
deal with such a question. And the Omaha reservation would be as good
a place as any for Mead to deepen the niche she had already carved out
for herself as an interviewer of women, whom most previous ethnographers had belittled if not overlooked. But this expedition, suited though
it was to the talents of Fortune and Mead, was a trial. Native Americans, for all their importance to most American anthropologists, had
never been a favorite subject of Mead's. Too many earlier ethnographers had spent too much time on reservations, which, lacking the mystery of the South Seas, were hardly terra incognita. From the start of
her career, Mead had known she would fare better doing field work in
places that either were more exotic or seemed so to Americans.

The three summer months in Nebraska in 1930, in which Mead
concentrated on women and Fortune on the visions of men, were
fiercely hot and grueling. Their informants, Mead wrote to Benedict,
were so "indifferent, unwilling and frightened" that she and Fortune
had "no way of checking up on material obtained from these people
for money, on what their fathers or grandfathers told them . . . religion of this sort could never have been gotten properly without a mass

of detailed evidence, without say a hundred visions of fathers and sons, and material on what they did with them. . . . Don't think I am a thankless wretch, please," she added. "And scold me if you think I deserve it and am overestimating the difficulties . . . I feel as if I had no sense of values left, when I try to evaluate this work. It has rained after a month's drought. That is one of the mercies."

Reo got some disturbing news that summer from his father in Paraparaumu, New Zealand. "We have had a year of utter slavery here," wrote the preacher turned dairyman, "with the extra work of cow disease. . . . Now worse has come. Mother left us on the 24th of last month so, subject to the unexpected, I shall never see her face again. She left with utter hatred of me as I did not actually see the poor soul go. So far as I can tell her mind was deranged, but it is difficult to say. We do not know where she is. . . . There is peace now in the house & we could do quite well were it not for the dread disease which entails dreadful work. . . . Of 4 [cattle] brought in all are diseased & 2 of them both very bad cases, unquestionably did not contract the disease here. It shows itself after calving & we cannot get them in calf again. Reo I must stop. . . . With best love to Margaret & yourself, Dad."

During those months Reo gathered material for *Omaha Secret Societies*, Margaret for *The Changing Culture of an Indian Tribe*. The Indians with whom she worked did not know they were being investigated but "believed I was merely killing time in idle conversation or attendance at ceremonies," as Mead would write. "For the most part, no notes were taken in the informants' presence but conversations were written up immediately afterwards. The one exception to this was the detailed reorganization of census materials which the informant believed I was doing for another investigator [presumably Fortune]. Such unawareness was essential to the successful prosecution of a study involving intimate details of contemporary life . . . The whole investigation is presented tentatively as a first step in the kind of analysis of primitive societies in the throes of transition."

In the book resulting from this largely unhappy time with the "Antlers," as she called the Omaha Indians to protect their privacy, Mead mused about her subjects in comparison with others whom she had studied: "When I first went to the Admiralty Islands," she wrote, "I was puzzled and annoyed by an invariable sequence which occurred in dealing with natives. If I gave them the most trifling gift, they would immediately ask for something else, and when that was refused, continued for half an hour to request different objects of varying value. This seemed particularly graceless behavior, especially when contrasted with the behavior of the Polynesian who, after elaborate thanks for the smallest gift, hurries away to prepare a return present.

"But in time I came to understand the apparent thanklessness of the Melanesian native, who is not accustomed to making gifts except along definite trade routes where return is assured. He did not understand why he was given anything. He was left with only two theories—either I owed him for some service which he had forgotten, in which case I was probably only paying him a part of what I owed him and he had better ask for the rest—amount unknown—or according to his categories I was . . . as mad as someone who distributed banknotes to a crowd.

"I had given him a fishhook—I might be insane enough to give him the lamp or the gun—there was no harm in trying it out. Hence his ingenious requests for everything in sight. The present day [American] Indian dealing with the national government has much the same attitude. He does not understand the premises upon which the government acts and so he believes anything to be possible."

Anthropologists and Indians used each other, Mead later contended. She deplored the sentimental attitudes toward American Indians, and the empty mock-heroic role thrust upon them by politicians.* Anthropologists studying other Indian tribes were also, at the very least, dispirited, and sympathetic with Mead's views of the "Antlers." "I wonder if any human planning could avert the Omaha tragedy here," Ruth Benedict wrote the following summer from an expedition to study the Apaches.

Mead no doubt wondered the same thing, but brooding was not her style. Her style was to get on with it, whatever "it" might be. She was developing a serviceable sense of timing, a fine stage presence, and a growing conviction that between any two well-met persons, or any two congenial trains of thought, she herself had to have been the essential link. She even became the godmother, or so its members assured her, of an amateur string quartet, two of whose members were married to Ash Can Cats. Fifty-two years later the quartet was still taking turns

* "Nobody played a more important role than Margaret Mead," said George C. Foster of the University of California at Berkeley, "in selling anthropology to the government. Charges of racism and colonialism are largely phony. I very much doubt that colonial history would have been any different had there been no anthropology at all. It's wrong for native Indians to accuse anthropologists of exploitation; there would hardly have been a nativistic movement at all without anthropologists, who hardly earned anything from what they published. I don't see that indigenous people anywhere in the world, except possibly in Vietnam around 1970, are worse off for anthropologists, and maybe in terms of developing their own identity they're better off."

•

rehearsing in each other's apartments, with only one change from the original membership.*

Mead's work continued to find public favor. *The Changing Culture of an Indian Tribe*, her account of the dismaying Nebraska field work, won high praise from one of her old professors in the December 1932 *Barnard Alumnae Magazine*. Clare Howard called the book "as fascinating as Jane Austen" and said she had always known "that Margaret Mead, '23, had what Lord Chesterfield would call an 'easy, insinuating manner' . . . [but] little I thought when I used to call upon her in the English novels course to explain the motives of *Jude the Obscure* or *The Vicar of Wakefield* that she would, in ten years, become an authority on the family life of the Melanesians and be accompanying her husband on an investigation of the social life of New Guinea."

In the spring of 1931, Mead was busy with plans to return to New Guinea. There was no question but that she would go with Fortune. Moody though he could be, especially in light of the contrast between her fame and his relative obscurity, his partnership was still crucial to her career. She needed him, as she would acknowledge in the foreword to her next book, *Sex and Temperament*, if she wanted to work with "people more savage and more inaccessibly located than I would have been able to reach alone." And Reo Fortune needed Margaret Mead, too, more than Luther Cressman had.

Mead rarely seemed to mention Cressman, who had put the church far behind him and whose life was becoming more settled as Mead's grew less so. While she was planning her third trip to the South Seas, he was preparing to become a father. Beginning his first term as a professor of sociology at the University of Oregon, in Eugene, he exulted in a telegram from Pennsylvania: "BLUE-EYED, BLOND-HAIRED GIRL ARRIVED AS ORDERED."

Cressman's responsibility in Eugene was to handle advanced research in social science and develop the field of cultural anthropology. It was Ruth Benedict, guardian of so many careers, who had guided him into archeology, which was to become his life work. At a 1931 convention of anthropologists in Pasadena, his old friend Benedict suggested that Cressman might make a study of the petroglyphs of eastern

* Mead rarely came by to hear the rehearsals. "Music wasn't her strong point," said Karsten Stapelfeldt, one of the quartet's violinists, "and neither was art. At the risk of sounding condescending, I had to explain to her the difference between Manet and Monet. Why should she sit through a whole evening of string music, when she had so much wisdom that had to be imparted to others?"

Oregon: if there had been occupation of great antiquity in the caves of the dry Southwest, why not also in the arid climate of Oregon, especially around the ancient lake beds? Four years later Cressman was named chairman of the University of Oregon's Department of Anthropology and Archeology. (Cressman is best known among anthropologists, next to being Mead's first husband, for having discovered in a cave the oldest dated artifact ever found in the New World, a 9,000-year-old pair of sandals whose wearer, he wrote, "did not look out on swirling dust devils or miles of alkali and sand flats, as we did that hot August day [in 1938], but on a great lake with wavelets lapping against a beach below the cave.")

Mead's energies were focused on her writing, and she paid close attention to the way it was received. *Growing Up in New Guinea* caused less stir than *Coming of Age in Samoa* had, but was generally applauded. A San Francisco critic remarked on the "diabolical delight" Mead took, in her second book, "in pointing out how little difference there really is between civilized man and his primitive brother," and called *Growing Up* "a contribution of utmost importance to sociology and to human life." Bristling at another reviewer's accusation that she had not understood the kinship system in Manus, she spent much of the summer of 1931 preparing a technical monograph—"the most detailed ever published," she said—called *Kinship in the Admiralty Islands*. Popular success was all very well, but Mead also craved the esteem and applause of her peers. Radcliffe-Brown was teaching a course at Columbia that summer, and Margaret and Reo enrolled in it, sat in the front row, and asked hard questions. Neither then nor at any other time in her life did Mead miss a chance to learn all she could from whatever authorities were at hand. "In the evenings," she remembered, "I wore my prettiest dresses and prepared the kind of dinners Radcliffe-Brown enjoyed."*

* She also tried to summarize Radcliffe-Brown's point of view, in a memo for Ruth Benedict: ". . . He believes in the sort of evolution which no one objects to, i.e. that societies were once simple and some have become complex, sometimes this history has repeated itself, sometimes not. He discusses this evolution primarily from the standpoint of what he calls *levels of integration*, or the size of the social group . . . throughout societies at these different levels of integration, many of the same structural relationships occur. . . . Brown says, study the simplest forms, not for origins but for clarity in understanding how they work.

"This assumes of course that society does work, or rather that societies do, that they must have a certain minimal stability to function well enough to keep their members alive and reproducing. Brown says we will find what the minimal stability is, and how the structures which support it, work. He

Radcliffe-Brown enjoyed these evenings, and later wrote to thank Mead for the hospitality and to congratulate Fortune on his Omaha monograph. "I regard him," Radcliffe-Brown said, "as one of the very few first-class anthropologists round the world. You see he has done so very much better than some of us ever expected he would, having in mind his original hardly adequate training and his apparently very firm attachment to certain preconceptions. Haddon had been a little doubtful as to how Reo would turn out and was very pleased when I told him my high opinion of the New Guinea work and Boas's approval of the Omaha."

For the next field trip, Reo's way, paved in part by help from Ruth Benedict, would be financed by a grant from the Social Science Research Council. Margaret's grant came from the Frederick F. Voss Anthropological and Archaeological Fund, willed to the museum by a mining engineer who had been enchanted with the drama and importance of field work. All Mead had to declare, to get this grant, was that she hoped to research the way sex roles were stylized in different cultures. With luck, what she learned would help her develop a new approach to the basic question of sex-linked biological differences.

Sex had not figured very prominently in Mead's study of the Omaha Indians, but it would in most of her future field trips, particularly the one she and Fortune set out for in September of 1931. Her husband's partnership in New Guinea would be a priceless professional boon.

---

claims that no one society can be understood by itself, but only when a large number of varieties of the same type have been studied. . . . He is primarily interested in social structure, and views the rest of society—i.e. art, religion, etc., from the standpoint of the structure. While this may leave untouched special problems within these fields, it does not rule them out by any too narrow definition."

CHAPTER TEN

"The Limits of Outrage"

QUITE EARLY in many field trips, Margaret Mead wrote to a young friend in 1969, it was common to "feel you understand everything and [that] there are—in effect—no mysteries. In primitive field work it comes at about two months. It doesn't last and is . . . followed by a period of despair, a sense that all is unknowable."

"You never can quite tell about Yabinigi," Mead wrote home in April of 1932. "He used to run amuck quite frequently, but people got tired of it and fed him soup made of dog's dung. Afterwards they told him what this soup contained and that he would be fed it again unbeknownst to him unless his mad fits were cured. That was a year ago and he has not run amuck since. Still, we do not let him have a gun at night. . . ."

Yabinigi and about ninety other primitive people, most of them much more placid than he, lived in the ridge-top village of Alitoa, sixty-six feet wide and as long as a block between two New York City avenues, in the steep and slippery northwest mountains of the Mandated Territory of New Guinea. Since the villagers' language had no word indicating their entire tribe or entire country, Fortune and Mead called them the Arapesh, after their term referring both to friends and to more distant personal connections.

Their country, Reo Fortune would write, "like most tribal countries of New Guinea," could be "traversed in a few days of hard walking." It was "approximately two days' walk long on the coast, two days' walk in inland depth, and it narrow[ed] to one day's walk long on its inland base. A traveller encumbered with baggage and porters takes about a day longer in any direction of traverse of the country." The villagers of Alitoa must have been startled, one December day in 1931, when up their steep hillside came 150 porters from another tribe, six of whom were carrying a large string hammock attached to two sturdy poles.

The hammock, covered with an umbrella of banana leaves, contained a resolute white woman whose chronically weak foot had prevented her from walking over the mountains herself. Margaret Mead, the cargo, was then about to be thirty and about to begin her fourth field trip. "She must have been absolutely terrific," said a scientist who marveled at the zest Mead still had in her seventies, when he encountered her at meetings, "when she was around thirty." As 1932 approached she must have been formidable indeed, although she would confess that being handed up and down the mountains had made her feel "a little seasickish," and, at times, "for all the world like a pig."

This hammock ride was the final lap of a journey that had begun three months earlier. Mead and Fortune had sailed from New York through the Panama Canal to New Zealand, where they visited Reo's family. Next, in Sydney, they visited the Kellys ("Carrie Tennant Kelly" was listed in the updated version of Margaret's will: she was to inherit the silver tea ball). In Sydney they also met a "lady reporter," as Mead wrote home, who had coined the phrase "gender consciousness," a subject then and always much on Mead's own consciousness.

From Sydney they went to Madang, Wewak, Marienberg, and finally Karawop, a plantation managed by some kindly Australians named Cobb, who helped Reo engage the men to carry the things he and Margaret would need for their next six months. Their intention had been to find the Abelam, a people living on the plains behind the northern coastal range of the Torricelli Mountains, who were said to build enormous triangular men's houses, and to have a rich ceremonial life. The carriers, however, had stubbornly refused to go any farther than Alitoa, and had left them stranded there, with their six months' supply of gear. Unable to proceed either into the interior or back to the coast, the anthropologists had no choice but to settle among a people who, as Fortune would complain, "haven't any culture worth speaking of—sisters-in-law are friends!"

But anthropology is full of surprises, as Mead would write in the 1950 edition of *Sex and Temperament in Three Primitive Societies*— her report (originally published in 1935) of this and her two shorter next field visits. As Mead put it, anthropology demands of those who practice it, among other qualities, "the openmindedness with which one must look and listen, record in astonishment and wonder that which one would not have been able to guess." Neither Mead nor Fortune could have guessed that they would be focusing on so forlorn a site as Alitoa, but they would make the best of it. "The way to do field work," Mead wrote home in July 1932, "is never to come up for air until it is all over."

Fortune would learn the language, which turned out to have eleven genders and twenty-two third-person pronouns; and he would publish, in 1939, an article called "Arapesh Warfare," a striking contradiction to Mead's own assertion in *Sex and Temperament* that "warfare is practically unknown among the Arapesh." She does admit, a few sentences later, that "although actual warfare—organized expeditions to plunder, conquer, kill, or attain glory—is absent, brawls and clashes between villages do occur, mainly over women." To Fortune, these "brawls and clashes" were quite something else: "Warfare," he would write, "was good Arapesh custom. It was distinguished from the sometimes heated quarrels between the turbulent clans of a single sovereign locality by its scale, its determination, and by its traditions and conventions."* Mead saw what she wanted to see; so, perhaps, did Fortune. Their differences "were not a matter of fact but of emphasis," said Paula Rubel, who worked with some Arapesh in 1974 in postpacification times, when the area had been brought fully under government control.

Margaret's and Reo's own outright brawls, or clashes, or wars, had yet to erupt. Mead's early letters home put a cheerful face on things. She and Reo stirred their photographic chemicals with a cassowary bone dagger. The weather was cooler than it had been in Manus or Samoa; they slept under two blankets, and were never unbearably hot. Altogether, the place was "easily the most pleasant . . . that I've struck" and the people were nicer than the Manus or the Omaha. "They never tire," she said, "of exclaiming how weak my hair is and how clean my hands." The children, who Mead said were raised to love and trust whomever they encountered, would "sit and . . . listen to the clink of my typewriter. They never go beyond sensation—the five senses, with sight and hearing only lightly exercised and the brain never." Adults would open their mouths wide to form spit bubbles, and they possessed, as few primitive cultures did, "the true kiss, that is, lip contact that is punctuated by a sharp implosion of the breath."

* Intertribal warfare was endemic. The ethnographer Anthony Forge recounted how Fortune and some Arapesh attended a meeting with some Abelam (among whom Fortune wished to study); somehow insults were traded and Fortune found himself quite alone with some angry Abelam, and hastily begged leave to go.

Fortune would disagree, but Mead would write (for a vastly larger audience than he would ever have) that rarely among the Arapesh was anyone very aggressive. People of both sexes preferred being chosen to doing the choosing themselves. They saw the world as "a garden that must be tilled: yams, dogs, pigs and children all had to be grown." When a baby was given a name, from one of its father's clans, "it looked up and laughed into its father's face." These people were "quite willing to talk to keep us amused, as talk seems to be what we want," but to Mead they seemed "ethnologically unobtrusive. They like to have us here as a neighborhood store, as it were. It is convenient to be able to get salt and matches and knives and pipes and beads whenever they wish." Since Mead's weak foot prevented her from joining Fortune in exploring the forbiddingly hilly terrain, she stayed put in the village and each day learned more about its inhabitants.

Why, she wondered, had the Arapesh developed so little in the way of art? Even if a small settlement did include an experienced artist, there was "a great casualness about details, a great willingness to substitute one element for another, a lack of emphasis on precision or form. . . . Quite understandably," she wrote, "young men of imagination live in a kind of low level terror that some essential detail will get away from them altogether." The only way for her to study artistic behavior was "actually to see an artist working," which could not happen often. But she was lucky, as she generally tended to be. She was able to collect several shieldlike bark slabs on which designs were made, and also to get some painting done on paper.

"It was only possible to get even this meager account by tracing the actual steps, the shifts and changes of plan between the painter and his helper." No sophisticated photographic equipment was available; "I had to record all the stages by hand, and—using water colors—paint in miniature each stage of the proceedings." When one such procedure was finished, Mead's miniature of a bark painting of a cassowary theme "naturally looked finer" than the large crude original in clay. The artist looked at what she had done and muttered, "Women, women." His manhood, Mead wrote, was so "sorely injured" that for several days he deserted the village.

Although Mead was to celebrate this culture as one which lacked "any contrasting ethos" between males and females, as "a strange anomaly in that it assumes men and women to be alike in temperament," the Arapesh did have customs which involved segregation of the sexes. Here, as in many parts of New Guinea, the "most dramatic representation of the separation of the reproductive functions of men and women was the tambaran cult." The tambaran, impersonated by flutes and whistles and other noise-making devices, was "the supernatural patron of the grown men of the tribe.

"Women and children must never see the tambaran. The little children," Mead wrote, "think of him as a huge monster, as tall as a coconut-tree, who lives in the sea except on those rare occasions when he is summoned to sing to the people. When the tambaran comes, one runs away, as fast as ever one can, holding on to one's mother's grass skirt, tripping and stumbling, dropping one's mouthful of yam, wailing for fear one will be left behind. The lovely sound of the flutes is getting closer every minute, and something frightful would happen to the [child] caught loitering in the village after the men and the tambaran enter it."

American parents on Christmas morning used to tell their children that Santa's reindeer had eaten the cookies left on the mantelpiece; Arapesh children were told, perhaps in a similar spirit, that the wreaths of red leaves left at the foot of each palm tree after the tambaran's visit were "the tambaran's anklets, which fell off as he stood beneath the palms. On the rain-softened surface of the *agehu* are large marks. One of the men may remark self-consciously to a woman or child that these are the marks of the tambaran's testicles."

Arapesh women had customs of their own concerning childbirth, puberty rites, and the dyeing of grass skirts. "The very sound of men's voices," Mead wrote, "will spoil the dye, just as the sound of women's voices will anger the tambaran." Old Arapesh men did not resent the waxing strength of the young men; they found it "their greatest source of happiness." Nobody, as far as Mead was concerned, seemed to stay mad for very long at anybody else. "No one here, except for very small children, ever maintains a mood of any depth or duration," she wrote. "We even have quiet days, ending up with a game of deck tennis before dinner." Amid all this harmony, she and Fortune seemed to get on better than they had in New York. Maybe the Arapesh couples set them a good example. Marrying, to the Arapesh, was a way "to become an integral part of another family, a family to which they will now belong forever, even after death." They avoided incest not so much because they thought it was shocking or horrible but because it was "a stupid negation of the joys of increasing, through marriage, the number of people whom one can love and trust."

Mead would write about the Arapesh, as she had of the Samoans and the Manus, in prose that was fresh and sometimes funny. "As the night falls and the chill of the damp mountain evening drives them all closer to the fire, they sit around the embers and sing songs imported from far and wide, which reflect the musical canons of many different people. A slit gong may sound far away and the people speculate happily and irresponsibly upon its message: someone has killed a pig or a cassowary; visitors have come and an absent host is being summoned; someone is dying, is dead, has been buried. All the explanations are offered as equally valid and there is no attempt made to sift their relative probabilities."

Mead's gift for description showed in her letters home, too. In April 1932 she wrote of bad storms "which make the thatch stand up like fur on the back of an angry cat." But where were the books her loved ones had promised they would be sending her? And later, "I repeat my cry for reading matter. Old magazines preferably. Novels aren't good, for one is tempted to finish them." Certainly there were no newsstands anywhere near Alitoa. Local news was "shouted from mountain top to mountain top in a long-drawn howl which resembles dogs baying at the moon."

She wondered what was happening at home, but, more important, she was homesick, and Ruth Benedict, in particular, missed her. "Oh, how I wish you were here to red pencil and suggest," Benedict wrote to her in the summer of 1932, as she was finishing *Patterns of Culture*. (Fortune, probably at Mead's suggestion, was reading Amy Lowell's poem "Patterns" at the time, which prompted him to ask his wife, "Is that why you and Ruth talk of patterns all the time?")

Now Fortune's *Sorcerers* had been published (as *Manus Religion* would be in 1935), and favorably reviewed. His books were received with respect but were not great popular successes.* Benedict wrote a separate letter to Fortune about *Sorcerers*, asking his help again and explaining why she wanted to add a chapter on his work to her book: "People need to be told in words of two syllables," she told him, "what contrasting cultures mean. . . . You have said it so well in your book that I can only sponge. . . . If you think it would be awful of me to take the words out of your mouth this way, cable me collect, just 'Don't,' and I'll understand."

"Do you realize what anthropology is," Benedict wrote Mead, "with you and Reo out of the country? Every one of them [other American anthropologists] is either riding some patented horse of his own and only interested in commendations of it, or they are too silly to pay

---

* *The Sorcerers of Dobu*, published in 1932, was still in print in 1984.

attention to." Margaret had written to Ruth about a book she thought she might do called *The Child in Culture*: a "swell" idea, replied Benedict, who marveled, "Think of anyone's having five cultures to draw on at first hand." When Mead came home, Benedict urged, she should "give a course in Methods—as you say, really METHODS this time . . . I don't know anyone who could give it half so well as you could." And Benedict was "glad you wrote about how strong a commitment you were getting to anthropology—as if you hadn't had it for some time, but then I know the difference, too. I've gone in that direction, too. You won't know what to make of my seriousness when you get back."

Mead and Fortune had had their moments of triumph: an Arapesh man "told Reo all about the nice brain soup which the warriors used to drink, brewed from the scooped-out brains of the enemy, although up to now they had been denying any touch of cannibalism"— a train of thought Mead did not pursue in her further writings, as Fortune did in his. "A census of the war records of individual, grey-headed old men," he wrote, "revealed the fact that approximately fifty percent of them claimed one or more war homicides to his credit."

By July of 1932, satisfied with their fruitful six months, Margaret and Reo were both eager to leave the Arapesh behind. Among them Mead had prepared to do what many would regard as the most detailed ethnography of her career, but she did not yearn to prolong the visit. While she was there, she wrote, "I had too much time to think—too many empty spaces." Unstructured time, all the rest of her life, was a prospect that would fill Mead with dread.

Arranging to leave was not easy, but after much confusion, "with unexpected good luck for this country," as Mead wrote, they found an owner of a pinnace, a small sailing ship, returning from Hong Kong with two suitcases, one of whiskey and one of gin, to be delivered up the Sepik River, which was just where they wanted to go. The Sepik, one of the world's great rivers, is as legendary as the Volga or the Mississippi. "In the mind of the most suburban Rabaulite and . . . the wildest bush native," Mead wrote, "the Sepik stands for mosquitoes, crocodiles, cannibals, and floating corpses." Previous explorers had named the river the Kaisereine Auguste Fleuve, and the Fleuve de l'Impératrice Auguste.

The Sepik area, in the northwest of what is now Papua New Guinea, struck Reo Fortune's Cambridge professor A. C. Haddon as "one of the most promising for ethnological research in the world"; the need for immediate investigation was extremely urgent; Sepik natives possessed "a remarkably rich culture for a savage community . . . [but]

we know absolutely nothing about their institutions, or their religion." Other foreigners, particularly missionaries, had their eyes on the Sepik, too. The sooner Margaret and Reo could get there, on the pinnace with its cargo of alcohol or by any other means, the more they could learn.

"The blessed thing about it," Mead wrote of the prospect of the pinnace journey, "is that we can go straight there without an interval of putting on white clothes and talking politely to all the other people who feel that the natives should be reserved for their special varieties of exploitation." And after they had seen something of the Sepik, Mead wrote to her former professor and employer, the sociologist William Fielding Ogburn, "we shall probably do an Australian tribe [which Radcliffe-Brown had suggested should be their next project] if our funds hold out. We are spreading them as thin as possible."

The choice of their next field site, Mead wrote, "was very simply determined. We selected the nearest tribe that was accessible by water which was unmissionized,* and which seemed to be least likely to have been extensively influenced, either linguistically or culturally, by either the Iatmul or the Banaro [tribes studied by previous ethnographers]. The most accessible tribe of this type was the Mundugumor, reported in the government records to have been well under control for over three years. They were located a half-day's voyage up the Yuat River, a southern tributary of the Sepik.

"We had never heard either of the tribe or indeed of the swift muddy river on which they dwelt. . . . A party of [labor] recruiters pass-

---

* Missionaries, Mead's later friend and colleague Geoffrey Gorer would write, were "almost wholly deplorable. With possibly the best of intentions they have made rogues out of honest men, self-seekers out of unselfish men, liars and perverts and neurotics out of men happily free from these defects . . . Christianity's intense insistence on individualism," Gorer would add, destroyed tribal feeling, and replaced tribal cooperation with chastity, "a poor substitute." Fortune had made a similar discovery among the Dobuans, who, he wrote, went to church, or sent their children there, "largely for fear of antagonizing the Mission, all the while keeping up full practice of their old pre-Christian customs."

"The mission's chief contribution," a later writer said, was "to sustain morale on the Station and win support in Australia"; it was obliged "to appeal no less persuasively to the pockets of its Australian patrons than to the hearts of its Papuan heathens . . . It was considered the business of the European to rule, the Islander to interpret, and the Papuan to obey . . . Missionaries 'rescued' children, took them into their homes, and bred them . . . towards a wholly fabricated status as an adoptive white—one whose appearance denies his loyalty. When they grew up, such children were likely to be scorned by Papuans and Europeans alike."

ing through Marienberg extended us their sympathy when they heard we were going up the Yuat and advised us to lay in a good supply of buttons, as the Yuat people had a liking for them. With this, and no further information, we landed our goods in Kinakatem, the first Mundugumor settlement, and the one that the government census books showed to be the center of the largest locality."

As the first white woman many people on the banks of the turbid Yuat River had ever seen, Mead would have been conspicuous no matter what she wore. Since the main sartorial problem was to fend off mosquitoes, her solution was to wear a large straw hat and, under her ordinary dresses, her husband's pajama bottoms. Luckily he had a good supply, and nobody cared if the legs belled over her shoes. The mosquitoes were no ordinary nagging little pests. The problem they caused, Mead wrote home, had "a clothing, an architecture, a closet economy all its own . . . the best plan is to spread one's possessions thin over endless shelves, so that everything can be found and grabbed before more than a hundred wounds are sustained. Bathing except at midday has to be done with a whisk in one hand."

Her letter did not hint of the more serious problems of her marriage. "Perhaps no other endogamous marriages," as she later wrote, "except those of two committed foreign missionaries or two stars of show business, present quite as many hazards. The members of a good anthropological team in a difficult field location are as interdependent as two trapeze artists or, to pick a loftier simile, as Alfred Lunt and Lynn Fontanne.

"It is, in retrospect, quite impossible to disentangle the threads of their expert perceptions, so as to say whose insight was more significant or who got the first clue to some unsuspected aspect of culture. . . . When marriages between anthropologists are based on marked contrasts in temperament and tempo, as is for many reasons most desirable, there is a further hazard in the way in which the cultural style, the physique and the habitat of a people may lock into the preferences of one of the pair and repel the other." Such unstable balances, she wrote, could lead to new tensions. Travel, even in the most efficient and civilized of circumstances, has been the undoing of many a pair. Of Margaret and Reo this much must be said: they traveled together as far as they could.

The Mundugumor, Fortune wrote to Ruth Benedict, were "a queer society. . . . I have a great conviction about societies not yet described that the limits of outrage are not nearly plumbed yet. . . ." Although

war, headhunting, and cannibalism had been outlawed three years earlier, the memory of that way of life was still vivid; "small children of
eleven and twelve had all taken part in cannibal feasts." It was not uncommon to see the bodies of much smaller children floating, unwashed
and unwanted, down the river. They are always throwing away infants
here, Mead wrote, because fathers could not be bothered to observe the
taboos associated with their survival. (Pronouncements like this, which
struck many of Mead's colleagues as offensively flippant, were becoming
part of her style.)

Babies were carried around in harsh, stiff, opaque baskets through
which they could see only narrow slits of light. Nobody cuddled or
comforted them when they cried; the most they could hope for was
that someone might scratch their baskets, which made a harsh, grating
sound. It was hardly surprising that they should grow up feeling
wronged, and planning wrong to others, in an atmosphere which Mead
found "riddled with suspicion and distrust." These people were a far
cry from the snuggling, cuddling, kissing Arapesh.

But there were some blessings to count, as Margaret and Reo settled in for what would be a three-month sojourn. They could drink, for
example, from glasses made of actual glass, rather than enamel cups,
and bake their bread in an oven, and use a grater made from a butter
tin. Boats that plied the Yuat could be relied upon to supply them
every month with two cans each of asparagus, cauliflower, and crackers,
a welcome variation from the indigenous diet. And the Mundugumor,
for all their meanness, could also be, as Mead went so far as to put it,
"charming." (This same paradox later confronted the anthropologist
Nancy McDowell, when she researched *The Mundugumor: From the
Field Notes of Margaret Mead and Reo Fortune*. In three extended
field trips to Yuat villages between 1972 and 1981, she found the Biwat,
as the Mundugumor now are known, to be just as "harsh and aggressive" on the one hand, and as "gay and charming" on the other, as
Mead had said they were.)

The Mundugumor were "even postponing their quarrels until we
leave," Mead wrote home, "a point which we—scientifically, of course—
do not appreciate. It takes adepts in hypocrisy to be sufficiently self-
conscious to think of what a front they present to the white man.*

---

* Reality, as Erving Goffman points out in *The Presentation of Self in
Everyday Life*, can have multiple and seemingly incompatible versions, sometimes expressed surreptitiously: Mead was learning that primitive tribes-
people could be just as perplexing in the impressions they "gave off," to use
Goffman's term, as their more "civilized" observers.

The Samoans would do it, but not the Manus, who are too sincere, or the Arapesh, who were too simple-minded, or the Dobuans, who could have thought of it but were too nasty. Haven't we a fine lot of different people to ring the changes on?"

For several weeks Mead kept a detailed record called a "Daily Diary," telling what went on every day in each of twelve households, and summarizing the major events in Kinakatem. Between November 15 and 20, she wrote in the diary, village life was disrupted by visits from a district officer, a labor recruiter, and passengers of a mail and cargo boat. Mead felt feverish during this period, quite likely from malaria, but fixed lunch for these visitors in addition to keeping up her regular ethnographic activities. "I am sure I shall start a suffrage movement among the more distant villagers who find me *talking place*—speaking the native language—an accomplishment of which the first white man certainly did not boast."

"I shall be 31 next week," she wrote home in December of 1932, after three months with the Mundugumor, "and I am not dispirited by the fact as I have gotten in quite a lot so far and I do not seem to be looking any older, though this climate is hard on the skin. I am a little thinner and I play quite a decent game of deck tennis. Think of me playing any kind of athletic thing fairly well!" Only later and elsewhere did she mention that, "in Mundugumor I had a good deal of fever and this, combined with Reo's unrelenting attitude toward illness, the mosquitoes, and the general sense of frustration over the people, made it a very unpleasant three months."

Fortune's attitude toward illness was radical and spartan, and more so all the time. "When we were first married," Mead said, "he had taken care of me very gently during my first attack of malaria [among the Manus] which is frightening because one gets so cold that it is hard to believe one will ever be warm again and stop shaking." But eventually her husband came to treat Mead's illnesses the same way he did his own, which she said was to "go out and climb a mountain, however raging his fever, in order to fight the sickness out of his system."

And only in 1935, when in *Sex and Temperament* she described her sojourns with them as well as with the Arapesh and the Tchambuli (whom they would visit next), did Mead publicly say how the Mundugumor took "frank, sadistic enjoyment of other people's discomfiture," and how their conversation, "especially about matters pertaining to sex, [had] the character of playing ball with hand grenades." Lovemaking, if it could be called that, was hardly joyous or languid: "Foreplay in these quick encounters takes the form of a violent scratching and biting match, calculated to produce the maximum amount of excitement in the minimum amount of time. To break the arrows or the basket of the beloved is one standard way of demonstrating consuming passion: so also is tearing off ornaments and smashing them if possible." If you wanted to ruin a neighbor's yam crop—and if you were a Mundugumor, as Mead described them, you would surely want to do just that—you had only to copulate in his yard.

All activities were fair game for "the coarsest, most Rabelaisian references." In sharp contrast with the Arapesh, whom Mead (though not Fortune) had found gentle and unassertive regardless of gender, both men and women among the Mundugumor were "expected to be violent, competitive, aggressively sexed, jealous, and ready to see and avenge insult, delighting in display, in action, in fighting. The Mundugumor have selected as their ideal the very types of men and women which the Arapesh consider to be so incomprehensible that they hardly allow for their occurrence." Forty years later, when organized sport had become popular throughout Papua New Guinea, Nancy McDowell noted that the Mundugumor, alone among groups she visited, had basketball teams composed of both men and women, and that "the women, in basketball terms, had just as much 'hustle' as the men."

But of course not all Mundugumor were aggressive. This society, like all those which Mead studied, needed its deviants; she thought so then, and many later sociologists came to the same conclusion. A man named Omblean, whom Mead called "the most intellectual informant we have ever had," was a misfit among the Mundugumor because he made a point of learning "every rule and every loophole through which intelligence could outmatch brute strength." Another misfit was a woman named Kwenda, "who was so consistently, stupidly, good-natured, devoted and natural . . . young, warm, and vigorous, that no man could want her." Omblean and Kwenda were among the exceptions who proved the rule.

For Mead's own part, she yearned for a gentler environment. It was among the Mundugumor, she later wrote, that she decided to have a child "no matter how many miscarriages it meant. It seemed clear to me that a culture that so repudiated children could not be a good culture." Fortune "didn't want any children at all and I didn't want him as the father of any children, because he would be too jealous," Mead told a friend. "I'd only married him when I was told I couldn't have children." Perhaps the doctor who had told her she could not give birth, during her marriage to Cressman, had been wrong. A new idea seemed to be taking shape: if a more suitable potential father someday presented himself, she might have a baby after all.

Meanwhile, Fortune's celebrated mind—the one thing about him that his wife thought she could still rely on—seemed to her to be failing. In this field trip, as always, it had been Fortune who decided which of them would do what. "I'd always accepted this," Mead said later, "because I could do anything, it didn't matter." But now Fortune's division of labor, far more extreme here than among the Arapesh, appeared to Mead to be ruining the work and further straining the marriage. "You do the children and the maternal culture and the language," he had told his wife, "because the language is nothing, and I will do everything else." Her job, they had agreed, would be to observe what she could of gender roles; his would be to prepare the official ethnography.

Although he never did get around to writing the ethnography, he apparently had intended to. In the letter to Ruth Benedict in which he described the Mundugumor as "a queer society," Fortune wrote, "I'm looking forward to being back someday—a great deal of work here yet though." Part of the work that remained to be done was figuring out the complexities of the Mundugumor kinship system, which decreed marriage patterns and exchange between generations. As Mead explains it in *Sex and Temperament*, this kinship system, likened to the different strands of a rope, was a terribly tricky thing to figure out. To her enduring disdain, in the middle of their stay in Kinakatem she "discovered that Reo had missed a clue" concerning kinship. The clue came from the terminology of children. Children were her assigned realm. Had she not picked up the clue, she said, it might have been overlooked altogether.

Her husband's failure struck her as "a flat contradiction of good scientific practice." But Mead made a mistake, too. In interpreting the Mundugumor concept of descent, says Nancy McDowell, Mead applied "an inappropriate label from today's point of view to a complex phenomenon." In context this does not seem surprising. Nobody is or ever was perfect; the point of all this is not that Mead and Fortune were fallible but that they were getting more and more on each other's nerves. "Of course I knew, after all those months in New Guinea, that I was living with a crank," Mead reflected many years later, but crankiness in the field was easier to accept, and more forgivable, than crankiness on the Upper West Side of New York. Fortune may have thought he had a crank on his hands, too. A letter he wrote to Malinowski in 1937 tells of having had a "psychopathological case" to nurse in mid-New Guinea, and of having had to get out, as it seemed the best thing to do to save Mead from a permanently deranged condition. "I suspect," Fortune's niece and executor Ann McLean added, "that both were correct in their appraisal of each other." Nancy McDowell, puzzled by the "mistake" that allegedly was "almost" made, doubts that "there is enough data or information to know exactly what happened. Mead and Fortune were both terrific fieldworkers, so who can be sure?"*

The teamwork between these two terrific field workers, it seems clear, was faltering. Their partnership, emotionally and professionally, was in trouble. Fortune's outbursts, Mead had figured, would be tolerable so long as they could manage to spend the bulk of their time in the field, where he was so inspired and diligent a worker. But could she still rely on him? And if she could not, was there any reason for them to continue together? Collaboration with the wrong person, in the field, might be even more trying than solitude. In any case, the Mundugumor culture was "so broken," she wrote much later, "that we decided to abandon it after two and a half months."

None of these glum thoughts appeared in Mead's letters home. She was either a very confused woman, around the time of her thirty-first birthday, or one who wanted desperately to protect her family and friends from knowing how she really felt. Of the Mundugumor, whom she would later describe in print as "loathsome," she wrote home comfortingly that, "It has been very pleasant. We finished up . . . quite happily and left them with gayer words and friendlier adieus than we had ever had from primitive people."

After these adieus the anthropologists, with the two hundred specimens of artifacts they had collected, headed for the mouth of the Yuat where it converges with the Sepik, to camp there for the night. Margaret suffered a nasty surprise. "The people had made a door to the latrine from a kind of palm frond that is edged with tiny thorns," she said, "and when I tried to open it, I ran hundreds of thorns into my hands."

With stinging hands, conflicting feelings and a husband who seemed increasingly truculent, Mead went on to Ambunti, the main government station 250 miles further up the Sepik, to join all the other whites stationed in the region for Christmas, 1932. After the holiday they planned to move on to an upper river field site. "News that

* Mead acquired Fortune's field notes in 1972 and 1973, intending to write the long-overdue ethnography but she never had time to finish. "When anthropologists criticize Mead," said McDowell, "they're after the wrong person; Fortune should take the heat, not Mead. She did five volumes on the Arapesh, but she only wrote popularly, in *Sex and Temperament*, about the Mundugumor. *There is no ethnography of the Mundugumor.* We can't evaluate her ethnography, since it doesn't exist, but we can evaluate her *work:* her Mundugumor work more than passes any test we can devise."

Bateson wouldn't be down," Mead had written in her diary on November 15. Fortune's fellow ethnographer and Cambridge alumnus Gregory Bateson, also at work with a Sepik tribe, was not expected to be part of the celebration. But, as it happened, he was.

CHAPTER ELEVEN

"The Closest I've Ever Come to Madness"

THE CHRISTMAS REVELERS at Ambunti drank a lot more than they ate. On hand were "seventeen men, who came from the most various backgrounds, and one other woman, who had just been released from prison for having killed her baby and somehow managed to get up the Sepik.

"Drinking went on all day, and our inexperienced little Arapesh boys, whom we had brought with us upriver, watched with astonishment the events that took place as dishes were smashed and furniture was pitched out of the door of one of the houses down on the flat. At ten o'clock at night our jovial, much-loved and alcoholic host, 'Sepik Robbie,' would say, 'We have had dinner, haven't we?' I learned to cadge large slices of bread and butter from Robbie's cook to fortify me during long dinnerless drinking." Offhand, these people seemed as unpromising as Mead's fellow passengers on the *Chitral* had seemed four years earlier, until among them she discovered Reo Fortune. This time she discovered the locally famous "Mr. Bateson."

"You're tired," said Gregory Bateson when he first saw Margaret Mead before the Christmas party in Ambunti. That alone endeared him to her. Reo and the Mundugumor had done little to meet her yearning for simple tenderness. Bateson, who stood six feet five and looked like an adolescent, had great charm, at least for women. A male Australian anthropologist who met him in Sydney called Bateson "the most physically unattractive man I've ever known," and one of his later American associates described him as "very homely, like a white Papuan." Men could not see the appeal of Bateson's "physical posture of puzzlement and bafflement, with arms and legs all twisted around each other." But several women, it was rumored, had left their husbands over Bateson, and others would consider doing so.*

* Even when he was struggling for breath in what proved to be his final illness, Bateson was handsome and charming, and wryly witty. "There are

154

Reo Fortune was also darkly handsome, and had a sharp and arcane wit—"How do you know when there's a hole in a whole?" he once asked. But by the time Fortune and Mead met Bateson in New Guinea, they had become disenchanted with each other, and Bateson struck them both as a source of diversion from their personal problems. The two men had been acquainted at Cambridge, where Haddon had given both his blessing in their Melanesian studies. Haddon, Reo told Margaret, "liked me, but [had] given Gregory his butterfly net." Under Haddon, back in England, Bateson would finish the master's thesis he was beginning when he met Mead and Fortune, "Social Structure of the Iatmul People of the Sepik River."

Bateson had abandoned an earlier plan to write about a dispiriting tribe called the Baining, on northern New Britain Island. In March 1928 he had left the Baining to seek the counsel, at Sydney University, of Radcliffe-Brown, who had bet his student Reo Fortune that Margaret Mead would never actually become his wife. In the fall of 1928, about the time Fortune and Mead were married in Auckland, Bateson had taken to the field again, for five more unhappy months of work with the Sulka, a coastal people who never entered the sea for pleasure: "I am the only regular bather in the village," he wrote to his mother. To his own surprise, while he worked with the Sulka, Bateson once became so mad, during a bout with tropical fever, that he shot a pig: an act which won him unexpected prestige. But "after all," as he wrote home, "these people are savage—their ways are savage, to a certain extent savagery here is a virtue—and its absence a weakness.

"My belly is full with this traveling and poking my nose into the affairs of other races," he also wrote during his Sulka field work. In mid-February of 1929, cruising past the Admiralty Island of Manus toward the Sepik, he had just missed what would have been a reunion with Fortune and an earlier first meeting with Margaret Mead. In the spring of 1930 Bateson had returned to England and, feeling out of place amid the "quasi-scholarship and quasi-wit" of Cambridge, had gone north to Yorkshire, where he spent a year as a paying guest on a farm, working on his ill-fated master's thesis.

---

a large number of ways of skinning a cat," he said during a 1979 seminar at the Esalen Institute in California, "and at a certain point you have to agree that the skin is on the outside and the cat on the inside." He made fun of the post-hippie jargon of the times, referring to "vibration" as "a word people use to fry eggs with," and, after showing a film he had made of Balinese dancers in a state of trance, he commented, "This is very close to whatever hypnotism is close to."

To the distress of his widowed mother, who rued the day he had caught "the travel fever" and "been embraced by Melanesia," Bateson had then returned to New Guinea and settled on the Sepik in the village of Tambunam, which he called "a wonderful place, about three quarters of a mile in length with a population of about one thousand—great big houses all set on high floors six feet from the ground." If only, as he had written to Haddon and to Radcliffe-Brown, he had a colleague to work with.

"I feel I could scarcely face another anthropological expedition without a partner," he wrote to his mother. When Mead and Fortune appeared in Ambunti for Christmas, after their grim time with the Mundugumor, Bateson was in scarcely better spirits than they were. Looking back later on the time when he met Margaret Mead, he described himself as "despairing, desperate, unfocused, not knowing what to do or why I was doing it. I'd already failed in a piece of field work with the Baining in New Britain." The Sepik, by comparison, seemed all but heavenly. "I discovered that on the Sepik River you could connect data. Iatmul can tell you things. They have rituals, and this stuff you can put in notebooks—this, believe me, was a great comfort, after the Baining, who I think are a little worse than the Arapesh in the degree to which they cannot tell you anything, and don't do anything, and nothing happens all the time."

Through his two older brothers, Bateson had already learned a good deal about despair. John, the eldest, had been killed in the Great War, and Martin, the next, had shot himself in the middle of Piccadilly Circus on John's birthday, under the statue of Eros, when he learned that the woman he loved would not have him. This left Gregory the only surviving child of the widowed Beatrice Bateson, whose husband William, master of St. John's College at Cambridge University, had been a biologist of great note and a founder of the science of genetics.

For all his self-doubt, Gregory Bateson was assuredly part of what the historian of science June Goodfield called "the circle of academic English families—the Darwins, Huxleys, Whiteheads, Mitchisons, Haldanes, and Hutchinsons, who all produced generation after generation of scholars whose interests were wide ranging and whose education had been intense . . . for the most part, their science was their religion and their offspring were expected to maintain their parents' faith."

These families were in their way aristocrats, "heirs to a great tradition, not measured in castles and wealth and hereditary titles, but in culture and education and I suppose a new kind of privilege. They have a deftness, a sureness of touch, an intellectual arrogance, surety, a confidence with which they walk and talk—a confidence which might be misplaced," said Goodfield, "but I have never read any of their writings where they admit they might be wrong. There's an old English saying that an Oxonian walks down a street as if he owns it, and a Cambridge man as if he didn't care who owned it." Mead with her American version of this same congenital confidence must have been delighted to recognize it in Bateson.

"At times Reo and I felt that Gregory was years younger than we were," she wrote. "At other times, however, Gregory seemed to be our senior. He had all the assurance of his English background and the intellectual certainty of his Cambridge education in the natural sciences." That assurance may have helped to save Gregory from suicide. "I had made one divinatory attempt on the river," he said, "to see if the answer would be to die, and God said no, you don't die this time, and then Margaret came along, full of enthusiasm." If a mentor is one who breaks a depression, Bateson said, then Margaret was surely a mentor to him.

At the time of this Christmas sojourn Mead presumably still held to the Episcopalian faith she had embraced at the age of eleven, but she may have kept this faith to herself upon learning that Bateson, for all his occasional allusions to God, was not a believer. As a schoolboy, when his fellow students had knelt for compulsory prayer, Gregory had followed the advice of his older brothers and knelt to repeat the alphabet eight times over. Faith in great works, his father had written, "is the nearest to religion that I have ever got . . . to set oneself to find out something, even a little bit, of the structure and order of the natural world is . . . a splendid and purifying purpose."

Soon after they met, Gregory showed Margaret his copy of *Growing Up in New Guinea*, and challenged her to clarify one of the points she had made there. Reo, listening to the animated conversation that followed, must have been reminded, perhaps uneasily, of the exhilaration of his own first meeting with Margaret, just after she had finished her work in Samoa. "As anthropologists do," Bateson wrote to his mother of his encounter with Mead and Fortune, "we began talking, and kept it up for 30 hours on end. The result has been a very odd party. Three garrulous anthropologists talking shop as hard as they could go, in the midst of tipsy New Guinea whites."

Margaret and Reo had thought of doing their next field work in Australia, among the aborigines, but Bateson's company made that prospect seem less appealing, and they decided to stay on in the Sepik. Two days after Christmas, Gregory took them in his motorized canoe to visit a tribe called the Washkuk, whom they considered studying. But the Washkuk, as Mead wrote in *Sex and Temperament*, "implored us not to come and live with them, because then they would obviously have to stay in their scattered villages to look after us, and they had just completed preparations for a long hunting trip . . . they seemed very much like the Arapesh [and] felt themselves that their lives would be hopelessly upset by our stay." The search must continue for a suitable tribe to study next, Margaret and Reo decided. Meanwhile the three had no choice but to spend that night among the Washkuk, who claimed to be expecting a raid from another tribe.

In case this menace should materialize, Reo covered the scene from inside the guesthouse with a revolver. He and Margaret and Gregory took turns sleeping on the floor of the improvised mosquito room. Once during that night, Mead would write in *Blackberry Winter*, "Reo woke to hear Gregory and me talking," and perhaps he felt as left out and puzzled as he and Margaret had made Luther Cressman feel in 1926, when she took so long to come down the gangplank at Marseilles. "There is much to be said," Mead continued, "for the suggestion that the true oedipal situation is not the primal scene but parents talking to each other in words the child does not understand. And by then Gregory and I had already established a kind of communication in which Reo did not share."

From Fortune's point of view, things got worse the next day. Bateson proposed a swim. Swimming had been one of his few pleasures in this stretch of field work, and since bathing suits had never been an issue, either here or by what Mead called "the bohemian standards of his university youth," this meant a swim in the nude, a prospect that horrified Fortune. "Reo came from a world in which the strongest Victorian values still obtained. It had been hard for him to cope with the fact that I had, after all, been married before and that when he married me he was, in his own view, taking another man's wife. And it was always hard for him to cope with rivalry at any level. The fact that he himself was enjoying Gregory's company as much as I was did not help at all."

Having ruled out the Washkuk, the Fortunes decided instead to study a people on the Aimbom Lake, 180 miles from the mouth of the Sepik, whom they called the Tchambuli. These people, known to later ethnographers as the Chambri, had an intricate art, an elaborate culture, and a beautiful location. Their lake, Mead would write in *Sex and Temperament*, was "so colored with dark peat-brown vegetable matter that it looks black on the surface, and when no wind stirs it resembles black enamel. On this polished surface, in still times, the leaves of thousands of pink and white lotuses and a smaller deep-blue water lily are spread, and among the flowers, in the early morning the white osprey and the blue heron stand in great numbers, completing the decorative effect, which displays almost too studied a pattern to seem completely real." As always, such field settings evoked Mead's freshest and most lucid prose.

Mead was grateful to find a renewed enthusiasm for work, and pleased that Fortune would no longer be her only companion. A few miles away, in the village of Palembei, Gregory Bateson had set up a new research site to continue his Iatmul studies. The two encampments kept in close touch; Bateson appointed one Palembei man to carry messages back and forth, and that messenger was kept so memorably busy that he could recall his routine to the British ethnographer Anthony Forge, a naturalized Australian, who worked on the same site twenty-five years later.

"Oleman," the messenger told Forge, "I used to paddle my canoe back and forwards every morning, noon and night." Sometimes Gregory himself would come for the evening, and he and Margaret and Reo would play a game called *bouts-rimés*, rhymed ends, a game Bateson thought showed how "fantastic" was the "infinite facility" of Mead's brain.* This was "a game of which poets disapproved," Bateson said, "but if you're not a poet, the objection is not so strong. We'd decide on a poetic meter, observing that it had a rhyme scheme like A-B-A-B or C-D-C-D, and go around the table supplying the final words. The only line I can remember writing myself is 'To catch the flies in Malinowski's grease.' "

Malinowski, of course, was the admitted master, and the conventional view of him, Bateson once said, "was that he was a horrible, detestable man, but a genius as an anthropologist. My view was that he was rather an amusing man, but a lousy anthropologist, a lousy theorist . . . [His] whole functional theory of human nature, that if you make a list of human needs, and then you dissect the culture on how it satisfies them—this seems to me to be absolute balls."

Reo Fortune remarked that Malinowski's practice was to grab natives "by the collar so they couldn't get away. . . . As they become independent you can't do this. This bullying technique is part of imperialism." But bullying seemed to Bateson to be part of Fortune's

* In one game of *bouts-rimés* Mead's last two lines said a lot about this very facility: "My pen leaps on, retracts, evades, until / My thoughts, inchoate, tumble to a spill."

and Mead's approach as well, when he saw them at work in the field. "I was at first shocked," he wrote to his mother. "They bully and chivvy their informants and interpreters and *hurry* them till they don't know whether they are on head or heels. But in the end I was converted and I am going to do some bullying too. . . . I spend hours feeling my way and getting into rapport with natives and it is all quite unnecessary. Also they plan their work while I very gingerly pick up what comes."

The three young anthropologists had plenty of time to compare their different ways of thinking and working. "Although Reo and I had far more sophisticated verbal techniques," Mead wrote, "Gregory had a sure sense of the technology of research." Anthropology, Bateson had written a few years earlier, was "all rather gentlemanly, rather scholarly . . . [it] was, on the whole, pretty thin." Parts of field work had always distressed him. Once during a field trip he missed an old woman's funeral, and he wrote to his mother: "I hate all that side of my work. I always feel that I am intruding when I try to learn about such things . . . I suppose the perfect anthropologist is as cynical as a newspaper reporter."

Mead, who all her life took unabashed delight in being observed, expressed no remorse about being an intruder, but she did admit to other shortcomings. A few years earlier she had boasted of speaking polished Samoan, but Tchambuli was apparently more humbling. "The dashed language," she wrote to Ruth Benedict on March 18, 1933, "is really awful. Learning five-syllable words and six-syllable names is very wearing, and it's a closed community of 540 people, too good a thing not to do in perfect detail, but a fair facer of a job . . . Today has not been such a good day, fussing around in the night with canvases to keep out a storm, a dark rainy morning, failure of scouts to report an event in Kilimbit hamlet, Tchuikumban so sleepy from staying up all night blowing flutes that he was useless for linguistics . . . a very horrible yaws sore to dress—half a toe eaten away and a horrible stench . . . horrible lot of gnats."

Three new languages to learn in so short a time, Mead wrote in *Blackberry Winter*, took their toll in her unconscious: "I would dream that I was standing outside a house, asking politely whether I might come in—and no one would answer me . . . only the nouns and verbs were in Tchambuli, the particles were in Samoan." But her worst troubles were not linguistic. Many years later, speaking of that time in New Guinea, she told a friend, "Reo later said he had burned himself out young and was therefore unable to give me a child, but he will not remember that he was able to make me pregnant, and gave me a miscarriage by knocking me down, and later said, 'Gregory ate our baby.'"

These months in New Guinea, as Bateson later said, were a great strain all around: "All three of us together were pretty well psychotic." All were violating the precepts of their upbringing. "The sons of distinguished Englishmen," as June Goodfield said, "did not just fall in love with someone else's wife—or if they did, didn't run off with her. In the old-fashioned Cambridge of William Bateson and the Darwins, behavior was Edwardian and Victorian; emotion and passion were well understood but the correct norms of public, outward behavior, too, were well understood.

"Gregory had been going through a period of very intense creativity and, suddenly emerging, was faced with an intelligent and stimulating person in the form of Margaret, whose needs also triggered his tenderness." Fortune's niece Ann McLean suggested that "Reo and Margaret and Gregory perhaps acted in the spirit of the freedom to which intellectuals had claim in the twenties, when they grew up, but in so doing may have done a disservice to their essentially prudish conditioning."

Even Mead, who if she was not impervious to stress could often appear to be, later said of this period, "We were all understanding too much. Everything was too clear. It was the closest I've ever come to madness. It was a rigid, boxed drama." More and more blatantly the situation was a triangle, with Margaret Mead at the apex. Relationships were not so different, as she perceived them, among the Tchambuli, whose gender attributes she was studying. They too lived in a "highly charged atmosphere of courtship in which no one knows upon whom a woman's choice will fall, each youth holds his breath and hopes, and no young man is willing to trust another . . .

"The course of true love runs no smoother here, where women dominate," she wrote, "than it does in societies dominated by men . . . What the women will think, what the women will say, what the women will do, lies at the back of each man's mind as he weaves his tenuous and uncertain web of insubstantial relations with other men . . . the women are a solid group, confused by no rivalries, brisk, patronizing, and jovial . . . yet the men are after all stronger, and a man can beat his wife, and this possibility serves to confuse the whole issue of female dominance and masculine charming, graceful, coquetting, dancing attention."*

* Mead's four months with the Tchambuli, said Deborah Gewertz, who on two much later occasions worked with the same tribe, "anticipates the work of many contemporary scholars," but Mead was wrong in failing to "push

Thinking back to the New Guinea tribes she had studied earlier, Mead generalized: "Although the Mundugumor seek to exalt the self, to bend other human beings to the service of the self, to exploit the weak ruthlessly and sweep aside the opposing strong, and the Arapesh seek rather to depress the self, their ideal man or woman being the individual who finds fulfillment in devotion to the ends of others, nevertheless the Arapesh and the Mundugumor are ultimately personal in their emphases . . . there is no feeling that the structure is so valid and beautiful that the individual should be subordinated to its perpetuation and elaboration, that the dance and not the dancer is valuable."

Not so with the Tchambuli, Mead would say; they "value primarily their intricate, delicately patterned social life . . . Neither men nor women are ideally concerned with personal ends in any way . . . underneath patriarchal forms women dominate the scene . . . but the actual dominance of the women is far more real than the structural position of the men." The Tchambuli, as far as she was concerned, showed "a genuine reversal of the sex-attitudes of our own culture, with the woman the dominant, impersonal, managing partner, the man the less responsible and the emotionally dependent person.

"We are forced to conclude," Mead reflected as she considered the three tribes she and Fortune had been studying, "that human nature is almost unbelievably malleable, responding accurately and contrastingly to contrasting cultural conditions." (This amplified the conclusion, supporting Franz Boas's ideas and refuting the ethnocentricity of the nineteenth century, which Mead had reached in Samoa.) The three tribes' differences, she said, sprang from culturally determined conditioning in childhood: "cultures are man-made, they are built of human materials; they are diverse but comparable structures within which human beings can attain full human stature." But why was it, she asked later, that "materialistic, bustling America and a materialistic, bustling tribe in the Admiralty Islands both produce hoboes, or why is it the individual endowed with a capacity to feel strongly who is maladjusted in Zuni and Samoa?"

Men, she noted, nearly always have more prestigious occupations

---

her own brilliant methodology to its obvious conclusion," which, in Gewertz's view, was that women's dominance, or lack of it, should be explained "in terms of the relationships through which they define themselves as persons. . . . Mead assumed that to change one's position in the hierarchy is to change one's nature. . . . Women neither wish nor need to play [the ludicrous games of men]."

than women, and when a man brought up to dominate women "encounters a woman who is naturally as dominating as he is himself, or
even a woman who, although not dominating temperamentally, is able
to outdistance him in some special skill or a type of work, a doubt of
his own manhood is set up in his mind." So it may have been between
Margaret Mead and Reo Fortune, who surely must have felt that she
was outdistancing him.* "Reo had a better ear than I have and Gregory
had a much better ear," Mead said many years later, "but neither of
them ever knew whose pig was dead. I always knew whose pig was
dead."

"There was vastly more growth in Margaret than in any of those
people she was associated with," the psychologist Rollo May said in
1979. "Fortune and Bateson were both technically odd, and Bateson
once told me, with a wry smile, that he and Harry Stack Sullivan were
both a little schizophrenic." The British anthropologist Meyer Fortes,
thinking back on Mead and her husbands, said, "it's clear that Margaret owed a lot to both these men, and that she gave a lot to them,
too, especially to Bateson, who was motivated—as she was—to great
generalizing ideas."

As the three anthropologists tried to ward off lunacy by formulat-
ing ideas, and working feverishly with their people, the completed
manuscript of Ruth Benedict's *Patterns of Culture* arrived, along with
her request for their comments. It gave them something to focus on
besides themselves and their daily work. Mead wrote a letter that her
friend Benedict found profoundly discouraging, explaining, "We're
really all you have to depend on to save you from the wolves, and
therefore we ought to say everything we can think of. So here goes,
and try to see me saying it, wrinkling my brows, and making awful faces
to get it clear, and ready to fly if I should say the wrong thing."

Mead suggested that Benedict should first decide "who you are
writing towards, read it straight through from the point of view of that
person, stopping to consider at each point his vocabulary, general information, and also his special knowledge. . . . It would be a bad accident

---

* People who cared about Fortune wondered all the rest of his life, and
afterward, why he never published his differences with Mead's and Benedict's thinking, which he seemed to feel more acutely with the passage of
time. His niece and executor, Ann McLean, suggests that Fortune felt out-
distanced "only in the sense of popular appeal. Reo's papers are peppered
with evidence of his confidence in his own professional judgment and his
misgivings about Margaret's. In my view, this is part of the reason why he
did not publish—part distaste for laundering dirty linen in public, and partly
that he realized the futility of taking on the media."

if your feeling for style and texture were to be spoilt by an accident of assembling miscellaneous source materials . . ."

If he had never met Margaret Mead, Bateson said, he would sooner or later have read Benedict's book without its having much impact on him. Since he read it at the same time Mead did, the manuscript's arrival was deeply important; "it led to the beginnings of what one could think of to do . . . We played typologies."

The typologies, according to Bateson, "pretty soon, for Margaret and me . . . became the central focus . . . the typology after all is a slice, a time section of a human being, of a culture, of a something or other, and the real problem is one of process leading to it. For me, that process was schismogenesis, the notion that there are progressive changes in relationships either of persons or of groups, and that those progressions are, in a sense, creative, evolutionary . . ." Schismogenesis—the origin of schisms—was to become one of the central, if to many most puzzling, ideas of Bateson's career.

Fortune was less enchanted with Benedict's manuscript, which incorporated her version of his 1927–28 work with the Dobuans. In an enclosed note, Benedict urged Fortune to make corrections on points of fact, "but not," he said in 1975, "on points of interpretation. As it was all interpretation, I didn't correct it at all. I was left no option but to send it back to her or to drop it in the Sepik River. I didn't drop it in the Sepik, so I sent it back. I didn't agree with the interpretation of it at all. Also, it was wrong on points of fact." But decades were to pass before Fortune could admit these objections to Benedict or even to himself.*

Benedict needed all the reassurance she could get about her book, and later barraged her publishers with suggestions to make it as popular as possible: "This seems too light a turquoise," she wrote when she first saw one jacket color. "I am clipping onto this letter a slip of paper that seems to be more nearly the right tone." She also urged that the price be as low as possible, to help make "culture" a household word among the "Macy shoppers."

Fortune was losing Mead, just as surely as Luther Cressman before him had lost her. She was growing besotted—as she had never been before and would never be again with any man—with the shambling,

---

* "Your book, Ruth, just to hand," Fortune wrote her when the final product reached him the following January, "looks very cheerful and magnificent. It looks fine—and you are really kind the way you take it and you say it all so well . . . It looks grand and I'm pleased all round." In fact, he was not.

gangling academic aristocrat Bateson, whose parents had agreed that
"to find an appropriate girl within their small circle of quasi-endog-
amous English intellectuals would be difficult" and that "to find a
suitable 'outsider' was nearly inconceivable." Could this determined
little American be the nearly inconceivable outsider? Could Gregory's
famous bachelor adventures be ending?

Years later, Bateson's Sydney colleague Ian Hogbin remembered
an evening during Australia's puritan days, when pubs were closed at
six and no drinks were served afterward except in the lounges of the
most expensive hotels. During one visit to such a lounge, "Bateson, the
most untidy man who ever lived, with holes in his trousers and flapping
soles on his shoes, attracted the attention of the waiter, who asked,
'Are you staying in the house, sir?'

" 'Of course I am,' lied Bateson.

" 'Do you mind if I have a word with the headwaiter?' Bateson did
not mind; the headwaiter arrived and asked his room number.

" 'Room 500,' said Bateson.

" 'But that's the housemaid's room,' said the headwaiter.

" 'Yes,' said Bateson, 'the one with the pretty blue eyes.' " He had
to go elsewhere to find his drink.

Mead, it was clear, was making Bateson for the time forget blue-
eyed housemaids and all other women; the two were falling in love.
"Both Gregory and I felt that we were, to some extent, deviants, each
within our own culture," Mead wrote in *Blackberry Winter*. He was
not stereotypically aggressive, as British men were supposed to be. She
was not indifferent to children, as American career women were supposed to be, nor did she fit the cliché of "the possessive, managing
American wife and mother. It was exciting," she wrote, "to strip off
the layers of culturally attributed expected behavior and to feel that
one knew at last who one was."

"If you're out in the tropics or the desert or anywhere else and
have a major idea," Bateson said years later, "the thing to do is pack
up and come home." In the spring of 1933, he and Fortune and Mead
packed up to leave the Sepik. "Reo and I cabled Boas that we were
coming home with immensely important new theoretical points," Mead
said, but they did not go home together. When the three reached Australia, they were all to go their separate ways, and Mead would not see
Fortune again until long after their divorce. When they arrived together
in Sydney, with Margaret flanked by her husbands present and future,
their Australian friend Timothy Kelly told his wife: "Here it comes, here
comes the triangle," and a triangle it assuredly, hopelessly was.

Margaret was the first to leave. After she had sailed for America, where she would summarize her "theoretical points" in *Sex and Temperament in Three Primitive Societies*, Gregory and Reo played chess, and next it was time for Gregory to leave by freighter for England, to work on a paper that would lead to *Naven*, a book about Iatmul transvestite rituals. Reo Fortune, who was not quite sure what he would do next, saw Bateson off, Caroline Kelly remembered, with a pineapple in one hand and a pawpaw in the other.

"This," Fortune said to the man who would succeed him as Mead's husband, "is extremely symbolic."

CHAPTER TWELVE

Between Conjugal Domiciles

BACK IN NEW YORK, only nominally married, and thousands of miles away from the man she loved, Mead was determined to win the widest possible audience for the ideas she had brought home from New Guinea. She had "a fine sense of what was current," as one of her colleagues put it, "and was often diligent in thinking about and publishing readable books and articles on what was coming up in the many shifting preoccupations of her lifetime." She welcomed the attention of the press. "NEW GUINEA SONGS ARE SOLD FOR A PIG," began a *New York Times* headline, which went on to say: "Woman Explorer, Back, Says Old Tunes Bring High Prices Among the Aborigines—THEY KILL GIRL BABIES—But Spare Enough to Do All Their Work—'Sweetest' of People, Even So."

This October 1933 article announced Margaret Mead's return to the American Museum of Natural History after "two years . . . with the Arapesh of the Prince Alexander Mountains, the Mundugumor tribe on the Yuat River, and the Tchambuli tribe on Aimbom Lake in what was formerly Kaiser Wilhelm Land and is now the Australian mandate of New Guinea. . . . The women shave their heads and bear burdens, while the men decorate their long hair with peacock feathers and strut about like lords," Mead was quoted as saying. "The reason that pigs constituted the chief currency . . . was that a pig was one thing that was infinitely divisible." Another article, headlined NEW GUINEA HAS ITS OWN PARIS, AS FAR AS STYLES GO, also quoted Mead: "A little coast community called Murik" was the place where "the very latest in grass skirts, shell jewelry and songs and dances are originated— the inland village buys the whole outfit—paying for it in pigs."

The idea got across: this Mead was a force to reckon with. A later article described her as "a slender, comely girl who danced her way into the understanding of the Melanesian people and became an adopted daughter and a sort of princess of the Samoans. When they anointed her with palm oil and indicated that a dance was in order, she did a nice hula and they declared her in—indicating the adaptability of the modern young woman if she just has a chance to step out."

Mead particularly liked stepping up to lecterns and before audiences, and went out of her way to look for speaking engagements. To one lecture agent she sent a memo called "Dope Which Could Be Used," suggesting "Adolescence Primitive and Civilized" and "The Relationship Between Culture and Temperament" as suitable topics for college audiences. She was an authority, she pointed out, "on comparative education, including studies of primitive adolescence"; *Coming of Age in Samoa*, now published in England as well as America, was recommended reading in many university courses.

Popular audiences might prefer something more earthy. "Private Life of Cannibals," perhaps? Or "Where Women Fish and Men Dress Dolls"? Or "The Gentle Savages"? Slides could be used to illustrate "Water Dwellers of the Pacific." Mead had lived, she said, "in parts of the world where no white woman has ever been," and in one place she was "trussed to a pole like a pig and carried in over the mountains," and "lived intimately with people just three years removed from cannibalism and head hunting." She also, she claimed, spoke five primitive languages and was "in general able to give a first-hand report of the private lives of savages."

In February 1934 a New York columnist joshed about Mead's report of field work among the Arapesh: "It seems that in this country if a man feeds you and you eat his food often enough why then pretty soon you are his property, just like he had bought a little calf and fed it until it grew up," so that the man would eventually be entitled to tell his wife " 'I grew your body, therefore I own you. Be quiet.' Of course, Dr. Mead says, she had her growth before she married this Dr. Fortune, and so he cannot own her but she is very little still . . . and what if she should suddenly grow two inches or gain weight or something, and then you cannot tell but what a scientific mind like Dr. Fortune's might figure out that replacement is as good as growth, and then all would be lost. Yours for Dutch-treating . . ."

Far from "owning" Margaret Mead, Reo Fortune was describing his feeling for her in language that sounds disturbed. ". . . I am not going to be any stage comedy edition of a Patriarch, without any real cultural supports. Better be beggar then [sic] owner of luv [sic] or wenshes [sic]—and dispense with the owlish gravities between one Owner Capitalist and another Owner Capitalist—instead beggar's freedom.

"I've told Margaret Mead so. Whether she's in or out of a beggar's Party I don't know. She's a bit intense for good party manners, and apt to go off being intense and vicious Matriarch of a Small One and Only Family—she may improve and stay, or go out—that's her business.

"I did not wish to complicate her business by living upon her—or try to influence her unfairly, or introduce beggary of money into a beggar's party proposal of another kind. . . ." This letter was posted from Queensland, on the north coast of Australia, in November 1934, and was addressed to Bronislaw Malinowski. After Mead left for New York and Bateson for Cambridge, Fortune had gone to London to study under Professors Malinowski and Charles G. Seligmann, and was now on a slow cargo boat bound again for Sydney. From there he would make another expedition, alone, to a particularly warlike and uncontrolled tribe of New Guinea highlanders. He would be working on his second two-year grant from the Columbia University Council for Research in the Social Sciences.

In another shipboard letter to Malinowski, Fortune confessed a "natural pique at seeing the young coming up like mushrooms, and [feeling] oneself stranded . . ." From Sydney, in late January 1935, Fortune wrote approvingly to Malinowski of Benedict's *Patterns of Culture* in spite of his real reservations and added, "If you knew Boas better you might like him for not being an old woman—I don't know why you prefer your English colleagues."

The most arduous field work of Fortune's life began among a

people of the Purari River, near its headwaters in the Mount Hagen region of the Mandated Territory. In April 1935 (at a time when Gregory Bateson was visiting New York), Mead wrote to Radcliffe-Brown that she had "had my first letters from Reo from the interior; he has to keep an armed force, is separated by guerrilla warfare from his nearest neighbour, and the verb has 39 parts. But he says the noun is alright, 'if you let it alone.'" His researches among this tribe, according to an unsigned memorandum which appears to have been written by Mead, were "concluded by their annihilation by a neighboring tribe. . . . He is at present working on some special problems of matriliny in the islands of Tabar and New Hanover, adjacent to New Ireland."

Barter Fortune described this period as Reo's work with "a particularly nasty interior tribe" called the Kamano, in Finintegu near Kainantu in the Eastern Highlands of New Guinea. No previous anthropologist had ever worked with these people. They were menacing, and Fortune was weakened by a bad bout of malaria. The story he rather incoherently told to his family when he returned to New Zealand was that his porters, like those who had left him and Mead with the Arapesh, had deserted and left him in a clearing surrounded by tall growth which concealed his would-be attackers.

Enfeebled though he was, he had the wit to put out four biscuit tins at the points of an imaginary square, enclosing his camp. Delirium and confusion followed. His diary, which he usually kept faithfully, was neglected for a full three weeks. The tribesmen did not, after all, attack him (deterred from doing so, perhaps, by fear of their own annihilation), but he returned home with "about seventeen nervous twitches which took some time to abate," according to Shirley Hinds, who was then Barter's wife. Reo, she said, seemed "wrecked in health and morale" on his return from the Kamano. "It was a pretty hostile crowd up there; it must have been very punishing."

After this, said Barter Fortune, Reo was never the same. The Kamano, and Margaret's departure, had changed him radically. "Up to the end of the Mead era," Barter said, "Reo was the most dynamic and physical individual who had entered my life," but now he was suffused with an "incomprehensible lethargy" that he never managed to shake off. Derek Freeman, who knew Fortune later, and who became Mead's most vehement critic, suggested that Fortune had "just dried up," and that the drying had a lot to do with Margaret Mead: "He had a primal scream in him, about Margaret, a scream that would have been heard around the world. It was agony." Others who spent time with Fortune in this period had similar memories. A colleague who often lunched with him recalled that he was "very cut up, rampantly bitter, difficult, edgy"; another perceived him as "eccentric to the point of paranoia," and "so deeply hurt that he tried to show that Margaret was all wrong in what she said."

Might Reo Fortune have turned out to be just as eccentric had Mead stood by him for the rest of his life? Those who knew them both were not sure. "She had already fixed his wagon for fair and for final," one old friend thought. "He was the brightest of all her husbands; he was smarter than Bateson, but he was much the most pathetic, too. Margaret simply ripped him to shreds. You don't have to do much to destroy a person, you know, if you have that person's affection." And for all their troubles, Margaret did have Reo's affection. Barter, defending Reo loyally, called him "the sort of bloke whom it would be absolutely impossible to break from without a tremendous bout of rationalization. He was incapable of giving cause. Incapable. He'd willingly have lain down and died for Margaret, had it been necessary. He was a man of self-abnegating loyalty, almost to a saintly degree."

Mead, at work in New York on *Sex and Temperament*, wrote in the preface that she expected Reo Fortune would amplify what she had to say there about the field work they had done together in New Guinea. "Among the Mundugumor and the Tchambuli," she wrote, "a larger share of the ethnographical work fell to Dr. Fortune. For this reason I have treated the Arapesh most extensively and in treating of the other two tribes I have given only the minimum of ethnological material that is necessary. . . ." He, she was suggesting, would fill in the gaps.

With a sad look Reo had told Margaret, the first time he held in his hand a published copy of his first major book, *Sorcerers of Dobu* (which was dedicated to Mead), "That's the last book I'll have done by myself; all the others will have you in them." This turned out to be true: her comradeship could be sensed in *Manus Religion* (1935), based on the 1928–29 Admiralties expedition, *Omaha Secret Societies* (1932), based on the miserable 1930 visit to Nebraska, and in his last work, *Arapesh*, a linguistic monograph, published in 1942. ("Arapesh Warfare," an article, was published in 1939.) Fortune never published a word about the Mundugumor.

Now, bereft of Mead's emotional support and her professional shrewdness—"she was the field work fund raiser *par excellence* of that era," as Barter Fortune said—Reo had to make do for himself. In another letter to Malinowski, he alluded to the William Wyse Student-ship, a Cambridge University research grant, and speculated that if the grant went to Bateson (which it did) it would be "a scandal of a common enough kind."

Her estranged husband's plight, insofar as Mead could comprehend it from thousands of miles away, certainly gave her no pleasure. On the contrary, perhaps because she had known from the beginning that their match was "profoundly unsuitable," it disturbed her very much. "She acted sad about him, and talked about people she wished he could meet," said Mead's old friend Deborah Kaplan. "She was a good person, even when what she *did* wasn't too good. As for Reo, although I thought he was very attractive and interesting, I couldn't vouch for his stability. I don't think he could have been easy to live with." Mead very likely wasn't so easy to live with either, but by her own lights she did her best to help those around her.

As she had once suggested a new possible wife for Luther, before she learned that he had found one for himself, Mead now tried to ease the path of her second husband. She confessed her dream for Reo in a letter to Radcliffe-Brown, in which she said that "finding [him] a place in the sun which he will feel is his place, uncomplicated by my presence in any way, is very near to my heart." If Reo Fortune could prosper, she would be delighted.

Another friend of Fortune's, who knew him well toward the end of his life, surmised that Mead had acted toward him as she did "out of ignorance rather than from an emotional need to devastate." And later Fortune did recover, at least in part. In 1937 he married his fellow New Zealander Eileen Pope, who had turned him down when he first proposed to her in 1924, and who went with him first to China, later to Canada, and finally back to Cambridge University where he was a lecturer.*

Gregory Bateson should have felt at home in his native Cambridge as a birthright member of England's scientific and intellectual aristoc-

---

* But at Cambridge, according to Mead, Fortune was resented by the established scientists, not only because of his unorthodox thinking but because he was a colonial. Between 1937 and 1939, Fortune lectured at Lingnan University, in Canton, where his work on Yao was aborted by the Japanese occupation. From there he went to South China. In 1942–43, he lectured at the University of Toronto, Canada. In 1944 he served with the Canadian Armed Services in the United Kingdom, and between 1945–46 as government anthropologist in Burma. In 1947, Fortune returned to Cambridge University as a lecturer at Wolfson College.

racy. But on his return there from Sydney in 1933, to join his widowed mother and to find his place in the donnish life he had rejected earlier, he felt more out of place than ever. Nobody seemed to care about the paper he was writing on the highly ritualized way the Iatmul of New Guinea had devised for dealing with tensions between the sexes.

This elaborate ritual involved transvestism, mock homosexuality, and elaborate dances. Bateson's paper on the subject later led to a book, *Naven*, published in 1936, which attracted as much interest as anything he would ever write, but Iatmul rituals were not of much interest to anthropologists among his countrymen in 1933. To the British school of social anthropologists, Bateson seemed a renegade. His confreres had little use for his growing conviction that the most precious tool science could have was, as he put it, "a combination of loose and strict thinking." His thinking, by their lights, had acquired too much of a loose American tinge.

Gregory was writing a lot of letters to New York, and getting many in return. (One of her assistants later found among Mead's papers a trove of passionate letters she and Bateson had exchanged during this period.) If the British anthropological establishment did not understand him, then Margaret most certainly and enthusiastically did. They made plans to meet again, along with his geneticist friend C. H. Waddington and Waddington's wife, Justin Blanco-White, who were vacationing in Ireland in the summer of 1934.*

Bateson's conversations with Waddington, Mead wrote in a journal article many years later, taught her "something of the way English biologists think. . . . They would pick their illustrations right across the field. One minute from embryology, the next from geology, the next from anthropology, back and forth, very freely, so that the illustrations from one spot illuminated, corrected, and expanded the one from another." But quite likely the central purpose of this trip, like that of Mead's 1927 visit to the museums of Germany, was to check on her instincts about a man she contemplated marrying.

Before and after her visit to Ireland, Mead contented herself with the company of old friends and the search for new ones. Many people who had been away from home as much as she had would have resigned themselves, however regretfully, to losing track of all but the closest of old friends, but not Mead. In the middle 1930s one of the Barnard friends she began to see again was Eleanor Rosenberg, who

* This reunion is mentioned only fleetingly in *Blackberry Winter*, and is covered in Mead's Library of Congress papers only with a roll or two of photographs.

lived with her parents on Riverside Drive and 101st Street and often invited her to dinner. Rosenberg's father shared Mead's fondness for the novels of Charles Dickens, which they once discussed at such length that Eleanor dreamed that the two of them were characters in *Nicholas Nickleby.*

Once Margaret phoned Eleanor at the last minute to invite her to supper at her apartment, and asked her to make a stop first at a store on Broadway to pick up a colander, which she pronounced "cullender." What, Eleanor wondered, might that be? When the store manager asked whether she wanted one with legs, she didn't know what he meant, which was embarrassing. "I could just as well have asked Margaret what she was talking about, but I didn't want to admit to her that there was anything I didn't know. You lived up to Margaret Mead, all her life. And it wasn't her fame or her reputation that made you feel that way. It was her personality."

Two more important friends who entered Mead's life in this interlude between field trips and marriages were Sara Bachrach and her painter fiancé Allen Ullman, whom Mead later described as "one of the few men I have ever known who could take three women out together and make each one of them feel contented, honored, and amused." Their friendship began dramatically, at the deathbed of a strikingly beautiful Barnard alumna named Eleanor Steele. "Eleanor used to call Margaret 'Little Angel Mother,'" a Barnard friend remembered, "and Margaret made a pet of her, made her an Ash Can Cat. She was beautiful and she was doomed: her father had died, her mother was dying, and she too knew she would die, of tuberculosis."

"She hadn't a penny in the world," said Sara. "I had to persuade a doctor to hire an ambulance at half price to get her to the hospital. Her problem turned out to be a staphylococcus infection, and three days later she was dead. We were all there: the man she had been married to, the architect who was her lover, and Margaret, who came out of her room to say, 'Come quick! Come quick!' so we could get there in time to stand at the foot of her bed and watch her die—twenty-eight years old, with braids the color of wheat."

Margaret might have been spared presiding at this particular deathbed, one friend said, if Eleanor had taken better care of herself: "She didn't wear her rubbers, the way she was supposed to. She wasn't like Marie Eichelberger, who also had TB but was very sensible—sensible and prim. Once a man wanted to marry Marie, but compared with Margaret, no man had a chance with her. Her devotion to Margaret was amazing.

"Margaret, if it weren't for Marie, would have had to stir her stumps and look after her own underwear, her own finances, shop for her own Christmas presents. Margaret pretended not to, but I think she resented it when Marie had to take time out to work at her own regular job, in order to make a living. Once Marie lent a book she thought was wonderful to Ruth Benedict, and Ruth, after a quick and disdainful look, could tell that by her standards it wasn't wonderful at all, and when Marie asked she said she 'hadn't finished it yet'—the worst comment she could possibly have made, since Marie had obviously read it at one sitting. But where would they have been without her?"

If Marie Eichelberger was self-effacing, Sara Bachrach Ullman was acerbic and exuberant. Mead needed both kinds of friendships. Marie took care of her; Sara made her laugh and relax. Meeting Sara Ullman at another friend's deathbed was, for Mead, a new example of the old pattern of loss and compensation: lose one beloved person—in two cases a younger sister—and find a new one right away. Soon the new friends were exchanging confidences. Sara told Margaret that the first time she saw Allen Ullman she thought, "My God, who is he, I'd like to have dinner with *him*," and did end up having dinner with him every night for the next thirty-four years.

A gifted pianist who also liked to write, she had more flair for helping others develop their talents than for exploiting her own, and if the others became famous, that was incidental. Years later, when Margaret Mead had become better known than she ever expected to be, she said that Sara Ullman was the only friend she had who would ask, "Margaret, how *are* you?" in a way that suggested she really wanted to know, and wasn't looking for some favor.

As methodically as Mead had once surveyed new classrooms and new bunches of playmates, she now assessed the cast of characters in American social science, to figure out who among them would be most worth meeting and how she could best get to know them. At a New York party in 1934 Mead met, for the second time, an unassuming-looking social scientist named Lawrence Kelso Frank, who told her about a big plan he had. He wanted to gather together a group of people representing different disciplines, so that they could develop an outline of everything then known about the teaching of adolescents. (Adolescence, which before Samoa had no special significance for Mead, was by now well established as one of the abiding themes of her career.) Frank's idea appealed to her immediately.

"The scheme was so large," she later wrote. "We were all to live for a month in the Hanover Inn at Dartmouth; there was to be money for the preliminary presentation of materials. It sounded like the most extraordinary daydream to me; he said nothing about how it was to be financed, simply that it would be done. After he left, I found a memo he had left behind with the name of the Rockefeller Foundation on the stationery." Frank was a man who handled other people's money, and saw to it that it went where he thought it could do the most good. His definition of "good" soared as high and spilled as wide as Margaret Mead's own.

At Hanover, Mead was as happy as a child at summer camp assigned ideal tentmates and a perfect counselor. Interdisciplinary convocations, from this point on, would be one of the sustaining delights of her life. The differing views of her fellow participants at first made them seem "an extraordinarily clashing group," as she remembered thirty-one years later, "which nothing could weld into a whole. Larry sat on one side, a green shade over his eyes, and most of the time let us argue. The outline that we developed—whose nickname was 'the cauliflower'—was never published; it would be pretty modern today."

This "multi-front operation," as Mead described it, was aimed at "pulling together all that we knew about human development as we would want to teach it in the schools"; it was "our first attempt to formulate all we knew, using the whole range of human sciences to do it." When she said "we" and "our" and "us" she referred to a heady cast of characters: Robert and Helen Lynd, who were then at work on *Middletown*; Lloyd Warner, a sociologist; John Dollard, author of *Caste and Class in a Southern Town*, who was working on his studies of frustration and aggression; Carolyn Zachary, who was organizing a Committee for the Study of Adolescence; and Alice Keliher, whose Commission on Human Relations was "meant to take the materials we had worked out at Hanover and put them into a form for use in the schools." With the psychiatrist Erik Erikson, Mead worked on a "zonal modal analysis, which led later to his differentiation of eight different stages of ego tasks."

Frank, from his position at the General Education Board and through the Progressive Education Association, had set up a Commission on the Secondary School Curriculum. Child development, to him, was a way of getting into a number of other fields that interested him, among them psychosomatic medicine. Frank "did not see the study of children as separate from the study of adults," Mead said in 1970. "He felt that we ought to be talking about *human* development, and not only of children. . . . One of the horrors of only talking about children is the extent to which there is no money to study children . . .

"And, of course, he also began doing a little work with geriatrics, and was interested in gerontology also. So he worked at the two ends of the scale. Nobody worked with the middle." Mead was filing away a few questions which would not greatly interest others until forty-five years later, when the notions of midlife crises and male menopause caught the popular imagination: Why did nobody deal with the problems of middle-aged men, including ways in which they might be related to early childhood diseases? And why, in that whole month at Hanover, had nobody mentioned death?

Her trip to Ireland in the summer of 1934 apparently persuaded Mead that she really wanted to marry Bateson, whom she mentioned with dissembled nonchalance in a letter the following February to Lloyd Warner: "Next month we seem due for a visitation from England as both Malinowski and Bateson will be here. Bateson is coming over particularly to see RB I believe and is giving some lectures in Chicago . . . [he] is going to give a lecture here at Ethnological Society and I imagine means to look in on you at Harvard. . . .

"I am giving a course at Columbia," this letter went on—it was her first teaching job at the university's Extension Division, which later became the School of General Studies—"and find it very hard to have to take the position of knowing more than people younger than I am. It is somehow so much easier to admit that one knows more than one's elders and betters, at least it might be interpreted as more of a credit to one's past." She was beginning to think, she concluded, that "the only possible way to see one's friends is to be on the same committee with them"—as befitted the daughter of Emily Fogg Mead, who liked houses with rooms big enough for committees to meet in. Later associates marveled that Mead not only put up with committee meetings but exulted in them; they became another of her subcareers.

"I have just reached that unfortunate 'committee age,' " she wrote to Ian Hogbin in Sydney, "when I get roped in all the time to help on these cooperative studies for which the Americans are so hopeful. Now it is Cooperation and Competition in 12 cultures. It means work for graduate students who need money, but it also means a lot of boredom. I have decided that boredom probably releases more poisons in the blood than fatigue. What do you think?"

The project that emerged from the Hanover Conference started in the winter of 1934–35 "in the middle of the depression," as she wrote, "with a minuscule budget"—so minuscule that one field worker, assigned the next summer to the brutally hot Western plains, looked wistfully through a store window at a twenty-cent sun hat she could

not afford to buy. But the task, Mead said, was "a new kind of seminar—we all shared each other's written reports and reacted, individually
and as a group, to the same shared materials."

The book that developed from this project, edited by Mead, is not
among her most compelling, but it helped to inaugurate what she and
Benedict called the "culture and personality approach" to social science,
as a "focusing point for bringing together the findings of several disciplines which were all dealing with different aspects of the socialized
human being." The student of culture, Mead wrote, would have to
"grapple with several problems which he has traditionally ignored . . .
[and] recognize each constellation of individuals as unique." This approach, she insisted, afforded "a common meeting ground where the
hypotheses of each discipline can be tested out and made relevant to
a more genuine social science." Publicly, as she made clear, Mead and
her collaborators were on the lookout for signs of "new movements for
the integration of the sciences dealing with human relations," though
Mead's private view of this approach soon became less sanguine. "I
hope the uncomfortable aura of the C and P [culture and personality]
research isn't gradually gathering around me like a miasma from a particularly swampy place," she wrote to Lloyd Warner in April 1935. "I
got into the infernal thing by accident and I shall be well and truly
glad when I am out of it."

Mead did a little recruiting for the *Cooperation and Competition*
project when she went to Smith College, in the summer of 1935, to
look in on a psychiatric social work program. She went with Carolyn
Zachary, from the Hanover group, who is credited with influencing
not only Lawrence Frank but the pediatrician Benjamin Spock and
the psychologist Gardner Murphy, as well as the Columbia University
"school of social engineering." Before they went to Northampton, Mead
wired a Smith social work student named Joan Maris, inviting her to
join her and Zachary for dinner.

"Imagine," thought Maris, "dinner at a hotel! Without white
sauce!" She not only got a good meal but a job offer, to work with
Mead, Ruth Benedict, Erik Erikson, and the psychoanalyst Karen
Horney on the research project. And how, Mead asked, was Maris
liking Smith? Well enough, Maris said, except for one teacher who
struck her as a terrible reactionary. Mead asked to be led to that teacher.

"You know," she told the teacher, "Miss Maris is very brilliant,"
which Maris said made the teacher "feel like a worm." Margaret Mead,
Maris added, "really did want to make everybody's life better. In old
Jewish ideology there's a notion that a good life is to make other people's lives better, and Margaret had a lot of that in her."

Many of the trains of thought Mead first encountered at Hanover found their way into *Sex and Temperament*, the report of her visit to the three New Guinea cultures.* In this book, as in her two earlier ones and in her later reports of field trips, she took pains to connect what she had seen abroad with what she found at home in America. In later years her ethnographic successors would quarrel with some of the conclusions she reached regarding societies in remote places, but fewer would argue with what she wrote about her own. About her own society Mead was remarkably prophetic. In fact, being a prophet, especially about America and Americans, was becoming another of her sub-careers.

In modern cultures, she wrote, "Women find themselves more and more often in a confused state between their real position in the household and the one to which they have been trained. Men who have been trained to believe that their earning power is a proof of their manhood are plunged into a double uncertainty by unemployment; and this is further complicated by the fact that their wives have been able to secure employment."

America impressed Mead as "a society in which hardly anyone doubts the existence of a different 'natural' behavior for the sexes, but no one is very sure what 'natural' behavior is . . . almost every type of individual is left room to doubt the completeness of his or her possession of a really masculine or a really feminine nature." America had bred "a generation of women who model their lives on the pattern of their school-teachers and their aggressive, directive mothers.

"Their brothers stumble about in a vain attempt to preserve the myth of male dominance in a society in which the girls have come to consider dominance their natural right." As a result, an increasing number of American men felt that "they must shout in order to maintain their vulnerable positions, and an increasing number of American women . . . clutch unhappily at a dominance that their society has granted them—but without giving them a charter of rules and regulations by which they can achieve it without damage to themselves, their husbands, and their children."

Mead in this book foresaw the waves of insecurity which from the 1950s onward would beset American women: "We must bear in mind the possibility that the greater opportunities open in the twentieth century to women may be quite withdrawn, and that we may return to stricter regimentation of women. . . . If we are to achieve a richer cul-

* "From the Hanover Seminar I learned how to handle the problems of character formation in what I now believe shall be described as a Neo-Freudian way," Mead wrote in 1962.

ture, rich in contrasting values, we must recognize the whole gamut of human potentialities, and so weave a less arbitrary social fabric, one in which each diverse human gift will find a fitting place."

In her preface to the 1950 edition Mead called *Sex and Temperament* her most misunderstood book, and she made clear the several reasons why. She had been accused of believing that there were no sex differences because she had written that her material from the field "had thrown more light on *temperamental* differences; i.e. differences among innate individuals irrespective of sex." In fact, she wrote, she had "wanted to talk about the ways each of us belongs to a sex and has a temperament shared with others of our own sex *and* others of the opposite sex." In addition, some readers had found unconvincing its premise that three societies in the same region were radically different with respect to their expectations of the genders. She had been accused, Mead noted, of finding what she had gone out to look for. But such coincidences, she insisted, were often the stuff of anthropology.

"Human nature," Mead concluded in *Sex and Temperament*, as she had said before, "is almost unbelievably malleable." This provocative book had no more enthusiastic admirer than the English writer Geoffrey Gorer, who appeared in New York in 1935, shortly after the publication of his *Africa Dances*, an account of a trip he made with a dancer friend from Dahomey to the friend's homeland. The book described dancing magnificently, and was both trenchant and charming: Gorer told of an odd knack he discovered, in the course of his trip, for reconstructing people's past lives, characters, and futures, by holding their hands. In Africa he also became clairvoyant, and was never disturbed by the climate, much preferring "the atmosphere of a perpetual vapour bath" to the irksome dry heat of the north.

Cannibalism, Gorer also wrote, did not deserve all the "pother" it had aroused. He found it "a somewhat barbarous custom . . . but less so than many European ones . . . As for eating a piece of my neighbour, I should almost certainly find it easier than seeing him killed or carved." Unlike "most Negroes," who "take their sex calmly and simply," the Dahomeyans had had forced on them "a system of sexual starvation which cannot be paralleled elsewhere in Africa," to such an extent that among a large part of the population "sexual perversion and neurotic curiosity were developed to an almost European extent."

The authors of *Africa Dances* and *Sex and Temperament* were destined to get together. "When Geoffrey arrived in the States," Mead said much later, "the only person he wanted to meet was me." As soon as they did meet they struck up a friendship that would last Mead's life, and they also became colleagues. Mead agreed with Ruth Benedict that Gorer, to judge by his African report, had the makings of a true anthropologist. His book made it clear that he shared their sense of urgency about locating and working with primitive peoples who in great numbers around the world already had been dispersed or destroyed by alien influences. "The few that are left relatively intact," he said, "will remain so for only a short time more." Really thorough field work, Gorer added, could not be done in less than "two or three years with a tribe under uncomfortable conditions." This criterion was so exacting that even his friend Margaret Mead would not have measured up.*

In Gorer's *Africa Dances* Mead and Benedict detected a "wonderful eye and ability to recognize patterns." That was one reason they recruited him to their vocation—at first so that he could help Benedict with a report on "Psychological Leads for Field Workers," for the National Research Council, which was to be finished in 1936. For four months of that year, Gorer would write, "Dr. Mead and Dr. Benedict devoted a great deal of their valuable time in putting me through a very intensive course of anthropological training," and introducing him to colleagues across the United States.

In a review of *Bali and Angkor*, published in 1936, the *New York Times* called Gorer a "clever and impatient" man who traveled "with his head as well as with his legs. He does not pretend to great learning, though he is always ready to offer sweeping pronouncements on life and human nature. . . . It is all interesting, if a bit cocksure." Gorer had gone to Bali "half-unwillingly," he wrote, "for I expected a complete 'bali-hoo'; picturesque and faked to a Hollywood standard; I left wholly unwillingly, convinced that I had seen the nearest approach to Utopia that I was ever likely to see."

Mead's curiosity about the Indonesian island of Bali was further piqued by accounts she heard from another new friend, Jane Belo, a

---

* Gorer was born in London in 1905, educated at Charterhouse and Jesus College, Cambridge, later studied at the Sorbonne and the University of Berlin, in 1934 wrote *The Revolutionary Ideas of the Marquis de Sade*, traveled extensively in Europe, Africa and the Near East, published *Africa Dances* in 1935, *Bali and Angkor* in 1936, a political satire called *Nobody Talks Politics* in 1936, and *Hot Strip Tease* in 1938. As a social anthropologist he went to the Himalayas to study the Lepchas in 1936–37, published *The American People: Study in National Character* in 1948, and collaborated with John Rickman on *The People of Great Russia: A Psychiatric Study*, published in 1950.

student of Balinese art and ritual. Belo, a member of a privileged New York family, had been living in Bali for the past three years with her composer husband Colin McPhee; she was back home in New York to visit her family and write up her findings. Mead helped to place two of her papers on Bali in the *American Anthropologist*. Bali, to judge by what Gorer and Belo were saying of it, sounded more and more enticing as a destination for Mead's next field work.

In the spring of 1935, as expected, Bateson came to the United States to give lectures at Columbia and the University of Chicago, and to see Margaret Mead. "Gregory Bateson had a very good time in Chicago with RB [Radcliffe-Brown]," she wrote in April 1935. "He's just got back to New York." There, apparently, Bateson and Mead decided to marry, as soon as three things could be accomplished. First, Margaret and Reo must be divorced. Second, Margaret and Gregory must think of a project they could work on together. Third, they must get it funded.

When Bateson returned to England, he and Mead traded excited letters: What about Bali? What about schizophrenia? What about studying the behavior of a native people in the Dutch East Indies? But how would they get their separate ways paid there? Miss Lucia (now Mrs. Sebastian Cabot), Margaret's devoted godmother, "contributed" $2,000—actually Mead had given it to her sometime before—for "another series of psychological and ethnological researches in the South Seas." Mead had arranged for this money to be funneled back to her project, and further help was lined up. Bateson, in England, was applying for the William Wyse Studentship that Fortune wanted also.

Mead did not want to go to Mexico again to divorce Fortune. If she went, people would probably guess why. Having no wish to call attention to her personal life, she engaged Ernesto Camou, the attorney who had handled her divorce from Luther Cressman, to appear on July 26, 1935, in Hermosillo, Sonora, "before the Court of Original Jurisdiction for Civil Matters," as the official document said, "to file a divorce complaint against Mr. Reo Franklin Fortune, then residing in the city of Sydney, province of New South Wales, Dominion of Australia, on grounds that: Since the month of August, 1934, my principal and her husband, whose characters proved mutually incompatible, separated and absolutely suspended all marital relations, due to the fact that the husband deserted, without justified reason, the conjugal domicile and went to reside in a city far away from the place where the said husband and wife established their residence."

Mead, said Camou, claimed "no alimony whatsoever, as she does not need same." The lawyer representing Fortune did not deny the allegations. The justice of the court accordingly ruled that the "unjustified abandonment (desertion) of the conjugal domicile" and the "de facto separation of the spouses with interruption of the marital relations for more than six months" constituted grounds for divorce; "therewith were dissolved the legal bonds uniting them by virtue of the marriage contracted by them in the city of Auckland, New Zealand, on October 8, 1928."

Mead could proceed with her plans. But she was concerned about the effect the divorce would have on Fortune, who unlike Luther Cressman had not designed a new life for himself. She took the trouble to make sure that Reo, when the divorce papers were served, would be staying with his and Margaret's closest Australian friends, Timothy and Caroline Kelly.

"She used us," Caroline Kelly later ungrudgingly remembered, "as a cushion, so that Reo could have someone to talk to when he got the news, and talk he did, for twenty-four hours, nonstop. He hadn't thought it would really happen. But Margaret, as my husband used to say, was a gentleman. Even when she seemed to be maneuvering, she tried to be kind."

Mead continued to worry about Fortune as she made plans for her trip to Bali. On October 12, 1935, she wrote to Radcliffe-Brown about a rumor she had heard that he would soon launch an anthropology project in China, a project which she suggested might be tailor-made for Reo Fortune. Fortune, she explained, was in desperate need; when his field grant expired next July he would have almost no money. The psychological effect of long years without recognition was taking its toll; an appointment of some sort would mean a great deal. Fortune had great respect for the Chinese, among whom his father had worked as a missionary. He also had a genius for language and, as she wrote in a separate letter to A. L. Kroeber, "a particular gift for probing the souls of certain kinds of primitive peoples. It's a combination of enormous persistence and a willingness to bear antagonism, while I tend to propitiate them and so perhaps see an overamount of their kinder sides." (This insight may apply to what some found Mead's remarkably gentle views of both the Samoans and the Arapesh.) In China Fortune could draw on greater reserves of tact and skill than might be imagined by those who had seen him only in his own culture.

Radcliffe-Brown answered Mead's letter encouragingly, adding that he had "succeeded in learning a good deal about China" and "made contact with practically everyone who is interested in anthropology or sociology. There is quite a little boom," he went on to say, "in what Malinowski has nicknamed 'functionalism.'" But what about Margaret? Would she, as Reo's wife, be wanting to go to China, too?

That question gave Mead a chance to break the news, in her return letter. She and Reo, separated since 1933, were now divorced. She had been keeping this information mainly to herself, she explained, because it was easier for her to look after Reo's publications and other affairs if people didn't know. She herself would be leaving in the middle of December for Indonesia, "probably" to Bali. She wanted to work on a special study of infants and to explore the possibilities of having a team of people, all of whom were interested in personality and culture, stay there for a year or so. She would be gone at least two years, and would use her time on the way over to do a new introduction and a new conclusion to *Cooperation and Competition in Primitive Societies*. Meanwhile, if Radcliffe-Brown had time, could he clear up a question in her mind? What exactly was meant by the phrase "social structure"? Did it refer to the actual relations between individuals, or the social forms which prescribed those relationships?

Radcliffe-Brown had discussed similar questions with Gregory Bateson when both were in Chicago in the spring of 1935. That fall Bateson was still in England, finishing *Naven* and lining up the William Wyse Studentship to finance his expedition to Bali. Mead applied for a Social Science Research Council grant of $1,000, a fifth of the total cost of an expedition to be made between April 1, 1936, and September 1, 1937, in Bali or Noesa Penida Island in the Netherlands Indies; her salary, she said, would be $2,225. She wished to study the relationship between character formation and culture "in a society," as she wrote in another letter, "where an individual's security depends on ties to a minute and accurate conformity to an impersonal pattern." She also wrote to Theodore Roosevelt, Jr., who had been governor general of the Philippines, to ask for letters of introduction to the governor general of Bali and some of Roosevelt's American friends in Batavia, capital of the Netherlands Indies.

Bateson and Mead had high ambitions: they hoped to establish a new relationship not only between themselves but between their own and other disciplines. They wanted to break down false barriers to bring about a new stage in thinking which they hoped would make better thinking possible. Before they began, Bateson did his best to prepare his mother for her daughter-in-law. "My chief feeling about the whole thing," he wrote to her of his marriage plans, "is one of relief. Partly relief at not having to go into the field alone . . . But there is deeper relief, too. As far as I can see my difficulties—in attempts at marriage and awkwardnesses in my relations with you—have largely been a result of inarticulacy, some internal clumsiness which makes me not see my own personal relationships frankly and sanely . . ."

His fiancée, he went on, was "small, very businesslike, and very quick intellectually . . . Is she a lady? Yes, if you will ever allow that term to be applied to an American. As a hostess she is smooth, and cosy, unfussy, gracious even. English of course she is not, but she is an anthropologist, and a good enough one to learn the points of English culture. No doubt—and she insists on this—you will have to give her lessons in English cultural norms . . .

"Her family are, she says, 'rationalistic, agnostic, Spencer-reading, New England Puritans,' and when I boasted of my five generations of atheism, she capped the tale with a statement that her great-grandmother was 'read out of' the Unitarium [sic] Church for heresy [he did not know, or say, that she was religious herself] . . . [she has] a good sound plain intelligent—almost female Darwin face."

By early February of 1936 the young woman with the good sound plain Darwinian face was aboard the S.S. *Tapanoeli,* bound for her fourth sojourn in the South Seas and her third (and Bateson's first) marriage. Her fellow passengers found her puzzling; for her it was a "weird and isolating experience" to travel with strangers "who knew nothing about me and my work and regarded the whole thing—a woman going off to study natives—as fantastic and reprehensible . . ."

The fellow passengers were doubtless unfamiliar with what Mead had been learning of Erik Erikson's eight different stages of ego tasks, the second of which was autonomy versus shame and doubt. The extreme of autonomy was "a pride sanction—delight in the approval of the admired." Geoffrey Gorer suggested the term "concern with renown" to cover the range of adult behaviors that fell within this category. His friend Margaret Mead was concerned indeed with renown, which was one reason why she had felt so misunderstood by the others on the ship. It would have been quite another matter, she said, "if I had said I was a schoolteacher going out to visit my brother who was a clerk in Singapore." She would then have been treated "with the gingerly roguery accorded a spinster in her thirties, but my place in the universe would be otherwise approved of . . . [but] the peculiar ambivalence of the traveling professional woman has a quality all its own."

She had written her parents, on the eve of her departure, that she and Reo were divorced and that this time she would be working alone in the field. They needn't worry about her, she said; Bali was safe and tame, with good medicine and transportation, and she would be able to work quite well. She was breaking the divorce news to them this way, she said, because she did not want to talk about it. Nor did she allude to her imminent marriage in a letter to Reo as her ship approached Singapore on March 3, 1936.

"This endless voyage is almost over," she told Fortune, "and the monograph [about the Arapesh] is almost done . . . It's been the most concentrated six weeks work that I have ever done, I think, about 150,000 words. . . . As I go over the material I am again convinced that the Arapesh culture was the hardest culture I have ever tried to tackle, so amorphous, so confused. To get any form out of it is a real job. . . . I have had no news of you for almost three months. Perhaps there will be mail in Batavia, there should be. . . .

"All day we have been anchored in a little harbour . . . among mangroves, and I could just see myself on shore, dirty, thin, disheveled regarding any boat as a palace. But at present I am fat, and I suppose clean, although I'd forgotten how sticky the tropics can be. And today we had our first pawpaw. . . . I am convinced all over again that Malinowski was perhaps the most thorough field worker God ever made. But he has no ideas at all; that's the difference between your field work and his. . . . In Batavia, I have letters to Museums and things but I have no idea what it will be like. I don't exactly look forward to all the strangeness.

"Well, here's luck, Reo." This letter makes no mention that "all the strangeness" would be considerably relieved by the tall, gangling Englishman who was to meet Margaret in Batavia and planned to marry her there.*

"For some reason," Bateson said later, "they wouldn't let us do it there. Charlie Chaplin had come through the Indies three weeks ahead of us, hoping to get himself married. His divorces and marriages were always news, and they didn't want to get a reputation there for that."

So it was in Singapore, on March 13, 1936, that Margaret Mead and Gregory Bateson were finally married, with a Cambridge anthropologist named Pat Noonan, then employed by the Singapore government, as Gregory's best man. Margaret then wrote another letter to her parents, telling them that the most extraordinary thing had happened:

---

* Fortune would not learn this news until the following month, in a letter from Bateson. In May 1936, visiting his family in New Zealand, he applied for a job as an ethnologist in Ceylon. That job apparently did not come through: in September he applied for a New Zealand job, in philosophy.

Gregory Bateson had taken a fast boat in time to intercept her in Java, persuade her to marry him, work cooperatively in Bali, and perhaps have a child eventually. He had grown up, as she had, in an academic home, with an intelligent mother who understood what his father was talking about. He had a beautiful scientific background, which she entirely lacked, and was a gifted photographer and logical writer; he would soon have a book to add to Emily Fogg Mead's "Holy Shelf" (of books by her loved ones and theirs).

From Singapore, Margaret and Gregory headed toward Bali on a boat that wound its slow way through the Indies and through the Macassar Straits. Largely because she had not had much to do, Margaret Mead had not cared much for her first honeymoon, with Luther Cressman on Cape Cod. Her second, with Reo Fortune, on the way from Auckland to Manus by way of Sydney, had been a little more purposeful. This third one, best of all, was joyously businesslike, with proofs of *Naven* for Gregory to read and a new field work methodology for both bride and groom to plan.

The bride also had a private plan. She intended to follow the advice of a medium whom Ruth Benedict had taken her to see—Mead always had an open mind, if not a downright soft spot, for representatives of the occult—in Harlem. This medium, hearing of the man whom Mead was planning to marry, could tell, sight unseen, that Margaret should "feed him chicken, for he's good clean through."

CHAPTER THIRTEEN

"The Batesons Are Not to Be Bullied"

I<small>F</small> M<small>EAD</small>'s first husband had been too predictable to suit her, and her second too erratic, she now had one who seemed her temperamental soulmate as well as her professional equal, whose view of the world meshed amazingly with her own, who could teach her things she longed to learn and who was eager, in turn, to learn what he could from her. Here they were, he thirty-one and she thirty-four, thousands of miles from either of their homes, just off the east coast of Java on the 2,905-square-mile Indonesian island of Bali. Later, the anthropologist Clifford Geertz would describe Bali as "perhaps the most richly stocked lumber-room of gracious and beautiful magical beliefs and practices in Southeast Asia." Its "network of back roads," to quote the Batesons' new friend and associate Colin McPhee, the composer and musicologist, "ran up the hills where, as you looked down towards the sea, the flooded ricefields lay shining in the sunlight like a broken mirror.

"The sound of music seemed forever in the air. People sang in the fields or in the streams as they bathed. From behind village walls rose the sound of flutes and cymbals as invisible musicians rehearsed at all hours of the day and night. Temples in a state of celebration shook with the heavy beat of drums, the throb of enormous gongs . . . in the hills, as you traveled higher and higher, among villages that lay farther and farther apart, the music, like the architecture of the temples, grew more austere, took on an air of increasing antiquity and severity. . . ."

McPhee also noted "a powerful, complex smell, acrid and pungent, of burnt feathers, fish and frying coconut oil . . . a daily smell, punctual and inevitable as the morning smell of coffee at home. It came chiefly from *sra*, a paste of shrimps that had once been ground, dried, mixed with sea water, then buried for months to ferment. It was used in almost everything, fried first to develop the aroma. It was unbeliev-

ably putrid. An amount the size of a pea was more than enough to fla-
vor a dish. It gave a racy, briny tang to the food and I soon found myself craving it as an animal craves salt."

Mead was elated to be commencing what she called "the perfect
intellectual and professional partnership in which there was no pulling
and hauling resulting from competing temperamental views of the
world."

Once, Erik Erikson writes in *Identity and the Life Cycle,* a passer-by
in Vienna asked Sigmund Freud what things he thought a normal person should be able to do well. Freud named two: *lieben und arbeiten—*
to love and to work. In July 1936, Erikson got a letter from Mead, who
later would become his and his wife's close friend, and who now at last
was finding for herself the joy of combining both work and love. "I suppose you have heard by now," she wrote at the end of this long letter,
"that I got married in Singapore, to Gregory Bateson." No doubt Erikson, whose psychological formulations Mead and Bateson were about to
apply, to bring about what Mead called "the most fruitful relationship
between cultural anthropology and psychoanalysis," was aware of this
news. In many circles the long-kept secret of Mead's divorce from Fortune to marry Bateson had caused gossip.

Bateson's and Mead's new project, which they expected would
take two years, was studying the cultural aspects of schizophrenia. By
Western standards the Balinese, given to trances, seemed far out of
touch with reality, but in their own culture, Mead surmised, "the ordinary adjustment of the individual approximates in form the sort of maladjustment which, in our own cultural setting, we call schizoid." The
expedition was largely financed by the American Museum of Natural
History, and the resulting monograph by the Committee for Research in
Dementia Praecox, a charity of the Thirty-Third Degree Scottish Rite,
Northern Masonic Jurisdiction, and the Social Science Research Council. If schizophrenia was on the increase, as statistically it seemed to be,
then there appeared to be an urgent need to learn which childhood experiences might predispose the condition and, as Mead wrote, "how
much predisposition can be culturally handled, so that it does not become a maladjustment."

Like many Mead projects, this one had been inspired in large part
by Ruth Benedict. In 1934, in an essay called "Anthropology and the
Abnormal," Benedict had written that science could not begin to en-
vision any "final picture of inevitable human behavior" without "a collection by trained observers of psychiatric data from other cultures." It
would have been hard to find observers better trained than Mead and

Bateson, or for them to find a culture more startlingly different from that of their homelands.

Few people on the campuses of Cambridge or Columbia, or in the hamlets Margaret and Gregory knew in Pennsylvania and Yorkshire, were much inclined to shift in and out of trances. An extended little finger in those places was not so much a sign of a radically un-Western attitude toward the body and its parts as it was an effort to look genteel while drinking tea. And, as Mead would write, "Where an American or a New Guinea native will involve almost every muscle in his body to pick up a pin, the Balinese merely uses the muscles immediately relevant to the act, leaving the rest of the body undisturbed. (Only in trance and in children's tantrums is the body totally involved.)" Between the ages of three and six in the lives of most Balinese came "a withdrawal of all responsiveness" which, once established, would last all through life.

Bali, Mead found, offered "the most extraordinary combination of a relatively untouched native life going along quietly and smoothly and in its old way with a kind of extraneous, external civilization superimposed like an extra nervous system put on the outside of a body . . . [where] an anthropologist is presented with an unprecedented situation—quick, easy transport between dozens of versions of culture. A journey that would take three days in New Guinea—and more than that to prepare for and recover from—is made here in an hour."

She wrote cheerful letters home: "The water buffalos are a beautiful gray, rather like ashes of roses, and the young ones are actually pink when they are scrubbed." The island "teemed with expressive ritual"; everyone, it seemed, was an artist or a dancer or both or willing, at the very least, to be part of a rapt and ready audience. "The shyest, most frightened people walk in boldly when they hear the sounds of singing and dancing."

Bateson and Mead at once encountered a community of exceptionally sensitive Europeans and Americans, friends of their friend Jane Belo, who had converged in Bali to enjoy and absorb its culture and art. Walter Spies, born in Moscow to a family from Dresden, had first come to Bali in 1927. He had lived primarily in Ubud and was studying art, drama, and dance. The former dancer Katharane Mershon, from Los Angeles, had moved with her family to a beach village, to learn about Balinese life and dance. It was Spies, Mead later wrote, on whom she "relied to guide my first steps, as he had guided those of so many other students of Balinese culture." When she and Bateson arrived, Spies was working with Beryl de Zoete on *Dance and Drama in Bali*.

Spies found them their house, their servants, and most of all "gave us our first sense of the Balinese scene."

For all the warmth of Belo's endorsement of the new arrivals, the other artists, aside from Spies, at first eyed the ethnographers warily. "The Batesons" (a term Mead did not seem to mind at all, as she had minded being called Mrs. Cressman) were scientists. Scientists were presumed to have an offensively cold, analytic approach. The esthetes, in turn, as Mead hinted in a letter home, made her think of "prima donnas" and "Medicis" and might, in their way, prove just as obnoxious as the Christmas revelers she and Reo and Gregory had encountered on the Sepik in 1932. Europeans transplanted to the tropics, for whatever reasons, tended to be difficult and gossipy. But here in Bali, at least, the gossip was "all in artistic terms," which made a refreshing change. Could it be that the artists and the anthropologists need not, after all, be enemies?* Apparently it could; soon the other Europeans were helping Gregory and Margaret to begin work on the film "Trance and Dance in Bali," which in time became an ethnographic classic.

Bateson had intended to work on the notion of *ethos*—a term he used to describe the characteristic spirit or prevalent tone of sentiment of a people or a community—which "had proved a useful conceptual tool" in helping him to understand the Iatmul, but now he and Mead were much too busily "engaged in devising other tools—photographic methods of record and description." He was also preoccupied with "learning the techniques of applying genetic psychology to cultural data," but the real reason he put aside the *ethos* idea was that "at some inarticulate level I felt that the tool was unsuitable for this new task." He and his new wife were assembling data, deliberately and otherwise, which they and people whose names they had not yet heard of would spend more than a decade unraveling.

"It seems to me," Mead wrote to a friend, "as if culture were rather like a cake of the ingredients of which we are ignorant, and the main thing is to get a big slice home, not give it chemicals to test whether it is made of butter or oleomargarine and in so doing wreck its consistency and then find that whether butter is used or not is scien-

---

* This community of Westerners had already formed a collective myth of what the Balinese were really like, which, according to the ethnographer Hildred Geertz, may have influenced the Batesons unduly. Balinese, according to this myth, were a gentle people, but thirty years later, in 1965, Geertz wrote, "tens of thousands of very ordinary Balinese villagers murdered tens of thousands of other very ordinary Balinese villagers." (The Mead-Bateson visit, however, occurred before the brutalities of the Japanese occupation of Indonesia and the subsequent civil war.)

tifically relevant. (Examples: Perry on Indonesia, Nordenskjöld on South American clothing, etc., material wrecked so that no one can use it.)" It was clear to the Balinese whom they were studying, Mead wrote, that "We belong to the caste of those who make books, and my arms are beginning to ache as if that were literally true."

Not until late at night did the ethnographers blow out their "multitude of tiny glass lamps in tall, slender chimneys," on the seventeen tables of the many pavilions of their house. Weary from long sessions of photography, they would wash their faces in the same water Bateson had used to process that day's batch of the 25,000 still pictures he was to shoot—23,000 more than he had planned. He had arrived with seventy-five rolls of 35-millimeter film but soon realized that would not be nearly enough. He ordered more film in hundred-foot rolls, which he cut himself and prepared on a rapid winder. No previous field workers had even attempted such ambitious photography; few who followed would surpass it.

Mead's head swam with what she described in another letter home as "a new and interesting type of fatigue . . . an endless procession of eidetic images passing under my eyelids," a fatigue which was "definitely associated with this very concentrated *looking* sometimes for 4-5 hours without stopping, at confused and colorful crowds." And after all the looking came the reporting. "We seem to spend our days covering unlimited numbers of sheets of paper with typing: even keeping track of them is a full-time job."

The newlyweds were tired, but even in bed, their only refuge from work, they were sometimes, and by their own choice, interrupted; villagers had been "sternly commanded to waken us for anything important," any ritual or ceremony that might contribute to their research. Life was intense. Having suffered miscarriages, Margaret was more determined than ever that eventually she would become a mother. She made do, meanwhile, with the babies of the Balinese. New babies, reincarnated fresh from heaven, were treated even before birth with respect due great age, and addressed with honorific terms. "Sir," a midwife would politely exhort, "please condescend to emerge, for we are cold and have no more betel nut. We should like to go home if you, Sir, would only consent to be born." This unctuousness lasted until the babies were 105 days old, when their feet were first allowed to touch the ground.

Much had to be learned about Balinese etiquette. "Anyone who visits a house where there is a new baby under 12 days old (if a later baby) or under 42 days (if a first child) becomes ceremonially unclean for a day," Mead wrote. "What is a day? The rest of the time after seeing a child until one has slept a full night in one's house. (Note: visit a new baby near the end of the day.) Can one go from one taboo house to another? Yes. (Note: visit new babies in bunches.)"

Everything strange frightened Balinese infants, even Margaret Mead, who by this time had dandled and studied babies in seven cultures, and never before had found it necessary to exaggerate her genuine interest into a parody of "cooing and gurgling." Unless she did this exaggerating, mothers would clutch their babies so tightly that they would scream. Geoffrey Gorer had said that Bali was the happiest place he had ever seen, but Mead did not agree. "Not an ounce of free intelligence or free libido in the whole culture," she wrote to John Dollard. "The whole culture is arranged like a sling, and most of the time the people swing in it, their knees barely gripping, working alone, without either punch or kick . . . Anything new or strange leads to total panic."

That was one "big point" she and Bateson noted. Another was "the idea of the separable penis. Old-fashioned Freudians' hair would stand on end . . . the idea [seems to] start with the mothers' habit of pulling . . . hard after urination, and later . . . just for fun. There is also genuine confusion between the front and the back of the body." Life here, she wrote, was "a rhythmic, patterned unreality of pleasant, significant movement, centered in one's own body to which all emotion long ago withdrew."

If he were going to Bali himself, Franz Boas had told Mead, he would study gesture, and so she did, trying to figure how gesture and trance and schizophrenia might be interrelated. When she held a Balinese hand and manipulated the fingers, it felt "perfectly limp, like the hand of a monkey or of a corpse." The Balinese were happy in huge, noisy, smelly crowds, but in the midst of such crowds they would often withdraw into a state Mead and Bateson called "awayness," in which "they are, for the moment, no longer subject to the impact of interpersonal relations." Their lives were not, like Western lives, punctuated with "commas and periods, the bar-lines and parentheses, in terms of which we habitually organize the on-going stream." Continuity, not logic, guided their thinking.

Dogs in Bali were a menace, best approached with a slinking, creeping walk and a switch held behind the back. It was better to creep from one house to another in the dark than to flaunt a lamp and risk provoking an all-night barking session or, worse yet, a bite. Mead was bitten once, as she came home through the chilly dawn after sitting up all night with a very sick child. She "burst into tears of helpless resentment," but then saw at once that such a failure of self-discipline was, like everything else, grist for her mill, and "must if possible immediately be used by the anthropologist as a stimulus point to discover what people will do when anger is shown in such and such a way."

Different hardships bother different anthropologists. Some object to poor sanitation, others to the rarity of solitude. Ann Chowning, recalling New Guinea field work, cringed at the memory of people's response when she told them she needed to get away to take a nap. "Fine," they would tell her. "We'll watch you."

In Bali, as in most of Mead's field sites, there was no such thing as a quiet moment alone. Bali was in no way a quiet place; wooden bells on cows' necks clattered softly all night, adding to a nonstop barnyard murmur that made Mead think of moments from her rural Pennsylvania childhood. Maybe she also thought back to the pageant she had talked her Barnard friend Deborah Kaplan into choreographing, where the Pennsylvania Dutch dancers were so inhibited they wouldn't even take off their socks. If only the people back home in Bucks County could see these Balinese pageants, acted out frequently in temple yards, showing the age-old struggle between the witch Rangda, who Mead thought seemed a rather motherly character, and the dragon Barong, about whom there was something possibly paternal.

At the sight of Rangda, during the pageants, a group of young men would fall into a mass trance during which they would stab themselves with daggers, called *krises*, but miraculously survive upon the arrival of the flamboyant Barong. Offstage, the Balinese were so exceedingly balanced and unemotional that Margaret and Gregory never could tell whether any two people were having a quarrel, but the pageants, with dazzling costumes and masks with bulging popeyes, fierce fangs and no inch of surface left unadorned, were compelling. "Trance and Dance in Bali," the film Bateson and Mead made of this pageant, kept them busy for two full months.

Without their trances, Mead wrote, the Balinese would lead dreary lives indeed, "fixed and rigid, foreordained but unguessed in advance." But trances, common also in Morocco, Kenya, Haiti, among certain American Indian tribes, and in the tales of certain early Christian saints, could endow ordinary people with powers both to create illness and misfortune, and to cure. The study of trance, and of Balinese history with its palimpsest of layers of influence from Buddhists, Hindus, Chinese, Javanese, Mohammedans, and the Dutch, held Mead's and Bateson's attention. So did their attempts to understand the complicated Balinese language, which had seventeen different levels of vocabulary. Bateson also had to master ancient ecclesiastical Balinese, but Mead's gender required her only to learn colloquial speech.

They had not come to add to the considerable body of erudite scholarship, most of it by the Dutch, which already existed on the subject of Balinese culture.* Here in Bali, as in their previous more primitive field sites, they relied mainly on their eyes and ears. Bateson was pointing his camera in all directions, and with excellent results. "He had the sense only good photographers have," said the gifted amateur photographer Karsten Stapelfeldt. "It's like target practice. The moment you've pressed the trigger you know whether you've hit the target."

Mead rarely lifted a camera, but in picture-taking her partnership was essential. She frequently drew her husband's attention to scenes he was too busy to notice for himself. And all the while she kept a meticulous running account, often without looking at the notebook she was writing in, of what was happening. They had come to learn all they could about posture, gesture, painting, and the symbolism of play and dance; nothing around them could be dismissed as irrelevant.

In June, after two months, Margaret and Gregory left their fellow Europeans and went to the remote mountain village of Bajoeng Gede, near Kintamani in the district of Bangli. Walter Spies had found a carpenter to build them a house there. They had chosen this "stepped triangle about 350 yards long and 250 yards wide with the temple at the elbow" because it "represented the lowest and dourest stratum" of the island's culture. Its ceremonial life was meager even compared with that of other mountain villages.

Had they been mistaken, the ethnographers wondered, to choose so simple and inarticulate a cluster of people? Most of the five hundred villagers were hypothyroid, sulky, and frightened, and, in Bateson's view, "incurably mild and unexciting." Among them, Mead wrote, her husband had "a little of the attitude of a man who comes in expecting a good stiff drink and finds himself put off with a coca-cola." But Mead, ever ready to find the bright side of things, pronounced the choice of this community "one of those lucky accidents that has accompanied me all my life." The widespread thyroid deficiency slowed things down so that there was "a simplification of action, but without a loss of pattern." Work among the villagers, few of whom ever left home, was easier than it would have been in a more complex place.

* They published no general ethnography of Bali. Mead and Bateson published a monograph in 1942; Mead published a monograph on Bali with Frances Cooke Macgregor in 1951.

And even so, she wrote home, living in Bajoeng Gede was a strain: "every word, grunt, scratch, stomachache, change of wearing apparel, snatch of song sung on the road or jest flung over someone else's wall is *relevant*." Mercifully, in trying to puzzle out the elements of Balinese culture, they could compare their own impressions with those of the other Europeans. Messages flew back and forth all over the island. Nothing could have been further from the loneliness she must have felt on her first field trip to Samoa.

Periodically she and Gregory would meet their fellow Europeans back in Denpasar, the chief town. Finding Walter Spies, she would write, "was very much like meeting someone in a round dance: from time to time, in the dance, one came face to face with him, joined hands lightly for a perfect moment, and the dance went on again, the partners separating on their separate tasks." Margaret and Gregory would return to Bajoeng Gede "very sure that we prefer our cool mountain top and no visitors and no motor cars, even if our village people are sulky and frightened and dressed in rags. At least we know them and can work ahead without fever or haste." Nobody they met anywhere on the island was more helpful than their twenty-one-year-old native secretary, I Madé Kaler—"Madé" is Balinese for "second-born"— whose steady devotion greatly simplified the whole Bateson-Mead enterprise.

This young man, Mead wrote home, "continues to amaze and delight us. . . . He isn't abashed or excited by anything in the world. He takes synchronized notes on ceremonies, keeps calendrical records of coming events, trims the lamp wicks, tacks black cloth on the shelves, makes Dutch, Malay, or Balinese translations of anything he is given, turns his mother into an informant when he goes home for a holiday, takes his bath in an icy stream three miles away at 6 A.M. so as to be always on hand, goes to Den Pasar and brings back 200 guilders, and takes down conversations as ungrammatically and brokenly as they occur."

Had there ever been such luxury? Certainly not in her or Bateson's previous field experience. Madé was "just about the nearest thing to perfection that God ever made." His cooperation meant that he and both his employers could work in absolute unison. One event observed by three persons simultaneously, Mead firmly believed, was far better than three events each observed by one. "For a ceremony in South Bali which you have never seen, even if you know all the people there—or at least someone does—the minimum to cover it all is about five persons, as there is one little rite going on outside the gate while another goes on under the bed and another in the house temple, and so on."

The villagers finally decided to trust the visiting ethnographers, in part because of the seemingly miraculous help they could offer to the sick. "Have we medicine to make the deaf hear, the old and halt walk quickly, the blind see and the decrepit lust for life again? When I dress a sore," Mead wrote, "the whole circle gathers to watch." Once she wrote home about "the most intelligent man in the village, the calendrical expert and the one man who really thinks about ritual . . . If he should die the village would be an intellectual wilderness."

When this man got sick, Mead gave him "salts and rhubarb and soda . . . and a hot water bottle made out of a clay Dutch gin bottle." He recovered. The villagers were awed. In time they came to treat Mead and Bateson less and less as allies of the Dutch aristocracy, whom they hated and feared, although they referred to Margaret as the "Njonjah," Balinese for "white woman," and to Gregory as the "Toean," the white man.

In late 1936, the Njonjah and the Toean had special visitors. Beatrice Bateson came from England with her friend Nora Barlow, a granddaughter of Charles Darwin, to meet her son's wife. (She had already sent Margaret some calling cards she had had made in England, engraved "Mrs. Gregory Bateson." After Gregory's mother died, it was explained, Margaret would be known simply as "Mrs. Bateson.") For the sake of their visitors, Gregory and Margaret leased the palace of the former Rajah of Bangli, which had three gold doors and rented for about nine dollars a month, and ordered up an opera. "It gives one a fine feeling of being a patron of the arts and lord of the manor combined," Mead wrote home, "to be able to order an opera."

During Beatrice Bateson's six-week visit she threw herself into the spirit of things. A lifelong atheist, who had never said grace even when all eyes around her were closed in prayer, she knelt for the first and only time of her life when she was required, in a religious ceremony, to present an offering. If it was for science, she apparently decided, it must be all right. She also appeared to approve of her daughter-in-law, and must surely have been disarmed by a nine-verse poem in her honor by I Madé Kaler. One verse went:

> Njonjah Biang we all love you
> But we don't know how we can show that to you
> Only God knows and he will probably tell you
> If not by day then in a dream of you.

Mead had to feign a taste for cremations and cockfights. Cremations, she wrote home, were "a most trying kind of spectacle. . . . The roads are already choked (by noon) with crowds of onlookers, who also help to churn the roads to mud. Some ten or twelve different kinds of archaic and noisy orchestras are playing. And finally, along the road to the cemetery, the high towers and big animals' coffins are carried by crowds of shouting, sweating, overexcited men who stop at stream crossings to splash each other and the onlookers, and who delight in dangerously tipping the 20-foot towers on which ride the corpse or the bones and some unfortunate relative of the dead. These are all taken to the cemetery, from which usually a stench of mud, people, decayed meat offerings and sometimes new corpses, and are burned up in a series of bonfires. . . . One comes away with a special stench in one's nostrils, very tired, and swears that one will never go to another cremation."

What a baby was to a woman—"something to play with, to toy with, to titillate and tease, to dawdle over, to carry about, to dress up and undress, to stroke and tickle—a fighting cock is to a man," Mead would write in *Balinese Character*. "Tomorrow," she wrote in one letter home, "perhaps Gregory will fight one of his new fighting cocks. We have two, and every day their special toilet is performed. They are bathed in onion water, they have sticks thrust into their eyes and their legs are painted with red pepper. They are here for all unoccupied male guests to play with by the hour."

Guests were quite often unoccupied. When any task was to be performed, the Balinese custom was for many more people to be present than were needed, and then to break the task down into small units. Balinese were also an "excessively dirty people," Mead wrote to Erik Erikson, "as unkempt as they are unforthcoming—with dirty clothes and dirty houses." They got rid of animal manure by pouring water on it so it would spread on the ground. They farted constantly, filled their dramas "with obscenities relating to sodomistic practice chiefly, & some anal jokes," and were intensely interested in small Chinese coins. They were "horribly embarrassed at any pictorial representation of heterosexual love making." Their religion reminded Mead of southern European Catholicism in that it was "largely negative in its working; there are things to be done & if you don't do them trouble will come."

Mead's idea of self-indulgence during field work was to write a letter. "I feel I am entitled to the dissipation of another bulletin," she rationalized in one note from Bajoeng Gede, having finished "ten days of meticulous recording of any tool change, sneeze, spit, wriggle, or exclamation by any one of the three" Balinese artists who had recently come to visit from another village. In another letter she said that "the combination of medicine, observation and theorizing which is necessary turns one into a sort of three-ring circus."

Two months after settling in Bajoeng Gede, Mead in a letter to Ruth Benedict commented on various stages of psychological development: "I've got my major clues, I think, on the superego formation and the latency point," but "after almost an entire day re-sorting and arranging clothes and medicines and such," her lungs were "full of bamboo dust and insect dung. This long fight against mildew and fungus and melted sugar coating on pills . . . is always tiring, and one always loses in the end."

Mead's accumulating ethnographic "points" were reported in later letters. "Ruth, darling," another letter began, ". . . We've had a good ten days since my last letter, with a nice point practically every day . . . I think I got a new displacement point this morning . . ." Many of Mead's letters went to psychologists and psychiatrists she had met in New York, chiefly through Lawrence Frank. One letter congratulated Karen Horney on her newly published book, *The Neurotic Personality of Our Time*, whose "creative hypothesis," Mead wrote, would "inevitably lead to more and better thinking, like a road that leads out from a confined little walled town on to an open plain, where there are many possible paths." Could it be said, this letter went on to ask Horney, that "the trap closes hardest" on the weak person, in any given society, who is "most temperamentally prone to accept or take seriously all the basic emphases of his own culture?"

Some of Mead's letters were hortatory. She cautioned her Barnard friend Jeannette Mirsky, who was making a short field trip to Guatemala to do field work on sibling rivalry, not to try to know her village too thoroughly in a month. "You can't get to know more than 100 people in that time," advised Mead (though others would argue that it took them a year to know 100). She also recommended wearing the native women's costume whenever possible. "If I had it to do over I would [wear native dress] in any remote spot." Dressing as native women did was helpful "in handling babies"; it lessened their fear and increased "your knowledge of the parts of the clothes they play with, how they search for the breast, what folds they hide their faces in, etc. . . . also gives you more understanding of posture, of what actions become automatic as parts of modest behavior, or avoidance of sitting in a splash of betel juice, etc. You would find you yourself are proportionally more comfortable the more you fit into the picture. . . .

"Remember," Mead advised her colleague, "a ceremony observed and never written up is a genuine waste of time. . . . You will tend to plan a full [day's work] for yourself, then someone will die, a baby will be born, there will be a riot, the cook will elope, someone will cut half their hand off, a visitor from the Carnegie [Foundation] will come, it will be a special feast day, your film will have to be packed up & sent if it is to catch a certain mail, & you will get a bit of disturbing mail from home. . . . Try to remember that you only have to provide about half steam, the culture will provide at least the other half for you . . . Have a swell time and write me a long letter when you get out of the field (not before) unless it helps to clarify your thinking, for you won't get an answer in time."

Most satisfactory of all her correspondents, Mead decided, was Geoffrey Gorer, who was off in Sikkim studying the Lepcha, when she wrote in June 1937, "You always answer the other person's points and you always make new ones to answer." In this letter she rued the effects of the "cheap tourist trade" on Balinese art: tourists, by placing such a premium on originality, had "perhaps overstrained the Balinese tendency to the fantastic and [that had] become confused with the occasional premium on pornography. . . ."

The content of Balinese art, Mead went on, "might be described as 'pickled affect,' the affects appropriate in the culture have been pickled in myth, and this myth is such a perfect constellation, that when acted out or painted out by individuals of Balinese virtuosity, the result is an art, but an art to which the individual executant has often contributed nothing but skill.

"Well," this letter ended, "now *you* say something!"

The Ash Can Cats, who had worried at Barnard how Margaret might sulk if they forgot her birthday, would have been relieved to see how she observed her thirty-sixth. On December 16, 1937, at 9:00 A.M., the Batesons and their fellow Europeans gathered to watch a pageant they had ordered themselves, an especially elaborate temple ritual, full of trances and apparent violence. It lasted for three and a half hours, and was performed by the 105 households of the village of Pagoetan.

At a similar performance the previous year, Jane Belo wrote in her book *Trance in Bali*, the priest who seemed to be in charge of the performance had shown his delight in meeting his first Westerners, ever, "by learning to shake hands, and so pleased was he with this new accomplishment that he would come up to [the Western guests] and shake hands time after time during the performance, walking away only to return again for the pleasure of returning the greeting."

That performance, given in a temple under enormous trees adjoining rice fields, had been so solid a success that "several different households of foreign inhabitants fell into the habit of taking their guests to Pagoetan as the best place to see a kris dance . . . it would sometimes happen that three or more trance performances would be ordered in a single week." Perhaps it was not entirely healthy for the participants to have such frequent trances and self-stabbings, but this show kept going on, Belo wrote, "and a most striking show it was," especially the one held on Margaret's birthday.

The more Western experts there were in Bali, the more pleased Mead was, so long as they were sympathetic. That winter she and her colleagues were planning "a great inter-disciplinary expedition, complete with endocrinologists and psychiatrists, which was to come . . . and have a headquarters at the Bando palace." Each visiting scientist would be taught about Bali, from texts and film, and then assigned a trained secretary-interpreter and a separate village to study. "We even took a three-year lease on the palace," Mead wrote. But even as slowly as news from abroad reached Bali—two months late, usually—awareness dawned that world war was looming, and that the three-year-lease plan would have to be scrapped.

Then Mead and Bateson came up with another idea. Before returning to America they would go back to New Guinea, where, for purposes of comparison, they wanted to test the field techniques they had been perfecting. If Mead had left Samoa with any doubts about how well she had succeeded, in what she tellingly referred to as her "work of apprenticeship," she was determined not to invite such doubts now, or ever. "We have been able to use so much finer techniques in Bali than any I have ever used before," she wrote to Franz Boas, "that I feel very definitely at sea in interpreting the results without some comparative material collected with the same care."

Mead elaborated: "Where before I occasionally made a sample of behavior over time which would run to two typewritten pages for an hour, we now have records of 15 typewritten pages and 200 feet of Ciné and a couple of hundred Leica stills for the same period. The recording is so much finer that I feel as if I were working at different levels from any work I've done previously." She knew that Boas thought she spent too much time in the field "in proportion to writing up," but she was all caught up with her field notes from the Arapesh expedition with Fortune, which "at the rate the Museum is going now won't be published before 1950." Since the Mundugumor and the Tchambuli were Fortune's ethnographic responsibility, not Mead's, there was no reason why a trip back to the Iatmul should not make eminent sense.*

* Reo Fortune had written Malinowski in August 1937 that he was learning "to *teach*, and hope yet to exercise my guts a little, saying a little more of what I think in future." He noted that Bateson, being in the field on the

When Mead and Bateson left Bali they were given a picture she described later: "Above, the shores of Bali with the Balinese showing theatrical grief and the Balinese volcano belching forth 'Goodbye and Good Luck,' in an elegant scroll design—and in English! In the middle of the picture a tiny ship with us in it, done correctly to scale as to our relative heights (which, when extended to our relative breadths, made me look like a kind of wooden toy), with me looking back towards Bali and Gregory waving excitedly to the Papuans in the lower front of the picture, who greeted us with waving bows and arrows and spears and proclaimed their savagery by wearing only G-strings and towering hair arrangements.

"In the lower corner was the Rabaul volcano (there'd been a big earthquake in Rabaul), belching forth 'Welcome.'" And then, when this gift had been accepted, the chief village priest asked permission from the village gods for the Toean and the Njonjah to depart.

In Soerabaja, Java, Margaret and Gregory had their teeth and cameras fixed, and tended to some business. She sent word home that "a Will and Deed of Trust providing funds for working up the materials in the event that both Mr. Bateson and I should die before this has been done" was lodged with her lawyer. Explaining in detail the results of the field work, she ended her letter to Clark Wissler, her boss at the museum, with thanks for his "judicious kindness" which made it "possible for me to work to my full capacity."

And then, on the Dutch ship *Maatsuycker*, the Batesons sailed in March 1938 toward Port Moresby, New Guinea, just as Hitler took over Austria. One of their fellow passengers, the Austrian Ambassador bound for New Zealand, was suddenly a man without a country. The next letter Gregory Bateson got from his mother counseled him to "take my advice and stick to the Sepik—unless Germans suddenly swarm over and bomb you. Europe is no place for intelligent young men" and Hitler was "terribly crazy and altogether amoral."

Their fellow *Maatsuycker* passengers, Mead wrote, were an uninspiring lot of "tenth-rate" tourists from Australia and New Zealand,

---

fellowship Fortune had coveted, could not "take Mead to Cambridge to undo him properly," presumably as she had "undone" Fortune in New York. In December 1937, working at Lingnan University in Canton, China (not the job Mead had asked Radcliffe-Brown to help him get), Fortune wrote Malinowski that he was "not favourably impressed with the Benedict-Bateson-Mead huddle in pseudo-psychological method, although I've been associated with them. . . ."

who in no way distracted her from correcting the proofs for *The Mountain Arapesh* (to be published in 1938 in Part 3 of *The Anthropological Papers of the American Museum of Natural History*), or Gregory from giving her lessons in Iatmul. Next, heading up the Sepik River from Rabaul on the *Montoro*, they met "two sisters [nuns] come to inspect their order, two Methodist missionaries who didn't drink anything, a huge Australian priest who looked like his German brethren and whose Queensland accent was like a blow in the face . . . a mob of miners who told one the names of imaginary public schools they had attended . . . and who solemnly discussed the charms, probably never seen, of Budapest, and an earnest-faced boy coming up to do two years at a lonely trading station in Papua."

Nor was that shipload to be their last experience with bothersome Europeans. Days after she and Bateson were resettled in Tambunam, Mead was complaining, in a letter home, of "a perfect plague of white men . . . seven separate pinnaces or schooners and seven evenings wrecked by Europeans to feed and talk to. But it's an accident and soon we will be lucky if there is a pinnace once a month which can bring stores." Later she wrote, "The descent of five government officials, including the Administrator, and three ships has left both us and the village too depleted in spirit to settle down to work."

Afterward Mead elaborated on such irritations: "My house would be filled with Iatmul people—men, women, and children—whose affairs were of the greatest interest and urgency to me. As figures of white men—identifiably white, not yet individually identified—appeared against the horizon, they looked like paper dolls, unreal figures in an unreal diorama.

"Then slowly, as they approached, their features would take shape as known or unknown people, and as they assumed reality, the Iatmul people, a minute ago my closest concern, would assume the flat, nonspecific appearance of paper dolls in their turn. This was the kind of price one paid sometimes, after weeks of speaking and writing and thinking in a native language, involving an almost physical wrench in order to come back to English."

The Tambunam villagers were a delight. Rhoda Métraux, a later American student of the Iatmul, described them as "aristocratic, well-fed, and the Number One people of the Sepik." Anthony Forge, who later followed many of Bateson's footsteps in the field, said he and Bateson agreed "that we preferred the spear-waving savages of the Sepik to the Balinese, who are beautiful on the surface, but what's going on underneath that surface is almost unspeakable, and when it breaks out every now and then, there's real violence."

Part of what Mead saw among the Iatmul made her think of home: "To turn suddenly from the quite unbelievable proportions of the Sepik into a narrow stream which flows between high banks, on which thinly leafed trees are set like worn-out sketches against the sky, where the lotus leaves are green when they lie flat and pink when the wind catches them, ruffling them up off the water which itself has a changeable pink and green powder on its darkness—this is to find one-self in a land to which one might conceivably belong." From Mead, by now a veteran of so many changes of scene, this was a high compliment.

In springtime, she wrote, "people live under their houses and one sees them most often in silhouette, part of the design made by the house posts, the platforms, the fishtraps and fish spears outlined against the Sepik which can be seen down each deep road—as one can see the Hudson through the crosstown streets in New York, only without any enclosing other bank behind to spoil the background." She was entranced by the "wide, wide open landscape with a half-sphere of sky overhead and the tossing white plumes of the elephant grass floating in the high grass plains, matching the clouds overhead."

One legacy of Mead's Iatmul sojourn was her enhanced appreciation of the solid floors of the world she had come from and would go back to. "You don't know how important it is to walk on a floor," she once said, "after you've lived in a house on piles for months, where the floor rocks and everything falls through it." In Tambunam, she and Bateson first stayed in a rest house whose floor was "made of loose pieces of beaten-down palm bark, laid on irregularly [and] not fastened down. Chairs go through the cracks, edges break off, tables dance every time anyone walks about, flashlights and glasses clatter to the floor at one end if a pig rubs against a house post at the other. The consumption of time and energy in adapting to such a floor is enormous."

But if their floor was a hazard, the bed where Margaret and Gregory spent most of their nights among the Iatmul made up for it. This was "an eight-foot square platform, on which a six-foot mattress is set, entirely surrounded by a big net, always tucked in, with a white canopy over it to keep out some of the dust and some of the insects (at that one spends five minutes picking up caterpillars, small spiders, swallow-tailed nits, mosquitoes, flies, borers, etc., which are always to be found speckling the bed when one climbs in)." Their neighbors were well aware of what they did. Life among the Iatmul, Mead wrote home, was "a little like planning how to live comfortably in a show window and at the same time keep up continuous observations of the crowd that gathers outside."

There were also scorpion bites, and death adders, with no known antivenom serums to fight them, and malaria—which afflicted them much of the time. Bateson suffered from malaria in Tambunam, but luckily, since this visit coincided with the dry season, there was not much for him to watch the villagers doing except hunt for crocodiles and argue about how to distribute the meat. Still, Bateson and Mead worked almost as hectically as they had in Bali.

Letter writing remained a luxury and an addiction for which Mead was all but apologetic, as others might apologize for eating too much ice cream or drinking too much gin. One of her letters was written as Bateson was cutting rolls of film in a black calico net, with all the lights out "except two small standing flashlights which stand at my elbow but outside the net, hidden in a kerosene box, and give just enough light to illuminate the keys of the typewriter." Keeping the flashlights inside the net, she said, would mean "too many mouthfuls of small insects."

"I've had a pleasant and recreational time writing this letter," she wrote to Gardner Murphy from Tambunam on September 27, 1938, "despite the fact that I have at least 200 pages of notes to type up . . . and . . . trying to develop and try out new field techniques and use them simultaneously with my own field techniques in the hope of developing field methods which will appeal more to the type of student which we need to send into the field."

Something important was happening to Mead as she and Bateson worked among the Iatmul. She stopped being just another ethnographer and assumed a place, which she would keep for the rest of her life, at the head of the pack—in the public eye, at least, if not always among her peers. Her apprenticeship years were now well over. For all her relative youth, she knew as much as anybody did about how to make sense of the ways of alien cultures, and she was eager to pass her knowledge along and around by any means she could think of. She was not there in the field just to write down facts, but to help reinvent anthropology, and to reassess its relationship with other disciplines.

Whatever naïve, careless, hurried, or shallow errors Mead may have committed in Samoa, at a time when so little had been known about psychological field work, she was now becoming expert in methodology. "It is significant," she went on in her letter to Murphy, "that Psycho-Analysts and Social Workers don't have any difficulty handling my results, but Anthropologists, more interested in forms than in people, do.* So I've decided it's wasteful to collect material by methods which other people won't use and therefore can't credit and I've set myself the task of overhauling the whole matter. . . . But it's hard to keep your mind on methods," she wrote, "when there is so much sheer work to be done. We have just two months longer here."

She was not so much complaining, she made clear, as rejoicing. Working with Gregory among his old subjects was "like sitting in a sedan chair instead of ploughing through bush." Freed from "the passionate listening which is necessary to grasp the whole grammar through unfamiliar phonetics"—that is, learning the language—and from the desperate need which anthropologists newly arrived at field sites usually have to unravel kinship and clan systems, she could "sit down and use my eyes to full advantage before their witness is complicated by much help from my ears. It's a very pleasant experience. And they are a swell people."

Mead, so joyously mixing love and work, was having a "swell" time, but she did not neglect her responsibilities as exemplar to other ethnographers. She scolded a promising young anthropologist named Buell Quain, who later killed himself in Brazil after having worked with an Amazonian tribe, for not having sent her a manuscript. "I am a very careful reader of manuscripts," she told him. "I comment on them with page references, in typescript, & I make my comments searching but constructive. . . . So you see you should have sent me the manuscript as I asked you to. . . .

"You don't put any personal news in your letter at all," she reprimanded him. "I don't know whether you are going into the field alone, where you are going, what kind of camera you have, whether you have any special problem, or anything. If I knew any of these things I could write a better letter. . . . I am completely sold on cooperative work," she had reminded him in a gentler vein a few lines earlier, by which she meant "not only at least two people working in the field simultaneously—but as often as possible both of them recording, in some way, the same event. . . .

"With all of you becoming South American experts," Mead concluded, "I see where I have my work cut out for me to keep up. Will I have to learn Spanish or will all your works do? I still have to learn

* The culture-and-personality school has always been disputed in American anthropological circles, and never did take center stage. It had never had much credence in Great Britain, France, the Netherlands and Germany. Many scholars feel that Freud's models cannot be applied to non-Western cultures without distorting them.

Dutch, which is quite enough ahead." Here Mead was being a little grandiose. Even her most fervent champions have not claimed that her many remarkable talents included a flair for languages. Few could assess authoritatively her command of the languages of the Samoans, Manus, Balinese, and the various New Guinea tribes she encountered, but several who closely followed her work spoke pidgin English, or Neo-Melanesian as it came to be called, and insisted that Margaret's pidgin, as they heard it, was merely passable. But pidgin or no pidgin, most critics generally added that they did not wish to carp. Mead, in their eyes, was still one of the most energetic pioneers of ethnographic field methods.

Mead's letters implored her colleagues for news of what they were learning. To Cora Du Bois, working on the island of Alor, east of Bali, Mead wrote from Tambunam on July 11, 1938, "You say you have very quarrelsome people. So have we. The village rings with shouted obscenities from morning till night. There are more quarrels here in a week than in Bajoeng in a decade . . . the trouble is (with so many quarrels going on all the time) that you can't hear or see any traces of the quarrel that wasn't, the anger that failed to flame.

"Therefore results on a culture where action, noise, anger, temper tantrums, self-directed acts of violence, penitential acts, etc., are common, will be incomparable with results on cultures where they are rare . . . we don't see any way around this impasse. Do you? . . . Do your people enjoy their quarreling? . . . The Iatmul are simply glowing & radiant after a successful yelling bout—and both sides tend to glow happily . . .

"They are the only people I have studied," she went on, "who laugh at the foreigner, when he gets it *right*. They do not laugh at mistakes. They laugh when other people *hit* the nail on the head, and they laugh when they themselves *fail* to do so . . . Do get your children to draw a man & a woman, together or in succession," Mead further advised Du Bois. "The man and woman, despite cultural stylization to draw on, gives amazing results on the faulty anatomical concepts of even quite large children."

The same day Mead wrote to Du Bois she also wrote to Ernest Beaglehole, famous for his studies of the Maori, and his colleague wife, Pearl: "As far as I know you and Cora Du Bois . . . are the only research workers interested in the study of children over a long period of time in a primitive society . . . [and] what do you do in the society where the babies cry all the time?"

She wondered too how the Beagleholes dealt with the way their subjects' behavior changed over a long period of observation. What happened when the parents of observed children became close friends of the observers? Could friends be good informants? And what of the question of health? "Even if one barred all questions of humanity and if medicine were not needed for purposes of rapport with the community, there is the problem of keeping alive the subjects of research. After one has invested six months of observation and several hundred feet of film in a child the child becomes very valuable, as well as usually an object of genuine affection and solicitude."

Mead missed one Iatmul childbirth, which she had hoped and planned for months to witness, having invested hours in "a false alarm set of birth pains" and a study of the whole family. She missed it because the mother simply went and had the baby "with no warning at all, out fishing! But," she added in this letter, to Geoffrey Gorer, "we have had an adult death, a child death, and a newborn infant death, that's a fair distribution, and I've seen one birth all the way through."

To this letter she added, "Just now we are most excited and interested about the way in which Gregory's point about the absence of internal sanctions within the group is reflected in the absence of internal sanctions within the personality also. It's extraordinarily pretty." Mead liked very much the words "pretty" and "point," and used them often, especially in correspondence with Gorer, whom she asked, in October 1938, "Don't you see that you are doing just what you have criticized the nineteenth century for doing, by concentrating your attention not on social process as such, but upon US NOW, you are really asking all over again the old question, how did they get from THEM to US, only you have phrased it the other way around, WHY DIDN'T THEY GET FROM THEM AT LEAST PART WAY TO US . . ." Although Mead drew from what she learned in primitive societies when she wrote and lectured about her own, she did not see primitive societies only in terms of her own. She saw them, and honored them, for what they were. "An adequate discussion of process," she wrote, "is what we need for an understanding of modern problems."

Mead went on to compliment Gorer: "I really don't see how you managed to get through such an enormous amount of careful work. It's a very useful vindication that intelligence is of infinitely more importance than length of stay or working conditions"—a conclusion which applied conveniently to Mead herself. Three days later she wrote to Gorer again, apparently about an expedition he was considering. "Denmark sounds like a good plan," she said, "but I'd like to have you work on the dignity of the primitive who knows nothing superior to himself, and whose knowledge compasses his entire culture."

Two of her Iatmul servants, Mead wrote home, were remarkable for their dignity: "Washoe, tall, proud, assured, and a little intimidating to me because I have never before had a boy who knew anything I didn't teach him . . . [and] for the table I have a brand-new extremely bright *monkey* named Mbetnda, all eyes and ears and intensity and eagerness, a delight after Balinese apathy about anything new."

But Mead and Bateson had not seen the last of Bali. An emergency there called them back. They had succeeded in gathering the necessary materials for many comparisons, one of which was "between the way the Balinese confined drama and action to the theatre, and maintained their everyday relationships placidly and evenly, never allowing children to contend even for a toy, whereas the Iatmul, who struggled and screamed and quarreled in real life, used their artistic performances to introduce moments of static beauty into their more violent lives."

Then, after eight months in Tambunam, "just as we were preparing to leave the field," Mead later wrote, "a witchhunt against homosexuals broke out in the Pacific which echoed from Los Angeles to Singapore. Many of our friends and associates in Bali were under attack. We had intended to meet Jane Belo in Sydney only to talk over with her plans for her own further research, but in the unsettled situation it did not seem safe for her to go back to Bali alone, so we returned with her for an additional six weeks' work."

And it was a good thing they did return, according to a letter Belo wrote to her mother on February 10, 1939: "The official who is the head of the South Bali district," Belo wrote, "has got a bee in his bonnet, to try to oust all the foreigners through the country, that is not immediately in Den Pasar, where he can keep an eye on our doings. . . .

". . . The Batesons . . . are not to be bullied, and I must say since they arrived we have been less pestered by the snooping police. . . . The Batesons are making my house their headquarters. You should see Colin's piano room filled with their stuff." Colin McPhee, Belo's former husband, had left Bali. Much of this commotion had to do with violations of Section 292 of the government's Criminal Code, which said: "Any person of age who commits fornication with a minor person of his own sex, whose minority is known to him or within reason should have been surmised by him, will be punished with imprisonment for a maximum of five years."

Belo went into more detail in a letter to a friend, saying that "police are in and out of our houses" as part of the "clean-up the government has been having of certain misdemeanors to which residents of these parts were prone. The method was to arrest and put in jail all suspects, pending investigation of their cases. Walter and four others have been in prison in Den Pasar since the first of January.*

"All of us who lived in a pleasant way have been investigated— police in and out of our houses, all our servants arrested and questioned. Of the 34 dancing girls in my village, all were questioned on my habits, down to a 3-year-old. . . . Colin had kept it a secret that we were divorced last July. . . . At least half the [European] people living in Bali have been asked to leave, or have left of their own accord, one dares not wonder why . . . the Balinese think the whole white caste has gone mad. . . . Thank heaven for the Batesons and their firm scientific reputations to back us up."

The Batesons, Belo wrote on March 9 to another friend, "came back for only a little over a month, to check up on some last points before going back to England and America, and as you can imagine there was a program full to the bursting for each day and night of their stay. To make it worse, Margaret came down with an attack of malaria tertia, brought from New Guinea, complicated with the most sinister gynecological complications, and had to be sent back to Sydney ten days before Gregory, who went this morning by plane. I am still a little breathless from the hyperactivity of their cooperation. . . .

"It's the idea of nobody having a right to their own private lives any more which is so hard to bear. But it seems to be catching on all over the world, and I suppose artists and scientists will have to end up by getting used to it."

A bonus of the revisit to Bali, Mead wrote, was that "the children whom we had been studying in detail over time were almost a year older and were again photographed." In her years of studying children Mead had had several miscarriages. Now another baby, unscathed by the "sinister gynecological complications," would soon be born in the United States, a short time before Margaret Mead turned thirty-eight. It was time to go home. "Gregory is too tall to sleep in a bed with a foot to it," Mead wrote to her mother. "We like a double bed best, but . . . the next best thing is two single beds, his footless, placed side to side."

* Mead later wrote of the artist Walter Spies that his "choice of Bali and of a continuing light involvement with Balinese male youth, seemed part of his repudiation of the kind of dominance and submission, authority and dependence, which he associated with European culture, and which could be revived in him when he encountered officialdom or rank. . . . The very disassociated impersonality of Bali gave him the kind of freedom that he sought."

CHAPTER FOURTEEN

"In the Center of the Planning"

Her fellow Ash Can Cats surrounding their celebrated friend, just returned from Bali, as she knitted for her expected baby.

FEW EXPECTANT MOTHERS since the Renaissance painters' apotheosis of the Annunciation can have glowed the way Margaret Mead remembered glowing in 1939. "I had the mask of pregnancy, very highly developed, with a special color on my cheeks. . . . I looked better than at any other time; people said I looked better and prettier." At a reunion of the Ash Can Cats, most of whom had children of their own, Mead arranged her old friends at her feet and all around her, as she sat knitting, for a photograph.

She learned for sure that she was pregnant on May 15. Gregory Bateson wrote the news to Jane Belo, and said he "found myself also full of a sort of joy for my own as well as for M's sake—odd, very

odd. . . . I keep her tied by the leg in our appartment [sic] while I go
to the Museum to work" assessing the Balinese movies.

On the Fourth of July, Margaret ventured to a party to watch the
fireworks over the Hudson, and when her hostess's mother beckoned
her aside to urge her to breast-feed her baby, Margaret assured her she
would. At that time many people still believed, as Gregory Bateson's
father had, that breast-feeding was obscene. Not for decades would
organizations like the Human Lactation Center and La Lèche League
arise to defend the practice. But Margaret Mead, who had been suckled
herself, needed no encouragement. Having spent so much of her time
in the past fourteen years watching primitive mothers nurse their children, she had every intention of doing so herself.

She did not, of course, just wait and glow and plan and grow. As
always, she worked. When Mead was invited to speak at a celebration
honoring the seventy-fifth anniversary of her alma mater, scheduled for
right around the time the baby was due, she hesitated only briefly.
"You're not going to have your baby at *dinner*, are you?" she was asked,
and she said she guessed not. Motherhood, before and after the fact,
was never to interfere with her work. The two commitments were to
coexist.

One day Florette Henri, the kind, bright, and loyal Barnard friend
who had edited Fortune's *Sorcerers of Dobu*, arrived at the Mead-
Bateson apartment to help, as she often had in past years, with secre-
tarial and editorial chores. She found Mead lying on her back with her
legs propped up against a chair: "the only posture," Mead explained,
"for a pregnant woman." Henri proceeded to take notes for the foreword
Mead was writing to *From the South Seas*, an anthology of her writing
about Samoa and the other Pacific societies she had studied.

"In 1939," Mead wrote in that foreword, "people are asking far
deeper and more searching questions from the social sciences than was
the case in 1925." New choices faced the man in the street. What kind
of a world should he want to build for his children and their grandchildren? "We are at a crossroads and must decide whether we go forward towards a more ordered heterogeneity, or make frightened retreat
to some single standard which will waste nine-tenths of the potentialities of the human race in order that we may have a too dearly pur-
chased security."

When the book and its foreword were finished, lectures had to be
planned for courses Mead would teach at Vassar, New York University,
Columbia, and Teachers' College. There were 26,000 still photographs,
22,000 feet of sixteen-millimeter film, and 1,200 carvings from Bali, all

to be catalogued. And there were a good many letters to go out. One letter, concerning Adolf Hitler, was sent to the White House, advising Mrs. Franklin Delano Roosevelt about the Führer. A film clip of Hitler had persuaded Mead that he was obsessed with building Europe. The war might be prevented, she suggested, if the President would "have a talk with [Hitler] in terms of building Europe." This suggestion may have been the first of Mead's many efforts to pass anthropological insights on to the government.

Another letter Mead wrote in the late summer of 1939, to her dear friend Ruth Benedict, had a devastating effect. This letter reached Benedict at the Blackfoot Indian reservation in Alberta, Canada, where she was directing a team of field workers, and it upset her so much that she had to spend three days in bed. She told her fellow field worker Esther Goldfrank what the trouble was: "Margaret," she said, "is furious." Mead's fury at Benedict, as Goldfrank understood it, had to do with a scandal among some members of the Columbia graduate Anthropology Department. A man married to one of these anthropologists wanted to leave her for another, whom Ruth Benedict knew well. He had traveled all the way from New York City to Alberta to ask Benedict's support. He hoped she would testify in court, if need be, that his wife had been unfaithful to him, so that he could get his divorce more easily.

Benedict agreed to do as her visitor asked. He returned to New York, where his wife, upon learning of his mission to Alberta, was incensed. If Benedict testified against her, she told Margaret Mead, she in turn would spread word publicly that Benedict was a lesbian. This would endanger Benedict's chances of being reappointed to the Columbia Anthropology Department after the sabbatical year she had just begun. The department was headed by Ralph Linton, who disliked Benedict as much as she did him, and who had made her last few semesters as unpleasant as he could. Mead's "furious" letter to Benedict, as Goldfrank understood it, upbraided her for taking such a risk.

When the summer was over Benedict went to California to continue her sabbatical, and Goldfrank came home to New York. As soon as she got there, Mead asked for her version of the Alberta visit and its consequences. "I can't understand Ruth," Mead told Goldfrank. The puzzling thing was apparently not Benedict's sexuality. For much of the time since she had separated from her husband, Benedict had lived with another woman, the young research chemist Natalie Raymond; "loving Nat and taking such delight in her," she had said, "I have the happiest conditions for living that I've ever known." What Mead seemed to disapprove of was Benedict's poor judgment in agreeing to involve herself in the divorce proceedings and in further risking the wrath of Linton, who might be expected to use any excuse to oust her from his department.

What this story helps to show, forty-five years later, is how Mead's power was expanding. Her letter to Ruth Benedict could reduce that esteemed and distinguished mentor, fifteen years her senior, to despair. By now the balance had permanently shifted. Once Mead had relied on Benedict for guidance; now it was the other way around. Now it was Mead, in this and all her other relationships, who called the shots, or at least she tried to.

Until 1939, Jeannette Mirsky and Mead, whose Barnard years had overlapped, had been friendly colleagues. Not only did they discuss anthropology but they went shopping together when Margaret needed clothes. Jeannette, daughter by her amused account of "the man who invented the housedress," had a flair for fashion and a tactful way of refraining from mentioning the defects in Margaret's figure. "You have such a lovely small waist," she would say. "I know where we can get some special skirts made for you."

This cordiality came to an end over lunch in late 1939, after Margaret passed to Jeannette a bit of romantic gossip. Jane Belo, back in New York, was about to marry Frank Tannenbaum, a professor of Latin American history. Tannenbaum, moreover, had been appointed to the faculty of Columbia.

"My God," Mirsky recalled exclaiming when she heard this news. "He must have kissed Nicholas Murray Butler's ass—Tannenbaum used to be a notorious radical."*

"Now, Jeni," said Margaret, looking her companion straight in the eye. "You know the law, don't you?"

"What law?"

"The law that young radicals in time become old conservatives."

"Then how do you place Papa Franz?" asked Mirsky. She was referring to Boas's response when, during the First World War, Butler had sent a questionnaire to all the Columbia faculty asking what they would do for the war effort. Boas had drawn a line through the question and written, "Mind my own business."

Mead fixed Mirsky with a piercing look, but Mirsky, to her sur-

* Tannenbaum had led homeless, unemployed people in demonstrations in New York churches in 1915–16; President Butler of Columbia was so supremely confident and imperious that he had earned the nickname "Nicholas Miraculous."

prise and pleasure, did not feel pierced. There had been a time when she accepted all Mead's "laws" as received wisdom, but that time was over. She had done her graduate anthropology field work in Guatemala, and written two acclaimed books, and "was beginning to have my own reactions."

If Mirsky's services as a fashion adviser were no longer available that didn't bother Mead much, because for most of 1939 she was wearing maternity dresses. One day during this period she phoned another friend to say, "Leona, for God's sake, you've got to come right up to the museum and see me, immediately, this afternoon!"

"That's going to be a little tough, Margaret," replied Dr. Leona Baumgartner, who later became commissioner of health for New York City, "because my mother has just arrived, and I've promised to spend the afternoon with her."

"Drop her off here at the museum and let her look at the exhibits," Mead said. "I'll only need ten minutes of your time." Ordinarily she was delighted to see Baumgartner's mother, to whom she was devoted, but the matter at hand was private and medical. Mead's question, as Baumgartner recalled, was this: Did she know of any New York doctor whom Margaret might engage who would allow her to deliver her baby in the squatting position?*

Mead herself knew of a doctor in England who would permit this unorthodox practice, but she was not optimistic about finding space on a ship. She and Gregory Bateson had decided that if their baby was a boy, they would raise him in England (where they had at first intended to settle, or so Fortune had written to Malinowski in 1937). "As to whether we will ultimately live in England or America," Mead wrote to a British colleague, "that depends on two things: whether we think we can do better work in England than America, or vice versa, and whether we can make enough money to live on in England. My earning power is pretty good in America; and in England Gregory would have the whole burden and if that meant giving so much time to some routine that he had no time for theoretical work, I don't think it would be worth doing. . . .

"We have made all our choices," the letter continued, "in terms of what seemed most likely to contribute to the advance of anthro-

* Ahead of her time in this as in many matters, Mead would have been gratified to read in a March 1981 issue of the *New Zealand Herald* of a "birthing chair," manufactured in Nebraska, which had become popular at, among other places, Lenox Hill Hospital in New York City. "It's embarrassing," a physician was quoted as saying in this article, "for us doctors in 1981 to finally learn what nature told us so many years ago."

pology, and barring the interruption of emergency situations when one's loyalty becomes, of necessity, more specialized in time and place, we will continue to do so. The only sacrefice [sic] which I am unwilling to make is the sacrefice of a chance to do the best possible work that we can do, during our remaining productive years. Appreciation and recognition do not matter, but having colleagues who are working along related lines, whose ideas one can use, and who can use one's ideas matter tremendously. Gregory had the opportunity during his six months over here to meet some of the best minds in America among the people who were working along related lines; they can and do use his stuff; he uses theirs. . . . The picture is very simple; we have to feed the baby, do what is needed by England in the present emergency, and do the best work we can. How can we do these things best is the only problem."

After the invasion of Poland by the Nazis on September 1, 1939, Great Britain and France declared war on Germany, and Bateson went home as soon as he could, to see what uses his country could find for his skills and talents. "This was the period of phony war," he said later. "Until Dunkirk, which was as important historically as Pearl Harbor, England was totally stuck in its own morale, and didn't know what to do." He was not sure what he should do himself, either, except to join a group of British intellectuals who nicknamed themselves "Tots and Quots," short for the Latin *Quot homines tot sententiae*—meaning there are as many opinions as there are people. Many of his colleagues in this informal group later became scientific advisers to the military.

"The important thing," Bateson once said and seemed always to believe, "is to have some data flowing through the system; it doesn't matter so much what the data are." But in this case it did matter. Which of the data he could consider would be most useful in the war against fascism? Home at Cambridge, his own and his father's and his grandfather's university, he went for advice to his esteemed professor Sir Frederick Bartlett, a Fellow of the British Royal Society and a specialist in psychology. Bartlett was not encouraging.

"What are you doing here, Gregory?" Bartlett asked. "You ought to be in America." Specifically, he suggested, Bateson should resume analyzing the materials he and Mead had brought back from Bali. Frustrated and restless, Gregory cabled Margaret on December 7, 1939, that he had applied for a permit to return to New York. The next day she cabled him that he had become a father.

A friend of Mead's claimed that she would have preferred to give birth on the Sepik River, where the babies stay with their mothers, but

Mary Catherine Bateson was born at French Hospital in New York City on December 8, 1939. The afternoon before, Margaret finished an article for the *Encyclopaedia Britannica*, which was a kind of family tradition; "my mother," Mead wrote to a friend, "finished a Britannica article actually in the hospital just before I was born." Of the children born that day in New York, few can have caused such commotion. The child's father could not be present, but enough others were to give the event the air of a Nativity pageant.

"For the record," Mead later wrote, "I never aimed at a squatting delivery for myself, only: 1) as little anesthesia as possible, 2) a film of the birth and 3) breast feeding adjusted to the infant's schedule." The delivery was delayed for ten minutes until the arrival of the photographer, and was witnessed by the obstetrician, several nurses (all of whom, at Mead's request, had seen the Bateson-Mead film "First Days in the Life of a New Guinea Baby"), a child development psychologist, a movie photographer, and the pediatrician Dr. Benjamin Spock. "It was rather silly to have me there to certify the baby's normalcy," Spock said four decades later,* but this particular baby would grow up to call herself, in her book *Our Own Metaphor*, "precisely the first member of the [Spock] generation." Her mother and Spock both belonged enthusiastically to what the historian William Graebner would describe as "a significant contingent of American reformers" who saw social psychology as a weapon against the threats posed by mass movements, dictators, and the destruction of community life. Fearful of "a twentieth-century version of savagery," they hoped to devise new approaches, or rediscover old ones, which would reduce social chaos by reducing insecurity in infancy and childhood. Spock's aim, in effect, was "to enlarge the playpen and put the parent inside—not as a boss but as a leader."

Medically classified as an elderly primigravida, a first-time mother past her middle thirties, Mead suffered an attack of malaria at the time of her delivery but instructed the hospital staff on how it should be treated. Twelve days later she took Cathy to the apartment of her devoted and elated friend Marie Eichelberger, who assumed the title "Aunt Marie," and later to her maternal grandparents' home in Philadelphia. There, at the age of six weeks, the child first met her father, who had gotten a work permit and had returned to the United States to join his family permanently. The Philadelphia visit ended soon afterward, perhaps in part because Gregory vexed his wife by "speaking of

---

* Spock unchivalrously told, several times in private and once on a television documentary, how "Margaret's nether parts—and she was never slim—were painted bright red with mercurochrome."

my father as a 'poor little man.' My father was six feet tall!" Margaret said. "But Gregory was feeling that all women henpecked all men—a passing bit of pure projection, but it made me feel absolutely infuriated."

When Benjamin Spock paid house calls on young Cathy, he observed that "Gregory would cower at the far side of the room; I scarcely knew he was there." Once when the baby reached for the camera her father had in his hand, her mother told him, "Don't worry, it won't hurt your camera." Mead believed, her daughter would write, "that if a child's experience of the rhythms of his or her body were not disrupted by artificially imposed feeding schedules, a natural equilibrium could be established." When the baby was hungry, the baby was fed.

"I didn't passionately love breast feeding," Mead later said, but friends recalled her "whipping open her blouse at the slightest whimper," and she herself told how, on the rare occasions when she and Gregory went out for dinner during the time she was nursing, "I would always order Port Salut cheese, because it was something quick," in case a phone call should summon her home at any moment to a thirsty daughter. The only real problem breast feeding brought her is referred to in *Blackberry Winter*: Margaret Mead's milk, as might be expected of one whose pregnancy had been so radiant, was too rich.

Resettling in Manhattan, the Batesons took the advice of Sir Frederick Bartlett and busied themselves cataloguing the film that led to the book which even Derek Freeman, Mead's most vehement detractor, would praise as an example of fine ethnography, *Balinese Character: A Photographic Analysis*. This work began in a parlor-floor apartment with a sunny back yard which they rented from Lawrence Frank at 72 Perry Street, between West Fourth and Bleecker streets in Greenwich Village. Frank and his Irish-born third wife Mary, who was thirty years his junior, occupied the rest of the house, along with five of Frank's children by his deceased previous wives and assorted servants and visitors, some of whom stayed around for indefinite periods. "There is some furniture," Frank wrote in his letter offering this apartment to Margaret, "enough to live, but with space for more."

Gregory Bateson's teenage British goddaughters, Philomena and Claudia Guillebaud, whose economist father was his colleague, arrived in America in July 1940, to stay, as his and Margaret's wards, for the duration of the war in Europe. They and a nanny and the nanny's daughter, also a teenager, were on hand to help care for Cathy. They also paid close attention to the Balinese pictures which Margaret and Gregory showed over and over, trying to decide how to organize their staggering wealth of material into a coherent book. Through much of

1941 and into 1942, they worked to winnow the still pictures down to 5,000, which Gregory enlarged, and from which were chosen the 759 pictures that appeared in the book published in 1942.

This combined household satisfied Mead's lifelong yearning for extended families, a yearning all the more pronounced after her time in Samoa and other Pacific cultures. It also guaranteed that Mary Catherine Bateson would never lack for caretakers. "Cathy," said one family friend, "had many mothers. Margaret was less elated with the actual warming of bottles than with the idea of having achieved motherhood." Other time-consuming matters were also on her mind. In 1940, in addition to her regular museum duties, Mead attended a winter conference at Vassar College, lectured on child psychology at New York University, accepted the first of her many honorary doctoral degrees—from Wilson College, in Chambersburg, Pennsylvania—and began a study that Frank had suggested, on psychosomatic medicine.

A sign outside Cloverly, the Franks' house in New Hampshire, warned: "PLEASE WATCH OUT FOR CHILDREN." No message could have been better suited to Mead's frame of mind, especially considering who the children's parents and their friends were. In the early 1940s and later, the Squam Lake region of New Hampshire provided many social scientists not only with an exhilarating change of scene but with surefire and nonstop shoptalk. Nearby were the summer homes of the sociologists Robert and Helen Lynd, the psychologists Gardner and Lois Murphy, and a number of other families of kindred professionals. Lois Murphy volunteered to find a house for Mead and Bateson to rent in the summer of 1940. The most they could possibly pay for the summer was $350, Mead wrote, adding that "Gregory thinks of getting a bicycle. We've absolutely decided that we can't afford a car."*

The teenage Guillebaud girls struck Gregory and Margaret as being far too reticent by American standards, so a game was devised to encourage them to speak up. Every time they failed to ask the meaning of a word they did not recognize, such as "schismogenesis," they were fined a nickel. "We only got a quarter a week in the way of an allowance," Philomena recalled, "so we began to pay attention and listen. It was a marvelous idea." Philomena also noticed, as many had before and

---

* That summer she wrote to her brother Dick and his wife about a birthday gift for their mother: a replacement for her "practically unusable" typewriter. "I can get her a Corona Zephyr de luxe, through the museum, for $34.75—a 20% discount," Margaret wrote. "If all four of us contribute [the purchase might be possible] . . . let me know . . . whether you want to come in on that."

would later, that Mead and Bateson had a way of using whoever was around them as subjects. "This was partly Margaret's fascination with seeing, you know, she hadn't had much exposure to the English, she was learning things about Gregory. . . . There were many, many cases when I would catch Margaret and Gregory sort of cocking an eyebrow at each other because one of us had said something which was interesting."

But it was not just on home ground that Mead and Bateson, during the early years of the war, saw eye to eye. They agreed that the war would inevitably widen and that this made it even more imperative to find new ways for nations and peoples to use power. Their richly extended domestic life was all very well, but both of them, after all the excitement of innovative field work with the Balinese and the Iatmul, needed more. Mead was even more partial than her mother had been before her to committee meetings, especially now that her gifts for organization and leadership could be applied to new and dreadful crises.

Bateson's motto for work, he said much later, was "Divide in order that you may not be conquered." Do not, in other words, put all professional eggs in one basket. A "patchwork of institutional ties," he was discovering, was the best way for him to work "within and between the hierarchies." One enthusiasm Gregory and Margaret shared was the Conference on Science, Philosophy and Religion in Their Relation to the Democratic Way of Life, which had first been convened in 1939 by the Jewish theologian Lewis Finkelstein and the writer Lyman Bryson.

This group's "promise of both high earnestness and unyielding discipline" was what made it attractive to the literary critic Van Wyck Brooks. The enticement for Bateson and Mead was the group's interdisciplinary approach to ethical problems. Their fellow conferees included Boas himself, the physicist Enrico Fermi, the classicist Moses Hadas, the Thomist philosopher Jacques Maritain, the Protestant theologian Paul Tillich, and Albert Einstein—exhilarating company.

Mead and Bateson missed this conference's organizational meeting, in September 1940, but were present the next year at the second, where Gregory read a paper, "On Social Planning and the Concept of Deutero-Learning." Discussing the ideological role of social sciences in wartime, he asked: "Are we to reserve the techniques to a few planning, goal-oriented and power-hungry individuals, to whom the instrumentality of science makes a natural appeal? Now that we have the techniques, are we, in cold blood, going to treat people"—as Martin Buber in 1923 had cautioned in his distinction between "thou" and "it"—"as things?"

Mead was beginning her next book, a study of contemporary America which she called *And Keep Your Powder Dry*. "The obligation of the scientist to examine his material dispassionately," she wrote, "is combined with the obligation of the citizen to participate responsibly in his society."* She also wrote that "Every social institution which teaches human beings to cringe to those above and step on those below must be replaced by institutions which teach people to look each other straight in the face." In her private life, too, Mead went out of her way to make sure that people could look each other in the eye. "She always seated us in a semicircle," said a California friend who sometimes visited Mead and Bateson in the early 1940s, "so we wouldn't have to crane our necks to see each other."

One of the Batesons' most earnest involvements was the Committee on National Morale, the American equivalent of the "Tots and Quots" group Gregory had belonged to in England. This assemblage of American intellectuals and scholarly refugees from Europe was founded by an oriental-rug collector and "intellectual entrepreneur," as Bateson called him, named Arthur Upham Pope. Pope, a man of great means and singular enthusiasms, was so impatient with America's ignorance of the art and archeology of Persia that he commissioned a seventeen-volume survey of Persian art.†

The Committee on National Morale, similarly fueled by Pope's enthusiasm, took full-page advertisements in the New York Times and sponsored talks over radio stations WNYC and WMCA. "Pope was out of the Persian business and looking for trouble," Bateson said, "and decided to promote the use of intellectuals in the coming war. He gathered together about fifty people including Margaret, myself, Ladi Farago [Ladislas Farago, the Hungarian émigré journalist], and Edwin Taylor, an international newsman who had reported the Spanish Civil War from Franco's side. All of us were supposed to think how intellectuals could be used."

"Upham Pope was a salesman, for all he could palaver," said Eliot Chapple, another committee member who in 1940, in collaboration with Conrad Arensberg, published a book Mead and Bateson found

* This double obligation would cause many tensions. It is exactly at the root of the accusations that Mead had gone out to the field, at least to Samoa, to prove Boas's morally superior social point that culture was determinant, though there is no inherent reason why objectivity and commitment cannot coexist.
† In 1943, when Pope was asked to give the annual Lincoln's Birthday address at Cooper Union, in New York, a New Yorker magazine account reported that he "presented the Great Emancipator in a rather Oriental light," barely remembering to work the President into his speech, which lasted more than an hour and a half, by noting that "Lincoln knew no Arabs, but he would have enjoyed meeting them, and they would have recognized him as a great sheik."

most interesting: *Measuring Human Relations: An Introduction to the Study of the Interaction of Individuals.* Pope got a five-thousand-dollar grant from the government to get a staff organized, with lovely girls turning out memoranda on everything. He'd go to Washington and come back and tell us of marvelous conversations—how [Secretary of the Interior Harold] Ickes and [Secretary of the Navy Frank] Knox had reported to the Chief, as F.D.R. was called, but nothing had happened. We'd all meet and allude to 'the Chief,' but nothing happened, and finally we said, 'Look, for Chrissakes, this is foolish; we'll go down to Washington and find out what the holy hell is going on.' "

This committee, Mead wrote, was "an attempt to mobilize what would now be called the 'behavioral sciences' for the war effort, with a core of those who had been concerned with the applications of psychology during World War I. Here many of those who were to play a part in psychological warfare and to work on problems of morale came together as volunteers to try to prepare plans which could be put into effect when war came." Its members, she wrote in *And Keep Your Powder Dry*, "realized that the older sciences of history, political science and economics needed to be supplemented by the newer disciplines of anthropology, sociology, psychology and psychiatry."

Her colleagues on this committee, she wrote, were "not caught up in the fashionable radicalism of the 1930s with its roseate views of the Soviet Union." Some who knew Mead in this and later periods of her life reflected with wonderment that she never seemed to be "caught up in" any politics, fashionable or otherwise, except for the undiluted patriotism which was encouraged by the Second World War.* As far as one friend who knew Mead at the time could recall, she never said a thing about the Spanish Civil War. (She did, however, congratulate the students who in the 1960s opposed the war in Vietnam, and she later publicly and militantly opposed nuclear war. The only presidential candidate she ever supported was Jimmy Carter in 1976.)

In any case, her committee associates, as Mead put it, were "spared the paralysis that crippled so many liberals who were stunned and confused by the Soviet-German pact" of 1939. They looked forward, instead, to "the application of anthropological methods to the study of modern societies," and felt scorn, Mead later wrote, for colleagues who "retreated to the ivory bomb shelters of minute and entrancing special-

---

* During the war, on a train between Washington, D.C., and New York, she encountered an acquaintance in Marine uniform, and asked how he was getting on. Oddly enough, said the Marine, he had been writing poetry. "Being a Marine," said Mead, "*is* a poem."

ist problems of kinship systems, templates and mentifacts," preferring to "come out into the marketplace, work in the dust of the traveled road . . . and try to ask the right questions, secure in the faith that, whenever in all his history man has asked the right question, he has found the answer." This combination of boundless energy and activist temperament helps to explain how incidental was Mead's choice of an academic career.

Gertrude Stein, on her deathbed in Paris in 1946, is said to have been asked, "What is the answer?" and is said to have responded "What is the question?" Mead, from the early 1940s on, claimed to know some of the questions: "How can we organize a society in which war will have no place? . . . What are the conditions in a culture, in its system of education, in its systems of interpersonal relationships, which promote a sense of free will?" And, further, "How can we analyze the problems of man's relations to man as we have analyzed the problems of man's relationship to nature?" This last, she held, was "the question that sets us free."

Naïve though it might have seemed, this question excited Mead as much as any she had encountered in her field work, and led to others: Could social scientists devise new ways to deal with allies and enemies? Could their theoretical knowledge be applied to raise the morale of American troops? Bateson, who at the time had no salaried job, was much involved in getting the Committee on National Morale to devise ways for its members to "use their scientific and intellectual professional skills, as distinguished from spy skills, cross-culturally." One thing they studied, in the words of their anthropologist colleague Philleo Nash, was "that literary form, 'the memorandum,' on which the government is based."

"We learned," Bateson explained, "about how memoranda are used in multiple hierarchies. If you want to get a message sent conventionally from me in this hierarchy"—he drew a picture to illustrate—"to this man in his, it takes a long time and is very ineffectual, which was why a lot of things didn't happen as fast as we would have liked them to. But we discovered there was no rule against sending draft memoranda.

"If you want to communicate from X to Y, you say to Y, 'I'm writing a memorandum, maybe you'll be interested, I'd like to incorporate your advice into the final version.' Then you have him read your 'draft,' get his comments, let him feel he has power, and throw his answer into the wastebasket, because with the draft memorandum you have achieved your aim." Another result of the efforts to puzzle out the labyrinths of

Washington led to a call from a government official at the Bateson-Mead household on Perry Street.

"This guy," Bateson told this author, "spent a day hearing about our very noble and liberal plans. We bombarded him all day, he settled into himself, screwed into his chair, and told us: 'Well, if you want to get something done in Washington, think of yourself as someone in an absolutely crowded elevator who wants to get to the other side of the elevator.

" 'You do this by leaning on the person just in front of you. They'll be unable to stand your contact, so you'll gain half an inch, and lean on the next person, and since nobody can stand being leaned on, you just keep doing this until you get to the other side of the elevator.' The guy, you see, very much disapproved of our having a plan as to where we were going."

Mead's *Blackberry Winter* is understandably vague about her "web of wartime activities." People who worked for wartime agencies either were not supposed to say exactly what they were doing or did not choose to. The most obvious thing to many concerned must have been the heady spirit of reunion and *Wiedersehen*, after the painful separations of the 1930s, of such close friends, regathering for so gallant a cause. Here they all were again on the same seacoast, and often in the same city: Mead, Bateson, and Ruth Benedict, who was on leave to the Office of War Information. Others who joined them often included Geoffrey Gorer, whom Margaret's brother-in-law Leo Rosten, working in Hollywood, recalled meeting there.

One day Rosten's secretary alerted him that a strangely dressed visitor awaited him outside his office. The visitor was "wearing broad sandals with no stockings or socks, violent green trousers, an orange shirt, and a planter's straw hat. He told me proudly," said Rosten, "that he thought he was being a good anthropologist: he had gone to a clothing store and told the salesman, 'I'm about to make a trip to Hollywood, and I don't want to stand out.' The salesman must have seen this as a chance to get rid of the worst schlock stuff he had—*nobody*, in Hollywood or anywhere, dressed like that."

Gorer, who in a tribal rite had managed to swallow an unborn mouse by pretending it was an oyster, had the full respect of Mead and Benedict. They were delighted especially with his "pioneering memorandum," a preliminary survey of "Japanese Character Structure and Propaganda," which was cosponsored by the Committee on National Morale and the Council for Intercultural Relations. This latter group was born over an informal meal after a session of the American Anthropological Association in Philadelphia, in 1940.

One of the diners on that occasion was the strikingly attractive Rhoda Bubendey Métraux, an honors graduate of Vassar College whom Mead came to regard as "the most distinguished woman anthropologist of her generation." Métraux and Mead would collaborate on many projects over the years, and eventually would live together, for longer than Mead ever lived with anyone else. This 1940 meeting, Métraux would recall, was held "at a time when we were fully aware that there would be no more professional meetings until after the war we had not yet entered. It was hoped that later such a group might become the basis for a Society for Culture and Personality."

This small group, the Council on Intercultural Relations, "gradually emerged," said Métraux, "as an independent identity with various linkages in the Washington years. For example [her husband] Alfred Métraux* and I were part of one cluster that was brought together by Margaret Mead, Gregory Bateson, Ruth Benedict, Philip D. Moseley, Geoffrey Gorer, and perhaps one or two others . . . this was only one of a number of such overlapping clusters."

Beatrice Bateson did not live long enough to see her only grandchild. Shortly before her death in April 1941, her daughter-in-law wrote to tell Mrs. Bateson that Gregory had "been working 15 hours a day, really giving all that his training and experience and mind and values could give to something which we feel may have a definitive connection with the outcome of the war. The task of mobilizing attitudes in this country so as to retain full vigour and avoid the paralyzing apathy-producing effects of propaganda is an enormous one." Gregory had "been in the center of the planning," Margaret wrote. "Everything that he hoped he would have a chance to do when he came back has worked out as if by magic. Right now he is dead tired out, living on a thin frayed edge of excitement, for he has had very little experience of big heavy pressure offices and lots of tiring conferences and deliberations."

Mead herself, it was clear, was more accustomed to such pressures. When she accompanied Bateson to a Smith College Conference of Topologists, between December 31, 1940, and January 2, 1941, they both made an impression on one of a select group of students who had been invited to meet the visitors. The student, a protégée of the sociologist Kurt Lewin, was Betty Goldstein, who later, as Betty Friedan, recalled

---

* Alfred Métraux, a distinguished scholar and a protégé of Claude Lévi-Strauss, was best known for his ethnological studies of South America—Chaco and Amazonian tribes—and for his work in Haitian and Easter Island anthropology. After his divorce from his second wife, Rhoda, he worked at the Musée de l'Homme and for UNESCO in Paris, where in 1963 he committed suicide.

that the two anthropologists were irreverently referred to as "God the Mother and Jesus Christ."

Bateson read a paper at that conference called "Equilibrium and Climax in Interpersonal Relations." He would also soon publish, in *Psychiatry Review*, an article called "The Frustration-Aggression Hypothesis." No doubt this had been discussed with his wife, who in *And Keep Your Powder Dry*, first published in 1942, wrote that she had returned to her native country "at the end of 1939"—actually in the spring—"to find all interest in pleasure practically wiped out, aggression held the center of the stage. Analysts, sociologists, psychologists—everybody was talking about Aggression and the stimulus to Aggression—Frustration," ideas that John Dollard had originated at Yale.

In May of 1941, Bateson and Mead both read papers—his on "National Morale and the Social Sciences," hers on "Anthropology and the Social Workers"—at the first meeting of the Society for Applied Anthropology, which had been newly founded at Harvard. One of this group's aims was to refocus the concern of anthropologists from distant primitive societies, impossible to visit during wartime, to nearby farmers and laborers.

In the summer of 1941, the 72 Perry Street household went en masse to New Hampshire. When Mead returned to New York that autumn, she was "asked to find out what I could"—by whom she does not say—about the movement called Technocracy, based on the idea that scientists and engineers should control the social system. This movement, Mead wrote in *Blackberry Winter*, "seemed to be turning into a form of Fascism." Its leaders included Howard Scott, who had been enamored of Margaret's late friend Eleanor Steele. "I invited Howard to dinner in a ground-floor apartment," Mead wrote, "leaving the shades up and wishing there were someone I could tell what I was doing." In those times, with the German-American Bund active in the Yorkville section of New York City, and real and imaginary Nazi agents around, Mead's air of mystery would not have been surprising.

On December 7 the Japanese bombed Pearl Harbor, and on December 8 the Congress declared war. Later that month the American Anthropological Association voted to endorse United States entry into the war. Margaret Mead was not opposed. "As an American, I hope we stay out," Mead had told an AAA friend. "As a human, I hope we go in."

These AAA meetings, one anthropology professor remembered, were "the only time I ever saw Margaret Mead take a back seat. . . . The dominant person there was Ruth Benedict, leaning on a mantel-

piece with her white hair, her birdlike face, a very commanding presence."
Although Benedict by then had formed her enduring personal alliance
with the psychologist Ruth Valentine, and had long since ceased to be
Mead's mentor, her presence was then and always commanding as far
as Margaret Mead was concerned. It was in 1941 that Benedict gave
Mead a book of thirty-three of her poems, handwritten, which "expressed the most recent personal choice," as Mead said, "of what she
liked best."

On December 8, Catherine Bateson's second birthday, Ruth Benedict gave Margaret Mead another sort of present: an official reason to
spend a lot of time in Washington. On behalf of the National Research
Council's Committee on Food Habits, Benedict was asked to invite
Mead to become the committee's executive secretary. "To the great
good fortune of the Committee," its official history says, Dr. Mead "accepted the post at first on a part-time, non-resident basis for the month
of January, 1942. On February 1, having been granted a wartime leave
of absence from the American Museum of Natural History, she came to
Washington to take charge of the office of the Committee on a full-
time basis."

CHAPTER FIFTEEN

Taking on Hitler and Hunger

TURNING FORTY, for most people, is an occasion for solemn stocktaking and potential self-pity. The *crise de quarante*, as the French call it, poses classic questions: Where am I going? What have I missed? Am I a credit to my profession? To my gender? Margaret Mead's fortieth birthday came nine days after Pearl Harbor, and if she found time to consider these matters at all, she must have felt reasonably satisfied with her answers. At last she was a mother; her bright and healthy daughter was now two years old. At last she was enchantedly married: "I love you, my darling, so much," she ended a September 1941 letter to Bateson. And at last, in a time of international emergency, the whole world's metabolism had caught up with her own; nearly everybody else was in as much of a hurry as she was.

Columbia University, her department head Ralph Linton told Mead in a letter, understood the exigencies of emergency work, and would cancel the second semester anthropology course she was to have taught in the Extension Office. There would be no need to "trouble" Gregory Bateson to take over the course for her, Linton said: "if he took it the enrollment would probably be diminished to the point where [the Extension] would lose money on it." The museum, which would promote Mead to associate curator of ethnology in 1942, also meanwhile granted her a leave of absence. She was free to go to work in Washington, where the administration was Democratic and her contacts were excellent; she had a pretty good idea of which people in which institutions talked to which others, and of what was going on overseas. "She was," said one of her colleagues, "a brand name." Her name, as she had promised her father it would be, was famous.

Magazine editors began exchanging memoranda asking whether it wasn't time for a takeout on this Mead person, who seemed to be attracting so much attention not only among her fellow anthropologists but in the general public as well. Radio audiences grew accustomed to the sound of her earthy, no-nonsense voice. Newspapers reported her honorary degrees and, in February 1942, that she received the first Gold Medal Award the Society of Woman Geographers had given anyone since Amelia Earhart, nine years earlier.

More and more often Mead gave speeches, and she noticed as she did so how her profession had affected her perceptions. She made note of what her audiences wore: whether she saw before her "a patriotic group of women, valiantly and self-consciously wearing last year's hats, or an afternoon group of women who are homemakers, or an evening group of women who, whether they are homemakers or not, don't do homemaking in the daytime." Superimposed on all this was a witty anthropological awareness that "these people," unlike those she had studied in the Pacific, were "completely clothed." Mead's speeches were widely quoted. When she said that a "social virus" of "systematized hatred" had begun to endanger the world, the implication was clear: if you wanted to fight a virus, didn't you need a scientist? And if the virus was social, should not the scientist be also?

W. H. Auden, who later became a friend of Mead's, wrote:

> . . . Thou shalt not answer questionnaires
> Or quizzes upon world affairs
> Nor with compliance
> Take any test. Thou shalt not sit
> With statisticians, nor commit
> A social science.

Mead and Bateson would have disagreed. Social science, in their view, was a hallowed thing and as useful a gift as mankind had at its disposal. At the June 1941 commencement ceremonies of the New Jersey College for Women, where she received an honorary doctor of laws degree, Mead gave an address called "Spontaneity as a Condition of Democratic Life." Science, she said, was a tool which had been abused in aid of fascism and apathy but now could be used for worthier ends. Propaganda, she also said, was "one of the discoveries which is bound to revolutionize the world" if it was used "to influence the behavior of human beings, to use the laws developed by social scientists instead of the intuitions of natural politicians." Gregory Bateson's thoughts were kindred. "It is more than ever urgent," he wrote, "for us social scientists to provide whatever shortcuts we can. . . . We do not know all the answers, but we must make our hunches available wherever they may be of some practical use." The proposition was clear: how to apply the power of social science to solve world problems.

From their field sites anthropologists streamed home to help, finding government work glamorous, but also at times futile. "If certain civilian researchers had been listened to," said Philleo Nash, "we could have been spared the atomic bomb and fire bombs. The anthropologist Clyde Kluckhohn was using ordinary social science techniques, interviewing Japanese prisoners of war for the Bureau of Overseas Intelligence of the O.W.I., and he learned that Japan was already so demoralized that fire bombs and the atom bombs weren't necessary."

Early in the Second World War Nash worked in the Office of Facts and Figures, on the recommendation of his old University of Chicago professor Harold Lasswell, who was an adviser to Archibald MacLeish. Mead, who had first met Lasswell in 1933, credited him with "contributing stimulating suggestions on methods of keeping track of interaction in the course of the conduit of ongoing events and on the specific role of the clarifier, a conference participant role which involved translating the assumptions and methodologies of different disciplines as an interpreter translates different languages." (For all the pride she had taken in writing her early popular books "in English!" Mead was bilingual: she could also express herself, when the spirit moved her to, in social sciencese.)

Lasswell's skills were useful in dealing with the race riots that erupted in Detroit in 1943. "All hell was breaking loose in Detroit," said Nash, "and we in our office were the only ones who were forecasting race riots." This they accomplished by the study of rumors. "The typical social science approach," he said, "would have been to conduct surveys, but we didn't work that way. What we did do was have information officers who appeared to be barflies hanging around to pick up rumors, and if we had ten information officers who came up with one rumor, we would give it some credence. Otherwise it was a matter of application of common sense, use of networks. We didn't like to do anything that *showed*. If it could be shown that the White House manipulated race relations, it would be assumed, wrongly, that it had to be for political purposes."

Washington, D.C., came to seem as vital a field rendezvous as Port Moresby or Rabaul. Mead, Bateson, Benedict, Rhoda Métraux, Geoffrey Gorer, and other colleagues such as Béla Maday and Philip Moseley, all of whom had top-secret clearance, would gather weekly to exchange information. These people, working for different government agencies, found plenty to talk about. Each agency had staff members "who were prepared," Maday said, "to use what those of us who were outside or in another agency were producing." The more widely these ideas spread, the more pleased the officials were.

"I leave ideas lying around like pencils," Mead once replied when someone asked if she wasn't afraid some of her thoughts might be stolen. "I *want* them to be stolen!" She could "dream up good ideas, solutions to problems, faster than anybody you ever saw," said Eliot Chapple. "But these were only good if somebody could judge what was the good ten percent or one percent of what she was saying. Half the time she couldn't tell the difference between lousy and good ideas." Mead's real strength during the war years and in later times as well, Chapple also said, was in the building of networks, cliques, and systems, in "perceiving which three or four people in any group would, when you got down to it, provide the clout.

"Her serious weakness was as a politician. She was so dispersed that she didn't have the follow-through to maintain relationships. She didn't stay with it. You've got to be able not only to get their ear but organize time, shift gears, develop relationships with poor characters from outer darkness. . . . She'd express herself forcibly and react so quickly that she didn't understand what the other person was trying to say.

"But she symbolized, for a hell of a lot of people, the relevance of anthropology to today's problems." She took seriously her membership on Mayor La Guardia's "I Am An American Day" Committee, and wrote a detailed letter to the mayor, after the Day, with seven suggestions about how the event, in Central Park, could have been handled better: the crowd should have been "welded together at some stage, preferably by singing," Mead wrote, and the police could have been "given some positive instructions as to how to explain the too-large crowds, such as: 'Twenty times the number we expected came,' etc., instead of just pleasantly saying: 'You can't get in. Keep moving.'"

Bateson, as 1942 began, was using anthropology in every new way he could think of to analyze and help defeat the enemy. At Columbia University, under the combined auspices of the Navy and the O.S.S., he was teaching a three-credit course, International Pidgin English 101C. His students were being sent by the Navy to the Pacific, to help produce what one friend referred to as "manuals on Micronesian culture, coconuts, chiefs and so on. Margaret wasn't particularly interested in these manuals or these analyses of countries. She did it, but what interested her more was the big outcome."

Much of the world was asking the question: What sort of people are the Nazis? Mead, to this end, sent Erik Erikson, in Berkeley, a full transcript in German of Hitler's latest speech, asking him to send "any good hunches" and references to the Führer's previous speeches. "There are a good many shakeups going on here in Washington," she wrote in her October 1942 letter, "and I would like to show such a memorandum to several people." At the Museum of Modern Art, three miles downtown from Columbia, Bateson analyzed in exhaustive detail a nine-reel, hundred-minute film called "Hitler Jungequex" which was brought to his attention by Leo Rosten. A week before its 1933 première in Berlin, the Führer himself had seen this film, which concerned a preadolescent Hitler Youth convert named Heini, his violent father, and his drudge of a mother. Bateson's effort was "to dissect out the relationship [between Nazis and enemies] and the whole range of phenomena—parenthood, adolescence, maturity, cleanliness, sex, aggression, passivity, and death— which are embraced by the Nazi view of life . . . and carried the stamp of official Nazi approval [and were popular with] Nazi audiences."

Bateson's fifty-two-page, single-spaced report showed how themes implicit in an artistic structure could be most effective, as propaganda, if they tapped the unconscious or semiconscious levels of audience response, or were based on "learning experiments which will demonstrate this more complex type of learning at an animal or human level." His study, which spurred on other thematic analyses of contemporary art, implied that European movies were as valid an object of anthropological inquiry as Iatmul rituals or Balinese dances. Bateson also wrote a *Yearbook of Civilian Morale*, and, in another paper, dealt with the problem of "organizing a hierarchical system in the American North."

The hierarchy that most concerned his wife, and best allowed her to hone some of the skills she had inherited from her mother, was the Committee on Food Habits, a branch of the National Academy of Sciences' National Research Council. Mead was indebted to the N.R.C. for having financed her Samoa expedition in 1925, but by the early 1940s, she said, the N.R.C. had become "a perfectly dead number . . . merely a holding company [which was] only allowed a few things in psychology, anthropology, and medicine—all the rest of science had moved over to [the Office of] Scientific Research and Development," under Vannevar Bush. Mead's job as Food Habits Committee executive secretary caused some of her male colleagues later to belittle her for being a "kitchen anthropologist"; others hinted that this work had been a front for other concerns. In that respect they were partly right. "When I went to Washington in World War II and was told I'd be judged by how much money I could bring into the Committee on Food Habits," she later said, "my response was, 'I'm not going to bring any money to it, or build it up into an empire, I just want to set it up so that it and I can get things done.'" In this aim she succeeded. The committee did get things done, and so did she.

The knottiest question of all, Mead wrote in a formal letter to Leo Rosten, filed but never mailed, was "what is to be done about 'rumors' which are actually based on real situations which it is impossible to correct. . . . As an example, there have been an enormous number of rumors . . . that the Government would actually [take] meat away from farmers, take the meat out of their freezer lockers, take the hogs which they wanted to kill for themselves. As such a policy is not contemplated at present, this rumor could be debunked with a good deal of profit, by some local rumor clinic device." From the Food Habits Committee evolved the Committee on Living Habits, the National and World Federations of Mental Health, and, after the United Nations was founded, UNESCO. "It didn't end up as a bureaucracy," Mead said of the original committee. "It ended in a point of view."

A similar point of view emerged from the new field of applied anthropology, a term coined in 1934 when the Bureau of Indian Affairs first found work for jobless anthropologists. In the depressed 1930s, these specialists had worked to stimulate small-group initiative and to foster community action on a local level. An "applied," in the jargon of the time, was someone more devoted to the applications of anthropology than to pure theory. The Society for Applied Anthropology was formed in the spring of 1941, and in 1942 Mead and Kurt Lewin set up a working relationship between her Food Habits Committee and his graduate department at the University of Iowa to make a series of experiments in changing food habits. With Mead's guidance, some of Lewin's young associates later helped establish a special O.S.S. training unit.

"Margaret wasn't an 'applied' except for the food thing," said Eliot Chapple. "In the food thing they used the neighborhood block association business. 'You know, Eliot,' she'd tell me, 'we really know the answers to these problems, part of which is forming block associations so that people on this side of the street can find out how people on that side of the street are dealing with what they can find to shop for and cook and eat.'" World hunger, in this period, was not so far off as many people supposed. The idea of sharing food with people in other countries was not popular; Mead used her knowledge of field work methods, said Rhoda Métraux, to help make it so.

Convinced that people should get the food most important to

them, the committee faced a variety of questions. Where should extra tomatoes be sent? Was it possible to remove the fatty, oily taste from wafers manufactured from the small trash fish called menhaden, a primary source of oil and fertilizer? Would people whose normal diet was rice take to emergency gifts of white flour? Would it break down the authority of parents to aim mass feeding programs at individuals instead of at families?

This committee met for two-day sessions once a month, to discuss problems of food and nutrition introduced by M. L. Wilson, director of extension services for the Department of Agriculture. Wilson, later Assistant Secretary of Agriculture, was also chairman of the federal task force which coordinated nutrition programs of all federal agencies for the "imminent" war effort. In a "preliminary memorandum" to Wilson, on August 7, 1942, Mead explained what the public had to learn. Housewives, for example, would have to be made aware of how their actions affected farmers: "It may be necessary to buy cheese in 1942 so that we will have beef in 1945, for if there is no market for dairy products, the farmer may sell his herd." The average urban housewife would have to stop feeling like "the helpless victim of the exploiting farmers" and be made to see that by buying foods the government requested her to, she was "exerting power," a power which could lead to "the sense of freedom and dignity which goes with spending money."

Good block leaders could help to strengthen the civilian defense structure by passing these ideas on to housewives, and making them feel they could help to answer such questions as: "If we were going to promise to feed Europe, shouldn't we give them something they would want to eat?" In this way, the scholar Joan Campbell said in 1980, Margaret Mead was twenty-five years ahead of her time in anticipating the need for a "systems analysis approach" to nutrition planning, and "to invent channels through which new findings can be readily translated into the meal planning of the woman on the farm, in the village, or on the street." Mead learned all she could about farm, village, and street. Whenever she could, she left her Washington headquarters to meet, inspire, and learn from workers in her vast new field, her native country. On one of these trips, in 1942, she went to the Deep South for the first time in her life, and felt, she later said, as if she were not in the United States but in New Guinea.

One stop during this trip, in a tiny town called Dewy Rose, Georgia, made a vivid impression on a pair of promising young Radcliffe nutritionists who were at work on their doctorates. Margaret T. Cussler and Mary L. deGive, then in their twenties, were visiting Dewy

Rose and two other nearby hamlets to research a dissertation called "Cultural Sanctions of the Food Patterns of the Rural Southeast," which was being financed in part by the Committee on Food and Nutrition. When Mead went to Dewy Rose to look in on these researchers, Cussler told the honored guest that she was reputed to be "the greatest woman anthropologist." The honored guest, Cussler recalled, "did not like that qualifying word 'woman' very much, but she gave us a lot of help. She taught us to apply field methods she had learned in the South Seas. She never was big on quantitative methods; she said you could learn all you needed to know from one person, if you covered that person extensively enough. She taught us that sometimes you might have to go back and talk to one person fourteen different times. We learned a lot, but that first meeting had a curious effect on me.

"It sent me to bed for a couple of days, because I never before had met a woman who was as smart as I thought I was." This was not the first time, or the last, when an encounter with Margaret Mead sent others reeling to their beds.

As she always had, Mead kept her eyes open wherever she went for possible recruits to anthropology. One of these was Joseph Neyer, a new Ph.D. in philosophy, who had studied under W. Lloyd Warner at the University of Chicago and had been declared 4-F by the Army because of flat feet. He had come to Washington, he said, "with a notion that my life would not be complete unless I somehow, sometime, spent eighteen months in a place like Borneo." Figuring that she might have a job for him, Neyer arranged to meet Margaret Mead, who was in fact at work on what sounded to him like an interesting project concerning the French-Canadian community in Maine.

"The money didn't come through in time, but for six weeks or so Margaret and I would have dinner, just the two of us, once a week. She urged me to become an anthropologist and counseled me about marriage. Her own marriage was good, she said, because she and Gregory Bateson shared their scientific interests. The main reason for getting married, she also said, was that married people had a chance to finish their conversations." When Neyer was drafted in spite of his feet, Mead asked him to write to her about the Army's social organization. He obliged, but when she saw him next, three and a half years later, she didn't remember who he was.

All this while she was gathering material for *And Keep Your Powder Dry*, her cursory portrait of America as she was rediscovering it, in which she explained her increasing "commitment to a theory of infinite malleability throughout human life." Geoffrey Gorer was much on her mind as she wrote it; she thought of him, she told him in a letter, as "the antagonist, the European observer whose brilliant misunderstanding of points in American culture has made me examine those points more sharply and come to understand where you are wrong. I feel like dedicating the book to my 'European social scientists friends without whose articulate misunderstandings this book could not have been written.'"

Mead wrote the book in 1942, in three weeks, during another summer near the Frank household in New Hampshire. *And Keep Your Powder Dry*, its author claimed, was a "pioneer venture," in that "no anthropologist had attempted to write about a major complex culture using the model of the whole culture that had been developed through the study of small primitive societies." It was as innovative as Bateson's study of the Nazi movie, and although A. L. Kroeber remarked when this book appeared that "a lot of people think they are discovering America," most critics liked it. "Until an authentic Martian arrives," said a reviewer for the Book-of-the-Month Club, Mead's "examination of America and Americans" was "about as close an approximation to a dissection by a man from Mars as we are likely to have." The review in *Reveille* applauded Mead for asking "such questions as, 'Why that chip on our shoulder?,' 'When will and when won't an American fight?,' 'Where lies the American strength and the American weakness?' and 'Why is it so important for us to think we're right?'" The most urgent task at hand, as Mead summed it up, was to build, "from a hundred cultures, one culture which does what no culture has ever done before—gives a place to every human gift."

To find a place for every human gift was an ambitious undertaking, and for Mead a kind of crusade. It was grandiose of her, many said in the early 1940s and kept on saying all her life, to think in such terms, but most of the time she was too busy to care. She traveled around discovering for herself the truth of the motto on every American coin in every pocket: *E pluribus unum*, out of many, one; the parts make the whole. She was astute in describing the special qualities of California, where she went to visit everyone she could think of, including her brother Richard and her sister Priscilla and their spouses. Priscilla's husband, Leo Rosten, author of the best-selling *The Education of H*Y*M*A*N K*A*P*L*A*N*, had been living in the Beverly Hills section of Los Angeles, writing screenplays under the name of Leonard Ross, when war broke out. Subsequently, as a member of the Office of War Information, he served as liaison between Washington and Hollywood, persuading government officials and studio executives to cooperate in making films to educate the public.*

In California, Mead discovered "the epitome of the fourth-generation attitude, the religious veneration of the newly manufactured solution, hoarfrost sprinkled on new-laid eggs." Not all Mead's prose in *Powder Dry* was so imaginative. Some of her passages betray the haste with which this wartime book was written, and belabor the obvious. It seems unremarkable to note, as she does, that "the behavior of those of us who live today carries traces of other behaviors, themes developed under other stresses." And someone, if not she herself, should have edited out sentences like "Our strengths and our weaknesses are the resultant of the choices . . . of those who have gone before us." But Mead is convincing about the ironic "trichotomy of those who are working too hard but enjoy what they are doing, those who are working—some of them too hard and some only lackadaisically—because they must if they are to live as well as exist, and those who are cut off from the chance to earn a decent living." Mead herself, it was clear then and always, chose to work much harder than most people would have dreamed of doing.

Those who clustered around her were hard workers, too. Mead arranged for Rhoda Métraux to be appointed to the civilian planning staff of the O.S.S., in order to study German civilian morale. (She regretted, Métraux declared in 1980, that she still was not free to say just what her O.S.S. work had been.) Mead was fond of Germans. Luther Cressman had some German ancestors, and so had Marie Eichelberger. Larry Frank, Mead's friend ever since the 1934 Hanover conference in New Hampshire, was on his mother's side a third-generation Cincinnati German.†

"Germans," Mead said, "get the roof mended." (Ruth Benedict had been advised by her grandmother that "in every marriage somebody has to get the roof fixed. Don't you be the one.") In the winter of 1942–43 Mead mourned the first German who had been deeply important to her, her mentor Franz Boas. Boas died at a luncheon he was giving, at the Columbia University Faculty Club, in honor of Professor

---

* Rosten later coordinated the beginnings of the social science division of the RAND Corporation, drawing up a list of social scientists to confer about how their techniques might be applied to problems of national security.
† Germans from southwestern Ohio may have an especially upright view of themselves. Peter Davis, in *Home Town*, quotes the mother of three trouble-prone young men in Hamilton, Ohio, near Cincinnati, who, asked why she thought they had so many problems, answered, "It beats me. Except for one English grandmother they come from good German stock on all sides."

Paul Rivet, who had been head of the Musée de l'Homme in Paris before the Occupation. Talk at this lunch had focused on the need to
combat the false philosophy of racism. Boas, said his biographer Melville Herskovits, made a comment on the need to press for the exposure
of racism whenever and wherever possible, and then, "without a further
sound, fell over backwards in his chair, dead."

Boas's last words, Mead wrote, were "I have a new theory of racism." What mattered more than his final statement was all he had said
over all the years since she had been a Barnard undergraduate—"a missile waiting to be directed." Mead's crucial and honorable direction had
come from her esteemed Professor Boas, whose *The Mind of Primitive
Man* some considered the Magna Carta of self-respect for the so-called
lower classes. Now that he was gone, forty-one-year-old Margaret Mead
was no longer a protégée. Now she was a mentor herself.

Mead spoke up always for the "lower classes," as Boas had before
her: "peasants," she once said, "are the only people who have simply
been taught that they cannot think." She could make herself at home
anywhere, and bristled when anyone implied, as people occasionally did,
that she had in her a streak of the snob. On her own time, however,
she gravitated toward people who were tall, elegant, and patrician. One
of her students was amazed at what a "superb interviewer she was,"
and how "in a very few minutes she had good social placement on me
and could tell just where I was coming from," perhaps because he
looked as if he and she might have the same ancestors. Mead always
felt at home among elite middle-class Americans. "I enjoy people who
look like noble members of the human species," she once said, and as
soon as she returned from studying noble Iatmul or noble Manus, she
was welcomed in houses in Australia and England and the United
States by people who had every reason to feel at ease in the world.

The war separated Mead and Bateson, as it did many other couples, for extended periods of time. In the summer of 1943, they both
left Perry Street, where their daughter was cared for by the Franks.
Mead was sent to England by the O.W.I. and Bateson was called to
Washington by the Office of Strategic Services to work as a "psychological planner." The English assignment suited Mead perfectly. "English
she is not," as her husband had warned his mother, but now she had a
chance to find out what his culture was really like. The assignment to
England taught her that "many things about Gregory which I had
thought were merely idiosyncracies were cultural." Studying a civilized
culture, she wrote a friend, was hard: "One of the blessed things about

natives [in primitive places] is that one really can't think of a great deal to say to them."

She also tried to figure out ways for "getting some decent social science done" in England. Officially she had been sent there to make new use of the expertise on courtship practices which she had been building since her return from Samoa. Her task on this trip, as Rhoda Métraux explained it later, was "to clear up a cultural misunderstanding about the American idea of a 'date.'" American GIs and their new English girl friends were not sure who was supposed to be aggressive toward whom, and who better than Margaret Mead to set things straight?

The trouble, as Mead explained in a pamphlet published in 1944 and called "The American Troops and the British: An Examination of Their Relationship," was that English girls had been raised to expect boys to do what American boys expected girls to do: impose restraints. Nobody, as a result, put on the brakes. Everyone, as a result, considered his or her partner immoral. "Everything got pretty well straightened out," Métraux recalled, "and we got some nice English wives."

In London Mead stayed in Chelsea, "in a tiny little house . . . which used to rise in the air and curtsey when the rocket gun went off. It was one of a row of tiny houses, and when there was a bad raid everybody on the street went to stay with the kindest woman, sure that no bombs would find her out. It was rather like going back to just post-college days, only with everyone dreadfully tired out from the war." To her hostesses, one of whom was Cathy's godmother, Mead wrote a thank-you letter that ended "Love and love and love," saying how amazingly exhilarated she had been by experiences everyone around her found draining. Gregory, on her return, had had to "get used to a wife who (1) can walk and doesn't insist on riding for a block or so, (2) smokes of her own volition and may even have cigarettes, and (3) knows a lot about England."

During this visit Mead also marveled at Scottish wheat fields, the Durham sunrise, the Devon countryside, and the ceremonious welcome accorded her by her British audiences, who assured her she had done "a grand job."* She was touched by "a women's gathering in a

---

* Mead's fame spread throughout the British Isles. An eminent Scots obstetrician, Sir Dougald Baird of Aberdeen, announced when he came to visit New York a few years later that there was one American whom he particularly wanted to meet: Margaret Mead. His friend Leona Baumgartner invited him and his wife, Lady Rachel, to dinner to meet Mead. Mead arrived late, went straight to the guest of honor, and said to him: "You're Baird! You're from Aberdeen! But have you ever delivered a woman in the squatting position?" Childbirth was never far from Mead's mind, but it wasn't

tiny church parlor in East Dulwich Grove as a tired, black-clad, middle-aged woman prayed, in a voice of unforgettable sweetness, that 'All those who are on holiday may be having a grand time.' "

In spare moments Mead confirmed some of the suspicions her husband had formed in America about the differences between the two cultures. The British, she would later write, "see the world as a natural world to which man adapts, in which he assumes no control over the future but only the experienced foresight of the husbandman or the gardener, who plants the best seed and watches carefully over the first green blades." American figures of speech, on the other hand, implied control and mechanism. The British countryside, she observed, was "not the place to do things in, it is a place to be in, and the young American has no practice at that kind of acute being."

Gregory and Cathy were delighted to see her when she returned to New York from England, Mead wrote Jane Belo, but not long afterward the family was parted again when the O.S.S. assigned Bateson to go as a "psychological planner" to Ceylon, India, Burma and China. He would be away for twenty months working on matters of psychological warfare. Since Stevens went to Asia too, his wife had room in her house in Georgetown, and it became Margaret Mead's Washington headquarters.

Margaret did not envy Gregory his work. The psychological warfare assignment, she later said, was "disastrous for him," whereas she had been lucky: "I was on the morale-building side, working with allies. The horrors of psychological warfare can come back and hit you in the face. If you break the trust of a people in their own government, by pretending the government is doing something which will destroy them, you have a destroyed people. You've destroyed trust that you need. Any conscious distortion of the truth does harm."

---

every evening that she got to meet an internationally noted expert on the subject. So insistently did she keep to the topic that her hosts and fellow guests tried in vain, among themselves, to switch to other subjects.

"Do you think," Lady Rachel asked her hostess as the dinner continued, "that we can *ever* get out of the pelvis?"

"Not for this evening," replied Dr. Baumgartner, who had known Mead for years, and she was right. When everyone went upstairs for after-dinner coffee, she said, "Margaret still did all the talking, and instead of letting Sir Dougald ask a question, told him all she had seen and done with deliveries in the South Seas.

"At length, when at last the Bairds had to go, Sir Dougald bowed to Margaret, kissed her hand, and said, as sweetly and politely as anything, 'May your next be a breech!' "

Mead, settling back in her chair, replied, "That's the first time a native ever put a hex on me."

Bateson's general task in Asia, as Georgiana Stevens understood it, was to "think up schemes to undermine the morale of the enemy," in particular, at first, by operating a radio station in Burma and Thailand. "We listened to the enemy's nonsense," Bateson said later, "and we professed to be a Japanese official station. Every day we simply *exaggerated* what they were telling people." The work discouraged him, because he did not know to what use the intelligence he collected would be put. In Burma he found a mummified left hand, which a certain family had owned for many generations, and when someone challenged his right to keep it, he had the wit to reply, "But the Japs collected it for me."

Bateson wrote to two aunts of how his two years were "dully wasted in India and Ceylon, trying to introduce a few anthropological ideas into the U.S. intelligence service, relieved by a period of fieldwork in [lower Burma] getting native reactions to the Japanese occupation and returning British raj. . . . What a mess it all is. Native supernaturalism all shot to pieces by materialism gathered from Oxford and Cambridge, and in its place a longing for some sort of supernatural structure." Calcutta appalled Bateson, who found it "the worst thing I know about the British Empire—a thousand Indian villages poured together, stuck together with cow dung, badly leached, with soil no good any more. The whole ecological fitting together of Indian agricultural life all got broken up, all the fault of the British Empire."

At one point during this miserable time, Bateson considered arranging to go to parachute school, so that he could be dropped in the middle of the night into Northern Malaya to look for an old Cambridge friend who had "gone bush" when the Japanese came in, and taken up with a native woman. "The theory was that we wouldn't get out," Bateson said, "so we'd wait there until the Allied Armies swept over Northern Malaya. I was depressed at the time, and this seemed a reasonable form of suicide. But then I found out that my friend's native woman lover had shot him dead."

While Bateson was despondent in Asia, his wife was energetic on the Eastern Seaboard, finding new uses for what she had learned in the Pacific. Since "our people were pretty green about that part of the world," as Georgiana Stevens said, Mead was "teaching a two- or three-week orientation course, so our people going there wouldn't make awful mistakes. She did some useful O.S.S. briefings, too, as well as keeping the food and nutrition study going"; she also gave at least one speech at Yale, at the Research Unit of the Institute of Human Relations, on "Administration of the Smaller South Sea Islands."

"She had a great talent," said Stevens, "for producing ideas and never mind how many secretaries it kept up all night. She and Ruth Benedict were both in Washington for several years. They and other social scientists had seminars in my house, but I didn't see much of them. I always left when they had seminars, and Margaret and I were both doing so many things that we'd meet only at breakfast.

"She never wasted a minute or a meal. All her meals were business meals, and why not? She'd take trains back and forth to New York, and her time was so calibrated that she probably wrote a book each way." She also wrote articles. In the spring of 1943 Mead wrote a piece for the *New York Herald Tribune* that connected the shortage of volunteer nurses with synthetic living. GIRLS PREFER ASSEMBLY LINE NOT ONLY FOR WAGES, the subheadline read, BUT BECAUSE OF LITTLE CONTACT WITH SUFFERING.

She would not have wanted to admit it, but her lengthening absence from her unhappy husband was causing Margaret Mead to suffer, too. That was one reason to keep frenetically busy.

CHAPTER SIXTEEN

"Peace, Queen Esther Victory Speaking"

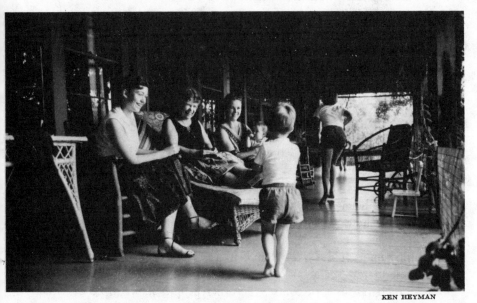

KEN HEYMAN

Many mothers over the years, among them Catherine Bateson (left), Margaret Mead and Mary Frank (later Perry), watched their children play on the porch of Cloverly, the Frank family retreat in New Hampshire.

IN DECEMBER 1981, when Dean Mary Catherine Bateson of Amherst College was interviewed on a television program about her mother, she said Mead had "tended to regret not being around more when I was a very small child." Certainly Catherine's mother was not around much during the war years. The 1943 Christmas holiday, Mead wrote to a friend, was the first time in two years that she had spent three uninterrupted days with her daughter, then just four. Mead and Ruth Benedict, as Georgiana Stevens recalled, would "commute from Washington on weekends, to see Margaret's daughter. I think Ruth Benedict was a lot more motherly, by nature, than Margaret was."

Since Cathy was very small, Mead told a reporter in 1944, she had been accustomed "to a mother who came and went irregularly . . . I think I lose something by that arrangement, but I'm pretty sure she doesn't." Mead never took basic physical care of her child, she once admitted, after the breast-feeding was finished: "I would have adored doing her clothes, but Marie [Eichelberger] cared about it more, so I let her do it"—somewhat, apparently, the way Tom Sawyer "let" his friends help him whitewash the fence. Eichelberger was foremost among the "roof menders," German and otherwise, on whom Margaret relied to "pick up the pieces and bridge the gaps," to quote Larry and Mary Frank's son Colin, who was born in 1941.

As soon as Colin could talk he was taught to call Eichelberger "Aunt Marie." He regarded her as "one of the kindest, least nasty people of my whole life—a WASP yenta who provided bridges at the right moments, and who had a sustaining image of Cathy and Margaret which Cathy and Margaret grew into." Born sixteen months after Cathy Bateson, Colin was brought up, in effect, as her younger brother. While her father was in Burma, or her mother between Washington, D.C., and Dewy Rose, Georgia, Cathy was safe on Perry Street under the care of Colin's parents and a steady stream of other doting adults, of whom some lived there and some made extended visits.

Mead, herself the product of an extended family, had admired big communal households even before her first field trip. The isolated nuclear family, she kept declaring all her life, was the worst possible place to bring up a child. Never would she have dreamed of bringing up her own child—especially an only child—without a great many people around. If possible, of course, the other people ought to be of similar mind and similar temperament. It was her great good luck that the Franks had established just such a household, and that a few blocks away lived Allen and Sara Ullman. Few families' interests could have meshed more closely. Mead would praise Larry Frank as one of the few people ever "who used foundations the way the Lord meant them to be used"; the painter Allen Ullman was a European by birth and in spirit; Sara Ullman had a sense of irreverent mischief as well as a mind Margaret relished. The Ullmans also had an only child, Martha, who was a year and a half older than Cathy.

The two households at 72 Perry Street were merged into what Colin Frank later called "an alliance against emotional problems, both personal and cosmic. That was a horrendous period both in the world's history and in the lives of my father and Margaret." The relationship between his father and Margaret, Colin said, was "very intense, caring, and nonerotic. Neither wanted to be the teddy bear for the other. They were the two co-energizers. They shared a very clear perception of family as a living segment of culture, a nurturant medium to foster thoughts and attitudes."

Of course there also had to be "someone to keep things from imploding," and that someone was Mary Frank, who was "terrifically strong physically and much stronger morally, in many senses, than my father. Her relationship with him and Margaret must have been much more sustained than they acknowledged. Her intensity and adoration relieved the aura of sadness my father had, from having been twice a widower, and gave him a kind of renaissance." Mary Hughes had grown up in the Bronx, where Colin and his brother Kevin, ten years younger, were taken regularly to visit the people they would remember as "our real relatives." Mary had first met the Franks as an N.Y.U. student when they hired her to help care for the older children.

It was suggested to Colin that he might wish to address his father's "co-energizer" as "Aunt Margaret," in the same spirit he called Eichelberger "Aunt Marie," but he declined. Margaret Mead did not seem to need that extra measure of "swaddling," as he came to refer to such support, which in his view served to "insulate the person from gut-level or straight feedback." The objects of such insulation, he said, are regarded as "very dear people, but users," whose "fervent true believers give them a protective coating, like royal jelly."

Why do swaddlers go to all this trouble? "So they can bask in reflected glory. So they can be part of the team, be included in the plans, have ownership, participation, co-authorship." All her life Margaret Mead attracted such people, with whom her relationship was rather feudal. In exchange for their loyalty, which helped her to deal with all manner of practical and emotional problems, they were assured of her protection.

"My name," she would tell such people, the way she told many others, "can open doors. If you ever need or want to use it, do. Don't hesitate."

Most people would have been amazed, Colin Frank said, to see how modest Margaret's quarters were in the merged Perry Street household. "She appreciated the high ceilings in her living room, but otherwise didn't pay much attention to her surroundings. She was obviously someone for whom the life of the mind was most important. What mattered most to her was intellectual stimulation, ceaseless energy, immediate support, and skillful listening."

One frequent visitor to Perry Street in the early 1940s was Eliot Chapple, who recalled that Cathy Bateson was "brought out on display in what seemed a very Victorian picture which the child, without being completely hostile, seemed to resent." Cathy's mother, absent though she often was, had firm ideas about child rearing. Disliking the sound of "Mommy," she insisted that her daughter call her "Mummy," and saw to it that there was something for the little girl to play with, or work on, in every room. Beneath the coffee table was a shelf with sand on it, where Cathy could play while the grownups had cocktails. Next to Margaret's dressing table was an easel, so that Cathy, who showed early talent as an artist, could paint while her mother got dressed to go out. When Cathy was four, her mother wrote, they once went for a walk on the Wellesley campus, during a conference on cross-racial and cross-ethnic relationships. Cathy was "climbing pine trees instead of keeping up with me. I said, 'You come down out of that pine tree. You don't have to eat pine needles like an Indian.'

"So she came down and she asked, 'Why do the Indians have to eat pine needles?'

" 'To get their Vitamin C, because they don't have any oranges.'

" 'Why don't they have any oranges?'

"Then," Mead wrote, "I made a perfectly clear technical error: I said, 'Because the white man took their land away from them.' " Cathy looked at her mother and said, "Am I white?" Yes, she was told, she was white.

"*But I didn't took their land away from them,*" said Cathy, "*and I don't like it to be tooken!*"

"She and Cathy had mental intimacy," Colin Frank reflected, "but Mead was not the cloth mother, as psychologists put it. She had no appetite or skill for day-to-day life. Face it, she couldn't have been the cloth mother and done all the other things she did in the world. I think she and Aunt Marie would both have been happy if Cathy had been born at age three with crinolines and Mary Janes." One ritual Margaret did perform was brushing Cathy's hair, and as she did so, she remembered, she "enlivened the tangles" by asking "was this pull a crocodile? An elephant? A rabbit?" Margaret's own curls meant a lot to her all her life, from the time her grandmother had confided in her, as she brushed them, about her parents; it pleased her to note of her daughter's hair, when Cathy was five, that it glowed "with a kind of texture that makes you feel it might be edible."

Family friends remembered that Cathy rarely cried. Once she wept in sympathy for two of her mother's friends who were angry as they all drove around New Haven getting lost. The women were angry because they had been excluded, on grounds of gender, from a lecture at the Yale Institute of Human Relations. Another time Cathy shed tears when she broke a glass snowball, the kind that creates a blizzard when it is turned upside down, given to her by two of her mother's associates. One of them remembered Cathy once asking her mother whether or not she should go to the bathroom, to which Margaret Mead replied, "There are some things you have to decide for yourself."

But Cathy's mother was not always self-possessed. "My father," Colin Frank recalled, "was one of the few men who could deal with Margaret in an open-handed way without her being put uptight. Sometimes she would come up for breakfast in a snit, and he would give her straight talk, and she would take it." The causes for these "snits" varied, said Colin: "She could be anguished if plans went awry. Maybe her dress wasn't right, maybe dinner wouldn't come out okay, maybe smoke would billow up from her kitchen. Sometimes she'd have a hissyfit over the projector, or the tape recorder, if a little person who'd been assigned to use it handled it wrong. She had no bent or love or time for mechanical or plumbing details."

"We might have a field day," Larry Frank once wrote to Mead, "figuring out why you make people mad, or why they get mad at you, and afraid of you." Although Mead appreciated his firm way when she was upset, she found him "extraordinarily empathetic," to the point of cowardice, in other contexts. "Being a foundation executive," she told another friend, "meant that Larry never had to express an opinion. He didn't want to take risks, wouldn't drive a car or go to movies or read detective stories, because doing these things gave him panicky pains in the stomach." He was, she said on another occasion, "an exceedingly motherly person—not feminine but maternal, feeding, nourishing." Colin, who grew up to become a psychotherapist, recalled his father as being "not exactly self-effacing, but I wanted him to take more credit; I wished he would say 'I *did that!*,' the way Margaret did. She was more self-promotional than he was, although not as much as she later became."

Mead's "jabbing, aggressive manner," Colin said, set the mood of the Perry Street household, and helped to generate "incredible amounts of work. She invoked and evoked the best there was in other people. She'd get them off their butts and tell them, 'Of *course* you can write this dissertation.' Thanks to her, they would turn out to produce much more than they would have thought they were capable of." There was never any lack of people who needed such jabbing; Mead's appetite for company, combined with Frank's, made 72 Perry Street a busy place. "But her busyness," said Colin, "was not as compulsive as it became later." She was not often alone. In solitude, as another friend suggested, "Margaret may have heard too many loud interior voices."

The noise on Perry Street was intergenerational and quite real. Mary Frank, since she was Irish, "treated my daughter beautifully," Mead wrote, "but she didn't love her quite as much as she loved her own son. So my daughter was beginning to learn that anger and love are the same thing, which she wasn't supposed to learn, because she wasn't Irish, after all. As in Kipling's poem, 'For when there are Irish, there's loving and fighting, And when we stop either, it's Ireland no more!' " On Perry Street there was always plenty of loving and fighting and commotion.

Much of the commotion was jointly produced by Cathy and by Mead's goddaughter Martha Ullman. "*Pull your voice down!*" Sara and Margaret would both tell their daughters. Martha's first remembered encounter with Cathy was in 1943, at Perry Street. Cathy was clutching the two Perry Street Persian cats, whom Gregory had christened Bathmat and Queen Victoria, and Margaret instructed her to "Put down those wretched cats and come say hello." Before long the two girls were as attached, and at times as antagonistic, as sisters.

"For a couple of only children," Martha remembered Mead saying, "they had more sibling rivalry!" Once when Martha kicked Cathy in the stomach her mother told her, "If you two children can't play together nicely, I'm going to have to separate you"—as dire a threat as could be imagined. Another time, when there was talk that Cathy might not be allowed to spend the night at the Ullmans', as had been planned, she and Martha both rubbed onion juice into their eyes, in a successful attempt to make themselves weep.

Perhaps partly because of the time she had spent discussing *The Mind in Sleep* with Reo Fortune, Margaret Mead considered a night without a dream a total waste of time. Cathy's easel was moved into her bedroom at night so that she could get up and paint what she had dreamed. (Allen Ullman gave Cathy painting lessons and encouraged her artistic talent.) One morning Margaret found a picture on the easel of "some really horrible-looking snakes," Martha Ullman said, which she, the visitor, had dreamed of and painted. "Until she found out that I had done the picture, Margaret was afraid Cathy must be in serious psychological trouble, because she was not afraid of snakes, as I was and am." (In her book *Male and Female* Mead wrote of how children "wake shrieking from their dreams of strange and terrifying animals that may destroy them.")

"We were all treated as test-tube babies," Colin Frank recalled. "We had all the advantages of social sciences—lots of leeway, lots of attention, protectedness and solidity. We were seldom fawned on but always made to feel precious. Margaret really fostered imaginative play—when I was three and Cathy was four we had a mock wedding. The idea was that if we learned how to organize fantasy worlds, we would grow up knowing how to deal with *the* world."

Colin had a more consistently progressive education than Cathy did. At first Cathy went with Colin to Bank Street School and later with Martha to the Downtown Community School. Mead was enthusiastic about the latter and a similar one, in Washington, D.C., called the Georgetown Day School, whose founding parents included her friends Philleo and Edith Nash. Both schools, she urged, should have nationality quotas and pay attention to rituals, as she had in her own childhood, like May baskets and Valentines.

But later, perhaps feeling that Cathy got enough permissiveness at home, Mead transferred her to Brearley, one of the most rigorous of New York City's schools for girls. When he was eleven or twelve, Colin said, he felt resentful "that my former colleague was turning into a socially aware Brearley girl who was learning to write on unruled white paper. Once when she had a slumber party I carved a bar of soap with what looked like hazelnut clusters and poured chocolate over it, to give to her and her friends, telling them, 'I just want you to enjoy.'"

In earlier years, when the school day was over at Downtown Community, Sara Ullman would pick up both Martha and Cathy. Their classmates' mothers would cluck, "Dr. Mead can't *possibly* be a very good mother if she doesn't come to get her own daughter," but Margaret had made a point, Sara remembered, of not employing a cook: "She could well have afforded one, but she said, 'If I had a cook I would be tempted to go to dinner conferences, but this way I have to come home to make dinner for Cathy.'" Instead of hiring a cook for herself, Margaret paid for a housekeeper to come three times a week to the Ullmans', so that Sara, who stayed at home, would have more time to give both girls the intelligent attention they needed.

"Peace, Ullmans' residence," that housekeeper would say when she answered the phone. "This is Queen Esther Victory speaking, and God's in His heaven." This greeting may have made Mead think of the medieval Julian of Norwich, who said all was well, all was very, very well—and all did seem enviably well with the "hearthiness" she had devised for her daughter and goddaughter. When Cathy came home from visits to this and other households she would point out differences between them and her own. Why, she asked her mother, did the Ullmans put their bread right on the table instead of on a plate? Because, Mead told her, Allen Ullman had grown up in France, where plates were not used for bread: "It isn't the custom." Just as the Iatmul differed from the Tchambuli, so could people on Waverly Place differ from those on Perry Street. In America, as Mead wrote, "The language of each home is different, there is a code in each family that no one else knows."

Margaret had Allen in mind, his daughter later learned, when she referred in her 1949 book *Male and Female* to an artist "with brightly shining hair and gleaming eye," who could "make a roomful of women feel more feminine because he has entered the room," who was "bred in cosmopolitan Europe, in a world where men play the most delicate musical instruments." Such a man, she said, could grow up free of doubts about his masculinity, in contrast to another man she portrayed, modeled on another real-life friend—who grew up homosexual even though he had been raised in the gun-toting, supposedly macho American West. Ullman's copy of *Male and Female* was inscribed "to Allen, who provided the necessary libido."

Although Sara Ullman unquestionably agreed with Mead about her own husband's charm, she admitted finding Mead's husband Gregory so attractive that "I'd have gone after him in a minute if he weren't married to my best friend." She was not exaggerating in calling Margaret her best friend: "Intellectually I couldn't help knowing, of course, that Margaret was a famous person, but I didn't think of her in that context. It had no bearing on our personal relationship."

In the summers the Ullmans would often join the Bateson-Meads, the Franks, and the other social science families at or near Cloverly. The games this group played, Catherine Bateson would remember, were planned by her mother to make sure "that the adults—the anthropologists and psychologists and mathematicians—would never be bored and the children would never be bewildered or ignored." Colin Frank grew up recalling "magic times" at Cloverly: "songs, talk, charades—classic charades with double meanings the adolescents could laugh at—square dances, picnics, rowing back and forth to the island in the lake, and Margaret showing Cathy fairy walking sticks, and Gregory building a water slide, and giving a raft the Balinese name for 'Floating Island.' "

Martha Ullman accumulated New Hampshire memories, too: "Margaret judged floats and parades and was very much a part of things. Some of the greatest times were when Margaret and Gregory were there—you could just feel her, as a spark, squeezing every ounce of participation into whatever was going on." One summer everyone acted out scenes from Shakespeare, with Cathy and Martha costumed in skirts Sara Ullman had got in Mexico, which on them looked like long dresses. "Gregory played Hamlet—my God, he was so handsome," said Martha, "and Mary Frank was Gertrude. Margaret, of course, was director. Another time we had to help hunt all over the stores in the surrounding small towns for yellow stockings because for some reason it was imperative that Malvolio wear yellow stockings. I tell you, attention was paid to detail."

During the time Gregory was away in Asia, Margaret confessed to a friend in a letter from Cloverly that she felt "very lonely and left out and without any role which is any use to anyone," especially during his "particularly bad periods of no letter writing." Until he came back, Margaret wrote, "I have, in a sense, no plans. Go back to work, placate all the people who haven't been in the war and feel rather sour about it, get my office sorted out and rearranged, perhaps actually plan to go to the theatre, and to exhibits, and even give a party or so, again. For it suddenly to be right to plan for pleasure—for adults—I find very disconcerting."

But when Gregory Bateson was part of the crowd at Cloverly—"ARRIVING . . . MIDDAY TOMORROW SATURDAY WITH MUSIC AND CHEESE," he once telegraphed—everyone had fun. Bateson had "the usual English upper-class indifference to children," as Colin Frank put it, "until they were out of the nursery, when he began to take an interest in them." He would put a whole peach in his mouth to see how they would react, and he was not above spitting watermelon seeds across a table.

This familial household extended in many directions and for varying periods of time to take in others. Nobody was exempt from being judged by its standards of excellence. People in it had no doubt that they were special, and this awareness, Colin Frank reflected many years later, was not without its problems. By his lights, the emphasis on achievement was excessive. He and Cathy grew up with the implicit question being not "How far do you think you want to go in school?" but "What will you get your doctorate in?"

When Margaret Mead learned, many years after Colin's boyhood, that he had then found her intimidating, she was "surprised," as he put it, "and even shocked." But more and more, as he wrote in 1980, "I'm seeing how the aura of Margaret took away from the value of ordinary life. . . . How much all of us bit players were there to make up for the sacrifices that she made," unwittingly accepting the sacrifices which "we were required to make in the process.

"Something about being a child was denied," he said, and as a result, "I can't get away from wanting to be the best. Is this a curse?" The best part of growing away from such a background, he said, was "being without the cool façade, the need not to appear to break stride or to sweat."

CHAPTER SEVENTEEN

"I Couldn't Keep Up"

PROFESSIONAL ENDOGAMY, Gregory Bateson once said, has its hazards. Shoptalk in shorthand is a luxury, but competition between spouses can be tense. "When two married dentists, or two married anthropologists, go off to play tennis," as Bateson put it, "they'll both feel much better if one sprains an ankle." He and Margaret Mead were not much for tennis, but they did go on walks. Sometimes when they had just finished a half-hour walk, Mead said, they would go right back to the place they had begun. They would take exactly the same walk over, so as to retrace their conversation along with their steps. "We were trying to work out what the links were," she said, "as we had moved from one place to another."

But after the Second World War was over, and as the 1940s wore on, Bateson and Mead walked more and more in different directions and at different speeds. One fellow anthropologist recalled seeing the two of them "walking down the enormously long fifth-floor corridor of the Natural History Museum, with Margaret always two steps ahead of Gregory and talking like sixty, her hands going like mad—she always talked with her hands as well as her voice. She took two steps to every one of Gregory's. He was behind her, very quietly nodding and agreeing, but she never looked back at all to see whether he was even there. Gregory was nearly a foot taller, but she was much the faster."

"It was almost a principle of pure energy," Bateson said of his marriage with Mead. "I couldn't keep up, and she couldn't stop. She was like a tugboat. She could sit down and write three thousands words by eleven o'clock in the morning, and spend the rest of the day working at the museum."

At the museum Mead was considered formidable. "Before I went to work for her there," one employee said, "I was warned that I would probably have a nervous breakdown, and it was easy to see why. Doors would slam, secretaries would weep, often there was someone in the hallways sobbing. Sometimes I could smell the tension in the tower before I even climbed the stairs to get there—I could feel it right through my skin."

One Monday noon in 1947 an angry woman stormed out of the southwest tower and down to Columbus Avenue to have lunch, alone, beginning with a Scotch and soda. Although it was not Frances Macgregor's custom to drink alcohol by herself, or so early in the day, she was fuming. Margaret Mead, who had given her five books the previous Friday and told her to read them sometime, had just now yelled at her for not having finished all five over the weekend. Who did Mead think she was, a flunky?

Mead of course knew perfectly well who Frances Cooke Macgregor was. "Here," she had said excitedly to Bateson when they saw Macgregor at a 1946 meeting, "is the girl I've been trying to seduce!" The seduction in question was intellectual, and it had succeeded. Macgregor had been persuaded to help Mead analyze the thousands of still photographs Bateson had brought home from Bali before the war, part of their effort to build a bridge between anthropology and the Gesell-Ilg approach to maturation—to see what links there might be between research done by field workers in remote places and studies of the growth of middle-class children conducted at Yale by Drs. Frances Ilg and Arnold Gesell. Child development, in Mead's view, ought to become "a major approach to the study of culture."

The project had been in her mind since the Vassar Summer Institute of 1945, when she heard Dr. Frances Ilg describe, "so vividly that my finger tips tingled, the motor-kinesthetic patterns peculiar to different stages of development." Ever since then she had been meaning "to explore the nexus between the rhythms of given temperaments and the way in which a culture institutionalizes these rhythms so that all individuals born within the culture, at varying cost, are also subjected to the same pattern of learning."

Exploring that nexus was a job for which Macgregor was well suited. A documentary photographer, uncommonly well versed in sociology and anthropology, she was the former wife of the anthropologist Gordon Macgregor (who had done field work in American Samoa a few years after Mead had—and, incidentally, had never in her hearing questioned Mead's work there). Frances Macgregor was also a tennis champion and an author; in 1941 she had written *Twentieth Century Indians*, with an introduction by Mead's museum boss Clark Wissler, and

in 1942 illustrated Eleanor Roosevelt's *This Is America*. After her master's degree, Macgregor was about to work toward her doctorate in
sociology when Margaret Mead, whom she had just met in that spring
of 1946, said, "If you do a book with me it'll do you a lot more good
than getting a Ph.D."

"I gave her four thousand pictures," said Mead, "and shut her
up in the tower for three days and she came out with an analysis of
Balinese hands." Macgregor was kept in an office with opaque windows that kept her from seeing that winter's huge blizzard begin, and
not allowed to talk on the telephone; "Margaret wanted me noncon-
taminated," she said, "with no interruptions, no communications.

"After the third day of looking at these pictures I began to see
some interesting things about hands and body postures, about the way
a child had been bitten by a chicken. I made some notes on a piece of
yellow paper and said, 'Here's all I have to offer you, Margaret,' and
then I heard her on the phone exulting: 'Gregory!' she said. 'Frances
has put her finger on the middle of Balinese culture!' " Mead's theory
had worked: "without getting any clues or stimulation from anyone,
operating completely alone, half the time not knowing what I was
doing, I made some suggestions about the cultural aspects of motor
habits and developments that fit into her larger theoretical scheme."
Macgregor thereupon became part of what Mead sometimes thought of
as an "orchestra" of people whose skills she was continually discovering, interweaving, and assigning to unexpected tasks—"Except I'm so
unmusical," Mead added, "that probably 'opera' would be a better
word—it includes the people that do the scenery."

Not until that Monday morning had Macgregor learned that even
prized members of Mead's orchestra-opera were not immune to her
stormy temper. "She didn't yell at *me* until that day, and I didn't know
that the reason she was so red in the face was that she really was mad at
her secretary—not at me. When she was bothered herself, I later
learned, she scolded you and put *you* on the defensive. Not knowing
this yet, I sat there over my lunch and thought: 'Do I need this? Am I
going to live in an atmosphere this difficult? And yet, if I leave after
just six weeks, nobody will believe I quit—they'll think I was fired.' "

After lunch, back in her office, Macgregor was still brooding about
all this when Mead came in, "with her arms crossed, like she did, and
a little-girl face." "Are you unhappy?" Mead asked.

"Yes, I am!" Macgregor told her. "I don't need this!"

"Do you think you need a psychoanalyst?" asked Mead, as she was
asking a good many other people in this stage of her life.

"Of course not," snapped Macgregor. What she needed, she made clear, was to be treated like the responsible and accomplished grownup she was. She thereafter made a point of being "very outspoken with Margaret—if I hadn't been, she'd have ridden all over me." And so they got on with the project that led to the book *Growth and Culture*.

For the year Macgregor worked at the museum, she was supposed to spend three days there a week, "but I actually spent ten," she said. "Margaret had my phone number and she never thought twice about using it, nights and weekends. It was tough and marvelous; I never had such training before or since." But a year or so later, when her work was done, the book still had no publisher.

"Well," Mead rationalized, "this is the atomic age—I guess nobody wants to read about the Balinese."

"So my department head won his bet after all," replied Macgregor.

"What bet?" asked Mead. On a trip back to Missouri to take the examinations for her master's degree, Macgregor explained, she had told her department head that she and Margaret Mead were working together on a book. He had bet her $50 that Mead would not finish her part of this collaboration. Mead, hearing this story, was appalled.

"Am I the sort of person people make *bets* about?" she asked. Macgregor resolved to keep quiet about the lack of a publisher, and did for some months.

"I wish you'd stop badgering me about that book," Mead said to her suddenly.

"I haven't said a word," said Macgregor.

"What do you think I am," replied Mead. "Nontelepathic?" But finally, in 1951, Putnam's, which had published Macgregor's book about American Indians, agreed to bring out *Growth and Culture*. Macgregor agreed to reduced royalties, so the book was printed at cost, and respectfully reviewed, and she and Margaret Mead remained close friends for the rest of Mead's life.

The level of excitement was high in the southwest tower of the museum, no matter what Mead's mood was. Her brain, Macgregor said, was "like a calculator, spewing out ideas. She was in a commanding position, committed to the idea that the concepts of anthropology were something the world should know about. No matter what tears and tantrums went on in that tower office, an air prevailed that everyone there was just dying to help Margaret, in however menial a capacity. Sometimes people there would boast: 'I just picked up her things from the cleaners!' "

One noon another employee, a girl of seventeen, wandered up to Mead's turret by chance. She was working as an assistant to the executive secretary of the New York Academy of Sciences, and from her desk, just outside the Hall of Dinosaurs, she made lunch-hour explorations to different parts of the museum. As she found her way up the spiral stairs to Mead's office, she saw a woman who appeared to her to fit the classic grandmother image.

"Come in, child," the woman said. Florence Blau, the child, did not know who this woman was. She could only see that the room she worked in was hopelessly cluttered, and that when she stood up she looked uncommonly short. She was also uncommonly inquisitive. Was Florence visiting the museum with her high-school class? No, Florence had finished high school before her sixteenth birthday and was working to help pay for her night classes at college. Then Florence returned to her own office to tell about the curious person she had met.

"Childie," said her boss, "that's Margaret Mead!" Florence Blau and Margaret Mead fell into a habit of having occasional lunches, and midafternoon tea with cookies. "She wanted to know all about my social life, and marveled that anybody in that day and age had the stamina to go to college at night. She told me my working days and going to college at night showed pioneer spirit that would become more and more prevalent. She was fascinated that my father was a night-club entertainer, and wondered how so many moves had affected my schooling"—which must have reminded Mead of her own itinerant childhood—"and how I could have finished school at such an early age. It had never occurred to me before that I had any more brains than the average brat. Only much later did I realize that she must have found these conversations as fascinating as I did.

"The great thing of my life at the museum was meeting Gregory Bateson, so large and gorgeous and macho. I never saw the two of them together, nor did I ever hear her talk about him. It was a big shock to me later to discover that they were man and wife."

They were not to remain so for long. This marriage, Bateson's biographer David Lipset wrote, "had slowly given way to its original alias, professional convenience. . . . Mead's inexorable fecundity and force of character no longer bolstered Bateson's intellectual and personal sprawl, as it had when they were both focused in the same research." Mead, Bateson once said, didn't forget anything. "She had total recall. I am, on the whole, inclined to think that it is a good thing to forget . . . it is an automatic way of deciding what is important."

"Gregory and Margaret," said their friend Harriet Harvey, "each needed a full-time caretaker." Gregory, said the psychotherapist Rollo May, was "not a guy you could push around. If you did, he'd tell a joke and act as if nothing had happened, but he'd move away. Margaret had a need to put everyone, including him, in his place. She would swing her broadsword and clip off ears and *then* communicate."

"Gregory's interest was in systems," said the anthropologist Lola Romanucci-Ross, "and Margaret's was in pattern. Her tendency was to generalize from 'data' to statements with global implications; one difference between them was that she could communicate and could make things clear to the general public. His interest remained in ideas." (At Mead's memorial service Bateson, who outlived her by a year and a half, said that it would be difficult indeed to assess specifically her contributions to social science, but that they were real.) In 1946, Bateson taught a course in anthropological theory at the New School for Social Research. One of his students recalled him as "tall and awkward and shy, without any stage presence whatever in front of a class of knowledgeable New York evening students.

"We struggled through the first two weeks' sessions together. At the third session, Margaret Mead came to the class and sat in the middle of the middle aisle of seats, squarely facing her husband. As Bateson struggled through his lecture, Mead would rise dramatically from her seat and correct him on a minor point.

" 'No, Gregory,' she would say, 'it was not *that* way at all. It was *this* way . . .' and then go on to explain in her wonderfully crystal-clear manner. This went on for two more weeks, and then Mead took over the class completely, this time from the front of the classroom.* Bateson did not return to the New School after that, and we knew that he and his marriage were definitely riding the greased skids to oblivion."

In the 1947–48 academic year, Bateson was a visiting professor of anthropology at Harvard, teaching a course about the peoples of Oceania and spending too much time, someone once heard Mead say, "gold-bricking" with his students. "He'd walk into class very shy," recalled the anthropologist Louis Dupree, "and put kinship genealogies on the blackboard for a number of minutes that seemed to last forever, and say, 'You obviously see . . .' and make some point that we didn't see at all. He left us behind at the starting gate; he was an abominable teacher. At the time his bag was psychoanalysis; he thought

* Not all Bateson's New School students were disenchanted: the *New York Times* book critic Anatole Broyard took the cultural anthropology course too, and recalled him as "a wonderful teacher."

we should all try it. He insisted that it had to be done by psychiatrists, though, and not by psychologists. He was very taken with Harry Stack Sullivan's theory of interpersonal relations—which included the idea that when people appear to be mentally ill, the thing to do is look to see who's around them. Sullivan spoke almost as turgidly as Talcott Parsons, of whom it was said that 'Parsonian' was so abstruse that it ought to be allowed for one of the two foreign-language requirements.* As Gregory kept emphasizing the need for psychoanalysis, I was tempted to tell him, 'You're *still* a fruitcake.' " It was rumored that Bateson's insisting on the importance of psychoanalysis for one and all was the reason he was not rehired at Harvard.

Bateson began analysis himself in 1946, when he was forty-two, "to sort of have a look at things," and became deeply involved. His analyst, whom he met through Mead, was Elizabeth Hellersberg, a Jungian who had studied with Karl Jaspers and who belonged to a close-knit group of psychologists educated in Germany. Hellersberg, to one member of this circle, seemed "distraught and flummoxed; she didn't give the impression of mental stability." Mead shared this view. "Gregory threw Elizabeth Hellersberg into such a bad panic," she said, "that the rest of us all had to spend our time rescuing *her*."

Hellersberg did not maintain the customary analyst's detachment from patients. She went along on a vacation to Nova Scotia with Bateson, another woman, and Karsten Stapelfeldt (who was divorced from the Ash Can Cat Pelham Korteheuer). On that vacation Gregory and Karsten spent much of their time taking pictures. "Photography," said Stapelfeldt, "seemed a fine, male occupation. Once when I was trying to get the proper focus for a picture of a shabby old cottage, I accidentally stepped backward into a pond where fishermen had been busy degutting their catch. I stood knee-deep in fish innards, and all the fishermen were crazy with laughter, which I tried to ignore as I walked into the sea to clean off the mess with salt water. Gregory stepped right into the water beside me, to inspect the sea anemones and the shellfish. What did he care if his pants were cold and wet?"

During his analysis with Hellersberg, Bateson once told Gotthard Booth, another analyst who was a friend of his and Mead's, about a dream he had had. His dream was of a two-part box, with a mother rat

---

* In 1944 Parsons had written to Mead saying he was "very glad that the fiasco here"—apparently she had been offered and then denied a job in the Harvard Sociology Department—"has not proved too bad a letdown for you. You are right that the woman question is not central to our major problem here just now and Clyde [Kluckhohn] and I had wanted you not as a woman but as a social scientist. In that connection our regrets are very severe."

in one part and her babies in the other. The baby rats kept trying to escape, and the mother would retrieve them and return them to their nest. The mother rat, Gregory told Booth, probably symbolized Margaret. "It's your dream," Booth told him. Mead, repeating this story years later, said there was often a mothering element in the way others perceived her: "Ruth and my husbands and other adults all had an incorrigible tendency to see me as mother, because I treat adults the same way my grandmother treated my parents." Total strangers, she also said, often came up to her to tell her she reminded them of their mothers, "no matter what their real mothers looked like or were like."

Mead, too, enthusiastically recommended psychoanalysis to almost everyone around her, including her staff at the museum. "The atmosphere there was so analytically oriented, it permeated everything," said Ellen Godwin, an employee in the early fifties, who for a while was the only person in the office, aside from the boss, who was not being analyzed. When her colleagues would come back from their psychiatrists and spend "hours talking over what had happened," she felt a little out of things. Not that she didn't have her share of difficulties, but "in Syracuse, where I came from, we didn't do that sort of thing." But finally she went to tell her problems to Mead, who at once arranged for her to see Gotthard Booth. "She said that for me it had to be a Jungian—it was so refreshing, the way she knew where everyone should fit in." Having Booth, "this wonderful, elderly man," as her analyst immediately raised Godwin's stock at the office, and taught her something about her boss: "Booth told me," said Godwin, "that he saw people whose problems included Margaret Mead."

For a certain period Booth and Mead met from time to time to confer about Bateson. When these sessions ended, Mead said, Booth wrote to tell her that he "felt very bereaved at being cut off so suddenly from my teeming inner and outer worlds." But however teeming her worlds were, Mead never underwent psychoanalysis herself. For the upper ten percent of the upper ten percent, she once contended, there is no analyst. Stapelfeldt remembered a night when he and Bateson finished a bottle of Scotch and decided, as many had before and would later, that Margaret Mead was unanalyzable.

"She was willing to try anything *but* psychoanalysis," said her colleague Fred Eggan. "It wouldn't have told her anything she wanted to know." Martha Ullman recalled Margaret's saying that some people needed to bury things, rather than drag them out, "and she didn't feel that anyone else had any business plumbing her own depths."* "She

* Her eminent psychiatrist friend Karen Horney could have had Mead in mind when she wrote in 1942, "A person attempting to analyze himself

should *not* have been an analyst/therapist," said Colin Frank, "because to do that she would have had to look into herself, which she clearly preferred not to do, was determined not to. For her it would have been like sitting on a tack. She and my father were always promoting analysis and therapy for others, but never for themselves. Maybe they figured that it was enough for them to be unblocked intellectually, which God knows they both were."

Nevertheless, analysts from time to time would beg Mead, she said, to give up anthropology and join their profession; all her life people marveled at her gifts as a teacher and helper of others. She rather marveled at these gifts herself. "You don't need an analyst," she told one troubled friend. "You can come to me." Her friend Sara Ullman phoned one morning in the late 1940s to say that something terrible had come up in a session with her psychiatrist. Was Margaret free to talk over the terrible news at lunch? For Sara, to whom she once concluded a letter with the simple command, "Be happier," Mead always found time. Hearing the details of Sara's problems, Margaret seemed relieved. "I thought you'd just learned that you had cancer," she said, "so I was figuring out what to do with Allen and Martha. What you need is a different psychiatrist"—whereupon, Sara said, "she arranged for me to go to one *hell* of a good one."

Lawrence Kelso Frank and Margaret Mead had been discussing psychoanalytic ideas ever since the 1934 Hanover conference. In 1940 Frank had assigned Mead to make a study of the existing literature on psychosomatic medicine, which she refused to publish until seven years later—that is, "until I could find out why half the Freudians said 'There's nothing new in this,' and the other half called it entirely false and a contradiction of Freud."

In 1948 Frank was chairman of the International Preparatory Commission that preceded the Second World Congress on Mental Health, which was to attract five thousand delegates from twenty-seven countries. The commission met in Roffey Park, south of London. "I was responsible for Larry being chairman of that commission," Mead said: Frank had never chaired an international meeting, and he "knew very little about international affairs, and we had very tricky ones on our hands. . . . I also had to work to see that they didn't turn mental

---

would simply fail to make any self-observations that would lead to insights as yet intolerable. Or he would interpret them in such a way as to miss the essential point. Or he would merely try to correct quickly and superficially an attitude conceived by him as faulty, and thereby close the door to further investigation."

health into a religion when nobody was looking." If the term "mental health" seemed vague and ambiguous, she later said, it should; it was "the name for a moving target for the welfare of the children of today and the children of tomorrow."

This meeting was to be more interdisciplinary, more international, and more ambitious than any ever held before. The twenty-five delegates at the ten-day Roffey Park preparatory meeting included Frank, Mead, Harry Stack Sullivan, and an Irish priest and scholar Eammon Feichin O'Doherty, who called the occasion the turning point of his own life. It drew "a collection of people in the world of mental health the like of which had never come together before or would since."

Still, "those whose chief interest is the mind," O'Doherty wrote later, "should also have a keen interest in the workings of their own minds, especially as this is revealed in their intra-group behavior. . . . Multidisciplined thinking demands that the corners be knocked off my too rigid schemata of conceptions by their clash with yours, so that I emerge not with, I think, a new concept—this seems to me to be psychologically repugnant—but with a drastically modified one. . . . My greatest anxiety for the future is that those who decry the existence of [interpersonal conflicts and tensions] may water down composite bodies like the IPC so that they become groups of prearranged yes-men, or mutual-admiration societies."

"We went off on a wild-goose chase," said another member of the IPC, "and brought down a crow. It is astonishing how wide in our own case was the distance between knowledge and insight; the lesson of the IPC was: You can call men and women together from all countries and all professions; and you will find them very willing to give time and energy, ingenuity and intelligence, and all the best things they have, and you may find yourself hampered by boundaries of the mind arising from national or professional training; but self-knowledge and self-discipline has not so far advanced that self-direction and all it implies may be expected to emerge spontaneously."

O'Doherty and Mead charmed each other. "He's a perfectly delightful creature," she remarked, "a many-sided, multi-faceted man who's a priest and a philosopher and a professor of psychology and a friend of all the young poets in Ireland—very perennially youthful with enormous ease in the world as a priest. . . . He'd put his arm around any woman without the slightest embarrassment." O'Doherty, then and later, found Mead "so bubbling with ideas, so overflowing, she was like a sculptor with a block of stone; she knew something was there but she couldn't say in advance what it would be. Her speech was like chisel

and hammer. We'd argue, she'd say, 'You're intolerable! Unpardon-
able!,' but with all her imperfections she was a great enrichment to me.
I learned so much, saw so much, and was able to give so much more to
my students because of the way she clarified things I had seen only
dimly before, and made them seem so luminous."

But for Mead the IPC meeting had painful moments. She must
have felt a little the way she had during sorority rush at DePauw: she
and some others were excluded from much of the planning. She must
have felt, for once in her life, peripheral. Harry Stack Sullivan, inventor of the phrases "interpersonal relations" and "significant other," had
had the nerve to try to "subvert his own creation," as Mead wrote, "by
selecting a small group of kindred spirits and taking them away from
the conference for a day and a night of private planning and revelry."
Sullivan picked three or four IPC people "and took them all for two
days to stay at an inn and get drunk and form a clique that would
wreck the conference," Mead said. "And so it was a pretty tough job
to keep that conference on any kind of an even keel, with Harry just
devoted to wrecking it, and I was determined he wasn't going to
wreck it . . ."

This schism, introduced into a conference that Mead said was "already overloaded with conflicting objectives," never did heal. Sullivan,
she remembered, had "started out attacking me and baiting me in every
conceivable way" at Roffey Park. "People thought we'd known each other
forever . . . that if we hadn't gone to nursery school together, that
we had at least been childhood sweethearts [but] of course we had
never met at all. So the whole group was pretty disoriented by his behavior. . . . He could be incredibly nasty.

"The turning point . . . came when he was sitting in the middle
of the room in a big chair drinking his seventeenth Scotch. And I came
along, and I pushed a little hassock next to him and sat on it, and he
said, 'All right, little dog,' and from then on he stopped fighting." He
was approving when Mead, the only person at the IPC who had read
all the reports submitted for the congress, "had them carried out and
stacked on the table behind me—piles and piles and piles—they had all
been bound alike so they looked very anal and impressive—and then I
[spoke of the contributions everyone had made]. When I came off the
platform, Harry looked at me and said, 'You can die now,' which meant
both, 'You've done a good job,' and, of course, 'Drop dead.' "

When the time came for the full-scale congress, Mead was her
confident self again, as she urged the thousands of delegates to influence the framers of society, and especially the writers of tax laws, to

pass legislation that would foster mental health. She also spoke in praise of guilt. Guilt, in her view, could be healthy when it made people pay taxes and prevented them from throwing banana peels in the street. In a democratic society, she said, guilt was a necessary thing.

To the conference the participants brought a lot of what were later called hidden agendas. Some were committed to seeing that mental health did not become a substitute for religion or ideology in their own countries; some had just the opposite aim. Despite these conflicts, Mead pronounced the meeting a success.

It was a good thing Mead's professional life was flourishing, because her marriage, the only marriage of her three that really mattered to her, was over. "She never left any of her husbands and families, she just got more of them," one of her later students observed, and while this view is not entirely inaccurate, it is a little sentimental. Cressman and Fortune parted from Mead more or less at her convenience, but Bateson left her at his. He left her, Karsten Stapelfeldt said, when she "became a statue," but that did not mean she wanted him to go. She did not want him to go at all, nor did she like not being in control. Losing him, Stapelfeldt thought, seemed to hurt her more than she could ever bring herself to say.

"This is going to be a rough year," Mead told one museum associate. "Gregory will be in Staten Island." He had left home, and their friends were not surprised. One day his Staten Island phone rang, with an invitation to a dinner party in Manhattan.

"It's a long way," Bateson demurred.

"But Margaret won't be there," said his hostess, thinking this information might lure him.

"Maybe not, but the network will."

Mead's network of friends and colleagues, most of whom were perceptive and talkative, was getting bigger all the time. Avoiding them grew harder and harder and, for Bateson, more and more necessary. Eventually he did what other men in Mead's life had done before him: he went as far away from her, in the continental United States, as he could get.

Gregory Bateson's office at Harvard had adjoined that of A. L. Kroeber, a founder of the Department of Anthropology at the University of California. Kroeber recommended Bateson to the Swiss psychiatrist Dr. Jurgen Ruesch, who was beginning a research project to study the psychology of communication at the Langley Porter Neuropsychiatric Clinic in San Francisco. Early in 1949, Bateson accepted Ruesch's invitation to go there to join in a study of human communication in psychotherapy. His initial work there, incorporating his interest in cybernetics—the science of control and communication in both animals and machines—led to other research into communication among other species, at first the otter and later the dolphin. What, Bateson wondered as he watched these animals, was play? "He roamed freely," the writer Barbara Bick said, "to integrate the disciplines of anthropology and sociology, psychiatry and the biological sciences, psychoanalysis and cybernetics, and most of all, communication and learning theories."

He considered these matters at annual conferences of the Josiah H. Macy Foundation, led by Larry Frank. Bateson's contributions to these meetings, as the cybernetician Heinz von Forster remembered, made considerable use of allegory as an explanatory device. Von Forster was asked to his first Macy conference on March 20, 1949, shortly after his arrival in the United States, to match his cybernetics theory with the conferees' data. "Look," he was told, "what you say is very interesting, but your English is abominable. We have a method for you to learn fast: you can edit our newsletter!" This idea was Margaret Mead's. The conferences, said von Forster, were "one big interruption—a free-for-all. Everybody would jump at one another in a very friendly way. If things were derailed, Larry would bring it back into line. Nobody cared whose ideas were whose; there was such generosity! It couldn't happen again; we'd have to invent it afresh." His colleague D. W. Harding suggested that "the open-mindedness of other professionals who gave [Bateson] scope could probably have been found during his lifetime only in America. Nowhere else could he have pursued his unorthodox lines of research with so much financial support . . . including support for research that failed . . . from official sources and scientific foundations."

Later Bateson lectured at the Veterans' Administration hospital in Menlo Park, and did research with schizophrenics and in family therapy. His 1956 paper "Toward a Theory of Schizophrenia" explained his view of what he called the "double bind," suggesting that schizophrenia can result when a child is given ambiguous instructions and then penalized no matter which way he reacts; whatever he does is wrong. Psychoanalysis, he thought, was for all its shortcomings "*the* outstanding contribution . . . to our understanding."

Bateson and Mead were officially divorced on October 23, 1950. The next year he married Betty Sumner, a bishop's daughter who was a psychiatric nurse. Mary Catherine Bateson went west on school vacations to visit. In 1951 she was introduced to her new half-brother John, named after Gregory's oldest brother. Two years later twins were born, named William and Anne, who lived for only a month. Personal sorrows aside, Bateson found the West Coast "a good place to gestate ideas. If you have a new idea in the East, they'll shoot it down, but if you have the idea in California, and nourish it, and let it get some feathers on it, then you can take it to the East and see if it can stand up."

Margaret's only brother Richard had settled outside Los Angeles with his second wife, Jessica, the sister of his first wife, Helene, who had died of cancer. Richard, whom Margaret visited faithfully, taught economics at the University of Southern California and became devoted to his step-grandchildren. It was "real nice," he wrote her in one letter, "to see so much of the baby."

The West Coast also agreed with Luther Cressman, still happily entrenched in Eugene, Oregon, where he was becoming more and more preoccupied with archeology. His career prospered; in 1942 the eminent Kroeber had complimented him on "the care and exhaustiveness of your study and on the way in which you have pressed interpretation to the limit of what the evidence allows without ever straining beyond it." The honest and faithful sharpshooter was now too delighted with his work, his wife, and their daughter to give more than passing thought to Margaret Mead. Margaret must have thought of Luther at times, but she allowed an account of her life in a 1951 edition of *Current Biography* to refer to "her first husband, the New Zealand anthropologist Dr. Reo Fortune." (From Bali, however, Mead had written to her mother asking to have Fortune's name deleted from her entry in *Who's Who in America*, where she had first been listed in the 1934–35 edition.)

Reo Fortune had also been on the West Coast of America, but he was merely passing through. In 1938 he and his second wife, Eileen, had stopped in Berkeley on their way from South China to Toronto, where he would teach at the university. The Fortunes had left China when the Japanese arrived, according to Richard Salisbury, who was later Fortune's student. They "arrived in California so penniless that they couldn't afford to ship all their luggage to Toronto, and so they stored some of it at a museum in Berkeley."*

• •

* Twenty years later, when Salisbury's work took him back to California, he wrote to Fortune, then in Cambridge, England, to say that the museum where he had left his things was to be torn down, and to ask what should be done with the luggage. In the flurry of correspondence that followed, it became clear that in spite of the passage of two decades, the Fortunes had an uncannily precise memory of exactly what was where in each of the suitcases they had left behind in California, and knew exactly what they wanted shipped to them in Cambridge.

Reo Fortune was a worry to those who cared about him. "As raw material for an anthropologist," Malinowski had written to Haddon in 1936, Fortune was "perhaps the most gifted of his generation. This at least is my opinion . . . he has done a great deal of extremely good field-work. He has considerable capacities for a theoretical grip of the subject. As far as I can see, he would probably restore the great tradition of Cambridge anthropology, if he would get the job there. At the same time, his defects are obvious. He is not a good lecturer yet, although I think he could develop into one. He has no experience of teaching . . ." Haddon agreed, in his reply, that Fortune could "not express himself clearly in speech and not too clearly in writing," and was a "very bad lecturer. . . . To be quite frank I doubt if he would stand much chance . . ."

The next year Malinowski had written to Haddon that Fortune had been "badly treated by destiny; he has the feeling that every man's hand is against him, and I feel that, if I fail to act on his behalf to the best of my ability, I shall be delivering the final thrust, so to speak." Field work, Fortune had observed in a letter to Malinowski, affected both the people who did it and the outcome of their work. "Is it not true," he asked, "that you can get a different type of scientific result by a different treatment of your field worker? Take one field worker— dip him in one culture once or repeatedly—one kind of result achieved. Take another field worker—dip him repeatedly in several very variant cultures—another kind of general result achieved. I'd not take particular credit for individual prowess, but I've had this latter treatment; and it does seem to me that it leads to a different type of result—in science. . . . Since I'm having a lot of varied field work invested in me I am in a sense like it or not, an administrative method on trial. Either you approve the type of scientific result so obtained; or you approve as a positive preference the one man one field and necessarily different type of result."

In Toronto, Fortune was vividly remembered, among other reasons, for an encounter with Thomas McIlwraith, head of the Anthropology Department, who was not a beloved figure; he "suffered a long list of junior colleagues," of whom "none lasted more than two years. All later went on to international recognition. Toronto's Anthropology Department was noted solely for those who left," said the ethnographer Edmund Carpenter, who is best known for his studies of North American Indians. "It was rumored Fortune got fired for suggesting, in class, that the unique human feature of face-to-face sexual intercourse might have influenced human development. I once asked McIlwraith if this story was true: in a hushed voice, he confided, yes," wrote Carpenter.

"That point can now be found in many introductory textbooks. Jacob Bronowski was fascinated that a subject he discussed over TV in the 1970s cost a scholar his job thirty years earlier."

On one occasion Fortune offered to fight a duel with McIlwraith, using any weapons they might choose from the Armor Gallery of the Royal Ontario Museum, where both had their offices. In making this suggestion, said Carpenter, Fortune was merely expressing "a widely shared sentiment. What makes the story amusing is the method. Fortune was a gentleman."

In 1947, Fortune had returned to Cambridge, where he lived for the rest of his life in a cottage he named Bonde Mteko. "You may be honest in your intentions about work," he wrote to Mead in July 1949, after she had written asking to see him there. "On the Sepik, however, you loved it so much you sat and looked at it for hours. You also put your private affairs first: and I am definitely not interested in any later rationalizations of your messianic message of 1932. It was mostly about 'southern' sweetness & light & 'northern' responsibility for power politics, and was a dishonest way of treating your private affairs. I do not care how you have rationalized it later— It was quite recognisable for what it was as it was. There is no question of handling that kind of thing in what you call poetic terms—or scientific ones for that matter. It is not serious that from any thorough point of view you have not made Arapesh history intelligible. It is merely unfortunate that since the Arapesh did a certain amount of killing to try to keep marriages stable, you should have played that particular point down. It looks like a reaction of your own personality: and not just inadequate field work— though I know it is the latter. . . .

"I trust that any real points if there are any you may have about work can be handled in an hour at most. Yours sincerely, Reo F. Fortune." In December 1949 he wrote her again: "Papuans believe in divinity incarnate in every birth, a redeeming atonement in every bloody death & other caused by sorcery, whereas Christians believe in one divinity revealed in one birth & in one violent death alone if they believe in revelation—Jews do not believe in Incarnation or in sacrificial redemption—not in Christ, anyway. The Arapesh said that they did not like married women running from one piece of taile [sic] to another— even if one is larger than another— They said that they used to kill people over divorce to propitiate the ghosts of their mothers and sisters, who would else lead them & their wives into temptation. Human sacrifice was a communication between profane remarks and religious remarks by means of the victim destroyed in ambush & war—as Hubert &

Mauss *Année Sociologique*—I think 1898 or 1899—pretend to believe in Hebrew & in Hindu gods equally—sacerdotal sacrifice establishing communication between a profane 'world' and a sacred 'world'—by means of a victim—2 worlds in that theory.

"There should be a general explanation of what the matter has been to make wars here or there. However, I am not sure yet what it is—are you? I was hurt at your saying it was persons of my temperament—the Arapesh & Gregory and your 'maternal' in contrast. Yours sincerely, Reo F. Fortune." Hers sincerely: Fortune was hurt, indeed, more visibly than either of Mead's other husbands, and not just by their professional disagreements.

In due course Mead established cordial relations with all her ex-husbands and worked to do so with their new wives, but this at first was difficult, especially in the case of Bateson. His departure, Colin Frank remembered, caused a "discernible thud. The whole Perry Street cosmos was jolted, but many positive things prevented that one event from being so devastating. At one level Margaret could realize, intellectually, that their relationship was special, had a span of time, was over, but [there was] the sting of being rejected, too."

"She didn't understand about men," said one Mead friend. "She didn't know you couldn't ride roughshod over them all the time. She didn't see that they couldn't take it. What she minded desperately, about Gregory, was that he and she could no longer work together. She didn't understand what it was he got from those girls." (There apparently had been other women in Bateson's life for some time.)

"Something about Margaret," said Francis Rawdon Smith, a scientist and the author of *Theories of Sensation,* who had known Bateson at Cambridge and later became his and Mead's close friend, "made men who fell for her think she could solve all their problems. It didn't work out very well for her husbands. Reo was the brightest and most pathetic, the one she clobbered most permanently. She didn't pull Gregory apart as much as she did the others.

"Not that he got off scot-free; he and she were both determined on success at the expense of scientific exactitude. Gregory, the son of the great biologist, abandoned scientific method. He felt, as Margaret also did, that the price of success was to be more spectacular than sound, by making more or less oracular, intuitive statements about things, some of which happened to be right.

"The competition for newspaper space, which those two people, under the same roof, both coveted, must have been intense."

CHAPTER EIGHTEEN

"The Most Brilliant Army Ever Assembled"

"SUCH CELEBRITIES, YET!" the poet Louise Bogan wrote in a letter to a friend in May 1948, just after a party at the New School for Social Research where she had encountered her old Barnard associates Margaret Mead and Ruth Benedict. "Ruth was looking old and beautiful," Bogan wrote, "Margaret as 'earthbound' as ever." The two women had indeed become celebrities. Mead's unswerving campaign to make her name and voice ever more public was reaping unexpected rewards, not all of them flattering. By expanding her focus so far beyond her original subjects, the South Seas and adolescence, she was beginning to invite caricature, and had inspired a bit of irreverent doggerel:

> Margaret Mead, Margaret Mead,
> Helps to fill our country's need,
> Thinks our culture is much lower
> Than the one that's in Samoa . . .

To Mead and Benedict the assessing and comparing of cultures was hardly a joke; it was one of the enduring aspects of their shared intellectual life. Benedict's 1946 book *The Chrysanthemum and the Sword*, an anthropological analysis of Japan, had won wider acclaim than any of her previous work, even *Patterns of Culture*. Without ever having set foot in Japan, in the course of her studies, which began with an assignment from the Office of War Information, she had learned enough, A. L. Kroeber wrote, to make one "proud to be an anthropologist."

Her new book, he said, showed "what can be done with orientation and discipline even without speaking knowledge of the language and residence in the country." It also, in Mead's view, "created a generally favorable attitude toward anthropological work on other modern cultures and demand for more work of the same kind. . . . It was the kind of book that colonels could mention to generals and captains to admirals without fear of producing an explosion against 'jargon.' "

Benedict distinguished between "cultures . . . which rely heavily on shame [like Japan] and those that rely heavily on guilt." A Greek Catholic friend of Mead's once told her he felt a personal responsibility for Hiroshima, and guilt about it, simply as a member of the human race. She did not feel that way at all. By her own "very Western Protestant ethics" Mead held herself accountable "for what I actually do and not for what other people do, and I have no sense of sharing in the great guilt of the human race." In her view there were two kinds of guilt: "the thing they call good guilt, which is like good aggression or good anxiety, and the bad kind, which can be confused with pathology or sin." The best way to approach the "overreaching fact and context to which all other contexts are subordinate," she said, was through what she called the " 'ought' factor"—to ask herself what she ought to do, "as a person so placed as I am in my capabilities at a given moment in the light of a general recognized mandate that it is the task of human beings at this moment to cherish and protect the lives of men and the lives of the world." More simply, *noblesse oblige.*

Mead took this task very seriously and methodically, with the help of Ruth Benedict. From its start, twenty-five years earlier, their friendship had been a constant and deliberate mixture of work and love. Each had read everything written by the other. Across continents and oceans and rooms, for all that time, the two had been exchanging theoretical ideas, love poems, and memoranda. They had marveled together at the Grand Canyon and the Sistine Chapel, and seen each other through many liaisons and the waverings of four marriages, three of them Margaret's.

Now, with the world in peril, they determined that anthropology should extend its boundaries, embrace other disciplines, and find all the applications it could. They saw no reason why anything should be off-limits for them. Mead had said in 1944 that she was "tired of working on such a large canvas," but now her aims were more grand than ever. Cultural anthropology, for example, could take on the witchhunt being led in the late 1940s and early 1950s against suspected Communists in government and in the intellectual and artistic world by Senator Joseph McCarthy of Wisconsin. The climate was such that "we were not permitted, believe it or not," a Voice of America official said, "to quote from the Declaration of Independence in broadcasts to Indonesia and mainland China." A federally run Institute of Psychiatry and Foreign

Affairs, designed and operated by cultural anthropologists, could counteract such bigotry.

Mead and Benedict, envisioning new and better bureaucracies, assessed those that already existed, to explore how museums and universities and government agencies could best be put to use. Maybe the same methods they had used during the war to educate housewives about food shortages, and before then to trace connections between gender and temperament, could be put to new uses. Maybe they could compare different styles of child rearing and the ways different nations acquired their characters so as to preserve what was best about nationalism and invent new and constructive uses for aggressiveness. Between them these dauntless women addressed such questions with whatever institutional funding they could solicit.

Where money was needed, they figured, money would somehow be found. They had always been good at finding it, and pragmatic about where it came from.* Benedict's expenses through Vassar had been paid by a scholarship from a benefactress whom she never met. Mead's career had begun, upon her graduation from Barnard, with the help of a $300 "no-strings fellowship" out of Ruth Benedict's own pocket. In 1946, when Benedict was awarded $2,500 by the American Association of University Women, that money was funneled into "little stipends," Mead wrote, "so that one student could go on studying, another could finish her dissertation, another could make a short trip back to the field."

To keep alive this chain of generosity and help finance work by deserving young anthropologists, Mead had founded, in 1944, a corporation called the Institute for Intercultural Studies. The IIS, which later was granted tax-exempt status, aimed to "create a climate of opinion of the importance of the cultural approach, to facilitate informal relationships between students of national character, to prepare and distribute reprints for those interested in developing or applying the cultural approach to contemporary international problems, to develop new re-

---

* In January 1946, Mead's fellow anthropologist Ashley Montagu wrote to ask whether she shared his concern that the Viking Fund, which annually gave some two million dollars for anthropological research, consisted of moneys that came from the "well-known Nazi sympathizer" Axel Wenner-Gren. Mead replied, "To say that because money has been badly come by it should not be used for a good cause seems highly sentimental. Perhaps all the more because it has been badly come by it should be used for a good cause. Because the man who made money oppressed the poor, fought labor unions, baited reds, fought the federal government, supported child labor, persecuted minorities, attended lynchings, etc., seems pretty irrelevant, and if his money finally goes to good causes instead of evil causes, that is a triumph for society, and possibly even for his conscience."

search and new research methods and to apply the cultural approach to problems of intercultural adjustment between and within nations."

Philleo Nash, who eventually became an IIS vice president, remembered the excitement of these early meetings: "Maybe the twelve of us around that table couldn't take care of the environment, feed the world, cure failure of the belief that democracy could solve its own problems. If you had reservations, that didn't prevent you from joining the discussion. We weren't a conspiracy, we were just having big thoughts." IIS meetings were held at various places around New York, but headquarters for records and office space were in Mead's tower at the American Museum of Natural History. Annual reports went to the museum administration.*

Mead and Benedict had in mind a specific scheme for postwar study of what they now began to call "cultures at a distance" and "contemporary cultures." The Office of Naval Research granted $100,000 to finance the study, which was based first at Columbia University and later at the American Museum of Natural History, and which would give anthropologists their biggest chance yet to relate what they knew to the needs of the government. The government, they thought, had been making shamefully little use of what they had to say about who America's future enemies might be, how to break down those enemies' morale and will to fight, and how to turn enmity into good will. This new project aimed to "develop a series of systematic understandings of the great contemporary cultures," as Mead said, "so that the value of each may be orchestrated in a world built new."

The builders of this new world symphony would of course be the Americans, and the first orchestrators would be the team of 120 people, assembled by Benedict and Mead, whose task was to interview émigrés from seven foreign cultures: Poland, Syria, France, China, the Soviet Union, Czechoslovakia, and the *shtetls* of Eastern Europe. The Navy's grant for Research on Contemporary Cultures, as the project was called, "had released a great burst of creative group effort," Mead wrote, "but it

---

* The IIS was originally supported by grants from such benefactors as Jane Belo Tannenbaum, and later by Mead's earnings from speeches and from not only some of her own books but those by Benedict, Colin McPhee, Buell Quain, and Edith Cobb, for whom she was literary executor. The IIS got the $50,000 advance for *Letters from the Field* (1977); half the $30,000 advance and all royalties for *World Enough*, which Mead and Ken Heyman published in 1975; the $1,000 advance for *Ruth Benedict* (1974), the advance and first-serial rights and royalties for *Twentieth-Century Faith* and *The Wagon and the Star* (1966), advances for *The Rainbow Book of People and Places* (1959), *Anthropologists and What They Do* (1975), *Continuities in Cultural Evolution* (1964), *The Golden Age of American Anthropology* (1960), and *An Anthropologist at Work* (1959).

had not essentially changed the style of work which had developed under Boas, in which each person gave as much as he could and was paid as much as there happened to be—or nothing if there was none." This new enterprise revived the spirit of Boas's "giant rescue operation."

These rescuers would try to find out the same sorts of things Mead had tried to learn in the field: How are children raised, what is a mother, what is a friend, what is a stranger, what constitutes a meeting, what is a family ceremony? This time, however, Mead would not be nicknamed Njonjah or Piyap, or risk malaria, or cross the Equator. This time it would be the informants who had done the traveling and who came to talk in grateful droves, from distant and endangered places about which they had plenty to say if only someone would listen.

All Mead's life she had had a weakness for one-line generalizations about nationalities, as about practically everything. Australians, she once informed a Sydney audience, were autocratic with their children because their society had no lower class. Eastern European *shtetl* residents, she once pronounced in the hearing of her brother-in-law Leo Rosten, were for some reason not given to suicide by jumping out of windows. Perhaps, Rosten ventured, this was because *shtetls* had few buildings high enough to produce fatalities.

Nevertheless everywhere she looked Mead thought she spied details to help explain how the characters of nations differed. In the summer of 1947, on the terrace of the Leopoldskron at Salzburg, "Great candelabra filled with lighted candles were set out for the Austrian musicians to play by," she wrote in *Male and Female*. "The American listeners could only half-attend for worrying and wondering about the candles—would they go out, would the musicians be able to see their notes as the candle flames wavered uncertainly in the light wind?

"Today we can no longer have candles on Christmas-trees, not because candles on Christmas-trees have become more dangerous, but because people no longer have the necessary habits to use candles safely, habits that include a sharp awareness of blowing curtains, or a child's loose hair. Perfect relationships between oneself and one's surroundings, between oneself and other people, depend upon this long, loving habituation; at first the infant's eyes, then those of the child, absorb the same patterns, as layer over layer of meaning is laid down in its mind, each layer being consistent with each other layer, however counterpointed or apparently contrasting." This was how cultures formed and evolved; one of the anthropologist's tasks, as Mead saw it, was to slice through and examine the layers, as the geologist looks at layers of the planet.

This new project, variously referred to as Culture at a Distance, the Study of National Character, and Research on Contemporary Cultures, would be the last in a lifetime of collaborations between Mead and Benedict, and Mead's first full-time collaboration with her younger colleague Rhoda Métraux and with Geoffrey Gorer, on whom Mead and Benedict had effectively conferred the status of anthropologist without portfolio in the 1930s. Gorer had been doing "more than any other anthropologist," Mead wrote, "to develop the study of National Character."

As early as 1941, at the Institute of Human Relations at Yale University, Gorer had been studying systematically the national characteristics of the Japanese. His research, lavishly encouraged by Mead, led to an April 1942 message signed "Gregory Bateson, Secretary," under the letterhead of the Council on Human Relations, at 15 West Seventy-seventh Street, the address also of Mead's museum tower. This letter, beginning "Dear Collaborator," enclosed "an abstract of a study of Japanese character structure, prepared by Mr. Geoffrey Gorer."*

The wartime Gorer reports had recommended that "neither the Mikado [Emperor] himself nor the abstract Throne should ever be attacked; indeed they should never be mentioned other than respectfully. Attacking the Mikado would be like attacking the Pope for medieval Catholics; it would merely excite anger against foolish sacrilege. Japanese society is inconceivable for the Japanese without a ritual head . . . If, however, the sacred dignity of the Mikado is admitted, then all the people with real, as opposed to ritual, power can be attacked in their every action, for bringing the Emperor into contempt, for trafficking in the Emperor's name, for betraying the Emperor and taking power for themselves."

Gorer had also recommended that the United States should adopt a "firm fatherly tone toward the Japanese." His suggestion was misinterpreted by the Office of the Coordinator of Information, which in a broadcast to Japan stated that "The United States is your father." The error, Mead recalled, "was ours. There is no 'firm, fatherly tone' in the

---

* "Who is 'the Council'?" Erik Erikson asked in his reply to this letter, which ended, "missing you all terribly." The council, as it described itself, had "recently been organized as a clearing house to promote the study of personality and culture in the various countries of the world. It will endeavor to bring together the scattered materials already collected by anthropologists, psychiatrists, psychologists, specialists in child-development, and others, and will study the ideas and assumptions implicit in the philosophy, religion, and arts of the different countries. These varied contributions are necessary to give a broad picture of the traditional culture in each country and to provide an understanding of the predominating character structure and personality of the various peoples."

United States such as Gorer, an Englishman, had wished to evoke. The best we could have done to carry out Gorer's intent would have been to say 'Talk to the Japanese as if they are fourth graders and you are fifth.' "

In the years after the war, Rhoda Métraux worked so tirelessly and happily on the national character project that she could recall it in vivid detail thirty years later. The Navy, she said, had insisted that "along with developing and making clear the techniques we had used for studies, we must train successors for ourselves. From war experience it was decided that, if possible, no group must have people only of one or two cultures. Every group must have people of the cultures being studied, both as a resource and for a critique of what other people were doing, and as actors on the scene in which they were presumably acting out their own culture."

The new team of 120, from fourteen disciplines and sixteen nationalities, had the zeal of Crusaders and the conviction, one observer said, that they were "the most brilliant army ever assembled." They should not get too smitten with quantifying, Mead warned them. "Man's humanity is denigrated," she said, "when human beings are treated as interchangeable ciphers in monolithic schemes in which, in human affairs, the distinctiveness of the individual human being is ignored or denied." Ruth Landman, who was hired for the project soon after her 1947 graduation from Vassar, recalled how Mead "could listen with the ordinary two ears and the third ear all at the same time, with all antennae out—and how she could pull together what was critical. Some of our informants spoke English quite badly and were overly excited; they hadn't had a chance to work properly for years."

Benedict, who had been hard of hearing since her girlhood, was too fatigued by the strain of this project to be much of a listener, either to her colleagues or to their informants. "She said very little, if anything," Landman remembered. "Her deaf ear was turned to the public; she deliberately had her office arranged that way. It was Margaret who ran the big seminars and generated the excitement in that wonderful cauldron of people, all of whom read everything everyone else did. She would launch and summarize the discussions, and these informants would sit wreathed in smiles at the idea of being understood, for the first time in years."

In many cases, Gorer wrote, "The informant's response is rather like Monsieur Jourdain's delighted discovery that he had been talking prose all his life; people are pleased to discover that their 'ordinary' life can be so deeply interesting to a stranger." Gorer was, he said himself,

a champion listener. His preferred way of "modifying my total ignorance," he wrote, was to hold long interviews with members of the society being considered. "I count the interview a failure," he said, "whatever the information gained, if it has not been for the informants an
interesting and stimulating experience, which they wish to repeat in the
near future." His method was "to take the fullest possible notes (I do not
know shorthand); I either have my notebook out at once, or use the first
excuse of a foreign word or phrase to bring it out of my pocket.

"I have acquired the technique of writing—almost illegibly to
others, I must confess—without looking down at the paper." In an early
letter to Mead, enclosing a rough draft of a two-hour interview with a
pair of Japanese women, he said his informants were "both Christians
and violently pro-Japanese, so I have to stop every ten minutes to say
that the information shows the Japs to be even more wonderful than I
had thought, and that it is all needed for making peace later."

In private Mead would sometimes chide Gorer. "You do hate the
Puritan character and the Christian religion, you are guilty about being
white, you are guilty about being happy—when you are," she had told
him in 1942, going on to say that his "strictures therefore have a very
different quality than mine, more acid, perhaps much more true. . . .
But I do want the contributions of all of us that are working together
to build up to something positive without the gravel in the machinery
which is introduced by things like that crack about religion which you
put into the Science, Philosophy and Religion meeting last year, which
went a long way to cancel out, for that audience, not only what you
had been saying, but also what I had been saying."

When others attacked Gorer, however, Mead rose to his defense.
Gorer's 1948 book *The American People* struck Alistair Cooke, who reviewed it in the *Manchester Guardian*, as an attempt "to psychoanalyse
a whole community," which Cooke considered "as perilous as brain
surgery. . . . In pretending to write about the Americans as ingenu-
ously as if they were the Samoans, Mr. Gorer's 'preliminary survey' fills
you with piercing doubts about the whole anthropological method. For
Mr. Gorer is a disciple of Malinowski and a colleague of Margaret Mead.
It makes you wonder if it's true what they say about the Trobriand Islanders."*

Gorer's most ridiculed and most celebrated idea, a product of the
1948–49 Research in Contemporary Cultures study, was his "swaddling

* *Time* would find Gorer's 1955 *English Character* "far less sweeping than
he was with Americans or Lepchas. Which suggests what can happen when
one man's Margaret Mead takes another Englishman's poise on."

hypothesis," a notion he had developed after repeated interviews with representatives of pre-Soviet Russia. Russian parents swaddled their babies, Gorer deduced, to make them stop kicking and go to sleep, but at what price? Babies tightly confined in swaddling clothes, he suggested, might be inclined to grow up to be suspicious and despotic. This new and sweeping preoccupation, which Mead shared, acquired a derisive nickname: "diaperology." Diaperology alluded to the vogue of describing cultures in terms of psychoanalytic theory. It referred in particular to the "swaddling hypothesis," explained in *The People of Great Russia,* which Gorer and John Rickman published in 1950, and which had stemmed from the original RCC study. The hypothesis, Gorer wrote, might help to explain how "the idea develops that restraint is unbearable; yet one has enormous strength and one must be swaddled in order to keep one from breaking things." One RCC group discussion of this hypothesis also touched on Balinese teething practices, Polish responses to crying babies, and American Indian cradleboards. A Russian woman present at this discussion said, "It is easy to handle a child when he is swaddled and stiff," though people "pitied the poor thing, especially in the summer." There was talk of movement, restraint, hyperkinesis, expressiveness in conversation, and of how often drunken Russians tended to walk upstairs on all fours. "We've got to pursue swaddling in every direction," Mead and Gorer had agreed, "including metaphors or any kind of figures of speech." This statement was not their finest moment.

In the spring of 1948, the expanded RCC project resumed the search for what Mead had described ten years earlier as "new social inventions which will be able to combine an aggressive character structure with socio-political forms which can use that aggression constructively." Funds for the expanded project were negotiated by Ruth Benedict with RAND. Dr. Nathan Leites, a member of RAND's scientific staff and husband of Mead's close friend the psychologist Martha Wolfenstein, coordinated the research of the nine project workers and two consultants.

This second Russian project, carried out at the Natural History Museum and known as Studies in Soviet Culture, would be a good way to provide work for more graduate students. "Even if almost all the senior people contributed their time," Mead wrote, "if everyone who could type did his own work, and if we used our apartments as bases, nevertheless more money would be needed if the steadily expanding work was to get done." Mead made it clear in *Soviet Attitudes Toward*

Authority, the 1951 book which resulted from this project, that she was "not only not a Russian specialist, but I do not speak Russian and I have been able to do only a minimal amount of interviewing or first-hand analysis of materials.

"I have had twenty-five years of experience working on comparable problems among primitive and contemporary people and several years of experience in relating researches of this sort to specific national and international problems. This book must be understood as an attempt to point up some of the implications of the work of the project team. The members of the research group are responsible for the selection of the concrete materials which have been used and for criticizing the contexts within which I have used them, but I alone am responsible for the theoretical phrasing, based as it is on the insights, research, and formulations of the members of the two Russian projects with which I have been associated."

The most remarkable thing about this book, as about many other Mead enterprises, is the scope of its ambition. It aimed to tackle questions that would perplex most of the world for most of the century: How could the Soviets be at once so suspicious and so trusting? Why did they need a political police force estimated to number a million and a half members? *Soviet Attitudes Toward Authority,* subtitled *An Interdisciplinary Approach to Problems of Soviet Character,* concludes with a summary of the weaknesses in two areas, in leadership and in the masses of the people, and with the suggestion that its findings be taken into account seriously by both contemporary and long-range planners.

It was a good thing swaddling was not more emphasized in this book. Since the hypothesis was highly debatable, said Harry Schwartz charitably in his *New York Times* review, "at least its omission is a merit distinguishing this book from other recent writing by the same author." Corliss Lamont in the *Annals of the American Academy* was also pleased that the hypothesis had been omitted from the book, but charged that the author had "swaddled herself in other theories which appear almost as farfetched," and accused Mead of overlooking, "unless perhaps by indirect implication here and there, the 177 minority groups"—other than the Great Russians—"that make up almost one-half of the Soviet Union."

The Study of Culture at a Distance, the 1953 "Manual" for the larger RCC project, also got mixed reviews. Much as Mead and Benedict professed to admire lean, clean English, this book was judged "high-blown, pretentious, and couched in the repellent jargon of social scientists." The *American Journal of Sociology* attacked the "often untestable and uncommunicable" emphasis on intuitive methodologies which "from any 'scientific' standpoint absolutely lack reliability," and found throughout the volume "an ambivalent note which seems to wish to communicate the 'scientific' character of the process, on the one hand, and the entirely individualistic, intellectual nature of the operation, on the other."

Cora Du Bois, who had visited Mead and Bateson in Bali and was now a Harvard anthropology professor, reviewed the RCC manual in the March 1954 *Annals of the American Academy* of Political and Social Sciences. Although the collection struck her as "somewhat incoherent," its "charming, penetrating and provocative vignettes" still constituted what she considered good reading. One reason the study of national character had not gained more acceptance among social scientists, Du Bois went on, was that it was not considered scientific. "The editors and some of the contributors would appear to agree," she said, "since there is frequent reference to the esthetic, intuitive, and perceptual gifts needed for such analysis. Whether in fact such capacities are any more irrelevant to science than 'intelligence' is certainly open to debate."

Nobody doubted Mead's ability to assemble "vignettes," to use Du Bois's word, which could charm, penetrate, and provoke. Nobody denied that she was intuitive and perceptive. Her prose, however, was losing some of its authoritative eloquence. In *Coming of Age in Samoa* she had won the public; in field reports, especially those concerning the Arapesh and the Balinese, she had won the esteem of her peers. But as the century's and Mead's own increasingly scattered forties wore on, two new and less beguiling strains were surfacing in what she wrote. *And Keep Your Powder Dry*, like several of her later books, had a slapdash, flippant quality, and now, with the nonsense about swaddling in *Soviet Attitudes*, she was proving how pretentious she could also be.

In 1948, at the age of sixty-one, after twenty-five years in the Columbia University Anthropology Department, Ruth Benedict was finally named a full professor. That summer, against the advice of doctors whom she went to see only reluctantly because Margaret Mead implored her to, she decided to go to Europe. She had bad hearing and an unstable heart, but she felt buoyed by a visit to her family and friends in Pasadena, and was determined not to miss a five-week UNESCO seminar in Podebrady, Czechoslovakia, on child education toward worldmindedness. On the way, she could see the landscapes of some of the countries whose character she had been describing from a distance.

An RCC worker was assigned to keep Benedict company on the eve of her departure and make sure she got to her plane on time. Leila Lee, whose chief responsibility had been to document all material and serve as a liaison between Columbia and the Office of Naval Research, had relished her duties on the project, as had most of her 120 teammates, and found the work "tremendously inspiring: I learned more in that group than I learned in all my college career." The night before Benedict left for Europe, she learned something new.

"I love my insomnia," Benedict told Leila Lee that night. "That's when I write all my poetry."

Benedict had not found much time for poetry in her daylight hours since the project began, nor would she in Europe. After the UNESCO seminar, she went to Poland and Holland and attended some international anthropological meetings in Brussels. In the second week of September, shortly after her return to her apartment on Central Park West, near Columbia University, Benedict suffered a coronary thrombosis and, as Mead wrote, "put all her effort into staying quietly alive until Ruth Valentine"—the psychologist who had been the last companion of Benedict's life—"got back from California." Ruth Valentine disliked flying and spent five days traveling east by train. Until her arrival, Mead and a small group of other close friends kept vigil. Valentine arrived the morning of September 17, and the two friends spent the afternoon talking. That evening Ruth Benedict died.

"If I can just live till I'm fifty," Benedict had once written in her diary, "I'll be peaceful." She had lived eleven years beyond that age, attracting more attention all the time. Her old adversary Ralph Linton, now teaching at Yale, was told that she had died of angina and said, "Goddammit, she can't even *die* of a woman's disease!" Another colleague said that she had been a sensitive, troubled, rich personality infatuated with death. Mead seemed to agree. Her friend, she wrote, "had always felt so strongly about the beauty of the dead that we brought our children to see her, giving them a protection which few children have today, in an acceptance that death is part of life." Colin Frank and Martha Ullman would remember Benedict's funeral all their lives as a solemn and momentous occasion, at which, Martha said, Margaret Mead had wept fiercely.

Mead was deluged with messages of sympathy, as if she were the chief mourner, but later she claimed not to have been undone by this or any other parting. "When people die," she said in her own last decade, "I have no sense that I have lost them. I mean, it's too bad they're not here. . . . I'd love to hear Ruth laugh again, the way she did when

I told her something ridiculous that had happened. . . . Sometimes I imagine writing her a letter about something happening now: how she would laugh at this, how Mother would feel about that. . . . They're all still here, in a way. They're all part of my life. I've lost the pleasure of their company, but I haven't lost them." The deaths of loved ones, Mead would have it thought, affected her, as had the pangs of adolescence, less gravely than they seemed to affect other people. Still, she must have felt a little unmoored. Her two most important teachers, one of whom had also been her steadfast loving friend, were dead, and her beloved husband was beginning a new life without her.

She sought comfort where she had always sought it, in her work.

PART THREE

Before we left for the field, Mead told me that if Manus turned out to be another cultural shambles—a slum culture, undermined and demoralized as a result of the drastic culture contact and change they had experienced—she would not write about it. What the world needed was a success story.

—THEODORE SCHWARTZ, 1984

CHAPTER NINETEEN

No More Top
on the Roll-top Desk

DURING ALL THE YEARS Margaret Mead had spent in her hidden tower office at the museum, she had worked at an old-fashioned roll-top desk. Desks like that would fetch fancy prices, a few years later, at Columbus Avenue antique shops, just across from the museum. Desks like that were heirlooms. Margaret Mead cherished most heirlooms, but this desk had no sentimental charm for her. Its roll-top only got in her way. Needing every inch of surface she could get, she marked her fiftieth birthday by summoning museum carpenters to saw the roll-top off.

What mattered most to Mead, at this time in her life, was getting rid of everything cumbersome. Behind her were three marriages; just ahead lay a new phase which it would please her to refer to as "post-menopausal zest." With deft skill she had fashioned unique arrangements with the two institutions that employed her, the American Museum of Natural History and Columbia University. If neither paid her what she was worth, or conferred on her enough status, they still lent her their prestige, which in both cases was considerable. They also, between them, allowed her the flexibility she needed to carve out her career as not just a teacher, not just a curator, but the best-known anthropologist in the United States and possibly in the world, whose pronouncements, on everything from South Pacific courtship habits to middle-American divorce rates, automatically made news.

On the new surface of her desk were notes for the classes she had begun to give at Columbia University Teachers' College (she had also lectured at Vassar, New York University, Stanford and the University of California, the University of Birmingham, and Harvard). Also on her desk, as on thousands of others, were copies of her tenth book, *Male and Female*, which Rebecca West described in the *New York Herald Tribune Book Review* as "a vast, turbulent book . . . turbulent because Margaret Mead is a genius of the prophetic sort." Toward the end of that book Mead declared, rather as Margaret Fuller in the previous century had proclaimed her acceptance of the universe, that: "I personally accept the culture within which I live and move and have my particular being as a way of life within which it is possible to work towards the welfare of all mankind in all places on the face of the earth.

"I accept the prophets who lament our blurred and imperfect vision. I accept the right of the revolutionary to challenge and break a society that cannot keep itself whole enough to stand against him. I accept the indomitable will to live of those who, bruised by demands greater than they can bear, demand joy, however slight and cheap, rather than sink into apathy and despair." The mood of Mead's nation was hardly one of Victorian certainty. Her fellow citizens were suffering, as she had noted in a speech in 1947, from "being asked to get up every morning and deal with every calamity in the world." The bomb had been dropped on Hiroshima; mushroom-shaped clouds had risen in New Mexico and off Bikini; the Soviet Union's capability was bound to catch up with America's. Who could tell what the future held, or how much future there would be?

Nobody could say, but Mead was willing to try. A problem that concerned her especially, she told an audience of women, was "to teach our children to nest in the gale, to have the habit of adjusting, to be pleased when they do adjust." Years later, after she used the phrase "nest in the gale" in Blackberry Winter, someone wrote to ask just what she meant by it. She answered: "Being able to be at home anywhere in the world, in any house, in any time band, eating any different kind of food, learning new languages as needed, never afraid of the new, sad to leave anywhere where one has been at home for a few days, but glad to go forward." She herself went forward wherever she was asked to go; motion in and of itself was coming to have a meaning for her. Maybe it always had.

Mead's abiding interest was in psychology, particularly the psychology of children. Children figured in many of her speeches: "We are laying a dreadful new burden on [them]," she told one audience: "They have to be a joy to us." The ideal place to bring children up, she said, was a town of five thousand diversified people but not, God forbid, a suburb. ("Don't ever learn to drive," she cautioned one goddaughter. "If you do, you'll have to live in a suburb.") Mead's best friends included several pillars of suburban communities, whom she frequently visited and unabashedly used as informants, as she always used everyone.

However relaxed she might seem, she was always, somehow, working. A suddenly "free" hour was no gift as far as Margaret Mead was concerned. When she found out, in the course of a two-week symposium, that a certain morning session had been postponed, she was furious. "How *dare* they?" she asked. "Do they *realize* what use I could have made of this time? Do they know I get up at five o'clock every morning to write a thousand words before breakfast? Why did nobody have the politeness to tell me this meeting had been rescheduled?" Empty time was something that seemed to alarm her.*

Since her return from Bali, Mead had been getting to know her native continent at least as well as she had learned the South Pacific, at first by making field trips for the Committee on Food Habits and later on all sorts of other expeditions. She went to Elmira College in upstate New York to be awarded another honorary doctorate, this time in science. She went to Antioch College, in Ohio, to dedicate a new eighty-room building for the study of human development. She paid repeated visits to Washington, D.C., her old wartime base, maintaining friendships and searching for new ways to influence public policies related to science.

As passionate about her own kinship patterns as about anyone else's, Mead traveled as often as she could to the West Coast, where her brother, her sister Priscilla, and several other relatives lived. Every year since the war she had made lecture tours which took her for two or three weeks at a time to California, where family reunions were sandwiched into a schedule that sometimes called for her to make several speeches in one day. These tours gave her a notion she needed of what far western audiences were thinking about, and helped her to plan her writing. Whatever was on other people's minds was likely to be on Margaret Mead's. "The way to write a book which will make the life of a remote island people meaningful to an American audience," she said, "is to lecture about it first . . . in as many parts of the country as possible, before I even begin to write."

She found every excuse she could to go to Philadelphia, where she regularly looked in on, and sometimes cooked for, her ailing parents. When Emily Fogg Mead died of a stroke in 1950, her grieving husband

* Some of her colleagues wanted to cancel an afternoon session of the American Anthropological Association convention on November 22, 1963, after President John F. Kennedy was assassinated, but Mead was among those who requested that the meetings continue. Her response to this assassination and to Senator Robert Kennedy's, in 1968, was to assign everyone she talked to, including her nephew Philip Rosten, to gather anthropological data about the public's reaction.

told—in a memoir that began "The Queen of our little group has left us"—of the pride his wife had taken in their children: not only in Margaret but in Richard, "who after a long struggle had achieved his heart's desire, a full rank teaching position"—in the business school at the University of Southern California—of Elizabeth's "gay warmth and affection, devotion to children," and determination to succeed as an art teacher, and of Priscilla's sense of order, devotion, and "skill with which she managed her large and complicated household"—which moved from California to Connecticut and New York—"and her social life." Priscilla Rosten, mother of three, was married until 1959 to Leo Rosten. Elizabeth Steig taught art in New York City public schools and later at Lesley College in Boston, and had two children.

Mead paid close attention to the details of the lives of those she loved but nothing, it seemed, was too trivial for her pronouncements. She spoke with equal fervor of bowling alleys ("one of the most beautiful creations"), of the importance of art forms requiring ephemeral materials, like food and flowers, and of Geoffrey Gorer's swaddling hypothesis. Now that her marriage to Bateson was over, Gorer was growing more and more important to Mead, professionally and personally. "I have not attempted to indicate the details of my indebtedness to his observations and analyses," she wrote in *Male and Female*, referring to their twelve years of cooperative work. *Male and Female* had begun with the Jacob Gimbel Lectures in Sex Psychology which Mead gave in 1946, in San Francisco, at the joint invitation of Stanford University and the University of California.

In Fort Worth, Texas, at a convention of the American Association of University Women, an organization revered by her mother and by Ruth Benedict, she told the fifteen hundred delegates that Americans, who never seemed able to get together on a national basis, should try on a local level to sort out what was bothering them. One thing that was clearly bothering and exciting them was sex, a constant theme in Mead's work. The 1948 Kinsey Report, *Sexual Behavior in the Human Male*, brought headlines for Mead as well as for its authors.

At a three-day symposium of the American Social Hygiene Association she criticized the report for handling sex as an "impersonal, meaningless act," for confusing sex with excretion and for missing its "emotional, spiritual and ethical sides." The Report, she said, "may increase the number of young men who indulge in 'outlets' with a sense of hygienic self-righteousness."

Though in retrospect the 1950s, the Eisenhower years, may seem a tame parenthesis in twentieth-century history, the decade looked frightening enough as it began. This may have been why Mead discerned in it "an attack of matrimony—an absolute panic, with everyone getting married." The "new ballet between the sexes," as she wrote in *Male and Female*, "no longer follows traditional lines," but was instead "a ballet in which each couple must make up their steps as they go along. When he is insistent, should she yield, and how much? When she is demanding, should he resist, and how firmly? Who takes the next step forward or the next step back? What is it to be a man? What is it to be a woman?"

These questions served to widen Mead's already considerable audience. She could not answer them, of course, but her flair for stating them so succinctly made them seem less threatening. More and more her name took on mythological overtones: Just think, people would say, even the great Margaret Mead has these matters on her mind! It was harder to be married in America, Margaret Mead said, than anywhere else, and if she said it, it must be so. Who would know better? Her happily alliterative name was becoming more and more a synonym for fresh common sense. She talked of "a series of pin-up girls whose breasts, tailored for love [were] explicitly not meant for the loving nourishment of youth." Undressing, she advised her fellow mid-century Puritans, would only increase anxiety; the more important thing to develop was "greater ease with our clothes on." (Her own clothes, many of them made by a dressmaker, were larger than they had been; she was growing increasingly plump.)

Neither gender, she emphasized, had any corner on bewilderment. Millions of women were "unmated and childless or left alone to bring up their children," while "so many men, restless and unsettled, wander over the face of the earth." And why were families in such trouble? That question, too, was unanswerable, but Mead was willing to venture a guess: part of the problem might be "the presence of so many unmarried and childless women in Western society." Such women might "mute the male's sense that women bear children, and he does not, and increase his feeling that women are imperfect men, castrated, incomplete, partial males, who can never be as important as he is because they lack his full equipment." And again, small wonder that complete sexual surrender was so uncommon among American wives: "Even before the girl has matured," Mead wrote, "she has been faced with the need for being the conscience for two, and at the same time playing gaily, deftly, a game that is never finished and at which she may always lose."

In the years of wolf-whistles and calls of "hubba-hubba," with everyone rushing to marry and then wondering why marriage had not brought happiness, these thoughts hit home, in all kinds of homes. Why was marriage so much less blissful than it was supposed to be? Many pondered this question, but it was Mead who dared to ask it publicly, in the first of eight lectures in a 1950 series at the New School called "Modern Women's Dilemma—What Direction Now?" Any woman, "unless she is deaf, dumb and blind," could find herself a hubsand, Mead pointed out, but if women continued "to cling to the archaic belief" that they had to find husbands superior to them, they would create "a group of men who get awfully nervous if their wives are any good."

Career advancement made men more desirable as spouses, but women less so. A career, as Mead defined it, was "something you would pay others to let you do if they didn't pay you." Her fellow professional women, she said, must help "to combine the necessary seriousness and the necessary familiarity of the new age so that we can function well, be at home as pioneers and keep our sense of urgency." Peril awaited women who tried to combine paid work with marriage. "Society seemed to throw its doors wide open to woman, but translated her every step toward success as having been damaging—to her own chances of marriage and to the men whom she passes on the road." Not enough attention was paid to "the great variety of human solutions to the problem of which men are to have which women, under what circumstances and for how long, and the less usual but modern problem of which women are to have which men." Society should busy itself with finding new ways "to give women a divine discontent that will demand other satisfactions than those of child-rearing." But never, in all her career as a writer, did Mead downplay the satisfactions of motherhood; she covered both sides of the street.

She had hurried to publish *Male and Female* before the news spread that the third of her own marriages was going the way of the two before it. The age of candor about the personal sorrows of public people had not yet dawned; Mead in the early 1950s was as reticent about her marital history as the Joseph P. Kennedys for a good while would remain about their mentally handicapped daughter Rosemary.

Maybe, Mead speculated, people who wanted to be married should be required to fill out forms, proving that they knew the names, occupations, and whereabouts of their prospective in-laws just as well as they knew of their own parents'. Maybe couples who wanted to marry should first have to wait for six months. In any case, as she had told a 1947 National Congress on Social Work, "a false idea of romantic love [was] wrecking the institution of marriage." Contrary to what the Moral Majority would claim later, it was an excess rather than a failure of faith that seemed to be doing marriage in; couples' expectations were not too limited but too large, which was why disillusionment was, and would continue to be, so hard to avoid. An Australian audience later heard her say, "If you ask many girls to list, in order, who they'd like to have near in an emergency, they'll mention their husband eleventh."

A good part of what Rebecca West in her review of *Male and Female* called Mead's prophetic kind of genius lay in the alchemy by which Mead cast her private troubles onto a public screen and turned them into lessons which others found useful and sometimes even entertaining. "A world in which people may reorient their whole lives at forty or fifty," she wrote, "is a world in which marriage for life becomes more and more difficult. Each spouse is given the right to and the means for growth. Either may discover a hidden talent and begin to develop it, or repudiate a paralyzing neurotic trend and begin anew. Ever since women have been educated, marriages have been endangered by the possible development or failure to develop of both husbands and wives." The phrase "she outgrew him" would in time become as commonplace an explanation for why a marriage ended as "he outgrew her."

Whoever outgrew whom, "The expectation of permanency [was] still great enough to brand every impermanence a failure, if not a sin, and also because to all the other insecurities of American life, insecurity of marriage [was] added." The "stigma of failure and sin," Mead wrote, must go; so also must "the indignities of divorce laws that demand either accusation or collusion." Americans did not know how to come to terms with sorrow over death or divorce, but they had better start learning: "Social practices must be developed so that the end of a marriage is announced soberly, responsibly, just as the beginning of a marriage is published to the world."

Male and Female, sharper and more eloquent than many of Mead's general books, is still provocative in 1984, though it is uneven. "Read *Male And Female*," said John Willey, who edited it and a number of her other books for William Morrow and Company, "and you'll find that Margaret was an atrocious writer when she tried to be conversational." But the book was well received when it appeared. Max Lerner, in the *New York Post*, called it "remarkable" and "brilliant," praising her in particular for asking "how divorce can be faced with dignity in a society in which it has become an established fact, but is still regarded with furtiveness and guilt." Mead's "knowledge of simple, stable cultures," said *Newsweek*, had "enabled her to take a cool-headed and frank approach to the complex, ever-changing sex roles of America." But her new book was not limited to Mead's own society; its point, as she told Harvey Breit in a *New York Times* interview, was "to show how many different kinds of women and men there are." Alluding to the Samoans, the Balinese, and the other cultures she had studied in the field, she indulged in one of her generalizations: "Many of the variations could be directly traced to 'the bottle and the baby carriage.' As long as the child is breast-fed and is hand-carried, you have one kind of society. If it is bottle-fed and carriage-pushed, you have another."

It may have been a relief for Margaret Mead to detach herself from what Marianne Moore referred to in her poem "Arctic Ox" as the "servitude and flutter" of marriage. "It suited her, after Gregory, not to have a man per se," said Colin Frank. "For her to share a bathroom with someone else would have been just too confining. The best thing about her was the way she kind of picked and chose bits of people, without having to perpetuate the myth that any one person would fill all her needs." What John Willey considered the meagerness of her private life seemed to him almost a matter of conscious decision, "as if she saw to it that she would always have ferocious deadlines, lectures, conferences that would protect her from personal entanglements."

Her staunch champion Wilton Dillon, who had been lured to anthropology in his Army days upon discovering *The Chrysanthemum and the Sword* at the Post Exchange in Tokyo, first met Mead and Métraux, as he would recall, "on a windy spring afternoon at the Natural History Museum where I listened for fifteen enchanting minutes to someone who turned out to be Rhoda." The following Christmas, Dillon was invited to slice the duck at Mead's traditional dinner, and thereafter was sent along to France, to do graduate work on the theories of the nineteenth-century anthropologist Marcel Mauss, with Mead's blessing and several letters of introduction.

Mead maintained her Paris friendships by stopping there frequently during the annual trips she began to take with Geoffrey Gorer, whose father had been a noted art dealer. Gorer, who had long since passed on to Mead his fondness for the expression "a pretty point," taught her what points to look for in paintings. On various holidays they visited W. H. Auden and his friend Chester Kallman in Austria, the museums of Florence, and Gorer's own house, with its marvelous gardens, in Sussex, south of London. One year they spent their vacation time together in New York City, pretending to be tourists. They arranged theater tickets, went to restaurants and museums, and tried, at Gorer's suggestion, to cross to the sunny side of the street, "but Margaret hated it," one friend said. "Margaret never liked what she called 'having a good time.'"

Gorer did not favorably impress all Mead's friends. In the opinion of one, he "had the misfortune to live in the same time as Auden and Christopher Isherwood and others who had similar sensibilities, but greater talents." Mead did not always agree with Gorer, either. And he took issue with her practice of choosing friends "primarily on the grounds of temperament," as she put it, "which means it doesn't make any difference whether they are high achievers in the public eye, or people who have no relation to the public at all." Gorer, she said, thought that "you should make friends with people of your own levels of public achievement."

Rumor had it that Mead considered marrying "Uncle Geoffrey," as she liked her daughter and Rhoda Métraux's son Daniel to call Gorer, but their relationship was apparently, and quite happily, platonic; it did not stop her from thinking, at least, of more intense involvements. "She could and did have good relations with men," said one of her friends. "There was something engaging about her, apart from her fame. She had liaisons, but she didn't want to get married."

Louis Dupree, who worked with Mead at the museum, wondered whether she ever really got close to anyone at all: "I had the feeling she was looking for a relationship like Nancy's [his wife's] and mine. She was plugged into us in so many ways; she would often ask, 'How's your married life coming?' But she herself never seemed to find that second person to tango with. My assumption was that she had love affairs up the kazoo, wouldn't hesitate to do her own number, wasn't going to lie around as a leftover. She had fame, she had enough money, she was relatively well off, but one thing seemed to elude her, the one thing she missed was the one plus one which equaled one. I used to wonder what really happened between her and Bateson, why their Bali rapport couldn't be transplanted into life in the United States, but you didn't question a giant like her; you didn't ask, 'How's your sex life, baby?' "

Never, by Mead's own admission, had she felt much of a vocation for intense, prolonged intimacy. "I've never known the kind of union," she once told her friend Jean Houston, "that made me want to exclude other people. I've only excluded other people if the person who loved me just couldn't abide my caring for other people. I would honor that feeling. But I've never wanted to belong to another person, nor would I ever want anyone to belong to me."

Margaret Mead exchanged frequent letters, most of them signed "Lovingly," with all the members of her original family. Sometimes she wrote to "Mother and Dadda," but often she wrote and posted separate letters, on the same day, to each parent. She was also an inspired practitioner of what some in her profession called "fictive kinship." Kevin Frank, ten years younger than his brother Colin, remembered his parents' friend Margaret most clearly from her many visits to Boston, after the Franks moved there in 1955. Sometimes she went up for annual open forums at Ford Hall where "desperate crowds would line up to hear what she had to say. Most adults are pretty dead; most children have enormous amounts of vitality and energy," said Kevin. "Margaret was someone with a real, riveted attention to what's happening now. Children can pick up at a glance if adults have ulterior motives or are patronizing; she wasn't like that. She had a genuine excitement about what I was doing."

And as Kevin Frank grew older he paid more attention to Mead's relationships with others. "She never worried too much about politeness," he said, "and she didn't give a lot of credence to niceties and unnecessary transition words like 'hello' and 'goodbye.' Unlike many social scientists, she got straight to the point. Her value as a social scientist was her ability to destroy and knock holes in some very fortified ideas, gloomy predictions, arbitrary limits as to what people could do.

"The strangest feeling I noticed in social scientists who would come to our house was some sadness—a longing for the formula, the concept, the doctrine, the observation that would be ultimately revealing, which the circular nature of conceptual reasoning makes it impossible to find—a longing to understand, yet perhaps a not complete awareness of why the whole thing seemed so frustrating. And there were tremendous sentimental journeys into the past—what Larry said, or what Gregory did at Cloverly in '48—as if you could resurrect the communion by resurrecting the memory. If social scientists had an imbalance, it might be to tend to live in their heads. Margaret, to some extent at least, lived in her guts."

As the 1950s proceeded, Mead, who had long extolled the merits of any group of people who could be called an "evolutionary cluster," entered into what someone called her "high clustering days." In *Male and Female* she had written that Americans were "a gregarious people, needing the presence of others to give us a full sense of ourselves." In this respect, as in a number of others, she was a consummate American, although her fellow anthropologist Ashley Montagu said she reminded him more of "regular secretary generals, of the sort the Royal Society had in the seventeenth century, who had the function of bringing together all the disparate work being done. She brought back that tradition, not only to anthropology but to a good many other fields."

Montagu was one of the dozens, probably hundreds, of acquaintances and colleagues whom Mead would bombard with clippings,

memos, and reminders. Once, when they met for the first time in several years, Mead picked up their earlier conversation, which had to do
with a Latin poem, exactly where it had been left off, without prelimi-
naries. Years might pass between her encounters with certain people,
but the people were still in her mind. She may not have wanted to get
too close to anybody, but she didn't want anybody she cared about to
drift too far away, either. Everyone should be where she could find
them, if she needed to. Since changes of scene and changes of company
were what she found most exhilarating, she rarely stayed put in one
place long enough to get on anyone's nerves, but as another friend, the
ethnomusicologist Alan Lomax, said of her, "If anyone really mattered
to her, that person had total access, any time, in a kind of frontier
loyalty."

In her biography of Bernard Berenson, Meryle Secrest wrote of her
subject that "only the daily assurance of an audience of fresh faces
could temporarily assuage his inner isolation." Mead, said one of her
associates, lived similarly. "I can't bear people who drop other people. I
don't give people up because they change," she once said. "One of my
friends says that the trouble with me is that I'm always making new
friends and never give up the old ones, so that there are too many. I still
have friends from the fourth grade, and I take on all the people that anybody I love has treated badly, and that's a very large number of wives and
sweethearts and discarded mistresses. You don't abandon any of your
children.

"I make, I suppose, an average of one new friend of importance
every two or three months," Mead had gone on. "That's five or six good
friends a year, without dropping any of the others. On the whole, I try
to introduce them to each other." Some of her friends, however, got the
impression that she tried to keep them apart. Her friendships reminded
one of her colleagues of "private fiefdoms: I always wondered why she
had so many orbits, gambits, and networks, some of which she tried to
connect and some not." An illuminating observation Mead's Barnard
friend Eleanor Rosenberg made, after five decades, was that "Margaret
did not talk of herself—always of you, of your friends, your relatives. She
would come by to see me when I lived on Morningside Heights and always let me treat her to dinner at the Terrace, which I was honored and
grateful to do, and we'd talk until late at night. She was deeply interested
in Barnard, its problems, its people. Once when I refused to admit that a
Barnard colleague's death could have been a suicide, Margaret called
later to tell me I was wrong."

Seldom, if ever, were Mead's friendships casual. "I have no real relationship in which you just sit and play cards and talk," she said. "Even with Rhoda [Métraux and Mead lived together after 1955 and worked together more and more closely] there's usually so much of an agenda. Normal married couples tend on the whole to spend a lot of time sitting around reading, or they used to, but I have almost none of that, because almost always, whoever I see I haven't seen for two weeks or two months or two years, so all encounters are intense. There's no time for casualness."

Kevin Frank, who grew up to help manage an upstate New York Zen monastery, spoke of the danger of institutionalizing a person who, like her, "led you to the common 'Aha!,' who perceived connections between facts leading to models, schemes, paradigms. You could almost talk of Margaret as a sort of priestess." But in the early 1950s Mead was thinking about preaching in a secular sense rather than a religious one. In 1950 the Australian Broadcasting Company asked its director of education, Charles Bull, to choose four people who would make a good team to give a series of lectures in Australia under the auspices of the World Education Fellowship. Bull, who had heard about Mead's rousing speeches in London two years earlier, at the world mental health meetings, called on her in New York and invited her.

"You know, Charles, it's a funny thing," she told him. "Just this morning Cathy and I were saying we'd like to go to Australia." And so they did, in 1951, with all expenses paid. Twelve-year-old Cathy was enrolled at the Frensham School, in New South Wales, and her mother toured the continent, delighting audiences, beginning new friendships, and renewing old ones. At a congress of anthropologists in Canberra, Margaret had her first meeting in years with Reo Fortune, who had been visiting his family in New Zealand on leave from Cambridge. Colleagues winced to think what might happen when, as one put it, "the two giants met again." They were reassured by the report of Raymond Firth, who was present at the reunion. "It's all right," said Firth. "He called her 'The Mater.'"

In New Zealand, Mead was snubbed when she tried to call on Reo's brother Barter. He resented her having worked on a project funded by the U.S. Navy, which had also funded research for nuclear attack work. "As a responsible and liberal scientist," he said, "she should have kept out of all that." But Mead did get in touch with the other Fortune in-laws, including a cousin who found her "so humane" and "so *large*."

Australia provided Mead with plenty of happy distractions. She had such a good time, one friend said, that she reconsidered settling there. "She could easily have gotten a chair here and she wouldn't have minded the climate; hardships never bothered her. She could have gone up to the snow or down to the tropics whenever she liked." And she found both friends and disciples. Paul Byers, an American photographer who attended all her lectures, became a protégé. Her old friends Caroline and Timothy Kelly, and Charles and Marjorie Bull, welcomed her warmly. And Professor Ian Hogbin at Sydney University gave her some fateful advice.

"It was I who insisted, who hammered and hammered and hammered at her," said Hogbin, "that she should return to Manus. Her previous idea had been that if she'd been there before, she knew all there was to know about it, all she needed to know." But now, hearing in more detail about the changes that had been wrought in the Admiralty Islands since she and Fortune were there in 1928—especially during and since the war—she changed her mind. A Manus politician named Paliau, she heard, was emerging as a major new leader. People in Manus, she was told, "were changing so fast, so unaccountably, that no one knew quite what was happening." An investigation of this rapid change, she was persuaded, "might provide a key to our understanding of similar, less rapid changes all over the world."

So began the plan for Mead's first postwar field trip. At an International Seminar on Mental Health and Infant Development in Chichester, England, in 1952, she showed her movies "Bathing Babies in Three Cultures." Reseeing these films can only have whetted her yearning to get back to the field. She had decided, she wrote, that "it was time for those of us who had given up our major task—studying primitive peoples as a way of throwing light on the processes of human society—for wartime work on problems of morale, communication among allies, and psychological warfare against totalitarian forces, to go back to our laboratories in the jungles, on the small islands, around the arctic fringes of the world. Our practice had outrun its theoretical base; we were overdrawn."

Mead got to work raising money, finishing her introduction to the anthology *Primitive Heritage*, with Nicolas Calas as her co-editor, which Random House would publish in 1953. Arranging for others to look after Cathy, she prepared for what she would describe as "one of the most astonishing and rewarding experiences that has fallen to the lot of man or woman in this century." Her plan was to see how Manus had been affected, as one of her irreverent colleagues remarked, by the fact that "the whole goddamn U.S. Army trooped through New Guinea in the war."

CHAPTER TWENTY

"A Little Minuet in Cotton Dresses"

Lenora Schwartz (later Foerstel) accompanied Mead on her 1953 return to Manus.

NOT SINCE her maiden expedition to Samoa had Margaret Mead set forth on a field trip, or any other kind of trip if she could help it, alone. There was no question of her going unaccompanied now, in 1953, to begin her first field work since she and Gregory Bateson had gone to Bali. For all her youthful energy, she was a woman in her fifties, and a gregarious one: she needed companionship. And for such a major expedition as her return to Manus (financed by field funds from the American Museum of Natural History and a substantial grant from the Rockefeller Foundation), the companionship had to be extraordinary. Whoever accompanied Mead would need the versatility of the young Reo Fortune and the resourcefulness of the young Gregory Bateson. Failing to find such a specimen among her own students, she conducted what amounted to a nationwide talent search, sending a circular around to the heads of all the major departments of anthropology in America.

A lean, intense, bespectacled twenty-five-year-old named Theodore Schwartz applied, at the urging and with the blessing of A. I. Halliwell, head of the Anthropology Department at the University of Pennsylvania. Schwartz listed "a very large number of skills and fields and interests—I was interested in linguistics, psychological testing, electronics, photography, cinematography, and I even specified an ability to repair equipment in the field. Anthropology attracted me," he said, "because it was the only way I could exercise such a diversity of interests."

Anthropology also appealed to Schwartz "for romantic reasons. I wanted to travel, and to see other peoples." Having written his master's thesis on labor migration in South Central Africa, he had hoped to go to Southwest Africa, perhaps under the sponsorship of the noted Africanist Professor Melville Herskovits of Northwestern University, who had been a student of Franz Boas. But funds were so scarce in the early 1950s that the prospects were slight for getting to any field. Interviewing Schwartz in Philadelphia, Mead had little difficulty persuading him to change his plans: "I'd have dropped anything," Schwartz said, "to go with Margaret Mead to New Guinea."

Originally Mead had been looking for two male companions, one a photographer and one an anthropologist, but that was before she met Schwartz's fiancée, Lenora Shargo, who became his wife in an Orthodox Jewish wedding in the fall of 1952. Lenora, who was nineteen, had never studied anthropology, and knew nothing of New Guinea except that it was nine thousand miles away. Nor, like her husband, had she ever been in an airplane or farther from home than to New York City. "But I knew other things. I knew all the great Russian writers, had read Tolstoy at age twelve, thought Uncle Vanya was my own uncle, and I knew all the artists. Margaret liked the fact that I was an artist and a dancer. She always surrounded herself with people who could dance." When people sat down Lenora noticed how much space they left between them. Lenora was observant and decisive; she could fix broken machinery; she had rare confidence. "My God, Lenora," Mead once said to her, "you're so flexible and secure that you must have had a lot of love in your life." This was true, said Lenora; "I was so flexible I could have gone to the moon."

Still, she and Ted had plenty to learn, and for six intense months, Mead taught them. She took them to the Gesell Institute in New Haven, to study techniques for administering projective tests: Rorschach ink blots, Thematic Apperception, mosaics, Stewart Ring Puzzles, Caligori's Eight-Card Redrawing Technique and Minnesota Paper Form Boards. In Philadelphia she taught them how to observe children in playgrounds, and to study their own families anthropologically. In New York they helped her shop and pack and mail supplies early, to avoid charges for excess baggage, and were shown how to operate cameras and tape recorders, and taught about etiquette in the places they would be going, especially in Australia.

"But, Mummy," said Cathy Bateson, "how can you ask her to call you 'Dr. Mead' when she'll be your best and only friend the whole time you're away?" "She'll have to, at least in Australia," said Cathy's mother, "because for the sake of the Australians, we have to preserve the hierarchy."

Nevertheless, Ted Schwartz remembered that "from the beginning it felt like family. That's the way Margaret was. To come into her life was to come in more or less for good." "To me," said Lenora, "she was like a permissive mother, who insisted that I learn to read, but never told me *what* to read." Yet Lenora did not call Margaret by her first name among the Australians, and she was reprimanded for exclaiming, "Is he gorgeous!" of a Melanesian in earshot of whites.*

In Los Angeles, the three had stopped to visit Richard Mead, whom Lenora remembered years later as "a nice, clean, but too placid man in a nice, clean house with a nice proper wife. He couldn't have been much older than fifty, if he was that, but he acted like an old, retired professor, and he didn't show much emotion." For the Los Angeles–Honolulu stretch of the journey, the three flew together, but Mead continued separately to Sydney, so that if one of their two planes should crash, the field work still could go on. On the plane to Port Moresby, she worried about an American woman passenger with a small baby. In the intense heat of New Guinea, Mead feared, the woman might not know how to keep the child comfortable.

In June of 1953, the trio arrived in Lorengau, the major settlement on Manus island. Lenora was scolded for not having brought a full-length evening gown to wear at a dinner there with Australian officials, though she had never owned such a gown in all her life. She felt per-

---

* Only twenty-seven years had passed since the White Women's Protection Act in New Guinea, which had decreed severe punishments for New Guinea men who made advances to white women. Evelyn Cheesman, who collected insect specimens in Papua for the British Museum, expressed a common enough attitude when she wrote in 1935 that "Women ought always to remember that they are dealing with animals. I have given offense to missionaries by using such a word, but far the best attitude to take towards natives is to look upon them all as a superior kind of animal. . . . 'All men are brothers' is a wonderful axiom to live up to, but it does not apply between savages and young women or children."

fectly comfortable in her regular dress at the party, but people could notice these things, Mead told her, and people could disapprove. Someone had disapproved, audibly, of Lenora's long, loose brown hair, which Margaret said should be tied up in a bun. Anthropologists, she told Lenora, ought to be as aware of their own cultural points as of those of the people they were studying; only prostitutes, she informed Lenora, wore long hair in Australia.

At last the group reached Peri village, Mead's 1928 headquarters, which again would be their base. "Margaret thought it was hysterically funny," Lenora said, "that I should say I couldn't 'find the culture.' Suddenly it came over me that I had *been in* the 'culture' from the moment I'd set foot on the island."

Soon after they arrived in Peri, a volcano erupted, which gave the Schwartzes a fine chance to show their mettle. Neither one of them, Mead said, "had ever seen an open wound, a birth, or a death. But the calm and expert way in which they handled the difficulties brought by the volcano in their first days in the field laid my anxieties at rest." Equable as ever in the face of disaster, Mead wrote home, "I have not decided whether this is a beneficent earthquake nicely timed to my special needs, as all the other earthquakes have been." Just so there wasn't a tidal wave, which would destroy the generator and the villagers' new houses, the earthquake resulting from the volcano was, in terms of field work, good luck: it showed how people reacted in an emergency. (It crossed Lenora's mind that the danger of a tidal wave might have been exaggerated by the local people for Mead's sake.)

Lenora did not know what to expect of her time in Manus, except that she was to do some trial mosaics, collect children's drawings to add to the collection Mead had begun in 1928, and administer a number of different projective tests. Altogether she and Ted and Mead would make a hundred half-hours of tape recording and shoot twenty thousand still photographs and 299 hundred-foot rolls of Ciné film. In childbirth scenes and other situations where photography was not feasible, Lenora made sketches and drawings to add to the voluminous field notes being taken. Mead, using her newly invented Neo-Melanesian shorthand, claimed she could take notes as fast as a man could talk.

Ted Schwartz felt let down when he first arrived in Manus. "After reading so many exotic monographs, so much classic ethnography, I was disappointed . . . It seemed so modernized, there were church services, village meetings resembling P.T.A. meetings, and court cases. The drums, the dancing, the ceremonial seemed gone—looked upon with disdain as 'the stinking ways of our ancestors.' "

That, of course, was the point. Manus's modernization, since Mead had described the place in *Growing Up in New Guinea*, was the reason she had come to study it again. When she and Reo Fortune had last been there in 1928, it was "a small cluster of stone-age headhunters . . . a mere two thousand nearly naked savages, living in pile dwellings in the sea, their earlobes weighted down with shells, their hands still ready to use spears, their anger implemented with magical curses, their morality dependent upon the ghosts of the recently dead. . . . A people without history, without any theory of how they came to be, without any belief in a permanent future life, without any knowledge of geography, without writing, without political forms sufficient to unite more than two or three hundred people." For money they had used dogs' teeth and shell beads.

Their "ceaseless economic endeavors," she had written, had been goaded by "a persistent fear of illness and death. Each man was expected by his Sir Ghost to keep up an appropriate amount of economic effort, in return for which his Sir Ghost would prosper his enterprises and protect his household." Each Sir Ghost, as Reo Fortune had written in *Manus Religion*, was represented by an ancestor's skull. But now, in 1953, the skulls had been hurled into the sea, along with the shell money, the dogs' teeth, the grass skirts, the mourning costumes, the dancing spears, and the baskets covered with rubber gum.

Now, Mead had heard, the people of Manus had become "potential members of the modern world, with ideas of boundaries in time and space, responsibility to God, enthusiasm for the law"; and were "committed to trying to build a democratic community, educate their children, police and landscape their village, care for the old and the sick, and erase age-old hostilities between neighboring tribes." Since Mead's first visit with Fortune, Manus had been a major staging area for the U.S. military. The troops who defeated the Japanese occupiers poured through the Admiralty Islands and treated the Melanesians not as objects of study but like brothers, Mead heard them say, and had given them what she would describe as "a passionate realization of what it meant to be treated—by civilized men, by white men—as people, people with individual names like anyone else."

From wood sawed in mills set up in the bush, "the Americans constructed miles and miles of barracks. The Americans knocked down mountains, blasted channels, smoothed islands for airstrips, tore up miles of bush—all with their marvelous 'engines.' . . . The Americans, she would write and Lenora Schwartz would verify, left behind not a single half-caste native child: no wonder the Manus were enchanted with what they called "fashion belong white man," or "new fellow fashion."

Growing Up in New Guinea had been much reprinted. Reo Fortune's photographs, including a winsome portrait of his and Margaret's grinning juvenile kitchen staff, captioned "Five Retainers," had been seen around the world. Now, as the 1953 visit began, those young retainers were mature men, eager to be part of the complexities of the modern world. The presence of Mead and the Schwartzes, one Manus leader told his people, meant that "everything you do will be recorded, filmed, put on tape . . . and *all America* will know whether we are succeeding in our new way of life."

"Two accidents of history—that we had chosen them and not some other tribe to study in 1928, and that Manus had been a major American staging area—were involved in this strange emergence of a group of erstwhile savages twice upon the world stage, once unconscious of their role, now fully aware of it." In the twenty-five years since Mead had last seen Manus, these villagers had made a leap, as she liked to phrase it, of something like four thousand years. Now they lived not in pile dwellings on stilts over the sea but in identical houses laid out in rows resembling streets. Now they wore Western clothes, marked time with calendars, lined up in queues, and longed restlessly for a place in the modern world. Mead, whose memories of the island in 1928 were still vivid, was uniquely qualified to put all this change into perspective. To study modern Manus without a background like hers, as Ted Schwartz later said, "would have been like studying embryology from scrambled eggs."

Mead's and Fortune's original work on Manus fully entitled her, she thought, to try to learn "how to treat this little revolution"—the changes that had occurred in Manus—"as a microcosm of what is happening all over the world, and how to select the details of life for a microscopic study." Making so dramatic a leap was no simple matter: "It is easier to shift from being a South Sea Islander to being a New Yorker—as I have seen Samoans do—than to shift from being a perfectly adjusted traditional South Sea Islander to a partly civilized, partly acculturated South Sea Islander, who has been given antiquated versions of our philosophy and politics, a few odds and ends of clothing and furniture, and bits and pieces of our economics."

And how had the people of Peri managed this feat? That question, she told the people, had brought her, with the Schwartzes, back to Manus. She had returned, she told them, "because of the great speed with which you have changed, and in order to find out more about how people change, so that this knowledge can be used all over the world."

The changes in Manus, aside from those the war had brought,

dated in part back to a 1947 religious outbreak called "The Noise," which had to do with the phenomenon of "Cargo Cults." Cargo cults, Mead explained in a letter home, were "the new New Guinea–Melanesian form of nativistic cult, at the core of which is a promise that the ancestors will return and after throwing out the white man or making them into servants, will bring all the white men's goods, the 'cargo.' Often these cults contain an apocalyptic element; only if the believers destroy all their present property, kill their pigs and dogs, and so on, can they hope to receive the cargo." Such a cult, Schwartz later wrote, "promised immediate parity with Europeans, through the supernatural intervention of Jesus, who would lead their own modernized ancestors into a wealth-laden reunion with the living. The cult subsided, leaving the movement with an assimilative program and an increasingly routinized native separatist church in its place."

The "movement" Schwartz referred to had one leader in particular. Paliau, the native Melanesian Mead had heard about in Australia, came from the island of Baluan and had a vision of a new world culture, to replace the obsolete local one. His vision had goaded the Manus into action. To avoid being beheaded, Paliau had collaborated with the Japanese military power and served as go-between for the Japanese army and the indigenous people in the maintenance of law and order. The new place in the sun he envisioned for Manus would combine mystical elements of reinterpretation of the Old and New Testaments, town planning, sumptuary laws, and an economic design for building a treasury.

"Some people felt that God had especially chosen Paliau to bring His Truth to New Guinea," Mead wrote, "after having watched first the failure of Captain Cook and then of the English, the Germans, the Australians, the Japanese, the Americans, to bring about the transformation of Manus man into the kind of society which Christ, by paying for men's sins, had made it possible for men to build." Paliau dreamed of leading a unified people toward a limited earthly paradise which could be attained realistically only through hard work and controlled behavior. Margaret Mead would "never, never, *never* have gone back to Manus, or done anything further there after 1928," said Rhoda Métraux, "if she hadn't heard about Paliau in 1951."

So now Mead settled down in Peri, her own and Fortune's original village. She dispatched the Schwartzes to the inland community of M'bunai, a day's trip away by foot and canoe, to study the Manus and Usiai people, who both lived there: it was a composite village. Once a week they came to Peri to dine, spend the night, "compare notes and talk, talk, talk about all we had seen," said Lenora. "First Margaret had thought of me as a wild animal in the woods, dancing with the people, but when she saw my notes, in which I elaborated on a system she had invented herself, she thought they were fantastic. She marveled that I could get the information I did. The reason I could was that I forged such strong bonds of respect with the people."

The Manus people liked Lenora and she liked them. "It made me physically ill," she said, "when Johannis Lokus, who kept our household going and who as a small boy had worked for Margaret and Reo, had to sleep in someone's kitchen when he went along with us to visit in Port Moresby." Mead's own relationship with the natives was more formal. "She was better at middle distance than holding close. As far as touch, Margaret was very careful"; she did not, Lenora said, visit the Manus people in their homes in the cities. Years later Mead asked another of her students, who was about to begin a field trip, how she was planning to bake bread.

"I don't like bread," said the student, "so maybe I won't bake it at all."

"But you must," said Mead, "to keep up white prestige!"

"She never ate with the Manus people," Lenora said. "When she ate, all the people of the village had to leave her house. (On a later trip Mead told a companion, 'They'll come in when *I* want them to come in.') She insisted on ceremony; she'd have a tablecloth and nice dishes. She trained everyone to leave when the tablecloths and dishes came out. The hierarchy between the anthropologist and the community was important to her. Except for Manus festivities, we were not invited to their houses, nor were they to ours. Basically, Margaret followed the mores of both the black and the white cultures of the time.

"She would always take a nap from one to three, and so did we. I had never taken midday naps in my life, but after a short time in Manus I realized I really needed this rest. You don't realize at first how much energy you have to put out to do that sort of work. Margaret taught me how to adjust by taking layers of sweaters off and then putting them back on. Margaret, who had had chronic malaria ever since Samoa, suffered from the heat more than I did." Malaria had afflicted Mead about a third of the time during her 1928 expedition to Peri. "Although I worked on the off days, and used even the bad days as an excuse for private conferences," she wrote, "still my efficiency was very much impaired." In 1953 things went better: "The three of us lost only about half a dozen days from very mild fever."

Heat and boredom, said Lenora, were Mead's only complaints. "She would get bored when the natives repeated things she already knew, and read detective stories. If she had been more physically active she wouldn't have been so bored." But physical activity had never been Mead's idea of diversion. "I have an ankle that goes to pieces," she once explained, "and I wear spectacles, and life's interesting enough anyway." Another problem, though Mead would certainly not have called it that, "was that her house was in the middle of all the activity in the village," said Lenora. "Ours, in M'bunai, was more private." Field work, Mead had cautioned the Schwartzes, "may destroy your marriage. All that intensity is hard on a couple." She spoke from experience; anthropology, Rhoda Métraux once said, often seemed "a contest in capacity for sheer survival." Mead's warning to the young couple proved well-founded. Ted's marriage to Lenora lasted five years.*

In 1981 Lenora Foerstel could vividly recall how embarrassed she had been, in 1953, when she had to take naked pictures of all the women in the village. One by one they lined up to take their clothes off to be photographed, front and profile. The men, meanwhile, were photographed by Schwartz. Lenora cringed at this invasion of the villagers' privacy but did not question the task. "I believed Margaret knew what she was doing. She didn't really believe that personality could be characterized by somatotypes, but that was one of the ways to test people, so of course she wanted to try it." Lenora became violently ill after taking these pictures, which the Peri people told her was divine retribution. She wasn't at all sure that they were wrong.

Mead's interest in somatotypes stemmed from a two-week International Symposium on Anthropology, sponsored by the Wenner-Gren Foundation, where she had befriended a beleaguered British physician named James H. Tanner. Tanner recalled having been "the youngest and least popular participant at the meeting," especially at one session where a number of prominent anthropologists were all arguing that all IQs were in effect equal.

"This was the era," said Tanner later, "when human differences were negated. I was particularly angry at a remark by Professor G. P. Murdock, at Yale, to which I retorted, 'The trouble with you people is that you don't seem to have that little bit of humanity that prevents you from kicking in the teeth someone whose IQ is less than yours. You fell that if people are different, they have to be bashed.' There was a

* Next, for nine years, he was married to his fellow anthropologist Lola Romanucci, who also became part of Mead's extensive longitudinal study of Manus when she went there with Schwartz in the 1960s.

fearful chill in that room, and just as everyone was getting ready to walk out for a break, Margaret came up to me and said, 'Young man, I think you're going to be in need of care and protection this afternoon—come and have tea with me.' She realized that I was friendless in that room, and she was the only one on my side."

Tanner was a student of W. H. Sheldon, author of *The Varieties of Human Physique*, which addresses the questions: "Do those who look most alike behave most alike? Does a particular sort of temperament go with a definite physique? Can we predict a man's likes and dislikes by measuring his body?" Mead was first introduced to these ideas by Gregory Bateson, who, in his Sepik work, used the temperamental classifications of Ernst Kretschmer. After the conference she had corresponded with Tanner, and had arranged to include somatotype research in her Manus field work.

When the somatotyping photographs the Schwartzes took of the Manus natives in 1953 were sent to Tanner, he observed that "the overwhelming thing was how extraordinarily mesomorphic these people were—they matched our Olympic athletes."

"Margaret herself," Lenora ventured many years later to Tanner, "was internally an ectomorph. She had internal movement which was never reflected outwardly."

"You mean like a thin man trying to get out?" he asked. "If she hadn't been so sensitive, she'd have been something of a bulldozer. Very reasonably she gave up on us when we didn't follow through on the pictures she sent us from Manus."*

Life in Peri village, for all the changes, was still demanding in 1953. There was much to be observed and done, including banking: "All day people make and return loans," Mead wrote, "varying from two sticks to ten sticks of tobacco—fifteen cents to seventy-five cents—which I solemnly record in a big book and solemnly cancel on return. Their love of trade, of working on credit, has not abated." Tobacco, in another form, prompted one of the most annoying interruptions of Mead's career. An urgent message summoned her to Lorengau, a seven-hour trip away by small launch in a bad sea, to return a phone call from

* Mead's friend and colleague Barbara Roll, previously Barbara Honeyman Heath, is still pursuing the somatotype studies, and with her photographer husband Fred Roll has sponsored several major expeditions to Manus. They have also published a lavishly illustrated book, *Stori Bilong Pere*, covering the genealogies of all the families in Peri village, which they presented to their friends there on a 1983 visit.

New York. The caller turned out to be not a member of her family with drastic news, as she had feared, but someone from Batten, Barton, Durstine & Osborn, the advertising agency, wanting to know what kind of cigarettes, if any, Dr. Mead smoked.

Mead's understandable irritation at having to leave her village was soothed by one circumstance: in Lorengau, just then, a man accused of having attempted to murder Paliau four years earlier was on trial. Mead thus had her first chance to study the popular leader at a near distance. Later, on his return from Lorengau, Paliau was delayed for the better part of a week at M'bunai, which gave the Schwartzes a chance to get to know him.

Mead's knowledge both of pidgin, or Neo-Melanesian, and of the Manus language complicated her burdens. "The mass of information, combined with endless reminiscing and anecdotes about everything that has happened in the last twenty-five years, assumes rather alarming proportions, and my typing gets way behind itself. I don't dare use tape because there is no chance to work over and revise—or, if one does, it takes as long." The natives seemed to remember her previous visit with astonishing clarity. They could recall how puzzled they had been to find that anthropologists would "come all the way there to live in a native house inferior to the kind of houses in which Europeans lived, with a floor made of slender split betel-palm trunks through which fountain pens and keys and chair legs slipped, sleep on narrow uncomfortable camping cots, eat food prepared by untrained little boys who burned the fish as they argued about who had more burnt tattoo marks on his upper arm, work eighteen hours out of the twenty-four in the steaming heat."

The natives' memory was phenomenal, except for one oversight: they could not call to mind how Mead had broken her foot when she was there in 1928. They remembered who had paddled the canoe that took her to the government station, who had donated the wood for her crutches, who made them, but not how the accident happened. It had happened, she told them, when she had slipped on a shaky temporary ladder in a doorless, stepless new house. After recounting this story, Mead pinned up a picture of herself on crutches, taken twenty-five years earlier, to remind the villagers of the one thing they had collectively chosen to forget, perhaps because of their own blame in the matter. As soon as they saw the picture, they all made haste to fix their own ladders. It was hard, Mead wrote home, to overestimate "the degree of sympathy and warmth that comes with [such] long acquaintance. I used to feel I knew many of the people with whom I worked—people like Fa'anotu in Samoa and our Arapesh boys and Madé Kaler in Bali. But this is different."

"It's all rather like a family gathering," she said, "with cousins one hasn't seen for twenty-five years." Some of the cousins were sickly, and Mead had to act as their doctor. Every morning she held a clinic to diagnose illnesses, and at all hours she dealt with medical emergencies. "There was seldom a day when I did not have at least one desperately sick person to keep track of. . . . I carried the continuous awareness of illness and death, not only as an anthropologist recording the events, but as the only therapist available." Some of her therapy was psychiatric. The vast changes since her previous visit to Manus had made depression and suicide common.

"What will it be necessary to say," she asked, "to the most promising and most crucial young man in the village who is still alive because he tried to hang himself with a piece of rubber tubing left over from the war which fortunately broke? How to [persuade him to] conquer his self-destructive, wounded pride and decide to live? All this requires a complete involvement—perhaps involvement is always measured by one's relative ability to act and to understand—such as I used only to achieve in trying to revive a drowned child or reduce the fever of a teething baby. But it is curious and wonderful to watch the way a changing ethic means a changing type of participation."

Their leader's stamina awed the young Schwartzes. "I mused on the need for a Manhattan Project," Ted wrote later, "to study the source of her energy, her creativity, and her appetite for and ability to encompass the complexity of very many lives within her own life and intellect." To Lenora it seemed that "Margaret did something with her viscera—she sat, unmoving, for hours, taking notes. She always knew what was happening behind the group, as well as in it. She internalized a lot, which could have been why she so often licked her mouth with her tongue, as if to bring her insides out."

But Mead's placid spells never lasted. Her temper was mostly directed at Schwartz, because, Lenora thought, "she assumed I was just obeying his orders and it couldn't be my fault." (Schwartz, who was to make at least seven more visits to the island of Manus, said in 1980 that he never was entirely sure why Mead had chosen him, and that he did not think he ever lived up to her expectations.) Margaret's anger, said Lenora, "was a powerful means of control. She would say she wished she could get us out of her hair, or that she could send us back." One of her tantrums erupted over what she took to be the Schwartzes' ingratitude when she offered them what for all she or they knew was "the only refrigerator in all New Guinea." Not wanting it herself, she had it sent to the young couple, but they didn't much want it either. Lenora, who had grown up in a Russian household with a samovar, found hot tea an adequate refreshment even so near the Equator.

Religion never came up in Mead's talks with Lenora, who had no reason to assume that her interest in the subject extended beyond a routine ethnological curiosity. Nor did the two women talk about sex. "She decided I was too sweet and innocent," said Lenora. "She characterized everybody and decided what she could and couldn't talk about with them. It was clear that she had had lots of sexual relationships herself, but she sensed, and she was right, that an experimental sex life was not my bag. I was brought up to be totally faithful, with the idea that the male would get sick if he had to go without sex for more than two days."

As Christmas approached in 1953, Mead ordered a huge cargo of special gifts from Sydney for the Manus people, and prepared to leave her young associates behind. "The process of being a good field worker," she once said, "is primarily discovering what you don't have to do." The Schwartzes, she decided, were now well enough trained to stay on until the following June to finish the project. When her departure day came, she had an idea.

"She thought it would be good," said Lenora, "for her and me to do a dance. At the time—though I look back on the scene with amused affection—I thought it was ridiculous, but of course she won, and so we did this little sort of minuet together, both wearing little cotton dresses."

And then, just as Mead was preparing to sail away from her second sojourn in Manus, a villager named Pokanau, who long ago had been her and Reo's houseboy, approached her with a valedictory word.

"Now, like an old sea turtle," he told her, "you are going out to the sea to die, and we will never see you again."

He could not have known how wrong he would be, or how often his old employer would return. Nobody could ever complain of Margaret Mead's work in Manus that she had just passed through.

CHAPTER TWENTY-ONE

"You Only Saw
a Fragment of the Iceberg"

PEOPLE AND IDEAS were what Mead most liked combining, but she also had a flair for making salads. "She would start with a dressing of oil, vinegar, lemon juice, mustard, salt, and pepper," her goddaughter Martha Ullman West remembered, "all beaten up in the bottom of a salad bowl. Then she would add capers, pimiento, fresh dill and tomatoes when she could get them, and salad greens. With this we usually had French bread and strong cheese. Margaret liked Gorgonzola, bleu cheese, Brie, Camembert, and Liederkranz. At the scent of Liederkranz Cathy and I would flee, holding our noses, but Margaret loved it."

KEN HEYMAN

Mead gave a salad-making lesson in Australia, on Christmas Eve 1953, at the end of her Manus field trip. Her pupils were her friends Marjorie and Charles Bull. The world, Mead was by this time convinced, had become "one great highway," with the dawning of "the age of the air . . . and in any inn along the way there must be room and welcome for each and every guest." The Bulls, chosen to welcome her as their Christmas guest, obliged with exemplary seasonal cheer, although the lady of the house, a social worker, needed to be asked: "Haven't you heard that there are six or seven kinds of lettuce?" In fact Marjorie Bull had not. "We were terribly simple people in Sydney then," she said, "with dreadful feeding habits," but that could be remedied.

"I will make the salad," said the incorrigible teacher, and she did so with a gusto that made up for the limited ingredients. This small cooking lesson was very characteristic of Margaret Mead. From the time in her Barnard days when she persuaded a classmate to choreograph her mother's Pennsylvania Dutch ballet, she was always a kind of choreographer herself, convincing people to try new things and showing them exactly how. "Here, go do it," she would say, and off they would go, farther than they had thought possible. She made them stretch, one said, and she dissolved their blocks. She endorsed, said another, and she emancipated. She also criticized. "If something went wrong," another protégé put it, "she was the first, second and third to tell you."

"Maybe at the back of it all," as Mead herself had written to Ruth Benedict in 1924, "I have a Puritan desire to make people fight their own peculiar battles," and so much the better if those battles had anything to do with anthropology. "Reo Fortune had been going to get further in psychology," one of his old friends said, "but Margaret turned him into an anthropologist, probably because she wanted someone alive to anthropology to accompany her into the field."

After this Australian Christmas, at Mead's request, Charles and Marjorie Bull drove her to the place on the South Coast where D. H. Lawrence had written his novel *Kangaroo*. "But she didn't want to linger there," said Marjorie. A glance was all she wanted or needed. Scenery—as many, including Mead's other Australian friend, Caroline Kelly, agreed—never moved her. "Our farm had a stupendous view, but whenever we reminded her of it she would just sit with her back to it, correcting papers, and say, 'Yes, I've already seen it.' But she loved Australia, always. After New York it was definitely her chosen base." Perhaps she declined to settle there because she agreed with D. H. Lawrence, a favorite author of Mead's and Gregory Bateson's, who wrote that if he "stayed here for six months I should have to stay forever—there is something so remote and far off and utterly indifferent to our European world, in the very air. I should go a bit further away from Sydney, and 'go bush.' "

Except for field trips—in her case an enormous exception—Margaret

Mead never "went bush" anywhere. The thought repelled her. "She hated the country," said Martha Ullman West. "She'd visit friends who lived there, to please the friends, but she was bored, as they well knew. She conceded that flowers were pretty—she prided herself, in fact, on her flair for arranging flowers—but plants and animals, as far as she was concerned, were dull. She was absolutely an urban person. What she cared about most were people, in the largest possible doses."

During Cathy's childhood Mead had taken to sending out photographic Christmas cards, showing her either with her daughter or at some remote site (once with a red arrow pointing to "MY ROOM"). These cards, with Mead's ever tinier and squigglier signature, went to a list of 521 addresses, from the South Island of New Zealand to the interior of North America, where they were saved and treasured for years. Some two hundred of those names represented what Mead thought of as her extended family, a group that in time encompassed her former husbands, their new wives, and all the households around the globe where she felt welcome. In some of these households there was talk of putting plaques in the guest rooms: "MARGARET MEAD SLEPT HERE." Keeping in touch with so many families, one friend said, "may have distracted Margaret from a pretty poverty-stricken life. Being a cast-iron monument, and having all those friendships, kept her busy, but after a few drinks she would relax and sometimes weep for the loss of Gregory."

Ted and Lenora Schwartz stayed in Manus until June of 1954, and headed home by way of Europe, where neither had been before. Over the next three decades after their divorce, they would return many times to Manus, with their later spouses and under whatever auspices they could manage. Margaret Mead had changed the courses of both their lives, as she had and would the lives of hundreds of others. It was said of Mead that she brought more young people into anthropology than anyone else did ever, convincing her recruits that they had chosen "the only occupation," as she once loftily described it, "that required strictly first-class people."

But the strains of field work, as Mead had warned, could be hard on even first-class marriages. Ted Schwartz was not pleased when Lenora received a telegram from Mead's child psychologist friend Margaret Lowenfeld inviting her to collaborate on a book about mosaic testing.* He was so displeased that he tore up the telegram, and he and

* Mead greatly admired Lowenfeld's work with expressive projective tests. "I learned more from her in two days," Mead had written to Gregory Bateson in 1948, "than from the whole rest of the summer put together. . . . She is rather an astonishing person, half Polish in fact, wholly Polish in character structure. . . ."

Lenora bickered their way through Europe to England, where Mead had arranged for them to be welcomed in London by Geoffrey Gorer and in Cambridge by Reo Fortune.

Not until much later did the young couple learn that Gorer's mother had died the day before they arrived. "He was heartbroken," said Lenora, "but he told us nothing about it. He gave us snails and pink champagne and saw that we had an elegant time. He was handsome and gallant, and I could understand how Margaret might have considered marrying him, but she later told me she couldn't imagine having to apply medication to his back, or sharing a bathroom with him or anyone else. She loved the way he treated her, though, and the places he took her. Who wouldn't?" Reo Fortune was just as welcoming when the travelers arrived in Girton, the village where he lived with his second wife, Eileen. He took them to his favorite pub. Lenora was honored and pleased to be Fortune's guest, but she found his conversation puzzling.

"I tried very hard to figure out how in one sentence we had got from New Guinea to cockroaches," she said. "Since I had not then read Freud, I didn't know he was free associating, dealing in what is called primary process." A student of Fortune's recalled his having "a bit of a stutter. His thoughts were six stages ahead of what he was saying, but if you listened carefully you could always find a thread there. The thread usually had to do with religious ideas—souls, transubstantiation."

Mead thanked Fortune for treating her young associates so kindly, in a letter of November 10, 1954, on museum stationery. Ted and Lenora, she told him, "had a lovely time, and it was a kind of bringing together of past and present for them, which was very much appreciated. . . . My book on Manus revisited [*New Lives for Old*, her account of the field work] is about ¾ done. . . . I am teaching a course in field methods this semester and enjoying it very much, but there are too many different kinds of students. Next year I am going to limit it to anthropology graduate students past the MA level, and really get some work out of them.

"Cathy flourishes—at present she is planning to combine writing and mathematics! Last year it was painting and biology. I plan to take her to Europe next summer to spend two months with a French family while I write somewhere—probably Ireland. It's always good to hear from you. Yours, Margaret." (Some of her letters to Luther were signed, "Love," but "Yours" was her customary ending when she wrote to Reo and, at least during the 1950s, to Gregory.)

Catherine Bateson, then just short of fifteen, was enrolled at Brearley School, where few of her classmates lived in Greenwich Village or had celebrated parents. Some of them found her aloof. She found some of them flawed, too. Whenever she was outspokenly critical of her contemporaries or her country, her mother would get angry. Such talk, Mead would tell her, was "a *bore!*" To show Cathy where she came from and what she stood for, she took her to family reunions of the Ramseys, Mead's paternal grandmother's people, in Winchester, Ohio.

The world authority on adolescence was delighted to have a resident teenager of her own flesh and blood. One Christmas card showed mother and daughter by the fireplace of their Greenwich Village living room, with Cathy holding up a phonograph record as if she were choosing the music for a party. Wilton Dillon was a chaperon for one party Mead gave for Cathy and her classmates. Dillon, whom Mead and Eliot Chapple hired to edit a *Human Resources Bulletin* in 1954, had become a virtual member of the family, as in time would his wife and their son.

After Lenora and Ted Schwartz returned to the States, Mead visited them in Ann Arbor, where Ted taught at the University of Michigan (later at the University of Chicago). Soon after their son Jonathan was born in Chicago, on October 11, 1955, a package arrived from a favorite establishment of Mead's, B. Harris Jewelers in New York, from which she always ordered engraved silver cups for babies and sentimental presents for grownups. Her taste, said the proprietor, Nathan Harris, a lifelong friend since the Ash Can Cat days, ran to antique things and crystal.

"Whenever Mead had any reason to speak or appear in Chicago," said Lenora, "she would be delighted for the chance it would give her to 'study Jonny.' She told me to be careful to pick him up as soon as he started to cry, because he was high-strung. I took her advice, and maybe that was why Jonny grew up to be unusually stable and calm." Mead could always find business to attend to in Chicago, or almost any other place she might want to go. The more her trips could combine the professional with the personal, the abstract with the concrete, the happier she was. On a March 1957 trip to Chicago she met Gertrude Hendrix, of Cloverdale, Indiana, whose professional interest in the early handling of horses and other animals paralleled Mead's in the early handling of human beings.

One consequence of this meeting was the filming in 1963, of the birth and early handling of a foal, and, the following year, of a filly, who was injured, and had to be killed after only eight days. Hearing this news, Mead phoned Hendrix to say "Well, you got your film, anyway," which Hendrix did not find very consoling. "But later, Margaret must have thought about what the catch in my voice meant," she said, "because she sent me a note to say how sorry she was about the little filly."

Mead's notes usually came straight to the point. In a few lines, which she often typed herself and did not read over for typographical and spelling errors, she could dispense either healing warmth or scathing scorn. One note, to someone whom she had obviously decided was not only a dimwit but a pest, was signed "Coldly, Margaret Mead." These messages were usually but not always answered. Ellen Godwin enjoyed the cards her old boss sent her later, but did not reply to them.

"Having worked in that office," Godwin said, "I knew how Margaret analyzed everything that came in—the paper, the handwriting, all the rest of it. Somehow I didn't want to subject myself to all that scrutiny. But when I was in Germany where my husband was stationed, and Margaret came there to speak in 1956 I naturally went to hear her, and later went up to the podium to apologize for not having written. 'We forgive people for things like that,' Margaret said. She was smiling; she seemed pleased to see me. I was more than pleased, I was enchanted, especially when she saw my son and said, 'Oh, I *knew* you'd hold him that way.' " (That son, too, got a silver cup from B. Harris.)

Mead did all she could for members of her giant extended family. For those whom she considered anthropologically gifted, she sometimes waived rules regarding graduate degrees. "Some academics were furious about Alan Lomax and Geoffrey Gorer," said the ethnographic filmmaker Timothy Asch. "Lomax, a protégé of the songwriter Woody Guthrie, had collected more material about American folk music than he knew what to do with. Mead gave him his lead and his structure and urged him to compare different song styles around the world, so he got into the club without a passport, without the discipline of a Ph.D., on the basis of his highfalutin theories and arguments."

One branch of her extended family was fathered by Ray Birdwhistell, whom she met when he was a doctoral student at the University of Chicago. To Birdwhistell, a friend said, Mead gave "enough recognition and support so that in time people would sit at his feet the way he had sat at hers." Mead called Birdwhistell's attention to one of the ideas of her late friend Edward Sapir, an idea that led to what in the late 1960s came to be called nonverbal communication or body language. "We respond to gestures," Sapir had noted, "with an extreme alertness and, one might almost say, in accordance with an elaborate and secret code that is written nowhere, known by none, and understood by all."

With the help of Mead and other mentors, Birdwhistell made it his life's work to decode this language of gestures by means of a discipline he named kinesics. This discipline sprang from his conviction that "body motion is a learned form of communication, which is patterned within a culture and can be broken down into an ordered system of isolable elements," as he wrote in *Introduction to Kinesics*, published in 1952. Actions, to put it differently, were at least as eloquent as words. "We must remember," Birdwhistell said in 1980, "that man talks for very few moments a day, but for hundreds upon hundreds of moments a day when humans are interrelated, they are passing important, transmissible information."

Birdwhistell's first wife, Miriam, recalled an occasion in Chicago "when Margaret sat right on the floor with everybody else, animatedly talking about the Hopi and the Navajo." Around this time the Birdwhistells and Mead had come to feel so close that they decided that if they were not technically kinfolk, at least they could and should become "kith." This the couple formally acknowledged by choosing "Mead" as a middle name for their second daughter, Nancy, and having the whole family formally baptized just as Margaret had arranged to be baptized herself when she was eleven.

Godmotherhood was no small thing to Margaret Mead. She made a point of being available when her godchildren needed her. Would you rather talk of the past, she asked one child whose father had suddenly died, or of the present and the future? "Good," said Mead when the child chose the present and future. "That's what I prefer to talk about, too." And when Martha Ullman suffered a youthful heartbreak, her godmother assuaged her grief by canceling her own plans and giving the girl a restorative lunch of egg rolls and vin rosé, along with the journals of Virginia Woolf and Katherine Mansfield.

That egg roll lunch was elegant, Martha recalled, with a glass of water and a glass of wine set at each place, as always when Mead dined at home in New York. She liked to serve ritual breakfasts of fried eggs, fried bread, sausage, and orange juice. For years she gave Christmas Eve dinner parties at which the menu included asparagus, Allen Ullman's steak with hollandaise sauce, and Colin McPhee's famous zabaglione. The guest list varied only slightly. One December 24 everyone at the party felt sad; something tragic had just happened to one of the regular celebrants. The absent person, said Joan Halifax, who was present, was "such a wild genius, with such tremendous charm and tremendous sexual energy, so brilliant, that a pall was cast over everything. We all looked out of the windows at the snow, and Margaret, though she usually led a consciously sacred life in the Protestant path, didn't even go to midnight [services]. Around midnight I went in one of the bedrooms to lie down, and woke from a deep sleep after a while to find Margaret kind of leaning over me, looking down at me. She took her glasses off and began to weep, and said nothing. It was a most spacious silence; I just held her. Neither of us could say a word.

"After a while she got up in a very proper way and departed, and somewhat later Alan [Lomax, with whom Halifax was then living] came and got me, and Margaret walked us to the door still not saying anything. So many people ran into her bristles, experienced her brilliance and her courage, but you don't hear so much about the spacious, silent compassion I felt from her that Christmas." But most Christmas Eves were more talkative: one year, Martha Ullman West recalled, a passionate discussion about love went on until four in the morning.

Mead tried never to miss weddings, christenings, holidays, or other gatherings of the several families she felt closest to. "She'd sleep on the living room Pullman couch, share whatever we had, and fall in with the tempo of our family life," said Miriam Birdwhistell. "Once she delighted our children by reciting Genesis 1:1 to them in pidgin English." Colin Frank had a similar memory: "I used to just beg her to speak to us in that curious, sing-song pidgin. She could be very funny. And she would let us know if she thought someone was a jerk, as not all adults would do. She wouldn't say so in so many words, but she would roll her eyes and purse her lips and wince, and shake her head in a slight tremor." Mead was as welcome at the Birdwhistells', who lived in Chicago and later in Louisville, Toronto, and Philadelphia, as she was with the family of Lawrence K. Frank, on Perry Street, at Cloverly, and, after 1955, in Belmont, Massachusetts. In 1955, Colin Frank said, his father had suffered from an acute sense of being tired of New York, "ground down by a lot of professional disappointments, and bad times financially. He was in a bad mood a lot of the time, in spite of the renaissance my mother's intense adoration had given him. So he took us all to Europe for three months, and then we resettled outside Boston, and Margaret and Cathy moved into Waverly Place with Rhoda and Daniel and the indomitable, fulsome, real Tulia."

Had the term "single parents" been coined in 1955, it would have applied to Rhoda Métraux and Margaret Mead. Daniel Métraux was six years old and Cathy Bateson was sixteen when Mead rented a floor of the three-story brick house Métraux had bought at 193 Waverly Place. Tulia Sampeur, a housekeeper whom Métraux and her husband had met during field work in Haiti, presided, neatened drawers, wrestled young Daniel to the ground on occasion, and, a childhood friend of the boy's remembered, made dreadful salads: "People would warn, 'Don't let Tulia make the salad. She'll beat it to a pulp!' " Margaret was grateful for Tulia (who, she wrote to a friend, spoke "no known language") in spite of her salads. She spoke, of course, Haitian Creole.

Domestic "hearthiness," as Colin Frank called it, was in all these cases mixed together with professional guidance and shoptalk. Being needed nourished Mead. "She was pleased when I told her once that I had dreamed of holding my hands out to her and saying, 'Oh, please help me,'" said Lola Romanucci-Ross. "Her preferred method of relating was with petitioners although she *said* she admired strong people who didn't need help—I keep thinking what D. H. Lawrence said, that true love can only exist between two people who are as eagles copulating in midair—but I'm not so sure Margaret wanted people to be like that."

Anthropology attracts different people for different reasons. "You can raid any other discipline," Ted Schwartz remarked in 1980, "and call it anthropology." Anthropology, said a like-minded museum colleague of Mead's, "feeds on crumbs from everybody else's table," which may account for the dubious reputation it has among some scholars of more formal disciplines. William Mitchell, who came into Margaret Mead's life in 1954, entered the field because he thought that philosophy, in which he had just received his master's degree, would be too limiting. "Philosophy didn't have data, details, ethnography—anthropology had everything. 'Everything,' as Margaret said when I took her course, 'is grist for anthropology's mill.'" That, said Mitchell, appealed to him, and so did "the relativistic point of view expressed in books by Margaret and by Ruth Benedict": the idea that different approaches are equally valuable, that European culture is not necessarily supreme.

The first time Mitchell went to see Margaret Mead "she was very busy, but she seemed to like talking to me. It was amazing how quickly she got social placement on me"—perhaps not so very amazing, since Mitchell obviously came of a background very much like Mead's own. "After about fifteen minutes she said, 'Bill, if you don't mind waiting while I make a few phone calls, you can stay for the afternoon.' I was delighted. She scolded me, though. She said, 'If you're going to be an anthropologist, you ought to be taking notes. You shouldn't trust your head.'"

After that conversation, Mitchell felt "an undeniable connection with Margaret that had an impact on my whole life. The connection was emphatic. She wouldn't have tolerated it otherwise." Was it love? "Of a sort, I guess, but love wasn't the point. The point was intervention. She would never hesitate to pick up a phone or help solve any problem she could for her friends or her students." One student, a friend said, "had a hangup about exams, always flunked them. Margaret arranged for him to have special take-home exams he could do in forty-eight hours. For people she bet on, she'd do anything."

Timothy Asch first met Mead in 1958, when he was a Columbia undergraduate who needed special permission, as she had once needed it herself, to enroll in graduate courses. He climbed to her museum tower to state his case. "After searching through that labyrinth for her office," he said, "I could barely see her for all the books on her table. Never having met me before, she asked me to sit down and tell her what was on my mind. My speech lasted only five minutes; I was terrified. She asked how old I was, how much money I needed, whether I was married, what was my plan. She planned my second and third and fourth years and my graduate life—field work after two years of courses. She was incredibly perceptive; her brightness really shone in her perception of events and of people's potential."

She kept that quality. Ten years later, a graduate anthropology student named Donald Tuzin spent a whole April weekend composing a letter asking her advice about the field work he proposed to do among the Arapesh of New Guinea, whom Mead and Reo Fortune had studied in 1932. Mead replied, suggesting a meeting at 1:00 P.M. on September 15. At that precise hour, without any word in the intervening months, young Tuzin appeared on her doorstep. Mead greeted him by saying she was not in the habit of making dates five months in advance without having them confirmed; nevertheless she and Rhoda Métraux were prepared for his visit. He was invited in for drinks and lunch.

The food and Mead's guidance about the Arapesh were exemplary, Tuzin said, but he did not feel quite at his ease. "My usual techniques for ingratiating myself with women their age," he remembered, "didn't work at all." Mead, many said, had her own effective "usual techniques" for ingratiating herself with young men, as well as with older ones.

"Of course nobody knew all of what she was doing," said William Mitchell. "Already, she was all over the place. Whoever you were, however important she made you feel, you only saw a little piece, a teeny fragment of the iceberg. When she was my adviser, in graduate school, she would tell me to come down to her office at 2:30 and ride with her in the cab to her dentist, and by the time she got to the dentist we would have solved two or three problems." When Mead moved into Métraux's house on Waverly Place, Mitchell and Paul Byers helped her pack and then reshelve her books. "Paul would plane and sand the bookcases, I'd kind of help, and we made a big party of it, with spaghetti and with one of Margaret's salads."

On Waverly Place, as earlier on Perry Street, Mead's quarters were comfortable and filled with paintings by her friend Allen Ullman and her sister Elizabeth Steig, but by most standards relatively simple. New York was only one of her several bases. "If you have an intense life in each of four places, even though you only get to them for, say, ten days a year," she said, "they're still all a part of your life, so that you have a large simultaneity that is different from living in one place and never in another."

Mead always lived intensely at the annual conventions of anthropologists, wherever they happened to be. Her colleagues found the meetings boring or intimidating; Ruth Benedict had complained in 1932 that they were "feebleminded"; but when Mead was around they were rarely dull. In late 1954, when the convention was in Detroit, she scolded her old associate Melville Herskovits in the middle of a speech he was giving. "Mel!" she said to him. "You're talking nonsense! Why don't you sit down?" Mead said this, someone remembered, as if they were at a small gathering of a few close friends, not in a large public auditorium filled with colleagues.

"She could be ruthless," said the ethnographic filmmaker Asen Balikci, "with Herskovits and Malinowski and many other men. If she disliked them and disagreed with them, she could devour them on sight—she didn't want any other big animals coming close."

Lesser-known colleagues could threaten Mead, too. Perhaps her irritation with Melville Herskovits, in late 1954, had something to do with a task Herskovits had assigned to his graduate student Lowell D. Holmes, then studying Polynesian ethnography at Northwestern University. The previous year Holmes had planned his first field trip, to Fiji. At the last minute, for reasons involving Fijian politics, his trip was canceled, and he had to find a new Polynesian destination. Herskovits, who for years had suspected that American Samoa might be more complicated than Mead had shown it in *Coming of Age*, suggested that Holmes might undertake a methodological restudy of the Manu'an island of Ta'u, where Mead had done her first field work. Holmes's criticism of Mead's work, Herskovits instructed, should deal with major issues, not trivial details, and should be made with "icy objectivity."

In theory Mead should have been pleased to hear of Holmes's new project. The tragedy of anthropology, she had said herself, was that

a given society should only be studied by one person, whose biases
would necessarily influence the results. No other anthropologist had
worked in Ta'u since she left in 1926. But not until Holmes and his
wife and child were settled in Ta'u did he write to tell Mead of his
project, and to ask her the real names of some of the girls who had had
"such bizarre sex histories." Mead's reply to his letter, Holmes said,
"was extremely skeptical and uncooperative. She wrote back that she
didn't know who I was, and that I should have had the courtesy to
clear my restudy with her before I left."

His project, so far as Holmes knew, was "the first methodological
restudy in anthropology ever conducted with the specific purpose of
evaluating the validity and reliability of an earlier observer's work." His
aim was "not necessarily to prove that I was right and that Mead was
wrong (if great discrepancies had been discovered), but to investigate
the 'personal' equation in ethnographic field work, that is, the kinds of
errors that might be made by particular people under certain conditions." How different would things look to a married man of twenty-
nine in 1954, accompanied by his wife and child, from the way they had
looked in 1926 to "a slip of a girl," the same size as and only a little
older than her informants?

"There is no such thing," as Mead had written in 1951, "as an
unbiased report on any social situation"; her bias was one thing and
Holmes's, unsurprisingly, was quite another. As an honorary *taupou*, a
ceremonial virgin, she had spent the better part of her time with very
young women; Holmes, given the chiefly title of Tuife'ai, "King of the
Cannibals," had access to the deliberations of the *fono*, the village
council. In American Samoa just as in, say, Evanston, Illinois, a society
seen from the perspective of female high-school freshmen would look different from the way that same society would look, studied three decades
later, from the office of the mayor. Holmes found Mead "overly protective" of her subjects, and thought she had taken too much artistic
license in the composite portrait, in her first chapter, of "A Day in
Samoa"; "she made it seem a beehive of activity," he said, "while most
hours of most days I was there you could have shot a cannon down the
equivalent of Main Street without hitting a soul."

Mead had found Ta'u people cooperative; to Holmes they seemed
competitive. She had reported that Samoans had no romantic love; he
"found their mythology full of some of the most romantic folklore I
had ever run across." Some of these discrepancies, he thought, may have
stemmed from the fact that Mead's chief informant, apart from the
girls she talked to, was "anything but typical—he was a Rosicrucian, in
fact—and I couldn't help wondering how valid his information had

been."* But Holmes concluded, in spite of their points of difference, that much of what Mead had reported from Ta'u was remarkably valid. He supported her conclusion on the basis of what he had seen in American Samoa in 1954 and learned about coming of age in the United States in 1925, that the Samoan experience would have been, as he put it, "immensely less stressful and traumatic."

Eventually Mead and Holmes became allies, but at first she took umbrage at his retracing of her steps. In the April 1961 *American Anthropologist* she reviewed Holmes's 1958 book *Ta'u: Stability and Change in a Samoan Village*, unfavorably. And in 1960, at the AAA meetings in Minneapolis, Holmes remembered that Mead had "cornered me and laced me up and down, said how dishonest I was, and what a poor job I had done. I was a brand new Ph.D. then, and this was tough for me to take. All the way home from that meeting I told my wife what I *should* have answered to Margaret Mead, but in a way I guess I should have been flattered. The only people she gave hell to, they say, were those she respected. She's nobody to have as an enemy, I can tell you that."

Mead wasn't really Holmes's enemy, though. Their common adversary, as time would prove, was Derek Freeman, who between expeditions to Borneo and his routine academic duties was spending all the time he could in his study in Canberra, storing up data to discredit both their portraits of Samoa.†

---

* Twenty-nine years later Napoleone A. Tuiteleapaga, the "chief informant" Holmes referred to, became a figure of brief world renown. This happened after Harvard University Press published the Australian anthropologist Derek Freeman's book *Margaret Mead and Samoa: The Making and Unmaking of an Anthropological Myth*. Based on a total of six years of field work over a span of four decades, mostly in Western Samoa but with a visit to Ta'u, Freeman's 1983 book aroused such publicity that the attention of much of the world was suddenly focused on all Samoans, especially outspoken ones, especially Tuiteleapaga.

Tuiteleapaga, after his encounters first with Mead and later with other ethnographers, was an old hand at being interviewed. He took it well in stride, early in 1983, when *Life* and the *Wall Street Journal* sent reporters to Samoa to get local reactions to the fuss over Freeman's book. He was quizzed at length about the "good-looking *palagi* [white girl]," as he called Mead, whom in 1926 he had befriended and served as an interpreter—but not, he said, as more than that. In 1980 Tuiteleapaga had published a book of his own, *Samoa Yesterday, Today and Tomorrow*, whose introduction he claimed had been written by Mead herself, "in her office in New York shortly after her death"—a neat trick, Lowell Holmes suggested in his review of the book. Whoever had written the introduction, Holmes said, had managed to reproduce the book's author's style of writing "almost exactly."

† Freeman's 1983 book on Mead's work, and the public reaction to it, is dealt with in the afterword.

CHAPTER TWENTY-TWO

"Teach Me Something!"

CLAUS MROCZYNSKI

TRUTH, KNOWLEDGE, VISION
—*inscription outside American Museum of Natural History*

IN LUMINE TUO VIDEBIMUS LUMEN
(In thy light shall we see light)
—*motto of Columbia University*

WHATEVER ELSE Margaret Mead was doing, and wherever she happened to be, she never stopped teaching. Whether her subject matter was the rag content of paper used for field notes or the lettuce used for a salad, she could no more help instructing anyone around her than she could help breathing. Colleges and faculties and classrooms were far from the only places to find students. She would have agreed with C. S. Lewis that "the ripest are kindest to the raw"; her eye was always out for young talent to nurse along, as she had been guided in her own youth by Franz Boas and Ruth Benedict, but nobody was too old to benefit from her instruction, formal or impromptu. Her Dublin colleague Feichin O'Doherty, the priest and psychologist, said that knowing her had allowed him to give immeasurably more to his students, "because of her clarification of my thought. She made luminous what I had seen before, but simply."

The cartoon picture of light bulbs symbolizing ideas keeps recurring in tales of Mead the teacher. Electricity lingered in rooms where her classes had met, it is said, for an hour after the class was over. Ken Heyman, whom Mead discovered in a Columbia classroom and took along to photograph several field trips, told a less metaphorical story about Mead and illumination. Visiting a primitive Bali village with her in 1957, he pointed out to her, with a laugh, some light bulbs the inhabitants had hung up: what use, he asked Mead, could these people possibly have for light bulbs?

"Just because in *your* society people only use them for light," she replied, "doesn't mean they aren't beautiful objects." Mead, Heyman said, "taught me how to look at things. She was remarkable with her eyes: we'd communicate almost extrasensorily, with just a nod or a look. She'd sit where the women sat, and although she was very unattractive, she could communicate so well with her eyes that even before they heard her speak, they'd be involved with her. She did something curious with her chubby little hands, too. She would sit with her palms up, as if to say, 'I come empty-handed, I carry no weapons, I am here to receive; show me.' It's quite uncomfortable to sit that way, but I saw her do it often, especially when she was talking to children."

"I am here to receive; show me," could have been Mead's motto wherever she went. In Australia, Marjorie Bull took her to visit a friend's quadriplegic nineteen-year-old daughter, who had hoped to be an anthropologist and still, despite her disabilities, was studying the subject. "In anthropology," Mead told the young woman, "we want to know what life is like from every point of view." She was everybody's teacher, but everybody was hers, too. When she assigned papers to her classes, she would implore them to "*teach* me something!" and when they obliged, she was delighted. When Mead invited Heyman to accompany her on the Bali trip, the young photographer was awed. "I didn't know how to talk to a genius then. I didn't even know how to talk to a friend. I was just a kid out of college, where I'd flunked courses. I knew so little of Asia that I barely liked Chinese food, when suddenly there I was washing in a Dutch bathtub in Indonesia that turned out to be a family's whole supply of drinking water for a week. Another time, when Margaret was given a piece of rotten awful pork with flies on it, I said, 'You're not going to eat *that*, are you?' and she said, 'You bet I am, and so are you.' But she drew the line somewhere. When a chief offered me his daughter, she said, 'Now, Ken!' "

Three kinds of students, Mead once said, were attracted to her classes: those who wanted her name on their records, those who wanted to hear her, and those who were seriously interested in anthropology. The last category, streaming through her classrooms and seminars, gave her many of the people who became her TAs—teaching assistants—at Columbia, and who helped to staff her turret office at the American Museum of Natural History. Her large lecture course, she said, was "designed to catch mavericks—people who don't know what they're looking for." Some students referred to these lecture courses as "Tuesday night at the movies"; one called them "immense travelogues, carelessly designed."

Mead could be and was lured away for terms of a week or a semester or a year as a guest professor at Emory, at Yale, at Fordham, at New York University, and at any number of other colleges and universities, but her chief allegiance was to Columbia. There she had taught her first course in 1940 at the Extension, which evolved into the School of General Studies, and held appointments more years than not for the rest of her life. In the spring term of 1966, typically, she gave three courses: G4172x, Cultures of the Pacific; G8272y, Methods and Problems in Anthropology; and G9352y, Seminar in Culture and Personality, a course for graduate students only. "I am sorry to have to limit my teaching to one semester next year," she wrote to her department chairman, Marvin Harris, on November 24, 1964, "but the exigencies of field work make it necessary, as conditions in New Guinea are so uncertain. I hope that the usual arrangements for my assistant can be maintained so that there will be a continuity in my work with graduate students while I am absent from New York."

Columbia never paid her more than a modest salary or promoted her beyond the rank of adjunct professor, but the university and its satellite Teachers' College suited her for other reasons. One was that the American Museum of Natural History, her career's official headquarters, was only a short cab ride away. The museum appeared to underrate her too; she was not made a full Curator of Ethnology there until 1964, but she was sent under its auspices to a lot of places she wanted to go, and allowed to carry on a good many extracuratorial duties in her tower overlooking Seventy-seventh Street and Columbus Avenue. Much of the business of the Research in Contemporary Cultures project just after the war, most of the affairs of the Institute for Intercultural Studies, and arrangements with Mead's various publishers were conducted from that office.

The museum gave her a headquarters for what one of her publishers called her "*apparat*—a system of aides who read her galley proofs and assisted her in all kinds of ways," and to whom she would make motherly phone calls at two in the morning to make sure they had got home safely, and again four hours later to remind them, as one *apparat* member recalled, "which nine things we were supposed to do first when we got to the office." The more Mead's enterprises sprawled beyond routine museum duties, the more she relied on these research assistants. "My needs are far greater for research assistants than they are for salary," she wrote in 1957 to the Menninger Foundation, where she was to speak. She asked that part of her lecture fee "be handled as a research grant, either through the American Museum of Natural History or the Institute for Intercultural Studies." For her *apparat* Mead sought women under thirty, a *New York Post* article reported, "with serious career intentions somewhere in the behavioral science field . . . intelligence at the Ph.D. candidate level . . . physical strength (the arrangements at the museum make the job physically exacting and there is a flight of stairs to be climbed) . . . height (a girl over five-foot-five has an easier time in this office)," and professional typing.

These young women constituted yet another of the *ad hoc* sororities Mead depended on all her life. The bond of these alumnae is strong: in the employ of "MM," as most of them called her, they read her galleys, designed her travel logistics, filed her papers according to her intricate color-coding system, and answered the hundreds of letters she got every week. When she made a serious new friend, as she claimed to do every two or three months, the new name was added to her Christmas card list. Later employees also kept on hand a supply of her queen-sized pantyhose, picked up her pants suits at the dry cleaners and her Dexedrine prescriptions from the pharmacy, and massaged her back, according to the instructions of her Chilean psychic healer, when she fell ill. ("If she'd been a man," said one employee, "I'd have had grounds for a lawsuit.") Most of them liked what they did. One spoke of her strong desire "to spare Dr. Mead any awareness of how much effort it took to make her life run smoothly. I wanted everything to seem to flow."

This museum office, where the decibel level was often fearsome, was Mead's most-used classroom, and an almost entirely female domain. She taught and mothered these young women who oddly, considering their youth, mothered her in turn. But few of them stayed around for longer than a couple of years. They weren't supposed to. "She kept hiring graduate students without minding the constant turnover," said Bridget McCarthy, who worked in the museum in the early 1960s, became Mead's first bibliographer, and later directed the Oregon School of Arts and Crafts. "She didn't want people who'd last. Temporary people, she said, helped her keep up with the times, and as soon as they were ready to go on to other, better things, she would urge them out.

"People who had imaginative ways to cope would flourish in that office," said McCarthy. "She was convinced that there always *is* a way, it's just a matter of figuring out what it is. She was very impressed, for instance, the day I came to work in a rainstorm wearing plastic bags over my shoes. You couldn't work in that office if you were going to make excuses. Why should an intelligent, educated, bright, white middle-class American have to make excuses? I'm not an anthropologist by any means," McCarthy said, "but I'll always be scheming the way Margaret Mead taught me to. I've often thought what a big influence she and Rhoda Métraux had on me. They taught me that the point is not so much to perpetuate yourself as to solve a problem and fill a need."

Ingenious employees and Mead's serious students got her meticulous attention. "Her comments on papers," said one of her graduate students, "were extraordinarily detailed. You felt when she was talking about someone else's paper that she was talking about yours as well." Students with personal problems were stunned when she would phone to ask how they were doing. She always made time to see them, and was especially attentive to students in the last stages of graduate school. She phoned a woman student preparing for the oral defense of her dissertation to remind her to wear a pretty dress. When Vincent Crapanzano was preparing in 1967 for his orals at Columbia Mead urged him to be sure and bring a map with him.

"I think," he replied, "that everyone knows where Morocco is." That, said Mead, was not the point. "Look," she told him, "there'll come a question you won't know how to answer, and the minute that happens, just get up and point out whatever you want to on the map, and they'll be so impressed they won't notice your confusion." But not everyone was so singled out, Timothy Asch said, or so charmed by Mead. "Oftentimes during Ph.D. orals she would turn on kids who didn't know their stuff. She'd sell them down the drain and expect them to come back, which some of them didn't. But what wonderful help she gave some of us! To potential employers she would say, 'I *know* you've got the money; I know all about that big grant you got last year from the government,' and force them to part with it for our sakes."

In between these commitments, and the total of fourteen field trips she made after her first 1925 expedition to Samoa, Mead taught regularly and with great gusto at two midwestern institutions. From 1946 on she went often to the Department of Psychiatry at the School of Medicine at the University of Cincinnati, and from 1959 to the Menninger Foundation in Topeka, Kansas. She was also an honored visitor, less regularly but just as zealously, at the Merrill-Palmer Institute in Detroit. Although Mead's parents both came from the Midwest, where she had visited relatives all her life, she found the region professionally as exotic and as fulfilling as Oz, probably because people there had the good sense to treat her as a wizard. Her associates there were generally midwestern, and therefore reassuring, but often exhilarating, too. Among them she could count on hearing shoptalk of the field she had nearly made her own life work in 1924, when she took her M.A. in psychology. "As the Irish speak of a 'spoiled priest,'" Mead once wrote, she "could be counted a spoiled psychologist"—one who had never really left the fold.

Blessed with what one of her friends, quoting T. S. Eliot, called "the sharp compassion of the healer's art," Mead had always sought others who had a gift for healing. Erik Erikson's ideas, she wrote, had interlocked with hers since the 1930s; when they both were guests at Cincinnati, a psychiatrist there remembered, "they talked nonstop for twenty-four hours." The hypnotherapist Milton Erickson, who shared Mead's interest in the phenomenon of trance, became her close friend too, and so did Martha Wolfenstein, with whom she co-edited *Childhood in Contemporary Cultures* in 1955. Long before her presidency of the World Foundation for Mental Health, Mead had been attracted to students of healing, among them all three of her husbands. Cressman had quit the ministry because he felt he could help people more by talking with them than praying for them; Fortune wrote of dreams and sorcerers; Bateson studied schizophrenia and practiced family therapy.

But professional healing is draining. It calls for uncommonly long, restrained periods of listening, with a focus rarely known in ordinary life. Although psychologists generally address themselves to weaknesses, and anthropologists to strengths, both listening processes are intense. That was one of the reasons Mead and the analysts understood each other, and also, Mead once ventured, the reason why analysts "went on having seminars until the day they died": after all that listening, they needed to talk, but not to just anyone. Mead was eager to hear what new theories preoccupied the analysts, who in turn, concerned as they were with pathology, must have felt refreshed by what Kevin Frank called her "ample personal reserves of optimism."

The analysts also treated her with a good deal more deference than she could count on from her regular colleagues. At Columbia someone once saw a fellow professor refuse to help her with what looked like two thirty-pound briefcases as she left Schermerhorn Hall. Mead once admitted to her friend Leonard Rieser, provost of Dartmouth College, that the reception he had arranged for her on a visit there was the kind she preferred: "royal." Who could blame her? At Cincinnati and Topeka, especially by the middle 1960s when Mead's visits to both had become a ritual, proper attention was paid. Parties were held in her honor. Bouquets and bottles of Scotch were left in her room. So were typewriters and paper and pencils, because she always had writing to do.

Writing requires privacy, which was dispensed to Mead in just the right doses on her visits to these institutions. Somebody always showed up to drive her wherever she wanted to go, which was everywhere. "Dr. Mead prefers being well-scheduled," one of her museum assistants once wrote to the Menninger office, "and of course parties, meetings, seminars and appointments with individuals are all appropriate." What was inappropriate were dull moments. These, during Mead's midwestern visits, were rare. At an especially uproarious Cincinnati cocktail party she once sat down so hard on a glass coffee table that she reportedly had to have 136 stitches where she had sat—a misfortune which did not prevent her from going ahead with her planned schedule the next morning, carrying a big fluffy pillow to sit on.

At both places Mead's hosts felt a little as if she saw them the way she had seen the Arapesh or the Balinese. "We were one of the islands she looked in on," said Dr. Harold Hiatt of the Cincinnati faculty. "We were another culture for her to study. What really interested her was the overlap between psychiatry and the anthropology of culture." Her Topeka associates felt the same way. "We were a tribe she liked to study," said Dr. Roy Menninger. "The mixture she saw here, of caring and intellectual ideas, seemed to her a model worthy of being copied. She was a great one for attacking parochiality."

Mead's instructions to the Menninger faculty were explicit. "Winter wives," she told them, was a shamefully demeaning name to give the spouses of temporary residents. A "phantom competitiveness" kept people from entertaining on even a casual basis. A "vicious two-class system," which separated clerical and maintenance personnel from professionals, must end, and why were there so few Jews around? "Okay," Roy Menninger remembered her saying, "you've built an organization here of people who can plough a straight furrow and sow a good crop, but what you need to get your thinking charged is more New York Jews." As Roy Menninger interpreted it, her view was "that a good marriage could be made between Eastern intellectuals and cornfed farmboys—there was no sense trying to tell her that corn came from Iowa, not Kansas. She was constantly fascinated by ideas that might be generated by this marriage: by this mixture, as someone described it, of Freud and friendliness." An exemplary mixture, by Mead's standards, prevailed at the Cincinnati Department of Psychiatry, founded and chaired by her old friend Maurice Levine, whom she had first met through her Cincinnati-bred Barnard classmate Esther Goldsmith Muegel.

Mead wrote that the reason she "liked to take a new idea, while it was still in bud and not yet ready to flower," to Cincinnati was the way "Maury Levine and the lively seminar of colleagues and students" would crowd together "in an antiquated and uncomfortable basement room, where the very walls sang with responsive interest." Levine shared her own disdain for hierarchical relationships between saved and damned, physician and patient, analyzed and unanalyzed. His life was "all of a piece, and his own roles, as physician, husband and father, teacher and friend, were permeated with the same sunny lucidity, the same perceptive tolerance for human weakness and the same imaginative expectation that somehow the humanness in other persons would come through."

A fellow member of the Menninger Foundation's Board of Directors, Deborah Szekely, had repeatedly but vainly invited Mead to be her guest at her celebrated and luxurious health spa, the Golden Door, outside San Diego. "Margaret and I always timed our arrivals in Kansas City so that one car could come to pick both of us up for the trip to Topeka," said Szekely. "It was a joy to hear her talk, and an extra joy to watch her in Board meetings, deliberately provoking arguments, and then sitting back, delighted that she had put people's gray cells to work.

"After one such outburst I said, 'Margaret, you can't possibly believe what you just said!' and she smiled and said, 'Of course not, but look at the processes that came about, the new ideas, the new thoughts.' She certainly kept everybody on their toes." What had drawn Mead to

Topeka in the first place was not so much any of the foundation's separate parts, but their sum, and the "air of urgency and excitement" that "kept a high flame burning"—a higher flame than the same resources could have produced if they were not interrelated.

"Daddy Menninger," said the founder's daughter-in-law, "believed that no matter what you do, you can do it better. That's a German idea"—and Mead's appreciation of Germans was abiding—"and a midwestern one, too. He also believed that once you found a good way to do something, you shared it. You lectured, you wrote, you *used* it. That's why there's such an atmosphere around here of research." Menninger's creed might have been Mead's own. "Her investment in this place was unambivalent," said Roy Menninger, whose brother Walter added that Mead was "keenly aware of this family, of its stresses, strains and myths."

At first Mead went to Topeka as a lecturer, but as Mrs. William Menninger said, she "soon promoted herself to being our superego. Only those who worked in it knew the foundation better. Sometimes she would upset my husband," Mrs. Menninger said, "by coming into his office or Karl's to pronounce on undercurrents and power plays that were always going on, and to say this was wrong, that was wrong. She was here, after all, to consult, and she was usually dynamic and provocative, in a constructive way."

After Mead's 1963 Topeka visit she scolded the foundation for "sending out men who after spending three years at the MSP [Menninger School of Psychiatry] have only the most rudimentary and vulgarized understanding of the Freudian theory of psychoanalysis." Ignorance of psychoanalytic theory, she said, could only lead to "a coarsening of the whole intellectual approach." Psychoanalysis, said Dr. Robert Stewart, a Cincinnati training analyst, was in the marrow of her bones: "Her command of psychoanalytic concepts was the equal of any professional's I ever knew." Wherever Mead went in the world, Leo Rosten said, she made it known that she wanted to meet the psychoanalysts, many of whom became her good friends, and some of whom at times felt that they got from her what they gave to their patients.

Dr. James Hamilton, the San Francisco psychiatrist, remembered an hour he spent with Mead in 1948, talking of the board exams he had to take to become accredited. He was nervous; he thought the board members' questions might unsettle him. Remembering that his friend Mead was "on a talking basis with several of the big shots in American psychotherapy," he asked for and was granted an hour of her time on the eve of his exams. "She went down the list of who was on the board, and told me what each one would ask, what their vulnerabilities were, and in the course of that hour she became *my* psychotherapist, and I walked into that meeting feeling one-up on those bastards.

"Ask her just about any question and you'd get a two-paragraph answer, analyzing the issue, and a third paragraph summing up what you should do. It was firm, definite, clear, and that was that."

In Topeka Mead told Doris Hunter, then Doris Gerlach, just what to do, too. Doris was a newly widowed young mother of three small children who had reluctantly decided, in 1959, that the only way she could support her family would be to take in a roomer. The roomer turned out to be Mead, on her first visiting professorship at the Menninger Foundation. Her luggage included a blindfold and earplugs, so that she could sleep through anything if she had to, and a narrow-spouted tea kettle which she filled and heated to steam all the curl she needed into her hair, which had not yet gone gray. When she knew that her hair was curly, Mead once told a friend, she always felt better.

In Doris Hunter's household Mead instantly proved the truth of what she had written to the Menninger office—"my most central interest is children"—by endearing herself to her hostess's twin daughters and infant son. "She really turned my world around," said Hunter. "I was never sure whether she was living with us or studying us—probably both. It doesn't matter. But I'll tell you one thing for sure: I loved her. We all did." Some evenings the roomer would ask the landlady for "a straight drink of Scotch," and Hunter would join her with "a good old Kansas drink from my college bootlegger days: bourbon and ginger ale," and the two women would talk. Anyone, Mead told Hunter, could make it alone. A husband wasn't necessary. "She often said, 'You do *not* need a man—I married a man, and it was a disaster, the way we competed.'" The necessary thing in Mead's view, no less in Topeka than in Samoa or New Hampshire or on Perry Street, was a big, dense, complex household.

"She always thought: the more people the better, the bigger the family the better," said Hunter. That was why Mead encouraged her landlady to establish what turned out to be the Menninger Foundation Family Care Program's first halfway house. Mead "thought it was so important for those patients to live with families, and if she hadn't made such an issue of it, I'd never have bought another house big enough to take in from two to five patients, which for me was gold-plated dynamite. Having those halfway people enabled me to support my kids."

When Mead and the halfway people were under Hunter's roof at the same time, that suited Mead fine. "She referred to herself as 'the other patient,' " Doris said. "After one of her stays with us she went off with the house key and sent it back with a note saying, 'This is the truest Freudian slip I've ever made.' " The troublesome question for the social scientist, as Mead had said in 1956, is "who is the patient." She was quite at home on the ambiguous boundary between insanity and mental health (as on most other boundaries), although she said she did not want "the interference with my life, relationship with my unconscious, that analysis would bring."

"[Mead] was a highly trained diagnostician herself," Leo Rosten said, "but she had a really shaky ego structure. She needed defenses and reinforcement against knowing herself. With the greatest affection, analysts and I would indulge Margaret in her fantasy that she didn't need to be analyzed." One reason analysis would not have suited her, said Mead's Cincinnati friend Robert Stewart, was that "she was much too action-oriented, and there is no premature cloture in analysis."

A surer place to look for action is in classes at a university. Classes, after an hour or two, are over. Classes at Columbia might contain promising young women like Rosalind Lippel, who was hired to work in the museum tower, where she stayed on after Mead's death until all her papers had been sent to the Library of Congress, and Nona Porter, who became one of Mead's Columbia teaching assistants and close friends. ("She got to choose her own TAs," said Porter. "That was part of her deal with Columbia. Otherwise they'd have been assigned according to need.") To Porter Mead once said, "I don't care if you have six husbands or not—and you probably will—or if you have twins. You've got to decide whether you want to be an anthropologist or not for the rest of your life. For several years you've spent entirely too much time becoming a woman and not enough becoming a person."

In her Columbia classes Mead met a parade of devoted followers like the elderly, beautifully groomed sisters Rita and Mary Niklas of Park Avenue ("We're both ballerinas," they said), who for years faithfully attended Mead's large lecture courses, and whom she inspired to travel to New Guinea. They remembered watching a helicopter descend along with a New Guinea woman who, never having beheld such a thing in her life, took it for a bird and put down a huge yam for it to eat—"the sweet, precious darling."

As the filmmaker Timothy Asch, the photographer Ken Heyman, and the anthropologist William Mitchell had all met Mead in her classes, so did the New Zealand ethnographer James Ritchie and the Montreal filmmaker Asen Balikci. Balikci said Mead "dispelled the prejudice against filmmaking, which in '59 and '60 was considered degrading." Mead's 1959 students also included Robert Suggs, to whom she was memorably compassionate during his oral exams: "I don't like the way they run these things," she told him. "The student feels too exposed. This time it'll be different. *You sit here*—and by the way, how's the boy?" (Suggs's newborn son had been ill.) William Carr also studied with Mead in the 1950s and "admired her teaching very much, then, because she made explicit the ethic of science, required intellectual integrity of us, made clear to us that everything is debatable, and that difficult though it was to detach yourself, in behavioral science, you had to try."

Carr and Suggs were both devoted to Mead until 1962, when she took issue with their response to a letter about disarmament that she and Rhoda Métraux published in the American Anthropological Association's newsletter. The letter implied that all anthropologists favored disarmament; Suggs and Carr retorted in a later newsletter that the women ought to have spoken only for themselves. Mead, Suggs said, later told him that if he did not retract his reply to what she had written, she would "knock your block off and ruin your career."*

"The fifties and sixties were palmy days for academia," said Robert Murphy, a professor of anthropology at Columbia. "That was the time of the baby boom; if we'd turn out a bright graduate student we felt like a high-school basketball team with a seven-four center." Undergraduates were another matter; Mead's interest in them, and in the anthropologically naïve general public, struck some of her colleagues as silly. "This was the mandarin period in academia," Murphy said. "There was

* She was not always nice to old friends. Joseph Neyer, the philosophy student Mead had befriended in Washington during the war, saw her again, for the first time in years, at a celebration honoring Lawrence Frank. Neyer arrived with the philosophy professor and popular lecturer Houston Peterson, for whom Mead had high regard. Peterson asked if she and Neyer had met. "Of *course* I know Joe," Mead said, and took Neyer's arm ("my moment of glory," Neyer called it) as they walked toward their seats. Neyer emboldened himself to inquire why Mead had asked for several copies of a July 1947 article he had published on international control of atomic fission. Without a word of acknowledgment or attribution, he knew, Mead had repeated several statements from this article, word for word, at a speech she gave at a London international health conference. Would she now admit, Neyer asked, why she had been so interested in his article? "Wouldn't you like to know?" Mead asked, a little flirtatiously.

enormous prestige for high arbiters and judges, leaders in what was becoming a potent political force in this country. The most successful academics were those who didn't teach at all, or who taught graduate students exclusively. The academy was invaded by horrible hubris, of which Margaret Mead had no part whatever.

"In the narrowest sense, in a very funny way, she was not ambitious. She didn't care so much about maximizing her position within her profession. What she wanted, instead, was to be effective. Most of us have much smaller reference groups: hers was the whole world." With the world as her frame of reference, Mead did not fuss much about academic details. She amazed her colleagues by enjoying committee meetings, but annoyed them by being too generous about handing out As, and also about helping favored students to sidestep tiresome academic hurdles so that some of them could "get into the club," as one had put it, "without a passport, without the discipline of a Ph.D." A guest course Mead taught at Yale in 1968 attracted six hundred students, the largest enrollment in that university's history. She was "bored stiff" that these students were all boys, she later said, but gave them all As and Bs anyway; she had no use for the custom of grading on the curve.

If the museum had forced her to retire, Fordham University would have made her chairman of the social science division of its Lincoln Center Liberal Arts Campus, but to Mead's pleasure, the museum did as she put it, "evict its curators." In one six-month period, reportedly, Mead was offered the chairmanships of the anthropology departments of both Fordham and New York University. "But why should she want to do that," an admirer asked, "when she could keep on being Margaret Mead?" More and more being Margaret Mead meant bending the rules so that she could do more or less what she felt like doing when she felt like doing it. And it is not so clear that she felt exploited by Columbia. She would have appreciated the retirement pension and health benefits of a full-time position, but the arrangement worked both ways. Twice Columbia offered her a full tenured professorship, in 1958 and again in 1963, and both times she turned it down. "We asked her too late," said Murphy. "It was like living with a woman for twenty years and then asking her to marry you, when she's already married to someone else. By the time we got around to bringing up the subject, she could make more money giving one lecture than we could offer her in a year."

The museum, said Mead's colleague and boss Harry Shapiro (who also on the side was an ill-paid adjunct professor at Columbia), gave her a freedom no other institution could match: "A full-time professor would have had to give four or five courses a year, and never have the kind of quiet and peace and independence she was allowed here. Her students appealed to her very much, but the museum was definitely her home." Home it may have been, but with her fellow curators and other museum colleagues, said Shapiro, Mead was only routinely cordial. "The other eight curators would all lunch together, but Margaret, who when she wasn't out of town or out of the country was physically detached, upstairs in her tower, rarely joined us." She was preoccupied with the public. In public, as Shapiro said, Mead "always talked with great conviction, assurance, and self-confidence. She was a missionary-like popularizer. Maybe she came to the museum convinced that her mission was to popularize anthropology, or maybe she talked herself into that idea after the fact, and invented the notion of using insights from primitive peoples and cultures to help understand our own."

But Mead was not an orthodox museum person. If it were not for her second and third husbands, one curator said, she would have been content to bring back "even fewer examples of weaving, matting, and basketry than she did. She emphasized other things nobody else noticed." Some of her museum colleagues found her humorless and imprecise. She was not amused when a tiny figure representing her was inserted, prankishly and briefly, into a model of Peri village, in Manus, in the Hall of the Peoples of the Pacific, nor did she exhibit any scholarly pedantry when someone asked her the provenance of a certain New Guinea mask. "Oh," she said, "just call it the Sepik basin," which was a little like saying it had come from somewhere—Minnesota, Louisiana, why be fussy?—along the banks of the Mississippi.

"Museums were a means to an end for Margaret," said her friend Karl Menninger. "She glanced at ours, when she came to Topeka, but what she really cared about were people—grotesque people, savage people, all people."

Many of Mead's close friends were seriously troubled. "I don't like neurotics," she said. "Obsessive neurotics who talk about the same thing for weeks and weeks are very boring. But I get along very well with psychotics, and I'm not afraid of them, either. In Manus, a boy under a palm tree was about to kill himself with a great big bush knife, and nobody would dare to stop him until I walked up to him and said 'Give me the knife.'" He gave it to her. "I've spent my life with depressed people," she once said. She got on especially well, she elaborated, with schizophrenics, whom she had no trouble understanding. "When Jane Belo would say, 'Today is red,' I'd answer, 'All right, what's tomorrow going to be?' 'Blue,' she would say. 'What's the difference?' I'd ask. 'Red days I can get everybody I want on the telephone,' she would answer, 'and blue days I can't.' "

So by temperament Mead was almost as much a therapist as a teacher. Her patients, like her students, could be found everywhere, even in her own family. One Sunday evening in Cincinnati, Mead dined with two of her cousins, a mother and daughter, in the Methodist retirement home where the mother lived. The daughter, unaccountably tired and sad, sat silent while her famous cousin talked to her mother. Quite suddenly Mead spoke three words to the daughter, words the daughter could not remember later, but which made her feel as if she had been slapped down like an unruly child. "I was so frozen inside that I didn't let on," she said. "I was afraid that if I did, I'd start to bawl."

By the Tuesday evening after that Sunday the daughter was "still in pieces—I'm a good sleeper as a rule, but for two nights I hadn't had any sleep at all. At 10:30 on Wednesday morning Margaret phoned my office to ask how I felt, and I broke down in front of everyone there to say, 'Margaret, how could you *do* that to me?' "

"You needed it," Mead told her. "I'm free for lunch, are you?" Over lunch her cousin said she hadn't understood what had happened. "I didn't *expect* you to understand," said Mead. "You needed it. You were depressed."

"But I don't *get* depressed," said her cousin, whereupon Mead just sat and smiled. "She'd done this deliberately," the cousin said later, "and it was just what I needed. That was her method, razor sharp. It got right through to you and curled your toes. When she came to Cincinnati she always saved Sundays, and sometimes Saturday afternoons too, for the family. We fascinated her just as much as she did us.

"In our family there's a lot of brains, but also a lot of people who can't take the pressure of work, and she wondered why that was." Her Ohio relatives, Mead once said, were "always in a terrible state, needing to be rescued from something or other." Once she arranged, through her Institute for Intercultural Studies, for the Cincinnati psychiatrist Jack Lindy to study these relatives. At a family reunion she introduced him to them and handed them a questionnaire: What did they do for a living? How much did they drink? How many children had they, and how far had they got in school? What she had in mind was "a study of five generations of a family in a small Ohio town where some members of the family got out and some were trapped by lack of education" but in which there seemed to be no intellectual difference between those who got out and those who stayed, which Mead said was "contrary to the usual expectation that it is the less gifted weaklings that are left behind in the little rural villages."

As much as Mead admired psychoanalysis, she would tell her students, it was only one of seven valid ways of getting insights. They could just as profitably study animals, infants, or primitive cultures; they could survive an extreme religious conversion or a psychotic episode; they could have a love affair with an old Russian. Her deliberate irreverence about such matters embarrassed some of her fellow academics. Anthropology, as Bronislaw Malinowski's daughter Jozefa Stuart put it, is "a worldwide cat club," and Mead did plenty to court the gossipy contempt of her narrower-minded colleagues, who were especially annoyed when she spoke charitably of—or in later years and worse yet consorted with—practitioners of such marginal disciplines as parapsychology and faith healing. "We still need our shamans, after all," said Mead in endorsing her friend Ralph Blum's *The Book of Runes*. Runes, ancient symbols which the Vikings used as an oracle, struck Mead as "part of living Western shamanism." Sagittarius, she was well aware, was her sign of the zodiac. Astrologers, mediums and psychics all could command her attention.

Mental health, Mead sometimes said, should not become a religion. She knew how to distinguish the one from the other. Doris Hunter was astonished at first to find that Mead went regularly, every Sunday morning she was in Topeka, to St. David's Episcopal Church. Part of her arrangement with the Menninger staff was that someone would give her a ride there every week.

"I'd never have picked it up from the language she used when she talked about other things," said Hunter, "but she was a real believer, I'm sure."

CHAPTER TWENTY-THREE

"Bishops May Not, but Anthropologists Do"

*The middle-aged leader must sanction the initiative of a com-
mitted following and an irreversibly united multitude, but who
will sanction him, the sanctioner?*

—ERIK ERIKSON
Gandhi's Truth

ONCE MARGARET MEAD told a friend of a good way she had thought of
to die: to be found on her knees in a church. The dead, after all, do
not seem out of place in churches. Whoever came upon her body there
would probably know what to do, and get it done, properly and fast.
Religion was much more of a comfort to Mead, for most of her life,
than many people who thought they knew her well suspected. "Prayer,"
she said, "does not use up artificial energy, doesn't burn up any fossil
fuel, doesn't pollute. Neither does song, neither does love, neither does
the dance." Several friends attested to her "need for the divine." She
went to church, she said herself, "not for God's sake, but for my own,
for the ritual and the repetition and the prayer, though I don't pray at
great length. I don't think it would matter to anyone else if I didn't go
at all."

At age eleven, in a carriage pulled by a galloping horse, she had
raced over the Pennsylvania countryside with her reluctant atheist parents to the baptism she insisted they allow her to have. In her sixties, in
jet airplanes, she rushed around the world to churchly councils and
meetings. In the years between, her faith had persisted pretty much in
secret; many of her friends took it for granted that she must be the
same sort of militant second-generation agnostic they were.

A Barnard classmate who never knew Mead to speak of any re-

340

ligious faith in fifty years deduced that "the church, for Margaret, must have been a center for her value system, her neighborliness." In part it surely was; Mead interpreted neighborliness on a far grander scale than most people do. But church for her was also a center for sacrament, for the transcendental. The transcendental is not something for which anthropologists profess a widespread need. One Mead student was surprised to find priests in his anthropology classes: "How could they be priests, I wanted to ask them, if they'd heard two anthro lectures? Anthropology wipes religion right off the map. But a year or two later I realized, hey, anthropology is *not* a contradiction of religion. Anthropology does not deal directly with human behavior, it is the study of universal parameters of human behavior—the study of a set of rules that can be acted out in all kinds of ways."

"Anthropologists," said Mead's colleague Ashley Montagu, "know more about religion than theologians do."* During the question-and-answer period following a talk Montagu gave at a fundamentalist college, he replied to one question by saying, "With all due respect, I am acquainted with several gods." Mead, Montagu added, was the only subscribing churchgoer he knew within his discipline. But Mead was, in the words of one of her several good friends in the clergy, "deeply and instinctively religious," without going out of her way to advertise her belief that "objective reality is discoverable, and that people are accountable for the use made of their lives in this world. As a young child she sought a connection for herself, not only a belief but a community. She never divorced herself from the need to be involved with the ordinary and sometimes irritating people who shared her belief." Between Margaret Mead and men of the cloth there was always an understanding, a sense of possible magic.

Luther Cressman, who married Margaret Mead in a rite of considerable pageantry in 1923, when he was newly ordained himself, had not found her much of a helpmeet in his work with parishioners, nor had she taken much interest in his anguished decision to leave the clergy. Grander, more anthropological concerns distracted her, as they apparently continued to through and beyond her next two marriages. Colin Frank, who spent most of his boyhood in the same house with Mead, was aware that she sometimes went around the corner to ser-

* Theologians would retort that anthropologists know a lot about the details of people's beliefs and habits of worship. Natural theology, Henri Renard wrote in *The Philosophy of God*, "deals with God the ultimate cause of being." Thomas Aquinas called it a divine science. Sacral theology is the study of supernatural revelation. It is difficult to imagine an atheistic theologian.

vices at St. Luke in the Fields on Hudson Street, and thought it odd
that "this highly rational person should be so religious." For a long
time, he said, he "poked at her faith as a kid with a stick would poke at
an iguana." Perhaps, Colin thought, she had bowed to the altar the
way Hermann Ebbinghaus had bowed to a portrait of Punch, for the
sake of order as much as for any other reason. Like his father, Colin
was largely unmoved by the Roman Catholicism of his Irish mother, as
by all organized religion.

But over the years, Colin said, "I came to believe in [Mead's] belief, in its strength and its genuineness. I think she believed in an order
which was given to the world through belief in God. Her study of other
cultures made her keenly aware of the unifying forces in ours, and made
her try to push people to be real participants. Maybe going to church
on Sunday mornings was a way for her to unify her feelings about her
own culture. Her feeling of having a place in our culture was strong. A
lot of religious people in her life were very supportive to her, and
helped her to anneal the intellectual and the spiritual."

In the years just after Mead's third divorce, she seemed to pontifi-
cate about how others should conduct their married lives. As a result,
said Colin Frank, she "paid a price of derision and venomous attacks by
people who didn't really know her. She craved some of the respectabil-
ity the church could give her, to make up for her misidentification with
primitive cultures. The myth of that misidentification had the momentum of a freight train—put on the brakes and it would stop, but not for
a mile. There were a lot of Margaret Mead jokes—Margaret Mead and
the Polynesian studs, that sort of thing—and maybe the church was a
helpful counterfoil to all that."

Quite likely it was. She could be a scold, she could drive her friends
in the church and out of it crazy, but she had an underlying tolerance,
which like her underlying common sense came to the rescue. She was
tolerant both of unbelievers and of the failings of the church.

Another reason Mead kept her religion to herself for so long was
that she knew how the society around her felt about divorce. Divorce
was not yet the distressing but chic epidemic it later became. Decent
people were known to end their marriages, in the forties and fifties, but
they didn't talk about it. The *Winnetka Talk*, a weekly publication in
a privileged suburb outside Chicago, warned readers away from certain
movies with the damning phrase: "Reflects the acceptability of divorce."
Mead did not feel sinful about her three divorces, but the time did not
seem ripe to call attention to them, either. In 1961, when she was invited to represent the Episcopal Church of the United States on the

Committee for Assembly of the World Council of Churches, to help plan an eight-year program of enormous international conventions, Mead demurred. She would love to, she responded, but was the committee aware that she was divorced? Might that not be a problem? To her great delight, it was not.

Luther Cressman mused in his ninth decade that it was just as well that his first wife never realized her childhood dream of managing a pastor's household. "Can you imagine," he asked with a laugh, "what would have happened to that parish?" He was probably right. The right size parish, for Margaret Mead, was the world.

That was what Mead saw coming, in the early 1960s: "a new period in the Christian approach to the world." The Christian churches, as the sixties began, were posing Mead's kinds of questions: questions concerning nuclear annihilation, religion's relationship with science and technology, the revision of traditional liturgies and rituals, the struggle for civil rights, and the tension between conservation and change. What should the church keep and cherish, what should it discard and replace? Big things were going on in the church. Christianity was being redefined, to give other religions and ideologies "the same respect, recognition and care we give ourselves." The ecumenical movement, a force after Mead's own heart if anything ever had been, was taking shape. "Ecumenical," from the Greek, means belonging to the whole world, and the early 1960s brought on an ecumenical time both for Christian churches and for Margaret Mead. The World Council of Churches and the Roman Catholic Church, inspired by Vatican II, leaned heavily on each other, working to find points of agreement.

"I don't think my religious sensibility has deepened with the years," Mead remarked around this time, "but ecumenicism deepened my participation and interest." The "social message of the Old Testament prophets in their ethics" had left her "perfectly contented," but now came an awareness that the brotherhood of man, as Mead saw it, was a question of borders: "There should be resting points, points of cohesion, on the frontiers between religions. When I say I am a Christian, it doesn't mean I am not a Moslem, not a Buddhist, not a Jew. It means that at the age of eleven I found Christianity a viable way of approaching the universe" and she found no cause to revise that approach. Much as she welcomed the ecumenical movement, she recognized its problems, especially those that might arise if it were taken to extremes. "People who screamed and cursed and condemned each other to hell ten years ago," she said, "are now sitting down ecumenically and claiming that a two-headed rainbow serpent is just as good a god as any other." That kind of thinking was too simplistic. "A great religion," Mead said, "provides an image of all humankind, an image sufficiently universal so that it can cross national, linguistic, and racial lines." She sought to bridge the gap between scientists and people of the church, who both, to quote her friend Archbishop Paulos Gregorios, had been "unforgivably arrogant—each presuming to have exclusive access to the knowledge of reality, and a capacity to state the truth verbally and finally." No statement on this subject, Mead knew, could be completely true or final. Before Vatican II, Mead wrote, the Christian churches had "pigeon-holed the members of the high traditional civilizations of Asia with the 'pagans' of the jungles and of the remote Arctic wastes." Now that such categorizing was officially obsolete, no one was more pleased than Mead.

She wanted no part, however, of the increasingly faddish revived art of meditation, transcendental or otherwise. The Maharishi Mahesh Yogi would not have found Mead a likely prospect for conversion. She had no use for the white light or the blue line or whatever it was that meditators claimed to see after they had repeated their mantras enough times. But she cherished the stillness she had found, from the start, in church. In Topeka, when he first saw his distinguished visitor, the Reverend Henry Breul of St. David's Episcopal Church thought, "My God, I'm being studied, like the Tikopia," but he soon learned that it was Mead the worshiper, not Mead the legend or Mead the observer, who knelt in his pews. "Onstage she was a Powerful Katrinka," Breul said, "but in church—at the early, pietistic service we used to call 'the me and Jesus kind of thing,' with no sermon, no music—she seemed a humble seeker after truth, a recipient, who liked the words: 'Be still, and know that I am God.' Maybe church was the only place she was still, the only place where she received." .

By the early 1960s, when the World Council of Churches had become one of the more extended and more admiring of Mead's many families, she was not only willing to admit her faith but eager to discuss it in appropriate precincts. As a member of the Commission on Church and Society she had the duty of attending seven consecutive annual conferences, and every year she endeared herself more to her colleagues. In New Delhi, in 1962, she was "wonderful and attentive," said the Baptist minister and WCC official Paul Abrecht. "About all the jargon that was exchanged, she said, 'It's very interesting to be here to see this really important work going on, and someday when I understand these terms you use, I'll know what it's all about.' Everyone howled." By the next year, in Geneva, Mead had mastered the dialect, and spoke it fluently in Holland in 1964 and England in 1965, when the committee members were quartered for their meeting at one of the less prepossessing colleges at Oxford University.

"Just to have a bath or a shave you'd have to walk down the court-yard to very simple hygienic facilities," said Abrecht. "You went down three flights, then six steps over, and three more flights up. Once I saw Margaret walking across the quad in her little nightie, with her cape over her, and I later told someone I had lost 150 pounds, in British currency, that morning." How, Abrecht was asked, could he have done that?

"You can't tell me," Abrecht replied, "that a picture of the noted American anthropologist in her nightie would sell for any less. . . .

"The next morning Margaret said, 'I don't know who brought us to this genteel English slum, but it must not have been anyone who had ever tried to empty a porcelain basin weighing twenty pounds through a window eighteen inches wide.' She had been trying to throw out her wash water." At the 1966 conference, in Geneva, Mead seemed to Abrecht to be in better form than ever; she foresaw the worldwide demonstrations that would erupt two years later. "Students of 1966, as she saw them, were giving a radical critique," said Abrecht, "and need-ing to demonstrate. She had the ability to be a kind of counselor to these kids, helping them, warning them against foolishness. She was quite effective, and when they made their march, capturing a lot of news space, she marched along with them."

In 1967, Abrecht's committee was asked to produce proposals for the WCC, whose central committee was "taken aback by all the talk of revolutions. Thanks to Margaret, we had been warned, and when the first student riots broke out in 1968, the WCC was abreast enough to foresee these problems. We looked pretty good." At the 1968 assembly in Uppsala, Sweden, Mead proved again, said Abrecht, "what a tremen-dous capacity she had to be at the center of every discussion, to know where the important leaders and problem people were, and where she should be." Archbishop Paulos Gregorios, who had long since become one of Mead's close church friends, marveled, "She could even upstage Gunnar Myrdal in his own country, claiming that if India dropped into the ocean, nobody in all of Sweden would care."

"It was nice to be together in Uppsala," Myrdal wrote to Mead in August 1968, "where we were even able to disagree publicly."

The 1966 World Council of Churches conference on Church and Society had impressed Mead particularly, as she would write in her last book, *World Enough: Rethinking the Future*. It was the first WCC meeting, she said, with "more than token representation from the developing world." Her own part in the struggle of the churches for a truly global perspective greatly impressed her WCC colleagues. One of them, a Scotsman, returned home to establish a local version of the Science and Religion Commission, on which he had worked with Mead, and another, a German churchman, said that his five days with Mead had caused him to see life more clearly than he ever had seen it before.

In 1964, when Mead was a visiting professor at Emory University, she asked Rhoda Métraux to go along so that they could continue to work together on a project. In Atlanta, as in most places Mead went, she quickly forged a firm new alliance. One of her first acts was to join St. Bartholomew's, the Episcopal parish near the Emory campus, whose pastor, Father Austin Ford, was to become one of the great friends of her life. If some of her colleagues at Emory could not decide right away what to make of Margaret Mead, this slender man with thinning ginger hair, a deep baritone voice, and a mischievous glint in his eye had no doubts. When he led a group of his privileged parishioners in a chorus of "We Shall Overcome," in the driveway of his parish house, Margaret Mead's unmusical voice could be heard among them. When she wanted to know what the Student Nonviolent Coordinating Committee was doing, and about other aspects of the southern part of the battle for integration, Austin Ford would explain to her. She admired Ford even more when he decided three years later to leave St. Bartholomew's to establish a "house-center" in the black slums south of Atlanta's stadium. He called his center Emmaus House; Emmaus, where the risen Christ appeared and was given food and drink, is a New Testament symbol of hospitality.

Ford also made her laugh, and, most endearingly of all, he argued with her. His new friend could be ruthless, Ford learned, and he was often on the receiving end of her quick tongue, "but I could give back as good as she could send it; she liked to have people snap back at her." He took Mead to visit the University of the South, in Sewanee, Tennessee, where he had gone to seminary. Sewanee struck Mead as having offensively snobbish values, and she told Ford exactly what she thought of it. They also tussled about social work, which Ford regarded as a bureaucratic sham, no more useful than a Band-Aid for a serious wound. Mead, whose dear friend Marie Eichelberger had been a professional social worker all her life, thought otherwise and said so vociferously.

"Margaret's arguments," said Archbishop Gregorios, "were a way of getting at reality, of testing you, of keeping a measure of honesty by bringing out some aspect of reality you hadn't thought of. She always had the upper hand. She always had a mass and then another mass of information to contradict whatever you might say." Gregorios, like Austin Ford, took delight in contradicting Mead and "seeing the way her ire went up."

The two priests also noticed, as many other people did, that Margaret Mead gave away a lot of money. "She didn't dramatize her charity," as Gregorios put it. "She never wanted her left hand to know what her right hand was doing." Mead paid frequent visits to Ford's Emmaus House, and from time to time saw to it that his mail included a check from some institution which had recently engaged her to speak, with a note explaining that Dr. Mead had requested that the money be sent to him. She often directed that her fees for speaking be paid in the form of a contribution to her museum, or to the Institute for Intercultural Studies. This was a sophisticated way of dealing with tax problems, to be sure, but it was also a way of helping young people starting out.

In 1967, in view of Mead's lifelong study of rites of passage, the Episcopal clergyman Father Bonnell Spencer persuaded her to become one of twenty or so consultants to his Subcommittee for the Revision of the Book of Common Prayer. Her particular job was to help with the section about Christian initiation: baptism and confirmation. Her task at first seemed small; Spencer asked only that she read a paper she had written about Christian initiation. "She made a vivid impression right away," said Spencer, when she came down from Columbia to General Theological on Twentieth Street, "sort of little and dumpy, with her funny forked stick. There was talk of possible reference to Noah's Flood—a flood, after all, was nothing if not a reference to water—and one of the bishops said 'Nobody believes *that* in this day and age.'"

"Bishops may not," Margaret Mead retorted, "but anthropologists do." As the group broke for supper, with Mead heading uptown to give a lecture, the others thought they had seen the last of her. But hearing them talk of their next meeting, she looked in her own little date book and announced what day would be convenient for her. In her six years on the committee, she missed only one meeting. On one occasion she scheduled her return from a New Guinea field trip so she would arrive in time. "If her church colleagues had expected that she, as an anthropologist, would feel detached from ritual in any form," said Spencer, "they soon learned that they were mistaken." Ritual, in Mead's view, was not to be relegated to the past. It was, instead, an exceedingly important part of life in all human culture, and people now needed what she called a "cosmic sense"—a sense of connection with the universal—as much as they needed to feel connected with their fellow human beings. Although she had been called to this committee as an anthropologist, the group she most enthusiastically seemed to be representing was the laity.

"Now wait a minute," she would interrupt Spencer's meetings to say, "you're getting way out of touch. I know what you're talking about, but nobody else will." Liturgically, said Spencer, Mead's contribution was not easy to trace. "It's hard to point to one passage and say, 'Here, this was hers.' In the discussions, though, she gave plenty. It was as much because of her as anybody that we were able to draw up a baptismal service in just one meeting, but by lunch of the second day we had done it. A lot of verbal fussing remained, but the substantial work was done." And it was Mead who fought to keep Satan, as such, in the rite for baptism. She wanted no modern dodge for the question, in the *Book of Common Prayer:* "Do you renounce the devil and all his works?"

Christian Howard, a leader in the Church of England laity, who met Mead at church meetings in the 1970s, considered her extremely effective. "She was capable of seeing religion as both a conserving element, honoring the unchangingness of ritual, rites, and the numinous quality of worship, and as a force for change. The church's danger is of being pulled apart between these two polarizations, with each side growing more and more acerb. We must stop and ask, 'What is the purpose of religion, of Christianity?' We can't classify it as just a religion—to do that is to dodge a lot of questions." Other associates also noticed what Miss Howard called Mead's "need for the divine." The ethicist Roger Shinn of Union Theological Seminary, who worked with Mead on the Church and Society Commission, said of her in *Christianity and Crisis* that she "believed in the local church as a community of trust, and . . . expected more of it—I must admit—than I." He had seen her kneeling at the communion rail where he served the bread and wine, and heard her move from her "blunt conversational style into the language of reverence without the slightest self-consciousness."

One Holy Week Mead scolded an Episcopalian among her assistants, who said she planned to appear for work at the museum tower, as usual, on Good Friday. "I think you need to take stock of your religious days," the assistant was told. Mead followed this advice herself. She never missed a service or communion at the WCC meetings, Paul Abrecht said, "and she was very critical if we didn't have high-quality worship. She wanted substance, and she insisted that we not slip in giving the spiritual dimension its due. She really sought, all the time, to deepen her own spiritual life. Once she said, 'If you don't provide communion at this conference, I'm going home.'"

This did not mean that she had ever had a religious experience, Mead herself said, "or any other experience that made me lose myself. Some people feel that sex and religion and esthetic experience are essentially one, in the end, but I believe they are quite different. . . . I don't have to experience religious or esthetic ecstasy, nor," as she said more than once, "have I ever known the kind of union that wanted to exclude other people." Far from excluding others, Mead wanted to infect as many of them as possible with her own passionate involvements. Some temperaments prune away what might be superfluous, others rake in everything that might prove useful; Mead was definitely a rake rather than a pair of pruning shears. She was a fisher, as feminists might choose to put it, of persons. That was why the church so appealed to her; it was "the one institution that does include both sexes and all ages, from infancy to death." For the sake of youngsters who had grown up hardly knowing what it was to repeat any experience more than twice, the church could modify and modernize rituals which had been hallowed by use hundreds of thousands of times over, without sacrificing their beauty.

For example, she said, St. Paul's Chapel at Columbia University might ideally be "transformed from a place of occasional, episodic use, a use tied to the calendar in obscure ways, into a place which has continuous use—twenty-four-hour use would be the most dramatic way of symbolizing its relationship to an open society." It might become a refuge offering help when the doors of the medical department were shut tight. It might provide sanctuary for the penniless, the hunted, the addicted. It might provide quiet, Mead wrote, for "the student who had flunked an exam or quarreled with a friend or lover"; it might be "a place in which judgment is suspended while *caritas* reigns, as well as a place where values can be tested, in thought and speech, and sorted out."

To move across disciplines as gracefully and deftly as Margaret Mead did, Christian Howard remarked, is no common thing: "She brought people together who would otherwise have been isolated." That was what Mead thought ritual accomplished, too. Ritual and worship are the outward signs of community. A good ritual, Mead wrote, is very like a natural language, one which has "been spoken for a very long

time by very many kinds of people, geniuses and dullards, old people
on the verge of dying and children just learning to speak, men and
women, good people and bad people, farmers, scholars and fishermen
. . . a language that carries overtones of very old meanings and the possibilities of new meanings." A ritual "must be old, otherwise it is not
polished . . . otherwise it cannot reflect the play of many men's imagi-
nations . . . otherwise it will not be fully available to everyone born
within the tradition. Yet it must be lively and fresh, open to new vision
and changed vision." Mead had specific suggestions. Why was divorce
not as openly acknowledged as marriage, especially in an age when people tended to marry so young and live so long? Should there not be a
tradition for housecoolings—as when the household at 72 Perry Street
disbanded—as well as for housewarmings?

Around Christmas 1966, Mead herself became a present, for an
Episcopal seminarian named Richards Beekmann. Beekmann was about
to finish his work at General Theological Seminary, but he had no
bishop to ordain him, and no diocese to work in. He was like a teacher
without a class or an actor without a stage. General Theological, where
Luther Cressman had studied forty years earlier, did not know what to
make of Beekmann's interest in the relationship between primitive religions and Christian eucharist. At the Museum of Natural History,
where he went periodically to do research in comparative religion and
cross-cultural studies, some friends asked what he would like for Christmas. More than anything, he told them, he wanted to meet Margaret
Mead. His friends arranged for this wish to be granted.

Beekmann was introduced to Mead late one afternoon near the
seminary, at one of the perennial havens of Margaret's life, the apartment of the devoted Marie Eichelberger, who seemed to him "a faithful disciple . . . happiest in the shadows." Over tea, Beekmann told
Mead about his problem and she seemed sympathetic. "It was important to her," Beekmann said, "that we met near GTS, where Luther
had gone, and that I had studied her second husband's book *Sorcerers
of Dobu*, which showed how interested he also was in the occult."

Mead said she would do what she could to help the young man,
but he had no idea how fast she could work. After tea he went across
the street to evensong at the seminary, and as soon as the service was
finished he heard Eichelberger calling: "Yoo-hoo! Mr. Beekmann! Margaret has taken care of everything—can you be in Wilmington tomorrow?" The next day the Bishop of Delaware, Brooke Mosley, who for
some time had been urging Mead to be present at a clerical conference
he was planning, offered Beekmann a job at St. John's Cathedral, in

his diocese. Mead described this arrangement as "whitemail." If Mosely would ordain Beekmann, then she would take part in his conference in the Pocono Mountains of Pennsylvania.

Beekmann was to pick Mead up, after a radio broadcast she had to do near Times Square, and drive her to that conference in the Poconos. With her staff in hand she waited for him, and climbed into his small stick-shift car for the trip westward. At five o'clock, at six, and again at seven, they thought they must surely be near their destination, but it was clear that they were lost. "We began to argue," Beekmann recalled, "like an old married couple."

"Richards," Margaret told him, "I've been up the Sepik and you've been across the Arctic—what's the matter with us that we can't even find our way through the Poconos?" (On a similar occasion she had scolded Napoleon Chagnon, veteran of many expeditions to study the Yanomamo of southern Venezuela. "Harrumph!" she had said. "You'd think that the world's most famous jungle anthropologist would manage not to get lost in downtown Washington!") Eventually Beekmann did find the conference of clergymen, where Bishop Mosely had prolonged the cocktail hour.

Later that evening a rather flippant young clergyman took issue with something Mead said about the difference between marriages and weddings. The sacrament of marriage, Mead had said, could exist between people regardless of their history or background, but a wedding, with all its pagan ritual of flowers and bowers and the giving away of the bride, was a one-time event. The flippant young clergyman said, "Well, *Miss* Mead, what would *you* know."

"I was embarrassed and horrified," said Beekmann. "I shuddered. But Margaret up and traced the entire history of matrimony, developing the theme canonically, theologically, and spiritually, for thirty-five minutes. I was overwhelmed, and so were most of the others there, and finally she stopped to ask, 'Will *that* satisfy you, young man?' There was great applause. Margaret was ruthless when confronted, but she loved it. This gave me great respect for her not only as a friend, whom I had already come to love, but as a church person."

Back in New York Mead found to her distress that she had left her favorite flashlight behind in the Poconos. Everywhere she visited, she said, people turned their hall lights off at night: without her flashlight, how was she to find her way to all those strange bathrooms? When Beekmann was ordained as a deacon (a standard six months before ordination as priest), he sent Mead a new flashlight along with a special vestment he had worn for the ceremony.

That gift, he felt, "forged the intimacy of our relationship. Without being very vocal about it, we both felt from then on that we could transcend time and space, that we would never be absent from each other's presence. She was one of the people with whom I had total, thorough, and explicit communication. She was the only person I've known whom I could disagree with but still be sure of her love, no matter what. From the moment I sat down to tea with her, at Marie Eichelberger's, she made me feel totally secure."

Perhaps because their profession put clergymen on a special plane, Mead was more flirtatious and feminine with them than she was with some others. "She always kissed me," said Richards Beekmann, "in a way that was not so much maternal as effusive and warm. It was wonderful to see the soft side of that fierce professionalism. She would tell me, 'You sit there, that's a *man's* chair, and let me get you a Scotch.' She always exclaimed over the little embroidered handkerchiefs and other presents I would give her. To me she seemed a tender, sensitive, feminine, sexual person who would wonder why women couldn't be women—she certainly was one herself."

But Mead had tensions with Beekmann, as she also had with Bonnell Spencer. Spencer disagreed with her preference for the old liturgy as opposed to the new. She also argued, at the Geneva meeting of the World Council of Churches, with a British canon who favored pure theory. Pure theory was all very well, she told him, "But what are we going to *do?*" Mead, in Beekmann's opinion, "tried too hard to make her religion practical. I tried too hard to be liturgical, ritualized, metaphysical. She saw religion as a force to fight world hunger, I saw it as a force to transcend. We would also argue about the ordination of women. When she came later to a conference I planned at Mercer Island, outside Seattle [where Beekmann was an assistant clergyman], she came out all in favor of women's ordination, which I was against. Theologically it's fine, but I just can't change my symbols that fast.

"I held my ground at a dinner party that night, expressing what I felt in my guts, not intellectually, and Margaret got up from her chair and stomped indignantly off with her staff, saying, 'Richards! You're incredibly dull!' But later, when we were leaving, as I gave her bottom a shove to help her into the Volkswagen van—she was pretty roly-poly— she said, 'You know, Richards, you're right. You're a priest, and you wouldn't want a woman in your male sanctuary any more than I would want a man to look through the drawers of my bureau.' " Mead, in the opinion of Christian Howard, "took both sides in the issue of the ordination of women. Both sides tried to get to her. Perhaps she didn't know which side she was on. She says in *Male and Female* that once the pattern is fixed, though patterns are not immutable, it's difficult to change."

Mead admired the King James Version of the Bible and was conservative about language and ritual, but she was not a contemplative or a mystic. The church's main responsibilities, she felt, were to banish hunger and to be alive to the world. For her participation in the conference outside Seattle, Beekmann had arranged to pay Mead a fee in addition to her travel expenses, which were all she had asked for, because, as he told her, he didn't want to use her. "You can only *use* a person," she answered, "when you're taking something from them that can't be replaced, so you aren't using me at all. There's nothing I wouldn't do for you—I'll always respond to your requests." And so she did, Beekmann said.

After Seattle Beekmann was assigned to an Oakland, California, parish which he found annoyingly complacent. His parishioners' "sense of outreach," he said, "was to allow the community bridge club to meet there on Thursday evenings. The vestry criticized me for allowing the parish to grow too much. They gave me a midlife crisis before my time." Beekmann decided to organize a Feast of St. Francis, in honor of the diocese's patron saint, the week of October 4, 1975, at Grace Cathedral. (St. Francis the nobleman-monk is a symbol of humility, gentleness, and a quiet, complex mysticism.) "My idea was to turn the cathedral into a lively spot and get enough attention to mobilize the parish and convince it that we can't just talk, we have to *do*." For eight months he and his staff worked on the feast, whose topic was to be "stewardship of mystery." The church, he hoped to help make clear, "had been so involved in meat and potatoes that it was forgetting its transcendental mission."

From all over the country people registered by computer to come to this conference, where Beekmann's old friend Margaret Mead was to be one of the big attractions. When she arrived in San Francisco, said Beekmann, "her biggest thrill was in seeing her friends the Eriksons. 'Don't you *know* who Erik Erikson is?' she asked me. 'He's one of the greatest men in the *world!*' She saw them, and some other old friends, and when she preached from the pulpit of Grace Cathedral it was packed to the gunwales. Everyone wanted to hear her."

Generally Mead did not like preaching because of the lack of response from the audience. People could not argue back to the pulpit, and passive audiences were not to her taste. She only preached to help her friends. Once, on three days' notice, she canceled all her plans and went up to New Haven to give a sermon in place of the Reverend William Sloane Coffin, who was then the Yale chaplain. One Ash Wednesday in Atlanta, Austin Ford remembered, Mead preached "about the importance of feeling responsibility to people we don't know yet and may never see, which led into the need for the World Council of Churches to oppose the proliferation of plutonium reactors. When the Council voted on that question," Ford recalled, "Margaret went through tremendous machinations to maneuver the votes to oppose plutonium."

Someone said of Mead that in another age she would have been a priest herself, but she did not warm to this notion. Late in her life she told a friend that of the three roles associated with the church—priest, prophet, and preacher—the only one that appealed to her was prophet, "because prophets give the idea that things need to be done which people ought to think and write and talk about." Also, she might have added, prophets attract the attention not just of one congregation but of all society, and after they have come and gone, nothing is ever the same. That is their reward for being without honor in their own countries.

After Mead's sermon in San Francisco, she and Beekmann and others in the procession marched outside, to stately music, through the cathedral's majestic doors, modeled after Ghiberti's at the Duomo in Florence. Medieval wooden ships and a huge hot-air balloon, with colorful stripes, filled the parking lot. The beauty of the scene, particularly of the balloon, overwhelmed everyone, Mead included.

"Margaret," Beekman told her, "you and I have been invited to ascend in that balloon over the city."

"Richards," she replied, "balloons are for children and fools, and you and I are neither."

Mead was not one to get carried away in balloons, real or metaphorical. Action suited her better. When one session of Bonnell Spencer's liturgical revision committee reassembled after a break for lunch, she rather suddenly said, "You know, I *like* this committee; I have such a good time!"

"I don't think," said Spencer, "that the Lord God Almighty could have given me higher praise than that."

CHAPTER TWENTY-FOUR

"These Tremendous Transferences"

KEN HEYMAN

MARGARET MEAD knew all she needed to about *moieties* and *affines* and *sibs* and *ujama* and *compadrazgo* and other technical terms of kinship, but she won more attention by talking, in plainer language, of families. The forthright ease with which she diagnosed and soothed the aches caused by families, as so many

All Mead's life she kept in touch with the Ash Can Cats (upper left), and her DePauw friend Katharine Rothenberger (right), and relied as much on colleagues like Gardner Murphy and especially Lawrence Frank (upper right) as if they were blood relatives.

aches are, was among the most endearing of her charms; the bold and generous way she defined the word "family" survives as the most enduring of her legacies.

When people had troubles with their families, Mead usually knew how to help them. Of course your family is driving you nuts, she would say. It's a nuclear family, isn't it? What did you expect? Nuclear families, isolating everybody as they do, are scarcely less dangerous than nuclear bombs. And of course you're disturbed about your own part in the divorce rate, but why add to your troubles by behaving as if divorce were wicked? Why is divorce a failure any more than death is? Where did the idea come from that everyone has to be married? Marriage, like parenthood, is a vocation, a call which some hear and some do not. Those who don't hear it should not pretend to, and nobody, married or not, should have children, as Mead had heard some people say they were doing, for no better reason than "just to get it over with." Society should wish childless people well, allow them to flourish in whatever contexts they may choose, and leave them alone. Not too alone, though. People Mead cared about were never left too alone. When one of her protégés left his wife for another woman, Mead declared that there were two possible interpretations: that he was a bastard or that he was having an identity crisis, and she preferred the second. But in acknowledging the man's second wife she by no means forgot his first.

"Life is good," Mead had concluded a letter to Erik Erikson in February 1959, "but terribly terribly thick, and full of prickly problems—other people's." Sometimes, Ken Heyman remembered, there seemed to be "forty or fifty people around Margaret all of whose husbands or wives had just left them. The first thing they'd all want to do was to go see her right away, because she was the one who could set things right. She was such a busybody, she'd run everybody's lives, but they loved it. Those who could take it loved it, anyway. Around the museum, with people she saw all the time, she could be a tough bitch, but with those whom she visited only briefly and occasionally, she had a marvelous, simple relationship."

When Mead got to an airport an hour before flight time, she would head for a phone booth and use the hour to call Léonie Adams, her Ash Can Cat friend since 1922. "An hour," she would say, "is about the time it takes to catch up with Léonie." Some of the ties Mead went out of her way to honor were more obscure. In an age when most people found it complicated to keep up with their present in-laws, let alone past ones, nobody would have held it against her if she had neglected her former husbands' relatives. Far from drifting apart from other former in-laws and distant relatives, she energetically sought them out, demanding to know how time was treating them. She always asked Luther Cressman what had become of his brothers, and in her second marriage she may have been a more inspired in-law than she was a wife. With the Fortunes, outside the little New Zealand town whose name meant "scrapings of an oven," most of Mead's encounters had been a pleasure for her and apparently for them as well. A snapshot of Reo's mother, Hettie, returned from her five months' mysterious absence, shows her with her arm around her older son's wife.

Mead had originally impressed her husband's brother Barter Fortune as "a most companionable and interesting person. She was establishing her footing in the world, making sure that the footing was good," but she did not put on airs; "she was capable of writing a newsy personal letter." Margaret and Reo had helped pay for Barter's university education, and had jointly proposed that he follow them into anthropology (a proposition they also made to Priscilla Mead), but he decided after two years of university study "that the circumstances of the economically depressed '30s demanded more attention to the state of contemporary man and society than to earlier states of mankind," which was to say he went into business. Shirley Hinds, Barter Fortune's first wife, recalled after Mead's death that "we were sisters-in-law for a very brief period, but she would look me up when she came back to New Zealand because she believed that womenfolk shouldn't bear grudges. She was right. It's true, as you get older, that people who have shared your background and family become more and more important." The cousin of Reo's whom Mead went out of her way to look in on many decades later said, "Oh, she was *large*," and it was clear that she was not referring to Margaret Mead's girth.

Mead was a conscientious daughter, granddaughter, sister, cousin, niece, grandmother, and godmother. Few family matters were beyond her scope. Addictions could not shock her, nor could roving-eyed husbands, grudges polished over generations to a high sheen, anguished vigils outside hospital emergency rooms and intensive care wards. She had planned funerals, she once told a florist who questioned her choice of a bouquet, on four continents, and she knew cremation pyres, requiems, and recitals of the *Kaddish* as well as she knew the cries of newborn infants.

One reason many women got depressed after their babies were born, she said, was that they lived too far away from close relatives. The cure for a family, she said over and over, was a family. "Children are having an awful time," Mead said in 1973, "living in quarreling houses, isolated, scared to death that their parents will get divorced, with nobody to rely on, no extra people, thousands of miles from their grandparents." Rituals and pageants were one way to help heal such woes. One of Mead's finer afternoons must have been that of her daughter's wedding, in June 1960, at St. Bartholomew's Church in New York City, to John Barkev Kassarjian, an engineer born in Syria of Armenian parents, whose father was a history professor in Beirut. Cathy and Kassarjian had met at Harvard while she was studying linguistics.

As many of the groom's family's friends as could arrange to be there saw the bride come down the aisle on the arm of her father, Gregory Bateson. So did nearly all the bride's kinfolk, most of the pair's friends from Harvard and Brearley and Israel and wherever else they had spent time, former cleaning women and housekeepers, all the people from Perry Street and Waverly Place days, museum people, Ash Can Cats, and Katharine Rothenberger from Indiana. Allen Ullman and Tulia danced the Charleston. After a honeymoon trip to the Middle East the young couple found a base in Cambridge, Massachusetts, which they left for a professional sojourn in the Philippines and, later, for an extended assignment in Iran. Each of these moves gave Mead a new and welcome place to pay visits when she traveled, as she increasingly did, around the globe. These stopovers delighted her, especially after the birth in 1969 of Sevanne Margaret Kassarjian, known as Vanni.

Mead wished her own parents could have had more time together in their relaxed and seasoned old age. Her father, who became gentler with the passage of time, outlived his wife by six years. Her mother had been pleased, once her own children were grown and gone, to have a new generation to instruct about such firm principles as the importance of the Democratic Party and the worthiness of such institutions as the American Association of University Women. Margaret inherited her mother's fondness for that group. "You're still here!" she exclaimed when she was asked to address an elderly AAUW audience in Connecticut. "I thought you all had died with my mother's generation, but here you still are." Mead's other favorite elders included her mother's sister Fanny Fogg McMaster, who marked her seventy-fifth birthday by giving subscriptions to the New Republic to all her nieces and nephews, declaring, "If I have to live in La Jolla, I can at least do this much to strike a blow for change." (At ninety, she gave a grand-nephew a subscription to The Progressive.)

Change was everywhere, in the headlines and in people's lives.

"We're having a new kind of revolt," Mead said in one speech: a revolt not of the enslaved and the exploited but of "all the people that are being done good to . . . In the past the professors knew best, the doctors knew best, the social workers knew best, psychiatrists knew best. There were great numbers of professional people who knew best and did good. Then the beneficiaries were supposed to be appreciative. And they've now become extremely unappreciative. And they're all insisting on getting into the act."

"The expectation of permanency is still great enough to brand every impermanence as a failure, if not a sin," Mead had written in 1949 in *Male and Female*, "and also because to all the other insecurities of American life, insecurity about marriage is added." Modern paintings showed fewer and fewer horizons, Mead said in a speech, quoting her artist sister Elizabeth, because people were confused about where they stood. Elizabeth, who taught art at first in New York and later at Lesley College in Boston, was divorced, having raised two children, from the cartoonist William Steig. Her and Margaret's younger sister, named Priscilla and called Pam, was divorced in 1959 from Leo Rosten. Priscilla had for years reminded one friend of "that Li'l Abner character who always went around with his head under a cloud." She gave frequent and elegant dinner parties at which, one of her guests said, she had a habit of "always serving one too few baked onions."

Priscilla, by all accounts, was the family beauty, but her beauty, said her daughter Madeline, brought to mind the "family curse": that bad things happened to each generation's pretty daughter. In April 1958 Priscilla wrote to Margaret, "I'm trying so hard to learn to be direct and simple . . . I do think I'm getting rid of 'Mrs. Hyde' really quite rapidly if this damn set of nerves and glands will just hold out . . . Lovingly, Priscilla—and I'd rather be Priscilla [than "Pam," presumably], I *like* her."

"I keep remembering your firmness as a child," Margaret wrote back, quoting the way her youngest sister in her very early years had asserted "I am Priscilla"—a firmness, Margaret's letter continued, "that somehow needs to get established again. All my love, darling . . ."

In 1959 Priscilla Rosten took pleasure in her children. She liked her son Philip's fiancée, and delighted in her daughters Peggy, who lived with her, and Madeline, who at seventeen had just been admitted to Radcliffe. That year she traveled around the United States making a series of visits to people who had mattered to her. But the visits, it turned out, had been farewells. On November 30, it was Margaret who discovered her sister in her apartment on Central Park West in New

York, and Margaret who cleaned up the blood, called the police, and arranged for Priscilla to be taken to the hospital where she died the next day. In overseeing all these matters, probably out of deference to her sister's family, Mead identified herself as "Mrs. Bateson." In a crisis, as Leo Rosten said, Margaret was always exemplary.

She had dealt with other suicides in the past, and had heard in detail about many more. Priscilla's death brought her grief, but not guilt. She did what she felt was right and did not brood; brooding was never her style. She seemed less upset by the loss of Priscilla, one friend remarked, than of their brother Richard, who died of pancreatic cancer in November 1975, when Margaret was in Africa. "The girls," Rosten said, "all lived in different worlds. They didn't seem to share very much. Maybe that was why Margaret got these tremendous transferences."

Part of Margaret Mead's brash genius lay in her skill at making what Rosten, alluding to Freud, called "transferences": shifting the feeling one originally has for a parent or someone else close to a therapist or friend or other central figure who appears in later life. Such transferences, for Mead, were frequent and intense. Her deep feelings were by no means reserved for the few with whom she was connected by blood or marriage. "I dare say it's very irksome occasionally," she wrote to her mother in 1927, "that I look at my family as impersonally as I look at people to whom I am unrelated, but you might remember also that my favorable judgments are also impersonal, and not based on any sentimental theories about blood being thicker than water.

"I am very fond of my family, as individuals," this letter went on. . . . "I know you have always resented the fact that I haven't cared about my family on the purely accidental count of blood relationship. Unfortunately, I fail to see that blood relationship entitles anyone to special affection. It is fortunate that I happen to feel a good deal of special affection for you all, so much in fact, that it is only upon occasions when my judgment happens to clash with yours, that you bring up the purely extraneous matter of 'being nice about my brother.' Being nice about anyone on such a count I would regard as pure dishonesty, and on the whole so would you.

"As far as my feeling for what you and Dadda have done for me, that also is a recognition of the affection and care you have given me as myself, in as much as it is given because I happen to be your daughter, I value it that much less. Anyway I don't regard the truth about any member of my immediate family as of such a discreditable nature that I have to 'be nice' and suppress it." Mead ended this youthful letter by saying she expected "we will have a very happy Christmas, one in which you needn't regard me as an alien, for I refuse to be one. I am just the catalytic agent which precipitates a large number of irrational loyalties, to the peace and well being of all of you, I trust."

The twenty-six-year-old catalyst who signed this letter grew ever abler, as time passed, to find room for new people in what she called her "constellations." Mead always made a point, she said, of finding her place in any constellation, and the more complex the scene, the better she liked it. Ultimately, her constellation became the whole world, the whole human race. In her life she practiced the lesson she advocated in her writing and her speeches: that we all ought to hasten not only to become our brothers' keepers but the keepers also of our neighbors, our countrymen, and also, in due course, our enemies. "Each time we have increased the number of those whom we would protect, whose death at our own hands we would call murder, we have increased the number of those who could become, in a body and overnight, without further identification, our mortal enemies whom it would be virtue to destroy," she wrote in 1957.

To become our enemy's keeper as well as our brother's was "something no men on earth have as yet learned how to be. And when we have learned, a new grade of evolution will be reached. For the relations between such peoples, who are of necessity the keepers of each other's children, no words that now exist will be wholly appropriate." What was needed was "the invention that will protect every member of the human species with the sanctions that once stretched no farther than a stone could be thrown."

Mead's own relationships stretched farther and wider and in more directions than any single friend could know. "She took care," her friend and colleague June Goodfield wrote, "that no one came too close, and even those fascinating books *Blackberry Winter* and *Letters from the Field* left unsaid as much as they revealed . . . She was pervaded by deep loneliness, and although she never admitted it, she was very vulnerable too. She cared immensely and gave generously, often to the point of being drained and impatient, but she rarely sought support. Everyone was her neighbor in the Biblical sense, yet she demanded far too much from those close to her."

"There was no pecking order within the family," said Mead's nephew Philip Rosten, "or, for that matter, between family members and more well-known figures. If you were part of Margaret's family (or the extended family of friends), you were of interest to her—be you a wandering student or a well-known author."

• •

The power of sisterhood, an amazement to some who first encountered it when the feminist movement was reborn around 1970, came as no surprise to Margaret Mead. Her own sisters, and then a succession of other sororities that only began with the Kappa Kappa Gammas of DePauw and the Ash Can Cats of Barnard, had long since made her aware of that force. But for all that she had predicted the movement's rebirth she and it were not quite sure what to make of each other.

The "which side are you on?" mentality, characteristic of a certain part of the feminist movement, offended Mead. Lady Rosemary, wife of the anthropologist Sir Raymond Firth, was nettled by the peremptory claims of feminists that Mead had been one of them, and by their efforts to link her with "the libbish eighties, the political go-go of the moment." Mead frequently made fun of the awkward usage of "chairperson," had no use for neologisms like "herstory," and asked, "What in thunder is gained by referring to God as 'she' except irritating people? All you get with a reversal is the opposite again." She did not, she said, envy penises; it was emphatically not her view that women should consider themselves substitute men, or that defloration and pregnancy should be thought of, as in some quarters they seemed to be, as enemy attacks or invasions.

Such thinking seemed to Mead naïve and beside the point; it made her impatient. "We women are doing pretty well," she said in 1976. "We're almost back to where we were in the twenties." Six years before the twenties began, Ruth Benedict had written in her journal that she saw "nothing 'new' about the whole [feminist] thing except the phraseology and the more independent economic standing of recent times," and observed that "restlessness and groping" seemed "inherent in the nature of women."

"Women don't have much power in this country," Mead said, "and they don't deserve to, either. . . . In a sense, I never was a feminist. I made friends with women, I stood by women, and if I was asked to do something that might improve the position of women in general, I did it. But I don't believe all these women fifty years old who haven't tried anything but marriage and children, who talk about how they've been discriminated against, because on the whole none of them have done anything else."

When someone in the audience at a speech Mead gave in Iran referred to her as one of the "foundresses" of the feminist movement, she denied it at once. The "foundresses," she said, were of her greatgrandmother's generation. "Everyone thinks everything was founded yesterday. Mrs. Friedan certainly thinks so." When Betty Friedan's *The Feminine Mystique* was first published in 1963, Mead told her goddaughter Martha Ullman West that the book contained "an interesting attack on me."

"Oh?" said Martha. "Are you going to review it?"

"It's not *that* interesting," replied Mead, but in fact the book irritated her. Friedan's sixth chapter, entitled "The Functional Freeze, the Feminine Protest, and Margaret Mead," says that despite Mead's "truly revolutionary vision" of what women might become, "increasingly, in her own pages, her interpretation blurs, is subtly transformed into a glorification of women in the female role—as defined by their sexual biological function," and that *Male and Female* had become the very "cornerstone of the feminine mystique . . ."

Mead's vision for others, Friedan wrote, "was of a world where women, by merely being women and bearing children, will earn the same respect accorded men for their creative achievements—as if possession of uterus and breasts bestows on women a glory that men can never know, even though they labor all their lives to create. In such a world, all the other things that a woman can do or be are merely pale substitutes for the conception of a child. Femininity becomes more than its definition by society; it becomes a value which society must protect from the destructive onrush of civilization like the vanishing buffalo."

In effect, according to Friedan, Margaret Mead claimed that "there were three classes of people: men, women—whose lot it was to stay home and bandage children's knees—and a very select company, including Mead herself, to whom the rules for the rest of women did not apply." Mead's intellectual position, as her Columbia colleague Marvin Harris saw it, was clear: wives, with very rare exceptions, should defer to their husbands' careers. "She would sound off on everything else," Harris said, "but never on the underrepresentation of women in our department. If she had, it would have been graven in one's memory. Margaret Mead was not the victim, ever, of anything."

Earlier Mead had belittled the "war between the sexes" as a passing and overrated invention of Madison Avenue, and said that there was nothing new about the tendency many New York men had to "picture women as rapacious monsters." All through history, she declared, whenever the relationship between the sexes appeared to be changing, men had "had nightmares that women were taking control." And another thing, all through history and all through the world: "The more uncomfortable we make the women, the more moral we feel."

Some of Mead's statements did seem to lend comfort to the enemies of feminism. She felt "a little cross now because my pension [from Columbia] is so low," she said in 1973; "I wasn't advanced as the men were—but I wasn't about to fight about it when the men in the department had a wife and child to support. I never had a chip on my shoulder about men." That she too had a child at least to help support was not, apparently, to the point. Mead's goddaughter Martha West and her brother-in-law Leo Rosten both said she did mind being no more than an adjunct professor, and, West added, she hated the discrimination against women at the Columbia Faculty Club. But she wavered in her public statements about feminism. "One of the things that worries me," Mead told a 1964 audience composed largely of physicists' and chemists' families in Oak Ridge, Tennessee, "is the younger group of scientists who know they shouldn't enslave their wives to housework, and so they have sloppy homes."

"One reason she ran afoul of the feminists," said Mead's perennial champion Wilton Dillon, "was her strong notion of what a *lady* was. She valued traditional background, overlaid with doing caring things. She was unabashedly a do-gooder, who believed in *noblesse oblige*." She also unabashedly enjoyed, as the song had it, being a girl. "I never wanted to be a boy," she said, "and I still feel that getting one of those obscure masculinizing diseases would be a fate worse than death." Far from resenting being excluded from male rituals in her field work, from Samoa on Mead took imaginative delight in studying women and children, and other matters which many men scarcely noticed. Let men do what they would and could; why not give them the driver's seat? She never learned to drive a car, much less ride camels or horses (or, for that matter, to swim). What always transfixed her was what the feminist Robin Morgan would identify as another feminine concern: "the interconnectedness of everything and women's alleged special ability to perceive this unity."

Feminine intuition, as Mead once defined it, is a matter of recognizing that the other person is different from oneself, and of paying enough attention to find out just what the differences are. "All the truth is there," she said. "All you have to do is listen to find it." In the view of her Swedish friend Tore Hakansson, "She was *more* than a feminist—she wasn't on the front lines of the movement, but then neither were Jane Addams and Sojourner Truth, and nobody can know what it cost them, or Margaret Mead, to achieve their independence."

It cost Mead plenty, she once suggested to the television newswoman Barbara Walters (whom she liked, as she did Johnny Carson, on whose "Tonight" show she was a frequent guest). "If the women's movement has done any harm," Mead once told Walters as they shared a taxi home from a dinner party, "it's to make it seem as if it all were easy. It *isn't* all easy!" The two women had been comparing notes, Walters said, "on how we'd both had some fame and some criticism, both of which are hard to take. We talked about what it was like to live alone and juggle too many lives, and how hard it is to bring up a child, especially a daughter, alone."

"You?" Walters asked Mead. "The most independent woman in the world? *You* have such thoughts as these?"

Yes, Mead said, she did have such thoughts.

But only once in her life, she said another time, had a man's opinion ever come close to interfering with what she wanted to do: when Edward Sapir tried to stop her, rather more because of what she called a "period clash" than on grounds of feminism, from going to Samoa. She went anyway, and inured herself in later years to the hostility she sensed from other men, mostly those in her own profession. "Men who would never begrudge success to women bicycle riders, women opera singers, women jugglers," she said, "begrudge it to me. Especially when they're drunk, they come to me and say, 'You have it all. It's not fair.'"

Although Mead denied being a feminist, she was an ally of the cause. The strength of her feminism, Colman McCarthy wrote in the *Washington Post*, came from "the criticism and balance she brought to the current renewal" of the movement, a balance which was "never reducible to bumper-sticker jargon." Mead's own example, as her *Redbook* editor Sey Chassler described it, was "that you can be what you set out to be, but first you must set out."

It would hardly have encouraged feminists to know that in 1959 Mead turned down the presidency of a large university, not only because she thought the time was not ripe for her to take this job but because "women make poor administrators." Still, those who wanted to regard Mead as a feminist heroine certainly could find support in some of what she said and wrote. "We must stop pretending that women live in a benevolent home where husbands never leave," Mead told a Florida audience. Uninteresting women, she once said, appealed to her far more than uninteresting men did, "because women think about more congenial things." Classes of women, she said, were more exhilarating to teach than classes of men. She opposed coeducation, she said at Radcliffe in 1969, because "twenty-four hours a day with boys can be appalling—it's bad enough to have to eat breakfast every day with your husband."

In Mead's private life, as one friend said, "she never understood about men," but some men felt that she did. "She was the quintessence of a woman," said the oceanographer and demographic scientist Roger Revelle, who first met Mead in London in 1960, over discussions about disarmament at a Pugwash Conference. "She was sexy. I never wanted to make a pass at her, but it certainly crossed my mind that someone else might want to. She could be coquettish. She had made herself into a legend and a character, and she loved it."

Women, Mead seemed to feel, needed more protection than men did. "She would help boys, in order to scold them and push them out for themselves," said one of her male students, "in a way that poor little girls couldn't be expected to push." One difference between men and women which Mead said was observable throughout history and in all cultures of the world was that "men in all-male groups are happy, whether they are in war parties, golf clubs, the army or the Boy Scouts. They like all-male society. Women, in all-female societies, are invariably sad. They talk about children who have died, lovers who have run off." Although Mead said this, she operated much of her own life, certainly her museum office, on a very nearly all-female basis. "She was always the Queen Bee, the Aunt Tom," said Friedan. "She played a considerable role in getting us all so preoccupied with 'fulfillment.' "

When the young sociologist Margaret Cussler (who had innocently angered Mead by saying she had heard her referred to as the "greatest *woman* anthropologist") wanted to dedicate her book *The Woman Executive* to her, Mead refused. "No," she replied, "they think I'm too aggressive anyway." Who "they" were she did not say, but it was clear that she craved their approval.

She craved their approval and she knew perfectly well that they were speculating about her own private life. It could not have been otherwise; other people's sex lives were such a running theme in what Mead wrote and said that concupiscent guesses inevitably were made about her own. It pleased at least one Samoan man, and several elsewhere, to claim her as a personal conquest, and many other people gossiped about her. "Just because she gave us theater tickets and was so generous with us," said the photographer Paul Byers, "people were always asking Ray Birdwhistell and Wilton Dillon and me if we were sleeping with Margaret." Ken Heyman, who was Mead's student in 1954 and later her photographer associate on field trips, said, "My mother wasn't sure that I ought to go, since Margaret had had so many husbands that I, at age twenty-nine, might be sexually maltreated."

Mead's three divorces suggested to some that she must be a home-wrecking vamp, and to others that she really might not care about men at all. Her long-time psychiatrist acquaintance Rollo May had no doubt she was androgynous. When Mead's Ohio cousin Martha Glardon asked her once what she thought of homosexuals, Mead paused for several seconds and then replied: "They make the best companions in the world." An ideal society, Mead declared at a 1974 conference, would consist of people who were homosexual in their youth and again in old age, and heterosexual in the middle of their lives. "What is new is not bisexuality," she wrote in one of the last columns on which she and Rhoda Métraux collaborated for *Redbook*, "but rather the widening of our awareness and acceptance of human capacities for sexual love."

Another of Mead's close friends contended that she "fell in love with women's souls and men's bodies. She was spiritually homosexual, psychologically bisexual, and physically heterosexual. She had affairs with both men and women—though never with two men or two women at the same time; in an eccentric way she had a very stern morality—but she wanted people to think there were many more of these affairs than there actually were; 'In our culture,' she said, 'it's good to have the image of the sacred whore.' "

In the late 1940s, when Mead had given an informal talk at a party given by the U.C.L.A. anthropologists Walter and Gale Goldschmidt for some of their graduate students, one guest in the audience raised her hand, in the question-and-answer period, to ask about Ruth Benedict's homosexuality and Mead's relationship with Benedict. "Margaret was miffed," said Goldschmidt, "but she kept her cool and handled the situation with marvelous grace, as if to ask the girl, 'Who the hell do you think *you* are?' "

"She had a problem with me because I was openly gay," said a woman artist who often saw Mead in the 1950s. "She often said she had never had anything against bisexuals, but it was clear she wasn't so comfortable about overt lesbianism. Was she a lesbian herself? I never thought so. Not everyone *is* sexual, you know. For some people, and I think she was one of them, work can take the place of sex."

"There's no doubt," said Leo Rosten, "that she spent a great deal of time with groups that included homosexuals, and that those groups found her simpático, but I don't think that was her own special bent. Pleasure, for her, was an interruption of cerebration. If she had a choice, I always thought, she'd rather exchange ideas than kisses." For the exchange of ideas, Mead knew of no sublimer forum than the conference. Other eyes might glaze over at the prospect of days in stuffy rooms with sealed windows, of plastic badges, endless panel discussions: Mead's did not. Conferences, for her, seemed a highblown species of that splendid ritual the family reunion. Each one offered a possible supply of exhilarating new cousins. At a conference she might meet Roger Revelle, or Buckminster Fuller, or Barbara Ward. Conferences were a way for her to help the world to confront itself. She rejoiced in the opportunity they gave people "to act as whole individuals, using all their senses as they seldom do in the narrower, more specialized contexts of professional and academic life." Her tower at the Museum of Natural History and her adjunct status on the Columbia faculty did not give her the wide platform she needed. At conferences she could be an *amateur*, in the French sense—one who argued and thought in larger contexts than narrow academic points. Cloistered for several marvelously focused days, exempt from the constraining routines of academia and home, free to grapple with cosmic issues, she was at her best.

We are talking here about a truly brilliant career, about one who picked and chose with exquisite skill: this from here, that from there. Goodbye, see you next year. Hello! Yes, it's me, with my cloak and staff, just back from São Paolo or Moscow or Delhi. Who else can give you what you can get from me? Who sidesteps resentments, cliques and cul-de-sacs of hierarchy better than I do, moving as I do between organizations? Cults and factions won't do. Everybody stay in this room till we talk things over. I'm here as an associate from another field, how could I be a threat? Shall we have coffee? A martini? You look as if you could use a friend, you poor brilliant young man. Let's talk. Maybe you'll become part of my network.

There was once a time, it is well to remember, when the word "network" was a straightforward noun, and not the banal verb it became (as the word "mentor" also did) in the late 1970s and early '80s, and during that time it was Mead's custom, Rhoda Métraux said, to develop networks wherever she went. On field expeditions, each member of her domestic staff gave her access to a different network of families. Every committee and council Mead belonged to at home might lead toward who knew how many more fruitful associations and networks. To deal with Mead on any level was to learn this, early on.

She often employed a wondrous facility for connecting the otherwise unconnected. Mary Catherine Bateson spoke publicly after her mother's death of her "ongoing relationships with several hundred people, in the later years of her life, as an attempt to maintain that sense of an interlocking whole, not to be cut off in an ivory tower in one part of the country. More and more it depended on her. She couldn't bring these people together . . . she kept trying to integrate friends who might never meet into a single world . . . she was continually constructing interrelated groups."

"Once you were a member of her family," said Alan Lomax, "you remained one for good. When she heard that I had lost part of my hearing in one ear she phoned at 2:00 A.M. to say, 'I've arranged an appointment for you with the best ear doctor in New York City. Your ears are precious; we must take care of them.'" Her professional associates sensed a similar concern. "I was very aware of the demands of the network," said Alan McGowan, who worked with Mead on the Scientists' Institute for Public Information. "I not only could ask things of them, but I had to respond to their needs, too. If I had a claim on them, through Margaret, then they also had a claim on me."

Philleo Nash referred to such networks as Mead's "alternate academy—a large number of individuals with whom she kept in constant touch by phone and mail, a wider array than any other scientist or politician or writer had access to." He also referred to these networks as her "maypole conspiracies," by which he meant an assortment of organizations, each of which might or might not know anything about the others, but whose activities, however unwittingly, all served the same grand aim, the aim Mead's younger friend Jean Houston had in mind when she spoke of "emerging paradigms."

No mortal could honor all the claims that arose from all the groups in Mead's "maypole," among them the midwestern psychiatric schools, the World Council of Churches, the United Nations, New Alchemy, New Directions, Planned Parenthood, the Human Lactation Center, and the Storefront Community School in East Harlem founded by her poet friend Ned O'Gorman, and her interest, spurred on by her friend Rudolf Modley, in developing "a language in which all the peoples of the world can really talk with each other," to say nothing of the numerous wary, conventional academics with whom she conferred at the American Anthropological Association, the American Association for the Advancement of Science, and all the other groups related to her own discipline.

In her work as in her life, Mead sought to have it not only both ways but all ways, and even to move at will between two camps which regarded each other, respectively and colloquially, as weirdos and pedants. Trouble could erupt when Mead's enthusiasms collided, as on occasion they were bound to. The self-styled "feisty innovators" of Robert Schwartz's Tarrytown Group, for example, must have seemed even more lowly than journalists to Mead's footnote-checking academic colleagues. Some of the latter must surely have cringed to read the brochure Schwartz sent out describing his Tarrytown Group as "a hidden university," established for "cutting-edge types" who were "at ease with the unexpected discontinuities common during such a time of major change." Schwartz, by his own admission "a guy who looks forward to sharing the fizz, the sparkle, the pop of new ideas," saw Mead as a congenial soulmate who was "trying to set up her own State Department."

Her young philosopher friend Jean Houston, a founder of the human potential movement, must have been harder for Mead's orthodox academic friends to figure out. She had impressive credentials. By the time she and Mead met in 1972 she had already given the William James lectures at Harvard, had written four books about behavioral psychology, and had taught at several universities. Born in 1939, Houston had graduated from Barnard twenty years later, studied philosophy and psychology and religion, taken a doctorate at Union Graduate School, and given workshops with titles such as "New Ways of Being" and themes such as "yeasting the metastructures of society." In early 1984 she was launching the "metacampaign" of a nonprofit organization called "The Possible Society," which she called "a secular evangelism to empower a new process so that newer, much deeper and more organic forms can arise. The issue of human survival," said Houston, "now rests on an expanded citizenry."

One of Mead's and Houston's first encounters was at a conference which they both helped to organize in Bath, England, in 1973, on education for women. During the conference, June Goodfield got into "a furious argument, no holds barred, with Margaret. We really went at it hammer and tongs, neither of us gave ground at all. You could see it in the faces of those students—they were horror-struck to find us so tough. I expect they had never seen anything like it. When the session broke for coffee Margaret and I, at opposite ends of the table, got up and immediately met in the middle of the room to give each other an enormous hug." When the discussion was over, Jacqueline Wechsler, the Hunter College president and former nun who was chairing the session, "put up both her hands as if toward heaven," Goodfield remembered, "and said, 'Praise the Lord. Students, mark this moment well. You have seen two women arguing passionately, without a shred of rancor, as men do all the time. We have not learned to do this, but we must.' "

Goodfield, Vanni Kassarjian's godmother and a close family friend, had felt much buoyed by Mead's support when her own marriage ended in 1972. Mead had a special compassion for younger women like Goodfield and Jean Houston. Houston, born the same year as Mead's own child and living just outside Manhattan, was available and admiring, and had a dazzling intellect to boot. "I need a daughter," Mead had told Houston gruffly when time came for Mary Catherine Bateson Kassarjian to leave for five years in Iran, "and I suppose that's probably you."

As time went by, Mead was in such constant motion that some who cared for her began to wonder whether she could stop if she wanted to. Mead's view, Houston said in summing up her friend's thinking, was that it was "all a question of citizens' volunteer associations, bands of angels, of empowered, loving, celebrational communities." It was also a question, as Mead sometimes put it herself, of "evolutionary clusters," only "she wasn't just a clusterer," as Houston said, "she was a swarmer." Mead's mind, said someone who gave her a battery of tests around the time she was fifty, was the least empty one he had ever seen. If there was any mysticism in her at all, she herself once reflected, it was simply in her tendency to "move with the tide of small events that seem to be deciding what to do next, with the general belief that the small events will give me the right cues. I follow the way the waves are rolling." In her case the waves often seemed tidal, and they rolled her just about everywhere, rarely to stay put for long. She was always eager to get out of here, however appealing "here" might be, and on to a new city, a new discipline, a new group that would provide abrupt and refreshing contrast with the one before.

Perhaps one two-week visit a year was ideal. In her growing reluctance to pause, Mead may have been fending off something more complex than the ordinary tedium nearly everyone experiences from time to time. In any case, she reconciled herself to a life of constant goodbyes, rewarded by the hellos that followed, and not always paying attention to what happened in between. The last thing anyone could have accused Margaret Mead of doing was wearing out her welcome.

CHAPTER TWENTY-FIVE

How the Legend
Got Her Cudgel

NAN MEAD BIRDWHISTELL, her middle name a tribute to her godmother Margaret, celebrated her sixth birthday on February 28, 1960. This Philadelphia gathering, like most rituals involving Margaret Mead, was a mix of generations and disciplines. In the Birdwhistells' twenty-room, three-story house, built in the 1820s, the guests assembled for a festive steak dinner, not only to honor the child but to talk of their work and of her father's. Ray Birdwhistell had been doing research in kinesics, the study of gestures, or "body language," as it was later called, since the 1950s. The Seminar in Communications Theory that he had led in 1954, at the University of Louisville, had brought together linguists, semanticists, and anthropologists, including Marshall McLuhan and his associates who came down from Canada. That seminar never really stopped.

Miriam Birdwhistell, at the time, was preoccupied with her roles as a wife and mother. She kept a close eye on the steak, so as to pull it from the broiler just when it was ready. But then she made a fateful decision, to be described in her forthcoming *Natural History of a Social Work Administrator*, which she told about in 1980 during the Cincinnati meeting of the American Anthropological Association. By 1980 she was immersed in her new life as professor of social work at the University of Virginia Medical Center, but she well remembered pulling the steak from the oven and, in so doing, spilling grease on the kitchen tile floor.

Figuring that nobody else would have occasion to come anywhere near the slippery spot, she wiped it with a paper towel and planned to clean it thoroughly as soon as dinner was over. Just as her guests were sitting down, a long-distance, person-to-person phone call came for Margaret Mead. A *Time* magazine researcher, at Rockefeller Center in New York City, needed to check a fact in a story just going to press. *Time* researchers who failed to check their facts risked being issued Errors Reports, a professional disgrace which such phone calls could help to avoid. These calls often came at inconvenient hours, and were resented, but not by Margaret Mead. Mead, who never had an answering service and whose home telephone number was always listed in the Manhattan directory, expected others to be as accessible as she was herself. Her own staff members were always to let her know how to reach them if she should need to, as she often felt she did need to, late at night, early in the morning or on weekends. She did not begrudge this call from *Time*.

But the noise of the Birdwhistell party was so distracting that she had to move from the phone in the library to another on the second-floor landing. Miriam returned to her guests in the dining room. Unbeknownst to her, Mead popped back down and told her host that the noise rising from the dining room made it impossible for her to hear. He directed her to the extension in the kitchen. Mead rushed there, slipped in the grease from the steak, fell to the floor, and knew right away what had happened. Once again she had broken "the ankle that goes to pieces," as she had referred to it in 1944 and many times later—the same ankle that had kept her stranded among the Mountain Arapesh.*

* She told Luther Cressman, in a letter written in the spring of 1960, that she had broken the same foot she had hurt in 1924, during their marriage,

In Philadelphia, as in New Guinea, Mead reacted to mishaps through a prism of her own. The fracture, to be sure, would prove to be a bore and an inconvenience. "The cast," a doctor told her when she complained of its heft, "does *not* weigh fifty pounds, it's your immobilized leg that *feels* as if it weighed fifty pounds." And when the cast came off, Mead made one of the most inspired decisions of her career as a public figure.

Uncle Sam's Umbrella Shop in New York, she learned, imported forked "thumb sticks," made of British cherry wood, from a cane and umbrella manufacturer in London. As soon as she tried such a stick, as high as her shoulder and cleft at the top in the shape of a Y, she knew she had to have one. Why should Margaret Mead use a cane? Canes made people look hunched and pathetic. Canes were for old ladies. Wonderful and admirable though old ladies were, Mead was not ready to be one of them.

What she was ready for was the exhilarating liberation of menopause. Mead claimed not to have finished menopause herself until she was sixty, but for years she had been an outspoken champion of postmenopausal zest. Postmenopausal women, unlike younger ones, who needed escorts, could range all through society, free to concern themselves not just with their own children but everybody's, free to say what they liked. "You're coming of age!" she reminded her United Nations colleague Mildred Leet. "People *respect* age! Learn to raise your voice! People will listen!"

Being listened to was of paramount importance all Mead's life. Stage fright, in old and young, was quite beyond her. "She gave me a lot of hints about speaking," said one of her fellow anthropologists. "She'd urge me to begin with something very startling, prove it was wrong, bring in something to make my points, say something outlandish, and be alliterative." Her speeches reminded Mead's priest friend Feichin O'Doherty of "machine-gun fire: she bubbled, knowing something was in there; she was like a sculptor with a chisel and hammer attacking a block of stone"—and someone else of a painting: "You'd find a dab of color here, a brilliant idea somewhere else, a sad, serious part in the middle,

---

but that this time the fracture was trimalleolar, involving the tibia and a foot bone as well as the ankle, and requiring a cast up to her knee. Cressman remembered the 1924 injury well: "I was sitting in our living room and she came limping in with a very handsome member of New York's Finest—I said, 'What *now?*' and she told me she'd been caught in a wind storm on Broadway in front of a taxi, so the officer brought her home. The next morning I took her to St. Luke's Hospital and got her foot treated."

and always some wit, always a little joke at the end, like, 'Thank you, Madame Chairperson.' "

As the featured speaker at the 1958 commencement exercises at the Oakwood Preparatory School outside Poughkeepsie, New York, Mead had discovered, rising to begin her remarks, that the senior class was seated behind her. She shifted the microphone around so that her back was not to the graduates but to their assembled parents, who included her friends Allen and Sara Ullman: "If I'm here to speak to the seniors, I'll speak to the *seniors*." Those graduating were elated to be hearing her, and so were all the disparate other groups who could entice her to address them, sometimes for large fees and other times as a labor of love. Between Mead and most audiences there was magic. An audience, when her spirits drooped, was just the thing to pick her up. "I'm so exhausted," she once complained. "If only I could give a lecture!"

Mead always got right down to the business at hand, and as best she could she looked her audiences straight in the eye. She bore in mind the advice her father had given her as a child about avoiding what he called the "lawn-sprinkler effect," by which he meant "spraying your words over an audience instead of looking one or two people in the eye." This, said Mead, was "the beginning of the *ex tempore* speaking which has made my life so much easier." She disliked reading from a prepared text, and having to announce months in advance what her topic would be. How could she know, until the time came, what she would feel like saying? By the time she had finished speaking, she said, she often had learned at least as much as she had taught: all lectures were part of teaching. Her friend Marshall McLuhan once told *Life* magazine that talking aloud to people gave him "lots of discoveries—I use statements as a probe, not a package." That was Mead's method, too.

Once Mead and New York City Public Health Commissioner Leona Baumgartner were both scheduled to address the annual meeting of the Junior Leagues of America, and each was eager to speak first so she could get on to her next appointment. On the platform they argued in whispers. Mead won: "Please, Leona," she implored, "I just *have* to get out of here." Baumgartner deferred. Mead took the podium to describe, among other things, some details of the pecking order among chickens. The audience, gradually discerning that this figure of speech concerned the pecking order being established right there before them on the dais, began to giggle. The giggles turned to laughter and applause. When Baumgartner's turn came to speak, she announced with considerable grace, "We've all had such a good time here that I think I'll cancel my talk."

No audience was beyond Mead. When a friend asked why she had agreed to address so stuffy a group as the American Medical Association, Mead replied, "Well, they're important, and maybe if I mention something good they've done, I can work in something else to provoke them." When she spoke to the Fragrance Foundation in 1976 she accused them of concentrating "on perfume and not on people," and asked why nobody was studying "what we are doing to people by blurring their sense of smell." The *Women's Wear Daily* account of this talk reported: "At diatribe's end, the grand old lady from Samoa, who says she wears nothing but Je Reviens, received a standing ovation. But what exactly did she say? Not much."

Her glibness was a mixed blessing. At Sydney University in the middle 1960s she ad-libbed a talk which could have been magnificent, a fellow anthropologist said, if only she had written it down. Once she gave a rambling, off-the-cuff speech to a group of adolescent psychologists which one member of the audience later edited for publication and sent to Mead for approval. A note from one of her assistants informed him that "Dr. Mead *never* consents to being edited."

The visit Mead made in 1964 to Oak Ridge, Tennessee, caused a great stir. "Possibly never in its history," the local paper reported, had "such a cantankerous speaker" appeared there. "This lady stood up there on the stage of the high school auditorium, looked a goodly percentage of the city's eggheads in the head, and suggested that, perhaps, they were a bunch of self-centered snobs." What were these elite scientists doing, Mead asked them, about bridging the considerable gap between themselves and their unskilled, uneducated Appalachian neighbors? "You behave just like any other Americans," Mead said, when some of these Oak Ridge residents talked back. "You just can't stand criticism." But she herself was not always graceful in the face of criticism. Heckling or booing could reduce her to tears. In Los Angeles, in the late 1950s, her fellow anthropologist Walter Goldschmidt had introduced Mead at a talk for a group of his students, for which she kindly charged no fee. Grateful, he recalled a talk he had given himself, some years earlier, at which the master of ceremonies had said, "I was asked to get either Margaret Mead or Ashley Montagu, but we don't have that kind of budget, and I'm sure you've all enjoyed Dr. Goldschmidt's talk anyway."

This gaucherie had so amused Goldschmidt that he ended his own introduction of Mead by saying, "And now, I give you the rich man's Walter Goldschmidt." Mead did not smile, "and then she went on," Goldschmidt said, "to give an unbelievably bad talk about what was wrong with American culture in general and American men in particular. The problem with American men, she said, was that bottle feeding had become so universal that men could suckle babies just as well as women could, which was why they were losing all their sense of adventure."

It pleased Mead that she could "talk Freud to the Freudians, Jung to the Jungians, behaviorese to the behaviorists," she told her much younger colleague Vincent Crapanzano. Crapanzano had been amazed, in the early 1960s, by a lecture Mead gave at the Army Language School in Monterey, California. Her audience, he said, was "incredibly bifurcated: half dedicated military men and half unusually bright language students. The officers heard one thing and the students quite another." Mead could impress any audience she wanted to, but the esteem of the public at large, in her quest for influence, meant more to her than that of her peers within anthropology.

Robin Fox wrote of Mead that "she was left over from the time when to be an anthropologist was, by definition, eccentric, and to be a famous anthropologist demanded a striking public presence. She never let her public down." As Marty Martin wrote in his play *Gertrude Stein Gertrude Stein Gertrude Stein,* "Genius is 'the art of becoming legendary.'" Mead's stick made her look so dashing, so invincible, and so legendary that she kept it, or a replacement from a ready supply of reserves, long after the ankle had healed. She needed the stick only on rough ground and for stairs, she wrote a friend, and she planned to get a trailing vine to drape on it for parties. It would go nicely, she added, with another proud new possession: a green-and-gold cape. She carried the stick all the rest of her life, and liked her first cape so much that she got two others, a red one and a blue one, both trimmed with black. For her, as for Batman and Superman, as Malcolm Kirk suggested in his book *Man as Art,* a cloak could seem to offer "wings of invincibility."*

For people who tried to figure Margaret Mead out, as people were forever trying to do, the stick was as provocative, and as ambiguous, as a Rorschach ink blot. How you interpreted it depended on who you were and how you saw her. She herself referred to it as her "pastoral rod": "Every society has some symbol that goes with a staff. In Israel I look like a prophet; in Greece, like Tiresias from *Oedipus Rex.* I can fit into their myths." Many agreed that it gave her the look of a bishop or a shepherd or, as one irreverent writer put it, "Big Bo-Peep." Others said

---

* Mead said she hoped other people who had weak ankles and knees would follow her example and use such sticks. "I don't want to be unique," she insisted. But sensible though the idea seemed, it was never widely imitated.

that Mead with her stick made them think of Zorro, of a witch, of Poseidon, of Neptune. The stick was referred to variously as a divining rod, a phallus, a dowser, and a shillelagh. "People look at the stick," Mead once said, "and ask, 'Do you use that to beat people with?' Imagine! I've never touched anybody with it, but they project: *they* could hit somebody with it, so they figure I must, too."

Winthrop Sargeant's 1961 *New Yorker* profile of Mead, "It's All Anthropology," referred to the stick as her "formidable-looking cudgel." Wherever she went, and there were few places she didn't get to sooner or later, the stick guaranteed attention. When a fellow anthropologist emboldened himself to ask what she meant by wielding it, she told him, "Any time I want to disguise myself, I'll throw it away." It suited her on one occasion to conceal the stick: on a tour of the Hermitage Museum in Leningrad, where it could not be left in the checkroom. Her gallant escort, the cyberneticist Heinz von Forster, hid it, during the tour, inside his own clothing.

The stick had practical as well as symbolic value. Mead could use it to "knock things off shelves, open transoms, cope with recalcitrant windows," hail taxis, edge her way toward a seat in a crowded subway, and, since she said it could support up to sixty pounds, it also made a fine impromptu coat rack in elevators.

She spent a lot of time in elevators, as in all other forms of transportation. "Someone on this elevator," she is supposed to have announced during one vertical journey, "has just had sex!" Two of Mead's closest colleagues deny that she could ever have said such a thing, but the story is widely repeated.

The anthropologist Warren Swidler, who one hot night was stuck with Mead and ten other colleagues in a stalled elevator in an apartment building near Columbia University, remembered long afterward how Mead "turned that elevator into a dwelling and a field," with the help of her friend Rhoda Métraux, who "told Iatmul stories while Mead tried to convince a flamboyant young man not to climb out the hatch to the top. We were stuck, if memory serves, just below the twelfth floor, where the party we were going to was," said Swidler, "so with a little shouting by the females, whose voices Margaret said would get a faster response than the men's, the police arrived before too long. Margaret suggested that all men with beards retreat to the rear of the elevator, because policemen didn't like beards, and we must look, from their point of view, as if we were worth saving." Mead's militant pacifist contemporary Dorothy Day issued similar directives to her followers when she led them to antiwar demonstrations: they were to wear neckties and jackets, to look more middle class. Appearances, Day and Mead both knew, could win or lose a hearing for ideas.

Long before she had the stick Mead had been stalking the world, watching over her flock, exhorting, and causing heads to turn with her implorings that science and society talk to each other. Not everyone responded to her sympathetically, especially not those of her fellows who went to and from their field expeditions, seminars, faculty meetings and classes without attracting anything like the attention which the press and the public paid regularly to Margaret Mead. If they themselves needed someone to turn on when "pure" scientists belittled their profession, Mead must have seemed a handy target. She "claimed much more for anthropology," said her younger colleague Ann Chowning, "than anthropology was in a position to deliver."

Some of her colleagues were angry when Mead hurried off a plane in Australia, before anyone else could exit, "So I can be photographed!" (She was not delighted when friends tried to protect her from an impromptu press conference in Christchurch, New Zealand. "I'm here," she said, "to be seen!") Some cheers were heard, at one anthropologists' banquet in early 1960, when it was announced that because of Mead's broken ankle she could not be there to deliver a scheduled speech. "There was real feeling," said one member of that audience, "that she was bringing discredit to the profession." Mead never managed to please all her scholarly colleagues.

But anthropology was only a part of the audience Mead aimed at. "She was an activator in her own society. She was a catalyst for social action: she used the power she knew she had to scare people into action. She would raise her voice and *boom*, she'd lift that stick and stamp it. Maybe it was an act." Act or not, it was effective.

She made herself fair game for all kinds of attention. In James Michener's *Return to Paradise*, a sequel to his *Tales of the South Pacific*, he portrayed "a remarkable woman . . . about fifty, sawed-off, dumpy, red-faced and scraggly-haired . . . an anthropologist," of whom a crude character says that " 'the most disgusting person you can meet is a woman scientist. They've ruined New Guinea, studyin' natives. They poison the Administration. . . . They want to make it coon utopia. . . . She was in the jungle, studyin' primitive habits—so she said. . . . No wonder she fills her books with dirty stuff about sex. She should know!' " The story's more literate narrator muses on the furor caused by this woman anthropologist's "superb essay on sex in ultra-primitive societies" and on how she had "fled her society to study the ultimate beginnings of sex, the cruel force that had so punished her. Somehow, in some strange way, she had triumphed over those early rejections and had found reassurance in the savage jungles of our first beginnings. She had become a woman loved by the entire world. But the jungle remained her home."

A 1963 satire by David Cort in *Monocle* magazine, headlined "MARGARET MEAD FOR PRESIDENT," suggested that "perhaps we have labored too long under the delusion that the populace seeks a Father Figure when, in fact, it longs for a Mother. And who is better suited to this role than Margaret Mead? The image of the lady professor dissolves and we are blinded by the vision of Cybele, Great Mother of the Gods, who knows all men's secrets. Since only a goddess is in a position to 'study mortal sexual behavior,' perhaps that is why, at the beginning of her career, Miss Mead hit on this subject, and has never let it go. . . . Her opinionizing becomes, itself, a sort of public sexual behavior."

The *Monocle* satire alluded to one of Mead's more flamboyant suggestions, first presented at a 1961 Denver meeting, that honeymooning couples of all nations ought to spend their first two weeks of married life in bomb shelters. The babies they conceived would be spared any danger of nuclear radiation and could grow up safe to carry on the human race. "If this statement had been made during the closing weeks of a presidential campaign," Cort wrote, "Miss Mead would have won the votes of all the young citizens who are convinced that their superior lechery entitles them to No. 1 citizenship and every sort of priority." Mead cared much less for this *Monocle* piece than for a 1959 "Close-Up" in *Life*, illustrated with pictures Ken Heyman had taken of her in Bali, in New York, and at Cloverly.

There were rumors that Mead had squelched an earlier profile because it mentioned the first of her three marriages, which she did not acknowledge publicly until *Blackberry Winter*. Sargeant's *New Yorker* profile called her "one of the world's important thinkers" and a "highly civilized woman" who was "anxious to bring her work to bear in a realistic way on the problems of the day." Although this profile was flattering, one friend said Sargeant disappointed Mead, "because he expected her living room to be full of things like spears and shrunken heads, and didn't listen."

Mead found time for local as well as national media. In 1960, during a visit to her friend Katharine Rothenberger at Lake Papakeechie in Indiana, she was interviewed at length for a page-one story in the *Elkhart Truth*. Headlined THIS No TIME FOR DESPAIR, the story quoted her as saying: "It's nonsense to talk of a third world war as if a fourth would follow. A third world war cannot be allowed to happen. . . . In 50 years, we will live in an entirely different world. Every generation must change together. Eskimos pushed their grandparents through the ice because they couldn't take them with them. We must not push ours through the ice of human unkindness by ignoring them in the change. . . . We are going somewhere we have never been. We will need a kind of president we've never had to do a job that has never been done before."

John F. Kennedy's administration, she told *Life* reporter Gail Cameron in 1962, was the first since Franklin Roosevelt's to be made fun of, in part because "it's the first time we've had a young couple in the White House. The cult of youth is important here, because Americans worship youth. For fifty years we've had movie stars as a guide for women and baseball players as a guide for men. No one is going to imitate a president or a first lady over fifty years old, because we don't like to admit that people get past fifty." The Kennedy Administration, she observed, gave America its first "son complex. Previously we'd always had a father complex." But the Kennedys, with their emphasis on youth, committed an oversight. The venerable New England elders Richard Cardinal Cushing and Robert Frost were conspicuous at the 1960 inauguration, which was all very well, but from then on, by Mead's lights, not much attention was paid to the wisdom of people of her age or older.

The cheering and idolizing and enshrining she received whetted Mead's appetite for more. But her fame, said Leo Rosten, left her uneasy. "Essentially she was modest," said Rosten, "and insatiable for reassurance. She grabbed every lecture opportunity, every seminar, every chance she could find for applause." This, Mead herself admitted, was true. "Even writing a book," she had said, "is, for me, a performance." All writers and teachers feel that way to some degree, of course, but Mead seemed to feel it literally and always, and the stick, her cudgel, made her performances all the more effective.

Mead had known just what to do when the accident happened at the Birdwhistells' house in 1960. Drawing on the presence of mind that had seen her through any number of crises in the field, she first asked a photographer in the party, Paul Byers, to take a picture of her as she lay on the kitchen floor. On grounds of chivalry Byers refused: he did not think she looked dignified. Mead wished he had more sense of history. "You always miss the important stuff," she told him. She got busy, directing two other guests to place a blanket under her, so that she could be slid onto it and carried to the living-room couch to wait while the back seat was removed from the station wagon, to convert it into an ambulance. Then she was rushed to the hospital, where the injured malleolus was X-rayed, and diagnosed as broken, to be reset the next day after the swelling had subsided, and put in a cast. She was released in time to make a second appearance at Nan's birthday dinner, where, ensconced again on the living room couch, she announced, "Now I'm ready for my steak and baked potato."

For the next six weeks, the library of the Birdwhistells' house became Mead's convalescent base of operations. Using her credit card, she dialed the numbers of all the people in all the places where she had been expected to appear in the early part of that year, to cancel—if she could not postpone—her appointments. This meant quite a lot of telephoning. "Next year," she had told *Life* in 1959, "is about completely frozen."

In a sense, from this point on, all her time was frozen. That was the price she paid, without complaint, for establishing herself as a legend.

PART FOUR

At the end, great confusion can be a mark
of greatness, too, especially if it results from
the inescapable conflicts of existence.

—ERIK ERIKSON
Gandhi's Truth

Elder Statescreature

Elizabeth Mead Steig with her sister at Lesley College in Boston in 1963.

TIME TURNS most of us into caricatures of our early selves. The unobtrusive, as they age, slink around more edgily than ever, fearful upon entering each new room that they may sit on someone's favorite chair. The cheerful get perkier, the quirky grow more crotchety, the serene more beatific. Margaret Mead, who had hungered all her life for acclaim, companionship, and a full schedule, got all three, in the last dozen years of her life, to a measure that even she must have found a little befuddling.

Since the Second World War she had consciously tried to reach "the widest possible audience," as her colleague Rhoda Métraux remembered, "partly to attract funds for research and partly because lectures and articles feed on each other in building up an audience." She wanted an audience and she had one, and it grew when television came into its own. Like John F. Kennedy, the first president to understand and exploit the power of television, Mead taught herself new tricks for establishing rapport with unseen audiences. One of these was to "put the audience in back of the camera and then focus your eyes—that's the difference between really looking in somebody's eyes and looking at that prompter." The more people could feel that she was looking into their eyes, the better.

No wonder it sometimes seemed that every ninth-grade teacher in America must be giving class assignments of letters to Margaret Mead asking advice and information about such maddeningly vague topics as how the world should be run. ("Most people just throw letters like yours in the waste basket," Mead wrote to the author of one such letter in 1968, "but I can't do that.") A joke began to circulate: What did Margaret Mead say when she was introduced to the Delphic Oracle? She said, "Hello, isn't there something you'd like to know?"

She kept learning herself, "all the time, through her pores," said Leo Rosten. "She had a brilliant flair for seizing ideas from children, colleagues, historians, and every other source that came her way. She was the greatest picker of brains I've ever known, the greatest girl reporter in the world." Even unlikely people, even those generally considered bores, could be her teachers: a bore, Mead believed, was "simply a person to whom one can find no tolerable level of response." "Don't you find these speeches boring?" she was asked in the women's lounge during a convention of anthropologists, to which Mead replied with another question: "Have you no interest in observing the ritual behavior in your own culture?"

She was punctilious about taking part in professional gatherings, and never if she could help it missed sessions of the anthropology classes she taught, but scholarship as such had not been her primary concern for years. In her field visits, ever since the 1953 Manus expedition, she had attracted as much attention herself as she focused on the people she had traveled across the world to observe. She, they were beginning to realize, was as much a phenomenon as they were. Film crews accompanied Mead on her later visits to Bali and Manus; a PBS-TV program showed her, huge in a sundress and a straw hat, telling a group of elderly men, in pidgin, that "Me no like sunny cooking you too much," and urging a roomful of schoolchildren to hurry up and learn to read.

These field visits, which few ethnographers make after the age of fifty, were important to Mead, but they were only part of the focus of her life. The focus of her life, not to put too fine a point on it, was the world. The widely publicized photograph of the planet earth, seen spinning in the galaxy from outer space, excited her and made her think of a thirteenth-century poem she had memorized as a child:

Late, late yestreen I saw the new moon
With the auld moon in hir arme,
And I feir, I feir, my dear master,
That we will cum to harme.

It was past time, Mead was convinced, for an expanded version of the "giant rescue operation" which Franz Boas had overseen in the 1920s. This time it was the planet that was imperiled, not just some disappearing distant peoples, and no one, in her view, could be exempt from helping with the task of salvation. She thought big. "I never get orange," she said in one of the film portraits made of her in the middle 1970s, "in dreams of prehistory." No wonder, with such vivid images in her head of prehistory and of doomsday, that Mead had so little time or appetite for the minutiae of scholarship.

She no more wanted to acquire a new body of knowledge, she declared, "than I want to learn to ski. I'm accustomed to extrapolating from a very small amount of complex material to the whole." What she did want was not to master every step of every discipline, but "access to new bodies of knowledge. I'm willing to take all the steps in my own discipline, though people don't always recognize that, but in other spheres I'm willing to take the highest level of abstractions at their face value. If I insisted on knowing all the steps, I couldn't move around analogically as I do."

She moved around in reality too, or, to be more accurate, she was moved. "Getting her where she had to go," said Colin Frank, "was like wheeling a giant brain around." For one who covered as many miles as Mead did, whose travels rivaled those of Air Force One when Henry Kissinger was using it, her own body stayed remarkably still. Fuel burned, continents and oceans sped by beneath her in the time it once would have taken her to traverse a single mountain ridge or a single bend of the Sepik, but during most of this activity she sat still. "She loved the dancer," the Baltimore psychologist John Money said of her, "but she did not dance." Except for what another associate called Mead's "silently kinetic tongue"—the tongue that darted in and out of her mouth like a snake's—she often did sit perfectly still. Such immobility may not have been good for her circulation, but it suited her temperament, and made possible her feats of globetrotting.

Once, uncharacteristically, Mead decided to change her schedule; she wanted to leave Toronto before her ticket said she could, and stalked with her cudgel into the airport to book herself an earlier flight for which, of course, she had no reservation.

"Sorry, ma'am," said the clerk at the airlines counter, "that plane's all full."

"But I'm Margaret Mead!" she replied, as if this information should assure an automatic waiver of the rules and rearrangement of the passenger list.

Usually others fussed over her logistics, and did battle when need be with travel agents. When Geoffrey Gorer and Mead took holidays together it was Gorer who made the arrangements and Mead who tried, though it did not come naturally to her, to "have a good time." Her idea of a good time was to keep on working. When she went away on business, her staff at the museum consulted with their counterparts wherever she was going to draw up a plan of exactly how she would get there, who would meet her, by what means and how soon they would convey her to her destination, how long and where she would stay, and when and how she would be home again.

After a long flight from Brazil to Kennedy Airport in New York, she was recognized by a bystander in the International Arrivals Terminal who made some joke about hoping she had not smuggled any cocaine into her suitcase. "What!" exclaimed her proper companion. "In Dr. *Mead's* luggage?" With that the customs inspector, who had seemed about to let her go by without opening anything, began methodically to look through every item of her luggage. He did so, he explained, not because he suspected her of any wrongdoing, but because "my wife would never forgive me if I didn't tell her what Margaret Mead takes with her on a trip."

Mead was good-humored about this delay, but once in a while, when things did not go according to plan, she was distressed enough to let fly such expletives as "Fiddlesticks!" or "Rubbish!" or "Nonsense!" (Taboos against four-letter words were vanishing fast in the swelling ranks of her admirers, but her own standards of speech remained Victorian.) If jet lag troubled her, she did not let on. Home at eight one evening from a visit to Switzerland, where the local time was three in the morning, she phoned a New York friend to suggest that they have dinner then and there. Even as a septuagenarian, let no one say of Mead that she wasn't a sport, or rather let no one fail to marvel at her energy, which she sometimes supplemented with 5-milligram Dexedrine tablets.

The more Mead became a citizen-philosopher, likened by her friend Wilton Dillon to Aristotle, the more anthropology became a sideline for her. She took on the job, Rollo May said, of being "the last of the nationwide people of wisdom, the way Nicholas Murray Butler had been in the twenties. She was a self-appointed queen, at whose feet young people would sit with great admiration, which was fine. But she had a need to put everybody in their place, to swing the broadsword like a Zen Buddhist guru." At some point in the 1960s the world had thrust onto Mead's shoulders what her fellow curator Robert Carneiro described as a mantle of omniscience. She accepted this mantle as her due and wore it with a flourish. It went well with the forked stick and cape, and added to her air of being a superwoman who knew everything and who also, knowledge being power, could do everything: not only omniscient but omnipotent.

There she was, this beaming, disarming, sternly loving grandmother, with a lap that looked ample enough for everyone to crawl onto and be rocked, soothed, and reassured that somehow, in spite of the perils of "the seductive quality of Western technology," which she said was the biggest problem facing mankind, all would be well. True, we lived in "the most crucial era since the age of fire," and must blaze our own trails into "a kind of civilization that no one has ever seen," inventing the model as we go along for a time in which "the whole ratio between energy and individual work will disappear." She was glad to be an American, she said, "because I think we can do more harm than any other country on earth at the moment"; better to be within such a society than outside it.

Children all over the world, she asserted, had "a new scream, a scream that imitates the machine . . . the amount of mechanical noise that surrounds us today is a brand-new problem." Population control was within reach: "it's almost time for us to tell the unconceived, 'wait a while, this is not a good time for you to be born.' " Everyone over twenty-five, she said many times from many platforms in the late 1960s, was "like an immigrant from another country"; the elders were the immigrants and the younger people, those born in this time, were the natives. For the first time in human history, there were no elders anywhere who knew what the young people knew: this was a doctrine to beguile the elders, flatter their juniors, and expand Mead's audience. *Redbook* asked her to make her monthly columns more timely and political, and so she did. She had become a messenger, then a prophet, now a high-class advice columnist. Most of the advice she dispensed was humane and sensible, if commonplace.

The more questions Mead was asked, the less she could resist giving answers. Was divorce so terrible? Was marijuana so dangerous? Maybe not, said Mead in widely publicized statements. The prohibition of marijuana, she told a Senate subcommittee in 1969, defending youth as she had for decades, was "far more dangerous than any overuse"; what we ought to be more worried about was the total breakdown in communications among doctors, which led to the prescription of lethal combinations of drugs for different parts of the body. The governor of Florida called Mead a "dirty old woman." She won more enemies by repeating, as she often did, that the longer people lived the less likely it was that their marriages would last for a lifetime, that people were asking too much of marriage, that divorce had become a moral act. In saying these things she was explaining, not exhorting, but many who heard her message felt the ancient impulse to turn on the messenger.

Not all her dreams for acclaim were realized. She was not invited, as she had broadly hinted she would like to be, to celebrate her seventieth birthday in the People's Republic of China. Nor was she consulted by government officials as much as she had expected to be during her four-month term in Washington, D.C., in 1973, as Fogarty International Fellow.* As one friend said, "She had assumed congressmen would sit at her feet and ask, 'Margaret, what should we do?' She thought her phone would be ringing off the hook with requests for her advice. But that didn't happen."

Another disappointment concerned the National Academy of Sciences, which did not elect her to membership until 1975, although she was indisputably the most publicly celebrated scientist in America. "Evidently she felt she should have got in twenty years earlier," said Fred Eggan, the first social anthropologist to be elected, who proposed Mead's name when he was on a temporary nominating committee with a relative handful of social scientists. Eggan's sponsorship finally got her in. Her fellow anthropologists as a group had never co-sponsored her. "She was thought bogus," said one of them.

Sometimes Mead knew what she was talking about, her peers thought, and sometimes, as her generalizations swept in a wider and wider arc, it appeared that she did not. On what grounds, for example, did she claim as she once did that "Americans are appallingly poor

* A fellowship by the National Institutes of Health.

lovers"? Which Americans? "She could go from the limited, the acceptable, the provable," said one of her colleagues, "and on to the universal, and by the time it was over, it was pure Margaret Mead." Her prestige added weight to her ideas. Some accused her of being the sort of leader who would first figure out which way the troops were marching and then get ahead of them. Her school of thought, it was said, could best be summed up this way: "The future lies ahead."

That wasn't entirely fair. Mead did superb work as president and then chairman of the American Association for the Advancement of Science, which gave her the most prestigious platform of her career. "She wanted momentum to gather for what she called the human sciences," said William Carey, whom Mead helped to persuade to take over the AAAS. "She felt that the AAAS had great potential for popularizing science, not just in the show business sense. She sensed that the arrogance of Western civilization was blinding us to the incendiary changes developing in the rest of the world, and the AAAS should accept its mandate to offset that arrogance."

Arrogance, Mead charged, was also rife in the smaller sphere of science. "The entire scientific world," she said, "is a hierarchy of snobbery. . . . Each science looks down on the newer ones, the newer ones being far more difficult and complicated than the old ones." Physicists, she charged, were the worst of all; hard sciences were "impossible—they can only work with one variable at a time." She juggled many variables and she risked trouble by being open-minded about such matters as parapsychology and unidentified flying objects. "I'm prepared to believe," she said, "that there are a large number of things going on in the universe that we don't know anything about." She should have had the courage, said her friend Archbishop Gregorios, "to pursue more deeply some of the contradictions many of us take for granted." She should have "questioned many of the facile conclusions people were likely to come to about bioplasmic energy, technicolor auras, Kirlian photography—she was one who was intelligent enough to deal with these things. The inner world fascinated her, but fear of professional misunderstanding kept her from writing or publicly thinking about it—she thought her professional colleagues might think she had gone gaga."

But proper attention was paid to Mead, at last, in the year she turned seventy-five. Appropriately, considering her patriotism, that was the nation's bicentennial. The AAAS, of which she was just winding up her three-year term as president, held an all-day celebration in her honor in Boston, where tributes were read by colleagues, students, and contemporaries, including the two Englishmen closest to her. Geoffrey Gorer was flown in from London, and Gregory Bateson came from Big Sur.

Gorer called the day "an occasion for celebration and thanksgiving for all Margaret has meant to her colleagues and to her country and to the whole world," and enumerated her gifts: the extraordinary range of scale, the enormous gusto in spite of which "she never gets mental indigestion," the extraordinary physical stamina, the love of words, the ability to use and enjoy all the gifts she was born with, and finally, as in the tale of Sleeping Beauty, a gift from the bad fairy: the promise that "nobody's ever going to be able to keep up with you."

Bateson spoke of Mead's "enormous visual and auditory greed for data," which, combined with "my own attempt to achieve laziness by way of rigor," had changed epistemology, in the last twenty or thirty years, from a philosophy to "a matter of observation and experiment." Lola Romanucci said that Mead had "taught me to be ever surprised by what is not at all surprising," and had a "spherical mind in a flat land." Robert Murphy said he would "rather comment on gravity than on the work of Dr. Margaret Mead." Renée Fox spoke about Mead's emphasis on the importance of interconnectedness, of how "in anthropology nothing one has ever seen or heard, smelled or tasted, is unconnected," which was why anthropology was "a good career for people who enjoy discovering unexpected connections, who expect to find life all of a piece."

"This," said Mead when her turn came to respond, "has been a love feast . . . I've been treated with extraordinary love and an enormous amount of undeserved praise, and I ought to be embarrassed, and I'm not."

Nor was she embarrassed by the fuss that was made on and around December 16, 1976. "HAPPY BIRTHDAY, MARGARET MEAD," said a full-page advertisement in that day's New York Times. The ad, paid for jointly by her first publisher, William Morrow, the American Museum of Natural History, and Redbook, where her monthly columns had been appearing since 1961, showed pictures of her at different stages of her career and announced a five-million-dollar fund drive for a Margaret Mead Chair of Anthropology at the museum. Contributions would be a fitting way of "giving something of lasting value in [Mead's] name: the only record we'll ever have of ourselves." Many reporters rushed to interview Mead around this time, and she was widely quoted, "I expect to die, but I don't plan to retire."

The thing she was still most afraid of in the world, Mead said at the AAAS party, was being bored. She had long ago determined to take charge of every hour of her life: "Empty time stretches forever. I can't bear it." Rather than ride alone in a cab to La Guardia Airport, she was driven by her student Mary Elder, who brought along a videotape machine Mead could hold in her lap to see the work Elder had been doing with midwifery. With other young colleagues she made breakfast dates for five o'clock in the morning. Only once did Jean Houston make the mistake of inviting Mead to the theater. She had loved going to plays in earlier years, but now she had less and less taste and time for Broadway, and even less, Houston thought, for small talk or girl talk. "There was no implicitness, no hanging out," said Houston. "Even after an extravagant meal, my one art form, Margaret would always eventually say, 'Now, Jean, the agenda!' Encounters with her were always an event."

Since most of Mead's encounters were with people whom she had not seen for two months or two years, there was always catching up to do, always intensity, and always others lined up to see her next. At last she had not only enough companionship but perhaps too much. When the incessant search for more sapped her strength, she restored her strength in her own way. Once she gave the keynote speech at a conference of librarians, one of whom, delighted to find that she was to sit next to Mead on the dais, held back during the cocktail hour before the lunch to let others talk to the guest of honor. This librarian, who realized that all her life she had been storing up matters she wanted to talk about with Margaret Mead, figured she would have the whole lunch hour to do so. But no.

"Look," Mead said to her when they sat down at the dais, "I didn't have any sleep last night, and I'm not very hungry, so I'm going to use this time for a little nap. I'll only be wanting dessert and coffee, so will you wake me then? Thank you." Thank you and good night, at 12:30 in the afternoon. On another occasion she woke from a restorative doze barely in time to "give a nice talk about Mrs. Roosevelt, and bawled us out," said someone in the audience, "because there weren't more of us. Why was it, Mead asked, that each of us hadn't brought twenty friends along?"

She was always glad to meet any other twenty people, as Lola Romanucci-Ross learned when she and Mead took a little break from their 1965 field work in Manus, in the Admiralty Islands. Manus, for all its ethnographic riches, offers little of the urbane, and Mead, as urban a woman as ever owned a passport, decided to go with Romanucci-Ross to Rabaul, which is the most cosmopolitan city in all Melanesia. Delighted with a respite from field work, Romanucci-Ross was looking forward to whatever pleasures an unplanned evening in the city might have in store. Mead, however, did not like the lack of plan, and fidgeted in her hotel room while her companion went out for an afternoon walk. "Whites find each other in places like Rabaul," Romanucci-Ross later said. "Somebody white found me on my walk, and mentioned a party, which I wouldn't have bothered with if I'd been alone, but I knew how Margaret would enjoy it.

" 'Can I bring a girlfriend?' I asked the man. 'Where from?' he asked. 'New York City,' I told him, and then I gave him my girlfriend's name.

" 'Oh my God,' said the man, 'hey, wait a minute,' and ran to phone his wife, returning to say that everyone around would want to be there."

"Well, Margaret," Romanucci-Ross said back at the hotel, "we've got a party."

That, Mead thought, was as it should be. For new people and new agendas she was insatiable to the point of arrogance. Primarily, as she had once wanted to rush to gather data about disappearing primitive civilizations, she now wanted to preserve the planet, and there was no time to lose. The main drawback of being Margaret Mead, she said, was "having to decide between too many things I ought to be doing . . . I have to go back to Manus, have to take my grandchild for a walk, have to go see old cousins, have to be human on every level. Choosing what needs to be done next is what worries me."

Why didn't she stay overnight? some friends in Chicago urged her. Why didn't she stop and relax? "I can't stop!" she told them. Her schedule was such a blur that she sometimes forgot where she was. Alighting from a plane in Philadelphia, she once absent-mindedly asked her taxi driver to take her to 211 Central Park West. That had been her address in New York City since soon after she and Rhoda Métraux had given their housecooling party and left Greenwich Village in 1966. Apartment 16J at the Beresford, on Central Park West, was bought in Métraux's name; the last thing Mead wanted was to be a property owner herself. "All those houses in New Guinea," she said, had "totally, totally exorcised my desire to own or build." She liked to describe herself as "a boarder in friends' houses," the chief friend being Métraux, whose interest in domestic details, luckily, was much more sustained than her companion's.

Mead much preferred doing other things. And she much preferred other people's houses to hotels. "When you displace people," she said, "you learn something about them." She especially liked displacing adolescents, whose bedrooms were full of posters and paraphernalia that helped her to decide, when the "generation gap" came along in the late 1960s, that this new generation of young people was "not having a good time. It's not a debauched generation at all. These young people are solemn even about their pleasures." As a house guest she was not hard to please. When Philleo Nash apologized for the state of the study–guest room where Mead spent the night under his roof, near his cranberry farm in central Wisconsin, she said, "Well, it's better than field conditions."

The trouble with housing in general, she said, was that "all our houses are built on the theory that people have three children who never grow up." Ideally, people would move in the course of their lifetimes, as their circumstances changed, from small houses to large ones and back to small ones again, all in the same community, a community being a four-generation collection of some five hundred people on whom one could depend to share one's griefs, hopes, and joys, who might or might not be blood relatives. At least fifty percent of the human race, she asserted, did not want their mothers-in-law within walking distance. Some of her best friends, like the English architect-planner Richard Llewellyn-Davies and the Greek Constantinos (Dinos) Doxiadis, were professionally concerned with where and how people lived.

Doxiadis derived what he named "ekistics," the science of human settlements, or the study of settlements as living organisms, from the Greek word *oikos*. He and Mead had met in 1963, when she heard him say that as many homes would have to be built in the next twenty-five years as had ever been built in history. Mead was fascinated. She became a regular member of annual week-long cruises Doxiadis organized on the *Semiramis*, a small ship that called at several Aegean islands. Mead, Geoffrey Gorer, Barbara Ward, Arnold Toynbee, Buckminster Fuller, and assorted other philosophers would cruise around conferring, for three or four hours a day, about how the world should be run.

In 1969, when Kevin Frank had just graduated from high school, he went along as Mead's guest on the cruise, on a grant from her Institute for Intercultural Studies. His fellow passengers, he remembered, were "people of such tremendous creative energy that even there on the ship they never really relaxed. There was always the sense that 'if we could only find that one unifying field theory of social science, it would be like the Lost Covenant of the Ark.'

"I tended to be a bit smug," said Kevin, "about all these very meaningful, very global people, wanting so much to have importance." At Delos, the last stop on the cruise, they would gather at the open-air amphitheater for a reading. Mead would have sat up late the night before, typing up a hundred-page document summarizing what had been said during the week. She would stand up with her staff, wearing her red cloak, while the crew from the ship held up flaming torches, and Barbara Ward would read the statement. These cruises, said Ken Heyman, were the one event in Mead's calendar that she wouldn't miss for anything. Maybe they made her think of the pinnaces going up the Sepik.

Shortly after Mead's seventy-fifth birthday her friend Robert Schwartz, who for years would keep advertising his Tarrytown Group as "a worldwide bunch of cranks and crazies co-founded by Dr. Margaret Mead," organized a three-day celebration in her honor at his conference center, summoning "thinkers and doers" from many places to pay her homage. "She asked me to do the party," said Schwartz. "I got the idea she'd missed ever having a really great birthday party." Several of the younger guests were invited because he thought Mead would appreciate their minds; as "presents" for her they were instructed to dress as such, with ribbons around their necks.

Those three days began with a gala black-tie banquet and continued with several earnest panel discussions, at which suggestions were collected to be sent to President-elect Jimmy Carter (who had sent his birthday wishes). Since Carter would soon have to sort out his administration's priorities, these suggestions were meant to help him. Guests were asked to make their suggestions "militantly specific. It will add to the chemistry of the interchange." Carter was gravely advised to supplement press conferences with "people's conferences"; personally read randomly selected letters from his constituents; celebrate the diversity of family and community life; observe the 55-miles-an-hour speed limit; turn off unnecessary lights at the White House; recycle commodities; rename a park for Franklin and Eleanor Roosevelt; reassure the electorate about legislation he planned to support; "review erosionary revisions of government regulations"; and put more emphasis on American folk traditions.

Several Tarrytown guests represented organizations into which Mead threw her energies after her retirement from the presidency and chairmanship of the board of the AAAS. At the opening Tarrytown banquet she was introduced by Michael Shower of New Directions, a citizens' lobby for international relationships and global responsibilities. "Originally we wanted her in a strictly honorary role," Shower said, "but she was full of beans and said no, no honorary title for her: she wanted real powers and responsibilities, or else we should forget it."

Mead told John and Nancy Todd, who were among the "presents" at her party, that their New Alchemy Institute would amount to nothing unless it opposed nuclear power more vocally. She was "opposed not so much to nuclear power," she told Alan McGowan, who in 1974 succeeded her as president of the Scientists' Institute for Public Information (which she and Barry Commoner had helped to found in 1963), "as to ignorance of its implications." Her chief role was to understand how a new technology could affect a society. "She thought social science should be included in all policies, technical and otherwise, [though] anthropology had ceased to be her chief focus after World War II," said McGowan, who considered Mead "probably the most generous person I've ever met. When a board member complained at a meeting that one of our ideas had been stolen, she roused herself up in her seat—it's amazing how tall she could look when she wanted to—and said, 'That's ridiculous! That's what we're in business for, especially at this Institute, to have our ideas stolen.'"

Mead wanted the world to be a better place and she wanted people to lead better lives, and if the means by which she sought to bring about these aims seemed naïve, or smacked of hubris and chutzpah, then there it was: when she received the Ceres Medal, commemorating the Roman goddess of the harvest, given by the Food and Agriculture Organization, she did not accept the award wholeheartedly until the citation was changed to take into account her contribution to the field of nutrition. She took all her involvements and connections seriously and critically. Some members of the AAAS planned to resign when Arthur Jensen, whose ideas were widely considered racist, was voted into membership in 1977. Mead, however, said, "I never resign from anything. I'd rather stay and fight from within. It's a great mistake to think that this is anything but an awful muddle."

She and muddles had a way of finding each other. "During the black power movement," said the anthropologist Napoleon Chagnon, "she thought race had so much vernacular symbolism that its existence, regardless of its uses by a lot of biologists and its many technical meanings, should be denied." Edward O. Wilson, whom Mead invited to dine with her on December 17, 1976, just after her seventy-fifth birthday, was nervous about the encounter: "Suppose the grand matriarch were to scold me," he thought, "for reintroducing genetics, social Darwinism, and biological determinism into anthropology?"

Wilson, author of *Sociobiology: The New Synthesis* and *On Human Nature*, had in Marvin Harris's opinion helped to "advance two propositions: one, social scientists are incompetent bleeding hearts who deny the existence of human nature; and two, hard-nosed, *real* scientists must assume control over the social sciences and reassert the importance of biological factors in human life." At the American Anthropological Association's meetings the previous month, left-wingers had moved to condemn sociobiology as fascist and racist. Mead, Wilson had heard on good authority, "was one of the most outspoken opponents of the motion, arguing that such a position is the antithesis of free inquiry" and asking, in effect, "Have we gone out of our minds?" The motion had been overwhelmingly defeated.

When Mead and Wilson met for dinner, he said, she "mentioned the dangers of allowing the sociobiological approach to be subverted to racism, but she was more anxious by far to find a common ground and to establish her own priority in analyzing genetic factors. In particular she cited the notion she had published [giving him references] that the members of each society are genetically diverse. According to her model, certain genetically based personality types predominate in a particular society and confer their distinctive traits. In other words, the biological and culturological viewpoints were not incompatible."

Mead was accused in New Guinea, to her chagrin, of not having told the people of Manus about Western racism when she first went back there in 1953. She was shouted down when she gave speeches in Manus and in Port Moresby, Papua New Guinea. A newspaper article was headlined YOU DON'T KNOW MANUS, MARGARET MEAD. She was accused of being among those Westerners who, having been deified by the social science establishment (though she had been more deified by the public) were "making a fortune ripping off the ideas, customs and tales of a people, telling their stories around the world." This charge was repeated in a "NOVA" PBS-TV program of October 1983 about the responsibility of anthropologists to their informants. But it is unjust to imply that Mead wished anything short of literacy for her informants: she wanted them to tell their own stories.

Still she could be oddly oblivious. To a largely black audience in the United States, she had used the word "pickaninny," explaining that in pidgin English, or neo-Melanesian, it meant what it had meant in the days of Stephen Foster ballads: "black child." The audience ignored the context and heard only the condescension. Mead was booed, and she burst into tears. "She had no business being that naïve," said Lenora Foerstel. "But she was even more naïve about South Africa—she thought apartheid was just a simple problem between the British and the Dutch: if the British and the Boers had just got together—perhaps with the help of a few astute American social scientists?—the whole trouble needn't have happened."

Foerstel, convinced that Mead felt Melanesians were superior to blacks in the United States, took pains not to introduce her to her friends in the black ghetto of Baltimore, "especially after the outrageous things she said to James Baldwin in A *Rap on Race*." That book is a transcription of a seven-and-a-half-hour "discussion of race and society," divided into three taped sessions, held in August 1970 and published a year later. Baldwin and Mead, who had not previously met, were both characteristically garrulous: "Wait a minute!" she tells him at one point. "Now just stop making faces and let me talk for a while. I was a child that both my parents wanted . . . I was told from the time I was born that I was totally satisfactory. I had a chance to be what I wanted to be and I have always been able to be what I wanted to be. I don't like Cadillacs, either. And I don't own one. I don't even own a fur coat [though in fact she did]. . . . You just think of the things that you suffered by," Mead goes on to tell Baldwin, "and most of them were created by Harlem. Now, your father. If you had had your father as a father but he had been white . . . He could have been, you know. There have been white preachers that were just as rigid as your father . . ." Mead was taking issue with Baldwin's assertion that he and she are "both exiles": she, she claims, is "absolutely not an exile. I live here and I live in Samoa and I live in New Guinea. I live everywhere on this planet that I have ever been."

Baldwin replies that he is "not at home here and never will be . . . I will never, never, never, as long as I live, be at home anywhere in the world." Mead at one point says, "Just plain fiddlesticks!" Baldwin says "Tsk, tsk, tsk." This apparently unedited exchange may have been provocative enough as a radio talk show, but it is nothing like the "extraordinary human document" the book's jacket claims it is, and its blathering tone offended many who were otherwise devoted to Mead, among them the poet Ned O'Gorman, who in 1965 opened a "storefront school" for poor children in Spanish Harlem. Mead, who was president of the school's board the year before she died, did battle for it in 1978 against city officials who tried to shut it down because O'Gorman had no teaching degree. O'Gorman loved Mead, was grateful, and considered her a great friend of his school and of blacks in general. Still, he thought A *Rap on Race* was "her lowest moment."

Few writers as prolific as Mead was can sustain for long the lively, clear language she achieved in some of her early work. Her books and speeches are uneven. Her most engaging writing is in her letters, now collected in the Library of Congress. Her correspondence with certain people is restricted, and some of it is not to be seen by anyone until 1999 (twenty-one years after her death), but hundreds of boxes of folders of letters, sorted chronologically, are wheeled out on carts in the Manuscript Reading Room, where thoroughly screened researchers, whose handbags and notebooks have been checked outside, are granted that delicious and usually forbidden privilege: reading someone else's mail. Even Mead's routine correspondence, spanning the time between her childlike diary entries and the haste of her late notes, breathes a passion and a spontaneity almost never sensed in the prose of social scientists. The prose of most social scientists, as Mead's Church of England friend Christian Howard observed, "feels drained, like the sky just at dawn and just at dark, when there's no color."

So it does; Mead chose a realm of work in which it was thought that "opacity equaled profundity," to quote Leo Rosten, "and jargon equaled philosophy." Perhaps in self-defense, she learned, as Winthrop Sargeant noted, to "write as technically and obscurely as anyone else." She could also write lyrically, and knew enough to scold students and colleagues who committed lumbering language like "neo-Malthusian" and "acceptive." Mead herself, for all the books she wrote, produced no masterpiece. In her autobiography, *Blackberry Winter: My Earlier Years*, she claims to "lay my life on the line," but there is a great deal about her life left out. Unpleasant matters are glossed over. She had a tendency, she admitted, to erase small misfortunes from her mind, but her book erases a lot of bigger misfortunes, too: her marriages, and their unravelings, are treated as casually as if they had been lunch dates.*

The book's tone calls to mind the seventh-grade adjective "conceited." From babyhood Mead was assured that "there's no one like Margaret." The second volume, hinted at in the subtitle, never got written, and once Mead tried to say why: "Success," she explained, "is boring. People don't want to read about success." But she missed the point. Successes like hers are not so much boring as complicated. Another autobiographical volume, Jean Houston thought, "would have taken too much discretion. Hers was the most complex life imaginable. She had so many fingers in so many pies, and was behind the scenes on so many levels, that her public image was just the tip of the iceberg." So it was. There were as many Margaret Meads as there were people who claimed her as their own.

No amount of commotion could stop Mead from writing. The "cumulative nature of reputation," she said, was one of the serious difficulties of the present-day world: "the more one publishes, the more

---

* But she wittily once said that the secret of successful marriage was to marry someone whose interests were the same as one's own: "I always did that and all my marriages were a great success."

requests one receives," which meant coming to terms as best one could with "the instability of a throwaway society." Mead seemed afflicted, as her friend Feichin O'Doherty put it, with "the desperate feeling that she had to keep on producing." Once when congested air traffic forced her plane to circle for hours over La Guardia before it could land, her only complaint was that she had run out of paper. On a much smaller plane, during one of Mead's visits to New Zealand, her host had gone to considerable trouble to have the pilot make a brief stop at one of the spectacular mountains in the South Island alps, so that Mead could see a glacier.

"*Glacier!*" she said. "Why should I want to get out of a plane just to look at a glacier? Who'll be there to *talk* to?" During a blizzard in Cincinnati, with six or seven inches of snow already fallen and more pelting down, with winds so high that police were ordering all traffic off the streets, Mead could only wonder, as a friend's car crept cautiously back toward her hotel, "Where *is* everyone?"

And now, visibly, she was spread too thin, trying too much, winding down. Famous all her life for the intensity of her attention—an attention that could confer a state of grace—she now sometimes appeared not to be listening at all. And the more she stopped listening to others, the more they stopped listening to her. The rapport that long had seemed to spring up automatically between Margaret Mead and almost any roomful of people could no longer be taken for granted. Philleo Nash, occasional master of ceremonies at Mead speeches in the years of her AAAS presidency, devised tricks to jolly her out of awkward moments at the lectern, but compassionate expertise like his was not always at hand. Alex Kotlowitz, a young New Yorker working at Emmaus House in Atlanta, noticed when Mead came there to visit that she didn't seem to ask him and his colleagues about themselves or the work they were doing there, but wanted to talk about herself. One of her museum assistants around this same time said: "She never asked us what it was like to be us; she just told us what it was like to be Margaret Mead—which was great, up to a point."

The failure to hear was not a metaphor. Like her revered mentor Ruth Benedict, and for that matter like a number of her own blood relatives, Mead suffered one of the most socially crippling of infirmities: she could no longer hear all that people around her were saying. Her hearing aid, especially when several people were talking at once, had a tendency to buzz and hum. After lectures she no longer took questions from the floor. All her life she had made the best of physical ailments.

Neuritis in college had inspired a poem. Malaria had not slowed her, even in childbirth. Stitches on her buttocks one evening were no reason to cancel her next morning's schedule. A chronically fractured ankle led to her most famous trademark, the forked stick. But deafness was another matter.

Her lifelong tendency to come straight to the point, a blunt and refreshing impatience, turned now to plain, and sometimes astonishing, rudeness. The education writer Jonathan Kozol, who had admired Mead's books for years, was excited at the prospect of being her fellow speaker at a Washington, D.C., conference, in 1977, on urban redevelopment. In Kozol's speech, which he had stayed up all night writing, he described the largest park in Boston, where he lived, as "a place of filth and fear and drugs and derelicts," and said it was much more important to spend money righting these wrongs than on elegant parks and shopping malls for tourists. Mead, who spoke next, never touched on the issue. "She did not appear to have prepared a talk," said Kozol. Instead she appeared "determined to create a confrontation despite my sense of reverence for her . . . I felt a bit shocked to see someone whom I had respected for so long playing a casual forensic game, trying to score small points."

The audience, consisting mostly of black leaders, shared Kozol's disappointment, and some surmised as he did that "she had been exploited by the lecture agency, [which] booked her to too many lectures at a time in life when people of her age and stature did not need such ephemeral rewards. . . . I felt that Dr. Mead should have been spared the indignity of being forced to speak without a speech, to argue without ammunition, to participate in a specialized conference with only general observations and abstractions. . . . I did not feel embittered, just a lot of quiet sadness. She did not need this."

But she did need it. She needed the money and she needed the activity. If she had stopped, she might have had to think about herself.

On a humid morning in June 1977, Mead was escorted into a canvas tent in the mall outside the Smithsonian Institution in Washington, D.C., where she had given a talk the previous evening at the Conference on Kin and Community. Now she was to have a look at an exhibit on families which had been prepared by some graduate students. The exhibit, plainly a labor of love, included the written, oral, and photographic histories of several families the students had been interviewing.

Mead approached the canvas tent holding her famous forked stick in one hand and her many-pocketed handbag in the other. She wore a chartreuse polyester pants suit and sandals. Except for the stick she looked to this writer, who happened also to be in that tent that morning, like any number of other frumpy grandmothers. When one graduate student remarked that the polish on Mead's toenails was chipped, another replied, "But imagine her having taken the trouble to put it there in the first place!" The students were awed that the most famous social scientist of the century, one of the world's most legendary authorities on kinship, was coming to see their project, and, they assumed, to beam and bless them.

She did not. "You think you've *invented* the family, don't you?" was what she had to say, almost in a snarl, when she saw the work the students had done. They did not seem to think any such grandiose thing, and their baffled hurt was plain to see. Perhaps at last Mead was bored by the homage of self-appointed surrogate grandchildren? Perhaps she felt fed up by the very subject of families? Perhaps, as always, she felt that she alone could interpret it to others? Or did she sense that something much more ominous was going on inside her? Whatever the trouble was, she didn't stop to brood. A few weeks later she was in Bali.

In July 1977, the young anthropologist Linda Connor was in an isolated village in central Bali to interview a faith healer whose life story was to be made into one of Timothy Asch's celebrated ethnographic films. Connor had deliberately cut herself off from the rest of the world, resisting even the temptation to go down to the next village for a swim. One afternoon an old taxi found its way up her road, and all the villagers rushed to tell her it was there. The cab door opened, a stick emerged, and the person holding the stick announced, "Hello, I'm Margaret Mead."

"Yes, I know," said Connor: who else on earth, she wondered, could it have been? Mead stated her business brusquely: she was on her way to visit her own old village, Bajoeng Gede, which was not far away, but she would like to talk with Connor: would the young woman come down to see her, if she had a free evening, at the Bali Beach Hotel? With mixed emotions Connor accepted this invitation a few nights later.

"Mead realized how strange it was for me to put myself in that hotel environment," she said, "after making such a point of avoiding such transitions. She asked about my work, was very understanding about my problems and sympathetic about my doing field work alone as a woman. She urged me to order whatever I wanted from the menu, but after eating just rice and vegetables for so long my stomach wasn't used to such food.

"We talked until quite late at night. Mead didn't seem to think Bali had changed much since her last trip back, in the fifties. After all, she said, it had been overrun then with tourism, too. I disagreed, but she was a very hard person to have an argument with. She wanted, and therefore managed, to feel that Bali hadn't changed, and whatever I pointed out about the new motorbikes, the new inroads made by the cash economy, the change from subsistence to wage labor, she didn't hear any counterargument. For her, everything socioeconomic and political was a backdrop that hardly got into the picture.

"She didn't seem worried that so much of Balinese culture had become a commodity, that the scale and context were all different, that the *kris* dance, in her time a very powerful black-magic ritual, was now run every hour on the hour for the sake of tourists.

"A couple of days later she came back to Bajoeng Gede with two Land Rovers full of ethnographic filmmakers and a still photographer, Beryl Bernay, all of whom raced around trying to film what was going on. Old ladies came crawling out to see who was here, and I was *commanded* by Mead to ask these people who their mamas were, and Beryl was *commanded* to take pictures of anything and everything. An absolutely decrepit old lady hobbled out from a lonely, deserted street, and Mead said, 'Beryl, *get* her. Get her!' as if the woman were wild game."

Mead, said Connor, was not walking well. "She seemed frail, and very snappy, blaming other people for little things beyond their control. Maybe her insistence that Bali hadn't changed had something to do with her fear of death. Maybe she wanted to feel that *she* hadn't changed, either."

Mead seemed to want Bali and the rest of the developing world to appear in the best possible light, which was one reason she had been so enthusiastic, from its beginning, about the United Nations. "People didn't realize how active she was at the UN," said her friend Glen Leet, with whom she worked on Non-Governmental Organizations, "and what a point she made of visiting all the department heads. She brightened up life there enormously. Her way of expressing things could seem outrageous, but eventually proved wise." The UN may have appealed to Mead, for all its faults, because no other organization spoke up as it did for third-world cultures.

Anybody who spoke against the UN, as the Australian-born novelist Shirley Hazzard had often done, would have Mead to reckon with, a reckoning that in Hazzard's case occurred on January 26, 1978, at the Cosmopolitan Club in New York City. She was summoned to meet Mead there for lunch. A blizzard the day before had made the city streets almost impassable, and Mead was almost an hour late. She did not apologize for keeping her guest waiting but came straight to the point: she asked Hazzard to take back some critical things she had written and said in public about the UN.

At a forum a few months earlier Hazzard had called the UN a "temple of discrimination" against women; in her 1975 novel *People in Glass Houses*, based on the ten years she herself had worked at the UN, she had satirized it as a wicked bureaucracy. She had no intention, she told Mead over lunch, of retracting these criticisms, which she felt were still valid. On the contrary, she said, at first politely, she meant instead to draw further public attention to "waste in UN expenditures, which are now running in the billions of dollars."

"I don't care how much they spend," said Mead, "and I don't care how much they waste."

"Can I quote you on that?" asked Hazzard.

"Listen," said Mead, whose "small, glittering eyes looked more and more dreadful" to her guest, "I've never spoken against anything. If you speak out, you just mobilize hostility. I never spoke out against fascism, I never spoke out against communism."

"You call that a proud record?" Hazzard asked.

"I'm telling you," Mead replied, "I never spoke against anything. I always speak positively. That's why I never had any trouble with the Attorney General's list" [of people and organizations suspected of being "subversive"]. Had she felt no obligation to object, Hazzard asked her, "when the UN suppressed news of famine in Africa, and nearly half a million people died?"

"Certainly not," said Mead. "People have to operate through channels. Sometimes they go right, sometimes they go wrong. 'Tain't that it's wicked, it's just the way the world is." Then Mead reiterated her point, which, Hazzard said, was "to persuade—or order—me to stop criticizing the United Nations in the press. Beyond this, I was to publish a form of recantation announcing that the UN was much improved and that my previous strictures no longer applied."

"That's the way it *was* at the UN," Hazzard was to say in her recantation, "but it's been reformed, and this is the way it is *now*."

"But that wouldn't be true," said Hazzard.

"It's just plain counterproductive to criticize the UN," replied Mead.

Hazzard, however, had no intention of taking back what she had said and written because Margaret Mead commanded her to. Mead, noting that her mission this lunchtime had not succeeded, "got up, with her boots flapping, and announced that she was leaving at once, because she had 'a lot of important things to do.'" Hazzard wrote in her journal that evening that her strongest impression of the meeting had been "of a woman carried away with ambition and aggression, and pounding her way with brute force." Calculation, Hazzard was convinced, "had played a fundamental role in Mead's rise to prominence . . . her egotism was ungovernable. Anyone who obstructed her path must be shouted down."

Many who knew Mead in this period could see her slipping. William Carey of the AAAS said that "she sensed that there wasn't a minute to be wasted . . . she tended to be somewhat impatient, especially with foot-dragging. She tended to be a little combative, to use shorthand and overemphasis in order to drive a point home.

"She also tended to be overtaken by flashbacks. Experiences and evaluations going back to the fifties and even earlier would come rolling into her mind, which didn't quite match the problems or situations we were trying to cope with in committee. . . . There was a great deal of anecdotal reporting by Margaret; she would make connections that bore on her own experiences, which nobody else in the room had shared.

"In some ways one almost had a literal, physical feeling, a sense that Margaret had drunk so much of life that it was spilling over. This could be confusing. With all the goodness and generosity that the woman had, she was not everybody's dish. She could seem arrogant, she could seem outrageous. I often had the sense about Margaret that what she really ached for was to have another go at it, at the whole thing.

"Endings, for her, were defeats. We hurt with her after she banged the AAAS gavel for the last time. What she felt, obviously, was, 'You roll through your three-year succession and then wham! You fall over the cliff.' She was no longer an officer, but I brought her to the Denver meetings as our special guest in 1977 and put her in a suite, and made it clear to her that as long as she cared to be, she was president emeritus of the AAAS.

"It was that year that she began to slow down. Her schedule was still very, very full, but she had to struggle. She had to make choices she hadn't had to make before when she simply, somehow, managed to do everything. There was no flagging intellectually, no dulling of outrage at nonsense, but I seem to remember that the passion of her rhetoric rose by several decibels. She was more cranky, more tired. It was more important than ever for her to make a point."

Mead had been aware for some years that she might at any moment lose her sense of timing and her ability to appeal to the country. She had reached the age where contemporaries' funerals happened oftener and oftener. In 1977, at a memorial service for her psychologist colleague Martha Wolfenstein, she encountered Wolfenstein's writer friend Marijane Meaker, whom she greeted by saying, "Oh yes, I remember you and your rambling mind. Martha had the least rambling mind I've ever known. I never could understand her friendship with you."

Wolfenstein had been one of Mead's several book collaborators. Now Ken Heyman, with whom she had done *Family* and *World Enough,* was preparing to join Mead on a third project, a study of aging around the world. The Soviet Academy of Sciences had invited them to record the work and leisure activities of the long-lived *dolgozhiteli* of the Caucasus. But Mead's strength was waning. The momentum she had relied on all her life was harder and harder for her to sustain. More and more she was a statue, a parody of herself, and statues, for all the esteem they command, cannot go anywhere. They cannot escape. It is their lot to stay put while circles of people gather to admire them, circles that can grow into crowds. They cannot tell the crowds to go away.

In the spring of 1978 William Carey began to understand that his dear friend Mead was "in a lot of trouble. That was the spring, when I talked to her on the phone, when she said, 'You ought to see me now. I'm sylphlike. *Sylphlike!*'"

CHAPTER TWENTY-SEVEN

"But This Is Different"

NOT IN MANY YEARS would anyone have thought of "sylphlike" as an adjective fitting Margaret Mead. At five feet two she had let her weight creep up to 175 pounds. On airplanes she sometimes had trouble fastening her seat belt. Overeating was one of the chronic hazards of her profession, and of her status as a national icon. Hostesses, awed to have her at their tables, served her generous portions of their favorite recipes, which often meant their most fattening ones, and from old habit she ate what was put before her.

The year 1977, with trips to Bali, Vancouver, Brazil, and Washington D.C., among other places, had been frenetic. Mead had grown increasingly snappish that year, but she looked well, and had made ambitious plans. She looked forward to visiting the Soviet Union with Heyman, to research their "upbeat book," as he described it, about aging. All Mead's life she had felt a special affinity for the elderly, and now she paid close heed to what felt different about being old. "When you get to be over seventy," Robert Schwartz once heard her say, "you get acclaimed for what you used to be blamed for." Also, she said, "people kiss you like you were a baby—not a kiss like a kiss, but a kiss like they were running for Congress."

As Christmas of 1977 approached, Mead and Rhoda Métraux decided to go to Emmaus House in Atlanta, where their friend Father Austin Ford would be sure to oversee the holiday with proper spirit and style. "Why aren't you more excited about our coming for Christmas?" Mead demanded of Ford in the second phone call to plan the logistics. He was not so much unexcited as overcommitted with seasonal duties, but he rose to the occasion. His guests took part in a visit from Santa Claus, a caroling party and several other gatherings, a reading of W. H. Auden's "For the Time Being: A Christmas Oratorio," and a splendid dinner ending with a plum pudding of Ford's own devising.

Mead had appreciated the pudding, but as the new year proceeded she had less and less appetite, even for her favorite cheeses, wines, and Scotch. When Ford visited New York City early in 1978 he had to urge her, as she in the past had urged others, to *"Drink, it would do you good."** Her refusal was firm, and seemed ominous. She had too many things she wanted to work out in her head, she told another friend, to drink alcohol. She took to ordering what she called a "special cocktail," Perrier water stirred with a spoon until all the bubbles had disappeared. More and more it became clear that Mead was not feeling well. She had said a few years earlier, to Jean Houston, "That mind of mine you say you want to study—you'd better hurry and study it soon." Houston's husband, Robert Masters, whose work is in psychophysical reeducation, had examined Mead and advised her that it was not her mind that needed attention but her body.

"Suppose," Houston suggested, "that there were people who cared about you and wanted you to have a good fifteen or twenty years more, not of deterioration but of quality life—and put in not a mandate but a strong plea, and told you how you could do it. Would you?"

No, Mead answered, she would not. But she did make one concession. Since it was her "responsibility to stay alive in this body at this time in history as well as I can, and if what you and Bob tell me to do will be a way, while I'm here, to make my brain work better, then I'll do your exercises."

This was no small concession: physical fitness had never much concerned Mead. The last time she remembered any exercise, she told Houston, was a game of shuffleboard aboard her friend Doxiadis's yacht some fifteen years earlier. From 1974 on, when Mead was in New York and could spare the time, she went twice a week to Masters's and Houston's Foundation for Mind Research, in Pomona, New York. The sprawling baronial house, lit like a Rembrandt painting and dominated by a huge Balinese carving, happened also to be the residence of the foundation's directors.

"In the work with Margaret we dealt with thinking processes and emotional responses, but on a body level, almost totally nonverbally, bypassing the conscious mind," said Masters. "I can sometimes uncover more basic and useful facts about a person's psychology during thirty minutes of work on this table than emerge during years of psychotherapy. Many people can't even let you turn their head from side to side. They

---

* In drinking as in many things Mead's tastes were eclectic, up to a point. She once considered changing to a different drink every year, "as a quick way of dating time," she told Jean Houston. "But I didn't like the different drinks well enough."

insist on 'helping' you by moving it. When they overcome such deep resistance, you may have altered their way of relating to the world, including other people."

Mead submitted to Masters's teachings in a studio from which Houston once heard "a bellow like a whale's," a bellow that caused the intrepid mistress of experiential workshops everywhere from Cairo to Santa Cruz to cower in her office, "wondering whether I was participating in the murder of Margaret Mead." But the sessions, said Masters, relieved Mead of her lifelong pain: "She'd been taught to disassociate herself from pain. She never knew she had the choice of *not* having pain. She got mad when it went away; she didn't want to believe that she had needlessly spent fifty years in chronic muscle pain. Some of the exercises I gave her caused her to sense her skeleton. I hadn't told her that would happen, but it did.

"She acquired as much additional awareness in several weeks as most people do in a year. She was easily the most intelligent person I ever worked with. When we began she was seventy-three, and could improve more quickly than anybody. But the idea that it should be pleasurable, that it shouldn't be hard, was difficult for her." For a while, after her visits to Masters, Mead's friends and colleagues remarked on how much better she looked, and also on a concurrent improvement in her disposition.

But these gains were visibly lost in 1978, which Austin Ford described as "a perfectly hellacious year." On March 20, Mead's twenty-two-year-old publications assistant, Amy Bard, wrote in her diary: "MM sounded real bad today. Tired, unenthusiastic. I wonder, is she on her way out? Is she finally getting old?" On April 12, Mead scrawled a note, apparently after talking with a physician, which Bard found later: "Mass on the body of the pancreas most likely represents a malignancy." But in May, Bard would recall, "she sat us down in the office and made six-month and five-year plans." Also in May, Bard and Roz Lippel and Carol Zwick were summoned to Mead's apartment to be told that although there was something medically wrong, something unidentified, Mead would plan no exploratory surgery, and would take no drugs that might affect her mind or the quality of her work. Business in the office was to go on as usual. The word "cancer" was not spoken.

When Dr. Walter Slote, a psychoanalyst who taught a course with Mead at Columbia, asked for her help with a classroom matter, her astonishing reply was, "How can you *ask* me such a thing, Walter, when you know how sick I've been?" Slote had heard nothing of any illness, but he began to understand when, in the last session of her class that spring, she asked if the students had any questions. When none were asked, she stormed out of the classroom saying, "All right, let it be on your heads!" which, Slote said, may have been the last words she ever spoke to any class.

Her colleague Robert Murphy, confined to a wheelchair because of illness, remembered a time that spring when he and Mead were in an elevator together in Schermerhorn Hall, where both their offices were. Quite uncharacteristically she bent down to give him a kiss, "as if she knew we both faced a kind of doom." But Mead did her best to maintain her schedule. On May 5 she celebrated Sun Day, a national event proclaimed by President Jimmy Carter, by taking part in a symposium where the other speakers were the ecologist Barry Commoner and the actor Robert Redford. But Philleo Nash, visiting New York from Wisconsin for the spring meeting of the Institute for Intercultural Studies, noticed that Mead had hardly had any appetite and that "she was very notional about wanting things she'd never liked before, like buttermilk." She accepted an invitation to an evening of slides of the Dalai Lama, and climbed up four flights to get there, but told her hostess, the writer Anne Fremantle, "I'm not supposed to eat anything."

Amy Bard sensed an air of death pervading the office, she wrote in her diary on May 22, but "the bottom line is that I don't believe it. I can't. The woman is too full of spunk. . . . When all is said and done, she does *not* carry grudges. She yells, she makes you suffer & when she knows you have suffered enough, she forgets. Apologies mean nothing to her because when you do something wrong, she doesn't want to let you off the hook. Essentially I respect the way she handles 'mistakes' . . . she's right—in what she said about me—American kids think you can apologize and everything will be OK . . ."

On a visit to La Maisonette, the best French restaurant in Cincinnati, Mead ordered nothing but "fluffy potatoes," the specialty of the house, on grounds that she had "a touch of flu." People were noticing more and more that she looked, as one of her close friends put it, "like a balloon with the air let out." At a party, seeing how slim her husband Marvin's colleague had become, Madeline Harris exclaimed: "Margaret! How did you do it?" At a meeting in June, when Ashley Montagu commented on Mead's weight loss, then some fifty pounds, she told him, "Don't laugh, I have anorexia nervosa." That was what one doctor had told her, and it must have sounded better to her, as almost any fate would have, than the kind of cancer that had killed her brother. Sometimes she said her trouble was diverticulitis. To a very few friends she admitted that cancer had been diagnosed, but she kept seeing new physicians, hoping for different opinions.

Mead made a trip to the West Coast, ostensibly to pay a visit to Gregory Bateson, who was thought to be in imminent danger of dying of lung cancer. Before she flew to San Francisco she telephoned Dr. James Hamilton, her psychiatrist friend whom she had known since the days of the Second World War, to ask for a private appointment. Mystified at this request, Hamilton was even more puzzled when Mead asked for his opinion. Being fifty pounds lighter allowed her to get around more easily, she told him, and in general she felt fine, but what could account for her loss of appetite? Did the diagnosis of anorexia nervosa sound plausible?

He certainly did not think so, said Hamilton. Anorexia, he told Mead, was "usually suffered by girls between the ages of seventeen and twenty-two who diet so intensely that they get their endocrinology all screwed up—it is a serious psychological disorder with endocrine complications. Someone seemed to have told Margaret that since she didn't have a goddamn thing wrong with her physically, her condition must be psychiatric."

"Margaret," he said to his old friend, "this is diagnosis by exclusion. Do you think there's anything in your life that represents a change over which you'd do some worrying?" Mead said she thought not; the weight loss had begun before the shattering news of Bateson's illness.

"Then," said Hamilton. "I don't accept this diagnosis. You ought to pursue the physical investigation further." That was the last he ever saw or heard from Margaret Mead.

Back in New York, feeling worse all the time and getting different reports from different doctors, Mead began making frequent visits to a psychic healer, a Chilean woman said to call herself the Reverend Carmen diBarazza. Margaret first met diBarazza with Bob Schwartz and Jean Houston. "Do you see more people in this room than we do?" Mead asked diBarazza. The healer, said Houston, replied that she did.

"Do you see the tall one and the short one with me?" asked Mead. Again the answer was yes. Those two people, Houston recalled Mead saying, were her "spirit guides—every tribe I've ever been to has seen them with me."

The Reverend diBarazza, June Goodfield was told by Mead, had told Mead that she had had an abdominal cancer which "had been taken care of," and "Margaret, who had every intention of living to be a hundred, who was totally interested in everything, who really did believe in the power of the mind, was prepared to examine this matter further."

"Carmen," according to Goodfield, "probably represented the Earth Mother idea. Margaret Mead, grandmother to the world, who helped everyone else, was unable to acknowledge that she, too, needed the same kind of warm, loving support she gave to others." Someone had to sanction the sanctioner, as Erikson had written of Gandhi, to comfort the comforter. "Carmen," said Goodfield, "had enormous, earthy presence, a pair of big strong arms and the sort of motherly bosom some might want to disappear into, representing a kind of comfort that presumably Margaret perceived she needed at this moment. Carmen looked like the big Mother Earth image of an opera singer, the kind who is always on the receiving end of 'your tiny hand is frozen.'

"Many of Margaret's friends," said Goodfield, "were most anxious lest anyone know that she, this public essence of rationality, went to a psychic healer. In that case, they were jolly lucky that the *National Enquirer* didn't find out.* But she really thought the combination of Carmen and will power could do the job." This new allegiance of Mead's was not out of character; she had written in a 1949 issue of the *American Anthropologist* of Ruth Benedict's "willingness to accept the currently discounted or hitherto unknown."

Mead was impressed enough with diBarazza to send Roz Lippel and a couple of her other museum assistants to her office, to learn how to perform her special back-rubs. When Mead's own sessions with the healer were finished, she would make use of keys she had to the apartments of several different friends around the city. These apartments were more welcoming than the one she still shared with Rhoda Métraux, who did not look with favor on diBarazza's new place in Mead's life.

"The last thing Margaret ever said to me was in Carmen's office," said Robert Schwartz. " 'I forgive you all your sins,' she said, 'for having introduced me to Carmen.' "

"What sins?" replied Schwartz.

"Even sins uncommitted," said Mead. In her declining months, said Schwartz, "Margaret and Carmen were as happy as clams together."

In the early summer of 1978, Mead's condition appeared to improve. "She was visibly better off in the months when she visited Carmen every day," said Schwartz. "Carmen probably extended her life by six months, and would have extended it even longer if Margaret hadn't

* In fact, the October 31, 1978, issue of the *Star* carried an article headlined FAMED SCIENTIST CALLS FAITH HEALER TO BEDSIDE IN BID TO BEAT CANCER.

disappeared," a judgment with which many of Mead's more medically orthodox friends totally disagreed, "but that summer she said in effect, 'Thanks a lot, Carmen, but what I really need now is a rest,' and went off to East Hampton."

East Hampton, which preservationists battle perennially to save from developers, is an exquisite seventeenth-century village on the east end of Long Island, a hundred miles from New York City. Mead went there as the guest of her friends Adelaide deMenil, a filmmaker and member of a Texas oil-well engineering family, and the anthropologist Edmund Carpenter. The pair had spent many millions of dollars improving a forty-acre tract of land, separated only by sand dunes from the Atlantic Ocean and with potato fields on either side. To this land they had moved five eighteenth- and nineteenth-century houses, each one meticulously restored. "She was so American," said Carpenter, "that I think it was like coming home, for her to be here." Hand House, which was lent to Mead, had been moved from the nearby village of Amagansett. Not only was it as restful a retreat as could be imagined, it had a spicy history. In 1935 Hand House had been ripped nearly to shreds by a group of Ziegfeld Follies girls rooming there for the summer, who had heard that somewhere inside it was buried treasure.

Another reason Mead went to East Hampton was that she needed more and more looking after. Rhoda Métraux had gone for the summer to her own retreat in northern Vermont. Elizabeth Steig came down from Boston to be with her ailing sister and Mead left the Beresford, where she and Métraux had lived for twelve years. She rented an apartment in the Alden, just across Eighty-second Street. Mead's museum assistant Roz Lippel had taken her friend Malcolm Lennox along when she went over to make sure that her boss was properly settled. Eying Lennox, Mead asked, "Is this male animal capable of putting casters on the legs of this bed?" Lippel said she thought he was. Mead had always been very conscious of the "male animals" who surrounded her bright, lively, and attractive employees, just as she had been conscious in the 1920s of the admirers of her fellow Ash Can Cats.

At the request of "MM," as they called her, Lippel and her colleague Amy Bard went along on one of the East Hampton visits. Their duties, always miscellaneous, came more and more to encompass practical nursing. "It was weird," said Bard, "to be taking such intimate care of someone I really didn't know all that well. I think she preferred having us around, instead of real nurses, because real nurses would have meant admitting that she was really sick. On the second of these visits, just after the Margaret Mead Film Festival at the museum, she was so sick after the long, tough ride out that we began to feel she might actually die on our hands; we thought, 'Hey, this is no joke, we have no medical skills.' We took shifts; we took turns going downstairs to fix the hot-water bottle and make her tea."

Mead's niece Madeline Rosten Lee went to see her aunt in East Hampton that summer, bringing along a male friend. "I'd heard so much about how awful she looked that I had to take someone with me who was not close to her, whose opinion I respected, to whom I could say, 'I'm just going to talk to her, *you* tell me how she is.'" On the day of this visit, said Madeline, her aunt was "very cranky. Hearing trouble was making her very nervous, and she couldn't write or work well, and they had her on some space-age protein diet in spite of which she didn't seem to object to watching the rest of us eat.

"True to form, she got very typically, thoroughly involved in the conversation. When my friend started to sound off about the dreadful conditions and public service mentality of the public schools, Margaret was furious. This dying woman, wasted by cancer, hauled herself up on that famous stick of hers and stood over my friend, who was sitting down, and told him: 'Look, I have seen schools in every country in the *world!*' Later my friend couldn't believe what he had done.

" 'My God,' he said, 'I was arguing about public education with Margaret *Mead!*' "

One hot day that summer Margaret's Barnard classmate Nancy Boyd Willey got a phone call from East Hampton, at her home in the nearby village of Sag Harbor. She was invited "not, as I had expected, for cocktails, but, since I was at home, alive, and had a car, to drive over and wait with Margaret so her hosts and their other guests could have a swim without leaving her alone. Her mind was just as sharp and clear as ever. We talked about conservation—'Bureaucracy,' she said, 'has *got* to be changed!'—and of her weight loss.

"She said doctors had told her she hadn't lost anything she wouldn't be better off without. She said she was still planning on a trip to New Guinea, and when I quoted one of my neighbors who'd said, 'Earth is the New Guinea of the universe'—which I thought was fairly amusing—she clearly didn't think so at all.

" 'I can *see* that you haven't read my books very carefully,' she said, making me feel just as inadequate as she always did when we were together at Barnard."

In early August Mead was an honored guest and speaker at the centennial celebration of the Literary and Scientific Circle of the Chautauqua Institution in upstate New York, where she had appeared several times before. The visit, Jean Houston recalled, was poignant: Mead had lost so much weight that even her nightclothes needed taking in, which Houston began to do. Joan Erikson, appraising Houston's work, said kindly, "You don't know much about sewing, do you?" and helped her to finish. "Margaret didn't want her clothes taken in," said Houston, "she wanted to grow back into them." Erik Erikson, Mead's writer friend George T. Land, Gregory Bateson and Catherine Bateson, on a visit from Iran, were there at Chautauqua, too. At her mother's request, it was understood, Catherine agreed during this visit not to come back to New York in the fall.

Every evening from seven to ten this group would gather on Mead's balcony to discuss the problems of the world. "It wasn't so much that Margaret was afraid of dying," said Houston, "as that she was passionate about staying alive, and finding out what new things were going to happen. As long as she could help people, as long as she felt she was needed, she whistled in the dark to keep up her courage. She got rosier and rosier in the cheeks as she said, one evening, 'You know that paradigm you people were talking about last night? I know what the answers are!' "

That evening, said Houston, "Something popped in me," and she began to orate almost ecstatically about how the present dark era would soon end, replaced with "a different way of being human and a different way of living on this earth."

Bateson and Erikson leaned forward closer to her, Houston said, as if to urge her on, but Mead interrupted them.

"Stop! Stop! Stop!" she shouted vehemently.

"I've got to go on!" said Houston, with tears of rage in her eyes.

"You will *not* go on!" said Mead.

"But I have to finish," said Houston. "I have to go to California in the morning."

"Then you should have asked sooner to make your statement," replied Mead, in what Houston recalled as a "sweet" way. What Mead sensed, Houston felt, "was that I was coming through with the new paradigm, which would bring her death."

But it wasn't a paradigm that killed Margaret Mead.

In late August, Mead made a trip very few people in her condition would have even considered. Her cousin Martha Glardon many months earlier had engaged her to speak at the convention of the American Correctional Association in Portland, Oregon. "I had talked to her several times in the spring and early summer," Glardon said, "and she told me she was having a lot of trouble with her stomach and couldn't eat much. She told me she felt like hell, and was very short-tempered, as only Margaret could be.

"I asked her to cancel the trip, but she insisted on going. She said she had to," in order to honor her speaking commitment and also, although she did not put it in so many words, to say goodbye to four people dear to her: her godchild Martha Ullman West, her first husband Luther Cressman, who would come to Portland by bus from Eugene to see her, and later, in California, to visit with Gregory Bateson at the Monterey home of Barbara Honeyman Heath Roll, with whom Mead had made a number of visits to Manus. This itinerary was even more elaborately crafted than Mead's usual ones.

"She ordered me to New York to travel with her," Glardon said, "and when I saw how she looked I almost fainted, and again wanted to call the trip off. She traveled in a wheelchair, because she couldn't walk, but she wouldn't hear of canceling the trip."

They flew first-class. Glardon put her seat back and Mead closed her eyes and stretched out. "She sat in a stupor most of the flight. She carried her own food—yogurt, Jello, and pudding—and every time she took a bite she would double up and lean her head against the back of the seat in front and gasp for a few minutes before she tried another spoonful. Then she would take a pill and sleep for a while. When we landed, the pilot and copilot came to hold her hand and say how honored they were to have her traveling with them."

Martha West was at the Portland airport to meet her godmother, and "when she was wheeled off that plane in a wheelchair I nearly collapsed into tears, even though I'd been prepared for the shock. Margaret could tell how shocked I was—there was no way I could hide it—and she said she'd had a terrible trip, been terribly nauseated."

The Saturday speech, including the question-and-answer period, lasted three hours. "She started out very slowly," said Martha Glardon. "Her tongue was thick and she was quite hoarse, but her mentality was all there, and she got a standing ovation." On Monday Mead spoke at a luncheon given by the International Halfway House Association, and again she did very well. "In fact she had perked up some, had makeup on, and even walked around with one crutch. The sociologists, psychologists, and criminologists in the group loved her; she was right down their alley."

Mead's godson-in-law Frank West, also in the audience, said, "On one occasion I was afraid she had lost the whole point, but in the last few minutes she brought it all together, and it was clear to her audience that she knew whereof she spoke. For a long time, I'm sure, Margaret did *not* believe that she was dying." When Ken Heyman visited her, soon after she returned to New York, she moaned, "Oh, Ken, I'm so sick—this disease has cost me $30,000." That, she said, was what she could have been earning by making speeches. "I can afford to be well and I can afford to die, but I can't afford to be sick," she said.

When Rhoda Métraux returned from Vermont late that summer, friends persuaded her and Mead to reconcile their differences, and Mead moved back to the Beresford.

Of the 23,000 Americans a year who get pancreatic cancer, fewer than one percent survive. By the time symptoms are felt and diagnosed, it is usually too late for treatment. Generally the first symptom is pain, which can come and go and may be intensified by food. Loss of appetite and weight follow, and so may nausea, vomiting, jaundice, depression, anxiety, and a premonition of serious illness. Mead, whose brother had died of the same disease, was unwilling to accept such a diagnosis. "Thinking she could buy five more years," said Austin Ford, "she didn't want to admit how sick she was."

There are many more ways of dealing with the knowledge of doom than there are beds in cancer wards. "Something in Margaret was so immensely controlling," said her friend Joan Halifax, "but her death was where she had to lose that control. She mastered so much of her life, but she never mastered death. Gregory Bateson, on the other hand, this great, funky, nonlinear old shoe of a mind and heart, came to know intimacy and human warmth, became so accessible, let people learn what he needed and let them give him immense amounts of it. Margaret's death was so *off*, it was a nightmare. It didn't feel clean."

Many who knew Margaret Mead would have expected her to behave in the style of her Cincinnati psychiatrist friend Maurice Levine, who wrote his staff a memorandum asking them to forgive him for dying, and urging them not to baby him. But open though Mead had been about adolescence and menopause, death was another matter. Maybe because she did not think word should spread of the possible imminent doom of one who relied on her mind, she kept her illness a secret. "She received the diagnosis of pancreatic cancer from three separate physicians," said June Goodfield. "Whether deep down in her innermost rational soul she ultimately knew that she had to accept this diagnosis is one of the things about Margaret Mead that we shall never know. She certainly refused to live her life as if she were under the sentence of death."

"Our biggest obstacle to treating MM," Amy Bard wrote in her diary on September 8, "is MM herself. She is powerful and controlling . . . one of the ways she controls is by pushing you almost to your breaking point and just before you are ready to crack, she says something nice & calls you back. She demands the absurd without hesitation, without second thought, almost makes it sound plausible."

"She was trying to manage her world," Bard later said. "She didn't know how to behave without her usual incredible control. Many of her relationships were based on her charm and her conversation, but she was losing that when she was so sick."

"I belong to the generation of children," Mead once told Jean Houston, "for whom survival was still relatively difficult. Most families had at least one child who died, if not four or five, so that those who grew up found it very hard to die, have very little capacity for dying." "This strong-willed woman," as Goodfield said, "so desperately believed that will power could bring her through this as it had brought her through so much else." Her plan for October through December, Jean Houston said, had been "to work with me on the completion of the notes for our study of her mind." But one October day Mead hemorrhaged so alarmingly that she was taken, in a state of semiconsciousness, to New York Hospital. Rumors quickly spread among the many who regarded themselves as members of Margaret's family. Pelham Stapelfeldt, who had kept in touch with Margaret since their days at Barnard, and who had noticed that she seemed "too tired to be anything but annoyed" at a surprise party, phoned Rhoda Métraux to ask what was happening.

"Margaret's just absolutely dead tired," said Métraux. "She's done too much; I have her in the hospital for fatigue. You can be sure that the Ash Can Cats would be the first to know if it were a matter of life and death." The news was kept from the Ash Can Cats and most of Mead's other friends, one of whom, a Philadelphia psychiatrist who never spoke to Mead after a "warm talk" in April, said with sorrow, "She didn't handle her death as well as she handled other parts of her life. I, for one, was excluded. She was very well protected by her cronies." Rhoda Métraux protected her friend as fiercely as she could; in a "Living Will" Mead drew up in 1962, Métraux had been named as the person whose role would be to "make whatever decision is consonant with my general interests" if Mead should lose competence to make such decisions for herself. This will specified that Mead was willing to be blind or deaf, to lose the power of writing or the power of speech, but not both. In October, Mead signed her routine last will and testament in her hospital room, with Roz Lippel and Barbara Sperling witnessing to attest that Mead was sound of mind as she signed her name.

Dear old friends, as well as admiring newer ones, were kept away from Mead's hospital room, where she was taking increasing doses of Darvon to relieve the exquisite pain. A note from Léonie Adams, referring to her and Mead's perennial sentiment about All Saints' Day, was never shown to the patient. Museum employees followed orders to say that their boss was "tired" and hospitalized but still keeping up with her work, which in fact she did as best she could. "When people asked me what was wrong I was told to answer, 'Nothing,' " Roz Lippel said. "I had to keep going in the office because I couldn't train anybody new to keep the momentum and the style going."

Martha West, phoning frequently from Oregon to inquire about her godmother's condition, learned that "a disgraceful number of people were crowding around for a last word on their project, a recommendation for their children to get into school, that sort of thing." Mead was not avoided, as many doomed cancer victims are whose friends in some irrational way think the disease might be contagious. Enormous numbers of people gathered around her, as she had urged them to all her life, but now she could not escape from one group to join another. Now she had to lie there and watch, when she was capable of watching, how circles within circles of resentment were developing among the people to whom she had mattered.

"It was awful, it was bad news," Madeline Lee said of all this excessive company, "but Margaret couldn't bring herself to say no to anybody, to cut herself off from all that she'd been part of. And a lot of people came because they wanted her to be something for them, to give them certain behavior. A lot of people hoped she'd turn into a sweet little old lady in a shawl. Well, she didn't."

Lee had gone to see her aunt shortly before her hospitalization. "Rumors were spreading that she might be quite sick, so I asked for an appointment—an audience. She was very cranky that day. She could be terrifying, she could be very mean, the tongue could descend very heavily. She asked about my sister, brother, father, and all kinds of things, and I finally interrupted to say, 'Look, that's not why I'm here. I'm here,' I told her, 'on family business. I think it's possible that you may be needing someone who'll do what you want done, and I'm offering to do it for you.' "

(Joan Halifax and Mead had a similar confrontation. "I could tell she really felt bad, and reminded her of work I had done with people dying of cancer, and intimated I would like to be helpful to her, and she said, 'Thank you, I appreciate what you're trying to do, but I don't want your help,' and there was nothing for me to say but, 'I hear that you need not to talk further about this,' and that was that.")

"You have no idea," Madeline Lee went on, "how bizarre it all was: Margaret was impatient with whatever was wrong with her—the word cancer was never spoken—because of the way it distracted her from the main event. She was impatient with everybody, including her doctors. It was my impression that she would change doctors whenever they wouldn't go along with what she wanted. But on this visit she denied that anything was wrong at all."

"I'm at the peak of my powers," Mead told her niece. "I'm perfectly able to argue with doctors and nurses myself."

"I understand that everything's under control now," Madeline replied. "I just want to make sure you heard my offer."

"I heard you," said Margaret. And then, after a long pause, she added, "Thank you."

"Margaret never seemed at any point to be saying, 'Enough! Now I want to die!' " said Lee. "She thought she was wearing out too soon, way before she had expected to, and she was *cross* at the idea." She was also cross when her daughter and granddaughter flew from Iran to visit, after a painstakingly considered call from June Goodfield. Mead did not want the child to see her as she was, and clung to diBarazza's faith that she might somehow have five more years to live, but Goodfield took responsibility for suggesting this final reunion, recognizing that "what was right for Cathy might not have been right for Margaret."

Mead, said Goodfield, "died exactly, in every respect, as she would *not* have wanted to. Ideally she would have been sitting up in her bed at home, surrounded by her students and friends, not in great pain, smiling beatifically, and giving them her last considered words. Alternatively, she would have liked to die in New Guinea, where she had hoped to go in December 1978. If I could have arranged a miracle, I'd have transposed her somehow to New Guinea. But she really felt that she could keep control of all events, including her own death. Moreover, she didn't really believe she was going to die . . ."

Remembering Mead's having said that "people should set the time when they die, so as to trouble other people as little as possible," and that she would like to take an overdose of sleeping pills and be found dead kneeling in an unoccupied church, friends considered spiriting her out to a church, but she was too weak to leave the hospital. The chaplain on duty in her ward, the Reverend Jean Sibley, said, "I would have been glad to minister to her more—some patients want to talk for an hour—but she never felt like talking. I was only sorry that I couldn't be more help to her."

Another visitor heard Mead say, "I just don't want that woman priest in here again." She did take communion from Father Austin Ford, who visited from Atlanta whenever he could, but the Reverend Sibley "got the impression," she said, "that a faith healer was there really a lot," and had "the feeling that *that* was the real religious thing for that time in Dr. Mead's life."

Mead's old friend Marie Eichelberger and her devoted young friend and former assistant Barbara Sperling, who had worked in her museum office for six years instead of the usual two, did their best, along with others, to recreate the vigil Ruth Benedict's friends had kept during Benedict's last days. Rhoda Métraux was rarely absent. Carmen diBarazza, Jean Houston, and her student Mary Elder, who had nursed Mead faithfully before her hospitalization, came to see her when they could. Many who wanted to visit Mead were not encouraged to. Leo Rosten had hoped to see her, but she asked him to talk with her on the telephone instead. He felt that the "charade of pretense around Margaret was unworthy of her, but we must allow people their defenses. If she needed that pretorian guard of ardent feminists around her, if she needed to cover and seal her simple emotions, then so be it. She was certainly very brave about physical discomfort."

"What have they found, doll?" Rosten asked Mead.

"You know doctors," Mead replied. "They poke around. If they found only one teeny little cancer cell, wouldn't they be happy?" Clearly she preferred to talk of other things, almost any other things, and Rosten's daughter Madeline did her best to oblige in this and any other respect she could think of.

"Margaret was under twenty-four-hour nursing care, but the nurses had to eat dinner, so I'd just sit there while they ate. I'd sit and read sometimes, but mostly just sit. It was an incredible experience. She once said, 'If you want to be an anthropologist, get yourself down to the nearest hospital and watch someone born and someone dying.' " But before Mead's life ended, there were plenty of lively matters to be dealt with.

"Since my job was to do what Margaret wanted done," said Madeline, "if she wanted to talk about going home next week, that was what we would talk about. I also thought it was important for her to have things to do, to feel she was still connected, so I went to appear on her behalf at a luncheon, to get some international UN award. Although she felt very sick that day, she dictated something for me to say, and in spite of all the nine million awards she had won earlier, she was touched and pleased and interested when I brought her the medal in the hospital a couple of days later.

"But on other occasions she wasn't pleased. Once she was very cross about something and said, 'All right, here's what I want you to do'—so I took out my notebook, knowing that anyone who didn't would be told, 'Write this down! And put a date on it!' Another time she said, 'You know, you and I make a very good team, Maddy. You'll do well, you'll carry on well.' She knew what a force she was, she knew what we were losing."

When a call came from President Jimmy Carter, Mead was under sedation and could not take it, but she later sent a message to the President that she considered the call "made," and that he should not spend any more of his valuable time trying to get through to her. Father Austin Ford visited, and once Madeline Lee brought the friend who had presumed to disagree with Mead about public education. "He just poked his head in to say hello, since Margaret was very ill that day," said Lee, "and she saw him and said, 'Hello, Stanley, I'm just gathering my strength for a good argument!'"

Glen Leet, Mead's colleague in United Nations circles, came when she was desperately sick, and she looked up and said, "What can I do for you, Glen?" William Mitchell passed through New York on his way from Vermont to an AAA conference in Los Angeles and disregarded advice that he ought not to "bother" Mead: "There was no way," he said, "that I was going to be in the same city with this dying woman and not go see her," so he made his way to the hospital room where she sat with her eyes closed, eyes that could scarcely see anyway, but when she heard his voice she said, "Bill! You know, I'm awful sick." He did know that, Mitchell said, and added that he was going to the AAA meetings.

"Have fun," she told him.

Toward the end, said Wilton Dillon, "she didn't look ugly, she looked young, like pictures of her younger self." At Margaret's request her photographer friend Paul Byers came from Westchester to give her a foot massage, which she afterward told him had hurt. "I got there just before they put her on a hundred milligrams of Demerol a day," he said, "and Carmen seemed to think the massage somehow messed up the energy."

One day Mead wakened from a nap to see Lucinda Steig Franceschini, another frequent visitor, along with Madeline Lee. "Hello, darlings," Mead looked up and told her nieces, "it's nice to see you. You both have the same haircut."

Jean Houston, whose travel schedule that fall was as busy as Mead's once had been, stopped whenever she could at the hospital. On one visit she asked Mead why she had been so angry at Chautauqua: "Was it that I was coming up with the paradigm?"

"Yes, darling," Mead replied. "I'm sorry." In their last conversation, a few days before the end, said Houston, "she asked me to tell her about all the places I had been in the past month, giving lectures and seminars. As it was quite a list, she responded in the pithiest way possible. She said 'St. Christopher,' meaning of course the saint of travelers, and wishing me, I think, his blessings. At that point she was in such pain that she had to use the most complete succinctness of her life."

A week before her death, Mead made a statement Madeline Lee found extraordinarily moving. "They finally found out what's wrong with me," she said. "It *is* cancer, and I want the world to know that. Now that they know what it is, they can start doing something to treat it." At last she acknowledged her illness and approaching death, and as usual, in spite of the small lie about the timing of the discovery, she wanted to be useful.

"You don't want to see her," Barbara Sperling told Ken Heyman when he came to visit. Sperling, who was pregnant, told Heyman, "I just hope Margaret gets to see my baby," which was not to be. Heyman looked in the room, saw Mead's feet, and did not go in. The next day, when she died, "I went down the hall sobbing, sobbing in the hospital chapel, and later on I figured out why—by discovering me, Margaret had given birth to me, as much as my own mother had."

In a phone conversation toward the end, Mead asked Austin Ford the number of a certain bill involving children's nutrition then pending before Congress. Ford replied that as far as he knew the bill had got beyond the stage where it needed a number.

"No wonder you can't get anything done," Mead told him, and hung up. But a few days later she said on the phone, "Come back again soon, we miss you."

"Well, Margaret, we've made it to another sunrise," said a friend who kept one of the all-night vigils. At 9:20 on the morning of November 15, 1978, the only other person in the room with Mead was her niece, who took her hand and said, "It's Maddy, and I'm here," which seemed, Lee said, "to allow her to die. To watch the death," she added, "was a great and rare gift."

On one of Mead's last nights, Austin Ford learned, she had told her nurse that she was dying.

"Yes," the nurse said gently. "We all will, someday."

"But this is different," Mead said.

"I Know She Can Hear Me"

KEN HEYMAN

Into thy hands, O merciful Saviour, we commend the soul of thy servant Margaret, now departed from the body. Her famous energy at last had given out. Her clothes were going to Emmaus House in Atlanta, her ashes would be buried outside the Pennsylvania church where she had been baptized at eleven and married, for the first time, ten years later. Now, at St. Paul's Chapel of Columbia University, for the first of numerous memorial services, 450 mourners were gathered, and many found the traditional Episcopal liturgy unfamiliar. *Acknowledge, we humbly beseech thee, a sheep of thine own fold, a lamb of thine own flock, a sinner of thine own redeeming.* Lamb, yes; somewhere in Mead there had always been the innocence of a child: chil-

425

dren, she had said, were her most central interest. And she was also, like the rest of us, a sinner.

Mead's "exquisite sense of timing," wrote her friend and colleague Vera Rubin, had served her to the end: she died on the opening day of the annual conference, this time in Los Angeles, of the American Anthropological Association: "By early morning word had spread throughout the meeting halls, with a sense of shock, that the familiar figure with the flowing red cape and the thumb stick would not be present to take her usual vigorous part in the proceedings." Soon the world knew. "I was angry at her for dying," said Larry Hirschfeld, a student of Mead's who heard the news during a field trip in Southeast Asia. "I'd heard that she was gravely ill, but I had no idea what a big event her death was; on the Armed Forces radio in Sumatra, on ABC, CBS, NBC, the UPI, the AP—over and over I kept listening to the story of her death. It was never left out of a single broadcast." In Papua New Guinea, where Nancy Lutkehaus was doing field work, she explained her grief by telling people her grandmother had died.

In Nigeria when she first heard the news, Constance Sutton was alone doing field work, and felt deeply bereft. Mead, for her, had been "the ideal mother. First I saw her as sexually neutral, but later she came to seem more and more feminine, she provided me with an incredible structure of self-esteem and support. She helped me, more than anyone, to realize that I could stand on my own two feet. She was more intellectually influential on me than I ever acknowledged. I'm a neo-Marxist, I wasn't doing her kind of anthropology, but she was willing to be a patron for anyone."

Students were there at St. Paul's Chapel, and professors, and curators, and Ash Can Cats, and employees, and relatives, and admirers who had never even met the deceased, and, to her own surprise, Mead's adversary Betty Friedan, who had accused her in *The Feminine Mystique* and elsewhere of "incredible vacillation" regarding the women's movement. Now, suddenly, Friedan was moved "to pay my respects. I felt that Mead, who was born twenty years before me, had gone as far as she could with feminism and that I, in reacting to her, took it a step further and was in a way her heir. I felt part of a procession."

Agnostic academics did their best to join in the verses of rousing Victorian hymns: "O'er moor and fen, o'er crag and torrent"; "To faithful warriors cometh rest"; "All is safely gathered in." On December 7, a service in the National Cathedral in Washington, D.C., was sponsored by the citizens' lobby New Directions, which Mead had helped to found. The congregation sang "O God, Our Help in Ages Past," and a kilted bagpiper marched alone down the aisle playing "Amazing

Grace." First Lady Rosalynn Carter left this service on the arm of someone wearing a yarmulke. At the larger of two later services at the United Nations, a representative of a group called the Temple of Understanding wanted to release a flock of doves, to symbolize Mead's love of peace, and was barely persuaded by Jean Houston that the doves might also make a mess.

At least nine other organizations held services in 1979, and in September a section of the park outside the Natural History Museum was formally named Margaret Mead Green. "Some called my mother a citizen of the world," the *New York Times* quoted Mary Catherine Bateson, "and I suppose she was. But she was also very profoundly a New Yorker. It is fitting that there will be a piece of New York bearing her name." This park was dedicated during the fourth annual Margaret Mead Film Festival. In Woods Hole, Massachusetts, the New Alchemy Institute made plans to dedicate to Mead a 230-foot ship, meant to head for harbors wherever food and help were needed. On the island of Manus a Community Center was dedicated to Mead in Peri village, where she was ceremonially mourned for five days. Village Councilor Peranis Paliau sent a cable: "People sorry of Margaret Mead's death. With sympathy, respect. Rested seven days. Planted coconut tree memory of great friend."

We brought nothing into this world and it is certain we can carry nothing out. On January 4, Rosalind Lippel took a subway downtown to Surrogate's Court to testify that "the decedent, Margaret Mead Bateson a/k/a Margaret Mead," on October 7 had been "of sound mind and memory and understanding, not under any restraint or in any respect incompetent to make her Last Will and Testament," so that Mead's estate, $222,081.67 after taxes, could be probated. Rhoda Métraux sold Apartment 16J and supervised a small, harried staff engaged in sorting out the fifty-year accumulation in Mead's museum tower, preparing some 500,000 different manuscripts, letters and other documents to be sent to the Library of Congress, and answering thousands of notes of condolence, by hand. The tower was not vacated until the following June 30.

Hundreds of people filed into the museum on the cold gray Saturday morning of January 20, 1979, for the largest of Mead's memorial services, where Ambassador to the UN Andrew Young was to present the Presidential Medal of Freedom, on behalf of Mead's friend Jimmy Carter, to her daughter. Gregory Bateson was present, too: he had come from his home at the Esalen Institute in Big Sur, California. He had not expected to outlive Mead: "I'll follow her soon," he had said when word reached him of Mead's death, but, perhaps with the help of his own faith healer, whom he described as "rather cute; I enjoyed my healer," Bateson had a remission from lung cancer and emphysema, and felt robust enough to make the trip east. His photograph had never been out of Mead's sight in her hospital room. When nurses moved her bed, they had to move his picture, too.

On the eve of the Saturday morning ceremony, Bateson and Philleo Nash and Wilton Dillon had made their way from Rhoda Métraux's apartment to the celebrated delicatessen Zabar's, three long blocks away in the howling wind off the Hudson River. Métraux worried about the effect this expedition might have on Bateson's health, but the splendidly named trio—Gregory, Wilton, Philleo—insisted. "We were hunters," said Nash, "going forth to bring back game."

"I don't know what I'm going to say," Bateson told Nash the next morning as they headed toward the memorial service.

"I think you're down for theory," said Nash.

"That's what I mean," replied Bateson.

"Just use your notes," said Nash.

"But I've lost them," said Bateson.

"Then you'll be fine," said Nash.

The crowd overflowed from the museum auditorium into smaller rooms outside, where the ceremony could be watched on TV monitors. In one of these rooms a small protest group made a fuss, accusing anthropologists of fascism, but most of the audience was reverent. A number of women present, as at most gatherings involving Margaret Mead, looked something like her, with bobbed gray hair and bespectacled beaming eyes. These women nodded knowingly when the television interviewer Barbara Walters told how Mead had confided that she, too, had sometimes felt lonely.

Buckminster Fuller, famous for talking on and on and on, was, for a change, remarkably laconic. "I know she can hear me," he explained when his turn came to speak. Then, looking upward, he added, "We love you, Margaret." Nash told how she had put the recognition she got as a person to work "to get respectful attention for the human side of 'our' science." The scientist Jean Mayer quoted Mead's statement that "people don't eat nutrition, they eat food." Andrew Young told how Mead had helped him understand his own "developmental process," and gave the Medal of Freedom to Mary Catherine Bateson, who walked and stood tall like her father but seemed to have inherited her mother's face and gestures and sure, deliberate way of speaking. Gregory Bateson said something many would echo later: that, theoretically speaking, Margaret Mead was hard if not impossible to pigeonhole. In years to come, he said, people would recognize that her contributions had been enormous, without being able to say quite why.

But in the months to come, they tried to. "I never thought that facts were particularly important to Margaret," said Dr. Roy Menninger. "She just didn't *need* facts. She could pick up patterns, observations, trends without them. She was, for me, an example of lateral thinking: she could put A and Q and X together in a way that nobody else would have thought of, pulling things out of their standard contexts and seeing them in *new* contexts."

"Her greatest forte," said Lenora Foerstel, "was getting the right minds together to explain how interdisciplinary ideas could dovetail. Her strength was her highly intuitive and unstructured ability to create intelligent relationships. Participant observation, before she came along, had been very rigid."

Wilton Dillon said that his friend Mead had "never said anything that was meant to last. She knew that theory was nothing more than the best explanation of facts at a particular point. She was an analyzer and an explicator, not a partisan." In the similar view of Mead's student Dorothy Billings, she had been laudably loath "to reduce her work to a litany, a battle cry, a slogan, a Ten Commandments." To the New Zealand anthropologist James Ritchie, she was simply "atheoretical." June Goodfield assessed Mead's contribution as "not so much a corpus of knowledge as sheer aliveness and vitality, and a living presence which could admonish, could prescribe, could help, could anger, could inspire—who could personify in all her strengths and weaknesses what it really was to be human and alive."

Others argued that Mead's greatest strength, professionally at least, had been her work with moving and still photography. Renée Fox, summarizing Mead's career in the *International Encyclopedia of Social Sciences*, hailed her and Bateson's "pathbreaking contribution" of using photography "not simply as ethnographic illustration, but as a detailed and rigorous form of cultural analysis." The ethnographic filmmaker Asen Balikci said at the 1980 American Museum of Natural History Film Festival that his debt to Mead was great. At critical moments in expeditions to film Eskimos and tribal Afghans, Balikci said, "I would step back and wonder how Margaret Mead would handle this."

"I was trying with her to help develop the Ethnographic Film Center," said Walter Goldschmidt in 1980, "and when hard meetings came along I'd think, 'Goddammit, if only I could get on the phone and talk to Margaret.' Her absence at the last AAA was more visible than anyone else's presence."

All Mead had ever done for photography, she claimed, was to encourage—though Lenora Foerstel called her "a better photographer than either Ted [Schwartz] or I." Still, it was Mead's film work, Asen Balikci said, that allowed her to record and transmit with unprecedented finesse "her *messianisme*—the cultural wealth of humanity, created after a hundred million years of strong and painful development, so that forthcoming generations would not be that much culturally poorer. It was that *messianisme* that sent her rushing to the field to assemble, collect, accumulate."

The most important thing Mead brought home from field trips was not rolls of film, or objects of art, but notes. With each field trip, she refined her note-taking techniques, distinguishing more and more precisely the events from the patterns they represented, and supplementing each record with letters home. Focusing on human beings, as Mead's ethnography does, it has, in the anthropologist Nancy McDowell's view, "a vividness unmatched and unrivaled in the professional anthropological literature." Mead's colleague Lola Romanucci-Ross marveled at her "serene certitude that all data collected by virtually anyone were increments to the understanding of culture."

Reo Fortune learned of Mead's death during a visit to his brother Barter outside Auckland, New Zealand. "That's two wives I've lost now," he said as he stared east toward the Pacific Ocean. When he returned to England there would be no one to greet him at "Bonde Mteko," his cottage outside Cambridge. (The meaning of "Bonde Mteko," if any, was a secret Reo kept to himself. "I wouldn't put it past him," said Barter, "to have chosen that name just to confuse people.") Fortune's thinking had never been easy to follow. At its best, his prose was, as a colleague wrote, "marvelously illuminating, carried by a terse style with an offbeat rhythm which at times merged effortlessly with the native rhythms of Melanesian speech . . . [and] revealing of a mind which moved towards discoveries in unconventional ways," but he had never advanced beyond the rank of lecturer at Cambridge University. His "wayward genius did not easily submit to the humdrum routine of teaching, the ebb and flow of Terms."

But toward the end of his life his students found Fortune lovable, and so did his friends' children, with whom he was willing to hide under tables in games of "Murder." He had "the air of having his hand caught in the cookie jar," said Harold Levine, who arranged to have the Anthropology Department at U.C.L.A. invite Fortune there to give some talks in 1979. That visit proved a delight; Fortune took pleasure in wearing shorts and a yellow baseball cap when he and his host went for walks along the beach at Venice.

Fortune was famous for his economies. He wrote on the backs of old manuscripts, watched for supermarket bargains, and pushed his orange Volkswagen by hand toward the pump to save on petrol. He was also ingenious. Caught without a raincoat at a party at the Cambridge Anthropology Museum, when the weather suddenly turned foul, he broke into a glass display case and helped himself to an Eskimo parka, which he put back the next day where it belonged.

His second wife, Eileen, had not shared the popular view that Margaret Mead had thwarted Fortune's career. Far from it. Once when Mead visited Cambridge Eileen Fortune asked her to stay and live with them, on the ground that Margaret could inspire Reo, as no one else ever had, to get back to his writing. That he never did resume it, Barter Fortune thought, was out of a kind of chivalry toward Mead. Much though he had come to differ with her version of their joint field work, angry as he had been at her, his abiding gratitude for her help had stopped him from contradicting her, in any big way, in print. "Kindness," said Barter, "was Reo's besetting sin. Had he been sufficiently bloody-minded to forget old loyalties, I am sure that he would have had it within him to enliven social anthropology considerably. But his conception of honor was puritan beyond belief."

In December 1979, Fortune fell down a flight of stairs in the library of Wolfson College at Cambridge University, and died of injuries a few days later. Gregory Bateson died of lung cancer July 4, 1980, at the San Francisco Zen (Buddhist) Center. His last needs were tended to with ceremonial devotion by a group including the Zen Center teachers and students, Bateson's third wife Lois, their nine-year-old daughter Nora, his ten-year-old granddaughter Vanni Kassarjian, and his forty-year-old daughter Mary Catherine Bateson, who wrote a moving memoir of her father's death.

"The other two have turned up their toes," Luther Cressman remarked when he heard of Bateson's death, "and Old Grandpa here is on television!" "Old Grandpa," as Cressman sometimes called himself, discussed his marriage with Margaret Mead on an "Odyssey" program in late 1981, and the following year on another television special, and wrote of it further in "The Golden Journey," his own memoir. Dorothy Cecilia Loch, his second wife, had died in 1977, but Sheeleigh, as she called him, sounded hale on his eighty-sixth birthday on October 24, 1983.

To friends old and new he gave a pamphlet he had had published privately, entitled "To You, from Cecilia," illustrated with pictures of his dark-eyed second wife on a trip to the moors, and showed his book *Prehistory of the West: Homes of Vanished Peoples*, about his pioneering work in the archeology of eastern Oregon. On its jacket is a picture of the famous 9,000-year-old sandal. From time to time, after their divorce, Cressman and Mead encountered each other at anthropology meetings. Once, in response to some remark she made, Luther said, "Well, that's the way the cookie crumbles."

"You really *are* a westerner, aren't you?" replied Margaret.

"What would I have said if I were an easterner?" asked Luther.

"Easterners," Margaret informed him, "say 'That's the way the ball bounces.' "

At another AAA meeting, Luther saw Margaret in the hall for the first time in years, and asked, "Can't we talk?"

"Not now," she said. "I want to go hear a paper."

"Go listen to the paper," he told her. "That," he said later, "really graveled me." But in subsequent years, largely at Mead's behest, they revived what Cressman referred to as "the ancient code of comradeship." He used that phrase in a 1983 letter to the Science Editor of the *New York Times*.

This letter, which brought Cressman more mail than anything he had ever written, was part of the debate over Derek Freeman's *Margaret Mead and Samoa: The Making and Unmaking of an Anthropological Myth*. The debate had erupted on January 31, when the *Times* ran a 47-inch story, starting on page one, about early reactions to Freeman's still unpublished book. "NEW SAMOA BOOK CHALLENGES MARGARET MEAD'S CONCLUSIONS," said the headline. "Two months before its official publication," the story began, "a book maintaining that the anthropologist Margaret Mead seriously misrepresented the culture and character of Samoa has ignited heated discussion within the behavioral sciences."

The story told of Freeman's charges that Mead, in researching *Coming of Age in Samoa*, had been gullible, naïve, and overanxious to help prove the theory of her mentor Franz Boas that it is culture, more than biology, that determines human behavior. Mead's exalted reputation, Freeman was suggesting, was therefore undeserved. The goddess with the cudgel had had feet of clay; the theories she made popular, sometimes blamed for a lot of the "permissiveness" of the past half-century, were in Freeman's view, to say the least, suspect. Freeman, since 1940, had spent a total of six years in the archipelago, mostly in Western Samoa, 130 miles from Mead's American Samoan village of Ta'u, and found that people there were just as troubled and troublesome as people anywhere, and that they resented being thought of as the lustful, slaphappy simpletons Mead had portrayed in *Coming of Age*. They had asked him, Freeman said, to set the record straight. This he claimed to have done, for the sake of the Samoans and for the sake of Science.

The most striking aspect of this whole affair was not Freeman's thesis, word of which had been spreading among anthropologists for years, but the public's response to the coverage in the *Times*. Had the article appeared on an inside page, or closer to April, when Harvard University Press had announced that the book would be published, the year 1983 would have been far quieter than it turned out to be for Freeman, for his fellow Samoanists, and for everyone who had any connection with the reputation of Margaret Mead. As it was, with the first article quickly followed by another, then by an editorial, then by an item in the Sunday "News of the Week in Review," the matter became an immediate international scandal. If the *Times* says something or somebody is important, as it had always said Mead was, the television networks and wire services and newspapers and magazines snap to and take notice. *Time* put the controversy on its cover. National Public Radio featured it on "All Things Considered." *Life* and the *Wall Street Journal* sent reporters to American Samoa.

Who was this New Zealand-born Australian, everyone wanted to know, who dared besmirch the reputation of the most famous and most revered woman scientist of the century? Could what he said be true? It was possible. Freeman had done distinguished work in Borneo and was regarded as a respected if moody and, in the case of his work on the Mead book, exceptionally dogged scholar. So: Had Mead lied? Had she been duped? If her work was not to be trusted, whose could? What time was it—what day was it, for that matter—in Australia? Phone calls from both hemispheres, day and night, broke the calm of Freeman's placid house near Australian National University in Canberra. Reporters wanted interviews. Harvard University Press, in Massachusetts, wanted to tell him that publication date had been changed from April to late February, that the first printing had been greatly increased and that Freeman should pack his bags to fly to the States. The freelance publicist Lynn Goldberg was hired to shepherd him around to the most influential of American television and radio programs, among them "CBS Morning News" and the "Phil Donahue" show in Chicago. On both of these Mary Catherine Bateson was also a guest.

"Gosh, Phil," she said in the course of the Donahue program, "I don't think of human beings as pies." Donahue, who apparently did, had asked what portion of each pie stemmed from nature and what from nurture: which was the determining factor in how we behaved, heredity or environment? Freeman called the question "silly"; Bateson and a third guest agreed. The third guest, who had recently published a book of his own called *Sala'ilua: A Samoan Mystery*, was Professor Bradd Shore of Emory University. Shore contended, before Donahue's vast audience, that Freeman's refutation of Mead had given the impression "of anthropology as a shooting gallery, not anthropology as a scholarly discussion . . .

"Margaret Mead was not completely wrong on Samoa," Shore said, "and that's the problem. She was incomplete. And when someone is incomplete you don't refute them, you correct, you add, and you also acknowledge what you have learned from them and what's—"

"That," said Mary Catherine Bateson, "is called science."

Neither of his fellow guests, said Freeman, knew what science was about. Few Americans, by his lights, did. After all his years of largely secluded research he seemed to be having too good a time on his publicity tour to care whom he insulted. ("Stop him, please stop him!" he said of a Columbia professor on a New York radio interview.) But Freeman's book, for all this commotion, was not having the effect he had predicted it would, one afternoon two years earlier in the garden outside his house in Canberra. He "rather supposed," Freeman had said that afternoon to this writer, that his book would cause Mead's reputation to "do a 32"—a phrase he learned in Anthony Burgess's *Joysprick*, concerning the work of James Joyce—which was to say to accelerate through space at the rate of a falling body, 32 feet per second per second. Mead's work, Freeman had predicted, would be forgotten, and so would she.

Instead, ironically, the work and the woman who did it attracted more attention than Mead had got even in the most bumptious periods of her lifetime. The conservative *Colorado Springs Gazette Telegraph*, in an editorial supporting Freeman, lamented the expenditure of "billions of tax dollars" on pointless social welfare programs "in pursuit of a theory that, by Freeman's standards, was drivel when Mead at the age of twenty-three apparently set out to prove her own preconceived notions, while ignoring her obligation to remain scientific."

Mead's old friends, and even some of her old detractors, were outraged. The fuss aroused by Freeman, Lenora Foerstel ventured, proved the same thing the previous year's defeat of the Equal Rights Amendment had proven, that "we can't tolerate a monumental woman figure." On the contrary, Freeman retorted, his own view was that "women are wonderful; anthropology should be the queen, not the king, of social science—the king would strut about, the queen would sit demurely. Women," he added, "have a special kind of common sense. Wisdom is always a woman. I'd be very relieved to find that God was a woman. I want to have a worshipful attitude toward women. They have so much to tell me that I can learn from no other source."

What a pity, many anthropologists said, that Freeman could not have leveled his charges against Mead's work when she was alive to defend herself. He had tried to, he claimed. He and Mead had met, in 1964, and corresponded; she had said in the appendix to the 1969 edition of "Social Organization of Manu'a," where she acknowledged the discrepancies between her Samoan findings and those of later field workers, that she looked forward to Freeman's further research. But not until 1981, Freeman said, well after Mead's death, was he granted access to what he said were crucial court records which proved his suspicion that American Samoa in Mead's time, no less than Western Samoa in his, was a far more violent and difficult place than Mead had said it was. This struck Lowell Holmes as odd: Holmes said he had not had any trouble getting access to those very records in 1954, and when he saw them they struck him as a joke: "They said that the Number Two cause of infant death was arteriosclerosis!"

Holmes of Wichita State, Shore of Emory, Melvin Ember of Hunter, Paul Shankman of the University of Colorado, and others from the hitherto obscure fraternity of Samoanists found themselves in sudden and urgent demand as the Freeman-Mead brouhaha continued throughout 1983, attracting unprecedented interest in both parts of the Samoan archipelago. Who was right about *moetotolo*, they were asked: Freeman or Mead? Was the practice a form of rape or a romantic game? Had Mead been cowardly to lodge with a U.S. Navy family? Was it fair of Freeman to compare a remote American Samoan village, in 1925, with an urbanized Western Samoan community of fifty years later? Penelope Schoeffel, in Sydney, had found that the first thing

Samoan children learn is a concept of shame. Eleanor Gerber, now in Virginia, said Samoans were famous for telling visitors what they thought the visitors wanted to hear. Who was right and who was wrong?

With gusto and before large crowds, Mead's Samoan work was reassessed at a Barnard College seminar in April, a gathering in May of the Society of Woman Geographers, an October forum at the University of Colorado, and a large panel in late November at the annual convention of the American Anthropological Association, where several papers were read, the most spirited of them by Annette Weiner and Theodore Schwartz. Beyond Samoa, said Schwartz, "what is at stake and not soon to be resolved is the epistemological nature and status of anthropology." Freeman's "badly written and deeply destructive" book, said Weiner, posed "only one penetrating question," which was whether it would "alter what people think about the value of anthropology."

"To undermine this value falsely," Weiner concluded, would be "to make us all prisoners of an old myth perpetuating the claim that human behavior is grounded in only one kind of truth and one set of values. Samoans wisely know better." Margaret Mead, Schwartz ended his paper, "was like no other anthropologist." By the standards of today, said Melvin Ember at Barnard, "Mead cannot be classified as a scientist but as a natural historian of human societies."

Also in November, at a Radcliffe Institute talk which chanced to fall on the fifth anniversary of her mother's death, Mary Catherine Bateson said that Freeman had simply not understood the difference between Margaret Mead's Samoa and his own: "He has forced upon us an elaborate argument, and drawn Boas into it with extensive and substantial distortions and misstatements about Boas's work"; he has "contributed nothing to our understanding," and, "worse than nothing, has given aid and comfort to those who hate Boas for the wrong reasons."

Boas, as Cressman put it in his letter to the *Times,* had had "a much more pressing problem on his hands" than using Mead to gather "information to support his idea of the greater importance of nurture over nature. . . . He had this brilliant, emotional, driving young woman-student, whose abilities he recognized and admired, insisting that he support her desire to do her first field work outside of North America like he would do for a man. . . . [Boas] knew his obligation to support his troublesome young student, to provide her an opportunity consonant with her training and let her then demonstrate her capability to perform as she had promised. He was fully sensitive to the trauma he would inflict on the girl if he frustrated her deeply rooted ambition. . . . If Margaret, in going to Samoa, wanted to prove some preconceived idea, [it was that] a woman, she, Margaret Mead, could be a professional anthropological field worker as well as any man of comparable preparation. . . .

"We are all indebted to her in some degree," Cressman concluded his letter. "Colleagues as scholars will correct her errors, the perspective of time establish her scientific worth, and we, her professional associates, will gain stature both professionally and personally if we rightly honor the remarkable young girl and the woman Margaret became."

Freeman deserves credit, Lola Romanucci-Ross wrote in *Reviews of Anthropology*, "for a remarkable effort in anthropological research; his meticulous care and patience are to be emulated . . . Margaret Mead was, among many other things, an enchantress. The uses of enchantment cannot be underestimated as generators of scientific knowledge."

But Mead was no more the tunnel-visioned cultural relativist Freeman suggests she was than he is a card-carrying biological determinist. She would hardly have disagreed with his conclusion that a new anthropology is needed, to transcend both extremes, and to make it clear that our troubles can no more be traced to our genes than to the towns we happened to grow up in. Maybe she wasn't entirely right about night crawling in Samoa. Maybe she was silly about how swaddling turned Slavs into despots, and deluded to think that her government would ever pay appropriate heed to the findings of social science. Certainly she was a careless speller. And she wasn't demure like the geneticist Barbara McClintock, who in 1983, at the age of eighty-one, won the Nobel Prize for her work with jumping genes on ears of corn, and who once apologized for being hoarse at five in the afternoon because she had not yet used her vocal cords that day. Mead's vocal cords rarely rested, and not all she said was judicious.

"Margaret loves the marketplace," said A. L. Kroeber, whom many regarded as dean of American anthropologists, but she was not just a merchant. "If you took the best ten percent that [she] has done," he also said, "you'll find it's more in quantity and better in quality than most other anthropologists."

Look at all she got right. Look how early she came upon the notions of cybernetics, body language, male menopause, trial marriages, and fashionable androgyny. Who of her peers aimed further and wider? And who was more generous? Her American optimism was fierce and fearless. If a humane thing had to be done, then someone should go do it, and here, if need be, was some money.

Academics will keep busy for decades assessing what Mead stood for. "A proper decoding of her ideology," said Asen Balikci, "would show she would reject military and economic imperialism, but not reject the cultural kind." Perhaps. But Margaret Mead unquestionably pioneered in the ethnography of women and children, in the application of psychology to field work in the study of national character, and in the refinement of methods. And she made her once arcane discipline seem not only glamorous but useful. "She viewed anthropology," said her fellow curator Robert Carneiro, "as a way of looking at problems, and not being defeated by them but solving them." Anthropology's task, as Mead saw it, was to focus attention not on structural arrangements but on human life in all its dignity, variety, and complexity.

"Her positive contributions," wrote L. L. Langness, "are monumental. Her influence, on the profession, on other disciplines and on the public are simply without precedent." Mead's greatness, wrote Reo Fortune's niece and executor Ann McLean, "consists in her having persuaded the contemporary American and American satellite public to examine critically their actions and attitudes and to contemplate, albeit briefly, the notion that there might be other ways of seeing and doing things that are equally viable."

"How much has this woman given us to think about," wrote Professor Jan Van Baal of the University of Utrecht, "concerning culture and concerning education, concerning the place of woman, and concerning change. Without her work we wouldn't even be able to discuss these problems the way we do now."

"She was supremely successful in almost everything she attempted," said Marvin Harris. "She knew how to manipulate people, how to develop and exploit networks of admirers, and how to use the media for image building. But her most solid contribution" was to raise "everybody's level of consciousness about cultural differences. The spread of the concept of culture as socially learned patterns of thought and behavior is a much more ecumenical theme than Mead's psychoanalytical ramblings and top-of-the-head psychologizing . . . Bringing the word about culture was Mead's mission. One might even say that it was literally part of her religion."

So teach us to number our days, the congregation read at Mead's Columbia service, *that we may apply our hearts unto wisdom.* Margaret Mead, through all her days, strove mightily for wisdom. She seemed guided always by the homely old saw she had quoted in a 1923 letter to Ruth Benedict: "Be lazy go crazy," which apparently meant that if busy equals good, then busier must be better yet. In Harris's estimation "she may have been the busiest, hardest-working incarnation of the Protestant ethic since Calvin."

Mead's sin, she once told Jean Houston, was greed: greed for new experiences. All her appetites were hearty. By conventional standards she moved around too much, ate and drank too much (could she have got so fat because she spread herself so thin?), wrote too much—her bibliography (with the introduction translated into Spanish and French) lists thirty-nine books (two edited and fifteen done with others), 1,397 other publications, and forty-three records, tapes, films, and videotapes. She had twenty-eight honorary degrees and won forty awards, and seemed genuinely pleased with each one. Some said she hoped for a Nobel Peace Prize, or a post in the Cabinet. For all her laurels, she did not rest, and rejection could hurt her as it hurts anybody. It could make her weep.

She meant at least as much outside anthropology as within it, especially to her friends in the clergy and in mental health work. The Reverend Theodore M. Hesburgh, president of Notre Dame University, said that his friend Margaret "struggled—with all her heart and great soul—back and forth between macrocosm and microcosm—for a world in which each gift will have its place." Dr. Roy Menninger said he would remember all his life a meeting with Mead in her New York apartment, at a time when he faced urgent problems regarding his family and his work.

"I spent two or three hours sitting across the table from her, with her little glasses perched on her nose, as she doodled, making a note or two, and it was one of the warmest, most intimate exchanges I've ever had with anyone in my life. Nearly always in this culture, when you engage in a moment that's truly intimate, one party or the other feels angry that he has shared too much. With Margaret that wasn't what happened. I had no feeling of being diminished. She never lost perspective. She got pulled into whirlpools, but she never gave the impression of being on the outside watching the poor fish struggle."

To have spent the better part of five years assembling different viewpoints of this woman, with all her contradictions, is to invite the simple question: "Well, do you *like* her?" The answer has to be, "which her"? The child Margaret and the elderly statue might have been hard to take. But Mead the undergraduate, with what the caption beside her Barnard yearbook senior picture called her "advanced idees," was another matter: Who wouldn't have welcomed a chance to ride with her from her campus to Greenwich Village in the 1920s, watching New

York from the top of a double-decker bus? She would have been fun to speculate with about the other passengers on the bus, or about any new roomful of people, at any point in her life, from the shores of Lake Papakeechie in Indiana to the banks of the Sepik in Papua New Guinea.

Many people relished and never forgot the discussions they had with Mead about such diverse matters as the Gesell-Ilg theory of maturation, the swaddling hypothesis, the importance of somatotypes, the relationship between the early handling of horses and the teaching of arithmetic to children. A more appealing Margaret Mead, to this writer, would have been the one who thought up games, at Cloverly in New Hampshire in the 1940s, to beguile two generations. Those summers on and near Squam Lake must have been wonderful, with the wild cries of loons in the background, bathing suits hanging on clotheslines, sweaters strewn around, and arguments about everything from how to get the government to listen to social scientists to trances in Bali to whose turn it was to pick the corn.

One of Mead's most endearing legacies was and still is the "family" she established during her daughter's wartime childhood, to supplement the one she was born to. The Franks, the Ullmans, and the more distant Guillebauds, not to say the unbullyable Batesons, bequeathed to their children, who in turn are bequeathing it to theirs, a sense of connection that endures, and impresses, to this day. Marie Eichelberger's funeral service in New York City on January 2, 1984, was a typically affecting reunion of this "family." Catherine Bateson helped prepare communion, Vanni Kassarjian, Mary Frank Perry, and Philomena Guillebaud read from the Scriptures. Mead the kinswoman, however hurried she was, always made time for those to whom she was related, by blood or by choice. Her Cincinnati cousin Martha Glardon "went through a period of hating Margaret because she was gone—in the family we'd been leaning on her for years. I miss her a lot more than I realized I would."

In Mead's sixties, renewed with what she called postmenopausal zest, she would have been an especially invigorating companion. In any low moment it would have been buoying to be able to phone her for a sure jolt of energy and purpose. "Come on," she'd have said, "it's not only possible, but it has to be done, and you alone can do it! What are you waiting for?" To have been a worker in one of her sororities, or a soldier in one of her armies, would probably have been in equal parts exasperating and exhilarating. Her scathing words could make strong women, not to say men, reel. Her loving attention, which Ruth Benedict in 1923 had found as restful as "a padded chair and fire place," must also have felt a little like a laser beam.

"I'm going to miss her," Mead's employee Amy Bard wrote in her journal, "and that's what hurts. She won't be around to love, hate, admire, get frustrated with, entertain. No more crazy stories and brilliant (though sometimes bizarre) pronouncements. I'm glad I got to spend those days with her at East Hampton. I was angry and frightened when I left and only recounted by negative emotions. Forgot how neat it was to get to know her a bit and let her get to know me."

"It's strange to think she's gone," said Louise Rosenblatt, whom Mead and Léonie Adams had asked to ride downtown with them on the Fifth Avenue bus from Barnard to Greenwich Village. "Since her parents lived to be in or near their eighties, I thought she'd be around as long as I was."

"One likes to be understood not in terms of fantasy," said Richard Sorenson, but as Mead had understood him: "in a way that hits home truly—which hardly ever happens."

"Even five years after her death I miss her," June Goodfield said in 1984. "She was my favorite kind of person, a gutsy pragmatist. No matter what the subject at hand, she had a capacity to go straight to its essence and say something about it that was original and highly illuminating. Sometimes, of course, she was wildly wrong, but more often than not I learned greatly from these moments, finding that the particular crystal had been shifted, that the light was refracting through the issue in a completely unsuspected angle . . . I miss, too, the forcefulness and the directness and the challenge implicit in this."

Receive her into the arms of thy mercy, into the blessed rest of everlasting peace, and into the glorious company of the saints. Amen. Yes. Receive her, cradle her, hold and enfold her. And the larger the company, of saints as of mortals, the more pleased she will be. Mead made some wonder, in the words of an Englishman who asked, when her death caused such a fuss, "How do you get on the list of the great and the good?" Mead got on that list, like the Republic for which she stood and like her Grandfather Fogg, whose motto was "Do Good Because It Is Right to Do Good," because she tried. She often messed up, sometimes badly, but she tried. For all her shortcomings, as Robin Fox wrote in the *New York Times*, she was "part of that long, informed, liberal, questing, progressive, courageous, challenging tradition of critical humane inquiry that is so essential a part of eternal vigilance." In a world where many are famous for no special good reason or for dubious deeds, Margaret Mead, all her nearly seventy-seven years, not only attracted but deserved the attention of the public.

Lord knows she meant well. And she did well, too.

Acknowledgments

As her friends and her Simon and Schuster associates well know, "Be Lazy Go Crazy" is at least as apt a motto for Alice Mayhew as it was for Margaret Mead. Her dedication to this project has been so complete that the book, in turn, can only be dedicated to her.

Her assistants, notably David Masello, Michael Gast, and Phoebe Rentschler, have been good-humored and efficient. Ann Godoff, particularly in her work with Maria Iano to assemble the pictures for these pages, has been inspired.

But corporate support, as Stewart Johnson predicted in 1979, goes just so far, and for the most part this enterprise has been a cottage industry, literally headquartered for six weeks in the winter of 1980–81 in a cottage at the MacDowell Colony, and for several extended periods in Sag Harbor, Long Island. During all these retreats, research trips elsewhere, and encampments in New York, I have relied on the matchless organizational skills and shrewd sympathy of Rosalind Lippel. Before she came along I was lucky to have the help of Cynthia Cannell and Leslie Weedin.

Early readers of portions or all of these pages, whose help has in some cases been enormous (and who are of course in no way accountable for any errors of fact or interpretation), include Joan Baron, Robert Carneiro, Eliot Chapple, Ann Condon, John Cox, Melvin Ember, Lenora Foerstel, Barter Fortune, Colin Frank, Hildred Geertz, June Goodfield, Jean Houston, Robert Howard, Irene Kubota, Madeline Lee, Nancy McDowell, Ann McLean, Jeannette Mirsky, Arthur Moore, Philleo Nash, Christopher Niebuhr, Paula Rubel, David Scherman, Bradd Shore, Nettie Terestman, and Martha Ullman West.

The staffs of the Alexander Turnbull National Library in Wellington, New Zealand, the Malinowski Archive of the British Library of

Political and Economic Science in London, the New-York Historical Society, the Menninger Foundation Archive in Topeka, Kansas, Columbia University and Barnard College libraries in New York, and the John Jermain Library of Sag Harbor have all assisted me, but my greatest debts for research help are to Mary Wolfskill of the Manuscript Reading Room of the Library of Congress, and to Jean Houston for giving me access to hundreds of pages of transcribed conversations she had with Dr. Mead.

Margot Adler, Charlene S. Baldridge, Gertrude Buckman, Alfred Connable, Ann Hooper, Daniel B. Jacobs, Suzanne Levine, Robert Littell Lowe, Fred Quinn, John Scanlon, Rosemarie Scherman, David Sills, Virginia L. Smyers, Edward Solomon and Frank Tuohy, among others, have led me to sources I might otherwise not have found.

For each of the three hundred or so people whose recollections of Margaret Mead I have been gathering since 1979, there must be four equally articulate others whom I would like to have talked to had time permitted. The interviews listed below were held throughout the United States, including three with neighbors from my own apartment building in New York, and during two trips abroad. Reo Fortune died shortly before an appointment I had to see him in England in January 1980; I went there anyway and talked with a number of his and his first wife's associates. (With Mead's third and first husbands I was luckier: Gregory Bateson was gracious during two visits I made to the Esalen Institute in California, and Luther Cressman has been generous with his time and attention, during several meetings on his coast and mine.) A March 1981 assignment from *Diversion* magazine, which led to a July article entitled "Margaret Mead's Other Pacific," made possible a journey to New Zealand and Australia.

Several people talked with me only on condition that their names appear nowhere in these pages, and some, whose names are listed in parentheses, I met not personally but through correspondence or over the telephone. A few of the interviews were brief, but nonetheless illuminating; others were held over several long sessions and evolved into friendships. To all I am grateful:

The Reverend Paul Abrecht, Léonie Adams, (June Adamson), Alexander Alland, Don Amador, Patsy Asch, Timothy Asch, Asen Balikci, Amy Bard, Gregory Bateson, Leona Baumgartner, August Becker, Richards Beekmann, Burton Benedict, Beryl Bernay, Dorothy Billings, Junius B. Bird, Miriam Birdwhistell, Florence Blau, Russell Bourne, Nancy Bowers, Emily Boxer, the Reverend Henri Breul, Richard Brickner, John Brockman, Noel J. Brown, Norman Brown, Marjorie Bull, Ralph Bulmer, Ruth Bunzel, Paul Byers, William D. Carey, Robert L. Carneiro, Edmund Carpenter, William

Carr, Robert Cassidy, Napoleon Chagnon, Eliot Chapple, Ann Chowning, Lambros Comitas, Carlton Coon, Vincent Crapanzano, Lee Cranberg, (George Cressman), Luther S. Cressman, Margaret T. Cussler, Mrs. Sherman Damon, David Dempsey, Harris Dillon, Virginia Dillon, Wilton Dillon, Robert DiPietro, Michael Dorris, (Cora Du Bois), Louis Dupree.

Ann Heidbreder Eastman, Gus Eckstein, William Edel, Monroe Edmonson, Ed Edwards, Fred Eggan, Joan Eggan, Mary Elder, Kenneth Emory, Jean Evans, Leslie H. Farber, Moishe Feldenkrais, Sir Raymond Firth, Lenora Foerstel, the Reverend Austin Ford, Anthony Forge, Meyer Fortes, Barter Fortune, George M. Foster, Robin Fox, Linda Bird Francke, Colin Frank, Kevin Frank, Josette Frank, Morton Freed, Ruth Freed, Derek Freeman, Anne Fremantle, Betty Friedan, (John Fryer), Ruth M. Galvin, Peter Gathercole, Ruth Garbus, W. R. Geddes, Hildred Geertz, Alice Gerlach, (John Gibson), Philip Gifford, Angela Gillian, Martha Glardon, Ellen Godwin, Augustus Goertz, Esther Goldfrank, Gale Goldschmidt, Walter Goldschmidt, June Goodfield, David Gordon, Paul Gottlieb, Linda Gottlieb, Ralph Graves, Metropolitan Paulos Gregorios, (Joel Grey), Barbara Guest.

Tore Hakansson, Ruth Strauss Hanauer, Marvin Harris, Harriet Harvey, Shirley Hazzard, Glenn Hendricks, Gertrude Hendrix, Florette Henri, Ken Heyman, Harold Hiatt, (Shirley Hinds), Lawrence Hirschfeld, Ian Hogbin, Lowell D. Holmes, Irving Horowitz, Jean Houston, Christian Howard, William W. Howells, Francis Hsu, Lawrence Hughes, Doris M. Hunter, Irene Hunter, Neal Hurwitz, John Hutchens, Bennetta Jules-Rosette.

Adrienne Kaeppler, Roger Keesing, Shelley Keesing, Caroline Kelly, Lawrence Kelly, Clive Kessler, Solon Kimball, Arden King, (Yasmina King), Otto Klineberg, Alex Kotlowitz, (Jonathan Kozol), Irene Kubota, Ruth Landmans, Daniel Lang, Percy Lee Langstaff, Jeanette Lappé, Marie Lawrence, Peter Lawrence, Leila Lee, Madeline Rosten Lee, Glen Leet, Mildred Robbins Leet, Harold Levine, Lucy Olga Lewton, Rosalind Lippel, Alan Lomax, Nancy Lutkehaus.

Frances Cooke Macgregor, Béla C. Maday, Deborah Kaplan Mandelbaum, Ruth Steinberg Manoff, Robert Masters, Rollo May, David McCurdy, Nancy McDowell, Alan McGowan, Ann McLean, Marijane Meaker, Karl Menninger, Roy Menninger, Walter Menninger, Mrs. William Menninger, Harold Meryman, Robert Mighell, Jeannette Mirsky, William Mitchell, Ashley Montagu, Arthur Moore, (the Right Reverend J. Brooke Mosley), Robert Murphy, Edith Nash, Philleo Nash, Joseph Neyer, Mary Niklas, Rita Niklas, Ben Nwose, the Reverend E. F. O'Doherty, Ned O'Gorman, Gonzalo Palacios G., (Helen Swick Perry), Anitra Pivnick, (Helene Pleasant), Nona Porter.

Dana Raphael, Roger Revelle, Edward Rice, Leonard Rieser, James Ritchie, Jane Beaglehole Ritchie, Dick Roberts, George Roberts, Lola Romanucci-Ross, Eleanor Rosenberg, Louise M. Rosenblatt, Abraham Rosman, Leo Rosten, (Philip Rosten), (Katharine Rothenberger), Paula Rubel, Vera Rubin, Richard Salisbury, Herschel Sarbin, Penelope Schoeffel, Robert L.

Schwartz, Theodore Schwartz, Barbara Seaman, (Irving Segel), Shari Segal, Harry Shapiro, Michael Shower, Chaplain Jean Sibley, David Sills, Bertram Slaff, Walter Slote, Francis Rawdon Smith, Michael G. Smith, Richard Sorenson, the Reverend Bonnell Spencer, Benjamin Spock, Karsten Stapelfeldt, Eleanor Pelham Korteheuer Stapelfeldt, Rexford Stead, Mrs. Harlan Stevens, Robert Stewart, Sarah Stewart, Leon Stover, Takeko Stover, Jozefa Stuart, Robert C. Suggs, Constance Sutton, Deborah Szekely.

Larry Tancredi, James Tanner, Lionel Tiger, Paul Tobias, John Todd, Nancy Todd, Donald Tuzin, (Heinz von Forster), Charles Wagley, Sherwood L. Washburn, Bennetta Washington, (Helena Malinowska Wayne), Winona Welch, Toni Werbell, Frank West, Martha Ullman West, Mary Linn White, Tim White, John Willey, Nancy Boyd Willey, Dorothea Willkie, Cathy Wylie, Marabel Young, Michael Young, Oliver Zangwill.

Notes

Notes refer to printed sources listed in the Bibliography
and to interviews listed in the Acknowledgments.

PART ONE

CHAPTER ONE

21
"We're the kind of people": Jean Houston, notes for "The Mind of Margaret Mead."

21
The motto of Emily's own father: Fanny Fogg McMaster, A *Family History*, p. 21, 8/14/81.

21
"In a sense," Mead recalled: A *History of Psychology in Autobiography*, p. 301.

22n
"My-father-majored-": Ibid., p. 295.

22
"She used to take me to weddings": *New York Herald Tribune*, Jinx Falkenburg column, October 23, 1949.

22
By the time: A *History of Psychology in Autobiography*, p. 301.

22
At four, "I": Houston notes.

22
"Most of the experiences": Houston notes.

23
"A fierce storm had just stopped": *New York Times*, December 17, 1901.

24
Philadelphia, Lincoln Steffens reflected: E. Digby Baltzell, *The Protestant Ethic and the Spirit of Class Authority and Leadership*.

24
This prospect did not entirely please: *Blackberry Winter: My Earlier Years*, p. 53.

24
Emily breast-fed Margaret: Ibid., p. 26.

24
"I loved the feel": Ibid., p. 54.

25
"It cannot be said": McMaster, A *Family History*, p. 32.

25
"Father was always attracted": Houston notes.

25
Mead appreciated his wife's: *Blackberry Winter*, p. 28.

25
Once he tried to escape: Houston notes.

25
"There are only two things": Irene Kubota interview.

26
Edward Mead, Margaret: Houston notes.

26·
There was never a question: Diary, Sept. 20, 1912, Library of Congress.

26
As a small child: *The Lactation Review* IV:1, p. 12.

26
These "fits" of anger: Houston notes.

27
"I spit on your hat": Ibid.

27
Nearly seventy years later: Nancy Todd interview.

27
Elizabeth "was born screaming": *The Lactation Review* IV:1, p. 8.

27
Still, Elizabeth's arrival: *Blackberry Winter*, p. 63.

27
In daydreams so vivid: Houston notes.

28
In a more evolved version: Houston notes.

28
"Wherever we were living": *A History of Psychology in Autobiography*, p. 300.

28
Unlike many cerebral women: Martha Ullman West interview.

28
Another constant daydream: *A History of Psychology in Autobiography*, p. 307.

28
Her notion, when she entered: Houston notes.

29
In 1980 Mary Catherine Bateson: Mary Catherine Bateson at American Anthropological Association convention in Cincinnati.

29
She also saw: Houston notes.

29
Every December 16: *Washington Post Book World*, May 26, 1968, p. 2.

29
The mistress of the house: Houston notes.

30
"I suppose that": Houston notes.

31
A contemporary, raised: Millicent Fenwick, "In the Days When Summers Seemed Endless," Op Ed Page, *New York Times*, August 14, 1981, p. A23.

31
"My name is Margaret Meade": Diary, May 14, 1911, Library of Congress.

31
"Miss Lucia kept a cow": Houston notes.

31
Margaret's maternal grandfather: McMaster, *A Family History*, p. 21.

31
By the age of ten: *A History of Psychology in Autobiography*, p. 300.

32
What she sought: Houston notes.

32
As he galloped: Houston notes.

32
"My highest hope": Diary, April 27, 1913, Library of Congress.

32
Mead could not quite remember: Letter to her grandmother, January 23, 1948, Library of Congress.

33
Margaret, obviously the smart one: Lenora Foerstel interview.

34
In an article: Library of Congress.

34
"Unless the setting star of Germany": *A History of Psychology in Autobiography*, p. 297.

35
"I never had to live through": Kubota interview.

Chapter Two

37
"I found the whole evening": *Blackberry Winter*, p. 94.

37
From home her brother wrote: Letter, October 19, 1919, Library of Congress.

38
"To realize the full implications": *Blackberry Winter*, p. 95.

38
She and Margaret were both assigned: Katharine Rothenberger interview.

38
Margaret also attached: Winona Welch interview.

40
Years later her composer friend: Letter from Colin McPhee, August 21, 1944, Library of Congress.

40
Manhattan, when she arrived: Anna Mary Wells, *Miss Marks and Miss Woolley*, p. 173.

40
"Those of us in the classes": Eleanor Rosenberg interview.

41
The Barnard campus: Helen Gahagan Douglas, *A Full Life*, p. 9.

41
The ideal woman of the 1920s: Alison Lurie, *The Language of Clothes*, p. 74.

41
The most convincing flapper: Pelham Stapelfeldt interview.

41
"These girls," Abbott was heard: *Blackberry Winter*, p. 103.

41
"She was a very unsophisticated": Lucy Olga Lewton interview.

41
"I didn't take my glasses off": Houston notes.

42
"I seem to remember": Nancy Boyd Willey interview.

42
"You *work* so hard!": Ruth Strauss Hanauer interview.

42
At examination time: Deborah Kaplan Mandelbaum interview.

42
"She gave off sparks": Nancy Boyd Willey interview.

43
Miss Latham, whose classes: Léonie Adams interview.

43
It was in this period: Houston notes.

43
"One of the things that's hard: Ibid.

45
Aggressive in her femininity: Ibid.

46
"I had one grand, glorious": Letter from Richard Mead, October 9, 1919,
Library of Congress.

46
"Margaret went to bed at ten": Mandelbaum interview.

48
"If you went to Barnard in those days": Jeannette Mirsky interview.

49
Maybe, one alumna speculated: Lewton interview.

49
It not only proved: Houston notes.

49
But one time her friends committed: Mandelbaum interview.

50
"You should have seen": Roger Revelle interview.

50
"If she had pointed to me": Richard Reeves interview.

CHAPTER THREE

51
Eventually Benedict was destined: *An Anthropologist at Work*, p. 68.

51
"I shall lie once with beauty": Ibid., p. 56.

52
"We have but this": Ibid.

52
"How of this": Ibid., p. 480.

52
Margaret, said someone: John Willey interview.

52
Anthropology seemed a new: *Continuities in Cultural Evolution*, p. x.

52
The mother of a classmate: Nancy Boyd Willey interview.

53
In 1891, after he began: George W. Stocking, *Race, Culture and Evolution: Essays in the History of Anthropology*, p. 170.

53
Boas did have a startling: *An Anthropologist at Work*, p. 4.

54
In 1919 he was censured: Stocking, *Race, Culture and Evolution*, p. 273.

54
Anthropology, Boas asserted: Judith Modell, *Ruth Benedict: Patterns of a Life*, p. 118.

54
To him, Mead said, anthropology: *An Anthropologist at Work*, p. 346.

54
Anthropology, wrote A. L. Kroeber: *American Anthropologist* 61 (1959), p. 104.

55
Boas's department, Mead wrote: *An Anthropologist at Work*, p. 344.

55
Her own guardian spirit: Ibid., p. 347.

55
"Your mask is getting thicker": Ibid., p. 540.

55
In anthropology Benedict found: Margaret Mead, "Ruth Fulton Benedict 1887–1948," *American Anthropologist* 51:3 (July–Sept. 1949), p. 458.

55
In her first year as a Vassar undergraduate: Kubota notes.

56
As a teacher, she: "Ruth Fulton Benedict," p. 458.

56
In Benedict's most halting lectures: Ibid., p. 459.

56
"They lean on my sense": Kubota notes.

56
Boas, Mead wrote, "spoke with an authority": *An Anthropologist at Work*, p. 4.

56
Boas, a later scholar said: Asen Balikci interview.

57
"I was the child Ruth never had": Houston notes.

57
"In March of 1923": *An Anthropologist at Work*, p. 67.

58
She wore the sling: Program for the pageant, undated, Library of Congress.

58
Once she confided: Letter from Barnard classmate Louise J. Schlichting.

CHAPTER FOUR

60
Mead could not have found: Letter from Edward Sherwood Mead, December 22, 1921, Library of Congress.

60
One of the reasons Luther: Houston notes.
60
"He'll be riding up": Ibid.
60
"But I want to get married": Ibid.
61
"You should have seen": Rosalind Lippel interview.
61
"I'm going to be famous": McMaster, *A Family History*, p. 68.
61
Luther spent the night: Luther Cressman interview.
63
She did not have time: Houston notes.
64
"Be lazy go crazy": *An Anthropologist at Work*, p. 287.
64
Intelligence tests, she said: *American Journal of Sociology* 31:5 (March 1926), p. 667.
64
"I don't like to think of you all alone": *An Anthropologist at Work*, p. 285.
64
"You could do this in Siberia": paraphrased in *Blackberry Winter*, pp. 127–128.
65
A New York businessman: Kenneth Emory interview.
65
Twenty-six years earlier: Edward Sapir, *Culture, Language and Personality: Selected Essays*.
65
Mead found the forty-year-old: *An Anthropologist at Work*, p. 286.
65
"It fills me with something like horror": *An Anthropologist at Work*, p. 53.
65
In Sapir: Letter from John Dollard, October 8, 1937, Library of Congress.
66
"Cultural anthropology, if": Sapir, *Culture, Language and Personality*, p. 150.
66
Pliny Earle Goddard, the museum's: *Anthropologists and What They Do*, p. 115.
67
Sapir implored Margaret: Houston notes.
67
With this in mind: Margaret Mead, Introduction to 1969 edition of "Social Organization of Manu'a" (*Bernice P. Bishop Museum Bulletin*, Honolulu), pp. xiv–xv.
68
That book, Mead wrote: Introduction to 1928 edition of *Coming of Age in Samoa*, p. 2.
68
Boas was beginning to work out: Stocking, *Race, Culture and Evolution*, p. 281.

68
He was also developing: Marvin Harris, *Sciences*, July–August 1983, p. 20.

70
"Samoa was not chosen": "Social Organization of Manu'a," p. 476.

70
They had their tasks: Introduction to 1928 edition of *Coming of Age in Samoa*, p. 5.

70
The "most important contribution": Letter from Franz Boas, July 14, 1925, Library of Congress.

72
On the contrary, as she had written: *An Anthropologist at Work*, p. 286.

73n
"You're certainly lucky": Luther Cressman interview.

73
"Of the heedless sun": *An Anthropologist at Work*, p. 88.

74
"Measure your thread and cut it": Houston notes.

74
"In the summer of 1925": *Letters from the Field*, p. 19.

74
"I don't know anybody who": Houston notes.

74
Talks with Sapir: Houston notes.

74
"As one emancipated young woman": Helen Swick Perry, *Psychiatrist of America: The Life of Harry Stack Sullivan*, p. 340.

75
"The young lad, twenty-eight years old": Luther Cressman, private communication, 1928.

CHAPTER FIVE

76
What she would learn: Grant application to National Research Council.

76
Mead's findings, Boas thought: Letter from Franz Boas, July 14, 1925, Library of Congress.

76
Between them, they worried: *An Anthropologist at Work*, p. 290.

76
Mead should watch out, Boas suggested: Letter from Boas, July 14, 1925, Library of Congress.

77
Much of what she would: *Blackberry Winter*, p. 138.

77
Her own formidable energies: Letter from Boas, July 14, 1925, Library of Congress.

77
"It's all true about the South Seas!": James Davidson, *Samoa mo Samoa*, p. 5.

77
In the late nineteenth century: Ibid., p. 4.

77
Henry Adams thought: Ibid.

78
In the spring of 1925: *An Anthropologist at Work*, p. 290.
78
Louise Bogan tried to console: *What the Woman Lived: Selected Letters of Louise Bogan*, ed. by Ruth Limmer (New York, Harcourt, Brace, Jovanovich, 1973), p. 93.
78
"I trust Margaret": Ibid., p. 93.
78
In Honolulu, on her way: "Social Organization of Manu'a," 1969, p. xvi.
78
"Picture me for these next": *Letters from the Field*, p. 22.
79
When she left Hawaii: Ibid., p. 23.
79
"Airplanes scream overhead": Ibid.
79
"I received a reasonably frosty": "Social Organization of Manu'a," p. xviii.
79
With a few unimportant exceptions: *Coming of Age in Samoa*, p. 262.
79
Ta'u, she told Boas: *Letters from the Field*, p. 28.
80
"The chief, Tufele, who is": Ibid., p. 29.
80
Furious rains in "drops": John Koffend, *A Letter to My Wife*, p. 134.
80
The air, Mead wrote home: *Letters from the Field*, p. 26.
80
The letters that mattered most: *An Anthropologist at Work*, p. 292.
80
"Develop all the expedients": Ibid., p. 301.
80
"Imagining what would have": Ibid., p. 202.
81
Nearly a century later: Linda Connor interview.
81
Not with the natives, who: *Coming of Age in Samoa*, p. 266.
81
Some critics would later: *Letters from the Field*, p. 29.
81
And so, when she arrived: Ibid., p. 36.
81
This household gave her: Introduction to 1969 edition of "Social Organization in Manu'a," p. 4.
81
Mead's first Christmas away: *Letters from the Field*, p. 41.
81
After even a few hours: Ibid., p. 39.
82
There were odd moments: Houston notes.
82
But the Navy-issue food: *Letters from the Field*, p. 26.

82
Just after Christmas: Ibid., p. 43.
82
Manu'a, she noted: *An Anthropologist at Work*, pp. 73–74.
82
Boas had warned Mead: Ibid.
82
One Sunday noon she wrote home: *Letters from the Field*, p. 38.
83
Very little of what Mead would report: "Social Organization of Manu'a," p. 5.
83
"Speaking on one's feet": *Coming of Age in Samoa*, p. 270.
83
"In Samoa I learned": *Male and Female*, p. 25.
83
"America excels": *Letters from the Field*, p. 35.
83
These required speeches: Ibid.
83
At times she had to try to rest: Houston notes.
85
"If shock is the result": *Coming of Age in Samoa*, pp. 133–134.
85
And though it was rumored: Ibid., p. 151.
86
To Samoans, Mead would write: Ibid., p. 99.
86
They told her of a curious activity: Ibid., p. 93.
86
In the moonlight, she wrote: Ibid., p. 19.
86
She would tell of: Ibid., p. 135.
86
She was satisfied that adolescence: Ibid., p. 157.
86
Samoans had no notion: Ibid., p. 105.
86
"Most men": Luther Cressman interview.
87
In future field trips: Houston notes.
87
Sapir's letter, as she recalled: Ibid.
87
"Oh, all the holes there are": *Letters from the Field*, p. 55.
88
As her Samoan visit: *Letters from the Field*, p. 51.
88
That book, to the satisfaction: *Coming of Age in Samoa*, Preface to the 1973 edition.
88
Her research, she said: Ibid.

CHAPTER SIX

91
New Zealand, she later said: Foreword to Ritchie, *Growing Up in New Zealand*.

92
Too poor to board there: Barter Fortune letter to Peter Lawrence, December 17, 1979.

93
Reo's spirit, which a friend: Peter Gathercole, obituary of Fortune in Proceedings of the Royal Anthropological Institute, January 7, 1980.

93
"In many ways innocent": *Blackberry Winter*, p. 158.

93
A man who studied: Richard Salisbury interview.

93
From Samoa she had written: *Letters from the Field*, p. 39.

94
"Are we to reject": W. H. R. Rivers, *Instinct and the Unconscious*.

95
"There once was a fellow": Letter from Barter Fortune to Peter Gathercole, June 10, 1980.

95
Their fellow passengers: *Blackberry Winter*, p. 161.

96
It was flattering: Houston notes.

CHAPTER SEVEN

99
She also found time: Letter to Kenneth Emory, March 24, 1928, Library of Congress.

99
Mead's month in Italy: Ibid.

99
The two women also: Houston notes.

100
"That Samoan eye trouble": Letter to Emory, March 24, 1928, Library of Congress.

101
Mead's boss, Dr. Clark Wissler: *Anthropologists and What They Do*, p. 116.

101
Her monograph: *An Anthropologist at Work*, p. 207.

101
"What would you have to say": Letter from William Morrow, 1927, Library of Congress.

102
Later Wilson wrote: Edmund Wilson, *The Twenties*, p. 95.

102
"What's this about Margaret": *What the Woman Lived*, p. 36.

102
So, not the least bit coincidentally: Letter to Emory, March 24, 1928, Library of Congress.

103
"Is it any wonder": Letter from Luther Cressman to Dorothy C. Loch, July 8, 1927.

104
On June 25, from Berlin: Letter from Mead to her mother, June 25, 1927, Library of Congress.

104
Margaret returned to New York: Letter to Kenneth Emory, January 24, 1928, Library of Congress.

105
He cautioned her, as others would: Letter from William Morrow, June 20, 1928, Library of Congress.

105
She claimed no alimony: Mead-Cressman divorce document, courtesy Luther Cressman.

106
The Admiralties would be: "An Investigation of the Thought of Primitive Children."

106
Anthropological rendezvous: *Blackberry Winter*, p. 165.

107
In August 1928 she revised: Will, Library of Congress.

PART TWO

CHAPTER EIGHT

111
"She isn't planning": Esther Goldfrank Wittfogel interview.

111
Before she left: Letter to Bronislaw Malinowski, August 9, 1928, Library of Congress.

111
He could cure it, he said: Letter to Bronislaw Malinowski, Sept. 10, 1928.

112
On the *Malolo:* Ibid.

112
"I can't *stand* the way you live": Interview with a Barnard classmate who wishes to be anonymous.

112
"And make a dash": *Blackberry Winter*, p. 168.

113
That book, the great Malinowski: Reo Fortune, *Sorcerers of Dobu*, p. xxii.

114
There they would begin: *An Anthropologist at Work*, p. 196.

114
Sex antagonisms were so strong: "Living with the Natives of Melanesia," *Natural History*, Jan.–Feb., 1931.

115
"But you've simply *got*": Caroline Kelly interview.

115
Certainly he seemed: *An Anthropologist at Work*, p. 309.
116
"I dreamed last night": Ibid., p. 310.
116
If there was a nervous air: Bridges, *Walk-About in Australia*, p. 40.
116
The next leg of their voyage: *Letters from the Field*, p. 62.
116
On their way north: Ibid.
116
On the way to Banyalo's: Ibid., p. 63.
117
Louise Bogan, who received: *What the Woman Lived*, p. 37.
117
"The ethnologist," Mead wrote: "Living with the Natives of Melanesia."
118
"When I arrived among": Houston notes.
118
This was old news to Mead: "Talk-Boy," *Asia* 31:3 (March, 1931).
119
The Dobuans, by his standards: Fortune, *Sorcerers of Dobu*, p. 211.
119
Mead's luggage: "Living with the Natives of Melanesia," p. 66.
119
In the back of her own mind: *From the South Seas*, pp. xi–xii.
120
But she found that despite: Ibid., p. 12.
121
The younger children: *Growing Up in New Guinea*, p. 19.
121
"The Manus are not aware": *Manus Religion*, p. 8.
121
"A tall, shaggy-headed sorcerer": "Living with the Natives of Melanesia," p. 70.
122
"The little bush monkey, naked": "Talk-Boy," p. 147.
123
"Rapport was a matter of seconds": Casagrande, *In the Company of Man*, p. 1179.
124
A story has been told: Meyer Fortes, "Anthropology and the Psychological Disciplines," in Ernest Gellner, ed., *Soviet and Western Anthropology*, p. 195.
125
Ruth Benedict had intimated: *An Anthropologist at Work*, p. 334.
125
Mead herself admitted: Houston notes.

CHAPTER NINE
126
In Manus, Reo and Margaret: *Letters from the Field*, p. 77.

127
"It was great": Letter from William Morrow, January 11, 1929, Library of Congress.

127
[Ellis and Malinowski quotes]: *Nation* 127:330 (Oct. 17, 1928), p. 402.

127
H. L. Mencken commented: *American Mercury* XV:59 (Nov. 1928), p. 379.

127
Mary Austin . . . wrote: *Birth Control Review*, June 1929.

128
A. L. Kroeber . . . wrote: Letter, October 11, 1929.

128
Mead replied that: Letter to Professor W. A. Brownell, March 10, 1930, Library of Congress.

128
"It is dreadful": *An Anthropologist at Work*, p. 409.

129
When Ruth was doing field work: Ibid., p. 94.

130
Her response was to resolve: *Blackberry Winter*, p. 183.

131
"I set the pace": Ibid., p. 184.

131
In January 1930 she wrote: Letter to Herbert E. Gregory, January 7, 1930, Library of Congress.

132
"I learned very early": Houston notes.

132
"If I'd started putting in": Ibid.

132
She scarcely knew the other: Houston notes.

133
"If we would go": *Blackberry Winter*, p. 189.

133
Their informants, Mead wrote: *An Anthropologist at Work*, p. 314.

134
"We have had a year": Letter to Reo Fortune from his father, October 8, 1930, Library of Congress.

134
The Indians with whom she worked: *The Changing Culture of an Indian Tribe*, p. 16.

135
"I wonder if any human planning": *An Anthropologist at Work*, p. 317.

136
Beginning his first term as a professor: Luther Cressman, unpublished manuscript, "The Golden Journey."

137
Bristling at another reviewer's: *Letters from the Field*, p. 101.

137
"In the evenings," she remembered: *Blackberry Winter*, p. 193.

137
"He believes in": Memo, July 19, 1931, Library of Congress.

138
"I regard him": Letter from Radcliffe-Brown, November 2, 1931, Library of Congress.

CHAPTER TEN

139
"You never can quite tell": *Letters from the Field*, p. 120.

139
Their country, Reo Fortune: Reo Fortune, "Arapesh Warfare," *American Anthropologist*, 41:1 (1939), p. 22.

140
"She must have been": Roger Revelle interview.

140
"A little seasickish": *Letters from the Field*, p. 103.

140
Next, in Sydney: Mead Will, October 22, 1930, Library of Congress.

140
Unable to proceed: *Blackberry Winter*, p. 194.

141
"The way to": *Letters from the Field*, p. 128.

141
Altogether, the place was: Ibid., p. 109.

141
"They never tire": Ibid., p. 110.

141
The children, who Mead: Ibid., p. 109.

142
They saw the world: *Sex and Temperament in Three Primitive Societies*, p. 135.

142
When a baby: Ibid., p. 36.

142
These people were: *Letters from the Field*, p. 109.

142
Even if a small settlement: *Technique and Personality: Three Lectures by Margaret Mead, Junius B. Bird and Hans Himmelheber* (New York, Museum of Primitive Art [Distributed by New York Graphic Society], 1963), pp. 9–10.

142
Although Mead was to celebrate: *Sex and Temperament in Three Primitive Societies*, p. 141.

143
"Women and children must": Ibid., p. 65.

143
"No one here": *Letters from the Field*, p. 113.

143
"We even have": Ibid., p. 117.

143
Marrying, to the Arapesh: *Sex and Temperament in Three Primitive Societies*, p. 92.

144
"As the night falls": Ibid., p. 6.

144
In April 1932: *Letters from the Field*, p. 117.

144
"I repeat my cry": Ibid., p. 128.

144
"Oh, how I wish": *An Anthropologist at Work*, p. 319.

144
"People need to be told": Ibid., p. 321.

144
"Do you realize what": Ibid., p. 319.

145
Margaret had written: Ibid.

145
When Mead came home: Ibid., p. 322.

145
Mead and Fortune: Fortune, "Arapesh Warfare," p. 27.

145
While she was there: *Blackberry Winter*, p. 199.

145
Arranging to leave: *Letters from the Field*, p. 124.

145
In the mind of: Ibid., p. 130.

145
The Sepik area: David Lipset, *Gregory Bateson: The Legacy of a Scientist*, p. 125. The quotations are from A. C. Haddon's "Report to the Electors to a Fellowship to St. John's College," unpublished.

146
"The blessed thing": *Letters from the Field*, p. 124.

146
The choice of their next: *Sex and Temperament in Three Primitive Societies*, p. 174.

146n
Missionaries, Mead's later: Geoffrey Gorer, *Africa Dances* (1962 ed.), p. 174.

146n
Fortune had made: Michael Young, "A Topology of the Dobu Mission," *Canberra Anthropologist*, September 1980, p. 87.

146n
"The mission's chief contribution": Ibid., pp. 91, 101.

146
"We had never heard": *Sex and Temperament in Three Primitive Societies*, p. 165.

147
The problem they caused: *Letters from the Field*, p. 130.

147
"Perhaps no other endogamous": Peggy Golde, ed., *Women in the Field*, p. 327.

147
The Mundugumor, Fortune wrote: *An Anthropologist at Work*, p. 330.

148
Although war, headhunting: *Sex and Temperament in Three Primitive Societies*, p. 167.

148
"They are always": *Letters from the Field*, p. 135.

148
It was hardly surprising: *Sex and Temperament in Three Primitive Societies*, p. 175.
148
The Mundugumor were: *Letters from the Field*, p. 135.
149
"I shall be 31 next week": Ibid., p. 136.
149
Only later and elsewhere: Houston notes.
149
"When we were first married": *Blackberry Winter*, p. 206.
150
A man named Omblean: *Sex and Temperament in Three Primitive Societies*, p. 229.
150
Another misfit: Ibid., p. 232.
150
It was among the Mundugumor: *Blackberry Winter*, p. 206.
151
"I'd always accepted this": Houston notes.
151
"I'm looking forward": *An Anthropologist at Work*, p. 330.
151
To her enduring disdain: *Blackberry Winter*, p. 205.
151
"Of course I knew": Houston notes.
151
A letter he wrote to Malinowski: Fortune to Malinowski, Malinowski Archive, London.
152
Of the Mundugumor: *Letters from the Field*, p. 137.
152
"The people had made": *Blackberry Winter*, p. 207.

CHAPTER ELEVEN

154
On hand were: *Blackberry Winter*, p. 210.
154
"You're tired": *Blackberry Winter*, p. 208.
155
"How do you know": Ian Hogbin interview.
155
The two men had been: *Blackberry Winter*, p. 164.
155
"I am the only": Lipset, *Gregory Bateson*, p. 129.
156
To the distress: Ibid., p. 134.
156
"I feel I could scarcely": Ibid., p. 132.
156
Looking back later: Bateson's talk at American Association for the Advancement of Science forum honoring Mead, 1975.
157
"At times Reo and I": *Blackberry Winter*, p. 12.

157
"I had made": Bateson at AAAS forum.

157
If a mentor: Gregory Bateson interview.

157
Faith in great works: "Gregory Bateson: Early Biography," in John Brockman, ed., *About Bateson*, p. 50.

157
"As anthropologists do": Ibid., p. 135.

157
Margaret and Reo had thought: Letter from Reo Fortune to Raymond Firth, November 11, 1931, Library of Congress.

158
From Fortune's point: *Blackberry Winter*, p. 211.

159
Sometimes Gregory himself: Bateson interview.

159
"My pen leaps": Note, undated, Library of Congress.

159
Malinowski, of course: Lipset, *Gregory Bateson*, p. 123.

159
Reo Fortune remarked: Ibid.

160
"I was at first shocked": Ibid., p. 136.

160
"Although Reo and I": *Blackberry Winter*, p. 212.

160
Anthropology, Bateson had written: Lipset, *Gregory Bateson*, p. 121.

160
"The dashed language": *An Anthropologist at Work*, p. 334.

160
"Reo later said": Houston notes.

161
Even Mead, who: Ibid.

161
They too lived: *Sex and Temperament in Three Primitive Societies*, p. 259.

161n
Mead's four months: Deborah Gewertz at Barnard College forum, April 8, 1983.

162
Thinking back to: *Sex and Temperament in Three Primitive Societies*, p. 265.

162
The Tchambuli, as far as: Ibid., pp. 279–280.

162
The three tribes': Ibid., p. 282.

162
But why was it, she: Ibid., p. 292.

162
Men, she noted: Houston notes.

162
"Only in the sense": Personal communication from Ann McLean.

162
"Reo had a better ear": Houston notes.

163
"We're really all": *An Anthropologist at Work*, p. 335.
164
If he had never: Bateson interview.
164
In an enclosed note: Lipset, *Gregory Bateson*, p. 137.
164n
"Your book, Ruth": *An Anthropologist at Work*, p. 338.
164
"This seems too light": Judith Modell, *Ruth Benedict: Patterns of a Life*, p. 211.
165
"To find an appropriate": Lipset, *Gregory Bateson*, p. 109.
165
"If you're out": Bateson interview.
166
"This," Fortune said: Caroline Kelly interview.

CHAPTER TWELVE

167
She had "a fine sense": Personal communication from Cora Du Bois, March 2, 1981.
168
Another article: *New York Daily News*, March 26, 1969; quoting a *New York Sun* article of 1939.
168
To one lecture agent: Memo, January 4, 1934, Library of Congress.
168
In February 1934: *New York American*, February 3, 1934.
169
"I am not going to be": Letter from Reo Fortune to Bronislaw Malinowski, December 1935, Malinowski Archive.
169
In another shipboard letter: Letter from Fortune to Malinowski, November 4, 1934, Malinowski Archive.
169
From Sydney, in late January: Letter from Fortune to Malinowski, January 28, 1934, Malinowski Archive.
170
In April 1935: Letter to Radcliffe-Brown, April 25, 1935, Library of Congress.
171
A colleague who: Confidential interviews.
171
Another perceived him: Oliver Zangwill interview.
171
"She had already": Francis Rawdon Smith interview.
171
"That's the last book": *Blackberry Winter*, p. 199.
172
In another letter: Letter from Fortune to Malinowski, March 19, 1935, Malinowski Archive.

172
She confessed her dream: Letter to Radcliffe-Brown, December 4, 1935, Library of Congress.

172
Another friend of Fortune's: Francis Rawdon Smith interview.

172
His confreres had: Lipset, *Gregory Bateson*, p. 148.

173
Bateson's conversations with: Lipset, *Gregory Bateson*, p. 149.

174
Margaret might have been spared: Confidential interview.

175
"The scheme was so large": Letter for Larry's Seventy-fifth Birthday, November 9, 1965, Library of Congress.

176
The differing views: Ibid.

176
Frank "did not see": Senn interview, p. 5.

177
Her trip to Ireland: Letter to Lloyd Warner, February 28, 1935, Library of Congress.

177
"I have just reached": Letter to Ian Hogbin, November 28, 1934, Library of Congress.

177
The project that emerged: Preface to 1961 Beacon Press edition of *Cooperation and Competition*, p. v.

177
One field worker: Jeannette Mirsky interview.

178
But the task: *Cooperation and Competition*, p. 518.

178
The book that developed: Ibid.

178
"I hope the uncomfortable": Letter to Lloyd Warner, April 1, 1935, Library of Congress.

179
"We must bear in mind": *Sex and Temperament in Three Primitive Societies*, p. 322.

180
Cannibalism, Gorer wrote: *Africa Dances* (1935 ed.), p. 316.

180
"When Geoffrey arrived": Houston notes.

181
Really thorough field work: Gorer, *Africa Dances* (1935 ed.), p. 245.

181
In Gorer's *Africa Dances:* Houston notes.

181
For four months: Gorer, *Africa Dances* (1962 ed.), p. viii.

182
"Gregory Bateson had": Letter to Lloyd Warner, April 1, 1935, Library of Congress.

182
Miss Lucia: Ibid.

182
Mead did not want: Ibid.
182
"Since the month": New York City Probate Court files.
183
On October 12: Letter to Radcliffe-Brown, October 12, 1935, Library of Congress.
183
"A particular gift": Letter to A. L. Kroeber, November 2, 1933, Library of Congress.
183
Radcliffe-Brown answered: Letter from Radcliffe-Brown, February 7, 1936, Library of Congress.
184
That question gave: Letter to Radcliffe-Brown, December 4, 1935, Library of Congress.
184
Mead applied for: Grant application to Social Science Research Council, Library of Congress.
184
She also wrote: Letter to Theodore Roosevelt, Jr., October 29, 1935, Library of Congress.
184
"My chief feeling": Lipset, *Gregory Bateson*, p. 150.
185
Her fellow passengers: *Letters from the Field*, p. 156.
185
Geoffrey Gorer suggested: *Cooperation and Competition* (1961 ed.), p. 519.
185
It would have been quite: *Letters from the Field*, p. 156.
185
She had written: Letter to parents, "On the Eve of Sailing, 1936," Library of Congress.
186
Nor did she allude: Letter to Fortune, March 3, 1936, Library of Congress.
186
Fortune would not: Letter from Fortune to Malinowski, April 20, 1936, Malinowski Archive.
186
Margaret then wrote: Letter to parents, March 1936, Library of Congress.
187
This medium, hearing: *Blackberry Winter*, p. 229.

CHAPTER THIRTEEN

188
Later, the anthropologist: Clifford Geertz, "Form and Variation in Balinese Village Structure," *American Anthropologist* LXI:6 (December 1959).
188
Its "network of back roads": Colin McPhee, *A House in Bali*, p. 10.
188
McPhee also noted: Ibid., p. 17.
189
Mead was elated: *Blackberry Winter*, p. 224.

189
Once, Erik Erikson writes: *Identity and the Life Cycle*, p. 102.
189
"I suppose you have heard": Letter to Erik Erikson, July 12, 1936, in Houston notes.
189
By Western standards: Margaret Mead with Gregory Bateson, *Balinese Character: A Photographic Analysis*, p. xvi.
189
"How much predisposition": Ibid.
189
In 1934, in an essay: *An Anthropologist at Work*, p. 283.
190
And, as Mead would write: *Balinese Character*, p. 17.
190
She wrote cheerful letters: *Letters from the Field*, p. 159.
190
The island "teemed": *Blackberry Winter*, p. 229.
190
It was Spies, Mead: Hans Rhodius, ed., *Walter Spies*, p. 358.
191
The esthetes, in turn: *Letters from the Field*, p. 195.
191
Bateson had intended: Gregory Bateson, *Steps to an Ecology of the Mind*, p. 108.
191
"It seems to me": Letter to Jeannette Mirsky, April 2, 1938, in Houston notes.
192
It was clear to the Balinese: *Letters from the Field*, p. 182.
192
Not until late at night: *Blackberry Winter*, p. 234.
192
Mead's head swam: Letter to Erich Fromm, March 28, 1937, from Bajoeng Gede, in Houston notes.
192
The newlyweds were tired: Houston notes.
192
"Sir," a midwife would: *Balinese Character*, p. 29.
192
"Anyone who visits a house": *Letters from the Field*, p. 165.
193
Everything strange frightened: *Balinese Character*, p. 29.
193
"Not an ounce": Letter to John Dollard, September 23, 1936, in Houston notes.
193
If he were going to Bali: *Letters from the Field*, p. 22.
193
When she held: *Balinese Character*, p. 84.
193
The Balinese were happy: Ibid., p. 68.
193
Their lives were not: Ibid., p. 255.

193
She "burst into tears": Houston notes.

194
Without their trances: *Balinese Character*, p. 5.

195
They had chosen this: *Letters from the Field*, pp. 168, 172.

195
Most of the five hundred: Lipset, *Gregory Bateson*, p. 155.

195
But Mead, ever ready: *Blackberry Winter*, pp. 232–233.

196
And even so: *Letters from the Field*, p. 200.

196
Finding Walter Spies: Rhodius, ed., *Walter Spies*, p. 359.

196
Margaret and Gregory would return: *Letters from the Field*, p. 195.

196
This young man: Ibid., p. 182.

196
Madé was "just": Ibid., p. 203.

196
"For a ceremony": *Letters from the Field*, p. 203.

197
"Have we medicine": Ibid., p. 171.

197
Once she wrote: Ibid., p. 179.

197
After Gregory's mother died: Letter to Emily Fogg Mead, August 29, 1936, Library of Congress.

197
"It gives one": *Letters from the Field*, p. 191.

197
During Beatrice Bateson's: Lipset, *Gregory Bateson*, p. 154.

197
"Njonjah Biang we": *Letters from the Field*, p. 195.

197
Cremations, she wrote: Ibid., 209.

198
What a baby was: *Balinese Character*, p. 24.

198
"Tomorrow," she wrote: *Letters from the Field*, p. 189.

198
Balinese were also: Letter to Erik Erikson, July 12, 1936, in Houston notes.

198
"I feel I am entitled": *Letters from the Field*, p. 174.

199
"The combination of": Letter to Karen Horney, May 30, 1937, in Houston notes.

199
"I've got my major clues": Letter to Ruth Benedict, August 9, 1936, in Houston notes.

199
"Ruth, darling": Letter to Ruth Benedict, October 1, 1936, in Houston notes.

199
One letter congratulated: Letter to Karen Horney, May 30, 1935, in Houston notes.

199
"You can't get": Letter to Jeannette Mirsky, April 2, 1937, in Houston notes.

200
"You always answer": Letter to Geoffrey Gorer, June 6, 1937, in Houston notes.

200
On December 16, 1937: Jane Belo, *Trance in Bali*, p. 131.

200
At a similar performance: Ibid., pp. 124–125.

201
That winter she: *Blackberry Winter*, p. 236.

201
"We have been": *Letters from the Field*, p. 213.

201n
Reo Fortune had written: Letter from Fortune to Malinowski, August 14, 1937, Malinowski Archive.

202
"Above, the shores": *Letters from the Field*, p. 215.

202
She sent word home: Letter to Clark Wissler, March 22, 1938, in Houston notes.

202
"Take my advice": Lipset, *Gregory Bateson*, p. 155.

202
Their fellow *Maatsuycker* passengers: *Letters from the Field*, p. 218.

203
Next, heading up the Sepik: Ibid., p. 219.

203
Days after she and Bateson: Ibid., p. 223.

203
"My house would be filled": Ibid.

203
Anthony Forge, who: Forge interview.

204
Part of what Mead: *Letters from the Field*, p. 230.

204
In springtime, she wrote: Ibid., p. 221.

204
"You don't know": Australian broadcast transcript.

204
In Tambunam, she: *Letters from the Field*, p. 220.

204
This "was an eight-foot": Ibid.

205
One of her letters was written: Ibid., p. 227.

205
"It is significant": Letter to Gardner Murphy, September 27, 1938, in Houston notes.

206
"I am": Letter to Buell Quain, 1938, in Houston notes.

207
"You say you": Letter to Cora Du Bois, July 11, 1938, in Houston notes.

207
"As far as I know": Letter to Ernest Beaglehole, July 11, 1938, in Houston notes.

208
Mead missed one: Letter to Geoffrey Gorer, August 6, 1938, in Houston notes.

208
"Don't you see": Letter to Gorer, October 17, 1938, in Houston notes.

209
Two of her Iatmul: *Letters from the Field*, p. 223.

209
They had succeeded: *Blackberry Winter*, pp. 327–328.

209
Then, after eight months: *Letters from the Field*, p. 155.

209
"The official who": Letter from Jane Belo to her mother, February 10, 1939, Library of Congress.

210n
Mead later wrote: Rhodius, ed., *Walter Spies*, p. 359.

210
Belo went into more detail: Letter from Jane Belo to "Johnny," February 10, 1939, Library of Congress.

210
Thank heaven for: Ibid.

210
A bonus of the revisit: *Letters from the Field*, p. 155.

CHAPTER FOURTEEN

211
"I had the": Houston notes.

211
Gregory Bateson wrote: Letter from Bateson to Belo, May 16, 1939, Library of Congress.

212
At that time: *The Lactation Review* IV:1 (1979), p. 7.

212
"You're not going": *Blackberry Winter*, p. 253.

212
"In 1939," Mead wrote: *From the South Seas: Studies of Adolescence and Sex in Primitive Societies*, p. xxiii.

213
One letter, concerning: Letter to Eleanor Roosevelt, in Houston notes.

215
"As to whether": December 30, 1939, letter, Library of Congress.

216
"The important thing": Bateson interview.

217
The afternoon before: Letter to E. J. Lindgren, December 12, 1939, Library of Congress.

217
"For the record": Letter to Leona Baumgartner, June 28, 1973, Library of Congress.

217
"It was rather silly": Benjamin Spock interview.

217
"Precisely the first member": Mary Catherine Bateson, *Our Own Metaphor* (New York, Knopf, 1972), p. 119.

217
The Philadelphia visit: Houston notes.

218
When Benjamin Spock: Spock interview.

218
"Don't worry": Philleo Nash interview.

218
"I didn't passionately": *The Lactation Review* IV:1 (1979), pp. 8–9.

218
"There is some": Letter from Lawrence Frank, "1939," Library of Congress.

219
"Cathy," said one: Georgiana Stevens interview.

219
"Gregory thinks of": Letter to Lois Murphy, May 10, 1940, Library of Congress.

219
"I can get": Letter to Richard Mead, July 1, 1940, Library of Congress.

219
"We only got": Lipset, *Gregory Bateson*, p. 163.

220
"Divide in order": Ibid., p. 275.

220
This group's "promise": Raymond Nelson, *Van Wyck Brooks*, pp. 236–237.

220
"Are we to": Lipset, *Gregory Bateson*, p. 167.

222
This committee, Mead wrote: *An Anthropologist at Work*, p. 557.

222
"Being a Marine": Florette Henri interview.

222
In any case: *And Keep Your Powder Dry*, p. xxvi.

222
They looked forward: Ibid., p. xxvii.

222
And felt scorn: Ibid., p. xxix.

223
"How can we": Ibid., p. 183.

223
Bateson, who at the time: Bateson interview.

225
This 1940 meeting: Rhoda Métraux statement at American University Seminar, March 1980.

225
Gregory had been: Letter to Beatrice Bateson, quoted in Lipset, *Gregory Bateson*, p. 166.

226
"As an American": Béla C. Maday, ed., *Anthropology and Society* (Washington, D.C., Anthropological Society, 1975), p. 44.

227
"To the great good fortune": *The Problem of Changing Food Habits*, National Research Council Bulletin No. 108, October 1943, p. 16.

CHAPTER FIFTEEN

228
"I love you, my darling": Letter to Gregory Bateson, September 1941, Library of Congress.

228
There would be no need: Letter from Ralph Linton, December 24, 1941, Library of Congress.

229
She made note: *And Keep Your Powder Dry*, p. 7.

229
When she said that "a social virus": Ibid., pp. 241, 246.

229
"Thou shalt not answer": W. H. Auden, "Under Which Lyre."

229
Science, she said, was a tool: *New York Times*, June 5, 1941.

231
"I leave ideas": Margaret Cussler interview.

231
His students were: U.S. Naval Administrative History of World War II, Vol. 1.

232
Bateson's effort was "to dissect": *The Study of Culture at a Distance*, p. 302.

232
Bateson's fifty-two page: Research on Contemporary Cultures Archive, American University.

232
Mead was indebted to the N.R.C.: *The Problem of Changing Food Habits*, National Research Council Bulletin No. 108, October 1943, p. 179.

232
"When I went to Washington": Houston notes.

233
The knottiest question: Letter to Leo Rosten, October 14, 1942, Library of Congress.

233
"It didn't end up": Houston notes.

233
In 1942, Mead and Kurt Lewin: *The Small Conference*, p. 113. *The Problem of Changing Food Habits*, paraphrase.

234
Good block leaders: Joan Campbell at American Anthropological Association Meeting, Cincinnati, 1979.

235
All this while: *And Keep Your Powder Dry*, p. 328.

236
Geoffrey Gorer was: Letter to Gorer, July 15, 1942, Library of Congress.

236
"It was as innovative": Vera Rubin interview.

236
"Until an authentic Martian": Book-of-the-Month Club review, December 1942.

236
The review in *Reveille*: *Reveille*, May 1943.
236
The most urgent task: *And Keep Your Powder Dry*, p. 256.
237
In California, Mead: Ibid., p. 101.
237
"Germans," Mead said: Houston notes.
238
Boas, said his biographer: Melville J. Herskovits, *Franz Boas: The Science of Man in the Making* (New York, Scribners, 1953), pp. 120–121.
238
Boas's last words: *An Anthropologist at Work*, p. 355.
238
Mead spoke up always: Houston notes.
238
"I enjoy people": Ibid.
238
The assignment to England: Letter to Jane Belo, January 8, 1944, Library of Congress.
238
Studying a civilized culture: Ibid.
239
She also tried to figure: Ibid.
239
Her task on this trip: American Museum of Natural History Margaret Mead Film Festival, 1981.
239
"Everything got pretty": American University seminar, March 1980.
239
In London Mead: Letter to Jane Belo, January 8, 1944, Library of Congress.
239
To her hostesses: Letter, December 10, 1943, to "Steve and Jolliffe," Library of Congress.
239
She was touched by: *And Keep Your Powder Dry*, p. xvii.
240
The British, she would later: *The Study of Culture at a Distance*, p. 349.
240
The British countryside: "A G.I. View of Britain," *New York Times Magazine*, March 19, 1944.
240
The psychological warfare: Houston notes.
241
Bateson wrote to two aunts: Lipset, *Gregory Bateson*, p. 175.
241
Calcutta appalled Bateson: Bateson interview.
242
In the spring: *New York Herald Tribune*, May 23, 1943.

CHAPTER SIXTEEN
243
In December 1981: "Nova" television program, December 15, 1981.

243
The 1943 Christmas: Letter to Jane Belo, January 8, 1944, Library of Congress.

244
Since Cathy was very small: *New York Post*, May 17, 1944.

244
Mead never took basic: Houston notes.

244
Few families' interests: Eulogy at funeral for Lawrence Frank, 1968.

246
Cathy was "climbing": *A Rap on Race*, p. 60.

246
One ritual Margaret did perform: Houston notes.

246
Margaret's own curls: Houston notes.

247
Another time Cathy: Margaret Cussler interview.

247
"We might have a field day": Letter from Larry Frank, n.d. (1940s), Library of Congress.

247
Although Margaret appreciated: Houston notes.

248
Mary Frank, since: *A Rap on Race*, p. 45.

250
The games this group played: *Our Own Metaphor*, p. 8.

251
During the time Gregory: Letter to Philomena Guillebaud, August 22, 1945, Library of Congress.

251
"Arriving . . . midday tomorrow": Telegram from Bateson, August 21, 1942, Library of Congress.

251
Bateson had "the usual": Colin Frank interview.

CHAPTER SEVENTEEN

253
"We were trying": Houston notes.

253
One fellow anthropologist: Sherwood Washburn interview.

253
"Before I went": Frances Macgregor interview.

254
Child development, in: Douglas Haring, *Personal Character and Cultural Milieu*, p. 356.

254
The project had been: *Growth and Culture: A Photographic Study of Balinese Childhood*, p. 198.

255
"I gave her four thousand pictures": Houston notes.

255
Macgregor thereupon became: Ibid.

257
This marriage, Bateson's biographer: Lipset, *Gregory Bateson*, p. 175.

258
One of his students: Personal communication from B. L. Stafford, July 10, 1979.

259n
In 1944 Parsons had written: Letter from Talcott Parsons, November 27, 1944, Library of Congress.

259
Bateson began analysis: Lipset, *Gregory Bateson*, p. 176.

259
"Gregory threw Elizabeth": Houston notes.

259
During his analysis: Ibid.

260
Mead, repeating this: Ibid.

260
When these sessions: Ibid.

260n
"A person attempting": Karen Horney, *Self Analysis* (New York, Norton, 1942), p. 33.

261
"Until I could find out": Houston notes.

261
"I was responsible for Larry": Helen Swick Perry interview with Mead, March 20, 1973.

262
Still, "Those whose": Fr. E. F. O'Doherty, *Psychiatry*, "Multidisciplinary Methods in Retrospect," p. 355.

262
"We went off": Ibid., p. 354.

262
"He's a perfectly": Helen Swick Perry interview with Mead, March 20, 1973, unpublished.

263
Harry Stack Sullivan, inventor: Ibid.

264
"She never left any": Dorothy Billings interview.

264
"This is going to be a rough year": Frances Macgregor interview.

264
"But Margaret won't": Georgiana Stevens interview.

265
"He roamed freely": Barbara Bick, *The Riddle of the Demon Mother*, p. 208.

265
His colleague, D. W. Harding: Ibid.

265
Psychoanalysis, he thought: Ibid., p. 213.

266
It was "real nice": Letter from Richard Mead, Library of Congress.

267
"As raw material": Letter from Malinowski to Haddon, July 7, 1936, Malinowski Archive.

267
The next year: Letter from Malinowski to Haddon, February 16, 1937, Malinowski Archive.

267
Field work, Fortune: Letter from Fortune to Malinowski, November 5, 1934, Malinowski Archive.

267
"It was rumored": Personal communication from Edmund Carpenter, November 27, 1982.

268
"You may be honest": Letter from Fortune, July 21, 1948, Library of Congress.

CHAPTER EIGHTEEN

270
"Such celebrities, yet!": Limmer, ed., *What the Woman Lived*, p. 261.

270
Without ever having set foot: A. L. Kroeber's review in *American Anthropologist*, 49 (1947), p. 467.

270
It also, in Mead's view: Houston notes.

271
Mead held herself accountable: Ibid.

271
By her own: Houston notes.

271
Cultural anthropology, for example: Voice of America.

272n
In January 1946: Letter from Ashley Montagu, January 19, 1946; to Montagu, January 22, 1946; Library of Congress.

272
In 1946, when: *An Anthropologist at Work*, p. 429.

272
The IIS, which later: Unpublished report, "The Institute for Intercultural Studies: Background—1940 Through 1978," April 2, 1979.

273n
The IIS got: Unpublished report, "Copyright and Royalty Information on Material for Which Margaret Mead Is Literary Executrix," January 1979.

273
The Office of Naval Research: *An Anthropologist at Work*, p. 443.

273
The Navy's grant: Ibid, pp. 436–437.

274
In the summer: *Male and Female: A Study of the Sexes in a Changing World* (New York, William Morrow, 1949, 1975), p. 256.

275
Geoffrey Gorer, on whom: *The Study of Culture at a Distance*, p. 8.

275
His research, lavishly: Letter from Gregory Bateson, April 22, 1942, Library of Congress.

275
The wartime Gorer reports: *The Study of Culture at a Distance*, p. 402.

275
Gorer had also: *About Bateson*, p. 181.

275
The error, Mead recalled: Ibid.

276
The Navy, she said: American University symposium, March 1980.

276
The new team: Asen Balikci interview.

276
"Man's humanity is": *The Study of Culture at a Distance*, p. 18.

276
In many cases: Ibid., pp. 79–81.

277
His preferred way: Ibid., pp. 81–82.

277
In an early letter: Letter from Gorer, "Tuesday" (late 1941), Library of Congress.

277
"You do hate the": Letter to Gorer, July 15, 1942, Library of Congress.

277n
Time would find: *Time*, November 21, 1955, p. 122.

278
The hypothesis, Gorer wrote: *The Study of Culture at a Distance*, p. 113.

278
A Russian woman: Ibid., p. 110.

278
"We've got to pursue swaddling": Ibid., p. 115.

278
"Even if almost": *An Anthropologist at Work*, p. 436.

278
Mead made it clear: *Soviet Attitudes Toward Authority: An Interdisciplinary Approach to Problems of Soviet Character*, p. 11.

279
Harry Schwartz charitably: *New York Times*, October 7, 1951.

279
Corliss Lamont in: *Annals of the American Academy* [of Political and Social Science], March 1952.

281
An RCC worker: Leila Lee interview

281
In the second week: *An Anthropologist at Work*, p. 438.

281
"If I can just": *An Anthropologist at Work*, photo insert following p. 280.

281
Her old adversary: Ruth Landman interview.

281
Her friend, she wrote: Houston notes.

281
"When people die": Ibid.

PART THREE

CHAPTER NINETEEN

285
Needing every inch: *Anthropologists and What They Do*, p. 117.

286
"I personally accept": *Male and Female*, p. 440.
286
Her fellow citizens: *New York Herald Tribune*, April 13, 1947.
286
A problem that: February 6, 1949, speech to Women's City Club.
286
She answered: "Being": Library of Congress letter.
286
"We are laying": *New York Herald Tribune*, March 15, 1950.
286
"Don't ever learn to drive": Martha Ullman West interview.
287
"How *dare* they?": Sherwood Washburn interview.
287n
Some of her colleagues: Vera Rubin interview.
287
"The way to write": *Anthropologists and What They Do*, p. 125.
288
"The Queen of": Memoir, n.d. (1950), Library of Congress.
288
She spoke with: *New York Times*, April 8, 1950.
288
"I have not attempted": *Male and Female*, p. 456.
288
She criticized the report: *New York Times*, March 31, 1948.
289
This may have been why: Houston notes.
289
The "new ballet": *Male and Female*, p. 4.
289
She talked of: Ibid., pp. 79–80.
289
Millions of women: Ibid., p. 6.
289
"The presence of": Ibid., p. 81.
289
And again, small wonder: Ibid., p. 291.
290
A career, as Mead: Ibid.
291
An Australian audience: Transcript of June 4, 1973, speech for Australian
Broadcasting.
291
"A world in which": *Male and Female*, p. 361.
291
Whoever outgrew whom: Ibid., p. 356.
291
The stigma of: Ibid.
291
Americans did not: Ibid.
291
Max Lerner in: *New York Post*, November 8, 1949.

291
Mead's "knowledge of": *Newsweek*, October 24, 1949.

291
But her new book: *New York Times*, October 30, 1949.

292
It may have been: Marianne Moore, "Arctic Ox."

292
They arranged theater: Houston notes.

294
Americans were "a gregarious": *Male and Female*, p. 328.

295
In her biography: Meryle Secrest, *Being Bernard Berenson*, p. 10.

295
"I can't bear": Houston notes.

295
"I have no": Houston notes.

296
"You know, Charles": Ibid.

296
"She could easily": Caroline Kelly interview.

297
"It was time": *New Lives for Old: Cultural Transformation—Manus 1928–1953*, p. 11.

297
Mead got to work: Ibid., Preface to the 1975 edition, p. x.

CHAPTER TWENTY

300n
"Women ought always": Evelyn Cheesman, *The Two Roads of Papua* (London, Jarrolds, Ltd., 1935), p. 222.

301
Neither one of them: *Letters from the Field*, p. 241.

301
"I have not decided": Ibid., p. 245.

302
When she and Reo Fortune: *New Lives for Old*, pp. xvii, 21.

302
Their "ceaseless economic endeavors": Ibid., p. 56.

302
Now, Mead had heard: Ibid., p. 21.

302
The troops who had: Ibid., p. 168, paraphrase.

302
"The Americans constructed": Ibid., p. 168.

303
"Everything you do": Foerstel interview.

303
"Two accidents of history": *New Lives for Old*, p. 186.

303
Mead's and Reo Fortune's: *Letters from the Field*, p. 257.

303
She had returned: *New Lives for Old*, p. 435.

304
Cargo cults, Mead: *Letters from the Field,* p. 247.

304
"Some people felt": *New Lives for Old,* p. 194.

304
"Never, never, *never*": Métraux statement at American University symposium, March 1980.

305
"Although I worked": Houston notes.

306
"I have an ankle": Lippel interview.

307
"All day people": *Letters from the Field,* p. 252.

308
"The mass of information": Ibid.

308
They could recall: Helen Swick Perry, "Selective Inattention as an Explanatory Concept for U.S. Public Attitudes Toward the Atomic Bomb," *Psychiatry: Journal for the Study of Impersonal Processes,* Vol. 17:3, August 1954.

308
"The degree of sympathy": *Letters from the Field,* p. 259.

309
"It's all rather": Ibid., p. 252.

309
"There was seldom": Foerstel interview.

309
"What will it be": *Letters from the Field,* pp. 260–261.

309
"I mused on the need": Theodore Schwartz, *Socialization as Cultural Communication,* p. viii.

310
"The process of being": Foerstel interview.

310
"Now, like an old sea turtle": *New Lives for Old,* p. xiv.

CHAPTER TWENTY-ONE

311
The world, Mead: *New Lives for Old,* p. 458.

312
"Maybe at the": *An Anthropologist at Work,* p. 286.

312
"Reo Fortune had been": Caroline Kelly interview.

313
It was said of Mead: *New York Post,* May 15, 1963, p. 43.

313n
"I learned more": Letter to Bateson, October 21, 1948, Library of Congress.

314
A student of Fortune's: Richard Salisbury interview.

314
Ted and Lenora: Letter to Fortune, November 10, 1954, Alexander Turnbull Library, Wellington, New Zealand.

315
Such talk, Mead: Library of Congress lunch, May 10, 1980.

316
To Birdwhistell, a friend said: Paul Byers interview.

317
"Body motion is": Birdwhistell lecture at American Museum of Natural History, October 4, 1980.

317
This the couple formally: Miriam Birdwhistell at American Anthropological Association meetings, Cincinnati, 1979.

321
"If you have": Houston notes.

321
Ruth Benedict had: *An Anthropologist at Work*, p. 326.

322
But not until Holmes: Holmes interview.

322
Mead's reply to his letter: Ibid.

323n
In 1980: Holmes, *American Anthropologist*, Vol. 84, No. 3, September 1982, p. 716.

323
But Holmes concluded: Holmes interview.

CHAPTER TWENTY-TWO
326
Three kinds of: Houston notes.

326
"I am sorry": Letter to Marvin Harris, November 24, 1964, Library of Congress.

327
The museum gave: John Willey interview.

327
"My needs are": Letter to Menninger Foundation, Menninger Archives, Topeka, Kansas, 1957.

327
For her *apparat*: *New York Post*, May 15, 1963.

329
"As the Irish": *A History of Psychology in Autobiography*, p. 295.

329
Blessed with what: June Goodfield interview, referring to a line from the "East Coker" section of T. S. Eliot's *Four Quartets*.

330
That was one of the reasons: Houston notes.

330
"Dr. Mead prefers": Letter from Barbara Sperling to Menninger Foundation, December 13, 1975.

331
"Winter wives": Letter to Menninger Foundation, 1963, Menninger Archives.

331
She "liked to take": Introduction to Maurice Levine, *Psychiatry and Ethics* (New York, Braziller, 1972), p. xi.

332
After Mead's 1963: Letter to Menninger Foundation, Menninger Archives.

336
She was "bored": Houston notes.

336
If the museum: Kubota interview.

337
"Oh," she said: Philip Gifford interview.

337
"I don't like": Houston notes.

337
"When Jane Belo": Ibid.

338
Her Ohio relatives: Ibid.

338
What she had: Letter to Daniel Métraux, September 18, 1978, Library of Congress.

339
They could just as: Houston notes.

CHAPTER TWENTY-THREE

340
Once Margaret Mead: Houston notes.

340
"Prayer," she said: *Christianity and Crisis*, December 11, 1978, p. 306.

340
She went to church: Houston notes.

340
A Barnard classmate: Eleanor Rosenberg interview.

341
"How could they": William Carr interview.

341
But Mead was: Austin Ford interview.

343
What Mead saw coming: Houston notes.

343
Christianity was being: Ibid.

343
"I don't think my": Ibid.

344
Before Vatican II: Houston notes.

345
"It was nice": Letter from Gunnar Myrdal, August 9, 1968, Library of Congress.

346
It was the first: *World Enough: Rethinking the Future* (Boston, Little, Brown, 1975), p. 100.

348
The ethicist Roger Shinn: *Christianity and Crisis*, December 11, 1978, p. 306.

348
"I think you need": *New York Post*, May 15, 1963, p. 43.

349
This did not mean: Houston notes.

349
That was why the church: *Christian Initiation* (Associated Parishes, Inc., 1970), p. 26.

349
For example, she said: Columbia University *Earl Hall Report*, January
1982.

349
A good ritual: Liturgical Conference transcript, 1965.

354
Late in her life: Houston notes.

CHAPTER TWENTY-FOUR

356
"Life is good": Letter to Erik Erikson, February 1959, Library of Congress.

356
"An hour," she would say: Pelham Stapelfeldt interview.

358
"Children are having an awful time": Kubota interview.

358
"You're still here!": Percy Langstaff interview.

358
"If I have": Madeline Lee interview.

359
"We're having a new": Ford Hall Forum transcript, Boston, December
1968.

359
"The expectation of permanency": *Male and Female*, p. 356.

359
"I'm trying so hard": Letter from Priscilla Mead Rosten, April 16, 1958,
Library of Congress.

359
It was Margaret: Personal communication from Philip Rosten, February 2,
1984.

360
"I dare say": Letter to Emily Fogg Mead, December 20, 1927, Library of
Congress.

361
"Each time we": *New York Times*, January 16, 1960.

362
"We women are": American Museum of Natural History press conference,
1976.

362
Six years before: *An Anthropologist at Work*, p. 132.

362
"Women don't have": Kubota interview.

362
The "foundresses," she: Victor Stoloff film.

363
Friedan's sixth chapter: *The Feminine Mystique*, pp. 137ff.

363
Mead's vision for: Ibid., p. 142.

364
She felt "a little cross": Kubota interview.

364
"One of the things": June Adamson, article in *Oak Ridger*, May 19, 1964.

365
"Men who would": Houston notes.

365
The strength of: *Washington Post*, November 27, 1978.

365
It would hardly: Frances Glennon notes for *Life* article, August 12, 1959.

365
"We must stop": Eckerd College Free Institutions Forum Lecture Series, 1975.

365
She opposed coeducation: Speech at Radcliffe College, 1969.

367
"What is new": *Redbook*, January 1975.

368
She rejoiced in: *The Small Conference*, p. 29.

368
Mary Catherine Bateson: AAA Convention, Cincinnati, Ohio, November 1980.

CHAPTER TWENTY-FIVE

374
"You're coming of age!": Mildred Leet interview.

374
"She gave me": Louis Dupree interview.

374
"You'd find a dab": Wilton Dillon interview.

375
"If I'm here to speak": West interview.

375
She bore in mind: *A History of Psychology in Autobiography*, p. 296.

375
Her friend Marshall McLuhan: *Life*, February 25, 1966.

375
Mead won: "Please": Leona Baumgarter interview.

376
When a friend asked: Kubota interview.

376
A note from one: Bertrand Slaff, M.D., interview.

376
Possibly never in: *Oak Ridger*, May 19, 1964.

377
She needed the stick: Letter to Colin McPhee, August 13, 1961, Library of Congress.

377
"Every society has": "Postscripts," *Chemical and Engineering News*, February 14, 1966.

378
"People look at": Houston notes.

378
Winthrop Sargeant's: "It's All Anthropology," *New Yorker*, December 30, 1961, p. 32.

378
When a fellow anthropologist: Heinz von Forster interview.

378
The stick had practical: Houston notes.

379
Some of her colleagues: Raymond Firth interview.

379
Some cheers were heard: Ann Chowning interview.

379
"She was an activator": Glen Leet interview.

379
She made herself fair game: James Michener, "The Fossickers," *Return to Paradise* (New York, Random House, 1951), pp. 407, 409.

380
A 1963 satire by David Cort: "Margaret Mead for President," *Monocle*, Summer-Fall, 1963.

380
Although this profile: West interview.

380
In 1960, during a visit: *Elkhart* (Ind.) *Truth*, August 31, 1960, p. 1.

381
John F. Kennedy's: Gail Cameron notes for *Life*, December 3, 1962.

CHAPTER TWENTY-SIX

386
Since the Second World War: American University symposium, March 21, 1980.

386
"Most people just": Letter, July 23, 1968, Library of Congress.

386
Even unlikely people: AAAS party, February 20, 1976.

386
"Don't you find": Romanucci-Ross interview.

387
She no more wanted: Houston notes.

387
Except for what: Foerstel interview.

388
"Sorry, ma'am": Peter Gathercole interview.

388
After a long flight: Slaff interview.

389
There she was: Personal communication from Richard Schuh, M.D.

389
True, we lived in: Ford Hall Forum, transcript, Boston, December 1968.

389
She was glad: Foerstel interview.

389
Children all over: Kubota interview for *Life*, February 25, 1969.

389
Redbook asked her to: Letter to Daniel Métraux, November 5, 1968, Library of Congress.

390
The prohibition of: *New York Times*, October 28, 1969.

390
The governor of Florida: *New York Times*, October 28, 1969.

390
"She had assumed": Philleo Nash interview.

390
On what grounds: Sherwood Washburn interview.

391
Her school of: William Carr interview.

391
"The entire scientific": Victor Stoloff movie.

391
"I'm prepared to believe": Houston notes.

392
Gorer called the day: AAAS birthday celebration in Boston, 1976, transcript.

392
Many reporters rushed: *New York Times*, December 16, 1976.

392
The thing she was: AAAS 142nd Annual Meeting, February 20, 1976, transcript.

392
She had long ago: Houston notes.

393
"Look," Mead said: Ann Heidbreder Eastman interview.

393
On another occasion: Rollo May interview.

394
The main drawback: Houston notes.

394
"I *can't* stop!": Fred Eggan interview.

394
Housecooling party: Letter to Sara Ullman, Library of Congress, June 7, 1966.

394
"All those houses": Houston notes.

394
She liked to describe: Ibid.

394
"When you displace people": Lenora Foerstel interview.

395
The trouble with housing: Australian broadcast, June 4, 1973.

397
Some members of the AAAS: *New York Times*, February 25, 1977.

397
Edward O. Wilson: Personal communication, February 18, 1981.

398
Mead was accused: Forestel interview.

398
To a largely: Ruth Bunzel interview.

400
Perhaps in self-defense: Winthrop Sargeant, "It's All Anthropology," *New Yorker*, December 30, 1961.

400
In her autobiography: *Blackberry Winter*, p. 5.

400
From babyhood she: *Blackberry Winter*, p. 29.

400
The second volume: West interview.

400
The "cumulative nature": *Margaret Mead: The Complete Bibliography, 1925–1975*, p. 12.

401
"*Glacier!*" she said: James Ritchie interview.

401
During a blizzard in Cincinnati: Harold Hiatt interview.

401
One of her museum: Lippel interview.

CHAPTER TWENTY-SEVEN

411
On a visit to La Maisonette: Harold Hiatt interview.

418
Of the 23,000 Americans: *New England Journal of Medicine* 301 (9) (August 30, 1979), pp. 482–485.

419
This will specified: "Statement of Intent," June 11, 1962, p. 2, Library of Congress.

421
Remembering Mead's: Houston notes.

AFTERWORD

425
Into thy hands: Funeral program, St. Paul's Chapel, November 17, 1978.

426
Mead's "exquisite sense": Vera Rubin article in *Human Organization* 38:2 (Summer 1979), p. 195.

426
On December 7, a service: Washington National Cathedral program.

427
Peranis Paliau, village councilor: Barbara Honeyman Roll, "Pere Mourns Margaret Mead," *Natural History*, 1979, p. 84.

427
On January 4, Rosalind Lippel: Affidavit, Surrogate's Court, County of New York.

430
Focusing on human: Nancy McDowell, "The Oceanic Ethnography of Margaret Mead," *American Anthropologist: In Memoriam Margaret Mead* (1901–1978) 82:2 (June 1980), p. 278.

430
Mead's colleague Lola Romanucci-Ross: "Anthropological Field Research: Margaret Mead, Muse of the Clinical Experience," ibid., p. 310.

430
At its best, his prose: Michael Young obituary "Reo Fortune (1903–1979)," *Canberra Anthropology*, September 1980, p. 107.

431
Once when Mead visited Cambridge: Houston notes.

431
His last needs: Mary Catherine Bateson, "Six Days of Dying," *CoEvolution Quarterly*, Winter 1980, pp. 4–11.

432
He used that phrase: "Dr. Mead's First Husband Comes to Her Defense," Science section, *New York Times*, May 3, 1983.

434
"Gosh, Phil": *Donahue Transcript* #03183, Multimedia Program Productions, Cincinnati, Ohio, p. 2.

434
"Stop him, please stop him!": Sherrye Henry radio interview on WOR, March 11, 1983.

434
In an editorial: *Colorado Springs Gazette Telegraph*, February 23, 1983, p. A10.

435
On the contrary, Freeman retorted: Telephone conversation with author, February 10, 1983.

436
Beyond Samoa: Theodore Schwartz, "Anthropology: A Quaint Science," *American Anthropologist* 85:1 (1983), p. 936.

436
Freeman's "badly written": Annette B. Weiner, ibid., p. 918.

436
"He has forced upon us": Personal communication from Ann Peck, December 18, 1983, concerning Mary Catherine Bateson's December 16 talk.

436
Boas, as Cressman put it: Science section, *New York Times*, May 3, 1983.

437
She wasn't demure like the geneticist: *Time*, October 24, 1983, p. 53.

437
"Margaret loves the marketplace": Interview with Sherwood L. Washburn.

438
"Her positive contributions": *Socialization as Cultural Communication: Development of a Theme in the Work of Margaret Mead*, p. 17.

438
Mead's greatness: Personal communication from Ann McLean, October 5, 1983.

438
"How much has this woman": Personal communication from Jan Van Baal to Luther S. Cressman, January 6, 1979.

438
"She was supremely successful": Personal communication from Marvin Harris, December 14, 1983.

438
In Harris's estimation: Ibid.

439
Mead's sin, she once: Houston notes.

439
The Reverend Theodore M. Hesburgh: Mead memorial service at the National Cathedral, Washington, D.C., December 7, 1978.

439
Dr. Roy Menninger: Menninger interview.

441
Mead made some wonder: Professor Alexander E. Campbell of Birmingham University.

Selected Bibliography

Badinter, Elisabeth. *Mother Love: Myth and Reality.* New York: Macmillan, 1981.

Baltzell, E. Digby. *The Protestant Ethic and the Spirit of Class Authority and Leadership.* New York: Free Press, 1980.

Baltzell, E. Digby. *Puritan Boston and Quaker Philadelphia.* New York: Free Press, 1980.

Bateson, Gregory. *Naven: A Survey of the Problems Suggested by a Composite Picture of the Culture of a New Guinea Tribe Drawn from Three Points of View.* Stanford, Calif.: Stanford University Press, 1965 (orig. publ. 1936).

Bateson, Gregory. *Steps to an Ecology of Mind.* New York: Ballantine Books, 1978 (orig. publ. Chandler Publishing Company, 1972).

Bateson, Gregory, and Margaret Mead. *Balinese Character: A Photographic Analysis.* Special Publications of the New York Academy of Sciences, vol. II, 1962 (orig. publ. 1942).

Bateson, Mary Catherine. *Our Own Metaphor.* New York: Knopf, 1972.

Belo, Jane. (Preface by Margaret Mead.) *Trance in Bali.* New York: Columbia University Press, 1960.

Benedict, Ruth. *The Chrysanthemum and the Sword: Patterns of Japanese Culture.* Boston: Houghton Mifflin, 1946.

Benedict, Ruth. *Patterns of Culture.* New York: New American Library, 1953 (orig. publ. 1934).

Berkow, Robert, ed. *Merck Manual,* vol. 2, 14th ed. Rahway, N.J.: Merck and Co., Inc., 1982.

Bick, Barbara. *The Riddle of the Demon Mother.* Washington, D.C., 1982, unpublished manuscript.

Birdwhistell, Ray L. *Kinesics and Context: Essays on Body Motion Communication.* New York: Ballantine Books, 1972 (orig. publ. 1970).

Boas, Franz. *The Mind of Primitive Man.* New York: Macmillan, 1946 (orig. publ. 1911).

Boas, Franz. *Rage, Language & Culture.* New York: Free Press, 1966 (orig. publ. 1940).

Bohannan, Paul, and Mark Glazer, eds. *High Points in Anthropology.* New York: Alfred A. Knopf, 1973.

Bram, Joseph, Colin M. Turnbull, Margaret Mead, Marvin Harris, and Saul K. Padover. *The Measure of Mankind.* Dobbs Ferry, N.Y.: Oceana Publications, 1963.

Bridges, Philippa. *Afoot in Papua*. Proceedings of the Royal Geographical Society of Australia, South Australia branch, vol. 25, 1925.

Bridges, Philippa. *Walk-About in Australia*. New South Wales, Australia: Hodder, 1925.

Brockman, John, ed. *About Bateson: Essays on Gregory Bateson*. New York: E. P. Dutton, 1977.

Casagrande, Joseph B. *In the Company of Man*. New York: Harper and Row, 1960.

Cassidy, Robert. *Margaret Mead: A Voice for the Century*. New York: Universe Books, 1982.

Chagnon, Napoleon A. *Yanomamö: The Fierce People*. New York: Holt, Rinehart and Winston, 1968.

Cobb, Edith. *The Ecology of Imagination in Childhood*. New York: Columbia University Press, 1977.

Cressman, L. S. *Prehistory of the Far West: Homes of Vanished Peoples*. Salt Lake City: University of Utah Press, 1977.

Cressman, L. S. *The Sandal and the Cave: The Indians of Oregon*. Corvallis, Oreg.: Oregon State University Press, 1981.

Dahlberg, Frances, ed. *Woman the Gatherer*. New Haven, Conn.: Yale University Press, 1981.

Davidson, James. *Samoa mo Samoa: The Emergence of the Independent State of Western Samoa*. Oxford: Oxford University Press, 1967.

Douglas, Helen Gahagan. *A Full Life*. New York: Doubleday, 1982.

Douglas, Mary. *Edward Evans-Pritchard*. New York: Viking, 1980.

Durkheim, Emile. *The Elementary Forms of the Religious Life*. Joseph Ward Swain, trans. New York: Free Press, 1965 (orig. publ. 1915).

Dyson, John. *The South Seas Dream: An Adventure in Paradise*. Boston and Toronto: Little, Brown, 1982.

Eddy, Elizabeth M., and William L. Partridge, eds. *Applied Anthropology in America*. New York: Columbia University Press, 1978.

Eliade, Mircea. *Rites and Symbols of Initiation: The Mysteries of Birth and Rebirth*. Willard R. Trask, trans. New York: Harper Torchbooks, 1965 (orig. publ. 1958).

Ember, Carol R., and Melvin Ember. *Cultural Anthropology*. Englewood Cliffs, N.J.: Prentice-Hall, 1977.

Erikson, Erik H. *Gandhi's Truth: On the Origins of Militant Nonviolence*. New York: W. W. Norton, 1969.

Erikson, Erik H. *Identity and the Life Cycle*. New York: W. W. Norton, 1980 (paperback ed.). Original monograph, *Psychological Issues*, vol. 1, no. 1. New York: International Universities Press, 1959.

Erikson, Erik H. *The Life Cycle Completed*. New York: W. W. Norton, 1982.

Firth, Raymond. *Human Types: An Introduction to Social Anthropology*. New York: New American Library, 1962 (orig. publ. 1958).

Firth, Raymond. *We, the Tikopia*. London: Allen and Unwin, 1957.

Fishel, Elizabeth. *Sisters: Love and Rivalry Inside the Family and Beyond*. New York: William Morrow, 1979.

Fortune, Reo. "Arapesh Warfare," *American Anthropologist*, 41:1 (1939).

Fortune, Reo. *Manus Religion*. Philadelphia: American Philosophical Society, 1935.

Fortune, Reo F. *Omaha Secret Societies*. New York: Columbia University Press, Columbia University Contributions to Anthropology Series, vol. 14 (repr. of 1932 ed.).

Fortune, R. F. *Sorcerers of Dobu: The Social Anthropology of the Dobu*

Islanders of the Western Pacific. New York: E. P. Dutton, 1963 (orig. publ. 1932).

Fox, Renée C. *Margaret Mead.* Reprinted from the International Encyclopedia of the Social Sciences, vol. 18. New York: Institute for Intercultural Studies, 1979.

Freeman, Derek. *Margaret Mead and Samoa: The Making and Unmaking of an Anthropological Myth.* Cambridge, Mass.: Harvard University Press, 1983.

Friedan, Betty. *The Feminine Mystique.* New York: W. W. Norton, 1974.

Gellner, Ernest, ed. *Soviet and Western Anthropology.* New York: Columbia University Press, 1980.

Gewertz, Deborah B. *Sepik River Societies: A Historical Ethnography of the Chambia and Their Neighbors.* New Haven, Conn.: Yale University Press, 1983.

Golde, Peggy, ed. *Women in the Field: Anthropological Experiences.* Chicago, Ill.: Aldine Publishing, 1970.

Goldfrank, Esther S. *Changing Configurations in the Social Organization of a Blackfoot Tribe During the Reserve Period.* Seattle, Wash.: University of Washington Press, 1966 (orig. publ. 1945).

Goodman, Richard A. *Mead's Coming of Age in Samoa: A Dissenting View.* Oakland, Calif.: Pepperine Press, 1983.

Gorer, Geoffrey. *Africa Dances.* New York: W. W. Norton, 1962 (orig. publ. Alfred Knopf, 1935).

Gorer, Geoffrey. *Bali and Angkor.* Darby, Pa.: Arden Library, 1979 (orig. publ. 1936).

Gray, J. A. *Amerika Samoa.* New York: Arno Press (Navies and Men Series), 1980 (repr. of 1960 ed.).

Grun, Bernard. *The Timetables of History: A Horizontal Linkage of People and Events.* New York: Touchstone/Simon and Schuster, 1982.

Hall, Edward T. *The Hidden Dimension.* Garden City, N.Y.: Anchor Books, 1969 (orig. publ. 1966).

Hall, G. Stanley. *Adolescence.* 2 vols. New York: Appleton, 1905.

Hamalian, Leo, ed. *Ladies on the Loose: Women Travellers of the Eighteenth and Nineteenth Centuries.* New York: Dodd, Mead, 1981.

Hardwick, Elizabeth. *Seduction and Betrayal: Women and Literature.* New York: Random House, 1974.

Haring, Douglas Gilbert. *Personal Character and Cultural Milieu.* Syracuse, N.Y.: Syracuse University Press, 3rd rev. ed., 1956.

Harris, Marvin. *The Rise of Anthropological Theory.* New York: Thomas Y. Crowell Company, 1968.

Heims, Steve J. *John Von Neuman and Norbert Wiener: From Mathematics to the Technologies of Life and Death.* Cambridge, Mass., and London: MIT Press, 1980.

Herskovits, Melville. *Cultural Anthropology.* New York: Alfred A. Knopf, 1964.

Herskovits, Melville. *Cultural Relativism: Perspectives in Cultural Pluralism.* New York: Vintage Books, 1973.

Herskovits, Melville, J. *Franz Boas: The Science of Man in the Making.* New York: Scribners, 1953.

Horney, Karen. *The Neurotic Personality of Our Time.* New York: Norton, 1937.

Horney, Karen. *Self Analysis.* New York: Norton, 1942.

Horowitz, Irving Louis, ed. *The Rise and Fall of Project Camelot: Studies in the Relationship Between Social Science and Practical Politics.*

Cambridge, Mass.: MIT Press, 1974.

Hymes, Dell. *Reinventing Anthropology*. New York: Vintage Books, 1974.

Inglis, Amirah. *Sexual Politics in New Guinea*. New York: St. Martin's Press, 1973.

Jung, Carl G. *Man and His Symbols*. New York: Doubleday, 1964.

Kluckhohn, Clyde. *Mirror for Man: A Survey of Human Behavior and Social Attitudes*. New York: Fawcett World Library, 1957 (orig. publ. 1949).

Koffend, John. *A Letter to My Wife*. New York: Saturday Review Press, 1972.

Koffka, K. *The Growth of the Mind: An Introduction to Child Psychology*. New York: Harcourt, Brace and Company, 1924.

Kroeber, A. L. *Anthropology: Biology and Race*. New York: Harbinger Books/Harcourt Brace Jovanovich, 1963 (orig. publ. 1923).

Kroeber, A. L. *Anthropology: Culture Patterns and Processes*. New York: Harbinger Books/Harcourt Brace Jovanovich, 1963.

Kuper, Adam. *Anthropologists and Anthropology: The British School 1922–72*. New York: Penguin Books, 1973.

Leslie, Charles, ed. *Anthropology of Folk Religion*. New York: Vintage Books, 1960.

Levine, Maurice, M.D. (Introduction by Margaret Mead.) *Psychiatry and Ethics*. New York: George Braziller, 1972.

Lévi-Strauss, Claude. *Tristes Tropiques*. New York: Atheneum, 1975 (orig. publ. 1955).

Lévi-Strauss, Claude. *The Way of the Masks*. Sylvia Modelski, trans. Seattle, Wash.: University of Washington Press, 1982.

Lichtman, Allan J., and Joan R. Challinor, eds. *Kin and Communities: Families in America*. Washington, D.C.: Smithsonian Institution Press, 1979.

Limmer, Ruth, ed. *What the Woman Lived: Letters of Louise Bogan, 1920–1970*. New York: Harcourt, Brace, Jovanovich, 1973.

Lipset, David. *Gregory Bateson: The Legacy of a Scientist*. Englewood Cliffs, N.J.: Prentice-Hall, 1980.

Lurie, Alison. *The Language of Clothes*. New York: Random House, 1980.

Lyman, Christopher M. *The Vanishing Race and Other Illusions: Photographs of Indians by Edward S. Curtis*. New York: Pantheon Books, 1982.

Macgregor, Frances Cooke. *Transformation and Identity: The Face and Plastic Surgery*. Oak Park, Ill.: Eterna Press, 1980.

Malinowski, Bronislaw. *Argonauts of the Western Pacific*. New York: E. P. Dutton, 1961.

Malinowski, Bronislaw. *A Diary in the Strict Sense of the Word*. N. Gutman, trans. New York: Harcourt, Brace, Jovanovich, 1967.

Malinowski, Bronislaw. *Sex and Repression in Savage Society*. Atlantic Highlands, N.J.: Humanities Press, 1953.

Mauss, Marcel. *The Gift: Forms and Functions of Exchange in Archaic Societies*. Ian Cunnison, trans. New York: W. W. Norton, 1967.

McCurdy, David, and James Spradley. *Issues in Cultural Anthropology*. Boston: Little, Brown, 1979.

McMaster, Fanny Fogg. *A Family History*. Privately printed. St. Joseph, Mich., 1964.

McPhee, Colin. *A House in Bali*. New York: John Day, 1944.

Métraux, Alfred. *Easter Island: A Stone-Age Civilization of the Pacific*. Michael Bullock, trans. London: André Deutsch, 1957.

Milner, George Bertram. *Samoan Dictionary*. London and New York: Oxford University Press, 1966.

Modell, Judith Schachter. *Ruth Benedict: Patterns of a Life*. Philadelphia, Pa.: University of Pennsylvania Press, 1983.

Monaghan, Patricia. *The Book of Goddesses and Heroines*. New York: E. P. Dutton, 1981.

Nelson, Raymond. *Van Wyck Brooks*. New York: Dutton, 1981.

Neumann, Erich. *The Great Mother: An Analysis of an Archetype*. Bollinger Series XLVII. Ralph Manheim, trans. Princeton, N.J.: Princeton University Press, 1974.

Perry, Helen Swick. *Psychiatrist of America: The Life of Harry Stack Sullivan*. Cambridge, Mass.: The Belknap Press of Harvard University Press, 1982.

Pocock, David. *Understanding Social Anthropology*. New South Wales, Australia: Hodder and Stoughton, 1975.

Quiggin, A. Hingston. *Haddon, the Headhunter*. Cambridge: Cambridge University Press, 1942.

Rhodius, Hans, ed. *Walter Spies*. Den Hoag: L. J. C. Boucher, 1964.

Rice, Edward. *Margaret Mead: A Portrait*. New York: Harper and Row, 1979.

Ritchie, Jane, and James Ritchie. (Foreword by Margaret Mead.) *Growing Up in New Zealand*. Sydney, Australia: George Allen and Unwin, 1980 (orig. publ. 1978).

Rivers, W. H. R. *The History of Melanesian Society*. Atlantic Highlands, N.J.: Humanities Press, 1968. (repr. of 1914 ed.).

Rivers, W. H. R. *Instinct and the Unconscious*. London: Cambridge University Press, 1920.

Rivers, W. H. R. *Social Organization*. New York: AMS Press (repr. of 1924 ed.).

Rose, Roger G. *A Museum to Instruct and Delight*. Honolulu, Hawaii: Bishop Museum Press, 1980.

Rosen, Sidney, ed. *My Voice Will Go with You: The Teaching Tales of Milton H. Erickson*. New York: W. W. Norton, 1982.

Sapir, Edward. *Culture, Language and Personality*. Selected essays; David G. Mandelbaum, ed. Berkeley, Calif., Los Angeles, Calif., and London: University of California Press, 1949.

Schwartz, Theodore. *Socialization as Cultural Communication. Development of a Theme in the Work of Margaret Mead*. Berkeley, Calif.: University of California Press, 1976.

Secrest, Meryle. *Being Bernard Berenson*. New York: Holt, Rinehart and Winston, 1979.

Sheldon, William. *Atlas of Men: A Guide for Somatotyping the Adult Male of All Ages*. New York: Hafner Press, 1970 (repr. of 1954 ed.).

Shore, Bradd. *Sala' Ilua: A Samoan Mystery*. New York: Columbia University Press, 1982.

Shostak, Marjorie. *Nisa*. New York: Vintage Books, 1982.

Silverman, Sydel, ed. *Totems and Teachers: Perspectives in the History of Anthropology*. New York: Columbia University Press, 1981.

Stanley, David. *South Pacific Handbook*. 2nd ed. Chico, Calif.: Moon Publications, 1982.

Stocking, George W. *Race, Culture and Evolution: Essays in the History of Anthropology*. New York: The Free Press, 1968.

Strachey, Lytton. *Eminent Victorians*. New York: Harcourt, Brace, Jovanovich, 1969.

Tuiteteleapaga, Napoleone A. *Samoa Yesterday and Today and Tomorrow.* Great Neck, N.Y.: Todd & Honeywell, 1980.

Turnbull, Colin M. *The Forest People: A Study of the Pygmies of the Congo.* New York: Clarion Books/Simon and Schuster, 1962.

Turnbull, Colin M. *The Human Cycle.* New York: Simon and Schuster, 1983.

Turnbull, Colin M. *The Lonely African.* New York: Clarion Books/Simon and Schuster, 1962.

von Hoffman, Nicholas, and Garry B. Trudeau. *Tales from the Margaret Mead Taproom.* Kansas City, Mo.: Andrews and McMeel, Inc., 1979 (orig. publ. 1976).

Wells, Anna Mary. *Miss Marks and Miss Woolley.* Boston: Houghton Mifflin, 1978.

Wilson, Edmund, ed. (Introduction by Leon Edel.) *The Twenties: From Notebooks and Diaries of the Period.* New York: Farrar, Straus and Giroux, 1975.

Winick, Charles. *Dictionary of Anthropology.* Paterson, N.J.: Littlefield, Adams, 1961 (orig. publ. 1956).

Selected Margaret Mead Books

And Keep Your Powder Dry. New York: William Morrow, 1975 (orig. publ. 1942).

An Anthropologist at Work: Writings of Ruth Benedict. Boston: Houghton Mifflin, 1959.

Anthropologists and What They Do. New York: Watts, 1965.

Aspects of the Present (with Rhoda Métraux). New York: William Morrow, 1980.

Balinese Character: A Photographic Analysis (with Gregory Bateson). New York Academy of Sciences, 1962.

Blackberry Winter: My Earlier Years. New York: William Morrow, 1972; Pocket Books, 1975.

The Changing Culture of an Indian Tribe. New York: AMS Press (Columbia University Contributions to Anthropology: No. 15). (Repr. of 1932 ed.)

Childhood in Contemporary Cultures (ed. with Martha Wolfenstein). Chicago: University of Chicago Press, 1974 (orig. publ. 1955).

Coming of Age in Samoa: A Psychological Study of Primitive Youth for Western Civilization. New York: William Morrow, 1961 (orig. publ. 1928).

Continuities in Cultural Evolution. New Haven, Conn., and London: Yale University Press, 1964.

Cooperation and Competition Among Primitive Peoples (ed.). New York: McGraw-Hill, 1937. Boston: Beacon Press, 1961.

Cultural Patterns and Technical Change (ed.). New York: New American Library, 1954.

Culture and Commitment: A Study of the Generation Gap. Garden City, N.Y.: Natural History Press/Doubleday, 1970.

Cybernetics: Circular Causal and Feedback Mechanisms in Biological and Social Systems, Transactions of the Ninth Conference, March 20–21, 1952 (ed. with Heinz von Foerster and Hans Lucas Teuber). New York: Josiah Macy, Jr., Foundation, 1953.

Family (with Ken Heyman). New York: Macmillan, 1965.

From the South Seas: Studies of Adolescence and Sex in Primitive Societies. New York: William Morrow, 1941 (orig. publ. 1928).

Growing Up in New Guinea: A Comparative Study of Primitive Education. New York: William Morrow, 1975 (orig. publ. 1930).

495

Growth and Culture: A Photographic Study of Balinese Childhood (with Frances Cooke Macgregor and photographs by Gregory Bateson). New York: Putnam, 1951.

An Interview with Santa Claus (with Rhoda Métraux). New York: Walker, 1978.

Letters from the Field 1925–1965. New York: Harper and Row, 1977.

To Love or to Perish: The Technological Crisis and the Churches (ed. with J. Edward Carothers, Daniel MacCracken, and Roger L. Shinn). New York: Friendship Press, 1972.

Male and Female: A Study of the Sexes in a Changing World. New York: William Morrow, 1975 (orig. publ. 1949).

New Lives for Old: Cultural Transformation—Manus 1928–1953. New York: William Morrow, 1975 (orig. publ. 1960).

People and Places. Cleveland and New York: World, 1959.

Primitive Heritage: An Anthropological Anthology (ed. with Nicolas Calas). New York: Random House, 1953.

A Rap on Race (with James Baldwin). Philadelphia and New York: J. B. Lippincott, 1971.

The School in American Culture. Cambridge, Mass.: Harvard University Press, 1951.

Sex and Temperament in Three Primitive Societies. New York: William Morrow, 1963 (orig. publ. 1935).

Soviet Attitudes Toward Authority: An Interdisciplinary Approach to Problems of Soviet Character. New York: The RAND Corporation/McGraw-Hill, 1951.

The Study of Culture at a Distance (ed. with Rhoda Métraux). Chicago: University of Chicago Press, 1953.

A Way of Seeing (with Rhoda Métraux). New York: William Morrow, 1974 (orig. publ. 1961).

World Enough: Rethinking the Future (photographs by Ken Heyman). Boston: Little, Brown, 1975.

Selected Margaret Mead Articles

"An Ethnologist's Footnote to *Totem and Taboo*," *Psychoanalytic Review* 17:3 (July 1930), 297–304.

"Social Organization of Manu'a," *Bernice P. Bishop Museum Bulletin* 76 (Honolulu, Hawaii, 1930; reissued 1969).

"Living with the Natives of Melanesia," *Natural History* 31:1 (January–February 1931), 62–74.

"Talk-Boy," *Asia* 31:3 (March 1931), 144–151.

"South Sea Tips on Character Training," *Parents' Magazine*, March 1932, 13, 66–68.

"An Investigation of the Thought of Primitive Children with Special Reference to Animism." *Journal of the Royal Anthropological Institute* 62 (January–June 1932), 173–190.

"Kinship in the Admiralty Islands," *Anthropological Papers of the American Museum of Natural History* 34:2 (1934), 183–358.

"The Mountain Arapesh. I. An Importing Culture," *Anthropological Papers of the American Museum of Natural History* 36, Part 3 (1938), 139–349.

"The Strolling Players in the Mountains of Bali," *Natural History* 43:1 (January 1939), 17–26, 64.

"The Mountain Arapesh. II. Supernaturalism," *Anthropological Papers of the American Museum of Natural History* 37, Part 3 (1940), 319–451.

"Principles of Morale Building" (with Gregory Bateson), *Journal of Educational Sociology* 15:4 (December 1941), 206–220.

"Museums in the Emergency," *Natural History* 48:2 (September 1941), 67.

"On Methods of Implementing a National Morale Program," *Applied Anthropology* 1:1 (October–December 1941), 20–24.

"When Were You Born?" *Child Study* 18:3 (Spring 1941), 71–72.

"Cultural Patterns and Problems of Morale." In *Abstracts of the General Lectures Given at the Vassar Summer Institute for Family and Child-care Services in War Time, June 22–August 1, 1942*. Poughkeepsie, N.Y.: Vassar College, September 1942, 107–108. (Mimeographed.)

Melanesian Pidgin English (assistant with Gregory Bateson, Phyllis M. Kaberry, and Stephen W. Reed to Robert A. Hall, Jr., primary author). "Special Publications of the Linguistic Society of America." Baltimore: Waverly Press, 1943.

"Anthropological Techniques in War Psychology," *Bulletin of the Menninger Clinic* 7:4 (July 1943), 137–140.

"Changing Food Habits." In *The Nutrition Front*. Report of the New York State Joint Legislative Committee on Nutrition. Legislative Document No. 64, 1943, 37–43.

"The Problem of Changing Food Habits." In Report of the Committee on Food Habits, 1941–1943, "The Problem of Changing Food Habits," *National Research Council Bulletin* 108, 1943, 20–31.

"The Role of Small South Sea Cultures in the Post War World," *American Anthropologist* 45:2 (April–June 1943), 193–196.

Introduction to Richard M. Brickner, *Is Germany Incurable?* New York: J. B. Lippincott, 1943, 7–13.

The American Troops and the British Community: An Examination of the Relationship Between the American Troops and the British. London: Hutchinson, 1944. (Pamphlet.)

A Bread and Butter Letter from a Lecturer. Los Angeles: Occidental College, 1944. (Pamphlet.)

"A GI View of Britain," *New York Times Magazine*, March 19, 1944, 18–19, 34.

"Why Not a Year of National Service?" *Parents' Magazine*, November 1944, 18.

Report of the Committee on Food Habits. "Manual for the Study of Food Habits," *National Research Council Bulletin* 111, 1945. Reissued 1962.

"Is It . . . Like Mother Like Daughter?" *House Beautiful*, October 1946, 124, 230–233.

"Masks and Men," *Natural History* 55:6 (June 1946), 280–285.

"Must Marriage Be for Life?" '47: *The Magazine of the Year* 1:9 (November 1947), 28–31.

"The Mountain Arapesh. III. Socio-Economic Life" and "IV. Diary of Events in Alitoa," *Anthropological Papers of the Museum of Natural History* 40, Part 3 (1947), 163–419.

"An Anthropologist Looks at the Report." In *Proceedings of a Symposium on the First Published Report of a Series of Studies of Sex Phenomena by Professor Alfred C. Kinsey, Wardell B. Pomeroy and Clyde E. Martin*. New York: American Social Hygiene Association, 1948, 58–69.

"Mental Health: A New Profession," *The Listener* 40:1028 (October 7, 1948), 511–512.

"The International Preparatory Commission" (with Lawrence K. Frank). In *International Congress on Mental Health, London, 1948*. Vol. I, *History, Development and Organization*. J. C. Flugel and others, eds. London: Lewis; New York: Columbia University Press, 1949, 74–89.

"The Mountain Arapesh. V. The Record of Unabelin with Rorschach Analyses," *Anthropological Papers of the American Museum of Natural History* 41, Part 3 (1949), 285–390.

"Ruth Fulton Benedict, 1887–1948," *American Anthropologist* 51:3 (July–September, 1949), 457–468.

"Cultural Contexts of Nutritional Patterns." In *Centennial: Collected Papers Presented at the Centennial Celebration, Washington, D.C., September 13–17, 1948*. Washington, D.C.: American Association for the Advancement of Science, 1950, 103–111.

"A New Control of Destiny." In *This I Believe: The Personal Philosophies of 100 Thoughtful Men and Women in All Walks of Life*. As written for Edward R. Murrow; Edward P. Morgan, ed. New York: Simon and Schuster, 1952, 115–116.

"Some Relationships between Social Anthropology and Psychiatry." In Franz Alexander and Helen Ross, eds., *Dynamic Psychiatry*. Chicago: University of Chicago Press, 1952, 401–448.

Foreword to Mark Zborowski and Elizabeth Herzog, *Life Is with People: The Jewish Little-Town of Eastern Europe*, New York: International Universities Press, 1952, 9–19.

"Expedition to the Admiralty Islands," *Natural History* 62:7 (September 1953), 334.

"Manus Revisited." In *Papua and New Guinea Scientific Society, Annual Report and Proceedings, Port Moresby, 1953*. Port Moresby: Papua and New Guinea Scientific Society, 1953, 15–18.

"National Character." In A. L. Kroeber, ed., *Anthropology Today: An Encyclopedic Inventory*. Chicago: University of Chicago Press, 1953, 642–667.

"Manus Restudied: An Interim Report." In *Transactions of the New York Academy of Sciences*, Series 2, 16:8 (June 1954), 426–432.

"Twenty-fifth Reunion at Manus," *Natural History* 63:2 (February 1954), 66–68.

Themes in French Culture: A Preface to a Study of French Community (with Rhoda Métraux). ("Hoover Institute Studies," Series D, Communities No. 1.) Stanford, Calif.: Stanford University Press, 1954.

"Different Cultural Patterns and Technological Change." In Kenneth Soddy, ed., *Mental Health and Infant Development: Proceedings of the International Seminar held by the World Federation for Mental Health at Chichester, England*. London: Routledge and Kegan Paul, 1955; New York: Basic Books, 1956, vol. I, 161–185.

"Commitment to Field Work." In *Gladys A. Reichard, 1893–1955*. New York: Barnard College, 1956, 22–27.

"The Concept of Mental Health and Its International Implications." In *Ninth Annual Report with Proceedings: Mental Health in Home and School, Papers Presented in Berlin, August 1956*. London: World Federation for Mental Health, 1956, 10–13.

"The Cross-Cultural Approach to the Study of Personality." In J. L. McCary, ed., *Psychology of Personality: Six Modern Approaches*. New York: Logos Press, 1956, 201–252.

"Mental Health, a Moving Target." In Josephine Nelson and Elizabeth M. Dach, eds., *Steps for Today toward Better Mental Health*. New York: National Health Council, 1957, 12–14.

"Do Women Like Other Women?" *Chatelaine*, August 1958, 13, 56–58.

"Growing Up in Different Cultures." In *Growing Up in a Changing World: Papers Presented at the Tenth Annual Meeting of the World Federation for Mental Health, Copenhagen, Denmark, August 1957*. London: World Federation for Mental Health, 1958, 7–14.

"Man in Space: A Tool and Program for the Study of Social Change" (with Donald N. Michael, Harold D. Lasswell, and Lawrence K. Frank), *Annals of the New York Academy of Sciences* 72, Art. 4 (April 10, 1958), 165–214.

"Apprenticeship under Boas." In Walter Goldschmidt, ed., *The Anthropology of Franz Boas*. ("Memoirs of the American Anthropological Association" 89.) *American Anthropologist* 61:5, Part 2 (October 1959), 29–45.

"Bali in the Market Place of the World," *Proceedings of the American Academy of Arts and Letters and the National Institute of Arts and Letters*, Series 2, No. 9 (1959), 286–293.

"A Letter from Margaret Mead," *Menninger Quarterly* 13:2 (Summer 1959), 12–17.

"Cultural Contexts of Nursing Problems." In Frances Cooke Macgregor, ed., *Social Science in Nursing*. New York: Russell Sage Foundation, 1960, 74–88.

"Weaver of the Border." In Joseph B. Casagrande, ed., *In the Company of Man*. New York: Harper and Row, 1960, 175–210.

"National Character and the Science of Anthropology." In Seymour M. Lipset and Leo Lowenthal, eds., *Culture and Social Character: The Work of David Riesman Reviewed*. New York: Free Press, 1961, 15–26.

"Brushes of Comets' Hair," *Menninger Quarterly* 16:2 (Summer 1962), 1–5.

"Where Americans Are Gods: The Strange Story of the Cargo Cults," *Family Weekly*, March 24, 1963, 4–5.

"Margaret Mead Answers: Questions about School Prayers, Happiness, Telepathy, etc.," *Redbook*, February 1963, 21–22.

"The Idea of National Character." In Roger L. Shinn, ed., *The Search for Identity: Essays on the American Character*. ("Religion and Civilization Series.") New York: The Institute for Religious and Social Studies; Harper and Row, 1964, 15–27.

"Memories of Walter Spies." In Hans Rhodius, ed., *Schönheit und Reichtum des Lebens: Walter Spies*. Den Haag: Boucher, 1964, 358–359.

"The City as the Portal of the Future" (with Elizabeth Steig), *Journal of Nursery Education* 19:3 (April 1964), 146–153.

"What I Owe to Other Women," *Redbook*, April 1964, 18.

"Consequences of Racial Guilt: Introduction: 1965." *The Changing Culture of an Indian Tribe*. New York: Capricorn Books/Putnam, 1966, ix–xxiii.

"Ritual Expression of the Cosmic Sense," *Worship* 40:2 (February 1966), 66–72.

"A Cruise into the Past—and a Glimpse of the Future," *Redbook*, February 1966, 30, 32, 34.

"Different Lands, Different Friendships," *Redbook*, August 1966, 38, 40.

"Alternatives to War," in "War: The Anthropology of Armed Conflict and Aggression," *Natural History* 76:10 (December 1967), 65–69.

"Homogeneity and Hypertrophy: A Polynesian-Based Hypothesis." In Genevieve A. Highland and others, eds., *Polynesian Culture History: Essays in Honor of Kenneth P. Emory*. Honolulu, Hawaii: Bishop Museum Press, 1967, 121–140.

"A Letter from Tambunam," *Redbook* August 1968, 22, 24, 26.

Introduction to Robert Gardner and Karl G. Heider, eds., *Gardens of War*. New York: Random House, 1968, vii–x.

"Lawrence Kelso Frank 1890–1968," *American Sociologist* 4:1 (February 1969), 57–58.

"Tribute to Dr. Erickson," *News Letter (American Society of Clinical Hypnosis)* 10:4 (June 1969), 1.

"A Conversation with Margaret Mead and T. George Harris on the Anthropological Age," *Psychology Today* 4:2 (July 1970), 58–68.

Introduction to Abraham H. Maslow and John J. Honigmann, "Synergy: Some Notes of Ruth Benedict," *American Anthropologist* 72:2 (April 1970), 320.

"Future Family," *Transaction* 8:11 (September 1971), 50–53.

"Field Work in High Cultures." In Solon T. Kimball and James B. Watson, eds., *Crossing Cultural Boundaries*. San Francisco: Chandler, 1972, 120–132.

"Dialogue on the Future" (with Roger Shinn), *Youth* 23:12 (December 1972), 2–15.

"My First Marriage," *Redbook*, November 1972, 50–52, 54.

"The Direction of Future Research in Papua New Guinea," *Man in New Guinea* 5:2 (June 1973), 7–8.

"Cathy, Born in Wartime," *Redbook*, May 1973, 38, 40, 43, 44, 47, 49.

"Margaret Mead." In Gardner-Lindzey, ed., *A History of Psychology in Autobiography*, vol. 4. New York: Prentice-Hall, 1974, 293–326.

"On Freud's View of Female Psychology." In Jean Strouse, ed., *Women and Analysis*. New York: Grossman (Division of Viking Press), 1974, 95–106.

"On Women" (interview with Irene Kubota), *Redbook*, August 1974, 31, 33–34.

"Our Lives May Be at Stake," *Redbook*, November 1974, 52, 54–55, 57.

Preface to Theodora M. Abel and Rhoda Métraux, *Culture and Psychotherapy*. New Haven: College and University Press, 1974, unpaged (6 pp.).

"From Poetry to Racism" (interview with Judy Lessing), *Thursday* (Aukland, N.Z.), June 12, 1975, 22–23.

"I've Always Been a Woman . . . I've Never Been an Imitation Man" (interview with Joan Wixen), *The Detroit Sunday News Magazine*, June 22, 1975, 12–13, 15–16, 18.

"Of Mothers and Mothering," *The Lactation Review* IV:1, 4–19.

Recent Articles Concerning Mead-Freeman Controversy

McDowell, Edwin. "New Samoa Book Challenges Margaret Mead's Conclusions." *New York Times*, January 31, 1983.

Wilford, John Noble. "Earlier Criticisms Surface in Reactions to Book on Dr. Mead." *New York Times*, February 6, 1983.

Milliken, Robert. "Was Samoan Sex Idyll a Myth?" *London Sunday Times*, February 6, 1983, 15.

Rebert, Isaac. "Culture Shock: Was Mead Wrong?" *Baltimore Sun*, February 15, 1983.

Bateson, Mary Catherine. "Of Margaret Mead, Her Critics, and Unhelpful Sensationalism." Letter to the editors, *New York Times*, February 13, 1983.

"Bursting the South Sea Bubble." *Time*, February 14, 1983.

"In Search of the Real Samoa." *Newsweek*, February 14, 1983.

Waugh, Auberon. "Paradise Regained." *The Spectator*, February 19, 1983.

Marshall, Eliot. "A Controversy in Samoa Comes of Age." *Science* 219 (March 4, 1983), 1042.

Turnbull, Colin M. "Trouble in Paradise." *The New Republic*, March 28, 1983, 32.

Angier, Natalie. "Coming of Age in Anthropology." *Discover*, April 1983, 26–37.

Rensberger, Boyce. "Margaret Mead: The Nature-Nurture Debate I." *Science 83*, April 1983, 28.

Sterba, James P. "New Book on Margaret Mead Dispels Tranquility in Samoa." *Wall Street Journal*, April 14, 1983, 1.

Howard, Jane. "Storm Over Margaret Mead's Samoa." *Smithsonian*, April 1983, 66.

"Samoa: Paradise or Hell?" *Life*, May 1983, 32.

"Dr. Mead's First Husband Comes to Her Defense." Letter from Luther S. Cressman to Science section, *New York Times*, May 3, 1983.

Freeman, Derek. "Of Denial and Animadversion: A Rejoinder to C. M. Turnbull." *Quadrant*, June 1983.

Schneider, David M. "The Coming of a Sage to Samoa." *Natural History*, June 1983.

Review of *Margaret Mead and Samoa: The Making of an Anthropological*

Myth, by Vera Rubin. *American Journal of Orthopsychiatry* 55:3 (July 1983), 550.

Holmes, Lowell D. Review of Freeman's book. *New York Academy of Sciences*, July–August 1983.

Cox, Paul Alan. Review of Freeman. *American Scientist* 71 (July–August 1983), 407.

Harris, Marvin. "Margaret and the Giant Killer: It Doesn't Matter a Whit Who's Right." *The Sciences* 23:4 (July–August 1983), 18.

Fisher, Helen E. Review of Freeman. *Science Digest*, October 1983.

Romanucci-Ross, Lola. "Apollo Alone and Adrift in Samoa: Early Mead Reconsidered." *Reviews in Anthropology* 10:1, 1984.

Index

McLean, Ann, 127, 151, 161, 163*n*, 438
MacLeish, Archibald, 230
McLuhan, Marshall, 373, 375
McMaster, Fanny Fogg (aunt), 22, 25, 26, 27, 33, 72, 358
McMaster, Mr. (uncle), 72
McPhee, Colin, 40, 182, 188–89, 209, 210, 273*n*, 317
Josiah H. Macy Foundation, 265
Maday, Béla, 230–31
malagas (Samoan expeditions), 83
malaria, 121, 122, 149, 170, 205, 210, 217, 305
Male and Female (Mead), 249, 250, 274, 289, 291–92, 294, 352–53, 359
  "feminine mystique" and, 363
  Rebecca West's review of, 285–286, 291
Malinowski, Bronislaw, 107*n*, 111, 113, 114, 122*n*, 124–25, 159, 177, 184, 186, 267, 321
  Coming of Age in Samoa and, 111, 127
  Fortune's correspondence with, 169, 172, 201*n*–2*n*, 215
Man and Superman (Shaw), 96
Man as Art (Kirk), 377
Manchester Guardian, 277
Mandelbaum, Deborah Kaplan, 43, 44, 47, 49, 58, 129, 172, 194
Mandelbaum, Mel, 129
Mansfield, Katherine, 91, 317
Manu'a group, 79, 80, 82
  see also Ta'u
Manus, 116–23, 149, 155, 283, 297, 300–310, 313, 314, 337, 386, 393, 398, 427
Manus Religion (Fortune), 114, 127, 144, 171, 302
Maoris, 91, 128
Marconi, Guglielmo, 23
Margaret Mead and Samoa (Freeman), 323*n*, 432–34
marijuana, 390
Maris, Joan, *see* Eggan, Joan
Maritain, Jacques, 220
marriage, 100, 143, 350
  Mead's views on, 40, 48, 58, 60–61, 113, 147, 235, 289–91, 306, 331, 333, 351, 356, 390, 400
  as pageant, 60–61

as vocation, 356
  weddings vs., 351
Marseilles, France, 89, 90, 96–97
Martin, Marty, 377
Masters, Robert, 409–10
Maugham, W. Somerset, 79
Mauss, Marcel, 292
May, Rollo, 163, 258, 367, 389
May Day, 39, 40, 71–72
Mayer, Jean, 428
"maypole conspiracies," 369
Mbetnda, 209
M'bunai, New Guinea, 304–5, 306, 308
Mead, Edward Sherwood (father), 21, 22, 34, 61, 70, 107, 130, 218, 358
  Cressman and, 26, 35, 60
  education of, 22*n*, 24, 25
  Margaret's correspondence with, 60, 185–87
  Margaret's education and, 36, 39, 60
  Margaret's relationship with, 24, 26, 27, 32, 92
  personality of, 25–26, 32, 35
  as philanderer, 21, 25
  wife's death and, 287–88
Mead, Elizabeth (Liza) (sister), *see* Steig, Elizabeth
Mead, Emily Fogg (mother), 24, 39, 42, 60, 107, 111, 177, 217, 219*n*, 358
  agnosticism of, 21, 31, 32
  death of, 287–88
  education of, 21*n*, 22*n*, 24, 36
  "Holy Shelf" of, 187
  humorlessness of, 24, 35
  Margaret's correspondence with, 82, 104, 185–87, 210, 360–61
  Margaret's relationship with, 24, 29–30, 33
  research of, 21–22, 64
Mead, Helene (sister-in-law), 266
Mead, Jessica (sister-in-law), 266
Mead, Katherine (sister), 27, 45
Mead, Margaret:
  academic relations of, 105, 316, 335, 379
  ambitions of, 14, 40, 61, 111, 184, 236, 336, 406, 437
  appearance of, 14, 22, 37, 41–42, 78, 124, 149, 168, 169, 185,